MORMON GOLD
Mormons in the California Gold Rush

- They came, some just before and some just after California became U.S. Territory (1846).

- They doubled the population of Yerba Buena and helped turn that placid, "ends of the earth" hamlet into a bustling San Francisco.

- They were involved in some of the first gold discoveries (Coloma and Mormon Island).

- They opened important trails across the Sierra and the Southwest.

- Some brought their families, built homes, and pioneered commercial farming in California.

- Many sent their gold back to help establish a currency for the infant Mormon settlement in the Salt Lake Valley, which without that help might have floundered.

SOME EARLY COMMENTS

FOR ANYONE writing on, studying, or curious about the California gold rush and the major role Mormons played in it, this book is pure gold! *Mormon Gold*, long out of print, has been a terrific standard for years–my copy is well-worn, dog-eared, and marked up–and this newly revised and updated edition is even better. Widely researched in primary sources, smartly organized, crisply narrated, marked with intrigue, epic in scope, insightfully mapped, sprinkled with appropriate analyses, contexted well historically, and with participants well-identified and tracked, this is must-have original scholarship at its finest. *Mormon Gold*'s back-reference material alone is worth the price of the book: name lists, subject index, and descriptions of five dozen Mormon-connected gold field locations.

MORMON GOLD skillfully fulfills its stated purpose to fully examine the "extended Mormon role in the gold fields." Beyond helping discover the gold at Coloma that launched the gold rush, Mormons became key participants in the expanding network of gold fields, including ones named Mormon Island, Mormon Bar, Mormon Gulch, Mormon Hill, and Mormon Ravine. *Mormon Gold* demonstrates that Brigham Young actually promoted the mining of gold by authorizing hundreds of Mormons to go into the gold fields including two dozen called on "gold mining missions" Readers will find *Mormon Gold* fascinating.

William G. Hartley, Professor Emeritus, Brigham Young University, former president Mormon History Association, award-winning biographer.

IN THIS NEW EDITION, scholar Lorin Hansen provides a masterful revision of a classic study. It includes important fresh research on a variety of topics, along with prolific illustrations and excellent maps, making this volume a significant addition to the literature about California's LDS Argonauts. Those with a personal interest will find here expert assistance in documenting gold rush era Mormon communities and the activities of Mormon gold seekers. Well written, and including new materials that add to our understanding of California during the 1850s, this is a work of great merit, essential for any library concerned with the Mormon historical experience.

Kenneth N. Owens, Professor Emeritus, California State University, Sacramento
Author of *Gold Rush Saints: California Mormons and the Great Rush for Riches*.

———————————————

J. KENNETH DAVIES, an economics professor and labor negotiator, became fascinated with Mormon mining enterprises and devoted great energy to researching and writing about the Latter-day Saint involvement in the gold rush before there was much in print on that subject. The resulting *Mormon Gold: The Story of California's Mormon Argonauts*, published in 1984, proved most useful to a generation of those interested in the subject. One invaluable aspect of his study was a truly insightful treatment of the Great Basin monetary system stemming from the gold brought from California. Davies and the publisher have engaged another respected historian of the California Mormons, Lorin K. Hansen, to somewhat revise and update the original book. Hansen has drawn on recent scholarship to update and improve the study and bibliography, has added numerous and most valuable illustrations and added and edited the appendices Davies had published separately elsewhere. Hansen's new edition is a most valuable contribution to Mormon and California history highly recommended to anyone interested in either or both subjects.

E. Leo Lyman, Professor Emeritus, Victor Valley College,
Author of *San Bernardino: The Rise and Fall of a California Community*; *The Overland Journey from Utah to California: Wagon Travel from the City of Saints to the City of Angels*; and *Amasa Mason Lyman: Mormon Apostle and Apostate*.

———————————————

MORMON GOLD filled a gap in my understanding of Mormon history. These authors sifted a lot of sand to gather forgotten nuggets into a significant new work. It's at its best when the steady flow of little facts immerses the reader in the lives of ordinary Mormon folk who dreamed, toiled, despaired and infrequently prospered in the goldfields of the American West."

J. Stanton Curry, Mormon history aficionado and Shareholder in the environmental law firm of Gallagher & Kennedy, Phoenix, Arizona.

———————————————

MORMON
GOLD

MORMON GOLD

Mormons in the California Gold Rush

Contributing to the Development of California and the Monetary Solvency of Early Utah

Second Edition

J. Kenneth Davies and Lorin K. Hansen

Granite Mountain Publishing Company
North Salt Lake City, Utah

MORMON GOLD: Mormons in the California Gold Rush, Contributing to the Development of California and the Monetary Solvency of Early Utah, Second edition.

Copyright © Granite Mountain Publishing LLC, 2010
All rights reserved.

ISBN 978-0-9830832-0-7

Printed in the United States of America
Cover design by Steve Hansen Designs

First edition published in 1984 by Olympus Publishing Company (978-0-9134202-0-1)

10 9 8 7 6 5 4 3 2

Copyright & Legal Department
Granite Mountain Publishing Company
900 North 400 West, Suite 12,
North Salt Lake, UT 84054

To order books, submit publication proposals for original works, or for customer service, please visit Granite Mountain Publishing Company's website

www.granitemountainpublishing.com

Library of Congress Cataloging-in-Publication Data

Davies, J. Kenneth, 1925-
    Mormon gold : Mormons in the California Gold Rush, Contributing to the Development of California and the Monetary Solvency of Early Utah / J. Kenneth Davies, Lorin K. Hansen – 2nd ed.
        p. cm.
    Includes maps, illustrations, bibliographic references, subject and name indexes.
    ISBN: 978-0-9830832-0-7 (hardcover : alk. Paper) 1. United States – History.
    2. Religion. I. Hansen, Lorin K. II. Title.
    Library of Congress Holdings Information is not yet available.
    Library of Congress Control No.: 2010939037.

www.granitemountainpublishing.com

CONTENTS

MAPS and ILLUSTRATIONS

MAPS

ILLUSTRATIONS

"Panning" for Gold on the Mokelumne

[From "How We Get Gold, From a Miner in the Year '49," *Harper's New Monthly Magazine*, vol. 20, issue 119 (April 1860) 600.]

PREFACE TO THE SECOND EDITION

IT HAS BEEN over twenty five years since I published the first edition of *Mormon Gold,* making available to the public for the first time a detailed history of the Mormon participation in the nineteenth century California gold rush. That work not only told the general story, but provided a detailed accounting of the individual personalities involved and elaborated on the importance of Mormon gold rush involvement to the monetary solvency of the new Mormon settlements in the Great Salt Lake Valley. I was very pleased by the warm reception given to that first publication.

Since the first edition was made available, there has been considerable additional research and publication concerning the Mormon story in early California. Because the first edition has long been unavailable and because of the recent research, I felt it was time to prepare a second edition of *Mormon Gold*, which would incorporate this new information.

Because of my personal situation, I was not able to prepare an updated, second edition myself. Therefore, I requested Gary L. Nelson of Granite Mountain Publishing to appoint someone to prepare the new edition and republish the work. Gary Nelson arranged for Lorin K. Hansen, who is very familiar with Mormon history in early California, to do the work. I was able, however, to follow the preparation and do editing on the entire manuscript.

I would like to express appreciation to Gary, Lorin, and all those who participated for their efforts in making the new edition such an inviting, complete work, and I commend the book to a new generation of readers.

J. Kenneth Davies

THE FIRST EDITION of *Mormon Gold* authored by Prof. J. Kenneth Davies and published in 1984 provided for the first time a detailed account of the Mormon participation in the mid-nineteenth-century, California gold rush. One reviewer, Brigham D. Madsen [*Dialogue: A Journal of Mormon Thought* 19:1 (Spring 1986): 181], considered it "readable . . . written with clarity . . . comprehensive . . . with a plethora of detail." He was impressed that so much could be discovered about the story and the hundreds of people involved "making the book a genealogist's gold mine."

A second reviewer, Samuel W. Taylor [*BYU Studies* 25:3 (Summer 1985): 130-132], praised the book for having "left no stone unturned in recounting all there is to know about Mormons and the gold rush," adding, "The depth of the research is incredible." Mormons have always been unusually diligent in keeping records, and Davies drew extensively from the diaries, journals, letters, autobiographical accounts, the Church manuscript history, and the Church financial records. He also made use of relevant contemporary accounts, census records, and newspaper accounts, etc. The result was an unusual, in-depth account of a fascinating period in Mormon and California history.

Through his in-depth research of both Utah and California sources, Davies was able to flesh out one of the more fascinating aspects of the story, the role of Mormons of the gold rush in keeping the fledgling Mormon community in the Great Basin financially solvent. It was a miracle that thousands of refugees could be driven into an inhospitable wilderness over a thousand miles from supplies and be able to set up instant, viable, self sustaining communities. As the pioneers moved into the Salt Lake Valley and spread out along the Wasatch Front, the supplies they brought with them were soon exhausted. In sending east or to the west coast for additional supplies to build their communities, any moneys they brought with them were also soon exhausted. Circumstances quickly reduced them to a very deprived existence running essentially on a barter system. It was essentially gold from the California mines that gave them the temporary currency which allowed them to continue commercial activities and to continue obtaining needed supplies.

It has been over twenty five years since the first edition of *Mormon Gold* was published. In that period there has been considerable additional research and publishing on topics related to the story. The book needed to be updated, and it has been my privilege to be given that task.

References and the bibliography, for example, needed to be updated. Some of the works referenced in manuscript form have since become available in published form. Also many significant works have appeared related to the story which provide useful information that needed to be incorporated into the text and referenced. The second edition has especially benefitted from the publications of Norma Ricketts, Will Bagley, David Bigler, Leo Lyman, and Kenneth Owens. Leonard Arrington has since written a full biography of Charles C. Rich. Davis Bitton has published one for George Q. Cannon. Leo Lyman has published one for Amasa Lyman. George Ellsworth and others have brought us the annotated diaries of Addison Pratt, Louisa Barnes Pratt, and Caroline Barnes Crosby. Michael Landon has published the annotated diary of George Q. Cannon for the years in California. Richard Bullock has published his account of the *Brooklyn* voyage and provided on the Internet biographical sketches of ship *Brooklyn* passengers. All of these specific works have been useful and are listed in the present bibliography. The *Bancroft Mormon*

Collection came available during the preparation of the second edition. I am sure that collection will grow and be a valuable source for future researchers and authors.

We should especially mention the book "*Gold Rush Saints: California Mormons and the Great Rush for Riches*" by Kenneth N. Owens. *Gold Rush Saints* is very accurate, written by an author thoroughly familiar with gold rush and Mormon Emigrant Trail history, and uses extensive primary source quotations. We would like to think that *Gold Rush Saints* and *Mormon Gold* are two essential works that should be read for a general understanding of the topic.

The present work tries to identify individuals involved in the gold rush and piece together their lives and interactions. It is extensively illustrated with portraits, landscapes, and maps. The second edition also adds background information. One of the problems of the first edition was that, to keep the work to a reasonable size, much of the name lists and account information had to be left out, separately photocopied, and privately circulated. Unfortunately this resulted in many of the people reading the work not having those appendices available to them. In this edition, those appendices are clearly labeled and attached to the ends of the appropriate chapters. To make room for these appendices and other materials, we have gone to a larger format.

As Sam Taylor pointed out, no book is perfect, and both reviewers offered their obligatory criticisms of the work. In both cases, the criticisms follow from the work being so comprehensive. For Madsen, the abundance of information made the text seem haphazard and repetitive. He suggested guideposts to keep the reader on a clearly marked path through the narrative. Correspondingly, Taylor expressed the view that sometimes a book is made successful more by what is left out than what is included. He wondered if maybe we wouldn't miss some of the information if it was left out.

I prefer Madsen's suggestion to Taylor's. I have tried to preserve the work as a comprehensive account. Following Madsen, we have taken some steps to improve the readability. For example, we have adopted a two column, open format and used other format features. I have added many subheadings as "guideposts" to more clearly mark the path of the narrative. We have used about a hundred-fifty illustrations and maps and placed them appropriately in the text to help the reader visualize the people and the geography of the text. Additional information has been added to some of the chapters. We added a chapter on the Mormon Emigrant Trail, since pioneering that trail, we thought, deserved more emphasis. In addition, we have added a time line near the end of the book (Appendix C), keyed to the text, to make it easier to keep in mind the flow of the story and the interrelation of events. Finally, we included a section (Appendix D) about the developing transportation and agricultural systems. In merely the decade of the story, California went from using two-wheeled ox carts to the beginnings of a railroad. We sketch out that explosive development and reference it to the text to add perspective to the events discussed in the text.

Actually, the reader should consider reading the final chapter (Chapter 25: Mormon Argonauts: Some Reflections) and the review appendix (Appendix D: Transportation and Agriculture as Background for the *Mormon Gold* Story) before beginning the main text.

One of the challenges in the present account is the variety of ways people spell names. In diaries, letters, trail rosters, and census records, spellings often vary. Individuals sometimes even spelled their own names differently at different times, for example Thomas Rhoades (Rhoads) and John C. Naegle (Naile). We try to be consistent in our own writing about these people, but let the spellings found in specific records prevail when they occur.

Of course, Mormons as a group are also referred to in various ways. "Mormon" is a popular expression for members of The Church of Jesus Christ of Latter-day Saints. For brevity, they are also referred to as Latter-day Saints, LDS, or simply as Saints. In the present work, all these variations are used. Whenever the word "Church" is used alone and capitalized, it refers to the LDS Church.

Davies attempted to follow the places and people in detail, and it is remarkable that so much of the story could be assembled. Unfortunately, the primary sources are limited, and there are still uncertainties and ambiguities in the story. Davies did some speculating to try to indicate the direction in which the information was leading. I have reduced some of this where I did not think it was especially useful, but I have left most of it in the text. When there is uncertainty, its presence is always clear, and I hope the reader will consider the speculation a positive aspect of the work.

I acknowledge with appreciation help from several reviewers. Leo Lyman re-read over half of the first edition and made many useful suggestions. Michael Landon, John Bascom, and Lila Bringhurst reviewed single chapters. Stanton Curry edited the work, concentrating on the first half of the book. Bill Hartley read some middle chapters and made valuable suggestions. Prof. Kenneth Owens read three key chapters and made important contributions. Prof. J. Kenneth Davies and Linda Thatcher reviewed and edited the entire text. I especially appreciate the help of Kathryn Marshall, who did touch-ups on previous maps, prepared additional maps, did digital touch-ups on some of the photographs, and did extensive editing of the entire manuscript.

Lorin K. Hansen

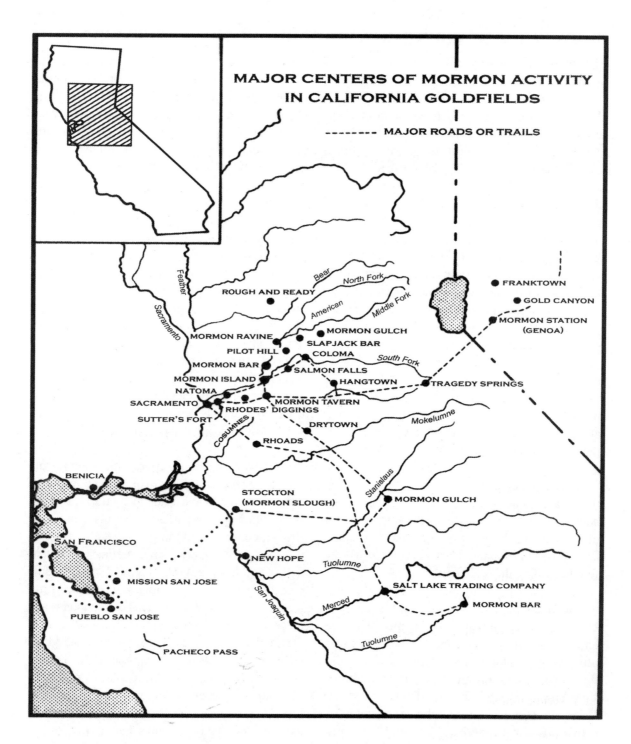

The deep involvement of the Mormon Argonauts in the California gold rush, lasting over a decade, is immediately made evident from the many Mormon names attached to early sites of the gold country.

Then Peter said, silver and gold have I none
but such as I have give I unto you.
　Bible, Acts 3:6

Introduction

WITH THE DISCOVERY of California's gold in 1848, and the subsequent rush of 49ers from all over the world to recover the nineteenth century equivalent of the mythical "Golden Fleece," the name "Argonaut" became applied to gold seekers, old and young, who ventured forth to California's El Dorado.

The ancient Grecian myth tells of a flying golden ram sent by the Gods to assist young Phrixus and Helles to escape from an unearned death at the hands of their father. As they flew over the straits separating Europe from Asia, Helles fell and was drowned. The ram flew on with its remaining passenger to the eastern shores of the Black Sea. There it was sacrificed and its golden fleece hung, guarded by a dragon.

Jason, a Greek nobleman's son, was sent by his king to retrieve the Golden Fleece. Accompanying him were fifty of the most courageous young men in the kingdom. Their vessel, the *Argos*, was built under the supervision of the Goddess Athena. Placed in its bow was a piece of mighty oak with the Delphic power to give guidance to the vessel's crew, the Argonauts, in their golden quest and ensuing adventures.

The namesake of the men of the *Argos*, the nineteenth century California Argonauts, was a diverse group. Among them, at once both typical and atypical, was a group of Mormons, that is, members of The Church of Jesus Christ of Latter-day Saints. They played a significant role in both the initial discoveries and subsequent mining of the yellow metal. The deep involvement of the Mormon Argonauts, lasting over a decade, is immediately made evident from the many Mormon names attached to early sites of the gold country. (See map on the opposite page.)

While the initial role of Mormons in the discovery of gold at Sutter's Coloma has been given adequate attention, their preliminary and subsequent activities have been relatively neglected by Mormon and non-Mormon, California, Utah, and Western historians. This neglect has probably stemmed from at least two reasons, one being Utah and Mormon oriented, the other being rooted in California.

Mormon and Utah Historians
Addressing the Gold Story

The neglect of Mormon and Utah historians comes no doubt from preoccupation with the Utah story, but perhaps also from the misconception of Brigham Young's actual policy toward gold mining. His public, negative attitude toward gold mining is well documented and well known. Almost unknown is the fact that he actually promoted the mining of gold under his direction and control.

There is no known evidence that Brigham Young's prophetic power included foreknowledge of the gold rush to engulf California in 1848-49. Nevertheless, forces he set in motion in 1845-47 resulted in several hundred Mormons being on site to participate in both the initial discoveries and the exploitation of the easy-to-get surface gold of those golden years. Once the gold was discovered, he was astute enough to take advantage of it, not only by sending gold mining missionaries but also colonizers who would make their fortunes from the labors of the gold miners.

The truth is that Brigham Young was more than a spiritual leader and pragmatic colonizer. He was also economically rational. Once he knew of the gold, he saw its critical need in the state of

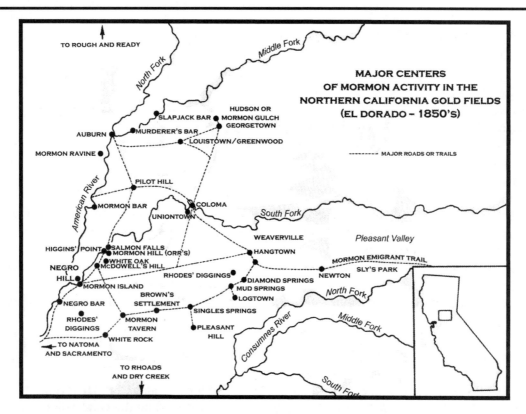

MAJOR CENTERS
OF MORMON ACTIVITY IN THE
NORTHERN CALIFORNIA GOLD FIELDS
(EL DORADO – 1850'S)

- - - - - - - MAJOR ROADS OR TRAILS

Deseret to serve as a medium of exchange, for use in external trade, and especially in the acquisition of capital. It would also be most helpful in support of a domestic money system.

But he at the same time was aware of the need for manpower to "make the desert blossom as a rose," and he knew the allure of gold, especially to an impoverished people. He had to keep the Mormon participation in the gold fields under control. He did it by publicly preaching against gold mining but at the same time confidentially calling, having called, or authorizing many of 19th century Mormon Argonauts, to go into the gold fields. He planned to receive their tithes and offerings in gold as well as to have them return home with their personal treasure troves. So important was this effort that two Mormon Delphic Oracles (Apostles Amasa Lyman and Charles C. Rich) were sent to California in 1849 to direct the work and collect the tithes. In the mid 1850s, Apostle Orson Hyde also became involved. His headquarters were located in Carson Valley (now in Nevada).

Later Mormon historians did not understand Brigham Young's actual policy concerning mining, and because they assumed an almost abso-lute power to obtain conformity to his will on the part of his followers, they were led to the popular but false conclusion that following the initial discovery of gold participated in by members of the Mormon Battalion in 1848, the faithful Saints left off mining. Therefore, only the unfaithful and apostates continued mining, and these were not worth writing about. The only Mormon subsequently involved in the gold fields who was known to any extent among the Mormon people was the notorious (to the Mormons at least) Sam Brannan who, while not a miner, made his fortune from gold miners, forgetting God and the Kingdom. He died a materially and spiritually impoverished old man, a perfect Mormon object story of the folly of following after the god of this earth—money, especially gold.

Less known was the story of George Q. Cannon (nephew of the next Church president, John Taylor) who was sent to California as the latter's personal gold missionary. He went on to become an Apostle and a counselor to four Church presidents, that is, a special couselor to Brigham Young and in the First Presidency for Presidents John Taylor, Wilford Woodruff, and Lorenzo Snow. While in his early years he disclaimed interest in gold mining as such, he acquired a personal fortune from the precious metal mining in Utah later in the century.

Because of the confidential nature of the calls of these gold missionaries, to admit that there were many faithful Mormons involved in the gold fields would apparently mean that Brigham Young had less than perfectly obedient people. To the faithful in later generations it meant their gold mining ancestors had defied their Prophet, an almost mortal sin and something to be hidden from coming generations. To the critics of Mormonism, it made Young appear less than the all-powerful tyrant they wanted him to have been.

California and Western Historians Addressing the Gold Story

California and western historians have probably neglected the extended Mormon role in the gold fields simply because they did not know about it. California's history was written after the body of the more active or practicing Mormons had left the state in 1857, when Brigham called his people home to defend Deseret against an "invading" U.S. Army. The call creamed off the most faithful and obedient of California Mormons—at least that is the usual assumption. Actually, there were many left behind who owned mines, businesses, and farms, who may well have planned to go to Utah after disposing of their properties but eventually abandoned such thoughts and remained.

Once the 1857 emergency was over, the need to "gather" became less critical, and by that time the Church leadership had apparently written California off. All Church leadership was removed, leaving the remaining California Saints without a Delphic piece of mighty oak to guide them. They were left to wander in a spiritual Sinai for forty years, but without a Moses or even an Aaron in their midst. Those Saints left behind, bereft of personal encouragement and direction from Church leaders, drifted away into apathy. Some became embarrassed or disillusioned as the practice of polygamy became well-published. Some became Josephites, that is, attached themselves to the dissidents left behind during the exodus west, who rejected polygamy, "gathering," and the leadership of Brigham Young. With waning attachment to Mormon roots, none of these were interested enough to keep alive the story of the Mormon Argonauts.

The Gold Story Reemerging

In the twentieth century Mormons began filtering back into California. With still an attachment and identification with the Church, they felt displaced from central Zion. Gradually, these Mormons formed an attachment also to the state. A sensitivity to Mormon roots in California developed, but a knowledge of those roots was at first superficial. By the time historians got around to writing California history, the prominent role of Mormons in the California gold rush era had either been swept under the rug or forgotten. Had it not been for the search for the exact date of gold discovery (a fact recorded and discovered in the diary of ex-Battalion member Henry Bigler, an obscure Mormon temple worker in St. George, Utah) the now well-known role of Sutter's Mormon workmen at Coloma might well have remained hidden.

The author's (J. Kenneth Davies') interest in the subject was provoked by his search for the history of Utah's workers. While attempting to identify the reasons underlying the historically uneasy relationship between Utah miners and Mormons, it was soon realized that Mormon antagonism toward miners found its roots in Brigham Young's public policy in the gold mining era. Thus began this inquiry which made necessary a re-examination of the role of Mormons in this exciting period.

The story that unfolded from the Mormon involvement in the California Gold Rush was one of Utah's first successful export industries. Over $80,000 in gold went through Brigham Young's Gold Accounts into the Mormon mint alone between 1848 and 1851—money used to support the Kingdom. Many thousands more of dollars, unaccounted for, remained in private hands to be used to buy supplies and capital goods. Had it not been for these 19th Century Mormon Argonauts the infant Mormon economy in the Salt Lake Valley might well have foundered.

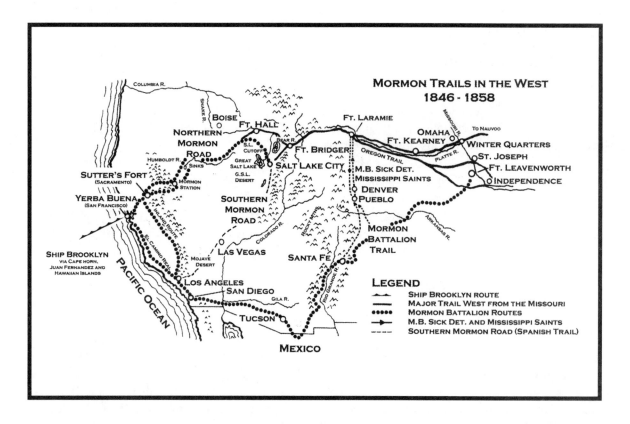

Mormon Trails in the West 1846 - 1858

Five Groups of Mormons Reached California before the Discovery of Gold:

1. William B. Ide and his family traveled the Humboldt and Truckee Route (Northern Mormon Road) and arrived at Sutter's Fort October 24, 1845.

2. The ship *Brooklyn* sailed from New York around the Horn and arrived at Yerba Buena July 31, 1846, three weeks after California was declared U.S. Territory.

3. Thomas Rhoades and his family followed the Truckee Route (Northern Mormon Road), crossed over Donner Pass about October 5, 1846, and settled southeast of Sutter's Fort near the Cosumnes River.

4. The Mormon Battalion, about 335 men (plus camp associates), blazed a trail through the Southwest and reached California January 14, 1847. They reached San Diego January 29, 1847, about five months after the arrival of the *Brooklyn*.

5. Jefferson Hunt and Orrin Porter Rockwell traveled the Southern (Spanish Trail) Route from the Salt Lake Valley to California in the fall of 1847 to obtain supplies for the Saints who had stopped their migration near the Great Salt Lake.

Awake, O kings of the earth!
Come ye, O, Come ye
With your gold and your silver,
To the help of my people . . . .
   Doctrine & Covenants 124:11

1
The Stage is Set

WITH THE ASSASSINATION of the Mormon Prophet Joseph Smith in 1844 and the increasing persecution of the Saints, the collapse of the Mormon dream of Zion seemed imminent. Nauvoo, their city of some fifteen thousand, was under constant mob threat. Outlying homes were being torched. Missouri had been abandoned six years earlier, and now Nauvoo was becoming increasingly untenable as a city of refuge. A new gathering place was needed for the faithful.

A new leader, too, was needed to supply the vision that Joseph had provided. Who his successor would be was not altogether clear in the 1844-46 period as numerous men rose to claim succession. The overwhelming majority of the Saints would choose to follow Brigham Young as the President of the Quorum of the Twelve Apostles, but his hold on the people was not as yet assured.

As the pressures on the Saints increased over the winter of 1845-46, they cast about for a land to which they could escape. Oregon and Vancouver Island held out great promise. Texas, too, seemed a likely home—it being the location favored by the popular Apostle, Lyman Wight.

Apostle John Taylor envisioned a new home in Upper California as seen in several verses from a hymn he authored. [1]

The Upper California,
O! that's the land for me,
It lies between the Mountains
and great Pacific Sea
        The Saints can be supported
        there;
        And taste the sweets of liberty.

We'll go and lift our standard,
we'll go there and be free,
We'll go to California
and have our jubilee,
        A land that blooms with endless
        spring,
        A land of life and liberty.

We'll reign, we'll rule, and triumph,
and God shall be our King,
The plains, the hills and vallies
shall with hosannas ring,
        Our tow'rs and temples there
        shall rise
        Along the great Pacific Sea.

Upper California at that time included the present states of California, Utah, and Arizona. It also extended sufficiently east to include the Colorado River basin, and therefore included also parts of what became Colorado and New Mexico. Taylor, however, was referring to Upper California as the land between the "Mountains and great Pacific Sea," a land of "endless spring," He wrote that "tow'rs and temples . . . there shall rise . . . along the great Pacific sea." However far inland Taylor's "Upper California" was meant to extend, he clearly envisioned Mormon settlements on the Pacific coast.

Interest in the coast was also indicated by Brigham Young's counsel to Samuel Brannan to go set up a printing press at San Francisco Bay.[2] It was also evident from Young's letter to Wilford Woodruff in England instructing him to send immigrants to the West Coast. [3] Whether the west Coast was to be their main destination or just a region of secondary settlement remained to be determined.

Because the Saints intended to settle in Upper California (on the coast or more inland), their interests soon became enmeshed with if not in conflict with those of the federal government. In 1846, the federal government, driven by a spirit of "manifest destiny," seemed determined to wrest Upper California from Mexican control. Washington officials had been deaf to Mormon pleas for help in Missouri and Illinois, However, with the Saints fleeing in large numbers into this area of federal interest, the Saints became unavoidably caught up in the drama of events that were beginning to unfold. They were to play a significant role in the development of the West.

According to Wallace Stegner, speaking of this Mormon migration as a whole, "The Mormons were one of the principal forces in the settlement of the west. Their main body opened southern Iowa, the Missouri frontier, Nebraska, Wyoming, Utah". Wherever they went and whatever they accomplished, by choice or by necessity, they moved with the frontier, hoping in the end to establish their Zion. The main body of the migration, of course, stopped at the Salt Lake Valley. But as Stegner adds, some went beyond the Great Basin and made contributions further west— "Samuel Brannan's group of eastern Saints who sailed around the Horn in the ship *Brooklyn*, and the Mormon Battalion [enlisted by the U.S. Government] that marched 2,000 miles overland from Fort Leavenworth to San Diego, were secondary prongs of the Mormon movement; between them,

they contributed to the opening of the Southwest and of California". [4]

Stegner lists the two main groups going to California, the *Brooklyn* Saints and the Mormon Battalion. However, some smaller groups arriving before the gold discovery should also be mentioned, for example, the William B. Ide and Thomas Rhoades families, as well as the Jefferson Hunt and Orrin Porter Rockwell party. We discuss all of these in the order they arrived in California.

William B. Ide and Family

Probably the first Mormons to reach California were William Brown Ide and his family. [5] Ide was born March 28, 1796 in Rutland Massachusetts. His ancestors go back to the Pilgrims. He had sparse schooling, but was a person of high intelligence. He learned the carpenter's and joiner's trade from his father. Ide married Susan G. Haskell of Northborough, Massachusetts in 1820 and practiced his trade in Vermont. In 1833 he decided to seek his fortune in the West and moved with his wife and then six children to Kentucky. Only a few months later he moved again to Madison, Ohio, about 20 miles east of Kirtland. Two more sons were born in Ohio.

Ide is presumed to have become a Mormon at that time, even though on one occasion much later he found it convenient to deny being a Mormon. In the records of the Church for August 12, 1838, he is probably the "Bro. Ide" who is recorded as joining a camp traveling to Zion (Missouri).

The Ides moved to Illinois and had a farm eight miles east of Springfield. In 1844, Ide was a delegate at the convention that nominated Joseph Smith as a candidate for president of the United States. [6] He was then called as an electioneering missionary for Joseph Smith to Vermont. [7]

Joseph was killed in 1844. Members of the Illinois State Militia said they had done it, and they would continue killing the Mormons until they were all killed or rounded up. Being Mormon living in such an outlying location as the Ides, east of Springfield, was not the safest of circum-

Oil painting of the ship *Brooklyn,* ca. 1840, painter unknown. The ship was built in 1834 by J. & M. Madigan in Newcastle, Maine. It was a fully-rigged trader with some cabin space 'tween decks for passengers. In 1846, the remaining cargo space between decks was converted to more cabins to accommodate some 238 passengers for the voyage to San Francisco Bay. At that sailing, the *Brooklyn* was well worn from eleven years of hard service. In 1849, at the beginning of the gold rush, the *Brooklyn* again sailed to San Francisco from the East, bringing some of the first gold seekers. *Courtesy LDS Museum of Church History and Art.*

stances at the time. In the fall of 1844, Ide started making plans to move his family to Oregon. The family built wagons that winter and in early 1845 moved to Independence, Missouri. They camped outside the city while making final preparations, along with many others who would make the trip to Oregon with them. They left Independence May 10, 1845. By June they were already at Fort Laramie, and by August they were at Fort Hall, in present day Idaho.

It was at Fort Hall they met Caleb Greenwood, an old mountain man who had been associated with John Sutter in California and who had just led a party eastward over the California Trail.

Greenwood claimed he was encouraged by Sutter to divert Oregon bound traffic into California. Promises of cheap land were made. Ide changed his mind about Oregon and decided to take his family to California. They became part of the Grigsby-Ide party (about 150 souls) who followed Greenwood into California. The Ide family, at that point, consisted of seven.

They went along the Humboldt and Truckee Rivers to Truckee Lake (now called Donner Lake). They were following the route that the Stephens-Townsend-Murphy party had gone the year before in taking the first wagons into California. They ascended the steep incline to the

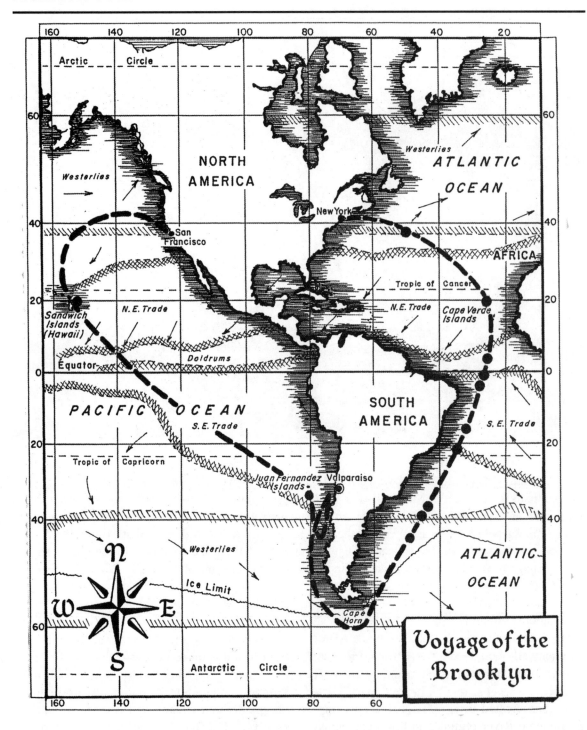

Map showing the route of the ship *Brooklyn* on its 1846 voyage to California. Dots on the dashed route show where eleven passengers and one crewman died. [Art work by Al Gregor.]

summit beyond the Lake, but only with the greatest difficulty. They went step by step getting oxen up first and hauling unloaded wagons up with the help of the oxen. The descent into the valleys of California was also difficult. This crossing led them into the valley of the Bear and American Rivers. The Ide party reached Sutter's Fort, according to Sutter's records, on October 25, 1845.

The Ides spent only about five days at Sutter's

Yerba Buena (San Francisco) in 1846-47. [Lithograph from *The Beginnings of San Francisco* (in two volumes) by Zoeth S. Eldredge (San Francisco: Zoeth S. Eldredge, 1912), 526.]

Fort before deciding to settle along the upper Sacramento River. Going north, Ide eventually began working for Josiah Belden, who owned the Rancho de la Barranca Colorado, a 17,000 acre grant about 140 miles up the Sacramento and about 2-3 miles south of what is now Red Bluff. He eventually bought the grant from Belden, and that became his permanent home.

Ide participated in the gold rush in the north Sacramento River region, [8] but is more remembered for his role in the Bear Flag Revolt of 1845-46 [9] and his role in the early government of Colusi County, where his ranch was located. Ide died in December 1852 while serving out what he intended to be his last term in the Colusi County government. He planned to retire and leave California, perhaps going to southern Utah where his Mormon son James lived.

The *Brooklyn* Saints

On December 20, 1845, in coordination with his plan to abandon Nauvoo, Brigham Young instructed the youthful and mercurial Sam Brannan to take Saints by ship to San Francisco Bay. Brannan responded and announced in the *New York Messenger*, a Mormon newspaper, that he had chartered the ship *Brooklyn* and would leave New York on the 24th of January. [10] Supplies were scarce in Nauvoo, and it was thought that Saints on the East Coast, therefore, could reach the West easier by sea. Some 238 persons booked passage, all but a handful being Mormons. Anticipating that they would be joined in California by other Saints traveling overland, they took with them enough agricultural and mechanical tools for 800 people, including three grain mills, turning lathes, saw mill irons, a printing press, and the beginnings of a library. Some of the goods aboard were on consignment, belonging to Mormons ex-

Samuel Brannan (1819-1889)
Samuel Brannan was born March 2, 1819, in Saco, Maine. He joined the Mormon church in 1833 and apprenticed as a printer in Kirtland. He traveled the country working as a printer, and finally was sent by the Church to publish the newspaper, *The Prophet*, in New York City. He was called by Brigham Young to organize an emigration by sea to San Francisco Bay in 1845. *Courtesy Bancroft Library.*

pecting to travel to California in 1846 with the anticipated overland vanguard of that year. [11]

The ship *Brooklyn* finally left New York on February 4. After sailing around the Horn and making brief stops at Juan Fernandez and the Sandwich Islands, the ship reached Yerba Buena (the future San Francisco) about six months later, July 31, 1846. Eleven passengers died on the trip and two children were born. (From family records, there is some indication that two more children were born that died shortly after birth.) The passengers reached the west coast just three weeks after Commander John B. Montgomery of the U.S.S. Portsmouth had raised the flag in the public square of Yerba Buena to declare that primitive hamlet U.S. territory. Therefore, they became the first ship load of immigrants into American California.

The new arrivals set up immediate accommodations—among the few buildings available, in tents, and at the neighboring Mission Delores. [12] More permanent homes were soon constructed. They essentially doubled the population of Yerba Buena, so (according to the historian, Bancroft) Yerba Buena became "for a time very largely a Mormon town." [13] Within a year they renamed the town "San Francisco," having it take on the name of the Bay. [14] The intent of the *Brooklyn* Saints had been to pool assets so that earnings of the next three years would go into a common fund which would be used to meet their living expenses as well as the need for capital.

Their imported supplies were limited and food was critical, so within a few weeks a group of about 12 families was sent out to establish an agricultural community. A suitable site was found in California's Central Valley, on the banks of the Stanislaus, about a mile above its confluence with the San Joaquin River. They called the new settlement New Hope. Hopefully this farming settlement would provide food for themselves and the main body of the Saints coming overland. [15] Separate from this group, John Horner explored possible farming sites in the East San Francisco Bay region and did test plantings. His most successful plantings were near Mission San Jose at the south end of the East Bay. [16]

Most of the *Brooklyn* Saints remained in San Francisco or at other Bay and Peninsula locations. In San Francisco, they established a school, began publishing the *California Star* (California's second and San Francisco's first English language newspaper), and started a number of businesses. They were a significant element in the community life of the Bay area in the pre-gold rush days of 1846-47.

Brannan also entered into business on his own, evidently using Mormon community capital and the tithing funds of the *Brooklyn* Saints, and later of some of the Mormon Battalion men, as the source of his personal capital. He purchased a river boat and established a store at Sutter's Fort in partnership with Charles C. Smith, a reputed Mormon immigrant who had been baptized in Nauvoo and apparently reached San Francisco aboard the ship *Toulin* in January of 1847. [17]

In the spring of 1847, much impressed by the favorable climate, terrain, and economic prospects of Northern California, Brannan headed east with three companions, Charles C. Smith and two others to guide the overland Saints on to California. [18] Brigham Young, having not yet reached the Salt Lake Valley, received Brannan none too cordially. He had little confidence in the young, brash 28 year old leader. Brannan had already exhibited some spiritual instability and had been disciplined earlier by a Church court for misconduct. In addition, serious charges of malfeasance had recently been registered against him by some of his co-religionists.

More importantly, the Prophet wanted a place desired by no one else, a place where Zion could be created in peace and isolation—hundreds of miles from its enemies. As Brannan described California to him, Young felt that California might not supply that kind of an environment. There the Saints would be in a minority. For their new Zion, the Salt Lake Valley seemed more attractive. In the comparative wastelands of the Great Basin they could be alone, essentially unhampered by their former foes. [19]

While disappointed, Brannan remained with the pioneers until after their arrival in Salt Lake Valley on July 24, 1847, hoping to change the Prophet's mind once he saw the desert country for which he was headed. Finally becoming discouraged by Young's intransigence, Brannan left for California as the pilot for a small Mormon party sent by Brigham Young. This party was led by Captain James Brown who, with other members of his party, had been among those detached from the main body of the Mormon Battalion before the Battalion had completed its trek to California. Those detached from the Battalion rejoined the overland exodus of the Saints and followed Brigham Young's vanguard pioneers into the Valley, arriving a few days later. Brigham Young directed Brown's party to report to the Army at Monterey and collect the back pay of those detached. In the Brown-Brannan party was its chronicler, Abner Blackburn. [20] Before reaching the Sierra Nevada, Brown and Brannan (fighting over leadership) broke up the party, Brannan proceeding on ahead of Brown.

Thomas Rhoades (Rhoads) (1794-1869)

Thomas Rhoades (Rhoads) was born in Muhlenberg, Kentucky about 1794. He married Elizabeth Forster. He served on the western frontier during the War of 1812. Rhoades lived for a time in Illinois, worked as a surveyor, joined the Mormon Church in 1834, and moved to the Crooked River area of Missouri. When the Mormons were driven out of Missouri, he surprisingly remained, perhaps not letting others know he was a Mormon. *Courtesy Bernie L. Rhoades.*

Upon his return, Brannan sowed seeds of discontent among his flock by being critical of Brigham Young's decision to remain in the valley of the Great Salt Lake. Brannan's disinterest, a flood and heavy mosquito infestation at New Hope, and the news that the overland exodus would stop at Salt Lake led to the disintegration of the New Hope colony during the winter of 1847-1848. By the time of the public announcement of gold in the spring of 1848, most if not all of the Saints had left the New Hope settlement. In addition, Brannan's brand of leadership spread dissension among the other Saints in California, especially among the Battalion men who questioned his authority over them.

Ed Fraughton's sculptured representation of the Mormon Battalion soldier. His twelve-foot monument, nick named "Charlie," was donated to the city of San Diego, California and is on display in Presidio Park on the bluff overlooking San Diego Bay. A replica is also on display at the Mormon Battalion Visitors Center in San Diego. The above photograph was taken with infra-red photography, giving the image an etherial quality. [The image is available only as a 366 × 480 pixel, 54-KB file and is reproduced here courtesy Ed Fraughton through Wikimedia.]

Thomas Rhoades and Family

The third group of Mormons and Mormon associates arriving in California before the gold rush consisted of the family and friends of Thomas Rhoades.[21] Rhoades, a native of Kentucky, born in 1795, had moved to Illinois in 1820 and was living in Edgar County when Mormon missionaries contacted him. He joined the Church in 1834 and shortly moved to the Crooked River country of Western Missouri. He was ordained an Elder in 1837. While apparently remaining a devout member of the Mormon Church, he and his family inexplicably remained in Missouri after the body of the Saints had been driven into Illinois in 1839. He was a landholder and owned a number of slaves.

In 1846, upon learning of the expulsion of the Saints from Nauvoo and possibly under the orders of Brigham Young, Rhoades gathered most of his family and some friends together for a move to Upper California, planning to join the Saints who, it was understood, would head west to some ill-defined location in California that season. He left behind his oldest son to manage his lands and slaves.

Crossing the Missouri River at St. Joseph the first part of May in 1846, he proceeded northwesterly across the Indian Territory of Kansas to Fort Laramie, where he apparently learned of the decision of Brigham Young not to continue further west that year. Rhoades, however, decided to continue on to California.

His exact route as he approached the Rocky Mountains is unknown, there being contradictory evidence. [22] Whichever route Rhoades took, he passed through Emigrant Gap in the Sierra Nevada and over what became known as Donner Pass about October 5, 1846. He settled down in the country east of New Helvetia (Sutter's Fort) in the vicinity of Dry Creek and the Cosumnes River. His older daughters soon married prominent non-Mormon pioneers in the area.

Several men of the family were involved in the liberation of California from Mexican control. Two, John and Daniel, distinguished themselves in the late winter of 1846-47 in the attempts to rescue the Donner Party, which was trapped in the deep snows of the eastern slopes of the mountains.

The following year, 1847, Rhoades lost his wife. In 1848, he and his family moved to the middle of the gold fields, maintaining a major claim on the border of western El Dorado and eastern Sacramento Counties. Family folklore maintains that Rhoades, with other close associates, actually discovered gold in 1847. While there is no documentation of this tale, a nagging question keeps raising its head. How could Rhoades have lived along the gold-laden rivers for over a year without seeing the gold that became so readily apparent in 1848? Of course, the same questions could be asked about the others living in the area.

How many of the Rhoades family group were Mormons is not known, the Church records of the period being very sketchy, but there is evidence that more than Thomas were numbered among the Saints. John, the oldest of the California sons, was considered a Mormon well into the 1850s. Some of the children were associated with their father and the Church after he moved to Utah in 1849.

Other overland immigrants of 1846 were the Wimmers. Peter Wimmer entered California in early October, 1846, with 14 families, about the time of the Harlan-Young party and the Rhoades family. Peter was married to Elizabeth Jane Cloud Bais, having married her in 1843 after the death of his first wife, Polly Harlan (daughter of George W. Harlan, a leader of the Harlan-Young party). Some of the Wimmer family, several of whom were Mormons, were on location for the discovery of the gold. [23]

Another overland group of 1846 consisted of the children of a Mormon widow, Mrs. Lavinia Murphy, who had been engaged by the Donner-Reed party as a washer woman to pay the way of her family across the country. She was supposedly in hopes of eventually joining up with the Saints. While Mrs. Murphy and some of the children died with many of the Donner-Reed company, several survived and were in California for the discovery of gold. One of these was Mary after whom Marysville traditionally was named. There is no known subsequent relationship of this group to the Mormon Church.

The Mormon Battalion

The fourth and largest of the groups coming to California was the Mormon Battalion. [24] On June 26, 1846, Captain James Allen (representing Colonel S. W. Kearny, U. S. Army, at Fort Leavenworth, Kansas) arrived at the Mormon's Mount Pisgah Camp in Iowa to raise several companies of men to serve for a period of one year. With strong encouragement from Brigham Young, a total of 499 men were recruited from the camps of the Mormon exodus scattered from Nauvoo to Council Bluffs. The army allowed for laundresses and other camp associates, so thirty-one of the men's wives (with a total of forty-four children in tow) decided to accompany the Battalion. Nine other boys joined the group and served as aides. Captain Allen led the group to Ft. Leavenworth, where one more enlisted, bringing the group to 500 men. Kearny's Army of the West was given the mission to take control of California. By the time the Battalion arrived, Kearny's dragoons had already left the Fort. The Mormon Battalion was assigned the task of opening a wagon road across the Southwest to allow winter travel and supply shipments to the coast. [25]

While the "Battalion Boys" were never required to shed human blood, they were not without their problems. Inexperienced and undisciplined to army life, and being a religious as well as a military group, they struggled with authority conflicts. [26] They also struggled against the "old school" heroic medicine, which at first was forced upon them. [27] Most of all they struggled with the enormous challenges of establishing the trail. The route had to be passable by wagons and at any one point not more than two encampments to the next water source. They left Fort Leavenworth on August 12, 1846, marched southwest to the Arkansas River and Fort Mann, arriving there September 16th. Between that point and southern New Mexico, approximately 165 men and women were detached for illness and other reasons, and were sent to Pueblo on the eastern slopes of the Rockies in present-day Colorado to await the anticipated westward movement of the body of the Saints. [28] Thus, by mid-November the Battalion had been reduced to the 335 men and four women who would make the 700-mile march across what constitutes the southern borders of present-day New Mexico, Arizona and California. [29]

Just five months after the ship *Brooklyn* landed at Yerba Buena, the reduced Battalion staggered out of the Imperial Desert, and on January 29, 1847 reached the Mexican village of San Diego on the Pacific shore. They had marched some 2,000 miles and had mapped out their wagon road.

Their regular army commanding officer, Lieutenant Colonel P. St. George Cooke, announced to the troops upon their arrival:

> History may be searched in vain for an equal march of infantry . . . . With crowbar and pick and axe in hand, we have worked our way over mountains . . . . Thus, marching half naked and half fed, and living upon wild animals, we have discovered and made a road of great value to our country. [30]

The experience with "crowbar and pick and axe" would stand many of them in good stead when they moved into what would become the gold mining country of central and northern California.

The men served several months more (to complete their enlistment) doing garrison duty in the Southern California area, and 317 were mustered out in July 1847. Seven men of the main body had died either on the March or while on garrison duty. Seventy-nine men, uncertain as to the plans of the main body of Saints (the vanguard of which was then in its final approach to the Great Salt Lake Valley) re-enlisted for an additional six months of duty in California [31] and are referred to as the Mormon Volunteers.

The 223 men who mustered out in July were anxious to join their families (then somewhere on the plains) and made preparations to travel north. The military structure had dissolved, but the men were still under their spiritual, Church leadership, with Levi Hancock as their leader. The over-all group was put under the operational direction of Andrew Lytle and James Pace. The group was divided into two groups called hundreds and in turn into four groups called fifties. One of the fifties was led by Jefferson Hunt. The group under the leadership of Hunt took the Camino Real route north through the Spanish missions of Santa Barbara, San Jose and others near the coast. The rest of the men, under Levi Hancock and then Lytle and Pace, took an inland route north along the "mother lode" foothills of the Sierra.

Joining up near Sutter's Fort or New Helvetia (present-day Sacramento), most of the men head-

Painting of the Mormon Battalion at the Gila River in Arizona by George M. Ottinger. The Battalion encamped there December 21, 1846, just a few days before crossing the Colorado River into Southern California 9-10 January 1847. They reached San Diego 29 January 1847. *Courtesy Utah State Historical Society.*

ed east, leaving just a few in the Northern California area. About a hundred men of those who had headed east over the mountains soon returned to rejoin the few left behind. They had been turned back by Sam Brannan and Captain James Brown, a leader of the Battalion detachees. Thus, 140 or so of the men were at work in California during the winter of 1847-48. The others who had gone East to meet their families, after the discovery of gold, returned as well, as will be seen later in this and subsequent chapters.

On March 14, 1848, the extended re-enlistment of the Mormon Volunteers serving in the southland ended. (Two of them had died during their re-enlistment.) After Jefferson Hunt (having gone north and then east) reached the Salt Lake Valley, he was sent with Orrin Porter Rockwell back to California to obtain supplies for the new Salt Lake community. They went by way of the Old Spanish Trail and Cajon Pass. Hunt and Rockwell returned to the Valley over the trail they had come, but at different times, Hunt in February 1848 and Rockwell in April 1848, both after

the Coloma discovery. About half of the released Mormon Volunteers went to the Salt Lake Valley with Rockwell. The other half of the Volunteers went north to the gold fields. [32]

Hunt, Rockwell, and Others

The final group arriving in California before the gold discovery consisted of a number of men (some already mentioned), for example, those sent to California from Salt Lake Valley in the winter of 1847-48 to secure supplies, the group associated with Captain Jefferson Hunt and Orrin Porter Rockwell. [33] Their story will be told in detail later. In addition, there were probably a few discouraged stragglers who left the Salt Lake Valley for California in the late summer and early fall of 1847. Also, a number of old-time Saints, moving independently of the Utah migration, reached California by the time of the gold discovery. [34]

A picture begins to emerge of the numbers of Mormons in California at the time gold was discovered in January of 1848. There were approximately 240 Mormon Battalion men and camp associates, 230 *Brooklyn* Saints, and several dozen Mormon overland immigrants located between the Pacific and the foothills of the Sierra Nevada—probably more than 500 in all. Most of the Battalion men were working in and around Sutter's Fort and into the foothills, as were most of the overland immigrants. A group of 40 or so of the re-enlisted Battalion Boys were mostly in the southern settlements serving as the Mormon Volunteers until March. The *Brooklyn* Saints were largely congregated in the Mission San Jose-Santa Cruz-San Francisco area. Those who had come from the Salt Lake Valley to secure supplies were less fixed in their locations. All of these groups would one way or another be involved in the golden events that would engulf the embryo state. To those who were generally believers in divine providence, their experience and the ensuing events seemed divinely ordained.

The Opportunity and the Irony

Whether by accident or providential design, these groups of Latter-day Saints were in strategic positions to participate in, and potentially profit from a major world gold rush.

The irony is that the Mormons had a negative policy towards precious metal mining. According to the Mormon economic historian, Leonard Arrington, in his *Great Basin Kingdom*, that negative policy was

> . . . hammered out in the 1850s and 1860s . . . based on the proposition that the building of the kingdom required the orderly balanced development of local resources by a unified people for the support of a permanent society. Mining and the 'gold fever' were not allowed to dominate the thought and activities of the Latter-day Saints. The disintegrating moral influence and social losses of the 'gold fever' were . . . important considerations . . . [as] was the fact that a permanent society could not be built upon mining. . . .

Finally, there was the purely economic consideration of whether mining

would pay . . . [which] it would not. [35]

But these were considerations that largely came after the fact—after Mormons had been both extensively and intensively involved in the gold fields of California.

At the time of the discovery of gold in 1848, there was no Mormon policy on mining because there had been little, if any, contact by the Church leadership and the body of the Church membership with that activity. While there were miners who were converted to the Church, upon gathering with the Saints to Zion they generally left that activity behind. There were, however, several influences antecedent to the gold discovery that would affect the eventual development of an ambivalent Mormon policy on mining.

First, in the Book of Mormon, sacred scripture to Mormons, time after time the ancient people of America had been blessed with riches—silver and gold—as the result of righteous living. However, this blessing frequently became a curse. One illustrative scripture reads:

> . . . many of you have begun to search for gold, and for silver, and for all manner of precious ores, in the which this land, which is a land of promise unto you and to your seed, doth abound most plentifully.
>
> And the hand of providence hath smiled upon you and most pleasingly, that you have obtained many riches; and because some of you have obtained more abundantly than that of your brethren ye are lifted up in the pride of your hearts, and wear stiff necks and high heads because of the costliness of your apparel, and persecute your brethren because you suppose that ye are better than they. [36]

The second influence came from events that took place in the 1820s when, as a young man, the Mormon prophet Joseph Smith was involved in looking for buried treasure—silver and gold. [7] This involvement was used by anti-Mormon writers to attack the credibility of the Mormon prophet and his claim to finding a gold record from which the Book of Mormon was translated. Some Mormons might condemn the search for gold and silver to avoid further such characterization.

These two influences were not sufficient to establish any formal doctrine or policy. That awaited a more direct kind of relationship with mining. Such an involvement took place primarily in connection with the California Gold Rush beginning in 1848 and carrying through to 1857 when many of the more faithful Mormons were gathered home from their far-flung colonies in present-day California, Nevada, Idaho and Wyoming upon the threat of an invasion of Utah by the U. S. Army.

NOTES

1. Carter, *Our Pioneer Heritage*, 7:597. Also Taylor, "The Upper California," 20:280.

2. Brigham Young to Sam Brannan, Letter, September 15, 1845, Smith, *History of the Church*, 7:444-45.

3. Brigham Young to Wilford Woodruff, Letter, Oct. 16, 1845, Brigham Young Letter Collection.

4. Stegner, *Gathering of Zion*, 7.

5. Details on the life of William B. Ide can be found in the following: Simeon Ide, *Life of William B. Ide.*; Willam B. Ide, *Who Conquered California?*; Rogers, *William B. Ide, Bear Flagger*; Walker, *Bear Flag Rising*; Warner, *Men of the Bear Flag Revolt*; and Hughes, "William B. Ide, Pioneer." No photographs or images of Ide are known to exist. His daughter believed that no photographs had been taken, but that he resembled his brother Simeon, only larger (Rogers, *Bear Flagger*, 89.) His brother Simeon is shown in Rogers, *Bear Flagger*, after 84.)

6. The *Nauvoo (Illinois) Neighbor* of May 22, 1844 notes that Ide was a delegate from Sagamon County, Illinois. The same information is found in Smith, *History of the Church*, 6: 389.

7. *Times and Seasons*, Vol. 5, No. 8, April 15, 1844 gives the list of the Electioneer Missionaries sent out to campaign for Joseph Smith. William Ide is listed for Vermont

8. Rogers, *William B. Ide, Bear Flagger*, 65.

9. Robert D. Parmalee maintains that Ide was motivated to lead the Bear Flag Revolt in hopes of rewards from Mormon leaders for having provided them with a sanctuary in their flight from Illinois. These claims are doubtful. He also claims that Ide's oldest son, James Monroe Ide, was an active Mormon from 1836-1878, dying in St. George. He says that his daughter Sarah joined the Church in 1878 with her second husband. Following Allen Fifield's lead, he asserts that most of the Grigsby-Ide immigrant company of 1845 were Mormons, residing at Sonoma where the revolt began, though this assertion also has not been verified. See Robert D. Parmalee, *Pioneer Sonoma*, 1972.

10. The story of that voyage is told in Hansen, "The Voyage of the *Brooklyn*," 47-72, and in Bullock, *Ship Brooklyn Saints*.

11. Several shipped goods on the *Brooklyn* anticipating repossessing them when they reached California overland. Among these were John Van Cott, John Neff, and Levi E. Riter and others. (Carter, *Heart Throbs*, 1946, 402.)

12. The subsequent story of the *Brooklyn* Saints from the viewpoint of Sam Brannan is told in Scott, *Samuel Brannan*; and Bagley, *Scoundrel's Tale*. See also Glover, *The Mormons in California.*.

13. Bancroft, *History of California*, 5: 551.

14. The *California Star*, 23 January 1847.

15. McCready, "New Hope." MA thesis; and Nash and Nash, In a Goodly Land, 1-13.

16. Horner, "Adventures of a Pioneer"; "Looking Back"; and "Personal History of the Author."

17. Bagley, *Scoundrel's Tale*, 197.

18. Bagley discusses who these two other com-

panions might be. See Bagley, *Scoundrel's Tale*, 198, note 8. Matt Harbin and Daniel Hunsaker have been suggested as the companions, and then dismissed. Joseph B. Chiles has also been suggested as one of the men. Chiles indeed was going east that year, but by the time he left Sutter's Fort in early July (as a guide to Commodore Stockton), Brannan had already met Brigham Young in the Green River area. Besides, if Chiles' biographer is correct, Chiles went east by the Santa Fe Trail. See Griffen, *Trail-Blazing Pioneer*, 65-67.

19. See Durham, Disco*urses of Wilford Woodruff*, 322-23. Brigham Young told some of the Battalion later, October 1, 1848, that the thought of leaving the valley felt like having vinegar rubbed into his eyes. Quoted in Golder, *The March of the Mormon Battalion: From Council Bluffs to California* (New York: The Century Co., 1928) 246.

20. Blackburn became associated two years later with gold discoveries in Nevada. He also became a California gold miner and, subsequently, a renegade member of the Mormon colony at San Bernardino. See Chapter 19. An account of his experiences can be found in Bagley, *Frontiersman*.

21. This synopsis largely comes from the self-published paper of the author, Davies, "Thomas Rhoads, The Wealthiest Mormon Gold Miner." (1980). See also by the same author, "Thomas Rhoads, Forgotten Mormon Pioneer," 81-95. Bancroft's *Pioneer Register* was used. Norma Ricketts has self-published work on the Rhoades family in California. In addition, Rhoades and Bowen have told a somewhat fanciful story of Thomas Rhoades in *A History of the Lost Rhoades Mines*, published by the authors in 1971.

This group is virtually unknown, though oblique references to them have been found. The early Mormon historians, Whitney and Roberts, completely neglected it. Even contemporary Mormon historians seem not much more aware of them. So shrouded in mystery are these people that their complete role in California is still uncertain. However, a significant role was played and, therefore, becomes a part of this history.

22. There were three possibilities: the first was the Sublette Cutoff which crossed present-day Wyoming north of Fort Bridger; the second took off northwesterly from Fort Bridger, joined the Sublette Cutoff, and then proceeded to Fort Hall in present-day Idaho and then west and south along the Humboldt or Marys River to the Truckee; the third possibility was the Hastings Cutoff that went almost due west from Fort Bridger down Echo Canyon to the Weber River in present-day Utah. At that point, two possibilities opened up -- one went over the Big Mountain and down Emigration Canyon into Salt Lake Valley. This was to be the route taken by the ill-fated Donner Party a few weeks later. The other possibility was down the tortuous Weber River into the valley of the Great Salt Lake. This was the route taken by the Harlan-Young parties, as well as several others that year. Near the Salt Lake, the two latter routes joined and went south of the Lake, across the Salt Flats and present-day Nevada, to the Truckee River and the Sierra Nevada in the vicinity of present-day Reno. It was known as the Hastings Cutoff. A safer route, the Salt Lake Cutoff, opened a year later. It went north from the Salt Lake Valley in the direction of Fort Hall, then cut west north of the lake, joining the Fort Hall route in the vicinity of the City of Rocks.

23. The Wimmer story is complicated by overlapping names. Peter L. was the son of Peter and Elizabeth Shirley Wimmer. The elder Peter had a son John and a son Jacob as well as Robert and several daughters. The mother joined the Mormon Church in 1832 and John joined in 1843. Two of the sisters joined the Church before 1846. Robert joined in 1847 and the father at least by 1858. One of these, Jemima Wimmer Powell, is credited by the family folklore of the Utah Rhoades with having discovered gold in 1847 while working for Thomas Rhoades' wife.

In many of the accounts of the discovery of gold at Coloma, a Peter Wimmer and his wife Elizabeth are included. However, Peter L.'s mother's name was also Elizabeth. Also referred to is a John Wimmer. Peter Jr. had both a brother and a son by the name John. It is not always certain as to which John, Peter and Elizabeth the various accounts refer.

24. The synopsis of the Battalion activities comes from the following sources: Roberts, Mormon

Battalion; Tyler, *Mormon Battalion in the Mexican War* ; Yurtinus, "A Ram in the Thicket"; Ricketts, *Mormon Battalion* (Ricketts emphasizes the story in context, extends the story beyond mustering out, and keeps an inventory of the individuals); Day, *March of the Mormon Battalion* ; Fleek, *Military History of the Mormon Battalion* (Fleek tells the story from the eyes of a military historian and ends the story when the Battalion ends, at the mustering out); Bigler and Bagley, *Army of Israel* (Bigler and Bagley relate the history from the basic documents.)

25. The more popular view is that the U.S. Army made the initial approach on the formation of the Battalion. Yurtinus, "Ram in the Thicket," shows that the Mormons made the first approach in Washington, D.C.

26. Campbell, "Authority Conflicts."

27. Divett, *Medicine and the Mormons*, 101-05.

28. As many as 50 percent of these Battalion detachees would become involved in the gold fields over the next few years. The use of the term "boys" is not descriptive of their ages, some of them being in their 50s. However, it is a term they frequently used to describe themselves and it will thus be used throughout this volume.

29. For the numbers and names associated with the various groups and subgroups of the Battalion, we will follow the rosters assembled by Ricketts. See her *Mormon Battalion*, 278-300.

30. Ricketts, *Mormon Battalio*n, 304; Bigler and Bagley, *Army of Israel*, 171.

31. Later extended for another three months. The story of the re-enlistment service of the Battalion members in San Diego is told in "The Mormon Volunteers: The Recruitment and Service of a Unique Military Company" by Yurtinus, "The Mormon Volunteers."

32. Somewhat related to the Mormon Battalion were the New York Volunteers. While a Mormon emissary was in Washington negotiating for the formation of the Battalion, Col. Jonathan D. Stevenson was authorized to recruit a regiment of volunteers from the State of New York to be sent to California for the war with Mexico. While the Mormon Battalion was being enlisted in Iowa in early July, Stevenson was enlisting men in New York—a total of 767 officers and men, possibly three of them Mormons or men who later became members of the Church—Andrew or Alexander J. Cox, a printer and member of Company C who founded the Sonoma Bulletin in 1852, Silas G. Higgins of Company C, and William H. Folsom of Company H. While a W. H. Folsom is listed as in the New York Volunteers, the William H. Folsom of this story may not have arrived in California until 1850. The first edition of Mormon Gold also lists Daniel P. Clark of Company B. (He is listed in *Bancroft's Pioneer Register*. However, there is also a Daniel P. Clark who came west with Amasa Lyman. These two identities have not been sorted out as of the publication of this edition.) The Volunteers embarked on several ships on September 25 and sailed for California. Rounding Cape Horn, they anchored off Clark's Point at Yerba Buena on March 5, 1847. They were officially mustered out of the service in August of 1848, though desertions to the gold fields had already decimated their ranks. Lynch and Clark, *New York Volunteers*.

33. See Chapter 4. The story of the Southern Route is reviewed definitively in Lyman, *The Overland Journey*. The story, particularly of those on that trail going to the gold fields in 1849, is told using the journals of some of those travelers in Hafen and Hafen, *Journal of Forty-Niners*.

34. This included Ziba Peterson (mentioned in the Mormons' Doctrine & Covenants) and his family along with Jesse and Joshua Hitchcock as well as John Killion. Peterson's story is told in Garrett, "Ziba Peterson: Missionary to Hanging Sheriff," 28.

35. Arrington, *Great Basin Kingdom*, 241-42.

36. *Book of Mormon*. Jacob 2:12-13.

37. Roberts, *Comprehensive History,* 1:82.

The Moment of Gold Discovery at Coloma depicted by William Henry Jackson.

Jackson (1843-1942) was a self-taught artist, first honing his painting skills in his youth as a photographer's touch-up artist. After achieving world recognition as a photographer, he returned to the paintbrush in his eighties. With a native talent and a photographer's eye, he recreated some of the memorable scenes in the history of the American West. Original in color. *Courtesy Scotts Bluff National Monument.*

And now behold my brethren . . .
many of you have begun to search for gold . . .
in the which this land, which is a land of promise
. . . doth abound most plentifully.
  Book of Mormon, Jacob 2:12

2

Gold at Coloma

THE FIRST OFFICIALLY recognized discovery of gold in Northern California [1] took place on January 24, 1848, at Coloma, the site of the construction of a lumber mill for John Sutter. [2] Working for James W. Marshall, the foreman, and present on that day were nine white men and one woman. Of the ten, at least six were Mormons, veterans of the Mormon Battalion march; one more of the men may have been a Mormon. Positively identified as part of the Mormon group were Henry W. Bigler, James Stephens Brown, William James Johnston, Alexander Stephens and Azariah Smith. A sixth man, known by the name of Barger and identified as a member of the Mormon Battalion, was also employed at the mill site. In addition to these were three more white men, Charles Bennett, William Scott and Peter L. Wimmer, Wimmer's wife, Elizabeth Jane, and a number of Indians. [3]

Azariah Smith's account of January 30, 1848, reads: "This week Mr. Marshall found some precious (as we all suppose) Gold, and he has gone to the Fort, for the purpose of finding out. It is found in the raceway in small pieces; some have been found that would weigh five dollars." [4]

Bigler's account of the gold discovery was more specific and was recorded at the time: "Monday 24th this day some kind of mettle was found in the tail race that looks like gold first discovered by James Martial [Marshall], the Boss of the Mill." [5]

Within a week of the discovery, Marshall took some of the ore to his employer, Sutter, and the two tested it, assuring themselves that it was indeed gold. William Johnston may have been a traveling companion of Marshall on this trip.

Keeping the Discovery a Secret

In June of 1848, Thomas O. Larkin, U.S. Consul in California, having just returned from the gold fields, wrote to the Secretary of State, James Buchanan. He asserted that "the discovery was made by some Mormons in January or February who for a time kept it secret." [6]

This assertion was apparently the basis for the common rumors that the Mormons had discovered gold and attempted to monopolize the mining of it. However, Rodman Paul observes that "While at Coloma, Sutter urged secrecy upon his employees, asked them to finish the sawmill, and negotiated an agreement with the local Indians to lease the land." [7] Larkin's assertion of Mormon secrecy may actually have been in connection with subsequent gold discoveries down the river at or near what became known as Mormon Island.

Following the initial discovery, the Battalion Boys completed the Coloma Mill in fulfillment of their agreement with Sutter and Marshall. However, they spent their Sundays and "oddspells" prospecting and sharing their findings with Marshall—at least for a while.

Bigler's immediate post-discovery diary entry reported as follows:

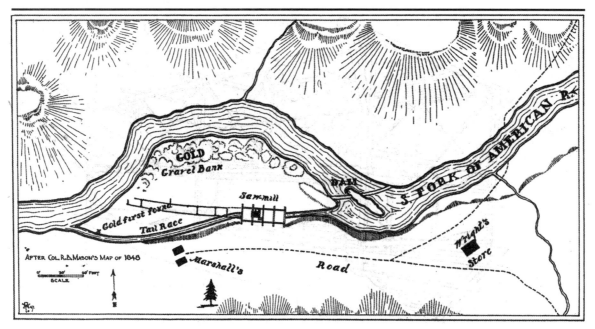

Map of the Coloma gold discovery site showing the locations of Marshall's sawmill, the tail race, and the spot where gold was discovered relative to the course of the South Fork of the American River. (From Robert F. Heitzer, "Archaeological Investigation of Sutter Sawmill Site in 1947", *California Historical Society Quarterly*, Vol. 26, No. 2 , June, 1947, 134-59) *Courtesy California Historical Society.*

Sutter's Sawmill at Coloma
From a watercolor sketch by Udo Schroeder.

The present structure, built a short distance from the actual discovery site, is a replica completed in 1968 based on existing drawings by Marshall, excavations of the original mill site, and an early photograph of the mill. This and other watercolor sketches by Udo Schroeder are available at the Marshall Gold Discovery State Historic Park, Coloma, California. *Courtesy of Udo Schroeder.*

Sunday (January) 30th "our metal has been tride and proves to be Goald. it is thought to be rich. We have pict up more than a hundred dollars woth last week." [8]

On the 6th of February, Bigler and Barger crossed the river to investigate an outcropping of rocks, taking with them nothing but their jack-knives, knowing nothing about washing gold, long or short toms, rockers or sluices. "Our only way" Bigler said, "was to pick it up grain by grain as we found it lying on the bare rocks . . . in the seams and creavices . . ." [9] By nightfall they had collected about ten dollars estimated by the use of wooden scales and a silver quarter which they figured was worth $4.00 in gold.

The following Saturday, February 12, Henry wrote:

> This afternoon I did not work be-ing tired & not verry well I took the gun & went a long down the Creek to hunt for ducks but in reality to look for gold. about a half mile down the Creek I discovered some Rock on the opposite side that indicated that gold was thare I soon took off my shirt & pants and crost over I soon pict up $1,50 cts worth bieing in the seems of the Rocks. but what is the worst of all it is on Capt Sutters and Mr Martials land for after the goald was found in the mill tail they leased a large scope of land of the Indians for 3 years and have sent to the Governor at Monteray to have it secured so I cannot have any claim on it. [10]

Having located more gold on Saturday the 12th, Bigler secretly returned to his mining on Sunday, the 13th, and again on the 20th, adding $24.00 in gold dust to his poke. This was at a time when wages were commonly $1.50 per day.

Azariah Smith's account of the weeks fol-lowing the initial discovery is corroborative. He reports that "odd spells and Sundays" were fre-quently spent prospecting and that gold was often found in the bottom of the mill race. However, his prospecting efforts were not limited to the imme-diate vicinity of the mill. He sometimes crossed the river to prospect down stream. His success in locating gold tempted him to spend full time in that activity, but at Marshall's request he post-poned leaving the mill for several days. [11]

On February 20, Bigler could contain himself no longer and wrote to his Battalion messmates (Jesse Martin, Israel Evans, and Ephraim Green, working on Sutter's gristmill at Natoma, five or six miles up the American River from Sutter's Fort), telling them about the gold but asking them "to keep it to themselves unless it would be some-one who could keep a secret. Mr. Marshall did not want it known until further development . . ." [12]

The Secret is Out

Sutter and Marshall wanted to keep the discov-ery a secret at least until the flouring mill could be completed, but their hopes were doomed. The news gradually became known. The talkative Mrs. Peter Wimmer, for one, "let the cat out of the bag," informing a teamster. He was made a gift of several dollars in gold which he had obtained at Coloma and used to pay for a bottle of brandy purchased from Charles C. Smith, the manager at Sam Brannan's store at the fort. Smith excitedly took the gold in to Sutter, who felt compelled to tell him the whole story. Smith then dutifully informed Brannan who came to the fort, leasing a larger building from Sutter to prepare for the gold rush he anticipated would follow. Brannan also opened branch stores at Coloma and at what would become known as Mormon Island. [13]

Bigler's claim to being the only one at Coloma afflicted with gold fever was overdrawn. Howev-er, some of the effects of the malady which would sweep California within a few weeks are elabo-rated by his account. He states that on February 22, making the excuse that he planned to hunt deer, he crossed the river intending to hunt for gold. His description of the day's activities belies the common belief of the ease with which the pre-cious metallic ore was found. He says:

> I felt very close in every crevice, and finally down near the waters edge, in the sand, I began to find it. Here I sat

James W. Marshall (1810-1885)

In 1845, Marshall went west to Oregon and then south to Sutter's Fort, where he worked as a carpenter. He served under John C. Fremont during the Mexican-American War. After the war, Sutter hired Marshall to locate a site and build a sawmill in the Sierra foothills. Some Mormons who had been in the Mormon Battalion were hired to assist him. It was in the tail race of this mill that he discovered gold. Like Sutter, Marshall was forced off his own land in the frenzy of the gold rush. He tried for a while to make a comeback with a vineyard at Coloma. Eventually he turned to gold mining in Kelsey, California. It was there Marshall died at age 74. *Courtesy Bancroft Library.* For a biography of Marshall, see Gay, *James W. Marshall: The Discoverer of California Gold, A Biography.*

all the balance of the day in one position, all hunched up, picking it out grain by grain, from the smallest particle up to a single nugget worth over five dollars. And laying it on the top of my cap with the point of my knife —when the first thing I knew, I could not see. It was dark and being so excited and without thinking, that when I arose to straighten myself, I yelled with pain. A person could have heard me quite a distance. I thought my back was broken. [14]

The news of gold spread slowly, often relayed by former members of the Mormon Battalion. James S. Brown, in his version of the spreading news, reveals that William Johnston, on "urgent" business, left Coloma for Natoma and the Mormon camps situated along the long millrace leading to the mill. "Then somehow or other the bag came untied and our old cat and all the kittens ran out, and to the camps they went, until everybody heard of the gold discovery. But like all great truths, people were slow to believe the story." [15]

Johnston's first hand news corroborating Bigler's letter brought some inquisitive "Boys" up-

stream. On Sunday, February 27th, Sidney Willis, Wilford Hudson, and a Mr. (Levi) Fifield, came into the Coloma camp, having received the word from Martin, Green, and Evans. On the pretext of hunting deer and visiting the men at Coloma, they had left Natoma. They arrived at dusk and spent the evening with the Coloma hands and a loquacious Marshall sharing their tales of gold.

The next morning while breakfast was being prepared, having been granted permission to hunt gold in the millrace, the three guests began to feverishly examine its banks. Within a short while, Hudson "picked out of the bank of the race with his butcher knife a nugget that according to our way of testing was worth a little short of six dollars." [16]

On March 2, Bigler, Fifield, Willis and Hudson left for Natoma, the first two by road, the others by way of the South Fork of the American River. When they were reunited a few days later, Hudson reported that they had found only a "few particles at one place only . . . that there was not to exceed 50 cents worth in very fine particles, so trifling a prospect in their estimation, that they had no notion of examining it any further." [17] However, Ephraim Green and Ira Willis, the latter a brother

Fiftieth anniversary of the discovery of gold at Coloma. From the left, present at the discovery of gold, Henry W. Bigler, William J. Johnston, Azariah Smith, and James S. Brown. Photograph taken at the 1898 Golden Jubilee in San Francisco. *Courtesy The Society of California Pioneers.*

to Sidney, kept encouraging them to return. After several days of coaxing and cajoling, they did return, the decision leading to the development of Mormon Island. [18] Bigler returned to the sawmill and "went to work as usual," and on March 11th started the mill up. The Boys had fulfilled their contract, at least at Coloma. [19]

On March 28th, Azariah Smith records that he received a letter from his father who had arrived on the shores of the Great Salt Lake the previous October. He makes no indication of just how his letter arrived so early in the season. The mountain snows of the High Sierra would have been almost impassable. It is possible that it had come west with the Mormon company that had left Salt Lake in November of 1847 via the southern route with Jefferson Hunt as guide and then brought north from Williams' Ranch in the south by some courier.

Whatever the route, Smith's letter indicates communication between Salt Lake and the gold fields as early as March of 1848. Included in a letter at that time from Brigham Young were instructions for the Battalion to come to Deseret as soon as possible.

With their contractual obligations completed as of March 11, the Boys at Coloma were completely free to prospect at will, bound only by the fact that Sutter had the rights to much of the land roundabout and they were obliged to share their findings with him. At least they thought he had the rights. [20] This encouraged them to range out into virgin and hopefully, unfettered land. March and April were spent feverishly ferreting out the gold from its hiding places, Bigler reporting that he usually extracted from $7.00 to $45.00 a day. However by Sunday, April 23, their consciences and/or physical exhaustion caught up with them, Bigler self-righteously and unfairly reporting: "Like Christians we kept the Sabbath day while a lot of the Gentiles came into our camp to look for gold but found none." [21]

Years later, Bigler reflected back on those early fumbling, back-breaking efforts to find gold on some flat land about a mile below the Coloma mill. He said:

> While working in the mines we must have worked under great disadvantages. I wanted badly to get an Indian basket, but some way or other failed,

John A. Sutter (1803-1880)

Sutter was born in Baden, Germany. He was educated in Switzerland and later served in the Swiss Army. Because of bad debts, he left his wife and children and fled to New York. By a circuitous route, he finally reached Yerba Buena in 1839 and managed to obtain a large land grant at the confluence of the American and Sacramento Rivers. He built a fort there and tried to turn his large land holdings into a personal empire. Sutter's Fort was the immediate destination for much of the early overland travel to California. That is where immigrants could buy or exchange labor for supplies. Sutter's family joined him in California after a twelve year separation. Gold was discovered at his sawmill, but in the frenzy of the resulting gold rush and his crushing indebtedness Sutter lost his large holdings. He eventually moved with his family to the East and settled in Lititz, Pennsylvania. He died at age 77, still petitioning Congress for restitution for losses in California. *Courtesy Bancroft Library.*

For a full, definitive biography, see Albert L. Hurtado, *John Sutter: A Life.*

and if I remember right, we had but one tin pan and that was a small one. I used a wooden tray that we had to knead our dough in. Elic (Alexander) Stephens dug out a wooden dish that he used to wash in, and we carried our dirt in sacks on our backs from some small dry gulches for five or six hundred yards to the river and washed it out. [22]

The Mormon quasi-monopoly did not last long. Bigler reveals that by the first part of May, "Californians began to come in thick and fast." The new breed of prospectors had little reverence for Sutter's land claims and "commenced mining wherever they pleased." [23]

The new influx was probably induced by Brannan's publicity stunt. According to Bigler, Benjamin Hawkins, a Battalion Boy, claimed to have been in San Francisco when Brannan "took his hat off and swung it, shouting aloud in the streets that gold was found, etc. The inhabitants of the place seemed to be panic-struck and so excited and in such a hurry to be off, that some of the mechanics left their work, not taking time even to take off their aprons." [24]

It is likely that the prospecting trips of Mormon workers at Coloma, downstream along the South Fork of the American River, took them up the numerous streams feeding into the river from the north. These explorations could have taken them into Greenwood Valley and to the vicinity of Pilot Hill and Mameluke Hill, (near the future Georgetown) on the northern slopes of which was located what became known as Hudson and/or Mormon Gulch. Their explorations could have even led them as far north as the Middle Fork. This area was to become a major location of Mormon gold miners through 1850, there being as many as 200 men there that year. [25] [26]

Sutter's Fort was located about a mile south of the American River on a rise above a slough from the river. It is presently in Sacramento, east of the civic center. Above: Sketch by Lieutenant Joseph Warren Revere in 1846, looking approximately north. *Courtesy Bancroft Library.* Below: View of the back of the fort, looking approximately south and showing the slough. From *Gleason's Pictorial Drawing-Room Companion*, Aug. 30, 1851, p. 288. *Courtesy California State Library.*

NOTES

1. Gold in small quantities had been mined by Mexicans near Los Angeles for years, but it had not drawn significant enough attention to produce a gold rush. See Bunje, *Pre-Marshall Gold in California*, vol. 2.

2. While many sources have been consulted in connection with the story of this chapter, for the first edition the source most useful was Paul's *California Gold Discovery*. A more recent detailed account of the Mormon participation in the Coloma discovery is found in Owens, *Gold Rush Saints,* Chapter 3, 91-124.

3. A few others had gone to the site with Marshall but had left prior to the discovery. See Owens, *Gold Rush Saints*, Chapter 3 for more detail.

Bigler was born in 1815 in present-day West Virginia. Joining the Mormon Church in 1837, he moved to Missouri in 1838. He served several short-term missions and joined the Mormon Battalion in 1846, faithfully maintaining over the years a diary from which the official account of the initial discovery of gold is generally taken. He died in St. George, Utah, in 1900. See Gudde, *Bigler's Chronicle*; and Bigler's Day Book and Diary. Also see Bigler, Memoirs and Journals; Letters concerning the discovery of gold; Journal; Diary of a Mormon in California; and History of the Discovery of Gold in California, all at Bancroft Library.

James Stephens Brown (not to be confused with Captain James Brown, also of the Mormon Battalion) was born in 1828 in North Carolina and moved with his family to Illinois. He joined the Mormon Church in 1844. He later wrote an autobiography which gives his version of the gold discovery. It is not as well accepted as Bigler's account. He died in Salt Lake in 1902. See his *Giant of the Lord*.

William J. Johnston was born in Ohio in 1824. He joined the Mormon Church with his family about 1838. He passed away in New Mexico in 1912

Alexander Stephens, the uncle of James S.

Brown, was born in North Carolina in 1813. Stephens was baptized a Mormon in 1841 or 1842 and moved to Nauvoo, working on the Mormon temple under construction. His demise came in Huntsville, Utah, in 1894.

Azariah Smith was born in New York in 1828, joined the Church in Ohio in 1837 and moved with his family to Nauvoo, Illinois in 1840. Together with his father, he enlisted in the Battalion and kept a personal diary from which came his account of gold. It, too, has not been as accepted as Bigler's account. His death was subsequent to 1903. Azariah Smith's journal can be found in David Bigler, *Journal of Azariah Smith*.

There is a great deal of confusion over Barger. Marshall, Brown, and Bigler refer to him as James Barger. Daniel Tyler, who later compiled a list of Mormon Battalion members, called him William W. Barger. The National Archives records list him differently as William, William W. and William H. Mormon records list no William W. or James Barger but do list a William H. Barger as living in Nauvoo with his wife in 1845. A plat of Salt Lake City in the early 1850s lists a William H. Darger (not Barger) as a lot owner. (Plat of Salt Lake City, 1850, Brigham Young University Archives. Based upon Pratt-Sherwood Survey of 1847). This may or may not have been Barger. And the Church Archives has a letter written by a Mrs. William H. Barger in 1848 from the Mormon Winter Quarters. (Letter of Mrs. William H. Barger, LDS Church Archives).

Peter L. Wimmer was a close associate of the Mormons before going to California and had been hired on as a general helper, responsible for the immediate supervision of the Indians. His wife was the cook. Born in Cincinnati, Wimmer had moved from state to state—Indiana, Michigan, Illinois and Missouri. Most of his family were converts to Mormonism, though there is no known record of his baptism. Wimmer is variously spelled as Weimer and Wiemer. He had come to California in 1846 in connection with the Harlan-Young parties which had preceded by a few weeks the ill-fated Donner Party. These parties, taking the Hastings Cutoff from Fort Bridger through the Valley of the Great Salt Lake, had crossed the dangerous Salt Flats of Western Utah. He may have been associated with Thomas Rhoades on the trip west. He remained generally friendly to the Mormons at least until 1857.

4. David L. Bigler, *Journal of Azariah Smith.*

5. Henry W. Bigler, Diary (Word in brackets is the author's).

6. Paul, *California Gold Discovery*, 37.

7. *Ibid.*, 41.

8. *Ibid.*, 62.

9. Gudde, *Bigler's Chronicle*, 99.

10. Paul, *California Gold Discovery*, 62.

11. David L. Bigler, *Journal of Azariah Smith*; Gudde, *Bigler's Chronicle.*

12. Gudde, *Bigler's Chronicle*, 101.

13. Paul, *California Gold Discovery*, 130.

14. Gudde, *Bigler's Chronicle*, 102.

15. Paul, *California Gold Discovery*, 173. The person responsible for leaking the news of the discovery of gold may have been Sutter himself. See Hurtado, *John Sutter*, 219-221.

16. Gudde, *Bigler's Chronicle*, 104.

17. *Ibid.*

18. See Chapter 3. Another version adds "all hands came very near leaving off work to turn our attention to hunting gold." (Gudde, *Bigler's Chronicle*, footnote, page 103.)

19. *Ibid.*

20. Sutter and Marshall made attempts to obtain the rights, but Sutter was told he did not have the authority to make treaty agreements with the Indians. See Hurtado, *John Sutter*, 222-224.

21. Gudde, *Bigler's Chronicle*, 109.

22. *Ibid.*

23. *Ibid.*, 110.

24. *Ibid.*, 111.

25. Wilford Hudson, who also played a prominent role in the establishment of Mormon Island, may have also been involved in gold discoveries in the area of what would become Georgetown, north of Coloma. In a recent book, Donald Dale Jackson tells of a miner by the name of Hudson who in the spring of 1848 showed up in Coloma with a mule loaded with gold. When he left, a large group of men followed him to a gulch that was so rich that a teenage boy later removed 77 ounces in one day to be followed the next day by another 90 ounces. Jackson, *Gold Dust*, 140-41. It is doubtful that the load of gold came from Mormon Island which was downstream from Coloma. It is possible that this was Wilford Hudson and that the gulch referred to was Hudson or Mormon Gulch, located on the north slope of Mameluke Hill.

26. Of the Mormons, Bigler, Brown, Stephens, and Smith moved to the Great Salt Lake Valley in 1848. Bigler was sent back to California the following year as a gold missionary for several months and was then called as a proselyting missionary to the Sandwich (Hawaiian) Islands. Brown went from Utah through the gold fields to the South Pacific as a proselyting missionary in 1849. Johnston probably remained in California following the discovery, being located in Diamond Springs, just south of Hangtown (Placerville) in 1850. He later rejoined the body of the Church in Utah. All of these appear to have remained faithful Mormons. In 1898, Bigler, Brown, Smith, and Johnston, the only known survivors of the initial discovery, were present at the 50th anniversary celebration in California—four old-timers generally described as being spry and hale despite their ages. Paul, *California Gold Discovery.*

Miners Working at Mormon Island

Contemporary (1849) sketch by Hiram Dwight Pierce, 1810-1881. View is from across the river, looking south. *Courtesy California State Library.*

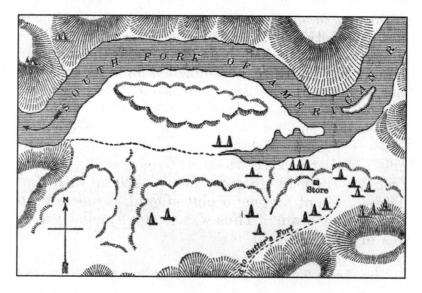

Map of Mormon Island showing that Mormon Island (actually, at lower river levels, a sand and gravel bar) was about twice as long as it was wide. The Island was reported to cover about one acre, that is, about 43,560 square feet. That means that the island was roughly 150 feet wide by 300 feet long. At lower river levels, the miners dug a ditch as an alternate pathway for the river (dashed line), separating the bar from the mainland. The town of Mormon Island developed south of the river and a little to the east. A trail to Sutter's fort and a store (the beginnings of a town) are shown at the lower right. [Image from Bancroft, *History of California* 6:48.]

And the gold of that land is good.
  Bible, Genesis 2:12

3

Mormon Island:
The First California Gold Rush

WHILE THE INITIAL GOLD discoveries were in the Upper Mines at Coloma and vicinity, it was not long until gold—apparently in very rich quantities—was discovered on a bar in the South Fork of the American River about midway between Coloma and Sutter's gristmill near Natoma. As reported in the previous chapter, about March 2, 1848 Sidney Willis and Wilford Hudson had detected gold at the site, but weren't overly impressed by the yield. A few days later they returned to retest and only then realized the richness of the find. They and their friends continued to mine the site. That bar and the general vicinity of the Lower Mines or Mormon Diggings became known as Mormon Island. Little excitement followed the initial Coloma discovery. Instead, it was to Mormon Island that the gold rush began. [1]

Bigler's Account

On April 8, 1848, Henry Bigler and Levi Fifield left Coloma and reached Natoma from a short trip to the Fort to find that several of their mates "were up river getting gold and had been for several days, but how they were making it, no one seemed to know" even though some of them had been down to the mill, reporting that "they thought the digging was going to be good." In retrospect, Bigler suspected that they had really been trying to play things down "until they knew that there was a chance for all." [2]

The following day [April 9] being Sunday, most of the Mormons came together to lay plans for going to Great Salt Lake. They decided that they would be ready to go the first of June, except for those men who were to accompany the *California Star* Express, organized by Brannan to take news of gold east, leaving April 15. [3] They also agreed to inform Sutter of their intentions so that he could arrange his affairs to settle accounts. (James or Daniel) Browett was commissioned to inform Sutter and to make arrangements for supplies desired as partial payment. Thus, this rich gold find was made just as they were preparing to leave California.

On April 10, Bigler, Brown and Stephens visited Sutter to settle up their individual accounts, but their employer, befuddled and frustrated by the impending events and short a bookkeeper, was unable to handle their request. The next day they headed for Coloma, intending to mine full time on shares with Marshall, who had agreed to grubstake them. Nightfall found them on a creek about 15 miles into the foothills from the flouring mill. Staying the night, they began prospecting the next morning using only their knives and two small basins used for drinking their coffee. Their take was about ten dollars.

They then struck out for the American Fork and followed it upstream a short distance where they found seven of the Boys [4] who that day had taken out $250 from the same spot as Willis and Hudson had made their original find in early March, the site that became known as Mormon Island. They were using what to Brown was an innovation, Indian baskets, with which they were washing out from $.25 to $2 a load. [5]

A View of Mormon Island (across the river looking south)

The island itself, the sand and gravel bar, is in the foreground and Mormon Island, the town, is over a low hill, back from the river. [The engraving is from *Gleason's Pictorial Drawing-Room Companion*, July 5, 1851, 148.]

As Bigler recalls, about that time one or both of the Willises went to Yerba Buena (San Francisco) on business, where they informed Brannan of their discovery. The leader erroneously assured them that he could secure title to the land for the Church. He advised all Battalion Boys to "go to work in the mine" and pay their tithing to him, which he would turn over to the Church. It was also agreed that Brannan would become a partner with Hudson and the Willises, sharing in their claim. [6] He evidently attempted to collect 30 percent from those working at Mormon Island—10 percent as regular tithing, 10 percent as his share for securing title, and 10 percent for a temple he maintained would be built in California

James S. Brown and Azariah Smith Accounts

James S. Brown claims that he worked one hundred days for Sutter, but "never received a farthing for it." However, he did not wish his readers to think Marshall and Sutter dishonorable. The fault lay in the fact that "people took advantage of them," undermining their business to the point of collapse. He said, "Every other enterprise [was] sacrificed in the rush for gold." California's gold rush was on, and the

Mormon Island, Sketch by William R. Hutton. *Courtesy Huntington Library.*

William R. Hutton, in his journal associated with the above sketch, *Glances at California, wrote:* "April 14, 1849, At Mormon Diggings all day. The South Fork has high, hilly banks on both sides & is a deep, rapid stream. The diggings are on a half island, low & covered with stones, & the gold is found several feet below the surface; it is all fine, scale gold."

Mormons were in the middle of it. "From 100 to 150 Mormons flocked to Mormon Island" to be followed by "people from every part of the United States." [7]

Brown traced the technological improvements in the prospecting for gold. From jack, butcher and table knives they progressed to pick and shovel, which they used to strip the soil from the bedrock. They then "conceived the idea of washing the sand and fine gravel in tin pans which, however, were very hard to get." Alexander Stephens then hollowed out a trough having a round bottom which they filled with the sand and gravel, running water over it to remove the soil. Finally, Stephens "commenced to rock the trough, which led to the idea of a rocker" causing the gold to settle to the bottom. An improvement was then made by placing the trough "on an incline so that the gold would work down . . . to the lower end." Brown was "under the impression that Stephens made the first rocker ever used in California. [8]

The last process identified was to "spread a sheet on the beach of the river, placing large stones on the corners and sides to keep it well stretched." The rich dirt was placed on the upper edge and water thrown over it leaving behind the gold scales which were periodically washed off into a tub. Using this method they averaged from $12 to $15 a day each, which was put into home-made buckskin pouches or wallets.

When Brown in 1893 wrote his account of the initial stages of the gold rush, wishing to have his story corroborated, he submitted it to the only survivors of the place and time within his reach—all Battalion Boys. He claimed that they all concurred in his story. [9]

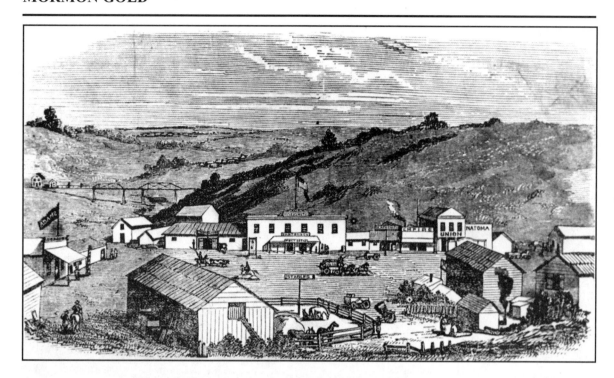

Engraving and Description of the Town of Mormon Island

"For two or three years past Mormon Island has occupied considerable prominence as a mining town. Many of its buildings are imposing in their appearance, and its trade of an active and somewhat extended nature. At this time it numbers perhaps a thousand souls,—has its excellent hotels, its numerous stage lines, express offices, banking houses, and trading posts. Its situation is on the south bank of the South Fork of the American River, in Sacramento County, two miles above the junction of the North and South Forks. It received its name from the community of Mormons which mined there in 1848. The surrounding country is broken and the diggings rich—to which water is conducted by the Natoma Company. Since the introduction of this water, last summer, this place has been improving rapidly. Negro Hill is on the opposite bank of the river, about a mile distant, and is approached by crossing Shaw's bridge, which is conspicuous on the left of the engraving."— *Steamer Union* (Sacramento) May 1, 1854. *Courtesy California State Library.* Shaw's Bridge (above the town and the sand bar) was built after a more crude bridge (below the sand bar) was washed away.

Not all "left off certainty" to mine. Some remained working at the Coloma mill or on the construction of the grist mill, hesitating to gamble on prospecting for gold. However, working for Sutter proved an even greater risk.

One of the Boys remaining with Sutter into April was Azariah Smith of the Battalion. He left Coloma April 11 to search for gold at Mormon Island and worked there with some success until April 23. He noted, "While there we have very good luck; I got there something near three hundred dollars. The most I made in a day, was sixty-five dollars after the toll was taken out, which was thirty dollars out of a hundred, which goes to Hudson and Willis, that discovered the mine, and Brann[a]n who is securing it for them. Before we came away, men, women and children, from the Bay, and other places in California, were flocking to see the gold mine, by the dozens, and by wagon loads." [10]

Like Brown, on April 23 Smith went to Natoma and down to the Fort to collect his back pay but failed to get anything. Nevertheless, he went to work "scraping the Grist mill head race." [11]

On April 30, Smith reported that he had made

Photograph of the Town of Mormon Island (looking eastward) *Courtesy Bancroft Library.*

Mormon Island was first settled by Mormon gold miners as a mining camp in February or March of 1848, shortly after the initial discovery at Coloma. Frequently, this "island," or sand bar on the South Fork of the American River, has been mentioned by gold era historians as the focus and the "spark" for the California gold rush, the discovery at Coloma remaining hidden longer. Apostle Amasa Lyman assumed active leadership of the Mormons mining at Mormon Island in 1849. However, by the time of the 1850 Census, few Mormons remained. This view is of the town long after Mormons were there in any numbers. The town was destroyed by fire in 1856 and was never rebuilt.

several more abortive attempts to obtain his pay, receiving "any amount of promises." Disgusted, he continued, "I think I shall quit scraping, and be looking for a fit out for HOME." [12] In the meantime, he went to work mining. In May he secured about $300.

Azariah was not the only one to quit. Years later Sutter wrote of this period: "So soon as the secret was out my laborers began to leave me, in small parties first, but then all left, from the clerk to the cook . . . only a few mechanics remained to finish some very necessary work . . . and about eight invalids, who continued slowly to work a few teams, to scrape out the mill race at Brighton. The Mormons did not like to leave my mill unfinished, but they got the gold fever like every-

body else. After they made their piles they left for the Great Salt Lake." However, he continued, "so long as these people have been employed by me they have behaved very well, and were industrious and faithful laborers and when settling their accounts there was not one of them who was not contented and satisfied." [13]

W. T. Sherman's Version of Events

William Tecumseh Sherman, later of Civil War fame, wrote in 1875 of his trip into the gold fields in June of 1848 with Colonel R. B. Mason. His version of the events appears to have become colored by the antagonism toward the Mormons which was in crescendo in the 1870s, although he himself had been quite friendly toward the

The gold separator, the rocker (also called a cradle), received its names from the fact that it had curved feet and could be rocked sideways using an upright handle. Gold bearing earth and gravel was placed in a top removable tray, which had an iron bottom with many small holes. When water was poured into the tray over its earth and gravel load and the machine rocked, the finer matter drained through the holes. The larger gravel and debris remained and could be discarded by removing and dumping the tray. Under the tray was a one or two stage incline with riffles or cleats. Lighter debris and water flowed over the riffles and out of the device. Gold particles, being heavy, tended to settle and get caught by the riffles. Periodically the riffles would be scraped. That final scraping could be cleaned to obtain whatever gold had been captured. [Lithograph from "How We Get Gold, From a Miner in the Year '49," *Harper's New Monthly Magazine*, vol. 20, Issue 119 (April 1860) 601.]

Mormons. He wrote that "some Mormons were employed by Captain Sutter at a grist mill he was building . . . six miles above his fort. All of these struck for higher wages, which he refused, and the two mills on which he had spent so much money were never built . . ." [14]

While Sherman claimed that neither the lumber nor grist mills were ever finished, the lumber mill was completed, producing the wood for most of the buildings constructed at Coloma. Therefore it may be assumed that Sherman was inaccurate in his reference to two uncompleted mills.

However, the Mormons do appear to have failed to complete the grist mill, though not without cause.

Newspaper Accounts

Through April, the Mormon Battalion Boys, a few *Brooklyn* Saints, and the family of Thomas Rhoades, along with the non-Mormon "old timers" of the area, had pretty free rein in the gold fields in and around Mormon Island. They had this free reign despite reports that had begun to circulate in the San

Francisco area as early as March 15 when the *Californian* published the following:

> GOLD MINE FOUND. — In the newly made raceway of the Saw Mill recently erected by Captain Sutter on the American Fork, gold has been found in considerable quantities. One person brought thirty dollars worth to New Helvetia, gathered there in a short time. California, no doubt, is rich in mineral wealth; great chances here for scientific capitalists. Gold has been found in almost every part of the country. [15]

Interestingly enough, this first account was not in Brannan's *California Star* but in its only major competitor, the *Californian*, California's first English newspaper. The fact that Brannan failed to break the news lends credence to the charges of a conspiracy by Mormons led by Brannan to contain the news of gold, though they by no means were the only conspirators.

Three days later, on March 18, Brannan's *California Star* was provoked into reporting the discovery of gold, obscured and confused by will-o-the-wisp rumors of coal needed for the steamship trade then opening up:

> THE MINERAL MANIA -- all not Coal that glitters -- The Philosopher's Stone never called into the field, and away from honest labor such a host of diligent bodies, as have the recent discoveries in the mineral kingdom, in California. Gold -- the veritable gold itself has been dragged forth, and now that it has been turned from the earth without sowing, we wouldn't be willing to risk a prediction where the excitement caused will cease. [16]

On April 1, The *California Star*, featuring a special edition published a more lengthy article on California's mineral wealth, which included some distortion of fact, if January 24, 1848 was the date of the first discovery of gold:

THE GREAT SACRAMENTO VAL-

James S. Brown
(1828-1902)

James S. Brown served in the Mormon Battalion and worked for Sutter at Coloma. He was present there when gold was discovered in 1848. He later was a missionary in the Society Islands (Tahiti) and in Great Britain. *Courtesy Pioneer Memorial Museum, International Society Daughters of Utah Pioneers.*

LEY -- It has a mine of gold and a probable estimate of its magnitude cannot be derived from any information we have received. It was discovered in December last, on the south branch of the American Fork, in a range of low hills forming the base of the Sierra Nevada, distant 30 miles from New Helvetia. It is found at a depth of three feet below the surface, and in a strata of soft sand rock. Explorations made southward, the distance of twelve miles, and to the north five miles, report the continuance of this strata, and the mineral equally abundant. The vein is from

Henry W. Bigler
1815 - 1900

Bigler served in the Mormon Battalion and was discharged with the others at Los Angeles. Most of the Battalion veterans went directly north to meet the Saints coming West. He and a few others were hired to help construct a saw mill for Sutter. It was Bigler's diary that provided the key documentation for the date of the gold discovery. Bigler served as a missionary to the Sandwich Islands, and later served again, the second time as the mission president. In his later years, he served in the LDS St. George Temple. He was known as a humble, unassuming man. *Courtesy Pioneer Memorial Museum, International Society Daughters of Utah Pioneers.*

For a biography, see Bishop, *Henry William Bigler: Soldier, Gold Miner, Missionary.*

twelve to eighteen feet thick in thickness. Most advantageously to this new mine, a stream of water flows in its immediate neighborhood, and the washing will be attended with comparative ease. [17]

This same issue published a note from an eastward bound private letter. This letter might well have been one written by Brannan and addressed to Brigham Young, who when he received it was on his return westward to Salt Lake from Winter Quarters with another company of Mormons. It might also have been written by S. G. Higgins, a Mormon member of the New York Volunteers then living in Sonoma. The letter-writer said:

> You will see plenty in the papers about mines. Already pickaxes, crucibles, and alembics are in requisition -- quite an active interest and excitement being felt among us on the subject. And without allowing any golden hopes to puzzle my prophetic vision of the precious metals, so soon as a sufficiency of miners, minerologists and metalogists find their way hither, and commence disemborging her rich treasures. Gold,

and quicksilver will be the principal products of this soil, several mines of each having already been discovered. [18]

Ricketts refers to this April 1 issue of the *Star* as a special edition, commissioned by the merchants of San Francisco. Brannan formed an overland mule train—the *California Star* Express—to carry copies of the special edition east. The Express consisted of ten men, at least six of whom were veterans of the Mormon Battalion. [19]

The April 1 issue of the *Star* was leisurely followed on April 19 by a brief item in the *Californian:*

> NEW GOLD MINE. -- It is stated that a new gold mine has been discovered on the American Fork of the Sacramento, supposed to be on the land of W. A. Leidesdorff, Esq., of this place; a specimen of the gold has been exhibited and is represented to be very pure. [20]

This mine was probably to the southwest of Mormon Island at or near what became Negro Bar and Folsom where Leidesdorff had a land

Francis A. Hammond
1822 - 1900

Hammond was a sailor on a Pacific whaler, but left that life at the Sandwich Islands because of an injury. He moved to San Francisco and became a shoemaker. In 1847 he became a convert to the Church. He was immediately caught up in the excitement of the gold discovery. Being more the business man than a miner, Hammond tried importing mercury to the gold region from the quicksilver mines in New Almaden, south of San Jose. However, he found business more profitable trading with the Natives. Later, he served twice as a missionary to the Sandwich Islands, served as a missionary again to Arizona, and finally to San Juan, (south east) Utah. He settled in Moab, Utah and helped colonize that region. *Courtesy Pioneer Memorial Museum, International Society Daughters of Utah Pioneers.*

grant. On April 22 the *Star* speaks of another gold mine, apparently upstream from Mormon Island:

> We have been informed, from unquestionable authority, that another still more extensive and valuable gold mine has been discovered towards the head of the American Fork, in the Sacramento Valley. We have seen several specimens taken from it to the amount of eight or ten ounces, of pure, virgin gold. [21]

This could have been at or near Salmon Falls, a few miles upstream from Mormon Island. On May 3, the *Californian* asserted:

GOLD MINES OF THE SACRAMENTO
> From a gentleman just from the gold region, we learn that many new discoveries have very recently been made, and it is fully ascertained that a large extent of country abounds with that precious mineral. Seven men, with picks and spades, gathered $16,000 worth in fifteen days. Many persons are settling upon the lands with the view of holding pre-emptions, but as yet every person takes the right to gather all they can, with out any regard to claims. The largest piece yet found is worth $6. [22]

And on May 6, after a visit to the mines to verify the stories of gold, the *Star*'s editor wrote:

> After a very pleasant, but brief sojourn in the Great Valley of the Sacramento, we have returned and resumed our labors, settled down in our chair again, physically refreshed and invigorated, and in mind abounding with reminiscences of all that we have seen and done while absent. Great country -- fine climate. Visit this Great Valley, we would advise all who have not yet done so. See it now. Full flowing streams, mighty timber, large crops, luxuriant clover, fragrant flowers, gold and silver. Great country this! [23]

According to Bancroft it was also at this

time that Brannan reportedly passed along San Francisco streets, swinging a vial of gold dust in hand and crying "Gold! Gold! Gold from the American River!" setting off the California gold rush. [24] However, the news of gold was already well on its way by that time, and Mormons and others had been mining gold for several months.

In San Francisco, after the *Californian's* first announcement of the gold discovery in late March followed by an announcement in the *California Star*, and after the *Star* Express edition and Brannan's stirring proclamation in April, the entire population of the city succumbed to a mania for gold. They began streaming out to the mines. By the end of May, there were so few readers left in the city, the *Californian* found it necessary to suspend publication. In their May 29 issue they printed: "To Our Readers: With this slip ceases for the present the publication of the *Californian* —"Othello's occupation's gone !" [25] (A Shakespearian line conveying: Farewell! It was great while it lasted.) The *California Star* suspended their publication June 14 for the same reason. [26]

Borrowman and Others at Mormon Island

The gold fever may have begun among members of the Mormon colony in San Francisco about April 8. John Borrowman, a Battalion veteran working there, records that on April 8 he received a letter from Henry Bigler. While he makes no mention of gold, the following day, Sunday, church meetings were dispensed with and Borrowman "spent the day visiting the Brethren." [27] If Bigler's letter contained news of gold, Borrowman cannot be accused of overreacting. On the succeeding days he worked at chopping, digging the foundation of an oven, and serving as a mason in building the oven. The following Sunday, the 16th, he wrote to Bigler and attended Church in the evening. The next week was spent working on the oven, making adobies and chopping wood. Not until May 13 did he finally leave for the gold fields.

Borrowman's diary appears to be the most detailed account of mining at Mormon Island in 1848. On his diary entry for Wednesday, May 10, 1848, appears apparently the first documentation of direct news of gold among the San Francisco Mormon colony, though some must have read or heard about it earlier from the *Star*. Heeding Samuel Brannan's counsel, Borrowman now wasted little time heading for the gold fields. However, before going, he attempted to collect $8.00 for four days of work for Origin Morey (Mowry) [28], a member of the *Brooklyn* Company who had become the owner of a river launch. Wages on land were then generally at $2.00 a day, but because the diarist had worked on a vessel or launch, the close-fisted captain figured he only owed him $1.00 a day as sailor's wages. He continued: "This evening Elder Brannan called a meeting & informed us of a gold mine being found by Brother Willis & gave his advice for all to go & work it." [29]

The following day, Borrowman made some purchases and in the evening an elders court, consisting of William Glover and either George W. or John J. Sirrine of the *Brooklyn*, heard the dispute between Borrowman and Mowry, deciding in the former's favor. Still not happy, Mowry probably paid in kind, transporting Borrowman on his launch to Sutter's Fort. Leaving on the 13th, they stopped at Marsh's Landing en route. Delayed by getting "out of course" and headwinds, they did not reach the Fort until the 16th.

Anxious to get at the gold, the passengers immediately hired a team to "take their luggage to the mountains where the gold mines is," themselves leaving the following day and reaching Mormon Island at sunset. There they found Brother Willis weighing the day's take, one man having acquired $128.00 that day.

Borrowman started mining with William Wood, of the Battalion, on May 18, digging $17 worth the first day. On the 19th, the two having mined $22 worth of gold, he was informed that Brannan & Co required 30 percent, leaving him only $8 for his share. On Sunday, the 21st, after shooting a quail, Borrowman attended a meeting of the miners "for the purpose of arranging our labor in the mines & it was agreed to form companies" of five men each, to work five square yards of land. He was placed in the company of James C. Sly of the Battalion.

The men generally worked Mondays through Saturdays, making from ten to fifty dollars a day.

Borrowman rested on Sundays, at least from mining. On the 30th, he spoke out "against paying rent [to Brannan] as [he] considered it an imposition." [30] Others, including William S. Clark [31] and the veteran Mormon missionary to the South Pacific, Addison Pratt (who was working in the mines to earn a poke for his projected trip to Salt Lake), also rebelled against Brannan's tax. Others no doubt also rebelled. Periodically Borrowman left off the backbreaking work of mining, going out to look for better diggings. He also began to purchase a few items for his homeward trip with his hard-won earnings.

On June 14, Borrowman engaged Francis Asbury Hammond to secure a fitout at San Francisco, weighing out $200 for that purpose. Hammond had reached San Francisco from Honolulu in 1847 aboard the "Currency Lass." Not a Mormon on his arrival in California, Hammond had been baptized on December 31 in San Francisco Bay. [32]

Hammond had not returned to Mormon Island by June 22, and Borrowman, impatient, went in search of a wagon. He found one that he liked, but was unable to find the owner to consummate purchase. On the 26th he went out to find a yoke of oxen but failed. He failed to record when or how he secured his fitout, but on July 19 reported that he spent the day fixing his wagon. Evidently Hammond had returned with the outfit but asked for what Borrowman considered extortionate pay for his services. Unable to resolve their differences, they called on Daniel Stark a member of the *Brooklyn* Company who had joined the Mormon Island gold miners to settle their dispute. According to Borrowman, Stark ruled in his favor but Hammond refused to accept the verdict. Borrowman's diary does not clearly indicate when the company left Mormon Island, but it must have been about the 20th of July.

Some others to reach Mormon Island in the spring of '48 from San Francisco were William and Jane Glover with three children, two girls, a boy (all from the *Brooklyn*), and a fourth child William Francisco Glover, born September 25, 1846 shortly after they landed in Yerba Buena.[33] William, Jane, and the three older children panned for gold. Jane would dig a hole in the sand to hold

William Francisco while the rest would take out the gold. They claimed to have taken out one and a half pecks of gold, which would be about twelve quarts. In the summer of 1849, they joined the "gold train" going back to the Saints in the Salt Lake Valley. [34]

Another Mormon who was possibly at Mormon Island was John Conrad Naegle (Naile) of the Mormon Battalion. His family claims that he was working in the millyard at Sutter's Mill when gold was discovered. Though this part of the story may be discounted, he allegedly mined about $3,000 in gold dust in about six weeks and planned to go to Salt Lake in 1848. If this account is reasonably accurate, he possibly mined at Mormon Island. [35] J. M. Horner of the *Brooklyn* was also involved at the Island in 1848. [36]

Across the river from Mormon Island was Negro Hill. Gudde and Gudde give Mormons the credit for making the initial discovery there, without naming the participants. It is likely that the following account by Henry Bigler deals with that particular discovery. Bigler revealed the exertions of Benjamin Hawkins, a Battalion man, upon learning of gold:

> When he and those who were with him arrived at the American fork a few miles below Mormon Island, they found a boat lying among some driftwood. They took it out and lashed it on a couple of horses and packed it a short distance up the river and crossed over the north side where they found a place that suited them. There they commenced work unobserved by anyone, for everybody was still farther up the river. At this time he said rockers began to be made, and one had been made above some-where and had escaped and floated down the river, and they saved it and in one day washed out between three and four thousand dollars. He told me there were five of them, namely himself, old man Haskel, and Fayette Shepherd. The other two, I disremember their names. [37]

Col. R. B. Mason Visits Mormon Island

In July of 1848, Col. R. B. Mason of the U.S. Army visited Mormon Island. In a letter written by him to the headquarters of the 10th Military Department at Monterey dated August 17, 1848, he noted that almost the entire male population of San Francisco had gone to the mines and he told of his trip to the gold fields, including Mormon Island, in the early summer of 1848. His company reached Sacramento on July 2 and he remained there to celebrate the 4th. He then visited "the lower mines, or Mormon diggings" where he found "about two hundred men . . . at work in the full glare of the sun, washing for gold, some with tin pans, some with close-woven Indian baskets, but the greater part had a crude machine known as the cradle." [38]

Mason then moved up the South Fork of the American River to Coloma, thence to Weber Creek and the incipient Weberville where Weber's store was located. He returned to the Lower Mines and then Sutter's Fort, reporting that the area was filling up with thousands of miners, scattered along the streams, taking out thousands of dollars worth of gold. [39]

Mason included with his letter gold specimens contributed by about 15 individuals. Among these were five men located at Mormon Diggings or Mormon Island, at least two and possibly three of whom were Mormons. [40] The colonel maintained that nearly all the Mormons were leaving for Salt Lake and "this they surely would not do unless they were sure of finding gold there in the same abundance as they now do on the Sacramento." This, of course, was pure speculation on his part. As many as one-third to one-half of the Mormons remained at Mormon Island. And the major motivation to go to Utah was not gold, but religious and familial.

It is not certain just how many Mormons remained at Mormon Island after the exodus of 1848. However, enough remained to maintain reasonably solid control at least until Apostle Amasa Lyman arrived in the early summer of 1849, and possibly longer. [41]

NOTES

1. An extensive account of mining at Mormon Island, using extensive quotations from primary sources is found in Owens, *Gold Rush Saints*, Chapter 4, 125-155.

2. Gudde, *Bigler's Chronicle*, 105, 106.

3. Norma Ricketts, "The California Star Express." Golden Notes, Vol. 28, No. 1, (Spring, 1982), Sacramento County Historical Society (also self published by the author). The five Mormon Battalion members known by name were: William Hawk, Nathan Hawk (William's son), Silas Harris (a nephew of William), Richard Slater and Sanford Jacobs.

4. Sidney and Ira Willis, Hudson, Jesse Martin, Ephraim Green, James Sly (and probably Israel Evans)

5. Gudde, *Bigler's Chronicle*, 107, 108.

6. *Ibid.*, 108.

7. James S. Brown, *Giant of the Lord*, 114, 116.

8. *Ibid.*, 115.

9. *Ibid.*, 117. Orrin Hatch, William S. Muir, George W. Boyd, H. D. Merrill, and Israel Evans.

10. Bigler, *Journal of Azariah Smith*, 115.

11. Paul, *California Gold Discovery*, 68-69.

12. *Ibid.*

13. *Ibid.*, 130-131. (Word in brackets is the author's).

14. *Ibid.*, 195.

15. *Ibid.*, 70.

16. *Ibid.*, 77.

17. *Ibid.*, 77-78.

18. *Ibid.*, 78.

19. Ricketts, "California Star Express"

20. Paul, *California Gold Discovery.*

21. *Ibid.*, 78.

22. *Ibid.*, 70.

23. *Ibid.*, 78.

24. Bancroft, *History of California*, 6:56.

25. *Californian*, May 29, 1848.

26. Publication resumed in November.

27. John Borrowman, Journals.

28. Two spellings, both pronounced as "Moe Ree," most often today pronounced incorrectly as "Mow Ree."

29. John Borrowman, Journals.

30. Ibid. (Word in brackets is the author's).

31. The story about Brannan's tax or tithing is verified by statements of William S. Clark, William T. Sherman and Addison Pratt, who refer to a 30 percent "tax" levied by Brannan. Bancroft says that William Sullivan Clark came overland in 1846. (Bancroft, *Pioneer Register*.) Borrowman first referred to Clark as "Brother" which term usually was limited to fellow Church members, but later referred to him as "Mister." He apparently was not a member of the Church.

32. Bancroft, *Pioneer Register*; Francis Asbury Hammond, "In Early Days,"

33. Glover, born in Kilmarnock, Scotland in 1813, emigrated to the United States as a young man, settling in Pottsville, Pennsylvania. He and his wife, Jane Cowan, joined the Mormon Church in 1842. With their three children (one of them named Joseph Smith) they were passengers on the *Brooklyn*. William served as a counselor to Sam Brannan, was a member of the first city council in San Francisco, and is said to have built the first school in that city. Sometime in 1848 the family joined the first gold rush to Mormon Island. Glover's subsequent liberality with his gold was presaged in his contribution to the gold being accumulated by Colonel Mason to be forwarded to Washington as evidence of the reality of the gold troves of California. He also responded to the call of the Church leaders to come to Utah with his gold in the Rhoades Company of 1849.

Shortly after his arrival in Utah, he deposited some $3,000 in the Gold Dust Accounts and made gifts of $50 each to Apostles Lorenzo and Erastus Snow, and F. D. Richards. Family tradition refers to the $3000 as a gift to the Church, however the record of his deposit shows it as "going towards the store" which would seem to indicate that he received credit toward future purchases from the Church storehouse.

Family tradition says that his "gift" left the family in "straightened circumstances." When he later told his wife of an opportunity to buy a small farm in Farmington, Jane presented him with $500 in gold dust that she had accumulated at Mormon Island. Carter, *Our Pioneer Heritage*, Vol. 3, 541-542; "Brigham Young's Daily Transactions in Gold Dust."

34. See chapter 11.

35. John Conrad Naegle, Biography.

36. Horner, with his bride Elizabeth Imlay, sailed on the *Brooklyn*. Upon their arrival at San Francisco, Horner proceeded to Marsh's landing near present day Antioch where he farmed for shares on land owned by Dr. John Marsh. That yielding poor results, Horner moved to the area of Mission San Jose, bought land, and began farming on his own. Discouraged by initial crop failures and attracted by gold at Mormon Island, John and Elizabeth went to that Mormon gathering place in 1848. Finding little gold, and John's having a bout with fever (ague) and shaking, they returned to farming near Mission San Jose. Horner soon prospered, reportedly becoming one of the richest farmers in California, his success largely based on the high price of agricultural goods induced by the gold rush. Liberal with his means, he built a school (which also served as a church), roads,

mills, a cemetery, and helped start two towns. He started a steamboat service between Union City in the East Bay and San Francisco and established a stagecoach line to connect the embarcadero at Union City to Mission San Jose. He also contributed significantly to the missionaries of the Mormon Church in the 1850s.

Because of a bank panic, being over extended, and having co-signed to help others get started, Horner lost everything in 1854. When the branches of the Church were shut down and the Saints were asked to move to the Salt Lake Valley in 1857, Horner chose to stay in California. He made important contributions to California agriculture, but he never fully recovered from his 1854 losses.

To start anew, Horner took his family to Hawaii and began working on shares for the Spreckles Sugar Company. In Hawaii he established his own sugar plantation and ranch. He became a prolific writer in the newspapers and was elected to the Queen's House of Nobles. One of his tasks in the House of Nobles was trying to put the kingdom on a good financial foundation.

In 1898 he published a book, *National Finance and Public Money*. In it he included an autobiographical sketch, "Personal History of the Author," 247-276. In modified form, it was also published in the Improvement Era, "Adventures of a Pioneer" and "Looking Back."

Horner added a hint that may explain the Mormon involvement at Mormon Bar, near Mariposa in John C. Fremont country. He said: "Some of our company" (it is presumed the *Brooklyn* Company) "volunteered and went down with Colonel Fremont to help finish up the work" of securing central California from the Mexicans. It is possible that these men were rewarded with the right to mine on his land grant. If so, it may have been Mormons from the *Brooklyn* who first discovered gold at the southern Mormon Bar. Horner, "Personal History," 250.

37. "Old Man Haskel" was probably Ashbel Green Haskell of the *Brooklyn*. According to the family and the Thomas Bullock gold train roster, Ashbel Green Haskell died while traveling with the Rhoades "gold train" back to the Salt Lake Valley and was buried in the Sierra. Carter, *Our Pioneer Heritage*, Vol. 3, 526-535. Shepherd, of the Battalion, was active for several years in the gold fields.

38. Paul, *California Gold Discovery*, 91; Mason report, August 17, 1848, Exec. Doc. 17, H.R., 31st Cong., 1st sess., 1850.

39. Mason reported that "gold is believed also to exist on the eastern slopes of the Sierra Nevada," a belief that proved to be true. Abner Blackburn, a Battalion veteran, and a number of companions discovered the precious ore in the Carson Valley the following year. Mason also says that he was informed "by an intelligent Mormon that it (gold) had been found near the Great Salt Lake by some of his fraternity." Mormon folklore credits members of the Bingham family with discovering gold a few miles southwest of Salt Lake, in what became known as Bingham Canyon, in 1848. That canyon became a major site for the mining of precious metals in the 1860s, and the location of the famous open pit copper mine, at one time the world's largest, with gold as an important by product. Paul, *California Gold Discovery*, 98.

40. William Glover (Mormon from the *Brooklyn*); R. C. Kirby (non-Mormon immigrant of 1846).; Ira Blanchard (possibly Mervin Simeon Blanchard of the Mormon Battalion; Levi Fairfield (probably Levi Fifield of the Battalion); and Franklin H. Ayer (non-Mormon immigrant of 1848).

41. A list of probable Mormons mining at Mormon Island is given in Appendices 3a, 3b, 3c, and 3d.

APPENDIX 3a (Note 3:41)
Mormon Battalion Veterans probably at or near Mormon Island, 1848.

Adair, Wesley
Allen, Ezra
Allred, James R.
Barger, Wm H.
Bigler, Henry W.
Blanchard, Mervin S.
Boyd, George W.

Borrowman, John
Browett, Daniel (James)
Brown, Ebenezer
Brown, James S.
Bush, Richard
Button, Montgomery, E.
Cory (Coray), William and wife
Cox, Henderson
Cox, John
Dennett, Daniel Q.
Dobson, Joseph
Duglass (Douglas), James
Evans, Israel
Fifield, Levi
Ferguson, James
Follett, William T.
Green, Ephraim
Harris, Silas
Hatch, Orrin
Hawk, Nathan
Hawkins, Benjamin
Holdaway, Shadrach
Holmes, Jonathan H.
Hudson, Wilford H.
Jacobs, Sanford M.
Johnston, William
Kelley, William
Knapp, Albert
Layton, Christopher
Martin, Jesse Bigler
Merrill, H. D.
Miller, Miles
Moss, David
Muir, William S.
Naegle (Naile),John C.
Park, James P.
Pearsons, Ephraim N.
Perkins, J. D.
Persons, (Pierson), Ebenezer
Pickup, George
Pixton, Robert
Prouse (Prows), William C.
Rodgers (Rogers) Samuel H.
Shepherd, Lafayette
Slater, Richard
Sly, James C.
Smith, Azariah
Stephens (Stevens), Alexander
Stoddard, John R.
Strong, William
Thomas, Elijah

Thompson, Samuel
Trueman (Truman), Jacob M.
Weaver, Franklin
Weaver, Miles
White, John S.
White, Samuel S.
Wier (Weir), Thomas
Willes (Willis), Ira J.
Willes (Willis), W. S. S.
Willes (Willis), Sidney
Wood, William

Source: The principal source for the names of these Mormons probably at Mormon Island and its vicinity in 1848 is Reva Holdaway Stanley, "Sutter's Workmen at Natoma." *California Historical Quarterly*. 1935, Vol. 14, 269-282. Other names have been added from numerous other sources collected by the author.

APPENDIX 3b (Note 3:41)
***Brooklyn* Saints and Other Mormons.**
Probably at Mormon Island and Vicinity,
1848

***Brooklyn* Saints**
Austin, Julius A.C. and family
Brannan, Samuel
Bullen, Newell
Burr, Charles C. and family
Glover, William and family
Horner, John M. and family
Robbins, Isaac R. and family
Smith, Robert and/or Orrin Smith
Stark, Daniel

Others
Behunin, Philo M.
Clark, Daniel
Clark, James
Hammond, Francis Asbury
Haskel, Ashbel Green
Higgins, S.G.
Pratt, Addison
Reid, John
Rhoads, Thomas and family
Smith, Charles C.

Source:
See Appendix 3a.

APPENDIX 3c (Note 3:41)
Deposits to Brigham Young's Daily Transactions in Gold Dust Accounts

December 10, 1848-June 23, 1849 (Likely participants in the Gold Rush of 1848)

Battalion Boys	Amount Deposited
Adair, Wesley	$29.43
Alexander, Horace M.	64.16
Allen, Rufus	6.13
Bailey, James	737.43
Barney, Walter	50.00
Beers, William	161.13
Borrowman, John	141.75
Boyd, George W.	29.40
Boyle, Henry	22.55
Brown, Ebenezer	119.20
Brown, James III	39.46
Brown, James P.	5.40
Bush, Richard	166.93
Campbell, Samuel	56.75
Canfield, Cyrus	29.73
Chapin, Samuel	117.13
Clark, Samuel	127.40
Curtis Foster	27.87
Decker, Zechariah	604.20
Dennit, Daniel Q.	34.30
Dobson, Joseph	56.63
Ferguson, James	640.06
Fifield, Levi	159.97
Follett, Wm. T.	255.00
Green, Ephraim	30.80
Hawkins, Benjamin	803.46
Hoffeins, Jacob	19.39
Holdaway, Shadrach	535.92
Hoyt, Timothy S.	64.00
Hunt, Jefferson	17.06
Hunter, Edward	47.56
Jones, David H.	106.00
Martin, Jesse B.	37.00
Morey, Harley	4.33
Murdock, John	3.00
Nowlin, Jabus T.	3.00
Park, James P.	23.40
Pickup, George	50.36
Pixton, Robert	17.59
Prows, William	47.39
Rodgers, Samuel H.	13.20
Shelton, Sebert C.	71.16
Shipley, Joseph	9.66

	Amount Deposited
Simmons, Wm. A.	126.20
Smith, Azariah	84.63
Smith, John L.	5.06
Steele, John	2.00
Strong, William	5.67
Thomas, Elijah	470.36
Trueman (Truman) Jacob	44.33
Weaver, Franklin	33.75
Weaver, Miles	61.00
Wilcox, Edward	50.00
Willis, Ira J.	48.33
Wood, William	16.56

Brooklyn Saints	Amount Deposited
Austin, Julius A.C.	19.83
Bullen, Newell	135.69
Burr, Charles C.	179.88
Robbins, Isaac R.	18.00

Others	Amount Deposited
Behunin, Philo M.	52.20
Hammond, Francis A.	71.50
Pratt, Addison	15.16

Source: "Brigham Young's Daily Transactions in Gold Dust," LDS Archives.

APPENDIX 3d (Note 3:41)
Additional Mormons arriving in Utah from the West in 1848, and therefore, likely participants

Allen, Elijah
Allred, Redick N.
Castro, James
Clark, Joseph
Clark, Riley
Collins, Robert
Dodge, Augustis
Evans, Wm. M.
Everett (Averett), Elisha
Forbush, Loren
Green, John
Hales, George
Hatch, Meltior
Hatch, Lewis
Hawkins, Benjamin
Hitchcock, Louis
Hoagland, Lucas
Hunsaker, Abraham
Hyde, William

The long tom, shown above, differs from the cradle in that the top tray (with perforated bottom) in the cradle is replaced with a long sluice with a riddle (or riddled plate) at the end. With the cradle, the upper tray must be repeatedly loaded, drenched with water and dumped. With the long tom, the operation is continuous. Gold bearing earth is shoveled into the sluice; water carries smaller matter to the end of the sluice and through the riddle plate holes; the wash drops into a riffle box (or incline with cleats); and as the water flows out with the small debris, gold tends to be caught by the riffles or cleats. Larger matter is shoveled out of the sluice at the riddle plate. The long tom could process about ten times the earth as the cradle with the same number of hands, so the long tom tended to replace the cradle. [Lithograph from *Harper's New Monthly Magazine* 20:119 (April 1860) 602.]

Johnson, Jarvis
Judd, Zadok Knapp
Lytle, Andrew
McCullough, Levi H.
Mesech (Mesick), Peter
Miles, Samuel, Jr.
Moore, Calvin White
Owens, James
Pace, James B.
Peck, Thorit
Pugmire, Jonathan
Rawson, Daniel B.
Raymond, Alonzo P.
Reed, Calvin
Roberts, Benjamin M.
Roberts, Levi
Rowe, William
Savage, Levi
Smith, Albert

Smith, Lot
Taggart, George W.
Tanner, Myron
Tippitts, John Harvey
Twitchell, Ancil
Wade, Edward Dans
Williams, Thomas S.
Winn, Dennis
Woolsey, Thomas
Zabriskie, Jerome

Source: Carter, *Heart Throbs*, Vol. 9, 469-521. (These names are in addition to names found in Appendices 3a, and 3b.)

**A view of the summit near the Mormon-Carson Pass Emigrant Trail,
showing the terrain through which the wagon trail was pioneered.**

The scene was sketched by an unknown artist from a daguerreotype by J. Wesley Jones.
[ca. 1850's]
Courtesy of the California Historical Society.

A good name is rather to be chosen
than great riches,
and loving favour
rather than silver and gold.
  Bible, Proverbs 22:1

4

The Mormon-Carson Pass Emigrant Trail

THE DISCOVERIES at Coloma and Mormon Island sparked an explosive rush for California gold from over the entire world. Yet many of the Mormons involved in those very discoveries— and among the first at the gold sites to gather the first easy yields—abandoned the gold fields before the gold rush hardly began. Such an incongruity reminds us that the story of the Mormon Argonauts is actually a story within a story. Their encounter with California gold was a landmark event in their lives, but it was secondary to what brought them to California in the first place, their desire to build a Zion in the West. So, for many, the search for gold was quickly set aside that they might regroup with family and friends in the Salt Lake Valley.

As related in chapter 1, the first attempt of the released Battalion in California to regroup with the main body of the Church occurred in mid-1847, before the gold rush, and was only partially successful. The second effort to regroup with the main body of the Church, involving both *Brooklyn* and Battalion Saints, however, resulted in one of their great contributions to the gold rush era, the opening of the Mormon-Carson Pass Emigrant Trail. That trail became a major thoroughfare into and out of California during the early years of the gold rush.

After the Battalion was discharged July 16, 1847, their first question was: Where would they find the main body of the Church? The discharged Battalion divided into several groups, to address that question in different ways.[1] The largest group, led by Andrew Lytle and James Pace, traveled up the California Central Valley, intending to either meet the main body of the Church in Northern California or travel east from there until they met them on their way west. They reached Sutter's Fort August 6. Brigham Young, of course, reached the Salt Lake Valley July 24, 1847, about two weeks prior and just a few days after the Battalion had been discharged. The Saints began settling in to build a Mormon Zion in the Rocky Mountains. So to reach the main body of the Church, the Battalion needed to go east.

Again, as also related in chapter 1, a second group of the Battalion, under the leadership of Jefferson Hunt, traveled north, nearer the coast, along the Camino Real. On reaching northern California, some of them sought work in the Monterey and San Francisco areas, but most of them reconnected at Sutter's Fort with those from the Battalion going up the Central Valley.

A third group, eighty-five of the Battalion (the Mormon Volunteers), re-enlisted for six months to position themselves better financially before returning, and they were stationed at San Diego. (Their subsequent history is discussed in chapters 5 and 6.) A group of fifteen soldiers were assigned by General Kearny to accompany his detail taking Fremont back to Fort Leavenworth for court martial proceedings. After that, they rejoined the Saints by retracing their trails west. A few others, at discharge, proceeded independently, some choosing to stay in California.

The two main groups from the Battalion meeting at Sutter's Fort continued on, taking the Truckee route across the Sierra. They took the same route that Brannan, Charles C. Smith, and two other traveling companions had taken earlier in the year. [2]

Brannan's earlier intent was to find Brigham Young and guide the overland Saints into California. He found Brigham Young, who by then had only reached the Sandy and Green River area of Wyoming. There Brannan conferred with Young and then assisted in bringing Battalion members of the sick detachments (who had wintered at Pueblo) into the Salt Lake Valley. Because of that task, Brannan arrived into the Valley three days after Brigham Young. Young was determined to settle in the Valley, but Brannan tried to persuade him to continue on to California. In his mind, how could they choose the barren Salt Lake Valley over lush California? Failing to persuade Young, Brannan returned to California in disappointment and disgust.

He began the return trip accompanied by Captain James Brown who led a small detachment sent by Brigham Young. Brown and his group had been part of the Pueblo detachments. They were to deliver a letter from Brigham Young to the Saints in California. Brown was also to settle accounts with the Army on behalf of the members of the Battalion sick detachments, since those detachments had not made it to California for the mustering out process. Antagonism developed between Brannan and Brown on their way to the coast. The conflict finally became physical and others had to separate them, According to Abner Blackburn, "Brannan and Cap Brown could not agree on anny subject. Brannan thought he knew it all and Brown thought he knew his share of it." [3] Brannan withdrew from the main party and preceded Brown's group along the Truckee route. (Charles C. Smith had already gone to California ahead of Brannan and Brown with the news of where the Saints would be settling, so Smith was the first to bring that news to California.)

The discharged Battalion, having reached Sutter's Fort, learned from Charles C. Smith about the Saints settling in the Salt Lake Valley. So they proceeded along the Truckee route, meeting the returning Brannan along the trail east of Donner Lake September 6, and Brown's group September 7. From Brannan they learned his low opinion of the Salt Lake Valley. From Brown they received Brigham Young's instructions. They were told that, unless they had supplies to sustain themselves the first winter in the Valley, it would be better if they would return to work in California, buy supplies, and come the next year. About half continued on to the Valley and some of those continued even to Winter Quarters to reach their families. The other half turned their supplies over to those going to the Valley and returned to California. [4]

John A. Sutter had employed some of Jefferson Hunt's Battalion group, who remained to work for him. Of the roughly one hundred Battalion boys returning along the Truckee route, about twenty went to San Francisco for work and the other eighty went to work for Sutter. Sutter employed the men in a variety of tasks. They worked as carpenters, shoe makers, tanners, blacksmiths, butchers etc. Some split shingles or clapboards. Some farmed. Some tended cattle or sheep. Some worked on a granary and gristmill at Natoma. Several of the men were hired to help James Marshall build a sawmill at Coloma. Some left Coloma for various reason, so that six were working on the sawmill and the races when gold was discovered there January 24, 1848 (Chapter 2).

That discovery was at first a loosely held secret, but it eventually spread and was finally announced by the *Californian* March 1, 1848. Also in early March, a few Mormons on their way back from Coloma to Sutter's Fort (alerted to possibilities of gold) discovered rich deposits of gold at Mormon Island (Chapter 3). Word spread quickly among fellow Mormons of that find, and soon many Mormons were panning and cradling for gold at Mormon Island. Brannan announced the gold in his special edition of the *California Star* April 1, and incited a stampede to the mines by his shouts on the streets of San Francisco about gold. [5] So, the search for gold had just begun when a few Mormons met Sunday, April 9 to discuss final preparations for a second try at joining the Saints in the Salt Lake Valley. Brannan was at the meeting.

Preparations for Emigrating to Salt Lake City

The northern route out of California that Mormons were experienced with at the time was the Truckee route. This took off in the Sacramento Valley from Johnson's Ranch and followed the Bear River into the Sierra. (Brannan had been over the entire route and the returning veterans over the first part of it.) They knew this would not be a viable route for their return. It would be extremely difficult even with just a pack train because of the necessary repeated crossings of the Truckee River and the presence of residual snow early in the season. An additional complication was they intended to take wagon loads of supplies and tools to the Valley. Because of that, they decided they needed to pioneer a new route over the Sierra. And why not? As the Mormon Battalion they had pioneered the southern wagon route to California over nearly impossible terrain. They felt confident of their ability to find and develop a more suitable route across the Sierra. Henry W. Bigler reported the meeting in his diary:

> The decision was that all be ready by the first of June, except eight who were ready and expected to start with an express next Saturday [April 15, *California Star* Express (chapter 5)]. . . . It was further decided that we send out a few men as pioneers before that time to pioneer out a route across the Sierra Nevada and if possible find a much nearer way than to go the Truckee route and thus shun crossing the very deep and rapid Truckee River twenty seven times. We were informed by Mr. Brannan we would have to do so if we went that route. The meeting also decided that Captain Sutter be informed of our intentions and time of starting for home, so as to give him time to arrange his business accordingly. It was also motioned and

carried that Mr. Browett be the man to inform him of our intended move, and also of what we wished as to the number of cattle and horses, and oxen, cows, brood mares and mules, etc. We would also take two small brass pieces (cannons) which we understood he offers for sale. We wished to get seeds of various kinds, as well as vines. [6]

It took Sutter a little time, but he settled accounts with Battalion workmen, giving them their wages in currency and kind, the latter including horses, mules, cattle, oxen and wagons. The men were eager to take colonizing supplies, so they also welcomed pay in the form of plows, picks, shovels, iron, seeds, and plant cuttings, etc. They also purchased the two cannons. Sutter recorded the settlement in his personal diary:

> May 15th. Paid off all the Mormons which have been employed by me, in building these Mills and other Mechanical trades, all of them made their pile, and some of them became very rich & wealthy, but all of them [are] bound to the great Salt Lake, and [will] spent their fortunes there to the glory and honor of the Lord! [7]

An advance company of Daniel Browett (the intended captain for the wagon train) and eight others had left May 1 to explore and establish a route for the emigrating Saints. They went east from Placerville, but only got as far as Iron Mountain before the snow was so deep they had to turn back. Clearly, it would be a couple of months before the company could get through. Henry Bigler and two companions began scouting for an appropriate staging ground for the assault on the mountains. Bancroft noted the preparations:

> They stopped in the midst of their success, however, and tearing themselves away from the fascination, they started on June 17 in search of a rendezvous where all the saints might congregate prior to beginning their last pilgrimage across the mountains. [8]

They decided on a staging ground about nine

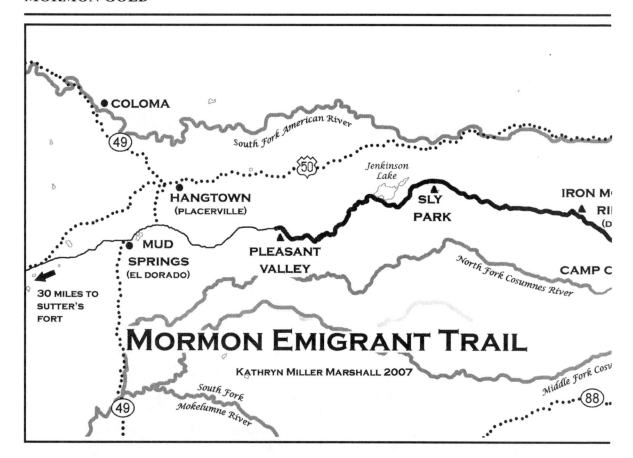

miles southeast of Placerville in a place they called Pleasant Valley. As they waited for others to arrive, they built a log corral to hold the accumulating animals. By June 21, pioneers began to assemble. On June 25, three of the original scouting party, Daniel Browett, Ezra Allen, and Henderson Cox set out again to establish the route through the Sierra. The pioneers kept waiting for them to return and guide them along the trail, but they never returned.

Pioneering the New Trail Begins

Interested parties continued to assemble at Pleasant Valley. [9] By departure time they numbered 45 men, and one woman, Melissa Coray. Melissa had marched all the way from Council Bluffs with her husband, 1st Sgt. William Coray, and both were part of the wagon train. The group was taking 17 wagons, about 150 horses and mules, and the same number of cattle. Also, they were bringing along the two brass cannon. Safety was a concern. All the men were armed. Discharged veterans carried their army muskets. Since their intended leader, Daniel Browett, had

not returned, the group reorganized themselves, choosing Jonathan Holmes as their President and Samuel Thompson as their Captain (Holmes providing overall leadership and Thompson responsible for progress on the trail).

The main wagon train left the Pleasant Valley encampment July 3, 1848 and moved to a new encampment at a beautiful meadow now called Sly Park (named after James C. Sly, one of the company). Bigler and Addison Pratt were left behind at Pleasant Valley to round up stray animals and rejoin the main group. In the words of Bancroft, as they moved out, "It was a strange sight, exiles for their faith thus delighting to honor the power that had driven them as outcasts into the wilderness." [10]

This first leg of the trip exposed the weakness of some of the wagons, so a stay at the second encampment gave them time to make repairs and wait for Bigler and Pratt to catch up. Actually, because of the severity of the trail, repairing wagons became a daily task.

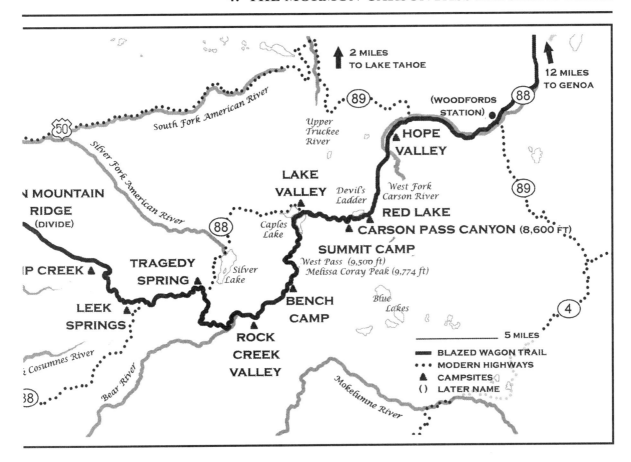

Not hearing from the three advance scouts, ten additional scouts were sent out to find the first and, through the original scouts or by themselves, establish the route for the wagon train. After nine days the second group of scouts returned. They had not found the previous scouts. They reported that the terrain was rough, with lots of brush and boulders, and very steep in places. However, they reported that, with some work, a wagon road could be built through it.

They were pioneering a road east following the divide between the South Fork of the American River and the Cosumnes River, making 8 to 10 miles a day. It is important to note the difference between following a divide or crest between two rivers when coming from the summit as compared to going to the summit. At the summit, the snow or water source is spread evenly, but the run-off reaches the foothills in just a few streams. This occurs because smaller streams coalesce into bigger streams. So in pioneering a trail from the summit, as one chooses a crest between two streams to follow in making the descent, as often as not that crest ends as the two streams co-

alesce. A wagon train coming from the summit must therefore descend one crest and climb to an adjacent one, or worse yet, try to follow the river bed in a canyon. Repeatedly choosing the wrong crests, and as a result repeatedly descending and ascending canyons, can make the descent very difficult. Choosing a crest in the valley and going to the summit, however, often results in that crest going all the way to the summit. It is no surprise, therefore, that this wagon train (pioneering a new route and going east) was able to establish a fairly reasonable route along a crest to the summit, but had more difficulty coming down the east side of the Sierra. [11]

On July 16 the advance road-making crew came upon a suspicious fresh grave near a spring. When the rest of the company reached the grave site, they were fearful that their advance scouts might be in the grave, so they opened it. To their horror they found the bodies of the three advance scouts, with wounds indicating violent deaths. A pouch of gold that belonged to Ezra Allen was found nearby. They re-buried the bodies, piled rocks over the grave site, and blazed a nearby tree

Memorial blaze at the Tragedy Spring grave site. The blaze reads:

"To the Memory of Daniel Browett, Ezrah H. Allen, and Henderson Cox, Who was supposed To have Been Murdered And Buried by Indians On the Night of the 27th of June 1848." *Courtesy of Pioneer Memorial Museum, International Society Daughters of Utah Pioneers.*

Grave site where Daniel Browett, Henderson Cox, and Ezra Allen were buried after being murdered apparently by Indians during advance scouting of the trail. *Courtesy of Dennis Holland.*

to inscribe the identity of the grave. That memorial blaze on the tree is now on display in the museum at the James Marshall Gold Discovery Park at Coloma. Allen's pouch of gold was taken to his wife. She had the gold fashioned into a wedding band. The site now appears on maps as Tragedy Spring.

From Tragedy Spring the Holmes-Thompson train followed a large 12-16 mile circuitous route around what is now Silver Lake and up what is now called Squaw Ridge to the summit. The summit, West Pass, was at 9,550 ft., and they crossed it going north about a mile west of a 9,700 ft. peak later to be named for Melissa Coray, the only woman of the party. (The peak was named in her honor by the U. S. Board of Geographic Names in October 1993.)

Bigler's vanguard group developed the road along Squaw Ridge. Part way up the ridge he recorded in his diary:

> July 22. Camp laid by, while myself and fifteen others worked a road to the top of the mountain; Some six miles from the top we saw several small lakes, some of which I was told abounded in trout. I passed over snow more than two feet deep and saw banks ten to perhaps fifteen feet deep. This day I gathered flowers with one hand and snow with the other. There were plenty of chickens in the timber resembling the prairie chickens. At evening we returned to camp tired and hungry, although we carried lunch with us. [12]

Reaching the Summit, Obstacles of the Descent

Reflecting on getting across the snowy summit, Bigler remembered picking flowers and watching prairie chickens. James S. Brown remembered the wagons continually breaking down on the rough terrain.

> When we reached the summit the wind blew as if it were the middle of November. As we crossed over we came to a large snowdrift; on the north side of the mountain our wagons rolled over the snow as if on marble pavement, but when we came to where the sun had shone in the latter part of the day, our wagons went down to the hub, and four were capsized and some of them badly broken. The others succeeded in reaching the bottom in safety. It took us till after dark to pick up the pieces and get them together to be ready to start the next morning. [13]

They were working their way down a long incline to two lakes at the bottom of what they called Lake Valley. Today, because of a dam the two lakes have become one, Caples Lake. The company camped at the lakes two days, resting and repairing wagons, while a group of scouts went out to determine the best route the rest of the way down the mountain. Unfortunately two of the most difficult stretches of the trail were just ahead of them.

They broke up camp on the third day and moved up a slope to Carson Pass, a secondary summit at 8,576 ft. elevation, where they encountered their first difficult stretch of the descending trail. There was no other way to go. From there the only way forward was to a precipice and down a steep (almost perpendicular) slope, a drop of about 1500 feet elevation to the shores of what is now known as Red Lake. The incline is now referred to as the Devil's Ladder. They were able to get to the bottom of the incline by unloading their wagons and lowering them by ropes wrapped around trees at the top. Some trees still bear the scars. Animals were maneuvered down the slope individually, some with packs to carry their other belongings.

Circled by high mountain peaks, Red Lake was found to be at the head of an eight-mile-long lush valley, crossed from Red Lake to the valley's end by a creek. They called these, respectively, Hope Valley and Pass Creek. The creek is now known as the beginning of the West Fork of the Carson River.

At the end of Hope Valley they came to what was the worst stretch of their trail, Carson River Canyon. To go further, they were confined to the

Melissa Burton Coray Kimball
(1828-1903)

Melissa Burton was married to William Coray at Mount Pisgah, Iowa in 1846, while they were part of the Mormon exodus from Nauvoo. She was 18 years old. William joined the Mormon Battalion and Melissa marched with him all the way to California working as a cook and laundress. William was discharged in Los Angeles, and they had a child at Monterey, The child died after only a few days. William and Melissa went to the Salt Lake Valley with the Battalion group pioneering the Mormon Emigrant Trail in 1848. Their second child was born shortly after reaching the Valley, and William died soon thereafter. Two and a half years later, Melissa married William H. Kimball, the son of Heber C. Kimball. Melissa had seven more children and died in 1903. *Courtesy Pioneer Memorial Museum, International Society Daughters of Utah Pioneers.*

stream bed, since the canyon walls were steep and several hundred feet high. The company camped for seven days while the men moved boulders and logs and tried to prepare a passable road, barely wide enough in many spots for the wagons. Zadock Judd recorded how they solved one of the more difficult problems of road construction—large boulders deposited in the stream bed by heavy spring run-offs and slides:

> We made good progress on our journey and left behind us a good road, until we got nearly across the mountains. In coming down a canyon we came to large rocks which were impassable with the wagons. They were from eight to ten feet high. We had no hammers nor drill with which we could do anything with the stone. It seemed almost an impossibility to go farther. Finally some one suggested that we build a fire on the rocks, and as there

> was plenty of dry logs and brush near, there was soon a good fire blazing on each rock that lay in our way. When the fire had died down and cooled off a little, we found that as far as the heat had penetrated, the rocks were all broken in small pieces, which were soon removed with pick and shovel, and another fire built with the same result.

> After building three or four fires, we found that the rocks were not much in our way, and we soon had a good wagon road right over them, and we were within a short distance of the old wagon road on Truckee River. [14]

After seven days, they covered about seven miles and had a passable road through the canyon. At that time fourteen LDS men in a pack train arrived—advanced elements of the Ebenezer Brown Company—having left the mines only

One of the more difficult sections on the Carson Pass Route, the steep incline from Red Lake to a summit near Carson Pass, is now referred to as "Devil's Ladder." Bark-stripping marks on some of the trees, caused by control ropes, can still be observed today (2009). *Courtesy of Dennis Holland.*

five days before. (Ebenezer had been a member of the California Volunteers.) The men of the Brown Company assisted the vanguard wagon train down through the canyon. Soon they were all out of the mountains and in Carson Valley. The main elements of the Brown company, traveling with the wagons, were close behind. They all came out of the canyon at approximately present day Woodfords, California.

Carson Valley and the Nevada Desert

The groups followed what they called Pilot River, which was still the West Fork of the Carson River. It took them north along the east foothills of the Sierra. At about the region that became Genoa, Nevada, the West and East Forks of the Carson joined. The groups continued following the Carson River north and then northeast toward the Carson Sink. They followed the river for four days and came to an easy passage through the low mountains to the north. They decided they were

probably also past the Truckee Canyon. So they turned and went northwest through an opening to connect up with the Truckee route. To take the first fairly level opening through the mountains or hills to the north they would have left the river shortly after what is now Silver Springs and gone approximately north along what is now highway alternate 95. If they took the second fairly level route through the hills, they would have continued a short distance further and taken a route approximately through Hazen, moving northwest. Both routes would have taken them to the Fernley area, at the bend in the Truckee River, where it turns north to eventually empty into Pyramid Lake. Since the pioneers record that they went to the Truckee on a northwest route, they probably took the second opening. [15]

It was soon clear there was no longer a reason for the two groups to travel together. The pack train could make better time alone. August 8 they separated, the pack train going ahead. Ten men

The rough terrain of Carson Canyon was the most difficult section of the trail pioneered across the Sierra by the Holmes-Thompson wagon train. The sketch is by Alonzo Chappel from a daguerreotype by J. Wesley Jones. [ca. 1850's] *Courtesy of the California Historical Society.*

from the original Holmes party joined them, including Zadock Judd and Francis Hammond.

The Holmes-Thompson party rested and August 14 began following the Truckee route northeast across the Forty Mile Desert. To avoid the heat of the desert, they traveled through the night, reaching the Humboldt Sink by morning. Again they camped to rest, and toward evening were approached by a train of eighteen wagons coming from the East. Presumably this was the James Clyman company. The Mormons told this westward moving company of the gold discovery, which greatly excited them. The Clyman company also learned of the new Carson Pass route and were eager to take it to press on to California and the gold fields. The next day, the Holmes-Thompson party continued on and met a second train going west, probably the Cornwall party. The Cornwall Company also was informed of the gold and the new Carson Pass route. The Clyman and the Cornwall companies retraced the Holmes trail, driving on to the Truckee and turning south to the Carson River. They became the first pioneers to use the Carson Pass route going west. [16]

The Holmes party continued on, moving up the Humboldt River. The next company they met going west was the Captain Samuel J. Hensley pack train. Of special interest to the Mormons was that this train had come from the Salt Lake Valley and had established a cutoff which would shorten the route to the Salt Lake Valley (now known as the Salt Lake Cutoff), which they took when they came to it.

Two days later they met a large company of forty-eight wagons led by Joseph B. Chiles. This was Chiles' fifth trip west. They too were excited to hear about the gold. According to Chiles,

MORMON EMIGRANT TRAIL/
CARSON PASS ROUTE
WOODFORDS TO
BIG MEADOWS

TO APPLEGATE - LASSEN TRAIL

BIG MEADOWS
[LOVELOCK (1868)]

Pyramid Lake

ancient Lake Lahontan

Feather River

Humboldt River

Humboldt Sink

Carson Sink
Alkali Flat

RENO (1868)   WADSWORTH

40 Mile Desert

CHILES CUT-OFF

Yuba River

Truckee River

FERNLEY

RAGTOWN

Stillwater Marsh-

DONNER PASS

OPHIR
TRUCKEE

Washoe Lake

VIRGINIA CITY
GOLD HILL
SILVER CITY

FALLON

North Fork American

American River

Lake Tahoe

DAYTON
EMPIRE CITY
CARSON CITY

FORT CHURCHILL   Carson Lake

GENOA
(MORMON STATION)

Walker River

LEGEND

Carson River

FREDERICKSBURG
WOODFORDS

TO PLACERVILLE & SACRAMENTO

Cosumnes River

KATHRYN MILLER MARSHALL 2009

▬▬▬ MORMON EMIGRANT TRAIL/
    CARSON PASS ROUTE
●●●● TRUCKEE RIVER ROUTE
▪▪▪▪ CHILES CUT-OFF SEGMENT
    OF MORMON - CARSON
    EMIGRANT TRAIL
★★★ SEGMENT OF ORIGINAL 1848
    HOLMES - THOMPSON ROUTE
    REPLACED BY CHILES
    CUT - OFF

The Mormon-Carson Pass Emigrant Route, showing its connections to the Truckee route of the California Trail. (Some modern cities and towns are added to reference the location of the trail.) The pioneering Holmes-Thompson group reached the California Trail as shown by the starred section of the Mormon trail. After Chiles, the California traffic going south to the Carson and the Carson traffic going north to the Humboldt river used the Chiles cutoff.

"It really ran us all mad." [17] Chiles also took the new Carson Pass route, but knew enough about the area from previous trips west that he didn't retrace the Mormon route all the way to the Truckee. Instead, after the Humboldt Sink, he turned southwest to reach the Carson River and the Mormon trail directly. From then on, this cutoff became the standard connection for Carson traffic east connecting to the Truckee route and for Truckee route traffic west taking the Carson route.

The advance party pack train of the Brown

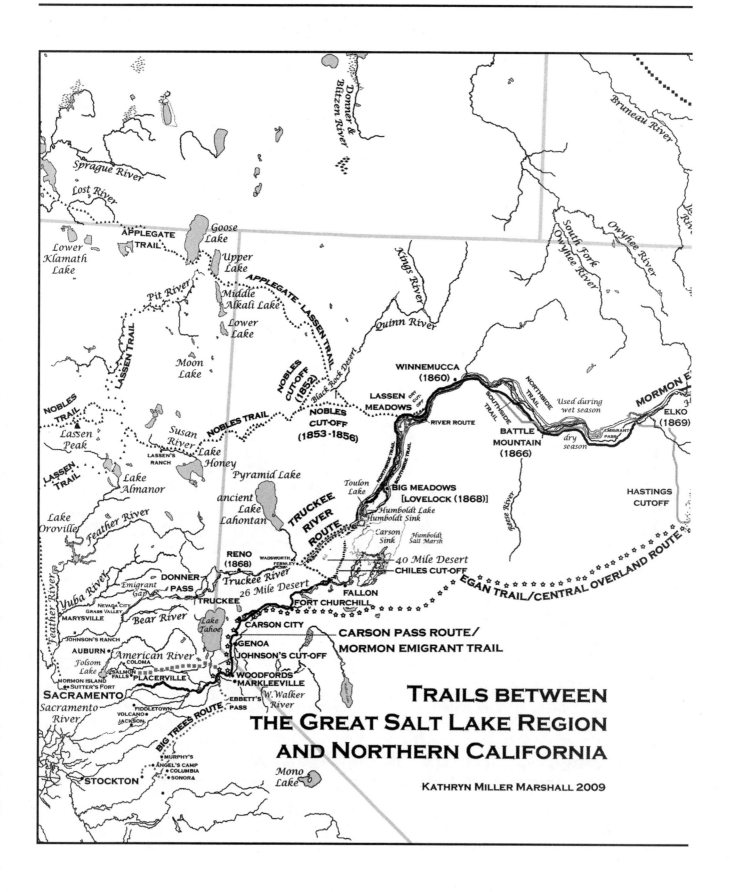

TRAILS BETWEEN THE GREAT SALT LAKE REGION AND NORTHERN CALIFORNIA

KATHRYN MILLER MARSHALL 2009

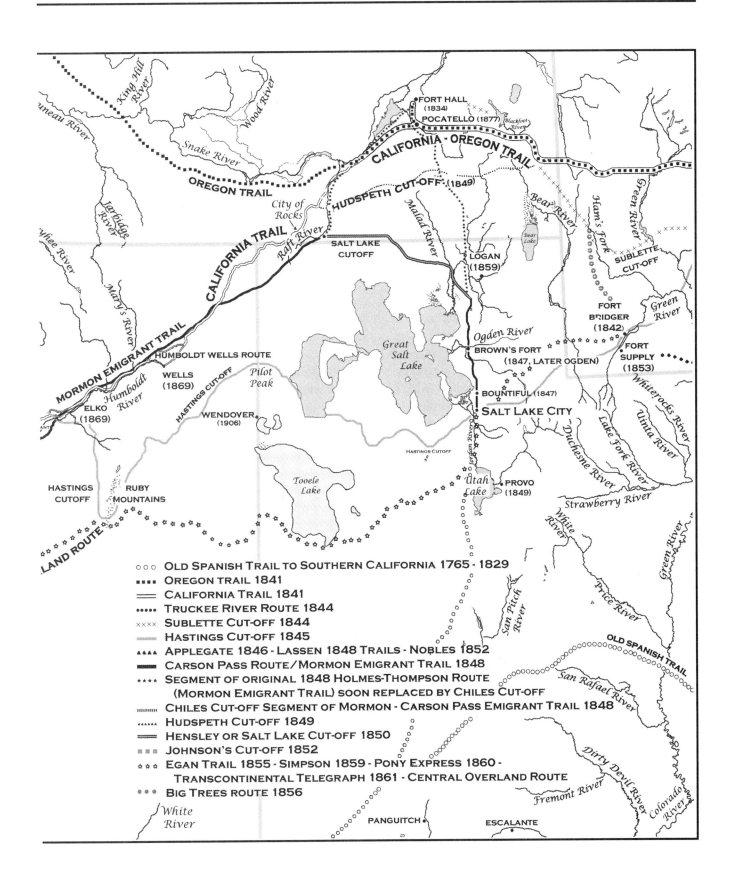

OLD SPANISH TRAIL TO SOUTHERN CALIFORNIA 1765 - 1829
OREGON TRAIL 1841
CALIFORNIA TRAIL 1841
TRUCKEE RIVER ROUTE 1844
SUBLETTE CUT-OFF 1844
HASTINGS CUT-OFF 1845
APPLEGATE 1846 - LASSEN 1848 TRAILS - NOBLES 1852
CARSON PASS ROUTE / MORMON EMIGRANT TRAIL 1848
SEGMENT OF ORIGINAL 1848 HOLMES-THOMPSON ROUTE
   (MORMON EMIGRANT TRAIL) SOON REPLACED BY CHILES CUT-OFF
CHILES CUT-OFF SEGMENT OF MORMON - CARSON PASS EMIGRANT TRAIL 1848
HUDSPETH CUT-OFF 1849
HENSLEY OR SALT LAKE CUT-OFF 1850
JOHNSON'S CUT-OFF 1852
EGAN TRAIL 1855 - SIMPSON 1859 - PONY EXPRESS 1860 -
   TRANSCONTINENTAL TELEGRAPH 1861 - CENTRAL OVERLAND ROUTE
BIG TREES ROUTE 1856

company, which left the Holmes-Thompson party at the Truckee, arrived in the Valley September 24. As the Holmes-Thompson party approached Salt Lake City, some elements of that company, eager to see their families, rode ahead and reached the city September 28. The main Holmes party reached the Valley October 6. The remainder of the Brown company, traveling with the wagons, also reached Salt Lake City October 6.

Subsequent History of the Trail

After the 1848 pioneering effort of the Holmes-Thompson company, there were three overland routes into Northern California for the gold rush: the Truckee, Lassen and the Carson. Because of the gold discovery, western traffic greatly increased in 1849. For every overland pioneer in 1848 there were 50 in 1849. [18] Of the three routes, Truckee had the bad publicity of the Donner party, and had the disadvantage of the 27 river crossings. The Lassen route to the north avoided high mountain passes but added several hundred miles to the journey, which had to be covered when supplies were low, the animals spent, and winter approaching. The Carson Pass route reduced the 27 crossings to 3, led into the center of the mother lode (Hangtown), and had a more even descending trail. However the Carson Pass route had the highest pass of the Sierra trails. (Hangtown was known as Dry Diggins before the hangings in 1848 and was incorporated as Placerville in 1854.)

Carson carried much of the gold rush traffic especially in 1849, 1850, and 1852. The total traffic in 1849 was on the order of 21,000, divided approximately equally between the three trails. Traffic was so heavy in 1849 the pasturage for animals became depleted late in the season. The traveler's own supplies often became depleted too at that stage of the trip and starvation was a frequent threat. Californians, learning of this, shipped out supplies to the incoming immigrants.[19] Mormon Station (on the present site of Genoa) in Carson Valley was established in 1851 for that purpose. Rumors of the great aid needed, especially on the Lassen route, shifted pioneers away from that route late in the season.

According to Soule and Stewart, [20] traffic increased to the order of 45-60,000 in 1850 and shifted more to the Carson route. Traffic was so heavy, casualties along the trail began to show. Travelers counted 9,771 animal carcasses and an estimated 3,000 abandoned wagons in the desert leading to the Carson River. A. W. Harlan reported that at his campground on the Carson there were 800-3,000 wagon remains with 2,000 more strewn along the river. Reports of the hardships of 1850 caused a drop in the immigration in 1851.

In 1852, however, a record number of some 52,000 immigrants went over the trails. The passage was made easier on the Carson by then because wayside supply stations developed both on the Carson Valley segment of the trail and on the western slope. John Studebaker (founder of the automobile line) set up a "tire-setting" shop near Red Lake.

By 1852 explorers also began to find and open easier alternate routes near the main trails. The most important alternate of the Carson Pass route was the Johnson Cutoff. That cutoff left the original trail near Carson City, Nevada, ascended a rather steep grade skirting the south end of what is now called Lake Tahoe, crossing Echo Summit at only 7,377 ft., and descending along the Peavine Ridge until dropping to the South Fork of the American River. This eliminated the Carson River canyon and Devil's Ladder difficulties and made the main pass over 2,000 ft. lower. As a result, after 1852, much of the Carson traffic shifted to the Johnson Cutoff, but there was still traffic on the original trail for the rest of the decade, particularly because the Johnson Cutoff became a toll road and the Carson Pass trail remained free.

Traffic continued to decline on the original Carson Pass trail as road improvements continued into the 1860s on the alternate route. Roadbeds were better cleared and smoothed. In some cases, blasting created new sections of the road that before were impossible, for example, on the old Carson Pass route near Silver Lake, in 1864 eliminating the need to ascend to West Pass to get from there to Caples Lake. So from the 1860s, not only did travelers find an easier passage over the Carson route, but back and forth freighting and coach travel became a common daily occurrence between California settlements and the Nevada Comstock region. More information on the subsequent history of the Mormon-Carson Pass Route is given in Appendix D.

NOTES

1. For more details on the story of the 1848 return of the *Brooklyn* and Battalion Saints to the main body of the Church, see Owens, *Gold Rush Saints*, Chapter 5, 157-199; and Ricketts, *Mormon Battalion*, Chapter 11, 205-227. Ricketts also published an earlier account, *Tragedy Spring*, 1983.

2. For an account of Brannan's trip to meet Brigham Young, see Bagley, *Scoundrel's Tale*, Chapter 7, 197-226.

3. Bagley, *Frontiersman*, 65.

4. A copy of the draft of the letter by Brigham Young to the California Saints can be found in Bagley, *Scoundrel's Tale*, 215-220.

5. Bancroft, *History of California*, 6:56.

6. Gudde, *Bigler's Chronicle*, 106-107.

7. Sutter, Johann August, *Diary of Johann August Sutter*, 1932, 47-48.

8. Bancroft, *History of California*, 6:51.

9. A history of the Mormon-Carson Pass Emigrant Trail can be found in Bennyhoff, *Emigrant Summit Trail*. Trail descriptions and topographical maps for various sections of the trail can be found in the following publications: Tortorich, *Hiking the Gold Rush Trail*; Tortorich, *Gold Rush Trail*; Fey, *Emigrant Shadows*; Fey, *Emigrant Trails*; Harris, *Overland Emigrant Trail*; and Brock, *Guide to the California Trail*. The probable make up of the emigrant companies going over the trail in 1848 is given in Appendix 4a.

10. Bancroft, *History of California*, 6:51.

11. Stewart, *California Trail*, 199-200.

12. Gudde, *Bigler's Chronicle*, 116-117.

13. Brown, *Giant of the Lord*, 122.

14. Judd, Autobiography, 17.

15. Bigler's northwest reference is in Gudde, *Bigler's Chronicle*, 120.

16. The trail encounters, interaction with pioneer groups coming the other way, are discussed in Stewart, *California Trail*, 201-216.

17. *Ibid.*, 205.

18. The subsequent history of the trail is summarized in Bennyhoff, *Emigrant Summit Trail*.

19. Lamb, "Emigrant Aid."

20. Bennyhoff, *Emigrant Summit Trail.* No page numbers. For the statements of Seoule and of Stewart, see section "Traffic Over the Route."

Appendix 4a (Note 4:9)

The Holmes-Thompson Company Leaving Pleasant Valley

Source for the following Information and Narratives:
Ricketts, *Mormon Battalion*, 222-25.

This company is reported to include forty-five men and one woman. The following list, compiled from many sources by Norma Ricketts, includes thirty-nine Battalion men and Melissa Coray, who marched with the Battalion. In addition, there were five non-Battalion men. It is assumed that the three scouts who mere murdered were not present and included when the forty-five and one were counted and reported.

G. Wesley Adair
James R. Allred
Henry Bigler
James S. Brown
Richard Bush
William Coray (Melissa, wife)
John Cox
Daniel Dennett
Joseph Dobson
James Douglas

Elijah Elmer
Israel Evans
William Garner
Ephraim Green
Meltiar Hatch
Orin Hatch
Jonathan H. Holmes
William Holt
William J. Johnstun
Zadock Judd
George Kelley
Jesse B. Martin
Daniel Miller
Miles Miller
David Moss
William S. Muir
George Pickup
Robert Pixton
Samuel H. Rogers
James C. Sly
Azariah Smith
Alexander Stephens
William C. Strong
Samuel Thompson
Jacob M. Truman
Thomas Weir
Ira J. Willes
W. Sidney Willes
O. G. Workman

The three murdered scouts were Ezra Allen, Daniel Browett, and Henderson Cox. The five men in this company who were not from the Battalion were James Diamond, non-Mormon; John Eagar, from the *Brooklyn;* Francis A. Hammond, the convert from San Francisco; Addison Pratt, returned from a mission in Tahiti; Philo M. Behunin, a twenty-year-old Mormon whose parents were in Salt Lake. How he came to be in California is not known.

Ebenezer Brown Company

The Brown company followed the Holmes company on the trail, leaving Pleasant Valley August 10, 1848. The company included men from the Battalion and families from the ship *Brooklyn.* There were forty-one men, twenty-five from the Battalion and the rest from the *Brooklyn.* "Phebe Brown and her son, Zemira Palmer, traveled with her husband, Ebenezer. She was the last of the three women who traveled the entire trip from Fort Leavenworth to San Diego, to leave California. The Browns went to the gold fields after he was discharged from the Mormon Volunteers in San Diego in March 1848."

Members of this party were not in the gold fields very long, and some not at all, but they left with "bags of gold nuggets." "Joseph Bates, who had worked at the Williams ranch [in Southern California] after discharge, was in the mines only four weeks and washed out $1,800."

Eleven of the packers who left the Brown Company after the summit are the following:

Joseph W. Bates
William Beers
Benjamin Brackenbury
Levi Fifield
Orlando F. Mead
Calvin W. Moore
Orrice Murdock
Benjamin Stewart (Came to California with James Brown)
John R. Stoddard
Miles Weaver
John Reed (Came on *Brooklyn)*

Battalion Veterans and Families in the main Brown Company

Ebenezer Brown,
Captain Phebe Draper
Palmer Brown (Wife of Ebenezer)
Elijah Thomas, 2nd Captain
James Park, II, 3rd Captain
Joseph Bates
William Beers
John Borrowman
Benjamin Brackenbury
Montgomery Button
Joseph Clark
James Ferguson
Lucy Nutting Ferguson (Wife of James; *Brooklyn)*

Levi Fifield
William A. Follett
Timothy Hoyt
Albert Knapp
Orlando F. Mead
Calvin W. Moore
Orrice Murdock
Zemira Palmer (Son of Phebe Brown)
William C. Prows
Benjamin F. Stewart
John Rufus Stoddard
Franklin Weaver
Christiana Rachel Reed Weaver (Wife of Franklin; *Brooklyn)*
Miles Weaver
William Wood
Phineas Wright

Passengers from the Ship *Brooklyn* with the Ebenezer Brown Company

Julius Austin
Octavia Lane Austin (Wife of Julius)
Louise Marie Austin (Child of Julius and Octavia)
Newton Francis Austin (Child of Julius and Octavia)
Edward N. Austin (Child of Julius and Octavia)
Newell Bullen
Clarissa Atkinson Bullen (Wife of Newell)
Andrew Bullen (Child of Newell and Clarissa)
Herschel Bullen (Child of Newell and Clarissa)
John Joseph Bullen (Child of Newell and Clarissa; born in San Jose after arrival)
Charles Clark Burr, (Brother to Nathan)
Sarah Sloat Burr (Wife of Charles)
John Atlantic Burr (Child of Charles and Sarah)
Nathan Burr, Jr. (Child of Charles and Sarah; born in California after arrival)
Nathan Burr (Brother to Charles)
Chloe Clarke Burr (Wife of Nathan)
Amasa Burr (Child of Nathan and Chloe)
Charles Clark Burr, Jr. (Child of Nathan and Chloe)
John S. Hyatt
Emmaline Lane
John Philips
Christiana Gregory Reed (Widow)
John Reed (Child of Christiana)
Hannah Reed Jamison (Child of Christiana)
John Jamison (Grandson of Christiana)

Isaac R. Robbins
Ann Burtis Shin Robbins (Wife of Isaac)
Wesley Robbins (Child of Isaac and Ann)
Joseph Robbins (Child of Isaac and Ann)
Margaret Robbins (Child of Isaac and Ann)
Isaac R. Robbins (Child of Isaac and Ann)
Orrin Smith
Amy Ann Dawd Hopkins Smith (Wife of Orrin)
Eugene Smith (Child of Orrin and Amy Ann; born in California)
Elizabeth Ann Smith (Child of Orrin and Amy Ann; born in California)
Eliza Smith (Child by Orrin's first wife, Werthy)
Henry M. Smith (Child by Orrin's first wife, Werthy)
Francis (Frank) Smith (Child by Orrin's first wife, Werthy)
Amelia Smith (Child by Orrin's first wife, Werthy)
Ellen Mariah Hopkins (Child by Amy Ann's first husband, Andrew B. Hopkins)
Emily Marilla Hopkins (Child by Amy Ann's first husband, Andrew B. Hopkins)
Daniel Stark

Also in the Ebenezer Brown company was Daniel P. Clark

The Marcus Shepherd Company

The Marcus Shepherd company was the third group to leave the gold fields during 1848. After discharge, Shepherd worked for a while in southern California before going to the gold fields. He and Benjamin Hawkins had discovered gold at Negro Bar across from Mormon Island. He was captain of his wagon train, but the names of his twelve companions are not known. "There were four men, however, whose arrival date in Salt Lake Valley coincides with Shepherd's arrival, so they may have traveled with him: James Bailey, James C. Owen, John Roylance, and William Kelley. Thomas Tompkins (of the *Brooklyn)* went to Utah in the fall of 1848. He could have been in either the Ebenezer Brown company or the Marcus Shepherd company."

Source for the above information and narratives: Ricketts, *Mormon Battalion*, 222-25.

THE CALIFORNIA STAR EXPRESS . . .

It would be utterly impossible at present to make a correct estimate of the immense mineral wealth of California. Popular attention has been but lately directed to it. But the discoveries that have already been made will warrant us in the assertion, that California is one of the richest mineral countries in the world. Gold, silver, quicksilver, iron, copper, lead, sulphur, saltpetre, and other mines of great value, have already been found. We saw a few days ago, a beautiful specimen of gold from the mine newly discovered on the American Fork. From all accounts the mine is immensely rich—and already, we learn, the gold from it, collected at random and without any trouble, has become an article of trade at the upper settlements. This precious metal abounds in this country. We have heard of several other newly discovered mines of gold, but as these reports are not yet authenticated, we shall pass over them. However, it is well known that there is a placero of gold a few miles from the Ciudad de los Angelos, and another on the San Joaquin. Several silver mines, specimens of which we have seen, have lately been discovered. This metal, it is said, is abundant in the vicinity of the Pueblo de San Jose, (now our most wealthy mineral district,) but it is said, also, to exist in many other sections of this country. Silver, as well as copper, we are informed, has been found near San Diego. Don Juan Bandini is the proprietor of a rich copper mine in that region. It is not yet in operation. We also learn that the country in the vicinity of Clear Lake is very richly provided with this ore. Sulphur abounds, especially in the Northern District, near Napa.

Facsimile of the first item about the discovery of gold in the special "Express" issue of the *California Star*, April 1, 1848, (Vol. 2, No. 13). This edition of the *Star* had four three inch columns per page and six pages. This paragraph comes in column five (outer column of page two) of a six column article titled "Prospects of California" written by Dr. Victor J. Fourgeaud.

*. . . and we did find all manner of ore,
both of gold, and of silver, and of copper.*

Book of Mormon, 1 Nephi 18:25

5

A Message of Gold to Brigham Young

AFTER ESTABLISHING the first pioneers in the Valley of the Great Salt Lake in the late summer and early fall of 1847, Brigham Young returned to Winter Quarters on the Missouri River to oversee the emigration of the next spring. He left a Stake Presidency and High Council [1] along with two Apostles, John Taylor and Parley P. Pratt, in charge of the precarious community. Gold had not been discovered when Brigham Young left that fall, but before his return he would have a full report of those events in California.

The Saints had recently arrived in the Salt Lake Valley, and in council, Apostles Taylor and Pratt concluded that additional supplies were needed by spring to avert disaster. When some of the discharged Mormon Battalion Boys arrived with their tales of California—especially of the southern settlements with their abundance of cattle and other foodstuffs—the Council decided that these settlements could be of great help. The substantial number of Mormon Battalion officers and men who had re-enlisted in the Mormon Volunteers under the leadership of Captain Daniel C. Davis were still in the area and could be of assistance.

Accordingly, on November 16, 1847, a group of men was called as a relief party under the leadership of Asahel A. Lathrop, a Captain of Ten in the immigration that year. With him as counselors were Orrin Porter Rockwell, one of Mormondom's most illustrious (some would say "notorious") scouts, and Elijah Fuller (also a Captain of Ten in the 1847 immigration). Their charge to secure "cows, mules, mares, wheat and seeds" [2] was put forth in two letters from the Church, one addressed to "Brother Workman," (probably Andrew Jackson Workman of the Battalion, sta-

tioned in Southern California [3]), the other to the "Saints in California," presumably the Saints in the north. The fact that two letters were prepared would seem to indicate that Church leaders intended both groups of Saints to be visited. There were also many letters carried between family members. It is very likely that many of the intended recipients lived in the north, again indicating a visit to the north. [4]

These two letters from the Church mention the names of only Lathrop, Rockwell and Fuller. However, a letter written years later by Jefferson Hunt's son, John, claims that the group consisted of 19 men with his father as the guide. Jefferson Hunt was the senior Captain of the Mormon Battalion. [5]

The relief party left the pioneer community near the shores of the Great Salt Lake on November 18, 1847, their return expected by the middle of February. They went by the only feasible route for that season of the year—south to the sometimes ill-defined Old Spanish Trail, then in a southwesterly direction to the southern settlements of Upper California. There were maps of the west which, though poor in detail, could have helped guide them. John C. Fremont's map was probably used. [6]

They reached the southern settlements in late December, a journey of about 6 weeks. After arriving there, the needed supplies (including two hundred or so head of cattle) were acquired and Jefferson Hunt departed on the return trip on February 14, 1848. Who his companions were is not known, though they probably included his family members, a few stray Battalion Boys discharged

THE CALIFORNIA STAR EXPRESS . . .

The Rio Sacramento is navigable to the head of the main valley.

It has a mine of gold and a probable estimate of its magnitude cannot be derived from any information we have received. It was discovered in December last, on the south branch of the American Fork, in a range of low hills forming the base of Sierra Nevada, distant 30 miles from New Helvetia. It is found at a depth of three feet below the surface, and in a strata of soft sand rock. Explorations made southward, the distance of twelve miles, and to the north five miles, report the continuance of this strata, and the mineral equally abundant. The vein is from twelve to eighteen feet in thickness. Most advantageously to this new mine, a stream of water flows in its immediate neighborhood, and the washing will be attended with comparative ease.

Facsimile of the second item about the discovery of gold in the special "Express" issue of the *California Star*, April 1, 1848. This paragraph comes in column four (outer column) of page three, in a section titled "The Great Sacramento Valley." No author is indicated, so it was probably written by Edward C. Kemble, the editor.

earlier but not having yet joined the Saints, as well as Asahel Lathrop and Elijah Fuller. Lathrop was to return to California with his family, probably by the following year, becoming a tavern keeper at what became known as Mormon Tavern.

Their return to the Salt Lake was not an easy one, pestered by Indians. They reached Salt Lake before May 15—a three month return trip. Their departure from California came only three weeks after the discovery of gold in the north, probably before they could have received the momentous word of gold.

On May 15, the Journal History (the on-going manuscript history of The Church of Jesus Christ of Latter-day Saints) records that Lathrop and Fuller "reported their trip to California." They had purchased cows at $6 a head, and lost a fifth of them on their return. They were 90 days on their homeward trip and were accompanied by 19 persons, including five hired Indians. Rockwell did not return with them. [7]

When did Rockwell learn of the Gold Discoveries?

Why had Porter not returned with the group? And what did he do until his return? The Journal History is silent on the subject. However, it is known that Rockwell and Shaw made an abortive attempt to secure a contract to carry the mail back to Salt Lake. [8] This goal might have led Rockwell to deliver (in the north) the letter from Brigham

Orrin Porter Rockwell (1813-1878)

Orrin Porter Rockwell was born in Belchertown, Massachusetts. Porter was one of the earliest converts to the Church and acted as first Joseph Smith's and then Brigham Young's personal bodyguard. Among non-Mormons he developed the reputation of a gunman to be feared. Legends of his notorious actions outgrew the man. His enemies called him "The Destroying Angel of Mormonism," and it was a reputation that no doubt served his purpose. On the sometimes dangerous travel between Salt Lake City and California, he was a welcome addition to many camps. In later years, he served as a lawman in Utah, and he died in Salt Lake City of natural causes in 1878. Schindler has written his definitive biography, *Orrin Porter Rockwell: Man of God, Son of Thunder*. *Courtesy Utah State Historical Society.*

Young and the Church High Council and any letters from Salt Lake to Saints in northern California. A return letter from James Ferguson to the Church, dated April 1, 1848, however, states that the official letter from the Church carried by Lathrop, Fuller, and Rockwell into southern California was delivered to Ferguson in San Francisco by Lieutenant Robert Clift of the Mormon Battalion.[9] Why had Rockwell not delivered the letter himself, and might he have been waiting for a response to carry back to Brigham Young and the High Council? Another letter written to James Ferguson, dated April 2, 1848, from William A. Kennedy of the New York Volunteers perhaps sheds some light on this. [10]

In this letter, Kennedy informed Ferguson that Rockwell had been arrested, along with Lieutenants Campbell [Canfield] and Barrett [Barrus] and Sergeant Myers, for "passing counterfeit

Courtesy Utah State Historical Society

Jefferson Hunt (1803-1879)

Jefferson Hunt was born in Bracken County, Kentucky in 1803. He and his wife, Celia, converted to Mormonism in 1835. They migrated with the Saints to Missouri and then to Nauvoo, Illinois. In Nauvoo, Jefferson became a major in what became the Nauvoo Legion. They left Nauvoo in the Exodus of 1846, and at Council Bluffs, Jefferson enlisted in the Mormon Battalion. He was commissioned a captain and assigned the command of Company A.

On discharge at Los Angeles in 1847, Jefferson led a group of the discharged veterans north to the Sacramento area and over the Truckee route to the Salt Lake Valley. Shortly after arriving in the Valley, he led a group back to California. over the Southern Route to obtain supplies for the fledgling Salt Lake settlement He led a large group of mostly non-Mormons over the same route in 1849. Years later he led another group to help settle San Bernardino. As a resident of San Bernardino, he represented Los Angeles County in the State Legislature and sponsored the legislation that created San Bernardino County. Jefferson then served as that county's first assemblyman. He left San Bernardino in 1857, to help the Saints in Salt Lake City defend against Johnston's approaching army.

In 1860, Jefferson settled the town of Huntsville, Utah (giving the town his name). While there, he represented Weber County in the Utah Territorial Legislature in 1863. He died in Oxford, Idaho in 1879.

According to a neighbor at Oxford, Jefferson " was tall, stately, with sharp features, a forceful character. The very air and even the earth seemed to move as he went on his way about his work. Stern, kindly hearted, all the elements of a warrior and a home man, a kindly husband and father were blended in his nature . . . He was noble, but not proud. He was a natural orator, convincing, with an overlow of well spoken language." (From the biography of Jefferson Hunt: Smith, *Captain Jefferson Hunt, 206-208.* For details of Hunt's political activities in California, see Sutak, "Jefferson Hunt: California's First Mormon Politician."

gold. The gold was coined into 5, 8 and 16 dollar pieces. The 16 is too large and the 5 & 8 too rough. Myers claimed to have received the gold from the paymaster." [11] These were probably Mexican counterfeits. David L. Bigler and Will Bagley have discussed the counterfeiting charges in more detail. [12] According to Bancroft, Canfield, Barrus, and Myers were tried individually by juries in Los Angeles in April. Barrus confessed, was found guilty, and was sentenced to one year in prison. Canfield and Myers were acquitted. [13]

Bancroft doesn't mention Rockwell, unless he is included in an additional statement about "Barrus and other Mormons" in the April entry for an 1848 summary. [14]

In any case, it would appear that Rockwell was in southern California in early April, but he could well have received some communication from Ferguson as a response to Brigham Young and the Church High Council, a response to be delivered by way of the southern route. The Fergu-

James Ferguson (1828-1863)

James Ferguson was born in Belfast, Antrim, Ireland on February 23, 1828. He converted to Mormonism in Ireland and emigrated to Nauvoo, Illinois. He left that city with the Saints moving west and, while emigrating west, enlisted in the Mormon Battalion as a private in A Company. He served under Captain Jefferson Hunt.

At discharge in Los Angeles, he had risen to the rank of Sergeant Major, the highest enlisted man's rank. He went to San Francisco and while there was married to Lucy Jane Nutting, who had been a passenger on the ship *Brooklyn*. He was a talented writer, was appointed official historian for the Mormon Battalion, and left us his assessment of the early San Francisco Mormon community in a letter to Brigham Young. James and Lucy mined briefly at Mormon Island and left for the Salt Lake Valley in 1848 in the Ebenezer Brown Company, riding double on a black stallion.

In Salt Lake City, James had a short career as a sheriff of Salt Lake County, as a Lieutenant in the Utah Territorial Militia, as a lawyer, and as an actor in early Salt Lake theater productions. (Played Hamlet in 1853.) He was sent on a proselyting

mission to Britain (particularly Ireland) in 1854. James, in his last years, drank alcohol to excess and, apparently because of that, died in Salt Lake City in 1863 at age 35. *Courtesy Pioneer Memorial Museum, International Society Daughters of Utah Pioneers.*

---

son response from San Francisco was dated April 1. This was at the time that the gold discoveries were becoming known, the *California Star*'s announcement of it being published, and the *California Star* Express being formed. So Rockwell could have learned of the gold through a return courier.

The charges against Rockwell must either have been dropped, or he escaped, as he left for Utah from the southern settlements on April 12. Rockwell had contact with Joseph N. Davis (who had been the captain of the Mormon Volunteers), John Y. Greene, and James Shaw (who had come down the trail with the original group, and had gone to work for a local rancher). [15] On April 12 Rockwell and these three left the Rancho Santa Ana del Chino in the southern settlements with about

25 of the Mormon Volunteers, including Henry G. Boyle, and John Jacob Riser, [16] both of whom reported on the trip. Rockwell and Shaw were the guides. Davis brought a wagon, which became the first wagon over the southern route. They arrived in Salt Lake on June 5 via Cajon Pass and the Spanish Trail. [17]

On June 9, four days after Rockwell arrived, the Salt Lake Stake High Council wrote to Brigham Young who had but recently left Winter Quarters on the Missouri River, saying:

> . . . and the brethren are in pretty good spirits . . . some few are disaffected and have got what we call the California fever . . . Orrin P. Rockwell has

Nathan Hawk (1823-1910)

Nathan Hawk was born October 29, 1823 in Washington Township, Putnam, Indiana. He married Elizabeth Conrad in 1843. Both of their families had accepted Mormonism. They had a first child in Nauvoo and left there in 1846, with the exodus west. Nathan enlisted in the Mormon Battalion along with his father, William. Both were privates in Company B.

In 1848, Nathan, William, and some others were hired by Brannan to carry his "Express" edition of the *California Star* to Brigham Young and points east. On his way east, Nathan and the others stopped in at Mormon Island and mined out some gold to show as samples along the way. Nathan delivered the message to Salt Lake and reached Brigham Young in Wyoming in mid July. The "Express" riders finally delivered the *Star* to a mail connection at Independence, Missouri, so the news of the gold discovery could quickly reach the east coast.

Nathan then took his family and returned to California, making it their permanent home. He continued to mine for gold, and Elizabeth gave birth to seven more children. Her parents also went to California and ran a hotel in Sacramento. Nathan and Elizabeth, according to family records, lived at times in Nevada City, Yolo, and Coloma. Nathan died November 17, 1910 in Yountville, Napa, California and was buried in Coloma. *Courtesy Center for Sacramento History.*

just arrived from California, in company with Captain Davis, and after he rests a few days intends to go to meet you.[18]

This communication raises all sorts of questions, three of which are:

1. What is meant by "California fever?" Could it possibly have referred to California gold fever?

2. If the message referred to gold fever, how could the word have reached Salt Lake so soon? Might Rockwell have brought it?

3. Does an eagerness of the Salt Lake leaders to communicate the arrival of Rockwell in Salt Lake, and his immanent personal visit to Brigham Young on the trail, indicate a rush to send preliminary information and the importance of the message he would deliver?

Thus, it is possible that the word of gold came into Utah via the southern settlements and the Old Spanish Trail in the spring of 1848. What more likely candidate for the honor of bearing such a message than the "Son of Thunder," Orrin Porter Rockwell? It has already been shown that the timing was possible. Rockwell had not left the Southern settlements until April 12—a month after the rumors were first published in the San Francisco papers and 2 1/2 months after the discovery in which several Mormon Battalion Boys had participated.

The California Star.

In proportion as the structure of a Government gives force to Public Opinion, it is essential that Public Opinion should be Enlightened.—*Washington.*

SAN FRANCISCO, APRIL 1, 1848.

IA STAR.

JRNAL,

d Interests of the
'ORNIA.

L BRANNAN.
. KEMBLE.

.
VANCE

over the fertile vallies of the Upper Pueblo, Napa, Sui' sun, and Sonoma, and you will at once perceive the advantages of these localities. Ere long when these beautiful vallies become thickly settled, they will represent, with their climate of eternal spring, those rare spots which when seen are never left without regret, depicted by poets as earthly paradises.

The progress of agriculture has ever been closely connected with the general history of every country. The system heretofore practised in California, and to

destined ere long to become the manufacturing metropolis, and the commercial emporium of Western America. We know no other country possessing superior advantages to this in regard to manufactures—our facilities in water power are as numerous and as good as could be desired. It would be tedious to enumerate our prospects for raw materials of almost every description. We have already mentioned a few—flour, cotton, hemp, wool, flax, leather, etc., besides minerals of almost every description, and we are constrained

its nominal wealth ɪ richest agricultural c nothing like a syst known; the produc be the spontaneous We want machinery plements, as well as of the husbandman tive kind, and totally the soil.

Central section of the nameplate and edition banner for the special, "Express" edition of the *California Star*. *From reprint, publisher unknown.*

If Rockwell knew of the gold, however, he wasn't sharing the information widely. John Jacob Riser, of the Mormon Battalion and the Mormon Volunteers, traveled with Rockwell, arriving June 5 in Salt Lake City. Yet Riser first heard of the gold discoveries two months later, as those of the Mormon Battalion started coming in to the Salt Lake Valley from the northern Humboldt route. [19] Perhaps Rockwell felt that if he told his company of the gold, many of them may have deserted his company to stay in California.

Porter reported to the leaders in Salt Lake. Captain Jefferson Hunt and Lieutenant George W. Rosecrans of the Battalion were chosen as the initial bearers of the good tidings to Brigham Young; they were scheduled to leave June 9. Probably accompanying them were John Young Greene, and Greene's cousin Joseph W. Young, both nephews of the Prophet. The Journal History records that Greene and Young reached Uncle Brigham's camp on July 11 "from the valley with good news." [20] There is no indication of what the "good news" was.

On June 21, Rockwell, with Captain Davis and others, left the valley carrying an epistle from the Stake Presidency to President Young who they found near Fort Laramie on July 20. However, as printed, it contained no hint of gold. [21] The following day Greene and two others were dispatched to the valley with the mail. [22]

The *California Star* Express Reaches Brigham Young

There is a second scenario for the communication of the discovery of gold. As already referred to, on April 1, about two weeks after the rumor of gold began to circulate in San Francisco but long before Brannan's public announcement, a group of ten men, including at least six Mormons, left San Francisco. [23] The men were employed by Sam Brannan to carry the April 1 edition of the *California Star* and private mail from California to the east to meet California and Oregon bound emigrants, as well as to Salt Lake and Council Bluffs. Of the six Mormons, the names are known for five: William Hawk, Nathan Hawk, Silas Harris, Richard Slater (all from the Battalion), and Sanford Jones. [24]

The *Star* was six pages 10 ½ by 16 ½ inches with four columns to a page. The special edition of the Star had only two paragraphs about the discovery of gold, modest coverage considering the world reaction it caused. One paragraph was buried in a long article by Dr. Victor J. Fourgeaud. The second one was in an article on page four about "The Great Sacramento Valley."

The type setting of the edition was almost completed when gold was discovered. The main purpose of the special edition was to "sell" California to prospective immigrants from the East.

Addison Pratt (1802-1872)

Addison Pratt was born in Winchester, New Hampshire in 1802. He felt a love for ships and the sea and at age nineteen began working as a whaler. At the Sandwich Islands, on one of his many voyages, he jumped ship and lived for six months in Honolulu, learning the native language. He returned to New England and, in 1831, married Louisa Barnes. They converted to Mormonism and migrated with the Saints to Nauvoo.

In Nauvoo 1844, Joseph Smith sent Addison to the Pacific again, to proselyte the native islanders. He went to the Society Islands (Tahiti), working there until 1847 when he returned to San Francisco. In San Francisco he assisted Brannan with the leadership of the Mormon colony, but not without some friction between him and Brannan. Addison left San Francisco for the Salt Lake Valley with the group pioneering the Mormon-Carson Pass Emigrant Trail in 1848.

In Salt Lake City, however, he was called by Brigham Young to return to the islands. He left with the Jefferson Hunt party taking the southern route to California in 1849. On reaching San Bernardino, he went to San Francisco, worked to obtain passage money, and sailed for Tahiti.. In 1850 his family left Salt Lake City to join him in Tahiti, taking the Carson Pass route and passing through the Mormon communities of northern California on their way.

In 1852 the Pratts returned to San Francisco and in 1854 they went to San Bernardino to establish a home. In 1856 Addison was sent again to Tahiti from San Bernardino, but stayed only a short time, coming back in 1857. The Mormon colony at San Bernardino was called back to Utah that year. His wife went, settling in Beaver Utah, near her sister. Addison stayed in California, living with his daughter, first in San Bernardino and then in Anaheim, permanently separated from his wife. He died and was buried in Anaheim in 1872. *Courtesy Utah State University.*

Dr. Victor J. Fourgeaud was given the whole front page and half of the second to lavish praise on the prospects of California, its climate, its soils, its rivers, etc. At the discovery of gold, apparently Brannan, unwilling to reset the paper, managed to give the gold discovery only those two mentions,

The group carrying the special edition with that meager report passed Sutter's Fort on April 15 with over 75 head of horses (the number they were to lose to the Indians and then recover in

the Sierra Nevada). They spent 23 days traveling only 40 miles of the route (probably the Truckee River which was "very high and rapid" at the time). In addition, the snow must have been very deep. A portion of the group reached Salt Lake about the middle of June. [25] Harris remained in Salt Lake while the Jacobs, Slater and Hawk traveled east to meet their families. The group left Salt Lake on July 9 and probably took with them the Council's communication of that date. They reached Brigham Young on July 27. [26] They no doubt left copies of the *Star* with Brigham Young.

Brigham Young (1801-1877)

Brigham Young was born in Witingham, Vermont in 1801. He became a carpenter and general tradesman and married Miriam Angeline Works. They were Methodists. He first heard of Mormonism in 1830, but studied it for two years before joining the LDS Church. He quickly rose in leadership roles, and at the death of Joseph Smith assumed leadership of the Church as president of the Quorum of the Twelve Apostles.

Brigham led the exodus west (in 1846) and after leading the first group of pioneers into the Salt Lake Valley (in 1847), had gone back to Winter Quarters to assemble a second group. It was there in December 1847 he was, by sustaining vote of the members of the Church, officially accepted as the prophet and president of the Church. And it was on his return to Salt Lake City (in 1848) that he first heard of the discovery of gold in California.

It was partly by the strength of Brigham's personality and character that the Mormons were able to sustain themselves in a remote, desolate wilderness, to colonize the Intermountain West, and at the same time to send proselyting missionaries to the far corners of the world. Brigham Young died in Salt Lake City in 1877.

Courtesy LDS Archives.

However, the personal report was probably more vivid and enthusiastic.

Nathan Hawk, in an interview with the *Sacramento Bee* in 1906, told of their meeting with Brigham Young:

NATHAN HAWK, *THE SACRAMENTO BEE,* 4 JANUARY 1906

Brannan procured [in trade at Sutter's Fort] all the 'dust' he could get, and returned immediately to San Francisco. He there worked off his boom edition of the *Star*, and secured a number of letters for me to take East, and returned several days later. The papers weighed eighty pounds. They were not much larger than a sheet of foolscap, but just bristled with glowing descriptions of the country, which Brannan declared was the long-sought Eden.

Brannan wanted the papers given to all immigrants [we] met, and he had packages addressed to every section of the Union. One larger than the others, I remember, was directed to the reading-room of the National Library in the City of Washington.

On our way back, there were twelve of us in the party, we met Brigham Young and his twelve trains, each one of them headed by an Apostle, in the Black Hills.

We stopped and talked with Brigham Young for quite a time. He was very anxious to find the conditions in the country we had traversed. I showed him the gold and asked if he would go on to California. He replied, 'No! I hope they will never strike gold in the country where we locate, for I do not want my people to go digging for their God.'

By the way, I forgot to tell you that the gold I took with me across the plains when I carried the first news of the discovery East, was dug out by myself and three or four of my comrades at Mormon Island.

My party arrived safely in Missouri, where my family resided. My companions, who went to different sections, and the papers of Brannan's that I put in the mails and sent on to their destinations, soon spread the news, and were the cause of the heavy immigration West in 1849.

In the mail they carried a letter from Samuel Brannan to Brigham Young dated March 29. [27] In this letter Brannan described the situation in San Francisco from his point of view. He did not write of gold, but was critical of Addison Pratt, veteran South Pacific missionary, whom he had called to preside over the San Francisco Saints, for his "want of natural stableness of purpose and firmness in decision and character." [28] He was also critical of Brothers William Coray, (James) Ferguson and (John) Borrowman, all Battalion Boys, for "interfering and opposing me in every move I made for the good of the cause." [29] Brannan also criticized Captain Jesse D. Hunter of the Battalion for an "impertinent" letter informing Brannan that if he wanted to hear first-hand the news from Salt Lake, via the letter to the Saints that had come by way of Rockwell, et al. earlier that year, he must attend a public meeting as Hunter "would not let the letter go out of his hands." This letter was undoubtedly the letter addressed to "The Saints" and carried north by Lt. Robert Clift. Whatever the facts and the reasons, Brannan was having difficulty holding the respect and allegiance of the Saints in California.

Brannan said that he was forwarding the letter addressed to "the Saints" and a file of the *Star*. He informed the Prophet that the *Californian*, the only competitor to the *Star*, had almost come under the control of Captain Hastings and that if it had, he (Brannan) would have owned half of it. He hoped to gain "control of public opinion" in the northern settlements "until the day of Manhood and independence." [30] It appears, from this and other evidence, that there was a close alliance between Hastings and the Mormons (at least Brannan).

Brannan's old argument for the settlement of California by Mormons was pushed when he maintained that "there is a powerful party in this country that wishes you to come here and take possession of the valuable lands in the country. On the subject though, I shall say no more." It would certainly seem that if Brannan knew of gold, which he did, he would have communicated that fact to Brigham Young whether by letter or by mouth. Who was this "powerful party?" Could it have been Colonel Fremont with whom some of the *Brooklyn* Saints were associated in Fremont's campaign in central California? Or was it the ambitious Hastings?

Also in the mail was a letter from James Ferguson dated April 1 from San Francisco and written to the "Presidency and High Council of the Stake of Great Salt Lake City." [31] Ferguson informed the Church leaders that the Battalion men had gone into the Redwoods on both sides of the Bay in the San Francisco area, and others on the "Rio Sacramento" and at San Jose. He was critical of Sam Brannan and his common stock company which had left "the many bereft and trodden upon, as they had always been . . . [while] the few who were the controllers and accountants of the firm, became rich and haughty."

Ferguson criticized Brannan's doctrine of amalgamation by which "several daughters of the brethren here had sacrificed their virtue and honor in disgraceful wedlock to sailors and vagabonds." He then informed the leaders that many had "a spirit of gathering and a desire to free themselves of the unholy influence" of the area, which made some (Brannan and his associates) unhappy. He said that it was the intent of many of the Battalion men and some others to meet in Sacramento on the 16th of July, "from which point all will start in masse, or as wisdom may order it." [32]

Brigham Young may have first heard about the gold discoveries in California from the Jefferson Hunt and George W. Rosecrans group on July 11, or from the Rockwell and Davis group on July 20. He certainly heard about the gold from Nathan Hawk and his companions of the "Express" on July 27.

Regardless of the source of the first word of gold reaching Brigham Young, his concern about the possible loss of man-power to California is seen in a communication to the Saints in the Valley. On July 17, six days after his nephews arrived from the Valley, Brigham Young wrote to Apostles Taylor and Pratt, who had remained behind in the Valley over the winter. Urging the Saints to stay put, he said that it was his advice that "they get cured of the California fevers, as quick as they possibly can, and let neither them, nor any other fevers trouble them any more, for I am well assured that if you do, the Lord will bless you and prosper you." [33]

The Saints in Salt Lake Valley first learn about the Gold

The *Journal History* includes items relative to the discovery of gold from members of the Mormon Battalion coming to the Valley in the summer of 1848. However, these entries were made years later from journals and reminiscences. The contemporary record is actually silent as to the actual notification of Brigham regarding the discovery of gold during his westward trek. It is also silent as to the Salt Lake Valley Saints learning of the gold discovery previous to the arrival of Brigham Young in September. However, Rockwell's group reached Salt Lake June 5. The *Star* Express had reached Salt Lake by the middle of June, and the first pack trains of 1848 bearing gold began arriving September 24. While some of the Saints had contracted "California fever" in June upon the arrival of Rockwell and the *California Star* Express, the Saints would have been less than human if some had not started to consider plans, at

least by September, for moving west into the new El Dorado.

By the time Brigham Young reached the Salt Lake Valley toward the end of September, escorted by Rockwell, a substantial number of the Saints already had their bags packed for California. The High Council tried to restrain the Saints, but some had already left. [34] Wholesale "desertion" in the Salt Lake Valley would have been disastrous to the plans of Brigham Young, who had been sustained as "President" only the previous December by action of the Saints at Winter Quarters. Similar action had yet to be taken by the Saints in the Valley. Young's official authority had not yet been fully established.

The crisis must have been considerably enhanced on September 28 when Mormon Battalion Boys and a few *Brooklyn* Saints began to arrive in the Valley heavily laden with bags of gold. For the Saints to see the Battalion Boys brandishing their wealth, telling of fabulous strikes they had heard of or in which some had actually participated, must have been devastating to the morale of the people.

On October 1, Brigham Young addressed the Battalion Boys, informing them of the reasons for the formation of the Battalion. He said: "There were some feelings between brethren who have been in the army and those not which are wrong. My fellowship is as pure to one person as another who has been preserved in the gospel covenants."[35] He also said that he had not wished the Battalion Boys to re-enlist and continued with the declaration:

> If we were to go to San Francisco and dig up chunks of gold or find it here in the valley it would ruin us. Many wanted to unite Babylon and Zion; it's the love of money that hurts them. If we find gold and silver, we are in bondage directly. To talk of going away from this valley for anything is like vinegar to my eyes. They that love the world have not their affections placed upon the Lord. [36]

Seeing the danger, especially after his arrival in

the Salt Lake Valley, Brother Brigham observed that the Sacramento Valley was an unhealthy place in which to live—that the acquisitions of gold would not be as valuable as food and drink and that to become wealthy in precious metals was to court degradation and ruin. He reminded the Saints that the Spaniards had looked for gold and had not only lost their greatness, but had almost lost their God. Moreover, the English colonists, who had paid attention to agriculture and industry, had waxed strong and become a powerful influence for good. Clearly Brigham's public policy of opposition to "running off" to the gold fields was beginning to emerge. However, the need to learn more about the gold also was realized. A few faithful, trustworthy men could be called on a mission to evaluate the situation.

NOTES

1. Local governing bodies of the Mormon Church.

2. Journal History. November 16, 1847, 3.

3. See Andrew Jackson Workman, Autobiography.

4. John Jacob Riser writes of many letters from friends. He received a letter from his brother in Salt Lake. See David L. Bigler and Will Bagley, *Army of Israel*, 399.

5. See Appendix 5a for list.

6. C. Gregory Crampton, "Utah's Spanish Trail," 382.

7. Journal History. May 15, 1848.

8. Harold Schindler, *Orrin Porter Rockwell*, 178-179.

9. Bagley, *Scoundrel's Tale*, 251-253.

10. W. A. Kennedy, Letter to James Ferguson.

11. Ibid. There were no lieutenants by the name of Campbell or Barrett, nor a sergeant by the name of Myers in the original Battalion—but transcriptions from handwritten material are often inaccurate. However, there were 1st Lieutenant Cyrus C. Canfield and 2nd Lieutenant Ruel Barrus, along with the 1st Sergeant Samuel Myers, in the Mormon Volunteers, discussed in the next chapter. If the event referred to above took place in Northern California as postulated, it would appear that at least some of the Volunteers were serving in the north in the spring of 1848 and, therefore, most likely involved in mining gold. Myers remained in California, at least until the fall of 1850. As Canfield made a deposit to the Gold Accounts in December of 1848, he may well have returned to Utah with Rockwell. (See Brigham Young Gold Accounts.)

12. David L. Bigler and Will Bagley, *Army of Israel*, 400-407.

13. Bancroft, *History of California*, 5:610-11.

14. *Ibid.*, 625.

15. Shaw was involved with Rockwell in the attempt to secure a mail contract and, as seen later, John Y. Greene was to become involved in what was possibly the first communication of the gold discovery to Brigham Young.

16. John Jacob Riser's account of the trip can be found in David L. Bigler and Will Bagley, *Army of Israel*, 397-400.

17. The Mormons usually referred to Cajon Pass as "Cahoon", a prominent Mormon name. Henry G. Boyle Diary and the Journal History for June 5, 1848.

18. Journal History, June 9, 1848, 2.

19. John Jacob Riser, Diary, copy in the author's (LKH) possession.

20. Journal History, July 11, 1848.

21. Ibid., June 21, 1848, 3.

22. Ibid., July 20 and 21, 1848, 2.

23. Ibid., April 1, 1848, 3.

24. Norma Ricketts, "California Star Express," 8.

For her source on this, Ricketts refers to Juanita Brooks, *On the Mormon Frontier.*

25. Silas Harris, Sketch, BYU Archives. The Express had probably split up either at the City of Rocks or Fort Hall, a number of the Mormons heading south to the Salt Lake Valley, the others continuing eastward along the California-Oregon trail to St. Joseph.

26. Journal History, July 27, 1848.

27. Ibid., March 29, 1848, July 27, 1848.

28. Ibid., Pratt was en route from a lengthy mission to the South Pacific but before leaving California spent a little time in the gold fields at Mormon Island.

29. Journal History, March 29, 1848.

30. Journal History, April 1, 1848.

31. That a response came by way of the *California Star* Express does not rule out that a duplicate may also have been sent by way of the southern route.

32. Journal History, April 1, 1848, Mormons encouraged marriage within the faith.

33. Ibid., July 17, 1848.

34. Ibid., September 28, 1848. The Battalion Boys reported that while en route they ran into a group of Mormons headed for California who were elated to hear of gold.

35. Ibid., October 1, 1848.

36. Eugene E. Campbell, "Mormon Gold Mining Mission of 1849," 20-21.

APPENDIX 5a (Note 5-5)

Hunt – Rockwell – Lathrop California Relief Party, 1847-48.

William Cornogg
Captain Davis (1)
Elijah K. Fuller

George Garner (2)
John Y. Green (3)
James Hirons, MB
Gilbert Hunt, MB
Jefferson Hunt, MB
John Hunt, MB (4)
Thurston Larson
Asahel A. Lathrop
Peter Nease, MB (5)
William Peacock
Elias F. Pearson
Eli Harvey Pierce
Orrin Porter Rockwell
James Shaw
A. Jackson Workman, MB (6)
Jake Workman (7)

Source: *Deseret News*, October 7, 1905.

(1) The only known "Captain Davis" of the Battalion who was already in California was Captain Daniel C. Davis. A "Captain Joseph Davis" and wife were Mormons in the gold fields in 1850.

(2) Garner was not on the original list but his name appears to have been added later.

(3) Nephew of Brigham Young.

(4) Not an official member of the Battalion; he accompanied it.

(5) An adopted son of Jefferson Hunt, he was not an official member of the Battalion, but accompanied it.

(6) Andrew Jackson Workman, a member of the Mormon Battalion, was not in the group when it left Salt Lake but probably became associated with it in California where he was stationed. He stayed in California for a couple of years, much of the time mining gold.

(7) Hunt lists "Jake" Workman. Two Jacob Workmans came to Utah apparently from the East in 1848, too late for this group. A Cornelius Workman came to Utah with the Rich Company in 1847. An Oliver G. Workman was in the Battalion.

Mary Ann Fisher Cheney
(1823-1851)

Zacheus, Mary Ann,
and Amanda Evans Cheney
(1818-1898) (1850-1926) (1833-1926)

The rush (or should we call it the stampede?) in 1848 of those in the general area of the newly discovered mines is illustrated by the stories of Mary Ann Fisher of the *Brooklyn* and Zacheus Cheney of the Mormon Battalion. In the summer of 1848 they looked in San Francisco for someone to marry them, but found the city essentially deserted. They tell their own story in a joint letter to her mother shortly after they were married:

To: Elizabeth Fisher of Uwchlan Township, Chester County, Pennsylvania.

From: Zacheus and Marry Ann Cheney, [Mission] San Jose August 21, 1850

Zacheus: " I had a very long and tedious march, enduring almost everything but death. We arrived in California in Feb. '47. I got my discharge in July and proceeded to San Francisco. I remained there till the Spring of '48 when I made the acquaintance of your daughter. We were married in July in the mines as there was no people at that time in San Francisco, or but few. We returned to San Francisco soon after we were married."

Mary Ann: "I have wrote to you about the mines several times and sent in one of the letters some of the gold dust just as I had washed it out myself -- something like $2 -- so you might see it. You might have all done well if you had come out here when the mines first broke out. There is still a very good chance for people that are industrious and saving. There are all sorts of people in California. The mining is not so good as it has been [Since it is not] so good as it has [been] we have moved from San Francisco and have been farming this summer."

Mary Ann gave birth to a child Christmas day, 1850, and died from complications a week later. Their child, Mary. is shown on the above right. Zacheus later married Amanda Evans, also of the *Brooklyn,* and they raised the child. (Hansen and Bringhurst, *Let This Be Zion,* 57-58.)

And their silver and gold,
as the prophets foretold,
Shall be brought to adorn thy fair head.

From Mormon Hymn "Oh Ye Mountains High"
(1985) #34.

6

The Mormon '48ers

THE NEWS OF GOLD spread throughout the reasonably tight knit Mormon community in Northern California in the spring and summer of 1848—slowly at first and then with increasing speed. In January, the Battalion members and the Rhoades family group directly involved in the discoveries were situated immediately in the gold fields. By April the Mormon colony in the San Francisco Bay area had heard of the discoveries and many were heading for the gold fields. Also in April, perhaps the Mormon Volunteers had heard of the gold and were becoming involved. (Most of them were in the southern part of the incipient state, but evidently some were already heading north.) Finally, by June those Mormons located in Salt Lake Valley were becoming aware of the gold in California. The story of the first two groups—those in the gold fields and the San Francisco Bay area—has already been detailed. This chapter deals primarily with the Mormon Volunteers in the south and the Salt Lake Valley Saints who led the way for the army of Mormon Argonauts from outside California that began to descend on the gold fields in the year of discovery—1848.

The Mormon Volunteers

At the expiration of their original enlistments, seventy-nine members of the Mormon Battalion re-enlisted as the Mormon Volunteers. [1] They were joined by three young men who had been officer's aids on the trip west, bringing the total to eighty-two. (Two wives and two boys also attached themselves to the group.) [2] They were stationed at San Diego, with a detachment at San Luis Rey. The enlistment of the Volunteers was to end on January 20, 1848, but their tour was extended two months, so they were discharged March 14. Thirty five of the men, who had appointed Henry G. Boyle as their leader, were determined to go to the Salt Lake Valley, getting as far as the Williams' Ranch by March 31. It was there that they met Porter Rockwell. If the news of gold reached any of the group, the information was not widely disseminated or at least believed. That group left April 12 for the Salt Lake Valley via the Southern Route, with Porter Rockwell as their guide.

While almost half of the discharged Volunteers accompanied Rockwell to Utah that spring, the others remained in California. Some of those staying went to work on Colonel Williams' "rancho" near present-day Chino. Even though the roster of the Volunteers is known, it is not known of a certainty all the names of those who remained in California. Appendix 6a presents a probable list. Also Ricketts lists a few that are known to have gone to the gold fields: Ebenezer Brown, Isaac Harrison, John C. Naegle, Lot Smith, John L. Wheeler, Andrew Work-

Andrew Jackson Workman
(1824-1909)

Andrew Jackson Workman (b. 1824) was living in Tennessee with his parents in 1841, when the family was converted to Mormonism. They moved to Nauvoo in 1843 and left with the Saints in the exodus west from Nauvoo in 1846. At Council Bluffs, Andrew enlisted in the Mormon Battalion, responding to a request by Brigham Young. He was discharged in Los Angeles and re-enlisted with the Mormon Volunteers for another six months. After his second discharge, Andrew worked in the mines until moving to Salt Lake City by the southern route out of San Bernardino in 1856. He married and returned to San Bernardino for a short time, going permanently to Utah in 1857. His first wife died, and he married again. He lived mostly in the southern territory and died in Hurricane, Utah in 1909. *Picture courtesy of the Hurricane Pioneer Heritage Park Foundation.*

man, Oliver Workman, and Jerome Zabriskie. [3]

Little is known of the activities of most of the Mormon Volunteers who remained. However, Andrew Jackson Workman fortunately kept a journal from which may be learned something about a number of them. [4]

Upon being mustered out of the Volunteers, in April of 1848, Andrew joined with 16 others in going to the Williams Ranch where they took a contract to construct four miles of adobe fence. In August, after the completion of about three and a half miles, they learned of the gold discovery. Workman recounts that some of the boys, after working awhile in the mines,

> brought some of the gold down and told us of the discovery and showed us some of the gold and we left our job and went up to the gold mines with those who had come down and told us about the gold. We started up in

August sometime and arrived there in twenty five or thirty days . . .

> We found some working in the mines. It was a few days before we got in to work. I did not make much for three or four weeks, nor did any of the company make much for three or four weeks, but we dug out quite a lot of gold. But it took a lot to board us when we had to give a dollar a pound for flour, and meat the same price and other things in proportion. I did not make more than two or three hundred dollars over the grub the first three or four weeks so I thought I would change my place and try to find better diggins (as we may call it). [5]

The route taken by these early Mormon Argonauts is not known, but the most direct way was through the San Joaquin Valley, either along the river or to the east of it along the foothills.

If the latter, they could well have been the un-named Mormons who reportedly discovered gold in 1848 at Mormon Bar in Mariposa coun-try and/or in Mormon Gulch some miles north in the Tuolumne River area a few miles west of the Mexican village of Sonora. Of course, the discoveries in the southern mines might also have been made by other former mem-bers of the Mormon Volunteers as they moved northward, or even by other Mormons coming down from the north or the Bay area.

Accompanied by Andrew's brother, Corne-lius, and about ten others, the company went about 50 miles north of Mormon Island, at first meeting with little initial success. Workman wrote that as luck would have it "my partner and I found a rich pocket of gold. He dug up the dirt with his pick and shovel, and I washed it in a tin pan that would hold at least eight or ten quarts and in two days I washed out about five thousand dollars in gold dust." They divided their money and started for home in November, 1848.

The group headed south. A few miles north of Mormon Island, Edwin Calkins took a short cut along an Indian trail and was never seen again. A search party was sent out, and an Indi-an was overtaken riding Calkins' horse. Justice was swift. The Indian was killed and the horse retrieved. Stopping for a few days at Mormon Is-land, rifles and ammunition were purchased and the group headed south to the Williams Ranch. They stopped at the ranch for a few weeks to get fitted out for the return to Salt Lake City. While at the ranch, Ebenezer Hanks [6] (who had been one of the Battalion members detached on the way west) arrived from Salt Lake City. He advised them that a company as small as theirs would be unsafe crossing the southern deserts because of the Indians.

Taking Hanks' counsel, the group decided to wait until a larger party could be formed. The Workmans and William and Hyrum Fellows went to work for Colonel Williams again. Un-fortunately, the five thousand dollars the Work-man brothers had accumulated was stolen while they were away at work. Not wishing to go to Salt Lake with nothing to show for their labors, they returned north in the spring of 1849. Af-ter six months of successful mining, the broth-ers purchased a string of 40 mules and engaged in teamstering with William Peacock. William was one of the Mississippi Saints who may have gone to California with Apostle Amasa Lyman that spring. Unfortunately for the Mormons, In-dians "got up too early" for them one morning, stealing the live stock. Unable to overtake them, the Workmans were broke again. Andrew pro-ceeded to San Francisco in the spring of 1850 and worked there for five or six months, but never received his pay. Making his way to the Mormon community at Pilot Hill, Andrew had good luck mining there until the spring of 1852. That year he took a steamer to San Pedro and joined the Mormon colony at San Bernardino. In 1855, Andrew finally made it to Utah. [8]

From either the Mormon Volunteers or their relatives, deposits were made to the Gold Ac-counts in the fall and winter of 1849-50 total-ing $4,023. [9]

Salt Lake Valley Expeditions

Despite Brigham Young playing down the in-cidence of "California fever," apparently some of the pioneers of 1847 headed for California that summer via the northern route. Who and how many is not known. [10] The valley's leaders attempted to stem the flow but with mixed suc-cess. In the meantime, Brigham Young reached the Salt Lake Valley in late September of 1848 about the same time that many of the Battalion Boys were arriving after their short but successful season in the gold fields. They brought with them both tales of gold and the physical evidence to support them.

The gold fever beginning to spread was a test of the leadership for resourceful Brigham Young. To have made a frontal attack on the problem, ab-solutely forbidding the Saints to go into the gold fields, would probably have been useless. Some other approach was needed. In his speech of Octo-ber 1, he let the Saints know how unhappy he was with talk of going to California to look for gold. However, he did not actually forbid the Saints to go. Some were already questioning his leader-ship and "inspiration" in rejecting the importun-ings of Sam Brannan the previous year. After all,

Brannan had proven to be correct. California was indeed a land of "milk and honey"— and gold! Pressure was building up among the Saints.

Brigham Young faced a number of additional problems:

1. While many of the Battalion Boys came to the Salt Lake Valley that year, one-third to one-half remained in California. Their manpower and especially their gold were needed in the valley.

2. The *Brooklyn* Saints by and large were still in California. They, too, were needed.

3. Tithes were being collected from the *Brooklyn* Saints by Sam Brannan and then apparently being retained by him. (Brannan had been called to preside over the group some time before and had not yet been released from that calling.) In addition, he was attempting to collect 30 percent from the gold mining Battalion Boys, over whom he had no clear authority.

4. There was no recognized, loyal, effective general Church leader in California.

5, Because of the lack of money, gold was needed to back a Mormon currency.

6. Gold was also needed to provide "foreign exchange"—money acceptable outside the Mormon common wealth.

7. Liquid capital was needed for projected economic enterprises and public works in Zion.

8. Most of the manpower in the valley was needed to cultivate the virgin lands if starvation was to be avoided.

9. With the arrival of increasing numbers of immigrants, and a poor harvest season, imported foodstuffs were needed to avert starvation.

President Young could release some of the pressure. He could allow the Saints to have their way—at least a little—and at the same time meet the needs of the Kingdom. The solution was to "send" some selected leaders on "missions" to California to evaluate the situation and to permit selected others to go with his blessings.

Such calls and permissions, if made public, however, might open the sluice gates. Therefore, no known public calls were made at the Conference of the Church held in Salt Lake City in October of 1848. In fact, no mention of gold was made, even though it undoubtedly was on the minds of many. [11] Perhaps the leaders' considered it "better to keep gold under wraps as much as possible." However, immediately following the bifurcated October Conference, at which Brigham Young was sustained by the Valley Saints as the Lord's Anointed, the president either gave permission to or actually called some of the men to go to California. But he did so carefully and secretly. They could go with his blessings only if they went "with his counsel."

In addition, somehow the Saints in California had to be brought under Church influence—if not control. Leaders were needed whose loyalty to the Church leadership was unquestioned. Those chosen had to be influential enough to win over a people who were fast losing faith in their existing local leadership. In California's "Babylon," the Saints were at risk of falling away entirely. One man alone was unlikely to be able to salvager the situation, but perhaps an infusion of loyal Saints could. Loyal tithe-paying Saints under good leadership could encourage others to tithe their increase, to send or bring their own gold with them to Zion, and to come to Zion themselves as circumstances permitted and required.

In the fall of 1848, at least two and perhaps three groups of individuals were either sent to California or went with Brigham's blessings. One left in October immediately following Conference, another in November. So secret were these groups, however, that their story has largely remained untold.

No direct record has as yet been found of the October group. Its existence can only be inferred. On October 19, 1848, Thomas Grover, a member of the Salt Lake High Council and father-in-law to Charles C. Rich, future Apostle to the gold fields, wrote to President Brigham Young the following:

Wagon train going west to the Gold Country across the California-Nevada desert.
Sketch by William Henry Jackson. *Courtesy Scott's Bluff National Monument.*

I wish to say to you I have concluded to go to California and have not time to call on you. I made my mind this afternoon and have to overtake the company as they are now gone. I wish to say to you that in going I have my family provided for and further I have nothing in view but the good of myself and the Kingdom of God and not withstanding I could not see you I want your blessing and prayers in going . . . I would be so glad to retain my standing in the council if you are willing if so if you will use your influence to that end I will feel grateful to you. I must close . . . I want your blessings now and while I am gone and (undecipherable) I be prospered I will bless you when I return. [12]

The letter itself is no proof of the existence of an officially called or approved company to the gold fields but the fact that one was called a month later, and the fact that Grover would be entrusted with Church tithing gold the next summer on his return to Utah, would indicate that he was not out of favor with President Young—that he went under counsel.

Grover's son later said that his father had gone to California for reasons of business with the *Brooklyn* Company, having sent goods to California that way. While camping in Lower or Southern California, Indians stole his company's horses and the men were forced to walk to Sacramento. His father joined others in mining until 1849 when "he returned to his family in Salt Lake Valley in connection with Thomas Rhodes" and reportedly turned over to the Church 100 lbs. of gold. [13]

It is not clear whose gold it was, but it probably was not Grover's. Grover was most likely associated with Levi Riter. Riter, from Pennsylvania, had entered the Salt Lake Valley in 1847 with his wife and three children. He also went to California in the fall of 1848 to secure goods. He mined for several months, also going to Utah in connection with Rhoades' Mormon gold train in the summer of 1849. [14] The California-bound company may have been captained and guided by the Battalion veteran, Ebenezer Hanks. Hanks, who was encountered by Andrew J. Workman in the winter of 1848-49, had just guided a group across the southern deserts. [15]

The fact that these three known men remained close to the Church would indicate that they had approval for their California trip (or trips). There probably were approximately 20 men with them. The names of the other members, of what was apparently the first organized and authorized group of Mormons going into the gold fields from outside of California, remain unknown. The lateness of the season dictated the use of the southern route. While some may have gone for reasons other than gold, the three known members ended up in the gold fields.

The members of the second group were officially called on a mission to California on November 26, 1848. [16] While the purpose of this mission was not specified, there is little doubt that the need for gold had something to do with it. The "call" was important enough that the apostolic stalwart, Amasa Lyman, was assigned to lead it, with the ubiquitous Orrin Porter Rockwell to serve as guide. Lyman had shortly before arrived from the East for a second time with a company of Saints from Winter Quarters. Rockwell had just returned from escorting Brother Brigham into the rapidly expanding City of the Saints at the Great Salt Lake, after having traveled the Spanish Trail the previous winter and spring.

The group consisted mostly of Mormon Battalion veterans, many of whom had just reached Utah that fall. How many had actually mined gold is not known, though some had been involved. [17] It is not actually known what happened to this party. Lyman, Sly, Boyd and Rockwell returned to Utah in the spring of 1849 via the northern route. Some of the group could have gone to Utah in the fall of 1848 under different, unidentified leadership."

NOTES

1. Journal History. December 31, 1847. The story of the Volunteers can be found in Yurtinus, "The Mormon Volunteers," and Ricketts, *Mormon Battalion*, 261-67.

2. These numbers are from Ricketts, *Mormon Battalion*, 261.

3. A list of those remaining in California is given in Appendix 6a. Ricketts' list of those known to have gone to the gold fields is from her *Mormon Battalion*, 265.

4. Workman was born in 1824 in Kentucky, his family moving to Tennessee where they were baptized by Mormon elders in 1839. After a short-term mission in 1843, the family moved to Nauvoo. Leaving that beleaguered city in the early spring of 1846, the family was in Mt. Pisgah, one of the Mormon camps strung along the southern border of Iowa, when Andrew and probably Cornelius or Oliver G. were recruited into the Battalion. The brothers completed the march to California. Workman, Journal. For Workman's list of participants, see Appendix 6b.

5. Ibid., p. 2. The principal known locations of Mormon gold miners "north of Mormon Island" in 1848 were Mormon Bar, Mormon Ravine up the North Fork of the American River, and Salmon Falls up the South Fork toward Coloma. However, if they were 50 miles from Mormon Island, they were well north of these locations. Other locations well to the north where Mormons were at least later congregated were Murderer's Bar and Slap Jack Bar on the Middle Fork of the American River, and what became known as Mormon Gulch (just to the north of the later location of Georgetown in El Dorado county.) Other possible locations were to the north of the American River and its tributaries, in the Yuba River country at what became known as Rough and Ready and Nevada City.

6. One of the Battalion Detachees, Hanks was to become one of the leading Mormon figures in the gold fields, in San Bernardino, and in southern Utah. As seen later, he may have been in the company of Levi Riter and Thomas Grover who also went to California that fall.

7. Peacock was one of the Mississippi Saints entering Utah in 1847. He was living with his wife and brother in Union Town, El Dorado County, in California in 1850. Workman's dates would indicate that Peacock had probably gone to California by the spring of 1849 when Lyman went.

8. Ibid. Workman and his brother, Cornelius,

were at Pilot Hill in El Dorado County in the fall of 1850. Also there were Benjamin F. Mayfield and Isaac Harrison of the Mormon Volunteers, as well as several other Battalion members and other Mormons. (See later chapters for details).

9. See Appendix 6c.

10. See Chapter 10 for a discussion of several other likely groups going to California in 1848.

11. Journal History, October 8 and 15, 1848.

12. Grover, Sketchbook, 2.

13. Ibid. The reference to a business mission may have been family justification for the venture to the gold fields. The 100 pounds of gold may be a gross exaggeration. There is evidence that Rhoades (Rhodes) did deposit about that much.

14. See the account of Riter in Chapter 11.

15. Workman, Autobiography, p. 3. Hanks would become one of the chief financiers of the San Bernardino Colony and leader of the group to settle Hanksville, Utah.

16. Journal History, November 26, 1848.

17. Including James Sly, Jesse Martin, Sidney Willis, and possibly Evans, Ferguson, and Davis. See Appendix 6d for members of the group.

APPENDIX 6a (Note 6:3)

Probable Mormon Volunteers Remaining in California – 1848

Bailey, Addison
Bailey, Jefferson
Barrus, Ruel
Beckstead, Gordon Silas
Beckstead, Orrin Mortimer
Bowing (Bowling), Henry (1)
Brown, Edmund L.
Brown, William W.
Calkins, Edwin R.
Canfield, Cyrus Culver (2)

Carter, Isaac Philo
Clawson, John Reese
Condit, Jeptha
Dayton, William J.
Evans, William
Fellows, Hyrum (3)
Fellows, William (3)
Fletcher, Philander
Harmon, Lorenzo F.
Harmon, Oliver N.
Harrison, Isaac
Hart, James S.
Jackson, Henry Wells
Kibbey, James W.
Lance (Lane))4), William
Lemmon, James W.
Mayfield, Benjamin F.
McBride, Harlan (Harlem)
Morris Thomas
Mowery, John T. (James) (5)
Myers, Samuel
Naile (Naegle), John Conrad
Park, James Pollock (2)
Riser, John J.
Runyon, Levi
Shumway, Aurora
Smith, Lot
Smith, Willard G.
Steele, George E.
Thompson, Miles (Jonathan M.)
Walker, Edwin
Watts, John S.
West, Benjamin
Williams, James V.
Workman, Andrew Jackson
Workman, Cornelius (Oliver G.) (6)
Young, Nathan
Zabriskie, Jerome

Source: List compiled by author from various sources.

(1) Not in all Battalion lists.

(2) Park and Canfield made deposits to the Gold Accounts in December of 1848 and January of 1849 but could have gone north in the summer of 1848 going on to Utah in the fall. However, if Canfield was one of those associated with Rockwell in coining gold, he may also have accompanied him to the valley.

(3) There is confusion over this person or persons, listed variously as Hyrum William Fellows, and as Hyrum and William Fellows. A William H. Fellows (age 1-9) is listed among the Pioneers of 1847, while a Hyrum W. Fellows was listed in the Battalion. Also, see later account in this chapter for a case for two men, Hyrum and William.

(4) While listed as William Lance on the Battalion rolls, this may have been William Lane, who would shuttle back and forth between Salt Lake and California over the next year or two. However, a William P. Lane, 16 years old, entered Utah in 1847.

(5) One Battalion list has John, another James.

(6) The Battalion list usually includes an Oliver G. Workman. However, Andrew Jackson Workman refers to his brother Cornelius. They were possibly the same person. However, Andrew had a brother, Cornelious Ceagar (Ceazer, Ceazar), born two years after him and another brother, Oliver Gaultry (Galtry or Gilbert), born four years after Cornelious.

APPENDIX 6b (Note 6:4)

A. J. Workman's Gold Company, 1848, of the Mormon Battalion Volunteers

Calkins (Corkins) Edwin
Carter, Isaac Philo
Fellows, Hyrum
Fellows, William
Fletcher, Philander
McBride, Harlan (Harlem)
Smith, Lot
Walker, Edwin
Workman, Andrew Jackson
Workman, Cornelius
Zabriskie, Jerome

Source: Workman, *Journal*, Brigham Young University

APPENDIX 6c (Note 6:9)

Deposits of Mormon Battalion Volunteers to Gold Accounts—1849-50

	Date of Deposit	Amount of Deposit
William Brown	10/29/49	$ 60.00
Albert G. Fellows (1)	10/28/49	199.00
Jacob Workman (2)	10/28/49	233.00
Loisa Calkins (3)	11/21/49	98.80 tithing
	11/23/49	889.20
Henry W. Jackson	11/20/49	125.00
	1/07/50	84.20
Jerome Zabriskie	11/20/49	330.00
Edwin Walker	11/26/49	84.00
	12/24/49	148.00
	3/04/50	293.34
Isaac Philo Carter	12/07/49	103.00 tithing
		934.20
Harlan McBride	2/21/50	192.00
Lot(t) Smith	2/21/50	250.00

Source: Gold Accounts, .

1 The father of Hyrum and William Fellows.

2 Probably a relative of Andrew and Cornelius Workman.

3 The widow of E. R. Calkins.

APPENDIX 6d (Note 6:17)

Lyman-Rockwell Party Called to California, Fall 1848 (Disposition uncertain)

George W. Boyd, MB (Mormon Battalion)
James Brown, MB   (1)
John Brown, MB?   (2)
Davis, MB?   (3)
Evans, MB?   (4)
Ewill, MB?   (5)
James Ferguson, MB
John E. (F.) Forsgren, MB
Joseph Horne   (6)
Henry Johnson, MB
Jesse B. Martin, MB
(Farnum) Kenyon (Kinion) (7)
James (C.) Sly, MB

Dan Smith   (8)
_____ Stoddard, MB?   (9)
_____ Swarthout, MB?   (10)
Sam Thompson, MB
(W.) Sidney Willis, MB

Source: Journal History, November 26, 1848.

(1) This was possibly Captain James Brown, a leader of a sick detachment of the Battalion. He had gone to California with Brannan in 1847 on Battalion business, and would therefore be a likely guide. However, it may also have been James S. Brown, one of the original co-discoverers of gold who reached Utah that fall. The latter was sent the following year on a proselyting mission to the Pacific Islands. There were also other Mormons by the name of James Brown.

(2) There were at least two John Browns associated with the Church at that time. One was a leader of the Mississippi Saints who came to Utah in 1847. The other was a member of the Mormon Battalion.

(3) Probably "Captain" Joseph Davis, who entered Utah in 1848 and ended up in California in 1850. Captain Daniel C. Davis of the Battalion, who frequented the California-Utah Trail, was the leader of the Mormon Volunteers stationed in California. However, he could have gone to Utah, returning in 1848.

(4) There was an Israel as well as a William Evans in the Battalion. At least Israel was at Mormon Island in 1848. William was a Mormon Volunteer and was a tithe payer in California in 1850.

(5) This was probably either John Martin Ewell or William F. Ewell, both of the Battalion and both of whom went to Utah from California in 1847. William was probably at Pilot Hill in California in 1850.

(6) Horne, originally from London, England, entered Utah with his wife and four children in 1847. He evidently sponsored a Gold Missionary a year later, if he did not actually go himself.

(7) Farnum Kinyon was a Captain of Ten in 1847. He died of cholera going to Utah from California in 1850.

(8) He came to Utah from England in 1848.

(9) This is probably either John R. Stoddard of the Battalion or Judson Stoddard, a member of Lyman's company to Utah in 1849. The latter was a friend and later business associate of Porter Rockwell in California in 1849-50.

(10) There were two Swarthouts in the Battalion—Hamilton and Nathan. There were also four Swarthouts who entered the Valley in 1847, George, Truman, Harley, and Charles.

Two sides of a five dollar gold piece showing the general pattern for coins minted in Salt Lake City from December 1848 through 1849. (22 mm diam.) Brigham Young commissioned John Kay in November 1848 to mint the coins from California gold. The emblems are the Phrygian crown (as a priesthood emblem), the All Seeing Eye of Jehovah, and the handclasp of friendship. Denominations were $2.5, $5, $10, and $20. The letters "G.S.L.C.P.G." abbreviated "Great Salt Lake City Pure Gold." The dies used for striking gold coins broke in December 1848, temporarily halting the minting process. *Courtesy Douglas Nyholm.*

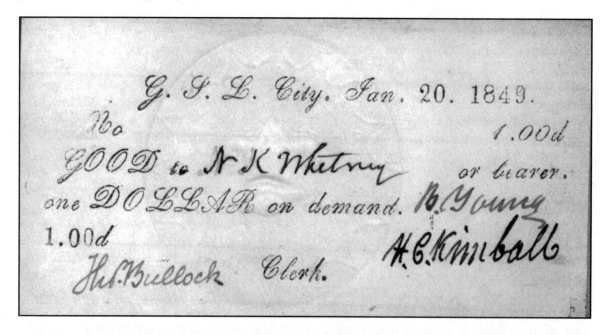

Typeset note circulated in lieu of gold coins. These were preceded by handwritten notes. No hand written notes have survived to the present.

While new dies were being obtained, handwritten notes and then typeset notes, authorized by Brigham Young, were circulated temporarily as a replacement for gold coin. After being signed, these were embossed with the seal of the Twelve Apostles, consisting of the Phrygian crown, the All Seeing Eye, and the letters around the edge of "PSTAPCJCLDSLDATW" (too faint to be seen in the above image), abbreviation for "Private Seal of the Twelve Apostles, Priests of the Church of Jesus Christ of Latter-day Saints, in the Last Dispensation All Over The World." They were issued in 50 cent, 1,2, and 3 dollar denominations. *Courtesy Douglas Nyholm.*

Now Hiram, the King of Tyre,
had furnished Solomon with . . . gold.
  Bible, I Kings 9:11

7

Mormon Valley Currency

AMONG THE MANY PROBLEMS facing Brigham Young and the fledgling Mormon Commonwealth in 1848 were the shortage of money, the lack of a viable money system and the deficiency of capital to meet the needs of an infant and growing community. These needs would soon be substantially met by the Mormon participation in California's El Dorado. [1]

According to Arrington about the only coin in the Valley for its first year was a $50 piece that Brigham Young brought with him. This was enhanced the following year (1848) by another $84 in coin brought into the Valley by President Young upon his return from Winter Quarters. [2] In addition, the Mormon Battalion Boys coming into the Valley in 1847 brought much more in Spanish and American coin with them, though probably not enough to satisfy the community's growing needs. The Lathrop Relief Company of 1847 may have taken some money with them to assist in making needed purchases. Nevertheless, money was short as evidenced by the appeal to the California Saints to assist the relief party.

The shortage of an adequate medium of exchange stifled trade, both domestic (within the colony) and foreign (with other parts of the country). This shortage was significantly reduced as the Mormon Battalion Boys, a few *Brooklyn* Saints and others coming into the Valley from California in the fall of 1848 brought with them much of their earnings in coin. They also brought

with them gold dust and nuggets they had retrieved from the stream beds of California. While constituting a temporary and partial solution to the economic problems associated with a lack of currency, this was a mixed blessing. With their bags of gold, they became a disruptive force in the days of dire community poverty. They served as a constant visual reminder of the gold to be found in El Dorado and of the poverty of the body of the Saints. Their stories assumed heroic proportions when illustrated by the physical evidence of success. Their gold must somehow be put to more positive use.

Minting of Coins Begins

Apostle Willard Richards, counselor to Brigham Young, was appointed the task of gathering up and weighing the dust and putting it into small paper containers with values ranging from one to twenty dollars. [3] The envelopes were signed by Willard Richards or Brigham Young, sealed with wax, and stamped with an official seal. [4] These could then be used for transactions without a continual re-weighing. This was only a stopgap measure, however. The real solution was to ask them to deposit their gold, and to receive back locally minted coin. John Kay, an English convert who evidently had some related experience, became the technician for converting dust to coin.

By what right did the Mormons engage in

Kirland Safety Society Note. In January 1849, responding to the increasing demand for currency, the Church authorized the reissue of the Kirtland notes. These were countersigned by Brigham Young, Heber C. Kimball, and Newell K. Whitney. As soon as the minting of gold coins was resumed, the coins were available to redeem the hand written, typeset, and Kirtland notes. *Courtesy Douglas Nyholm.*

The 1850 five dollar coin (still 22 mm diam.) was a slight redesign of the 1849 coin. On the front, the priesthood emblem changed slightly, a halo was added, and nine stars were added around the central emblems. There were no coins struck after 1850 until 1860. *Courtesy Douglas Nyholm.*

what was and is normally a monopoly power of government? Was Mormon coinage not a counterfeiting operation? The Constitution specifically gave the right to coin money and regulate its value to Congress.

It must be remembered that, at that time, despite the provision in the Constitution, there was no adequate national currency, nor was there a national banking system. Each state had its own banking laws and systems, and each bank issued its own paper currency—bank notes, usually fractionally backed more or less by a motley array of domestic and foreign gold and silver coins. The domestic coins were mostly privately minted.

Moreover, Utah itself was in a political and economic limbo. It was part of contested territory during the Mexican-American War, unorganized U.S. territory after the signing of the Treaty of Guadalupe Hidalgo (February 2, 1848), the provisional State of Deseret after March 1849, the Territory of Utah after September 9, 1850, and the modern state of Utah not until January 4, 1896. While there were U.S. troops in Western California, there were few, if any, in Utah, the term of enlistments of the Battalion detachments having expired in July of 1847. The only de facto government between the Sierra Nevada and the Continental Divide was that of the Mormons, headed by Brigham Young. They arguably had a common law right and responsibility to issue money. This right was not denied them until the Civil War when all privately issued money throughout the country was taxed out of existence and outlawed.

It was too late in the season to travel, and therefore to secure either specially printed paper currency or professionally prepared dies for gold coinage from the East. The most generally acceptable form of money was coin. Therefore, the first effort to create a money system was the minting of gold coins using crude, homemade dies.

The first recorded receipt of gold by the gold office (later called the "Mint" and the "National Bank") was from Ebenezer Brown, a Battalion veteran who, on November 23, 1848, "paid in tithing six ounces of gold dust and six dollars; total $100," representing earnings of $1,000. [5]

Evidently the rate per ounce was $15.67.

Two days later, Brigham Young, John Taylor (a senior apostle), and John Kay prepared the design for the contemplated gold coin. The inscriptions for the coins were "Holiness to the Lord," with an emblem of the Priesthood on the front and on the back "Pure Gold" and the value, surrounding two hands representing friendship. [6]

During the month of November "several small companies of Battalion brethren arrived from California; some brought considerable gold dust." [7] By the 9th of December it was observed that the "faith of many of the Saints was sorely tried and some of them grew weak and wanted to return to the States and others wanted to go to the gold mines in California to dig gold, while many were willing to suffer the loss of all things for the Gospel's sake and for the testimony of Jesus." [8]

On December 10, 1848 regular deposits of gold dust began to be made to "Brigham Young's Daily Transactions in Gold Dust" account book. [9] As an essentially theocratic society existed, Brigham Young acted as the fiduciary agent for both the Church and state. The accounts were frequently in his name, although he was acting in behalf of both the religious and secular communities, as well as on his own account.

The first and only recorded deposit on the 10th was that of William T. Follett, of the Battalion, who deposited 14 1/2 ounces of dust. Two days later, Kay delivered 25 pieces of gold coin valued at $10.50 each for a total of $262.50 [10] which must have been coined from Follett's $232.00 and Brown's $100.00. [11]

In the first two days of operation, 18 of the 25 $10.50 gold pieces were paid out. John Kay, the minter, received five pieces on the 12th, a fact not recorded in the gold account. Brigham Young received the other 20 coins, paying out 18 and evidently retaining two of them. All of those receiving gold coins (Young and Kay excepted) made deposits in excess of their payouts, the balances being retained in their accounts until later withdrawals. For example, Follett made his next withdrawal of $69.50 on January 30, totaling the $232.00 deposit of December 10. [12]

The 1860 five-dollar gold coin (still 22 mm diam.) was minted in a new design. The lettering on the front of the new coins was from the Deseret Alphabet, translation being "Holiness to the Lord." The coins were similar to U.S. $5.00 gold pieces of the time. The Mormon version was minted only in the $5.00 denomination (the meaning of 5D on the back). In 1864, the U.S. Government outlawed the minting of coins or printing of currency by private firms and associations, and the Mormon minting of coins ceased. *Courtesy Douglas Nyholm.*

On December 19, 1848, Brigham Young received from the mint 21 more gold pieces, reduced in value to $10.00 each. Sixteen of them were paid out. [13] The disposition of the other five is not known. Only the payout received by Sister Bent was not specifically covered by a deposit. A total of $593.26 in deposits was received that day. [14]

On December 22, "Many of the brethren came to the office to exchange gold dust for hard money, but no business was done on account of Pres. Young not having any coin." [15] The crucibles had been broken, and minting had stopped. This same day several men deposited dust which was not actually weighed out until January 3, 1849. [16] It was apparent that more crucibles, this time professionally prepared, would have to be ordered from the East. The lack of coin created an emergency.

Authorization to Issue Bills

On December 27, "Thomas Bullock made out four notices calling the brethren together on Thursday to regulate the currency." [17] On the following day, at 10 o'clock a.m. a meeting was held "for the purpose of regulating the currency, at which a vote was taken authorizing Pres. Young to issue bills . . . . Thomas Bullock opened a box of paper to make bills, Pres. Young giving him the necessary instructions as per size, number, etc." [18] Hosea Stout recorded that this important meeting "called this morning for the purpose of consulting the practicability of issuing bills of credit or notes to answer for currency for the time being as the gold dust cannot be coined for the want of crucibles at present. The gold dust to be deposited with the President and no more than the amount to be issued in bills, which plan was agreed upon." [19]

This policy of not issuing bills valued at more than was deposited in gold was followed until March 1, 1849, when the payouts came to exceed the deposits. From that time until the end of September, there was insufficient gold to back the currency issued. This development is discussed later.

The next several weeks were spent by the top leadership of the Church in overseeing the preparation and distribution of paper, Valley currency. Typically, Brigham Young issued orders, with clerks Thomas Bullock and Robert Lang Campbell cutting the paper (approximately 2 in. by 4 in.) and writing out in longhand the $1, $3, and $5 bills. They were usually signed by Brigham Young, the Presiding Bishop, Newell K. Whitney, and Thomas Bullock, with Heber C. Kimball (one of Young's counselors) signing some. Even Sundays were frequently spent in the money making activity. Once the bills were signed, they were embossed with the private seal of the Twelve. This seal had the three pointed Phrygian crown, the all seeing eye, and the following initials around the edge: P.S.T.A.P.C.J.C.L.D.S.L.D.A.O.W. which stood for "Private Seal of the Twelve Apostles, Priests of the Church of Jesus Christ of Latter-day Saints in the Last Dispensation All Over the World." [20] While the first of these "white notes" were hand written, a printed version was soon introduced.

The first bill, a one-dollar note, was issued on January 1, 1849 to an unnamed person. The following day, Brigham Young, Apostle Amasa Lyman, and Thomas Bullock, spent the entire day "paying notes to depositors and receiving gold dust." [21]

Stout recorded on January 2, 1849: "Today the National Bank commenced its operations and those who had gold dust were depositing it in the Bank at a rapid rate. It seems to take well among the people. I was there awhile and today received $25.00 of it for a rifle.[22] Stout did not receive his $25 from the Gold Account directly as he is not found listed there. The table Appendix 7b shows the deposits and payouts, as well as the accumulations of dust and notes and the net gold or notes through June of 1849. Its significance will be discussed later.

The issuance of January 2 must have almost used up the existing supply of Valley currency as January 4 and 5 were used by the same men in preparing another issue. According to Arrington, this second issue, dated January 5, 1849 with a total value of $1,217.50, mostly in 50 cent and one dollar bills, was made and paid out, although the Gold Accounts shows but $967.26 paid out. [23]

On Saturday, January 6, the "High council met and among other actions decided that the Kirtland Bank bills be put into circulation for the accommodation of the people, thus fulfilling the prophecy of Joseph that the Kirtland notes would one day be as good as gold." This issue consisted of the unused currency of the Mormons' defunct Kirtland Anti-Banking Society in Kirtland, Ohio, which had collapsed in the Depression of 1837. [24]

On January 8, 1849, President Brigham Young spent all day in the office fixing up his new press to print "white notes" and preparing for use of the Kirtland money. The following day he, Heber C. Kimball, and Newell K. Whitney "signed bills after which President Young pressed the bills in his new press and afterwards signed off the Kirtland bills. In the night Thomas Bullock worked alone putting his private mark on the bills." [25]

The crude hand press broke down but was repaired in time for operations on January 10 when the Kirtland bills "were handed out for circulation together with other bills." The next several days were typically spent by Brigham Young "in the office weighing gold dust and delivering out bills." The January 17 Journal History entry had a humerous and intentional "typo." It reads: "This was a clear gold day in G.S.L. City." [26] The word "gold" was typed, with a pen and ink change to "cold." Evidently, they were very conscious of both.

By January 19, 1849, the last of the bills were issued and President Young and Thomas Bullock spent the day on the "first type-setting in the Valley." The following day, President Young's nephew, Brigham H. Young, "was engaged in printing bills all day on the press." [27] The issue bore the date of January 20, 1849. Arrington claims that this printed issue consisted of 3,329 notes in denominations of $.50, $1.00, and $3.00, and valued at $5,529.50.

From January 25 to 30, with Sunday off, Young, Whitney, and Bullock spent each entire day signing the bills coming from Angell's press. Brigham Young had said that more bills would be ready in a week. That week had passed and on the 30th, "Several persons called at the office but only a little business was done as the bills, on account of Heber C. Kimball's sickness, were not ready for delivery, nor had Newell K. Whitney signed enough bills to pay off all." However, the following day "President Brigham Young and Thomas Bullock were engaged paying out bills. Newell K. Whitney signed over 400 bills; the office was full of people all day." [28]

Evidently the "Valley Notes," white notes and Kirtland notes, were not universally accepted even in the Valley. For example, the short supply of beef was especially troublesome at the time. Mormon herds had not yet had a chance to build up and the attempt to bring cattle across the deserts from the west coast and the over-grazed trails from the east had not been very successful. So short was beef supply that some licensed butchers felt they could refuse to sell "for anything but gold dust or coined money."[29]

This refusal called forth two responses from the Church-civic leaders. Brigham Young preached a sermon on Sunday condemning such an attitude and a letter was sent to the butchers threatening the loss of their "butchering business" if they "refused to sell meat for the paper currency." Hosea Stout reported that after several days, "There is again beef in the market to be had for paper money." [30] He credited Brigham Young's sermon for the change of heart, but one suspects that the threat of the loss of the license played a significant role. [31]

Gold Account Balance

The receipt of gold and the payout of Valley currency became routine in February, so routine that the operators of the Gold Accounts may not have been aware that the total value of the notes was beginning to exceed the total value of the gold. The Table in Appendix 7b shows the receipts and disbursements to and from the Gold Accounts for December 10, 1848, through June of 1849. It may be seen that through February there was over 100 percent reserve or gold backing for the money issued. However, beginning on January 30, a decline in the reserve began, which continued unabated through the rest of the period, with a negative balance appearing on March 1 and steadily worsening thereafter. It

is interesting that the Gold Account itself ceased to summarize receipts and payouts as of February 26, 1849, the figures from that point being reconstructed by the author (JKD).

On March 6, President "Brigham Young spent the day in his office weighing gold dust, paying out bills and delivering out lots to applicants." [32] The managers of the financial affairs no doubt realized the problem of over-issue of paper money, and that to reduce the payout of such, acreage was sometimes distributed in the place of paper money. The granting of "lots" became a routine operation.

There appears to have been some concern in the community concerning the precarious position of the Gold Accounts. On March 9, the First Presidency found it necessary to reassure the people by issuing a General Epistle which vaguely stated: "Money is very abundant, owing principally to the gold dust accumulating there from the coast, upon deposit of which bills have been issued by the presidency." [33]

The need for Valley currency and the shortage of gold reserves was probably a factor in the call of Elders Lyman and Rich to California. Called in March, Lyman was to leave shortly after April conference with Orrin Porter Rockwell and about 20 others, some of whom had spent time in the gold fields the previous spring. Rich did not leave until the fall. While those Lyman and Rockwell took with them are not known, a likely group consisted in part of the tried and tested Captains of Ten of 1847. This could explain why almost 50 percent of those men ended up in the gold fields. Other likely groups were the Mississippi Saints with whom Apostle Lyman had been closely associated since 1847, and the family units associated with the members of the Mormon Battalion who had come west with Lyman in 1847. Both of these groups provided about 50 percent of their numbers to the gold fields. Lyman's mission was apparently to secure all of the gold possible, as fast as possible, and send it back post haste to Brigham Young.

If the Valley currency was intended to be fully secured by gold, how did the accounts develop an imbalance? The reason is that the Accounts served more than an exchange function. They also served as a savings institution in which some kept their surpluses albeit not for very long periods. The resulting increase of reserves until the end of January possibly caused the managers of the fund to over-optimistically miscalculate. Seeing that those surpluses could be used elsewhere, more profitably than sitting idle, they put them to work, much as any bank would do, except that no interest was paid or charged.

The breakdown in the sanctity of the 100 percent reserve began on December 19, 1848, when Sister Bent received two gold coins, with no evidence of her having made any deposits. As she never repaid the money (at least according to the record), it was in effect a gift. Once the departure began, there were other departures. For example, Andrew Cahoon, upon his return from a mission to Great Britain in 1848, deposited on January 2, 1849, $27.53 in dust but received $30.00 in paper money, smaller denominations possibly not being available. He repaid the difference of $2.47 on April 2 so that this constituted an interest free, albeit short and small loan. Others had the same privilege, though the loans were usually of the same character. [34]

Another type of departure is seen on January 17 when William Castro, a Battalion veteran serving as a mail carrier, was given $5.00 for postal service. This was repeated the 27th. Others also were paid for postal service. William Clayton, who wrote "Come Come Ye Saints," received $25.00 on Feb. 20 and March 1, no explanations being given for the payouts.

These were small departures. Of much greater consequence were the disbursements to Church leaders. On June 12, 1849, Heber C. Kimball, a counselor to Brigham Young, began to receive sizable amounts of money for which at least equal deposits are not recorded. During the period in question, he deposited $5.00 in dust but received $485.00 in paper money. Over the period, Newell K. Whitney, the Presiding Bishop, received $401.00 depositing but $2.26 in dust. Brigham Young deposited $883.58 receiving $1337.55, though some of this was paid to others by his order, probably for goods and services. Clearly the fund was also being used

to support some of the leaders of the Church or compensate them for their services.

Brigham Young's Gold Account of 1848-49 evidently served several purposes, which while useful in and of themselves, probably also helped produce the imbalance of the gold accounts in March, 1849. The fund provided:

1. An exchange for dust, gold and silver coin and paper money,

2. Transfer payments (gifts),

3. Interest free loans,

4. A source of payment for various services and goods provided the Church,

5. Support of several General Authorities,

6. Funds for government operation,

7. A repository for tithing funds,

8. A repository for savings accounts,

9. A source of foreign exchange,

10. A backing for paper currency, and

11. A source of gold for the minting of coin.

Not only was currency being paid out without the receipt of a corresponding value in gold, but also gold was being paid in for other than the receipt of currency, for example for credit or for land. In any case, while there were departures from 100% reserve, according to Arrington, the Salt Lake Valley Notes were secured by at least an eighty percent reserve. And the excess was amply secured by anticipated receipts. There were no doubt some who were concerned, and preferred not to turn over their gold dust or outside coin for notes, However, others accepted that there was sufficient reserve and that the notes could be redeemed as soon as gold dust was coined again. At least in one case, even an "outsider" found the notes acceptable. [35]

Minting Starts with New Dies

The Mormon Mint was evidently intended as a permanent and important operation in April of 1849. A letter to Apostle Orson Pratt in the East from the First Presidency included a request to send all kinds of help including "more mechanics of practical operators in smelting, assaying, mixing, compounding, dividing, subdividing and proving all sorts of metals and minerals and have them bring all tests and apparatus they will need to operate them." [36]

By April 23, 1849, "four sets of dies for the gold pieces" had arrived well on their way before the above letter was written. On that date John Kay took the dies into the Prophet, who had spent the afternoon weighing gold dust and distributing lots. He tried them out, making impressions from all of them. [37] However, they do not appear to have been put into use at that time. Perhaps there was insufficient gold to warrant their immediate use or there may have been a defect needing correction. Whatever the reason, payout entries for this period indicate that notes were being paid for the dribbles of dust coming in, as well as for withdrawals of past deposits.

A new development began to show up toward the end of April. Some of the Battalion Boys and others began to pay their tithing in notes rather than gold. Some were demanding gold for their notes. On April 10, Benjamin Hawkins of the Battalion turned in $468.00 in notes, demanding and receiving $468.00 in gold. [38] If all holders of notes followed suit, the bank would be in real difficulty.

Valley currency had little if any use other than in the Valley. When business, whether private or Church, was conducted outside the Mormon Commonwealth, gold was needed. John M. Bernhisel was a frequent agent for the Church in the East. He would soon be headed for the national capital with a petition for the creation of the State of Deseret. On May 2, having spent some time with Brigham Young, he "brought in $600.00 in paper money to be redeemed, the cash to be sent in the fall to the States." [39] Financial obligations on the west coast itself were frequently met directly from the gold accumulations of Apostles

Lyman and Rich who would both be there by the spring of 1850.

How much gold came into the Valley as the result of the gold mining of 1848? Those known to have come from California deposited a total of about $6561.00 for an average of $102.50 per depositor. About 100 other persons deposited a total of about $1786.00 for an average of $17.86 per deposit. In addition, Apostle Amasa Lyman deposited $132.95 and Brigham Young deposited $160.38 in dust and coin. Also a number of the deposits consisted of tithing apart from other deposits of those tithe payers. This added income totaled about $4560.00, which evidently was retained by the tithe payers. Thus in total, at least $19,103.00 in dust and coins appears to have been brought into the Valley between October of 1848 and June of 1849. In addition, many probably brought in additional gold for which there was no accounting made in the public accounts. Certainly, the inflow of gold into the Valley constituted a significant "cash income," probably far exceeding any other source, and possibly more than all other sources combined.

Both the Gold Account and the Journal History entries relating to gold were essentially dormant for the summer months. However, by July 3 emigrants on their way to California from the East began to enter the Valley. Parley P. Pratt, an apostle, records that "Emigrants now came pouring in from the States on their way to California to seek gold. Money and gold dust was plenty, and merchandise of almost every description came pouring into our city in great plenty." [40]

In September 1849, there were new developments. The destruction of paper currency began and the minting of gold coins commenced using the professionally prepared dies. On September 10, 1849, Daniel H. Wells, Aide-de-Camp to Brigham Young, and Thomas Bullock "spent the day in the office destroying paper currency; they tore up and burned between three and four thousand dollars [41] in preparation for the new issuance of gold coins. Two days later, Bullock and John Kay were "engaged at melting gold dust and rolling bars." [42] These two men were to remain the principal mint employees. They frequently were personally supervised and, on occasion, even assisted by Brigham Young himself. As the operations of the mint began before the arrival of the Mormon gold train toward the end of September, it must have used dust remaining from the previous season, unless some unrecorded gold deposits took place.

In design, the new coins were similar to those of 1848. The $10 coins spelled out Pure Gold and on all other 1849 and 1850 denomination coins the GSLCPG was utilized. [43] The melted gold was rolled into bars of various diameters, depending on the intended value of the coins. They were then cut and stamped. The minting did not proceed without difficulty, though the nature of the problems is not always clear. One problem appears to have been that on occasion the gold became brittle rather than malleable. On September 21, Bullock and Kay were instructed by Brigham Young to remelt the defective brittle bars, along with scrap gold, into an ingot to be sold rather than coined. [44] The mint then appears to have suspended operation.

Another problem perhaps associated with the brittleness was in preparing gold with the proper fineness or purity. It was at first prepared without alloy but silver was soon added. This produced coins with greater hardness and therefore with less wear. Also, silver being of less value than gold, it paid for the cost of the minting operation and probably gave a profit (seignorage)—a common practice. However, too much alloy must have been added for the Mormon coins soon gained a reputation as "debased," "spurious" and "vile falsehoods." Their value consequently dropped outside the Great Basin, circulating at a discount of as much as 25 percent. This in turn began to hurt Mormon credit. [45]

On September 28, 1849 the Mormon Gold Train arrived from the west coast under the captaincy of Thomas Rhoades, a Mormon immigrant of 1846, with about $3,000 in gold dust and $1,280 in coins collected by Apostle Lyman from the California Saints as tithing and contributions. The train had left the gold fields on July 14 with Thomas Grover, a former member of the Salt Lake High Council, in charge of the Church money. In addition Rhoades reportedly brought $17,000 in his own gold and William Glover, a

Brooklyn Company leader, at least $3,300 in dust and coin. [46] Other members, including Levi Riter, also brought unrecorded amounts of California earnings. The mint could now operate again, restarting on October 1st.

A special account for Thomas Rhoades (Rhoads) began on October 9, which showed him depositing $10,826.00 in dust. The detailed disposition of this deposit is shown later. It may be summarized by the fact that by December 24, 1849, $4,324.35 had been disbursed to a number of individuals for supplies, building materials and services rendered, including construction of a home, the contract for which was $1,101.00. While the Gold Accounts refer only to $10,826, Brigham Young later referred to Father Rhoades with his $17,000 in gold as the wealthiest Mormon to come from the gold fields.

Dust was received by the mint on October 3 and new coins paid out. The following day "considerable gold" was deposited. [47] While mentioned in the Journal History, these operations are not recorded in Brigham Young's gold dust account book, nor is there any record for the period between October 9 and October 27. On the latter day a new account book was opened, simply entitled "Brigham Young." [48] Lacking the simplicity and clarity of the earlier record, it continued until July 20, 1851. [49]

Not all large transactions were recorded in the account. For example, the Journal History records that on November 7, $6,000, presumably in gold, was exchanged for silver, a fact not reflected in the account. [50] On December 7, Brigham Young and Thomas Bullock "went to the mint and weighed upward of a thousand dollars worth of gold dust for Bishop (Isaac) Higbee," who presided over the Utah Valley Saints. He received "coin for the same." This transaction, too, was not recorded in the account book. [51]

The operation of the mint over the next several months was important enough to be referred to frequently in the Journal History, often being the only notable thing mentioned. [52] Typically, the entries refer to Bullock and Kay spending the day melting gold, rolling bars, cutting them into coins of $2.50, $5.00, $10.00 and $20.00 denominations and stamping them. An unusual entry was made on January 22, 1850 reading "Dr. Blake (a member of Stansbury's government survey party) was engaged in evaporating the acids from the $5.00 gold pieces." [53] Was he instead "sweating" the coins, reducing their gold content and pocketing the "evaporate?" By March 15 of 1850, the old dies must have become defective for on that date Brigham Young gave instructions for "casting new dies." [54]

The need for more monetary gold became clear during the spring. The struggling Mormon economy was typically exporting more gold than it was receiving. A letter of April 23 from the First Presidency to Elders Lyman and Rich in California revealed: "The various movements east, last fall and of the merchants this spring have considerably reduced the circulating medium of the Valley for the time being, but it will be of short duration." [55]

After the non-Mormon, eastern firm of Livingston and Kinkead opened for business in Salt Lake City, the demand for eastern goods was so great the firm essentially depleted the local coin circulating and a great deal of the unminted gold dust. In 1850, Brigham Young went to their store to watch them load up their teams for the trip East. According to the Church historian, their wagons were "loaded with more gold dust than had come to the mint that fall. In one box there was as much gold as a man could carry and there was a box of silver that required three men to lift it into the wagon." [56]

It may have been this shortage that induced the practical Brother Brigham to send more "gold diggers" to California that spring to reduce the "short duration." The problem worsened as the Mormon gold coins reached the markets and were judged "debased." The devaluation of Mormon gold coins was admitted with the announcement in the Journal History that "The $20 gold pieces coined in the Valley were passing in St. Joseph for $18.00" [57] a discount of 10 percent.

In contrast with the previous summer, the mint was kept in operation in the early summer of 1850. August and September were, however, quiet. With the arrival of Lyman the first part of

October, the entries in both the Journal and the Gold Accounts picked up but only briefly. The relatively easy-to-get gold from the stream beds of California was about gone. A new kind of highly capitalized mining was taking the place of the gold pan and rocker.

Between October 1 of 1849 and the end of June of 1850, at least $25,841 had come into the Valley from California, far in excess of the amount during the same period of the previous season. By July 20, 1851, the amount entering the Valley had reached about $71,133 for this period. [58]

The use of the gold as shown in the second volume of the Gold Accounts was much the same as for the earlier period but on a much grander scale. In addition to being used in minting gold coin, there was a significant increase in the income received by the General Authorities. However, in the latter season, they deposited large amounts of gold dust, much of it undoubtedly secured for them by the gold missionaries they had sent to the gold fields. The death of Valley currency is not recorded in the Journal History, but according to Arrington probably occurred by the early part of 1852. However, before ending this period of gold coinage, the Deseret News took a final shot at detractors of Valley currency: "[I]f Valley coin in exchange, is not as valuable as goods, at the current prices offered in our market, we recommend our friends to keep their coin, and not insult their neighbors with such miserable trash as virgin gold." [59]

The Demise of Mormon Money

The demise of the Mormon money system was probably occasioned by several converging developments.

1. The gold missions commissioned by Church headquarters were abandoned. This abandonment probably came because of the increasing difficulty of getting surface gold and because of the loss of manpower to the "Flesh-pots of Babylon."

2. Not only were no more men sent into the gold fields after the spring of 1850, but the strong counsel of the General Authorities was now to return to Deseret. The more transient Saints, those

with fewer California ties, and those most obedient to counsel left the gold fields in 1850-51. Therefore, the inflow of gold dust was greatly diminished.

3. While some faithful Saints remained behind in Northern California, there was no General Authority, nor even a recognized local leader or Church organization, to collect tithes and offerings there.

4. With the gold rush, monetary gold became more available from traditional minting operations of the U.S. Government.

5. Mormon farmers and ranchers were beginning to produce surpluses which could be sold for gold, silver or traded for other goods and services.

6. Mormon money had become anachronous. Its depreciation made its circulation difficult and negatively affected external Mormon credit, something that was still very much needed for the orderly development of the Mormon economy.

7. Utah came under the governance law and domination of the United States Government. To continue to mint gold coin gold or print currency would risk charges of counterfeiting.

In 1861 the new Utah territorial governor, Alfred Cumming, issued a prohibitory order stopping the minting of gold coins in the territory. After that, most of the recently minted 1860 gold pieces were exchanged at the U.S. Mint for U.S. gold coin. Then on June 8, 1864, Congress passed a law forbidding the private coinage of gold. [60]

There is little question that California gold played an extremely important role in the Mormon economy. The time devoted by Church leaders to the receipt, weighing, and coining of gold and the issuing of gold-backed currency for an extended period is persuasive evidence of its importance. In fact, it played a critical role in the economic development of Deseret as well as in the personal lives of the Church leadership. Without the substantial infusion of gold, the community's growth would have at least been limited, if not stopped. Had it not been for the Church's

early negative overtones designed to discourage manpower loss, later generations might well have looked on the California gold rush as a divine intervention to aid the Saints in their efforts to create a new Zion. It is little wonder that Church leaders became so involved with gold, but it created an apparent contradiction with their publicly expressed attitudes and an ambivalence toward gold in the Mormon community.

NOTES

1. Detailed reviews of the monetary system of the beginning Mormon community in the Salt Lake Valley can be found in Arrington, *Great Basin Kingdom*, also his articles "Coin and Currency" and "Mormon Finance." A more recent review with illustrations is Rust, *Mormon and Utah Coin*, which must be used with caution, because it uses many illustrations of forgeries without so designating them. A copy with errata corrections is recommended. A better recent review is Nyholm, *The History of Mormon Currency*, 2004. The latter will soon be replaced with an expanded edition. The process of making gold coins is discussed in Kagin, *Private Gold Coins.*

2. Arrington, *Great Basin Kingdom*, 438 (footnote 69).

3. Ibid., 55, from *Deseret. News Weekly*. May 1, 1897.

4. Rust, *Mormon and Utah Coin*, 38.

5. Journal History, November 23, 1848.

6. Ibid., November 25, 1848.

7. Ibid., November 30, 1848.

8. Ibid., December 9, 1848. While Haight, the diarist from whom this excerpt was taken, was not a General Authority nor Church Historian, this entry, and others selected for the official Journal History of the Church, would play an important role in the development of the Mormon attitude toward gold mining.

9. Brigham Young's Daily Transactions in Gold

Dust," hereafter abbreviated "Gold Accounts," Vol. 1. See Appendix 7a for a summary.

10. Journal History, December 12, 1848.

11. Also on December 12, the first day of full scale operation of the gold office, payouts were made to William T. Follett, $52.50; James Craig, $10.50; William Beers, $21.00; Asahel A. Lathrop, $31.50; Ephraim Green, $10.50 by I. J. Willis; and Daniel Dennitt, $10.50.

Of the above group, Follett, Green, Beers, Willis and Dennitt were Battalion Boys. Lathrop has already been discussed, though where or how he secured the $92.19 he deposited is not known. Craig entered the Valley in 1847. It is not known how he obtained the $15.87 he deposited. It may well have been received in payment for some service or goods going to one of those coming in from California.

12. Brigham Young, Gold Accounts, January 4, 30, 1849. On December 13, "Pres. Brigham Young, John Kay and Thomas Bullock, (one of Brigham Young's clerks) received gold dust," the receipt of which is not recorded in the Gold Accounts for that day. On the 15th, $1567.69 1/2 in deposits of dust were made with payouts in coin totalling $52.50. The payouts (all more than covered by deposits) were made to Shadrack Holdaway, MB $31.50; Ephraim Green. MB by I. J. Willis, MB $10.50; and Asahel Lathrop, $10.50. Ibid., December 15, 1878, and Journal History, December 13, 1848.

13. See Appendix 7b.

14. Ibid., December 29, 1848.

15. Journal History, December 22, 1848.

16. Brigham Young, Gold Accounts, December 22, 1848 and January 3, 1849. Charles C. Burr and Newell Bullen of the *Brooklyn*; Philo M. Behunin; and Samuel Chapin, of the Battalion.

17. Journal History, December 27, 1848.

18. Ibid., December 28, 1848.

19. Hosea Stout, Diary, December 28, 1848. Brooks II:339.

20. Journal History. December 29-31, 1848; January 1-5, 8-12, 15-19, 22, 12, 1849 and Arrington, *Great Basin Kingdom*, p. 51.

21. *Ibid.*, January 1, 2, 1849.

22. Hosea Stout Diary, January 2, 1849. Brooks, *On the Mormon Frontier*, II:339.

23. Arrington, *Great Basin Kingdom*, 56 and Brigham Young, Gold Accounts, January 5, 1849.

24. Journal History, January 6, 1849. For an excellent discussion of the collapse, see Hill et al., *Kirtland Economy Revisited*. The re-issue consisted of 256 notes valued at $1,331. Already signed by Joseph Smith and others, they were countersigned by Brigham Young, Heber C. Kimball and Newell K. Whitney and were in $1.00, $3.00 and $5.00 denominations. (Arrington, *Great Basin Kingdom*.)

25. Journal History, January 8 and 9, 1849.

26. Ibid., January 8-17, 1849.

27. Ibid., January 19-23, 1849. However, because of a flaw, the printing was stopped. There were no more receipts or payouts until January 24, when the bank began operating again.

28. Ibid., June 30 and 31, 1849.

29. Josea Stout, Diary, February 4, 6, 1849. Brooks, *On the Mormon Frontier*, II:341-342.

30. *Ibid.* and Journal History, Feb. 2, 1849.

31. Lewis Meyers was a butcher in the Salt Lake Valley at that time. (He was one of the Mississippi Saints associated with the Crow family.) If he was involved, he was probably trying to accumulate portable assets. He soon emigrated to California.

32. Journal History, March 6, 1849. Emphasis, author's.

33. Journal History. March 9, 1849.

34. Brigham Young, Gold Accounts. See dates in text.

35. Arrington, "Coin and Currency," 66-67.

36. Ibid., April 12, 1849.

37. Ibid., April 23, 1849.

38. Ibid., April 10, 1849.

39. Journal History, May 2, 1849.

40. Journal History, July 3, 1849.

41. Ibid., Sept. 10, 1849.

42. Ibid., Sept. 12, 1849.

43. Douglas Nyholm, personal communication.

44. Journal History, Sept. 21, 1849.

45. Arrington, *Great Basin Kingdom*, p. 71-72.

46. See Appendix 7c for the noted entries made for William Glover on October 2, 1849.

47. Journal History, October 3 and 4, 1849.

48. Gold Accounts, Vol. II. This second volume of the Gold Accounts, entitled, "Brigham Young," covers the period October 27, 1849, to July 20, 1851. It will be referred to as Gold Accounts #2.

49. See Appendix 7d.

50. Journal History and Brigham Young, Gold Accounts #2, November 7, 1849.

51. Journal History and Brigham Young, Gold Accounts #2, December 7, 1849.

52. There were single entries on Nov. 7, 19, 22, 28, 29, 30; Dec. 7, 19, 21, 27 of 1849; Jan. 12, 22; Feb. 21, Jan. 12, 22; Feb. 21, 23, 25; Mar. 5, 12, 13, 14, 15, 16, 21; Apr. 1, 4; June 17, 28; July 9, 12, 13; Oct. 3, 4, 18, 19; Nov. 14; Dec. 20 of 1850

53 Journal History, June 22, 1850.

54. Ibid., Mar. 15, 1850.

55. Journal History, April 23, 1850.

56. Discussed in Arrington, "Coin and Currency," 73-74; Quotation is from Journal History, October 22, 1850, used by Arrington.

57. Journal History, May 28, 1850.

58. Appendix 7d.

59. *Deseret News*, January 10, 1852.

60. Rust, *Mormon and Utah Coin*, 89.

John C. Naegle (1825-1899)
Courtesy Heber and Genevieve Moulton.

John C. Naegle was born in Bavaria, Germany and immigrated with his parent's family to Indiana. He had a brother, Conrad, who converted to Mormonism and joined the Church. John also joined. The Naegle brothers went to Nauvoo, arriving shortly after the Prophet was killed, and shortly after that left Nauvoo in the Mormon exodus west. John joined the Mormon Battalion and later the San Diego Mormon Volunteers. After discharge, he went north and panned for gold.

John Naegle was a large man, 6 ft. 2in., and had correspondingly large feet. So when his shoes wore out in the gold fields, he had to go to San Francisco to have a special pair made. While there, he learned of John Horner's farming success in the Mission San Jose area. He visited the area and bought a farm with gold he had saved from his mining operations. John rented his farm out to Jonathan and Caroline Crosby (who had just returned from their proselyting mission in Tahiti) and went east to bring his parents west. He brought his parents as far as the Salt Lake Valley and returned to the West Coast alone. There he sold his farm for a good profit and emigrated back to the Salt Lake Valley.

Upon arriving in the Valley, John paid a thousand dollars in gold as tithing, another thousand for the building of the temple, and more to the Church's perpetual immigration fund to help bring the poor to the Valley, a total of $3000 in gold. According to family tradition, he was told by Edward Hunter, then the Presiding Bishop of the Church, "Brother John, you have paid more gold into the Church at one time than any other man in the Church." He would seem to compete with Thomas Rhoades for that distinction, but perhaps there are some nuances of the stories we are not aware of.

John was in the process of establishing a home in Lehi, Utah, but was called to help settle the Touquerville area in Southern Utah and set up wine and cotton industries. Mormons believed in abstaining from alcoholic beverages (the Word of Wisdom); however, more important at that time was whether the money they spent on it left the Mormon settlements. Currency was scarce. So if citizens insisted on buying wine, they needed a wine industry, to keep money spent on wine in the territory. Mormons still used wine for the sacrament (communion) in the temples, but not in the quantities John Naegle was to produce. He regularly sent barrels of "Naegle's Best" to be sold in Salt Lake City. He shut down his wine operation only when wine could be produced and shipped in by rail from the West Coast cheaper than he could produce it. He also raised horses and cattle.

Information comes from Naegle, *Life of John Conrad Naegle*. 2003).

APPENDIX 7a (Note 7:9)
Receipts and Disbursement
Brigham Young's Daily Transactions in Gold Dust
December 10, 1848-June 30, 1849

Date	Received	Cumulative Total	Paid Out	Cumulative Total	Net
12/10-12	993.75	993.75	136.50	136.50	8572.50
12/15	567.69	1561.44	52.50	189.00	1372.44
12/19	593.26	2154.70	150.00	339.00	1815.70
1/2	133.64	2288.34	1035.61	1374.61	917.73
1/3	1817.17	4105.51	1.50	1376.11	2729.40
1/5	346.21	4451.72	967.26	2343.31	2108.41
1/6	--	4451.72	49.00	2392.37	2059.35
1/7	1548.29	6000.01	--	2392.37	3607.64
1/8	191.23	6191.24	81.50	2473.87	3717.37
1/10	89.00	6280.24	745.35	3219.22	3061.02
1/12	132.03	6412.27	503.33	3722.55	2689.72
1/15	456.26	6868.53	200.51	3923.06	2945.47
1/16	5.68	6874.21	188.24	4111.30	2762.91
1/17	179.92	7054.13	83.30	4194.60	2859.53
1/19	102.11	7156.24	25.13	4219.73	2936.51
1/24	34.17	7190.41	57.43	4277.16	2913.25
1/31	210.07	7400.48	601.12	4878.28	2522.20
1/31	103.71	7504.19	1447.36	6325.64	1178.55
2/4	102.19	7606.38	311.91	6657.55	948.83
2/7	14.00	7620.38	173.33	6830.88	789.50
2/14-20	179.92	7800.30	375.21	7206.09	594.21
2/26	295.57	8095.87	673.17	7879.26	216.61
3/1	--	8095.87	661.87	8541.13	(-) 445.26
3/6	151.82	8247.69	175.88	8717.01	(-) 469.32
3/12	53.90	8301.59	133.90	8850.91	(-) 549.32
3/17,19	17.06	318.65	335.00	9185.91	(-) 867.26
3/26	25.00	8343.65	505.86	9691.77	(-)1348.12
4/2	89.17	8432.82	196.38	9888.15	(-)1455.33
4/10	47.00	8479.82	570.20	10,458.35	(-)1978.53
4/18-30	--	8479.82	276.50	10,743.85	(-)2244.03
May 1-28	20.00	8499.82	302.00	11,036.85	(-)2537.03
June 1-30	25.00	8524.82	522.00	11,558.85	(-)3034.03

Source: Compiled from Brigham Young's Daily Transactions in Gold Dust.
LDS Church Archives.

APPENDIX 7b (Note 7:13)
Recipients of Mormon Gold Coins
December 19, 1848

Sister Bent,	$20.00	Shadrack Holdaway, MB,	$10.00
Jacob L. Workman,	$10.00	Ira N. Spalding,	$10.00
David H. Jones, MB,	$20.00	Cyrus Canfield, MB,	$10.00
Alexander Neibaur,	$20.00	James H. Rawlins,	, $10.00
Azariah Smith, MB,	$10.00	Rufus Stoddard, MB,	$10.00

APPENDIX 7c (Note 7:46)
William Glover's Gold Account
October 2, 1849

American Coin	2623.85
Dust	676.16
	3300.01

Pay towards the store $3000.00	
Due him in Valley coin 300.01	
Paid William Glover by (to) Lorenzo Snow	$50.00
Paid William Glover by (to) Erastus Snow	$50.00
Paid William Glover by (to) F. D. Richards	$50.00
Paid B. Young the above	$3000.00
Received from B. Young the above dust	376.16
William Glover balance above dust	300.00
Paid Wm. Glover by (to) L. Snow, E. Snow & F. D. R.	150.00

Source: Gold Accounts.

APPENDIX 7d (Note 7:49) TABLE 7-2
GOLD DUST DEPOSITS October 28, 1849-July 20, 1851

	Received		Received
October 28	$1037.00		
29	658.00	July 6	$23.80
November 1	986.90	18	272.35
2	503.35	August 2	7.00
5	500.14	10	170.00
6	41.35	12	258.50
12	260.25	17	140.00
13	92.50	20	255.65
16	190.00	26	33.95
17	2.68 1/2	September 9	1.15
20	918.50	11	87.15
21	1106.66	17	12.50
22	23.80	23	4.15
24	32.75	October 1	4209.95
26	313.80	3	1101.03
December 1	476.15	4	643.50
5	51.20	5	614.75
6	35.30	7	1528.55
7	1038.00	14	314.77
10	11.95	25	588.80
21	485.17	November 8	1947.25
24	272.00	12	559.80
31	57.31	19	11,281.10
January 3	790.00	26	30.00
4	367.00	December 11	11.50
7	84.20	14	10,240.00
8	207.00	16	2.50
20	180.00	Feb. 1, 1851	266.50
23	10.69	March 10	240.00
February 14	5.00	31	38.53
15	3588.63	June 9	618.50
18	500.00	July 20	38.75
21	620.40		
March 4	150.00	Total	$57,257.57
7	293.34		
9	2758.20	add: 10/02/49	3,300.01 (Glover)
12	656.48	10/09/49	10,826.00 (Rhodes)
25	36.66	TOTAL	$71,133.58
April 1	601.00		
12	849.90	Source: Reconstructed from Gold Accounts.
25	235.00	Vol. 2, LDS Church Archives.
30	4.25		
May 1	60.00		
4	258.08		
27	1.50		
June 1	330.00		

[COPY RIGHT SECURED]

MORMON

WAY-BILL,

TO THE GOLD MINES,

FROM THE

PACIFIC SPRINGS,

BY THE NORTHERN & SOUTHERN ROUTES, VIZ. FORT HALL, SALT LAKE, AND LOS ANGELES INCLUDING,

SUBLET'S, HUDSPLETH'S,

AND THE VARIOUS CUT-OFF-

ALSO--FROM LOS ANGELES TO ST. FRANCISCO BY COAST ROUTE, WITH THE DISTANCES TO THE DIFFERENT RIVERS IN CALIFORNIA--TOGETHER WITH

IMPORTANT INFORMATION TO IMMIGRANTS

BY JOSEPH CAIN & ARIAH C. BROWER

G.S.L. CITY, DESERET
W. RIHARDS, PRIGNTER

1851

Facsimile of Mormon Way Bill, written by Joseph Cain and Ariah C. Brower, printed by W. Richards. The original was 4 by 6 1/2 inches. As stated on the back cover, "This Way Bill is printed on colored paper, being the most endurable, and will not wear out by being creased or carried in the pocket."

I did teach my people
to work in . . . gold.
   Book of Mormon 2 Nephi 5:15.

8

Mormon Guides to the Gold Mines

THE INFLOW OF GOLD into the Mormon Commonwealth from California's Mormon Argonauts was not the only benefit or source of income to the community to be traced to the gold fields. Mormons also played a key role in getting people from the east to the gold fields. They served as guides both from the western outposts of the United States scattered along the Missouri River through the Rockies to either Fort Hall or Salt Lake, as well as from those outposts to the gold fields, whether by the northern Humboldt River route or the southern Old Spanish Trail. They also maintained numerous supply stations and river ferries along the way. In addition, for those unable to afford a personal guide, they published at least two written guides to the gold fields, which probably provided far more help to the gold seekers than financial gain to the producers.

The first such guide was prepared between the summers of 1848 and 1849 by Ira J. Willis (Willes), veteran of the Mormon Battalion and former gold miner. He had left California for Utah with other veterans in the summer of 1848 following a spring of gold mining in the area of what became Sacramento, Sutter and El Dorado counties. His brother, Sidney S. Willis, and Wilford Hudson (both Mormon Battalion boys) are usually credited with having made the second major gold strike in California at what became Mormon Island on the lower American River.

Despite their successes, many of the Mormon miners decided to rejoin their families and the body of the Church that summer. Wishing to avoid the Donner Pass with its inconvenience (27 crossings of the Truckee River) and bad reputation because of the Donner tragedy, upon leaving that spring they decided to pioneer a new route. They gathered together at Pleasant Valley east of Weaverville (Weberville) southeast of present-day Placerville. While waiting, they made a number of gold strikes and left there July 4, 1848. Willis traveled in connection with this party. [1]

Ira J. Willis Guide to the Gold Mines

Willis kept notes of his trip, and these became the basis of his "Ira J. Willis Guide to the Gold Mines." After rejoining the traditional California Trail north of Carson Valley on their way to Utah, they encountered the west-bound wagon train of Captain Samuel J. Hensley and later a train under Captain Joseph C. Chiles. The Mormon group followed along the California Trail to the City of Rocks and then cut southeast to Salt Lake City on what became known as the Salt Lake Cutoff.

After his return home, Willis prepared a handwritten guide which was to be copied and recopied. Apparently there was no other detailed "way bill" available at the time for the area between Salt Lake and the gold fields. Willis' Guide became

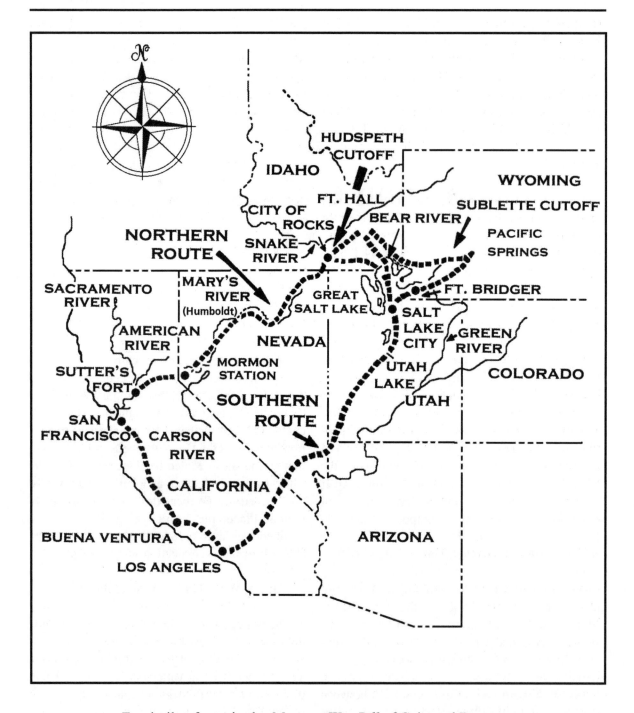

Facsimile of map in the *Mormon Way Bill* of Cain and Brower,
showing the trails covered by their *Way Bill*.
Courtesy of Kathryn Marshall

standard fare for two years until it was superseded by a second Mormon guide. While numerous errors were found in the only known original copy extant (now located at the Huntington Library in San Marino, California), it still served a useful purpose. Known travelers to use the guide were J. Goldsborough Bruff in 1849, William T. Coleman in 1850, Sarah Royce, Madison Moorman and McDiarmid. [2]

The Guide, as transcribed by Irene D. Paden, marks a trail that begins at Salt Lake going north to the Bear and Malad rivers and a warm spring (now Honeyville, Utah). The trail headed west and north to the City of Rocks (Steeple Rocks) and "the Old Road" or California Trail. It followed along Goose Creek, through Hot Spring Valley, to a branch of the Marys River (the Humboldt). [3] The trail crisscrossed the river several times as it headed west to the Sinks. From the Sinks it went to the Truckee, via the Hot Springs, bypassing the shorter but drier Chiles trail. At the Truckee, it went south over the hill to the Salmon Trout Creek (actually the Carson River), up that river to Red Lake and Lake Valley and Carson Pass and down the mountains through Rock Valley, Leek Springs, Camp Creek and Pleasant Valley with its gold mines, and finally Sutter's Fort, a distance of 862 miles.

The Cain and Brower Mormon Way Bill

A second much more extensive and detailed guide was prepared by two former California Mormon gold miners, Joseph Cain and Ariah C. Brower, a copy of which is currently in the Bancroft Library at UC Berkeley. Published by Willard Richards, counselor to Brigham Young, in Salt Lake City in 1851, it was one of the earliest printed Utah publications other than the *Deseret News*. The title page is represented in the leading illustration of the chapter. On the back cover is the note:

> This Way Bill is printed on colored paper, being the most endurable, and will not wear out by being creased or carried in the pocket

Brower was born in New York State in 1817. A printer by trade, he entered Salt Lake on September 29, 1847, as a Captain of ten in the Edward Hunter Company. He brought with him his wife, Margaret, and three children 1, 5, and 7 years of age. He subsequently moved to California with his wife and probably his children. He was in or near Salmon Falls in 1850, where he maintained an inn, and where Apostle Amasa M. Lyman and Apostle Charles C. Rich dined with them in May and July of that year. Brower became one of the early printers in Utah, becoming foreman of the print shop of the *Deseret News* and head of the fraternal association of Printers of Deseret. [4]

Cain was born in 1824 on the Isle of Man. He returned there as a missionary in 1846 after joining the Church. Returning from his mission, Cain entered Utah in 1847 at age 25, with his wife Elizabeth, in the Edward Hunter Company. In the fall of 1849, he was called to go to California, evidently sponsored by Willard Richards, as one of the Flake Company of gold miner missionaries, thereby becoming acquainted with the southern route. He traveled with the company to California via the Old Spanish Trail and then northward via the missions of the Camino Real to the gold fields. He probably went first to Mariposa, in the southern mines, to which Flake himself went with most of his company. While not listed among the tithe payers there on May 1, 1850, he was listed by Apostle Lyman as a transient member of the Church, his name appearing among others who were tithe payers at Mariposa.

On June 20, Cain met with Elders Lyman, Rich, Hunt, Egan and Hunter, all of the top Mormon leaders in California, at Lathrop's Mormon Tavern on the Placerville-Sacramento Road. He also was visited by Lyman and Rich on the 30th of July in Greenwood Valley, returning to Utah with either Lyman or Rich that year. On October 1, 1850, Willard Richards deposited $260.00, having received it from "J.C.," probably referring to Joseph Cain. [5] Cain became postmaster in Salt Lake from 1854-55 and, with Brower, assisted in the publication of the *Deseret News*. He died of consumption on April 20, 1857.

Neither Cain nor Brower deposited gold to the Mormon Gold Accounts on their return. However, President Willard Richards did with eight entries totaling $1543.50 ranging from $25 to $300, between October 1 and November 19, 1850. Some of this gold may well have come from these two men.

The *Deseret News* of January 25th, 1851, published the following prospectus:

> MORMON WAY BILL. Pointing out the distances and describing the various routes from the Pacific Springs to California, and thence to the various goldmines, is about to be issued from the Deseret press, by Cain, Brower and Co. These way bills will be forwarded east the first opportunity, and sold to emigrants traveling west; so that merchants, mechanics, millers, bakers, those keeping boardinghouses and all who choose can have the opportunity of advertising their goods, wares, merchandise, cattle shops, or whatever they may have for the benefit and use of emigrants in said Way Bill, on reasonable terms, if presented to the proprietors within ten days from date.

> N.B. Merchants and others who are going to the States this spring, wishing to take some of the above Way Bills along with them to sell to emigrants, will do well to hand in their orders immediately for the number of copies they want. [6]

The *Deseret News* for February 22, 1851, again announced the availability of the Way Bill "now completed and for sale at the Post Office; price one dollar for a single copy. Thirty percent discount will be made when an individual buys them to sell again."

The Cain and Brower Way-bill starts at Pacific Springs, northeast of Fort Bridger. At that point there were two routes open to travelers. The left hand fork took the traveler to Fort Bridger, down Echo Canyon and eventually to Salt Lake. From Salt Lake the traveler could then head north and then west on the Salt Lake Cutoff to the City of Rocks on the California Trail. At Pacific Springs the wayfarer could have taken the right hand road, Sublette's Cutoff, to either Fort Hall where supplies could be obtained, or to the soda springs if a short cut was desired. These routes joined the Salt Lake Cutoff near the City of Rocks. From the latter area, the route went south to the Marys or Humboldt River. At Kanyon Creek, "passable only in the early part of the season because of high water," the emigrants were warned that if they valued their lives they should:

> Keep in not less company than 25 armed men, with vigilant watch by day and night; if not, they will lose their animals and most likely be murdered in the bargain; guards had better keep a strict watch in the night, or they will be shot from the thick brush which is all the way down Mary's River. No man, woman, or child should leave the company, under any circumstances whatever, for the brush conceals the Indians, who take advantage of persons who are a little way behind their train; this advice will suffice for the whole of the river to the sink of Mary's river, and if emigrants do not take it and profit by the same, they never will get to the end of their journey. [7]

Following the same route as Willis' Guide, the travelers were warned, upon reaching the Carson River, to "look out for Indians up Carson Valley." The road went to Mormon Station, over Carson Pass, down to Pleasant Valley and Weaverville (Weberville) "the first small town you come to, and the beginnings of the Gold Diggings." The road then led to Sacramento by way of the Mormon Tavern.

At that point the Way-bill noted distances to various parts of the mines from the Mormon Tavern. One road went north to the North Fork of the American River, a distance of 35 miles. However, the authors advised emigrants to head south, the northern mines being too crowded. They said that "there are many of the southern diggings yet good." They advised the Argonauts not to go to Sacramento as they would be only "throwing away valuable time, having to come back as far as the Mormon Tavern if they were going to any of the mines north of the North Fork.

Lathrop's Mormon Tavern

Mormon Tavern, first established by a Mormon named Morgan and operated by Asahel A. Lathrop of the Mormon Battalion. Persons in the picture are mostly of the Jaeger family, later owners of the property. The Mormon Way Bill ends the California route at Mormon Tavern and gives the distances to destinations in various directions from there. The history of Mormon Tavern can be found in John N. Wilson, *These Lonely Hills*, available in the California State Library, Sacramento, and in the El Dorado County Museum, Placerville. *Courtesy Museum of El Dorado County.*

The directions and distances are then given to the southern mines, via Stockton and the Marsedes (Merced) store, probably the store maintained by the Salt Lake Trading Company under Howard Egan on the Merced River. [8] This route avoided the very difficult mountainous area between Sonora and Mariposa, but also missed the Mormon Gulch and Sonora mines. The road then went to Mariposa and as far south as King's River, another hundred or so miles.

The editors advised emigrants, without wagons and going no further than the Merced store where they could buy provisions at reasonable prices, to take no more than 50 pounds of provisions from Stockton "as it is troublesome work traveling over steep mountains looking for diggins and having to pack tools, bedding and provisions." However, if they intended to go beyond the store, or Mariposa at the most, they should take provisions for one or two months as the cost of freighting goods was very high.

In addition to the northern routes to the gold fields, the authors gave the details for the southern route. As the travelers on this route approached the Santa Clara Road in the southern part of the Mormon domain, they were warned to "look out for Indians." The route then took them to the Las Vegas (Vegas) springs, the Mojave desert, Cahoon (Cajon) pass, Williams' Ranch and the Pueblo de Los Angeles. The suggested route then went via the Spanish missions to San Francisco.

The editors suggested that emigrants not attempt to take their cattle beyond Fort Hall or Great Salt Lake but to exchange them for others, or horses. Cautioning that worn out cattle could not make it to the trip's end and citing the sacrifice of "thousands of cattle and horses" along the way to California, they pointed out that the road to Fort Hall and Salt Lake "is comparatively a railroad, to the one from thence to California." The emigrants were advised not to load themselves down with tools as these "can be purchased cheap in California." They were also warned that they must get over the Sierra Nevada mountains before the 10th of October because of snow which began to fall about that time, a tragic lesson learned from the Donner-Reed party.

It was suggested that pack animals be loaded with hard bread and dried beef. "Clothes can be bought in Sacramento and Stockton, as cheap as in the States." They said that men could "get to good diggins, which will average $8 to $16 per day" and could secure all the clothes they wanted "with one or two day's work." They advised: "After the emigrant settled on his winter diggins, he had better secure provisions enough to last him until April; together with pickles, vinegar &, (etc.?) as a preventive to the scurvy." [9]

Appended to this guide are eight pages of advertisement including the following:

Irvin Stoddard -- Meals, horses Cattle, Pack-saddles etc.

B.F. Johnson -- everything needed by the traveler from pack animals to drugs at the "Sign of the Collar."

Martin H. Peck – Blacksmithing.

A. L. Lamoreaux -- Blacksmithing, feed and fresh food.

A. Neibaur -- surgeon dentist from Berlin, Prussia, also

"A constant supply of the best matches" made by Neibaur.

M. Cannon -- Daguerrotype Miniatures.

Livingston & Kinkead (formerly of St. Louis) General Merchandise.

George Gibbons & Co. California Bake House Meals and food.

H. Chaight -- Hotel with Blacksmith shop.

S. Hotchkiss, M.D. Dental Surgeon.

Wm. McBride Blacksmithing.

A. B. Lambson Blacksmithing.

T. S. Williams Food, animals and supplies.

Beach and Blair -- Ale and Ice, Salmon Trout

S.M. Blair Residence for Sale.

McVicar & Barlow, Watchmakers and Jewelers.

The advertisements are then followed by a Way-bill for the Oregon Trail by way of Fort Hall and going as far as The Dalles.

It would appear that the two Mormon guides were probably among the best available --- at least in 1849-1851. They certainly must have played a significant, if inexpensive and little recorded, role in the gold rush of those years. In addition to these written guides, unrecorded numbers of trail-wise Mormons served as personal guides for those parties that could afford them. And others maintained numerous way-stations and ferries along the routes west.

Some maps, discussion and views of the development of the Mormon-Carson Emigrant Route from the Mormon Argonaut period and into the next decade are presented in Appendix D (page 364).

NOTES

1. Henry Bigler, *Bigler's Chronicle*, 112-14.

2. See Irene D. Paden, ed. "The Ira J. Willis

Guide," 193-204. The guide was transcribed by Paden from an original at the Huntington Archives. A copy of the transcription is in the LDS Church Archives. Willis settled in Lehi, Utah Territory in 1849, and married. He died December 5, 1863. See Appendix 8a for a copy of guide.

3. While there are both Marys and Humboldt Rivers in Nevada, travelers frequently used them interchangeably referring to what is now known as the Humboldt.

4. Davies, *Deseret's Sons of Toil*, 53-70.

5. Gold Accounts.

6. *Deseret News*. January 25, 1851.

7. *Mormon Way Bill, Deseret News*. January 25, 1851. All remaining quotes in the chapter are taken from this source. (Word in brackets is the author's.)

8. See Chapter 15 for details.

9. Lorenz, "Scurvy in the Gold Rush."

APPENDIX 8a (Note 8:2)

BEST GUIDE
to the

GOLD MINES
by

Ira J. Willis G. S. L. City

Way Bill of distances, camping place, rivers, hot springs &c on the Route from G. S. L. City to the Gold Mines

	Miles
To Bear River, crossing the Weber 4 miles this side of Capt. Brown's Roadometer Measure (Good camping at short distances)	84.
Thence to Malad or Mud Creek	3.
Thence to the 1st Warm Spring	6.
Thence to the 2nd good camping	14.
Thence to the Spring in the Mts. good camping	12.
Thence down Deep Creek cross at the Bend	6.
Thence down Deep Creek good camping	6.
Thence to Spring in the plains poor	10.
Thence to Cajiers (or Cajius) Creek good camping at several places in sight on left	26.
Thence Up Cajiers (or Cajius) Creek, good camping	9.
	176._
Thence to the Old Road near the Steeple Rocks (probably at the city of Rocks)	176.
Thence to Goose Creek over a hill	10.
	192.
Several camping places from the Steeple Rocks to Goose Creek.	
Thence Up Goose Creek, good camping	22

To the Hot Spring Valley	13.
To the 2nd Spring (good camp)	5.
through the Valley	32.
Found good camping places none of them are more than 10 miles apart	
Thence To a Branch of Mary's River [1] good camping through a kanyon crossing the Branch	8.
9 times camping	8.
Thence to Mary's River good camping all along	10.
Martins Fork of Mary's River good camping all along	60.
	359.

Thence over a hill through a kanyon to where you	359.
strike Mary's River again	20.
(good camping & good in the Kanyon)	
Then to a pass in the hills where you cross the	
River twice good camping all along	72.
Then to the next crossing of Mary's River	
good camping all along	46.
Then over a drive without grass or water	14.
Then to the lower crossing of Mary's River good camping	14.

Then to the lower camping place on the River, grass scarce	26.
Then to a Slough, grass scarce poor camping	15.
Then to the Sink of Mary's River grass & wood scarce	20.
	586.

The best water here is in a slough that passes through	
a bend & a narrow Bluff. Here also you may find a	586.
new track [2] on your left that Childs (Chiles)	
intended to make last fall which may be nearer	
& less distance to do without grass & water.	
By the Battalion route from the Sink to the hot Springs,	
no grass, poor water	20.
Thence to Truckie River, good camp	25
(Should be 631)	622.

The road forks here. [3]	
You will take the left hand road to	
Salmon Trout (Carson) river good camp	25.
Childs (Chiles) road if made comes in at this	
or the next camping place.	
Then turn to the right and cross a bend good camping.	15.
Up the river good camp	8.
Cross a hill to the river good camp	12.
To Pass Creek Kanyon good camping every few miles	42.
through Pass Creek Kanyon	5.
	738.

Thence to Red Lake or the foot of the dividing	738.
Ridge. Califa. Mts.	11
	749.

Good camping nigh by

Then to Lake Valley,	good camping	6.
Then over the highest Ridge (Carson Pass) to Rock Valley,	good camping	
Then to the Leek Springs,	good camping & good by the way	13.
Then to Camp Creek	poor camping	10.
Then down the ridge and then you arrive into a valley two miles on your left grass plenty		16.
Then to Pleasant Valley Gold Mines		12.
		816.
Then to Sutters		55.
	(Should be 871)	862.

Truckie & Salmon Trout are not the same
river but Mary's, Ogden & Humboldt are.

Source: Best Guide to The Gold Mines. Copy at Baldwin Library, San Marino, California.

1. The Marys River is a tributary of what is now known as the Humboldt which was referred to by both names.

2. At the Sink of the Mary's or Humboldt river, two choices were available. Emigrants could travel due south on the Chiles road through forty miles of salt wasteland to the Carson River at or near what became known as Ragtown, a few miles west of present-day Fallon. The other option, the one described by Willis, was to continue along the California Trail southwest, passing the hot springs and hitting the big bend of the Truckee at or near present-day Wadsworth (or Fernley). The Mormon Trail then struck south, over the low hills, to the Carson River at or near Silver Spring where it was joined by the 40 Mile Desert road.

3. The right hand fork followed the Truckee River over Donner Pass.

Amasa M. Lyman (1813-1877)

Amasa Mason Lyman was born in Lyman Township, New Hampshire. He converted to Mormonism when he was nineteen, and rose rapidly in the Church in roles of responsibility and leadership. Lyman was ordained an apostle in 1842 at age 29. He was a regent of the University of Nauvoo, a justice of the peace, and a company captain in bringing groups to the Salt Lake Valley. He helped establish western settlements and served ten years in the Utah Territorial Legislature.

In 1850 he went on a mission to California to conduct Church business, gather tithing, and encourage the sending of gold to the struggling community in the Salt Lake Valley, returning in September of that year. In 1851 he and Apostle Charles C. Rich led a company of settlers to Southern California, where they established the San Bernardino colony. That settlement functioned as a way station and trail terminus for winter travel to California. In 1857, members of the Church at San Bernardino were called back to the Valley to help defend against Johnston's army approaching Salt Lake City. In later years Lyman had a falling out with the Church over the doctrine of the Atonement, for which he was excommunicated in 1870. He died at Fillmore, Utah, in 1877. For a definitive biography, see Lyman, *Amasa Mason Lyman, Mormon Apostle*, 2009. *Courtesy LDS Archives.*

He said there was a book deposited written upon gold plates, giving an account of the former people of this continent.

Pearl of Great Price -- Joseph Smith 2:34

9

Amasa M. Lyman and the Mormon Apostolic Gold Mission

WHILE FOR SOME REASON Apostle Amasa M. Lyman's mission call to California and the gold fields in the fall of 1848 had been postponed, by spring of 1849 it had become evident that such a call could no longer be delayed. Brigham Young's Gold Account (Deseret's "National Bank", so called) was in serious difficulty.

On March 26th "it was decided to send Elder Lyman and Orrin P. Rockwell on a mission to California with an epistle to the faithful Saints, and also to preach the Gospel and look after the interest of the Church and the Saints, and to return with those who might be coming to the valley in the fall." [1] On March 31st, it was concluded that Lyman and Rockwell should "take a mail to the Pacific Coast immediately." The Church leaders also discussed "the propriety of sending a good responsible man to settle on the Pacific coast at or near San Francisco bay." [2] They did not envision that person as being Lyman as he was expected to return to Salt Lake that fall. This call went to the neophyte Apostle but seasoned Saint, Elder Charles C. Rich, who did not actually depart until the fall.

Roster for the Lyman-Rockwell Party

The Lyman-Rockwell party was reconstituted at conference time in April of 1849. It consisted of 20 men, but the members of this party are unnamed. Four groups of the pioneers to the Salt Lake Valley in 1847 provided especially large proportions of their numbers to the gold fields. Contrasted with the 15 to 25 percent overall of the Pioneers of 1847 who went, these four groups had the following record as probable migrants to the gold fields: [3]

1. Of the 39 Captains of Ten, 15 (or 38 percent).

2. Of the 15 adults in the Crow Company, 13, (or 87 percent).

3. Of the 12 family units of the Mississippi Saints, five (or 42 percent).

4. Of the 19 detached family units of the Battalion, 12, (or 63 percent).

A few of these are known to have gone other than with Lyman. Some went to California as individuals, others of them going as family units. Many, if not most, were in California at the time of the 1850 census, which was conducted in the fall and over the winter months of 1850-51. [4]

The Captains of Ten, having shown evidence of loyalty and skill on the trail, served as likely candidates for the trip with Lyman. The Mississippi Saints and Battalion families had been closely associated with Apostle Lyman since 1847. At Fort Laramie, Lyman had been dispatched south to meet them and escort them into the valley. Many had settled in the Cottonwood area south of Salt Lake on land assigned to Lyman. A good many of the southern Saints would help Lyman and Rich in the settlement of San Bernardino in 1851. [5] These groups, therefore, constituted a most likely source of recruitment to the gold fields in the spring of 1849.

Lyman left Salt Lake on April 13th. One of his wives, Eliza Marie Partridge Lyman (left behind in Salt Lake) recorded that "Br. Lyman started for California . . . left us, that is, Pauline, Caroline and I [his wives] without anything to make bread -- it not being in his power to get any." However, she observed that "the family at Cottonwood have some." [6]

Though left destitute, friends and relatives came to the rescue of Lyman's wives, (Eliza, Pauline and Caroline), providing them with flour and corn. And Lyman did not leave them to forage for themselves. On October 3rd Eliza informed her diary that household supplies reached them, having been sent by Lyman from California with a man named Frederic. Divided among his several families were coffee, sugar, tea, and all sorts of cloth.

While there were those who went to California in the spring of 1849 with Brigham Young's blessing or permission, there were those who went contrary to his wishes. The problem is that it is difficult to distinguish among them.

The pressures for movement from Deseret to California had begun to mount in the late winter. On February 24th, Brother Robert Crow, the patriarch of a large family, had presented a petition signed by himself and seven others, asking permission from the Presidency and Council of the Church to go to the California gold mines to dig gold. The request was denied, Crow being counseled to stay in the valley and raise grain. [7] However, Crow was in the gold fields with the other members of his family the following year.

On Sunday, February 25th, President Young, provoked by the "corrupt" and "rebellious souls" going to California, advised them to do so and

> not come back, for I will not fellowship them . . . If the people were united I would send them to get the gold who would care not more about it than the dust under their feet, and thus we could put Millions into the Church and gather the poor." [8]

It would appear that Robert Crow and family may have gone to California in a state of rebellion. However, arriving there, he stayed close to Elder Lyman and to the Church, being very receptive to missionaries in the gold fields as late as 1856-57. In addition, in response to H.G. Boyle, a number of his family members left their homes in the latter year, migrating to San Bernardino and Utah. What may well have happened is that once the decision was made to send men and families to California that spring, the Crow family members were recruited by Lyman. The Orrs, the Harmons and the Hanks (probable California emigrants of that year) stayed especially close to the Church over the next several years. They also may well have joined the Apostle.

John Brown, a leader of the Mississippi Saints, discussed in greater detail in the next chapter, was of the opinion that Lyman and company were sent to California to keep disgruntled expatriates "from poisoning the minds of those who were in that country who had never been" to Utah. [9] These would basically have been from among Battalion members and *Brooklyn* Saints who had stayed in California although others are known to have gone by way of the traditional Oregon-California Trail.

The concern with any "unauthorized" exodus is seen in the Journal History entries of that spring, most of which were taken from diaries of various individuals. On March 17th, Patty Sessions reports, "there are some people here who are about to leave for the gold mines. Some for other places, but most of them have the yellow fever."[10] On March 21st, "eight wagons and families left for Ogden on their way to the gold mines." [11] On March 22nd, "Three wagons passed President

Willard Richards' corral . . . on their way to the gold mines." [12] As seen later, Abner Blackburn, one of the Battalion detachees, his brother, Thomas, and probably ex-Lieutenant George W. Rosecrans of the Battalion and his family, along with several others, were among those leaving Utah for the gold fields that spring, apparently without the blessings of the Church leadership. (These members at least later became disaffected.)

Rockwell had responsibilities other than merely accompanying Elder Lyman. Recently appointed a deputy marshal, Porter carried with him a warrant from President Heber C. Kimball for the arrest of Hiram Gates and Levi Fifield who reportedly kidnapped Rockwell's daughter. [13]

In addition to the General Epistle from the Church leaders, Lyman carried with him an unusual letter to Samuel Brannan from Brigham Young. After assuring Brannan that the man "who is always doing right has no occasion to fear any complaints" and referring him to Apostle Lyman for any further questions, the Church leader said with a undertone of sarcasm that he was glad to hear that Brannan "was pushing every nerve to assist and sustain him." Referring to the *Brooklyn* leader's rapidly accumulating wealth, the Prophet said that he expected $100,000 in tithing if he had accumulated "a million to tithe." [14]

Young then went on to say that once he had settled his tithing, Brannan should not forget the leader's "destitute" circumstances, requesting a gift of "twenty thousand dollars in gold dust," adding that such an amount was "but a trifle when gold is so plenty . . ." He then requested that the Californian send an additional $20,000 to divide between his two counselors, Elders Kimball and Richards, adding that Brannan would then have their "united blessing . . ."

In a final paragraph, Brannan was counseled to "deal out with a liberal heart and open hands making a righteous use of all your money" and the Lord would bless him with "rich treasures." If not, his "hopes and prospects will be blasted . . . and no arm to save."

Departing for California and San Francisco

The Lyman-Rockwell party departed Salt Lake on April 12, 1849, taking the northern route, and arrived at Sutter's Fort on May 25th. According to Schindler, Lyman headed for San Francisco to begin collecting tithes from the Saints residing there. Schindler also indicates that Rockwell went right to the "diggings." It is assumed that Lyman at this time delivered the letter to Brannan from Brigham Young. Given the content of the letter and the importance of Lyman's trip for gathering the tithes, it is likely the subject of collections did come up with Brannan. In any case, they apparently departed on good terms, despite the strong tone of the letter. Lyman wrote Brigham Young about how he was approaching Brannan, at least at first. In a letter from Sacramento, July 6, 1849, he wrote, "I saw Mr. Samuel Brannan and his partner Mr. Stout. I think that Samuel will do some good thing for the Church if he is let alone. I design pursuing a course with him that will allow him an opportunity to do all the good he may have the means or disposition to do." [15] Schindler's observation that the first known collection attempt was not until January 8, 1850 may be referring to the reporting of a final more confrontational approach. [16]

Most of the *Brooklyn* Saints and many of the Mormon Battalion Boys had been paying tithes to Brannan who, until the arrival of Lyman, was the only acknowledged, albeit challenged, leader of the Saints in California. However, by the time Lyman arrived, Brannan was evidently marching to a different tune than Brigham Young's. He reportedly refused to give up the tithes collected. Of course the actual tithes had already been spent on his multitudinous, and to some, "nepharious," business ventures and were therefore not readily available. He also apparently refused to give up the records of tithes and offerings at the time, doing so a year later. [17]

Lyman in the Gold Fields

Lyman did not spend all of his time in the comparative ease of San Francisco, being found on the "North Fork" (probably of the American River), by September 19th when he wrote to the First Presidency. [18] He received a letter of instruction

Mormon Bar on the North Fork of the American River

John M. Letts visited northern California in 1849 by way of the Isthmus of Panama. He toured San Francisco, Sacramento, and the mines, writing about the experience and sketching scenes along the way. This scene, sketched at Mormon Bar, later lithographed, is where he first tried mining with a "machine," presumably a rocker. (From *California Illustrated*, by John M. Letts.) *Courtesy Bancroft Library.*

(dated November 2, 1849), by way of Bro. George W. Hickerson, associated with the Pomeroy train, as well as a copy by way of Capt. Howard Egan, the leader of the Salt Lake Trading Company. Details of these groups leaving Salt Lake in the fall will follow in later chapters.

In the letter, Lyman was instructed that "the proper time and place for paying labor tithing is when and where labor is performed." This meant that "the brethren who are digging gold" should tithe "weekly, semi-monthly or monthly according to circumstances"—preferably every ten to sixteen days. Lyman was informed that "This is an important part of your mission to collect tithing so that the public works shall not languish."[19] Instructions were given for money to be paid certain individuals out of the tithing. The brethren were instructed that on their return they should

bring their gold dust, "rather than foreign coins as our mint is in good condition and in active operation at home."

Referring to the groups of Mormon '49ers leaving for the goldfields that fall, the Church leader said that "nearly or quite every man who has gone from here this fall to the diggings has gone in good faith and feeling" and all were expected to go to Lyman for "council and instruction." Lyman was advised that he would then be in a position to "combine the strength of the brethren to their mutual advantage."

From Lyman's letter of September 19th was addressed from the "North Fork," it would appear that he was at the time someplace other than at Mormon Island which was on the South Fork of the American River. Perhaps he was at Mormon

Bar, Mormon Ravine, or even Murderer's Bar and Slap Jack Bar, the latter two actually on the Middle Fork branch of the North Fork. However, he spent much of his time at Mormon Island.

J. M. Letts, a non-Mormon miner at Mormon Bar in 1849, wrote three years later somewhat critically of his experiences with the Mormons. He said that his neighbors in 1849 "were mostly Mormons, headed by Amasa Lyman accompanied by Porter Rockwell operating under an alias, Scofield." [20] Referring to Rockwell's supposed attempt several years earlier on the life of Governor Boggs of Missouri, who had emigrated to California in 1846, Letts said that Boggs and his two sons (upon hearing of Rockwell's presence) "were supposed to be in search of him" and that Rockwell accordingly was always well armed and had with him a guard dog. He also wrote that Rockwell was well admired by the Mormons, "keeping him informed of the whereabouts of the enemy."

The Mormon "community" at Mormon Bar was apparently unusual compared with the stereotype of Mormon communities. Letts maintained that that Mormons "here were a good set of fellows, somewhat reckless, fine horsemen, fond of sprees, and an occasional fight . . . They were all hardworking and fond of gambling. They had all been to 'Salt Lake,' (also not true) and considered it their country and home, many of them having left their families there."

While Letts does not give a date for this involvement at Mormon Bar, his reference to Lyman, Rockwell, and the Boys as having been in Salt Lake, though inaccurate, would indicate that he was speaking of late 1849 or early 1850. Because of Lyman's known activities after December of 1849, it is believed that Letts must have been referring to the latter half of 1849. It is important to note, however, that the Mormons were apparently still in the majority even though substantial numbers had left in the summer of 1848.

Letts continued with a description of the mining operations at Mormon Bar in what must have been one of the earliest attempts at using hydraulics, but in reverse of the usual placer mining technique. Under Lyman's direction, ("his word was law,") a canvas hose was made to pump water out of the holes, the hope being that gold would have accumulated in the bottom. However, the experiment proved "disastrous," at least financially.

As so frequently has happened in the history of the Mormons, their cohesiveness, if not clannishness, earned them the ill-will of non-Mormons. It is understandable that they, having been the first on the scene, would have viewed the Bar with a certain proprietary interest—much to the displeasure of the non-Mormon latecomers. It is also within reason that they should have been resented. Letts continued his story, telling how he felt the Gentiles were victimized by the Mormons because (as he saw it) "The 'faithful,' having a majority, had it all their own way; and they managed as seemed best calculated to victimize the 'Gentiles'."

He continued saying that the Mormons, "having canalled and worked the bar, knew every foot of it." They wanted each man to be allowed any ten feet he desired. Latecomers wanted to draw lots. Lyman proposed the former method of distribution and, because Mormons were in a majority and followed Lyman's dictates, he won out. When the vote was cast, there was a mad rush, the Mormons securing the richest claims.

However, according to Letts, he outsmarted them. Knowing nothing about the bar he "followed the 'Prophet' and his satellites," taking the next spot above them. He was able, he said, "to remove as much as six to eleven ounces of gold on some days."

Rockwell in the Gold Fields

Porter Rockwell found an easier way to obtain gold than to go through the grubby, backbreaking labor of mining it. Schindler claims that Porter went almost immediately after his arrival in June to Murderers Bar, a few miles east of present-day Auburn, about a mile above the juncture of the North and Middle Forks of the American River (and on the Middle fork) where he opened a bar or saloon. [21]

He is also reported to have opened an inn at Buckeye Flat, and is known to have had a tav-

Mining at Murderer's Bar, on the Middle Fork of the American River.

Murderer's Bar was named for murders committed there in the early gold rush period. The victim's remains were discovered by prospectors. Mormons mined at Murderer's Bar and also Slap Jack Bar a short distance up stream.

Most of the early gold mining was done at river bars ("placers" in Spanish.) Miners soon recognized that the gold that had been eroded out of the mountains for centuries, was deposited in these bars, along with the gravel and silt. The rivers were essentially giant flumes, and the river bars of gravel were essentially sections of "riffles." These bars would form, especially at turns of the river where the water would slow on one side or the other and develop eddies, causing the silt and gold to settle. The gold would gradually work its way down even to bedrock. When they had finished mining the bars, miners (when they could) would divert the rivers and mine the river beds.

At Murderer's Bar, there was a giant cleft in the rocks cutting across the river. Miners felt that cleft could be filled with gold. So the miners built a giant flume to divert the water. If they were going to do it for the cleft, why not an entire section of the river? So the flume was constructed a mile long. Water wheels in the flume were used to pump out water and to help bring up the sediment to the miners, who would then use sluices and rockers to separate out the gold. The first flume was no sooner built than a cloudburst produced a wall of water racing down the canyon. The flume was washed out and it floated downstream. It was then rebuilt. (See Robie, "At Murderer's Bar," 3-6.) [The illustration is in the Robie article, but is originally from *Harper's New Monthly Magazine*, vol. 20, issue 119 (April 1860), 603.] Much gold was taken out of Murderer's Bar. The first three prospectors (converted sailors) "began to mine with pick and pan and on the first day took out twenty-nine pounds of gold. They worked their claim a little over one month and then went back to San Francisco with over five hundred pounds of gold valued at $105,000." (Peters, Autobiography, 97.)

Rockwell operated his Round Tent Saloon at Murderer's Bar. Charles C. Rich, at Slap Jack Bar just up stream, called some Mormon miners to leave the mines and go on a proselyting mission to the Sandwich Islands (Hawaii). George Q. Cannon was one of the miners called.

Rockwell's Rifle Contest

Sketch by Dale Bryner in Schindler, *Orrin Porter Rockwell: Man of God, Son of Thunder,* 1983.
Courtesy University of Utah Press

ern located where Deer Creek crosses the old Sacramento-Placerville Road between Shingle Springs and Mormon Tavern. In addition, Schindler records that Rockwell also maintained the "half-way house" on the American River between Sacramento and Mormon Island. [22] He must have been a very busy entrepreneur.

While Letts maintained that Rockwell was known as Scofield, Slater, (an anti-Mormon writer) [23] claims that he operated under the name of Brown. Achilles, [24] another anti-Mormon writer, refers to him as using the name of James B. Brown. The use of the pseudonym "Brown" is corroborated by the diary of Louisa Barnes Pratt, a devout Mormon on her way to join her missionary husband, Addison Pratt, in the South Pacific. A member of the Mormon Huntington Company, on July 16, 1850, west of Weaverville (Weberville) she recorded: "Camped in an oak grove near Brown's a fictitious name for Porter Rockwell." [25] This identification also establishes the location of Porter's second hostelry as being on the road between Placerville and Sacramento.

The general location of Rockwell's fourth hostelry, between Sacramento and Mormon Island, is also supported by the account of Jonathan and Caroline Crosby who were in the Huntington Company with Louisa Pratt. As the group approached Sacramento, Caroline and Jonathan Crosby noted that Rockwell was seen selling whiskey to the miners. In Jonathan's "Biographical Sketch" they add that they "Went on to where Porter Rockwell & another man in Co. were keeping a licquer shop, we camped a day & sold our teems & waggons to P. Rockwell . . . but we had the use of them to take us to Sacramento & Porter sent a man along to take the teems back." [26]

While Rockwell's involvement in the whiskey trade may seem incongruous with the 20th century image of Mormons, it was no singular aberration. A substantial number of Mormons operated hotels, inns, or taverns in the gold fields. Reference has already been made to Lathrop and his Mormon Tavern. Cannon reports that two Mormon Battalion Boys, William Squires and Jeptha Condit, opened a tavern on the road between Sacramento and the Mormon Tavern. [27] Reference to

Jonathan and Caroline Barnes Crosby
(1807-1892) (1807-1884)
Courtesy Utah State Historical Society.

The Crosbys converted to Mormonism in Canada and followed the Church from Kirtland, Ohio to Nauvoo, Illinois, and to Salt Lake City. From there they accepted a call to do missionary work in the Society Islands (Tahiti.) Returning from Tahiti, they lived for a time in San Francisco, then near Mission San Jose, for awhile in San Bernardino, and finally settled in Beaver Utah.

Louisa Barnes Pratt
(1802-1880)
Courtesy Utah State University.

Louisa lived with her family in Canada before moving to New England, where she met and married Addison Pratt. The Pratts heard about Mormonism from Jonathan and Caroline Crosby. They too joined the Church and followed the Mormons from Kirtland, Ohio to Nauvoo, Illinois. From Nauvoo, Addison was sent on a mission to the Society Islands. Louisa went west to Salt Lake City. From Salt Lake, Louisa was sent with Caroline and Jonathan to the Society Islands. Both families returned together, the Pratts going to San Bernardino. Louisa settled with the Crosbys in Beaver, Utah. Addison stayed in Southern California and lived with their daughter.

more tavern-owning Mormons will be found in later chapters.

Rockwell evidently operated in partnership with others, perhaps explaining his ability to keep several operations going. Schindler claims that Porter was in partnership with a Mormon, probably Judson Stoddard (who operated under the name of Jack Smith), at Murderers Bar on the Middle Fork running the Round Tent Saloon. He

states:

In 1849 a main street crowded with makeshift buildings of all descriptions made up Murderer's Bar. Rockwell ran the Round Tent Saloon amid this confusion and hauled in whisky from Sacramento by pack train. Arriving at a hill overlooking the bar, he would loose a blast on a bugle carried for the

Sacramento during the Inundation of January 1850

Lithograph by Casselear and Bainbridge. The view is from above the Sacramento River, across Front Street, and looking eastward down "J" Street. The Brannan owned City Hotel is the three-story building mid block to the left of the beginning of "J" Street. The American River flows from the far distance and enters the Sacramento River a short distance off the picture to the left. Sutter's Fort is about two miles up "J" Street and to the right. *Courtesy Bancroft Library.*

purpose, and his partner, Jack Smith, at the Round Tent would reply by firing a signal shot to miners up and down the river that `business' was about to begin. [28]

Schindler also recounts another story about Rockwell, this one at Halfway House. He reveals:

Things moved smoothly for the quiet Mormon (Rockwell) until one day when another trading post operator, an ex-battalion member, challenged him to a shooting contest.

When word spread that 'Brown' and Boyd Stewart were going to shoot at targets for a prize of $1,000, Half-Way House found itself playing host to hundreds of garrulous miners. Stewart hailed from Columbia, California and had distinguished himself during the Mormon Battalion march by his inability to stay out of trouble.[26] He knew who Brown really was, a detail Rockwell came to regret.

The rifle match took place in the afternoon, and when the scores were tallied, 'Brown' was declared winner, and the $1,000 in dust and nuggets was turned over to him. This was all the reason necessary for a celebration, and before an hour passed the plaza at Halfway House was the scene of perhaps the wildest whiskyfest ever staged in the gold fields. Stewart, stung by defeat, turned to the drunken mob and shouted Rockwell's identity for all to hear. Not a few men in the horde of miners were Missourians and Illinoisians by birth. Many others harbored grievances over their treatment by Mormons in Zion. In their stupor, they shouted threats of reprisal against the man they

Sam Brannan's City Hotel
(Cropping of illustration on page 132)

The first floor of the City Hotel consisted of a lobby, a bar, and a dining room. The second floor had individual first-class rooms. The third floor was an open area with tiers of bunks around the walls and a large washbasin in the middle of the room. Hastily constructed in 1849, the hotel quickly became outdated. It was torn down and replaced by another structure in just a few years. Two structures to the right is the Eagle Theatre, site of the beginnings of professional theater in California. *Courtesy Bancroft Library.*

knew as the Destroying Angel and surged forward to offer him a taste of camp justice. According to Achilles, it was only with a great deal of luck that Rockwell managed to avoid being caught and hanged. [29]

Regardless of the truth of this tale, some of it coming from unfriendly sources, Rockwell was ready to leave California with Charles C. Rich when he started out on his return to Zion in October of 1850. As far as is known, that would be the last that Porter, the rather unorthodox Mormon frontiersman, had to do with the gold fields of California, though he did later return to San Francisco for a visit.

To San Francisco and Sacramento

Meanwhile, on January 8, 1850, Lyman and Rockwell visited Brannan. The following interchange purportedly took place:

Said Lyman, "We've come for the Lord's money."

Replied Brannan, "Give me a receipt from the Lord and you can have the money." [30]

This version of events is purely folklore. It is known that Lyman visited Brannan on that date, recording it in his diary, but Lyman does not refer to Rockwell being with him, neither does he say

what his business with Brannan was. Nor does he record any sort of negative reaction by Brannan to his visit. [31] If Rockwell did visit Brannan with Lyman, and if the above conversation did take place, Rockwell must have remained uncharacteristically quiescent. If he was such a desperado, as he is usually made out to be, one can hardly conceive of Brannan getting by with such a retort.

On Saturday the 19th Lyman "travelled to Sacramento on the 'Senator' "meeting (John S.) Fowler, a business partner of Brannan, in the operation of the City Hotel. Upon their arrival, Lyman was lodged at the Mormon-owned hotel, Sacramento's first. The flood waters which had inundated the area were receding, as observed by Lyman the following day. On Monday, the Apostle visited Captain (Jesse D.) Hunter, [32] a Battalion leader "who with his family was living on raised floors above the (flood) waters."

On Tuesday, they went by boat to the Fort, a couple of miles up the American River and thence by foot to the camp of Dan P. Clark [33] and D. (Darwin) P. Richardson and M. (Marcus) L. Shepherd, both of the Mormon Battalion. From there he visited with (William L.) McIntire and (George W.) Rosecrans, also of the Battalion, at whose house he lodged. Lyman returned to Sacramento and the City Hotel on Sunday, January 28, 1850.

The City Hotel was Sacramento's first. a three

story wooden structure, it faced the riverfront and is prominently pictured in the drawings made of Sacramento's Embarcadero in 1849-50. It was started in June of 1849 and completed in September, being built by Sam Brannan (with John Fowler as his partner) from materials left over from Sutter's flour mill at Natoma. The mill had been started by the Battalion Boys but abandoned the previous year when the gold rush began. The hotel's cost was reportedly $100,000. [34] On the 4th of July of 1849, a celebration dance was held in the recently begun building. Two hundred men are said to have vied for the attention of but 18 women, the men having paid $32.00 a piece for the sport. As the Rhoades family in the area had a large number of girls, and Mormons were not adverse to dancing, it might well have been from among these that some of the 18 were recruited.

The Fowler referred to by Lyman and the John Fowler mentioned by Miller [34] was probably John S. Fowler, one of the original Mormon pioneers of 1847 who was said to have gone to California in 1848, never returning to Salt Lake. [35] (He had sent his wife Jerusha and his four children on the *Brooklyn*. One child died on the voyage.) Bancroft reveals that John S. Fowler, an immigrant of 1847, was the second Alcalde (Mayor) of Sacramento in 1848-49, dying in Sacramento in 1860 at 42 years of age. [36]

As Brannan secured most of his original capital from the Saints in California, the City Hotel might well have been considered a Mormon hostelry, though it was publicly in Brannan's name. This may be the reason it was so frequently used by Lyman and later Apostle Rich.

Statehood for California and Deseret

On January 29, 1850, Elder Lyman was in the San Francisco area [37] and there met General John Wilson in the belated joint attempt of Presidents Zachary Taylor and Brigham Young to secure statehood for the combined California (what became California plus what was then called Deseret).

Apostle Lyman forwarded tithing funds in July of 1849, and he was in the area during the political maneuvering preceding the California Consti-

"Married Mum?...No Sir!"

In 1850, at the beginning of the gold rush, only about 8% of the California population was female. The male/female ratio was about even for those under 15, and women tended to prefer living in the cities. Therefore, women were rare in the mining towns. As a result, their appearance at the mines created considerable stir as the lithograph illustrates. *Courtesy Bancroft Library.*

tutional Convention to be held in Monterey. The Convention was called and districts identified on June 3, 1849, a week after Lyman's arrival. Delegates were elected on August 1 from eight districts of the incipient state. Two of these areas, San Joaquin and Sacramento, included most of the gold fields, four delegates being elected from each. Evidently none of these delegates were Mormons. The Mormons were apparently not politically involved in this development, tending to keep themselves separate from the community at large. Had they realized the position the church leadership would subsequently as-

Replica of the first Statehouse of California (San Jose)

The first Legislature of California met in the original structure in December 1849 to organize and prepare to make application for statehood. *Courtesy San Jose Public Library.*

sume, they would probably have been very busy in those elections. The few Saints remaining in San Francisco and San Jose fared no better in terms of representation. Not even the ambitious Brannan, whose policy it was to "mingle with the world," was a delegate. However, J. A. Sutter and L. W. Hastings, two friends of the Mormons, were elected along with others to represent the Sacramento district. [38]

The Constitutional Convention was called to order at Colton Hall in Monterey on September 1, 1849. Five days later the Church leadership addressed a letter to Lyman instructing him to get involved. However, this effort was far too late. The letter would have taken about 90 days to reach Lyman. The Convention completed its work on October 12th, adjourning the following day. So the letter could not have reached him in time to be of any influence. Nevertheless, the letter does indicate something of the thinking of the

Church leaders on some of the questions raised by the convention. [39]

Lyman was informed that a proposed constitution for the Mormon "State of Deseret" had been drafted and a memorial sent to Congress requesting recognition. The Church leaders informed him that General Wilson, who was on his way to California to serve as the General Indian Agent, had stopped by as a special emissary of the newly-elected President Zachary Taylor, whom the Mormons had supported in the elections of the previous year. Taylor wanted California to enter the union but was fearful that Congress could become so embroiled over the slavery issue that it might stop the effort. He, therefore, wanted to see it come into the union as a state, "leaving it in the power of the people to say whether it shall be a slave or a free state, and thus taking the bone from the Congress."

According to the letter, President Taylor preferred to see two states in the west, but because of the "sparseness of population," such was not possible. Because of the gold rush, the Southerners in California were seen as a roadblock to the admission of California except as a slave state but hopefully Mormon "influence . . . should . . . counterbalance that of the slave-holders, and thus settle this troublesome question. It is therefore their (the national leaders) policy to seek our influence, and we need not add it is our policy to use theirs."

Admitting a negative first reaction to General Wilson's proposal for amalgamation of the two sides of the Sierra Nevada into a single state, Lyman was informed that Wilson and Young had worked out an arrangement whereby Wilson, with the aid of Lyman and the California Mormons, would propose a single state for the two areas but that the constitution should include an irrevocable proviso by which the state would automatically divide into two separate states at the beginning of 1851, "each having their own constitution, and each becoming a free sovereign and independent state without any further action of Congress. This was to be a "back door" approach for Deseret to become a state, and Lyman was warned that there could be no deviation from that point.

Perhaps regretting the tenor of the Church president's earlier letter needling Brannan, as well as with an ambivalent feeling about Rockwell, they added:

> We need not say that it will be advisable for you to get Samuel Brannan, with the Press (the *California Star*), and all the influence you can collect around you to carry out your designs. We should be glad, if circumstances do not render it expedient to act otherwise, for Bro. Porter to act with you in the delegation, but as you are present, and know best whether there would be feelings and excitement in relation to him or not, we leave the matter for you and him to act according to your judgement for the public good.

Should the convention fail to act as the Mor-

Peter H. Burnett
California's First Governor.
Courtesy Bancroft Library.

mon leaders wished, Lyman was instructed to bring his "influence to bear against them, and enter a protest against any amalgamation on any other terms. And it would be advisable for you to get as many of our friends to sign a remonstrance against their incorporating any of this country, and send it forthwith to Washington."

Recognizing the tenuous nature of the "alliance" between President Zachary Taylor and the Church, the First Presidency of the Church added that should the "slave question, by any means, become settled before our admission into the Union, politicians might feel themselves more independent and our interest might not lay so near their hearts."

In reference to a problem that would come to

characterize the long term negative relationship between miners and the Mormons, they continued: "Our miners population is the only serious objection to our admission to Union, independent of Western California." [40]

Recognizing that they were being "used" by the national political leaders and that permanent amalgamation of the two Californias would not be in the interest of the Mormons, they suggested that should the petition which had already been sent fail, "the one here proposed will catch us, and before the yoke of the consolidated state can reach over the Sierra Nevada and fasten on us, 1851 will arrive, and the yoke will be broken. Thus while government is using us to save the nation, we are using them to save ourselves . . ."

Looking for justification for seeking eventual separation from California, the Church leaders maintained that "independent of gold diggers" who were really only "transients," Mormons outnumbered non-Mormons two-to-one or five-to-three. They failed to recognize that the hundreds of Mormons being sent to California that fall, as well as most of them already there, were no less transients.

Lyman was then instructed that, regardless of what happened with respect to the politics, he was to "increase a righteous influence over the people and government every day and thus secure the rights and privileges belonging to us, for we expect to hababit [inhabit] that country as well as this, and want our share of good in common with the great whole."

The last sentence above would seem to indicate that the intention of the Church leadership at that time still was permanently to inhabit Western California as well as Deseret. It may well have affected the decision implemented a month or so later when several groups of Mormon gold missionaries were sent from the valley into Western California.

While belated, the Church leaders' concern about the convention was not misplaced. In fact, probably the most hotly and long debated issue at the convention was the question of the eastern boundary of California. [41] The debate on this

question began on September 22, 1849. There were two basic proposals presented. One called for the eastern boundary to be at the Sierra Nevada mountains. This was the proposal of the Committee on Boundaries. It was strongly defended by Sutter, but more especially by L. W. Hastings. The other proposal was to establish the boundary at the Rocky Mountains, including all of present day Arizona, Utah and Nevada in the State of California.

There were four basic issues:

1. Should an area specifically not included in the boundaries set up by the acting governor, be included, thereby disenfranchising all of the Mormons in the area of Salt Lake?

2. Could a government including such a far ranging area be efficiently administered?

3. Would Congress accept the reduced boundaries?

4. How would the decision affect the slavery question?

On September 24, 1849, when the first vote was taken on the committee's recommendation for reduced boundaries, it was voted down, a substitute motion incorporating the extended boundary being accepted on a nineteen-to-four vote. But many of the delegates evidently had not yet arrived.

The question was reopened on October 8 and debated hotly for three days. One of the main arguments against the reduced boundaries had been that Congress would not accept them. A compromise proposal was made providing for the Sierra Nevada boundary but with the proviso that should Congress refuse to admit California with that boundary it would be the Rockies. This motion was passed with a thirty-two-to-seven vote. The actual Constitution submitted to Congress called for the Sierra Nevada boundary.

The Journal history records the late arrival of Lyman with General Wilson: ". . . to represent Deseret in forming a temporary coalition with

California to sue for admission into the Union as a free and sovereign State, not arriving in California in time to attend the convention held there." [42] By the time of their arrival, the Constitutional Convention at Monterey had written the constitution, approved it, and adjourned. The citizens of California approved the constitution and elected Burnett the new governor in a special election. The new government convened at the new capitol in San Jose, December 22. The new governor, Governor Burnett, was inaugurated, various offices filled, and the boundary of the state again discussed. When the Mormons arrived, they presented "a long communication to Governor Burnett on the subject, indicating the policy Deseret was willing to pursue." [43] Burnett listened to the Mormon delegation and reported the following to the Legislature: "I cannot in the solemn discharge of the duties imposed upon me by the position I occupy, recommend you accede to the proposition made." [44] California applied for statehood on the basis of a Sierra Nevada boundary. The Mormons were told that the Legislature could not re-address the issue at that time.

In other words, Mormon help in California statehood efforts was not needed. The proposed California state constitution was forwarded to Washington on March 12, 1850. While Mormon hopes for an early Mormon state were destroyed, at least the desire not to be included permanently in California was realized. Western California was admitted into the Union as a state without Deseret by action of Congress on September 9, 1850.

On February 8, 1850, Lyman sailed to Los Angeles with Jesse D. Hunter and Charles Crisman, [45] probably hoping to intercept Elder Charles C. Rich. Lyman arrived at San Pedro on February 20th, hearing there that Brother Rich had left the area a month earlier, going to San Francisco overland. On March 2nd, Lyman set sail for San Francisco, escorting 30 or so members of the Huffaker party he found at San Pedro, only to find waiting a message that Brother Rich had already gone to the southern mines. [46]

Waiting in San Francisco for Rich to return and beleaguered by the thirty (sometimes "wild")

boys of the Huffaker Party, who were undoubtedly impatient to get their hands on some gold, Lyman finally decided to escort them to the gold fields via Sutter's Fort. The group left San Francisco on April 1st aboard the steamer *El Dorado*.

On the way, still on the extended Bay and approaching the mouth of the Sacramento River, the vessel put in at Benicia where fortuitously Elder Charles C. Rich, returning by steamer to San Francisco from the southern mines, landed at about the same time. The two Apostles were finally reunited.

NOTES

1. Journal History, March 26, 1849.

2. Ibid., March 31, 1849.

3. The statistics and lists have been developed from the author's files of Mormons known or believed to have been involved in the gold fields. See Kate B. Carter, *Heart Throbs of the West,* Daughters of Utah Pioneers, 1947, Volumes 8-10, for lists of Mormon immigrants from 1847-49. (See appendix 9a for lists.)

4. California Census. 1850.

5. Arrington, "Mississippi Mormons," 50.

6. Eliza Marie Partridge Lyman, Diary, (Words in brackets are the author's.)

7. Journal History, February 24, 1849.

8. Ibid., February 25, 1849.

9. John Z. Brown, ed., *John Brown*, 103.

10. Journal History, March 17, 1849.

11. Ibid., March 21, 1849.

12. Ibid., March 22, 1849.

13. Journal History. April 11, 1849. Levi Fifield was one of the Battalion Boys who had been in on the mining of gold at Mormon Island. Gates had

entered Utah the previous year. He may well have been one of the co-founders of Greenwood in El Dorado County.

14. Journal History, April 5, 1849, 3-4.

15. Amasa Lyman to Young and Council, 6 July 1849, Young Papers.

16. Schindler, *Rockwell*, 193.

17. Campbell, "The Apostasy of Samuel Brannan", 157-167.

18. Letter, Amasa Lyman to the First Presidency, September 19, 1849.

19. Letter, First Presidency to Amasa Lyman, November 2, 1849.

20. J.M. Letts, *California Illustrated*, 95.

21. Schindler, *Rockwell*, 192.

22. Slater, *Fruits of Mormonism*, 77n-78n. Schindler, *Rockwell*. This was possibly at or near Mills Station (Hangtown Crossing) where the White Rock Road intersected the Mormon Island Road.

23. *Ibid.*

24. Achilles, *Destroying Angels*, 14.

25. Ellsworth, ed. *The History of Louisa Barnes Pratt*, 116.

26. Jonathan Crosby, "Biographical Sketch" July 17, 1850.; Lyman, Payne, and Ellsworth, eds. *No Place to Call Home*, 110-112.

27. Cannon, Diary. October 23, 1850.

28. Schindler, *Rockwell*, 192-97.

29. Robert B. (Boyd) Stewart of the Battalion is known to have been in the gold fields the next year. This may have had reference to the famous Columbia Mine in Tuolumne County near Mormon Gulch. He may have been one of the elusive discoverers of gold at that spot or even at the Mormon Gulch to the south. However, the reference to Columbia itself is a bit early, the gold of Columbia reportedly being discovered in 1850. Boyd was called on a mission to Oregon in 1850. While with the Battalion, he had been punished for failing to salute an officer and for sleeping on duty.

30. Schindler, *Rockwell*, 193. Other authors place the exchange at other times. However, the tale is apocryphal, no documented source being identified. An extensive discussion of the apocryphal story can be found in Bagley, *Scoundrel's Tale*, 287-300.

31. Amasa Lyman, Diary; Campbell, "History of the Church in California," 160-163.

32. Captain Hunter had been an officer in the Mormon Battalion, taking his wife and daughter with him on the Battalion's march. After his discharge he was named an Indian Agent in California. He was shortly to leave for San Diego, probably under Church direction, where his wife would eventually die. He remained in California after 1857 when the Saints were called to Deseret.

33. This was probably the Dan P. Clark that came west with Lyman in 1848, not the Dan P. Clark who Bancroft lists in his Pioneer Register as a veteran of the New York Volunteers.

34. Miller, *Guide to Old Sacramento*.

35. Carter, *Heart Throbs*, 8:404.

36. *Ibid.*; Bancroft, *Pioneer Register*, 746.

37 Lyman, Diary, January 29, 1850.

38. *California. Constitutional Convention*, 1849. Report of the debates by Browne, 5, 478.

39. Letter, the First Presidency to Amasa Lyman, September 6, 1849. Church Archives.

40. Ibid. It is uncertain as to who "our miner population" was, there being no known sizeable mining operations in Deseret at that time.

41. Browne, *Convention of California*, pp. 167-200, 417-458.

42. The story of the Mormon delegation and the proposal to include Deseret is in Lyman, "Larger than Texas (1849 proposal for uniting Mormon Deseret and California to form one state). 18.

43. Journal History, January 31, 1850, 10.

44. *California. Legislature.* Journal of the Proceedings at first Session, 435.; For a discussion of the Constitutional Convention and the first Legislature, see Ignoffo, *Gold Rush Politics.*

45. Hunter and others evidently went on to San Diego, with Crisman and others settling on the Williams ranch. Crisman may well have been one of those accompanying Lyman to California the previous spring.

46. Lyman, Diary.

APPENDIX 9a (Note 9:3)

Pioneers of 1847
Possible Mormon California Migrants with
Lyman-Rockwell Company
Spring of 1849

1. Captains of Ten

Barton, Asa
Boyes, George
Brower, Ariah C.
Cherry, Ebenezer
Fairbanks, John B.
Gardner, Archibald
Gates, Jacob
Kinyon, Farnum
Lathrop, Asahel A.
Leffingwell, William
Orr, Thomas
Pierce, Robert
Smith, James
Taylor, William

2. Crow Family Unit

Crow, Robert
Crow, Elizabeth
Crow, Benjamin B.
Crow, Harriet
Crow, Elizabeth J.
Crow, John McHenry
Crow, Walter Hamilton
Crow, William Parker
Crow, Isa Vinda Exene
Crow, Ira Minda Almarene
Myers, Lewis B.
Threlkill, George W.
Threlkill, Matilda Jane

3. Mississippi Saints

Harmon, James, wife
Mathews, Benjamin
Mathews, William
Roberts, John and family
Sparks, George, W.

4. Mormon Battalion Detached Family Units

Brown, James
Brown, James P.
Button, Montgomery and family
Chase, John
Hanks, Ebenezer and wife
Hunt, Jefferson--his family
Kelley, Nicholas
Shelton, Sebert C. and family
Steele, John
Tubbs, William R.
Wilkins, Dave
Williams, Thomas S.

Source: Carter, *Heart Throbs of the West,* 1947.

Sacramento City, 1849. View looking east across Front Street and down J Street from the Sacramento River waterfront. Lithograph by George V. Cooper. Noticeable are the many trees in the city. The big hole in the middle of J Street may have been from the removal of one of these trees. Recognizable mid block to the left of J Street (overlapped by a ship's main mast) is Sam Brannan's City Hotel. Second small structure to the right of the hotel (adjacent to the larger, corner building) is the Eagle Theatre, site of the beginnings of professional theater in California. *Courtesy Bancroft Library.*

Early Sacramento (looking south) showing Front Street on the left and the Sacramento River on the right, with the levee in between. Image was published by Forrest and Borden on an 1850 lettersheet. Lettersheets of the era were stationery, printed with woodcuts and lithographs, for miners to write home on. They were the forerunner of the modern picture post card. *Courtesy California State Library.*

I'm willing to be chastened and bear my daily cross;
I'm willing to be parted from every kind of dross.
Endure the fiery furnace, Till free from guilty stains,
Till all alloy is melted and naught but gold remains.

From Mormon Hymn "Farewell to Earthly Honors"
(1948) #35

10
The Pueblo Saints

IN THE LATE WINTER of 1845-46, the call to "Come to Zion" seemed to mean to come to California. The *Brooklyn* Saints were on their way via an all-sea route. The main body of Saints, from Nauvoo and its environs, were headed across Southern Iowa. They went inspired by John Taylor's poem, "The Upper California, O That's Land for Me." Scattered Saints were being issued calls to head west, to meet up with the main body someplace in Indian Country —west of the Mighty Missouri. In addition, the Mormon camps across Southern Iowa would furnish that summer several hundred men and a few women for the Mormon Battalion. The *Brooklyn* Saints reached their goal as did most of the Battalion. A few of the others also made it, but over a hundred Mormons from among the Mississippi Saints, the Crow family from Southern Illinois and a hundred or so Battalion detachees spent the winter at Fort Pueblo on the eastern slopes of the Rockies, a couple of hundred miles south of Fort Laramie.

On April 8, 1846, under instructions from Brigham Young, a company of Mormon converts left Monroe County, Mississippi, for an intended meeting in Indian country with the main body of Mormon expatriates, then headed westward across Southern Iowa. The group consisted of about 43 persons in 19 wagons and was under the immediate leadership of William Crosby. The Mormon leadership sent John Brown, a kinsman of Crosby by marriage and a veteran Mormon

missionary, to assist in bringing these Mississippi Saints to the main body heading west. [1] En route the contingent was joined by 18 members of the Crow family from Southern Illinois, but originally from Kentucky. [2] They, along with Battalion members with whom they would sojourn that winter at Fort Pueblo (Colorado), would play a significant role in Mormon involvement in the gold fields.

When the Mississippi Saints reached reached Independence on May 26th, they discovered the country astir with rumors. They were hearing that ex-Governor Boggs of Missouri, who had left for California with the Russell train on May 12th, had been intercepted by Mormon marauders and murdered. Not being known as Mormons, they were advised (because of the marauders) to keep off the trail. They, nevertheless, moved out, joined by a few non-Mormons who wanted the protection of a larger party as they traveled the Oregon Trail through the Indian country of Kansas. Several days later, their companions discovered with whom they were traveling and withdrew only to rejoin them later. Their fear of Indians was greater than their discomfort with Mormons.

About three weeks before the Mississippi Saints reached Independence, the Rhoades family left St. Joseph, on the Missouri River to the north, led by Thomas Rhoades. Rhoades, like Crow, had come from Illinois and before that, for a week or two and then proceeded on to California, possibly having learned that the Saints were not going to continue their westward march that season.

Three weeks behind the Rhoades company, the Mississippi Saints and the Crows had also hoped to meet up with the Saints along the Platte. They proceeded along the south bank, supposing that the others must be someplace on the other side of the river. Reaching Ash Hollow, southeast of Fort Laramie, on July 1 the Mississippi Saints were informed of the absence of Mormons on the trail. (The Rhoades company evidently had been more successful in keeping their identity secret.) And evidently, the main body of the Saints had not reached that far west. Brown recorded that, "There was considerable dissatisfaction in the camp. Some were in favor of turning back . . ." A few miles below Laramie they met a Mr. John Reshaw, [3] who was headed south to Fort Pueblo. The season was late, too late to make it to the Pacific slope, and they did not wish to stay at Forts Laramie, Bridger, or Hall to the west. They decided to accompany Reshaw, heading south on July 10, and reaching the fort on August 7th. They found the fort occupied by several mountain men with their Mexican and Indian wives and families. During the fall, the occupants were joined by 150 or so sick and/or disgruntled detachees from the Mormon Battalion.

When spring came in 1847, the Mississippi Saints, along with the Battalion detachees and their families, [4] were ready to join the main body of Saints. The advance company of the Saints had taken up the march from Council Bluffs on April 8th. Brigham Young, on learning that the main body of the Pueblo group had not yet arrived at Fort Laramie, dispatched Apostle Amasa M. Lyman to hurry them along.

While the Crow family entered the valley of the Great Salt Lake on July 22nd, two days before the ailing Brigham Young and the main body of the advance company entered on the 24th, the main body of the Mississippi Saints and Battalion families entered the valley on July 27-29th, under the leadership of Amasa M. Lyman. The Apostle was accompanied by Samuel Brannan—helping

Robert and Elizabeth Crow
(1794-1876) (1795-1870)

The Crows had a large family, lived in Mississippi, and joined the Mormon Church in 1838. When they heard the Saints were going west, they formed a wagon train, mostly of immediate and extended family members and headed for the Oregon Trail. They wintered in Pueblo and were among the first to enter the Salt Lake Valley. Most of the family went to California and lived out their lives there, some in the vicinity of Auburn. *Courtesy Pioneer Memorial Museum, International Society Daughters of Utah Pioneers.*

Kentucky. They, too, were probably moving west under instructions from Brigham Young and also headed for a planned linkup with the main body of the Saints in Indian Country someplace along the Platte River. They reached Fort Laramie by June 15th. The Rhoades party waited at Laramie to account for their close, personal relationship, as well as that between Lyman and the Mississippi Saints which seemed to prevail over several years. Brannan had intercepted the main pioneer company in Wyoming country, attempting to persuade Brigham Young to settle on the Pacific slopes. Failing in his primary mission, he may well have decided to attempt to win over to his cause more pliable converts, especially from among his traveling companions.

While Brannan apparently failed in this likely objective at the time, his first-hand tales of the virtues of California, including its lush crops and salubrious climate, apparently made lasting impressions. They would later be recalled after two difficult years of pioneering effort. They would be remembered especially after Brannan's news of the gold reached the valley in June of 1848, to be followed by the hard evidence of gold carried by the returning Battalion Boys in the fall of 1848 and in 1849. Many, if not most, of the Mississippi Saints, initially settled in Holladay, a few miles south of Salt Lake, on land assigned to Elder Lyman, continuing to maintain close ties with the Apostle. They struggled with the privations of the supply-short winter of 1847-48. They heard rumors of the discovery of gold in California throughout the summer of 1848 and became titillated by the tales and the evidence of gold when the Battalion Boys began to reach the valley in September. To make matters worse, they suffered through the cricket-plagued growing and harvesting season of that year, receiving almost nothing from their hard labors.

In the fall they began to hear rumors of men being called and others given permission by their leaders to go to California. One company was called to go with their own apostle leader of 1847, Amasa M. Lyman. The group may have included John Brown of the Mississippi Saints and James Brown of the Mormon Battalion. However, Lyman did not go that fall. An extreme winter in 1848-49 convinced many of the Southern Saints, not used to a frigid climate, that sunshine, laced with gold, was better than snow and starvation.

Toward the end of March they learned that Lyman had been called again to go on a mission to California, with an "epistle to the faithful Saints and also to preach the Gospel and look after the interests of the Church and the Saints." [5] Many undoubtedly let the Apostle know that they were willing to "sacrifice all" to follow him again, this time to Western California.

Unfortunately, there is no known record of those who went with Lyman when he left the valley of the Saints on April 12th with Porter Rockwell as his guide and companion. However, there is strong reason to believe that some of the Crow family, Mississippi Saints and Battalion detachees accompanied him, as they were in California by the late winter of 1849. [6] In addition, family accounts and traditions claim that some did go to California in the spring of 1849—with or without the blessing of the Prophet.

On February 24, 1849, Brother Robert Crow presented a petition for himself and seven others requesting permission from the Presidency and Council of the Church to go to the California gold mines to dig gold under the sanction of the authorities of the Church. [7] Permission was denied, at least at that time, though that decision may have been rescinded when Lyman was called. The fact that the Crow family was on good terms with the Church later, at least for some time, would seem to indicate that they may have gone with the blessing of Brigham Young, though the same may not be said of all who went that spring.

Whether going by "call," permission, or in defiance of Church discipline, the Mormon Argonauts of the spring of 1849 split up when they reached California, going in different directions. However, substantial numbers of them were concentrated the next year in El Dorado, Sutter, and Sacramento Counties. They were joined by more friends and relatives from the South. It is interesting to follow some of these Pueblo families and their associates through the next few years.

The Crow Family

In 1850, the aging patriarch Robert Crow and his wife, Betsy Elizabeth, were located above Sacramento City on the American River in Sacramento County with their son Walter H. Another

Henry G. Boyle (1824-1908)
*Courtesy Pioneer Memorial Museum, International
Society Daughters of Utah Pioneers.*

Henry G. Boyle joined the Mormon Battalion
on the Mormon trek west in 1846 and, on dis-

charge in California, joined the Mormon Volunteers. His service in the Volunteers completed, he went to Salt Lake City by the Southern Route with Porter Rockwell in 1848.

Boyle came back to California in 1851 to help found the San Bernardino colony. To try to help pay off the mortgage of the San Bernardino colony, Boyle went on an unsuccessful gold mining mission in 1855 to the Kern River region. Immediately after, again to obtain funds for the mortgage, he was sent to Northern California to ask the help of the northern Mormons. While in the North, he was called to do missionary work among the northern settlements, serving until 1857, after which, he went back to San Bernardino. He sold out in San Bernardino and went back to Salt Lake City in 1857.

Boyle served on missions for most of his life, completing a total of fourteen. He was a missionary to the Southern States, serving from 1867-1878, and 1875-1878 as the mission president. Returning to Salt Lake, he was elected Chaplain to Utah House of Representatives in 1878. He was sent on a mission again to the Southern States 1879-1881. On his return, he was again elected chaplain to the Utah Legislature.

Boyle died in Pima, Arizona in 1908 at age 84.

Crow family, headed by James R. Crow, was at the same location. A son, Benjamin B. Crow, [8] a miner, was living with his family in the Mormon enclave at Greenwood in El Dorado County. Living with the family was Jesse Brown, a Battalion detachee, who was working at the Tin Pan Alley. Benjamin hosted Apostle Lyman on August 1, 1850, shortly before the latter started for Utah. Eight doors from Benjamin was his brother-in-law, George Threllkill, with his wife Jane Crow Threllkill and several children. William Crow, a butcher, was also living at Greenwood with Lewis B. Myers, also a butcher and formerly of Deseret.

By the time Lyman left for Utah in the summer of 1850, Robert Crow had evidently decided to remain in California. In a directive dated July 31, 1850, at Lewisville (Louisville), California, he authorized Amasa Lyman to "sell or convey all my right, title, and claim to my farm on Weaver (Weber River in Utah) together with my 4 houses north of Ogden or rent them as he may see proper . . . I also authorize him to settle for me for braking up the farm south east of Salt Lake City -- near Chase's saw mill -- . . . including all debts -- and money due me -- as my only lawful agent." [9] The paper was witnessed by a Mormon, Bradford W. Elliott. [10]

Nothing more is known of the Crows until 1857, when a missionary, Elder Henry G. Boyle, visited them. On January 14, 1857, after preaching in the Odd Fellows Hall in Secret Ravine, near Auburn, Elder Boyle, accompanied by Benjamin Crow, stayed at the home of Brother Hamilton Crow, where the missionaries "were warmly received and well used . . . (and who thought) this is a good family . . . " On the 15th the missionaries went to Father Robert Crow's, spending the evening with him. Boyle reported, "I like Father Crow, and I think his daughter Araminda is a good girl, and also Mr. Timkill's (Threllkill's) wife, one of his daughters." [11]

The diary of another missionary, Elder Frederick Hurst, [12] refers to a "Father Braim Cram" (Crow) as leaving San Bernardino for Utah in November of 1857. With him were his family. Evidently the trip bore marital fruit as Ira Minda Almarene Crow later married Francis M. Hamblin of Santa Clara. [13] Several of them are found on the records of the Reorganized Church in San Bernardino in 1867. [14]

The Harmon (Harman) Family

Probably also associated with the Crows as they left Utah in the spring of 1849 was the family of James Harmon. [15] Upon reaching Salt Lake in 1847, James had set up a blacksmith shop in partnership with Dimick Huntington, one of the Battalion detachees who had also wintered in Pueblo. They took up land in Holladay, along with other Mississippi Saints.

The family reportedly first settled in the Sacramento area in 1849. It may have included Oliver N. and Lorenzo F. Harmon and a daughter, Eliza. On May 28, 1850, Elders Lyman and Rich visited Brother James Harmon then some 30 to 35 miles up the American River from Sacramento, probably in Long Valley or Mormon Ravine near Auburn in Sutter (later Placer) County. The Apostles returned on June 11th and 12th, staying with the Harmon family in their hotel, the Homestead House. Apostle Rich, whose diary refers to the Harmons as Hammond, returned to the Harmon's residence on August 12th. While the Apostle collected tithing from others, the Harmons were not

included at that time. Rich visited the Harmons again on October 3rd, staying with Benjamin F. Mathews, another of the Mississippi Saints, this time collecting substantial tithing from both Harmon and Mathews.

James engaged in placer mining, while his wife Mary ran the hotel, which became a gathering place for Mormon missionaries when proselyting activities took place several years later. In 1851, James returned to Mississippi, evidently to bring west a daughter who had remained behind; but he contracted a fever while crossing the Isthmus of Panama and died in Auburn in September of that year.

The widow Polly (Mary Ann) Harmon remained at Homestead House, frequently visited by missionaries in 1856-57. References to her are found in the diaries of Henry G. Boyle and Frederick Hurst, proselyting missionaries. On January 8, 1857, after visiting with Hamilton Crow (spelled Crone in the transcript), Benjamin Crow, and Jesse Brown, Boyle visited the Long Valley House belonging to Father Robert Crow, and the Homestead of Widow Harmon. While at Auburn, widower Boyle stayed overnight on the 9th at the Harmon's hotel getting "an introduction to a mining tunnel." The following day he "had an interesting conversation with Eliza Harmon." On Sunday the 11th, Boyle and his companion, William H. Shearman, "scored it to the luke warm saints at the Homestead House." Their preachments seem to have had a positive influence, Boyle hearing "some of them say they were going to be rebaptized." [16]

Oliver N. and Lorenzo F. Harmon were residing together at Buckeye in Yolo County, to the northwest of Sacramento and west of the Sacramento River, in 1856 and 1857. Boyle gives repeated reference to them and their assistance in his missionary work. They were rebaptized [17] on September 15th of 1856 and Lorenzo was ordained an elder on December 31, 1856, at the time of the organization of the Buckeye Branch. The Branch was presided over by Hezekiah Thatcher, a fellow Southerner. Lorenzo was called to serve a mission to Oregon at a Conference of the Church held April 6 and 7, 1857, in San Francisco. Oliver

N. Harmon served as the sergeant of arms of the Thatcher Company, leaving California in July of 1857 for Utah.

Widow Mary Ann Harmon also moved out that year, going to Carson City (Eagle Valley) in Nevada where she purchased a cattle ranch. She temporarily remained there after the general Mormon exodus from that area, going to Utah in 1859 accompanied by her three youngest children. Two of her older daughters remained behind. She settled in Centerville, Utah, where she passed away in 1898. [18]

The Sparks and Roberts Families

Another closely related group of Mississippi Saints of 1847 consisted of George W. Sparks and family and his sister and brother-in-law, John Roberts. Sparks was born in either Monroe County, Mississippi, or in Alabama, in 1819. He married Luana (Lorena) Roberts (Roberds) in 1842. Both families wintered at Pueblo and moved to California in either 1849 or very early in 1850, being found in Diamond Springs in El Dorado County in September when the census was taken. Sparks was listed as a merchant. The family folklore indicates that Sparks gave the community its name. Associated with them was the John Roberts family consisting of Roberts, his wife Martha and six children two to 14 years of age. The youngest was born in Utah, the others in Mississippi.

The Sparks family spent the winter of 1850-51 in Diamond Springs, operating a boarding house, evidently in addition to a merchandising business. The family then moved to Suisun Valley (west of the Sacramento River in Mendocino County) where they lived for a year or so, moving next to the Russian River near the coast. They were there, along with the Roberts family, when missionary work opened up in 1855.

Sparks was farming on Dry Creek four miles north of Russian River in the summer of 1855 when Elder Henry G. Boyle, a Battalion veteran, and David Holladay, a Mississippi Saint, reported them as "all well and doing well. They were glad to see us and used us kindly. This family feels better than any I have seen in this part of the coun-

try yet." Living nearby was the family of John Roberts. However, according to Boyle, the latter "have no good feelings for Mormonism, although they are friendly enough." [19]

While there was some initial and even periodic questioning of the devotion of Sparks and Roberts to the gospel, they and their wives, along with William Prouse (a Battalion veteran) and his wife, were either baptized or rebaptized by the missionaries. Sparks participated in raising money for the San Bernardino colony, and participated in the formation of the Dry Creek Branch of the Church in the spring of 1857. The Sparks and Roberts families emigrated to San Bernardino in May of 1857, Roberts being in charge of the company. [20]

When the call came from Salt Lake for the San Bernardino Saints to gather to Zion (Utah), in the fall of 1857, George Sparks elected to remain behind. He eventually became the owner of 5120 acres of land in San Diego County. [21] He became associated with the large branch of the Reorganized Latter Day Saint Church in San Bernardino, being the branch president in 1867. John Roberts was a member of the branch of the Reorganized Church in San Francisco in the 1866-68 period, being one of six elders in that branch. [22]

The Battalion Detachees

Montgomery E. Button, a Battalion detachee moved to California by 1850, settling with his family near the Southern Mines of Mariposa County. He may not have been a miner, as he was included in the census with only farmers, ranchers, and teamsters. [23] He was listed as a member of a Quorum of Seventy of the Mormon Church while in California.

It is not known just when the Sebert C. Shelton and Mayfield families went to California, but a number of them lived together at Pilot Hill, El Dorado County, in 1850. Living next door was Harriet Mayfield with a 10-month-old daughter, Eliza E. Grayham. Andrew Mayfield, and Lysander Woodworth, a detached member of the Battalion who had wintered in Pueblo, were living with her.

Sebert Shelton evidently had some problems with individuals in the Church, one of whom was a Brother Brown. This may have been James Brown who seems to have had difficulty with more than one of his fellow religionists, much of it over the disposition of back pay of the Battalion detachees which he had collected in California in 1847. Shelton was counseled by Brigham Young in 1850 to "do right, live in peace and (this) above all things (earn) the spirit and blessings of God, that you may obtain an exaltation in his Celestial Kingdom, for the favor of good Saints is better than gold, and the favor of God is more precious than costly pearls." [24]

In another letter written the same day by William Clayton for Brigham Young, it was called to Shelton's attention that his tithing account had been neglected, it being suggested "that it would be better to have it settled up before you leave . . . as tithing is about the most important and the first part of a man's duty ought not to be deferred, but in all cases it ought to be attended to punctually. We need all the tithing there is due to carry on the public works this season . . . "

Both the Mayfields and the Sheltons received the missionaries kindly in 1855-57, assisting them in their missionary efforts as well as housing and feeding them, helping with their laundry, and furnishing them with transportation. From "Old Brother Shelton," the missionaries learned of other "old Mormons" in the country, being taken by the old man to see some of them. Among these was Captain William Leffingwell, a High Priest and Captain of Ten in 1847 who had lived with or by the Sheltons at Pilot Hill in 1850. Moses Martin, an excommunicant, and George W. Oman, of the Mormon Battalion, lived nearby. Through the Mayfields, Boyle also became acquainted with S. G. Higgins, formerly of the New York Volunteers and Sonoma. Sebert Shelton died at his home in Stony Point on August 10, 1857. His widow became associated in the Reorganized Movement, being a member of the Petaluma Branch in 1866-68, along with the Omans and Harriet Mayfield.

A Battalion detachee, Ebenezer Hanks was one of the small company of Battalion detachees sent to California with James Brown to secure the back pay of the others detached. After returning to Utah, he stayed until 1849, when he and his wife Jane went to California. The 35-year-old Ebenezer settled near Salmon Falls on the South Fork, possibly New York Ravine, which enters the South Fork a short distance below Salmon Falls. They established an eating house which Jane ran while he mined for gold. Hanks evidently returned to Utah over the winter of 1849-50, being there in the spring when he made deposits to the gold accounts. His wife was not well, but President Young did not let that deter him in issuing Hanks a mission call to the Society Islands. In a letter written on April 22, 1850, Hanks was told by Brigham Young that if he went, taking his wife, she would regain her health. He was also told, "I can freely say that it is the will of the Lord you should do this and also help the brethren who are going there with your means, and by complying you shall be abundantly blessed and prospered on your mission."

While he did not go on the mission, upon his return to California that season Ebenezer was not too busy to be involved with Elders Lyman and Rich during the summer. Nor was he so obsessed with the desire for money that he forgot to tithe, but contributed several hundred dollars in tithing. He became one of the chief financiers of the San Bernardino colony, investing more than $25,000 between 1851 and 1855. He went to San Bernardino in December of 1855, leaving his wife behind for awhile, returned to the north in October of 1856, and then finally moved to San Bernardino in 1856 or 1857. He returned to Utah in 1857 when called by the Church leaders, and settled in Parowan as a member of the Iron Mission. In 1882 he moved to the area later named after him, Hanksville (a supply center for silver miners in the 1890s), where he died in 1884.

Thomas S. Williams was a sergeant in the Battalion, being detached at Santa Fe with the sick detachment and spending the winter at Pueblo. He became involved with Brannan after the latter's meeting with Brigham Young in the summer of 1847, being with him when they met up with the Battalion detachment on its way to the Great Salt Lake. It is uncertain when he went to California again, but it was probably subsequent to June

8, 1850, when he returned to Utah with mail from the eastern states.

On October 14, 1852, Brigham Young sent a letter of counsel to Williams located at Sacramento. It was mostly about business. Williams was counseled on how to sell Church cattle. He was advised not to hold on to them at a high price too long, that it would be better to make a little profit than lose it. He was advised not to accumulate or carry about large sums of money, but was to forward it frequently to Salt Lake City. Finally, he was to pay his tithes and make no permanent investment that would tie him if he had to suddenly flee.

The Pueblo Saints, consisting of the Crow Family, the Mississippi Saints and the Battalion detachee family units (close to 50 percent of whom went to California Gold Fields) constituted a substantial portion of the Mormons who remained in California after the general exodus of 1857. And a number of those eventually became lost by the Utah-based Mormon Church when they joined with the Reorganized movement of the late 1860s. Their story seemed to support the fear of Brigham Young that the search for gold might well lead many away from the fold. Perhaps it was as much the lure of an "endless spring" which attracted and kept them as it was gold itself.

NOTES

1. Arrington, "The Mississippi Saints." Also, Brown, *Autobiography of Pioneer*, 66-68. See Appendix 10a for list of these Mississippi Saints.

2. See Appendix 10b for list of Crow family group.

3. Brown, *Autobiography of Pioneer*, p. 68, variously recorded as Reshaw, Kershaw, and Richards.

4. See Appendix 10c for list of detached Battalion family units.

5. Journal History, March 26, 1849.

6. See the 1850 California Census.

7. Journal History, February 24, 1849.

8. One census index lists him as Benjamin Croso. Another variation of the Crow name was Cram. Much of the data to follow is taken from the census for the various counties of California in 1850.

9. Amasa Lyman, Papers.

10. Elliott ran for El Dorado County Recorder in 1850.

11. Henry G. Boyle, Diary, January 14, 1857. (Words in brackets are the author's.)

12. Frederick G. Hurst, Diary.

13. This was possibly the Brother Hamblin, an Indian missionary, who was in the company of Saints leaving San Bernardino. Other members of the Crow family settled in Nevada, California and Oregon. Jacob Hamblin was a prominent Mormon missionary to the Indians in Southern Utah.

14. Membership Records, Reorganized Church of Jesus Christ of Latter Day Saints (RLDS). Copy in author's files.

15. Harmon was born in Boonesboro, Kentucky, in 1801, while Mary Ann B. Smithson, his wife, was born in South Carolina in 1808. The couple had lived in Alabama and Monroe County, Mississippi, where they had joined the Church and had five children. They wintered in Pueblo in 1846-47.

16. Boyle, Diary, Jan. 11, 1857.

17. A rebaptism does not necessarily designate apostasy, as it was a rather common ritual in the early LDS Church, often being representative of a re-commitment to the kingdom.

18. Carter, *Our Pioneer Heritage*, 2:449-451.

19. Boyle, Diary, August l, 2, 1855.

20. Ibid., April and May, 1857.

21. *Illustrated History of Southern California,* 717.

22. Membership Records, RLDS.

23. California Census, 1850.

24. Brigham Young, Correspondence, April 20, 1850. (Words in brackets are the author's.)

APPENDIX 10a (Note 10:1)

Mississippi Saints, 1846-47

Dowdle, Absalom Porter
Gibson, George Washington
Harmon, James, wife
and daughter
Holladay, John David
Kartchner, W. D.
Mathews, Benjamin
Mathews, William
Roberts, John and family
Smithson, Allan
Smithson, William

Source: Kate Carter, *Heart Throbs of the West,* 8:412-413.

APPENDIX 10b (Note 10:2)

Crow Family Company, 1846-47

Chesney, James
Crow, Robert (1)
Crow, Elizabeth Brown (2)
Crow, Benjamin B.
Crow, Walter Hamilton
Crow, John McHenry
Crow, Walter Hamilton?
Crow, Isa Vinda Exene
Crow, Ira Minda Almarene
Crow, Elizabeth

Crow, Harriet
Crow, William Parker
Little, Archibald
Myers, Lewis B.
Therlkill, George W. (Threllkill) (3)
Therlkill, Matilda Jane Crow (3)
Therlkill, Milton Howard
Therlkill, James William

(1) Father of group
(2) Mother of group
(3) Married

Source: Carter, *Heart Throbs of the West,* 8:412-413.

APPENDIX 10c (Note 10:4)

Battalion Detached Family Units, 1846-47

Adams, Orson B.
Brown, Captain James
Brown, James P.
Button, Montgomery E./family
Chase, John
Hanks, Ebenezer
Higgins, Captain Nelson
Hirons, John
Hunt, Jefferson family (1)
Kelley, Nicholas
Shelton, Sebert C. and family
Sharp, Mrs. Norman (2)
Steele, John
Smith, Mrs. Milton (2)
Stillman, Clark
Tubbs, William R.
Wilkins, Dave
Williams, Thomas S.

(1) The family of Capt. Jefferson Hunt who had stayed with the Battalion.
(2) Widows.

Source: Carter, *Heart Throbs of the West,* 8:412.

Thomas Rhoades (Rhoads) (1794-1869)
Courtesy Bernie L. Rhoades.

Thomas Rhoades was born in Muhlenberg, Kentucky. He married Elizabeth Forster, and served on the western frontier in the War of 1812. After his military service Thomas moved to Illinois and worked at surveying and construction on a national pike going west to the Mississippi River. While working on that project, he became acquainted with Mormonism and joined the Church. The Mormons, at the time, were relocating from Kirtland, Ohio to the Missouri frontier. So Rhoades moved to the Crooked River area in Ray County, Missouri. He may not have been public about his Mormon connections, because when the Mormons were driven from the state the Rhoades family remained.

The Rhoades family, however, were part of the Mormon exodus to the west. Because of their location, they followed the Oregon Trail out of St. Joseph, Missouri, and hoped to overtake the Crow family and the Mississippi Saints, with whom they had connections. The Rhoades party outpaced both the Mississippi Saints and the main Mormon companies, arriving at Fort Laramie before learning that the lagging Mormon companies would stop for the season at Winter Quarters. Rhoades decided to keep going and his group reached California by way of the Truckee route in October 1846.

The Rhoades family settled between Dry Creek and the Cosumnes River, southeast of Sutter's Fort. Members of the family were involved in the Bear Flag revolt and the Donner Party rescue. In 1849, at the invitation of Apostle Amasa Lyman, Rhoades took his younger children (his wife had since died) and led the gold train back to the Salt Lake Valley. The rest of the family remained in California.

When through the fiery trial thy pathway shall lie,
My grace, all sufficient, shall be thy supply.
The flame shall not hurt thee; I only design
Thy dross to consume, and thy gold to refine.

From Mormon Hymn "How Firm a Foundation"
(1985) #85

11

The Rhoades Mormon Gold Train

THE SUMMER OF 1849 saw thousands upon thousands of gold seekers headed west from numerous fitting-out stations along the Missouri River. The principal routes lay through Fort Hall in present-day southern Idaho and Salt Lake City. At Salt Lake, the spring and early summer travelers headed north; those in the fall headed south. The northern route joined the Fort Hall road at the City of Rocks near the Nevada-Utah-Idaho border and then proceeded west along the Humboldt and its tributaries in present-day Nevada. Upon reaching the Humboldt Sinks one route headed south across the salt desert to the Carson River; the other proceeded to the Truckee where the trail split again, the south branch heading south to the Carson River, the other heading west up the Truckee to Donner Pass. These Argonauts, their dreams filled with golden riches, were shocked to find a Mormon wagon train headed in the opposite direction, bound for Salt Lake, the City of the Saints. The latter's possession of some $30,000 in gold was bound to whet their appetites and confirm the stories of golden wealth in California but it also piqued their curiosity. Why would those foolish Mormons be leaving the land of gold? [1]

Upon arriving in California at Sutter's Fort on May 25, 1849, the most immediate responsibility of Elder Amasa Lyman had been to gather up what gold he could and send it back to the Salt Lake Valley, in dire need of gold for its money system. He set about the task and by July 6th had collected $4,152 in tithing and donations. [2]

The tithing and contributions averaged $188.73 per person and ranged from $5 to $600. Fifteen of the 21 who contributed $100 or more also gave $500 or more. This money, $2,872 in dust and $1,180 in American coin, was deposited with Brigham Young on October 1, 1849. [3]

Not only did Lyman collect tithes and offerings, he also induced several wealthy gold miners to emigrate to Zion, taking their gold with them. On July 6th, he wrote Brigham Young that he anticipated sending the collected gold and money in the care of Thomas Grover. Grover had come to the California gold mines via the southern route the previous winter. The Church "supercargo," traveled under the captaincy of the aging Thomas Rhoades who had come west over the northern route in 1846. Rhoades had been eminently successful in his gold mining ventures and was to take much of his accumulation with him to Salt Lake City.

In the same company was William Glover of the *Brooklyn*. A counselor to Sam Brannan, he had become disillusioned with the spiritually declining leader. Glover along with his wife, had

William Glover (1813-1892)   **Jane Cowan Glover (1816-1896)**

William Glover was born in Kilmarnock, Ayreshire, Scotland. Jane Cowan was born in Cle, Lanarkshire, Scotland. They married in Scotland in 1832 and, soon after, emigrated to Albion, Nova Scotia, Canada. In Albion, William worked as a coal miner. They immediately began a family, but unfortunately, of their first seven children four of them died not long after their birth. They emigrated to Pottsville, Pennsylvania where they heard the message of Mormonism and joined the Church. They took passage on the *Brooklyn* going to California in 1846. William had leadership ability and was elected to San Francico's first town council. He was put in charge of the Saints when Brannan went East to meet Brigham Young. William also helped build the first school in San Francisco, worked in business with Sam Brannan, and ran a boarding house.

In 1848 the Glovers went to Mormon Island and worked the placers for gold. William gathered several thousand dollars in gold, and Jane gathered some of her own outside her cabin, which she put away for emergencies. They joined the Rhoades gold train going back to the Salt Lake Valley. William turned over his gold to the Church when they arrived. They bought a farm in Farmington with the additional gold that Jane had gathered and saved.

William served on a mission to England 1852-54 and was given charge of a group of Saints emigrating to Utah from Liverpool. He was active in the local dramatic productions and local brass bands.

William married two other wives, Zelnora Snow, who had come on the *Brooklyn*, and Margaret Lockheed. Both William and Jane died in Farmington, Utah. At the time of William's death, he was the father of 26 children, 73 grandchildren, and 11 great-grandchildren. *Photos courtesy of Jack Marshall.*

Hervey Green (1806-1875)

Hervey Green was born in Lake Pleasant, New York. He joined the LDS Church in 1831, only a year after the Church was organized. He was with the Church in Kirtland and in Missouri. He married Sally Ann Pickard and they had two sons, Henry and Ammon. She died on the plains of Missouri giving birth to twins. The twins also died.

Hervey at times acted as scribe for Joseph Smith and was President of an elders quorum in Far West, Missouri. He was an active missionary, serving in New Jersey and Michigan, and campaigned for Joseph Smith when Joseph was a candidate for the presidency. He introduced Charles C. Rich to Sarah Pia, recommending her as a wife. Charles and Sarah soon married. So Hervey was close to the Rich family.

Hervey then married Rich's sister, Jane Ann Rich, and they had two girls. They lived in Nauvoo, left with the exodus west, had another daughter at Winter Quarters (Nebraska), and arrived in the Salt Lake Valley in September 1847. In 1849, Hervey and his oldest son, Henry, took mail to California and returned with the gold train. He taught school for a short time in Farmington, Utah. Jane Ann gave birth to a son in the Salt Lake Valley and Hervey went again to California with his two sons by his first wife. In California, Hervey for a time co-owned a hotel in Salmon Falls with Hezekiah Thatcher.

Hervey moved to Mission San Jose, farmed part time for John Horner and taught school at the first English speaking school in Alameda County. He moved to San Bernardino and remained there

when the Saints, responding to the request of Brigham Young, returned to Utah. His son Ammon, however, moved with the Saints to Utah.

Hervey joined the Reorganized Church of Jesus Christ of Latter Day Saints and did missionary work for them. He became President of the Northern Slope District, covering 20 counties in California. In 1875 he died in Linden, a few miles east of Stockton. *Courtesy Community of Christ Church Archives.*

---

also been successful in his gold mining activities. [4] Years later, he produced a short account of the Mormon gold train. Also included in the gold train were: Samuel G. Ladd, Levi Riter, Hervey (Harvey) Green [5] and others.

The Mormon gold train organized for departure July 14 in Sacramento. [1] The movement of

the eastward bound gold train was documented by the incredulous accounts of several westward bound trains of gold seekers. On August 4th, a westward bound emigrant, James Pritchard, recorded that he met the eastward moving Rhoades leading a group of Utah-bound Saints, some of whom were from the *Brooklyn*. Rhoades, strangely loquacious, plied them with information about the mines in California. [6] The following westward moving companies met the Rhoades company traveling northeast along the upper reaches of the Humboldt River toward Fort Hall: the Fosters on August 25, the Caldwells on August 27, the Goulds on September 3, Bruff on September 4-6, the Boston Pack Company on September 5th, and the De Wolfs on September 8th. [7]

The Bruff account gives some interesting detail, including some apparent misinformation about Sam Brannan. On September 4th Bruff camped nearby a "Mormon train of 8 wagons, with several women and children, and plenty of stock" reportedly led by Sam Brannan. Mistakenly claiming that Sam Brannan commanded them, he said they were headed for Salt Lake from California. He walked over to the Mormon camp "and obtained much information about California, from an aged man, who seemed to be an honest follow." The old man was "Mr. Ths. Rhoads." He continued, "One of them had a fine specimen of crude gold, which he exhibited to one of my men." [8]

Bruff was the leader of one of the unfortunate companies to travel the Lassen Road into Northern California that year. He may have been unwittingly misled by Rhoades who "had not travelled Lassen's Road but was intimate with many who had . . ." However, Rhoades also informed him of the details of the "Truckee and Mormon or Carson River routes. [9]

It seems strange that the usually secretive Rhoades, who had kept his presence in Illinois and Missouri so well hidden, who kept the same anonymity on his westward migration in 1846, and whose activities were not well known in California, should become so well documented on his trip to Utah. It could be that the westward bound emigrants were exceptionally curious and prying as to the reasons behind people leaving California when they and so many others were so anxious to get to the gold fields.

Some of the details of the Mormon gold train are given by William Glover, emigrating with Rhoades and his "barrel of gold" to the valley. He wrote "In the Spring of `49' myself and a few others gathered up our effects and started for Salt Lake. While at Sacramento buying our outfits we met Amasa Lyman. He wanted me to go to Southern California to settle and spend my money. I told him 'no' I had started for Salt Lake and I was going. He told me then to go and I would get the [k]nots knocked off me." [10]

Glover maintains that as they traversed the mountains a company of 13 men, "armed to the teeth with some picks and spades" would pass and repass them every day, "professing to be prospectors hunting for gold." The Rhoades company camped near one westward moving company, (which had had some contact with this group), a member of which warned them that they were in danger from the supposed prospectors. Upon reaching Carson Valley where Mormon Station was established that year, the packers finally turned back. Glover reminisced: "They had murder in their hearts, but the Lord put a hook in their jaws that they had no power to molest us. We went on our way rejoicing and praising God that he had spared our lives and the little means we had (as much as $25,000 to $30,000) for a better purpose."

Glover's narrative indicates one of the dangers of the trail—the possibility of being robbed. It also indicates the early part of the route used over the Mormon Emigrant Trail through Carson Valley to the Humboldt River. It may have been the first wagon company to make the eastward passage over the route since it was pioneered the previous summer by members of the Mormon Battalion. In addition, it indicates that some miners may have been deserting the gold fields of California as early as 1849, looking for richer diggings in other areas. For example, gold was discovered in Carson Valley that year by Abner Blackburn and company as they traveled west. The gold train reached Salt Lake the last of September, Glover "praising God that He had preserved us through all the varied and trying scenes of a long, tedious, and perilous journey . . . ."

An account of Levi E. Riter, written by his son, W. W. Riter, in 1917 tells of Riter's involvement. [11] The father had emigrated to Utah in 1847 but had gone to California in the fall of 1848 in an abortive attempt to collect goods (or compensation) he had sent on the *Brooklyn* in the care of Samuel Brannan. He was also the agent for John Neff and

Thomas Grover (1807-1887)

Thomas Grover was born in Whitehall, New York. At age twelve, he began working as a cabin boy on a barge on Lake Erie. Eventually he became captain of a freighter working northeastern waterways. In 1830, Thomas purchased a farm in western New York. In addition to working the farm, he was a Methodist preacher.

Through interactions with Joseph Smith, he was converted to Mormonism and joined the Church in 1834. He resettled in Kirtland, helped build the Kirtland Temple, went to Missouri, served on the Far West High Council, and finally settled in Nauvoo. Thomas was on the Nauvoo High Council, was on the general staff of the Nauvoo Legion, and was a bodyguard for Joseph Smith. He was on a mission to Michigan when he felt impressed to return immediately to Illinois, arriving just after Joseph Smith was killed. He helped escort the bodies of Joseph and Hyrum back to Nauvoo.

Thomas was one of the first to leave Nauvoo on the exodus west. He operated a ferry to help the Saints cross the Platte river. He arrived in the Salt Lake Valley in October 1847 and was appointed to the Salt Lake High Council.

In the fall of 1848 he was sent to California by the southern route to conduct Church business. He then went to northern California and mined for gold. He returned to Salt Lake City by the northern route in the Rhoades' gold train, bringing gold of his own, plus gold sent by Apostles Rich and Lyman.

He served the Church in many roles, including a mission to New York when he was 67.

Thomas's first wife died and he remarried. When plural marriage was introduced, he eventually married four more wives. He died in Farmington, Utah at almost age 80. *Courtesy Pioneer Memorial Museum, International Society Daughters of Utah Pioneers.*

John Van Cott who had likewise shipped goods in 1846, anticipating at that time that the Saints would settle on the coast.

Riter was unsuccessful in either securing the goods or being compensated for them, but while in California mined for gold from the Merced River in the southern mines to Feather River in the north. With a few thousand dollars in gold dust, he joined the Rhoades' Mormon gold train.

Riter's story differs somewhat from that of Glover. His son, agreeing with Glover, said that Riter and Green took off from the group before reaching Fort Hall hoping to reach Salt Lake in advance of the rest of the party. However, while Glover makes no mention of Riter and Green taking gold with them, Riter says, "There was a man in the party by the name of Green, who was bringing with him some six thousand dollars in gold dust, which had been collected from the Mormon members of the Church in California as tithing.

Green determined also to come along (with Riter) and bring this gold-dust with him."

This story seems to be at odds with other accounts. First of all, there was only a little over $4,100 in tithing and contributions, and Thomas Grover is believed to have been in charge of the Church money. However, to continue with Riter's story, after leaving the Fort Hall Road (Oregon-California Trail), Riter and Green were attacked by Indians during which attack "Green took his sack of gold by one end and father (Riter) grasped the other. They started to save themselves as best they could. After going some distance they could not agree as to what course they should take. The sack of gold would be too heavy for either one of them to carry, so they dropped it in a gully, carrying in their memory, as well as possible, the spot, so that they could locate it later." The two men split up, Green returning to the main group, Riter being rescued by an emigrant train and returning to the Rhoades gold train. After reaching Salt Lake, Riter "got some of them (Mormon emigrants) to go with him and they found the sack of gold, also his overcoat, the watch and some few other matters which the Indians had not had time to return and obtain." On November 5, 1849, Riter paid $147.64 in tithing, indicating personal earnings in California of almost $1500.00. [12]

The arrival of Captain Rhoades' gold train in Salt Lake appears to have caused little public comment. There was no newspaper at the time, but even the Journal History, said little. The latter does reveal that a wagon train with 14 men arrived from California on September 28, 1849. No mention was made of the names of the men nor the women with them, though it does say that some were from the *Brooklyn*. [13]

The names of Thomas Rhoades and several others with that train are identified in a letter from the First Presidency to Apostle Amasa M. Lyman, dated September 30, 1849, in which the names of Green, Grover, Rhodes, Glover and Ladd are revealed. In this letter the Church leaders acknowledged "the receipt of funds sent per Capt. Rhodes, and say unto you go and prosper, and may the Lord be with you. We wish you to say unto Bro. Samuel Brannan that we wish him to immediately gather up all the means he can say, two,

three, four or more thousand dollars, and come to this place, for we wish him to go east, and make his arrangements to carry on business at this point instead of that; that he may do good, and be useful to the cause where he can live in peace." [14]

This letter indicates that Sam Brannan did not go to Salt Lake, Captain Bruff notwithstanding. A letter of the First Presidency a few days later addressed to Amasa M. Lyman, Charles C. Rich, and Samuel Brannan in California also indicates that Brannan never arrived in Utah (if he ever left California). It appears he had not yet been completely "written off" by the Church leaders. The letter also pressed Lyman to "collect all the tithing you can and forward every safe opportunity." In addition, it suggested that "every tenth day should be required of Mormon gold miners, as well as a tenth of all proceeds of a man's business." Such a labor "assessment was also being carried into effect" in Salt Lake City. [15]

The arrival of the Rhoades gold train, while unannounced, nevertheless produced a beehive of activity at Church head quarters, which also served as governmental offices. The primary use of gold at that time was in coinage, which was being recommended. The gold from the Mormon gold train was immediately fed into the smelting operation of the Mormon mint. The importance of the gold operations is evidenced by the eminence of the men involved, including Brigham Young, John Taylor, Charles C. Rich, Thomas Bullock, John Kay, and Willard Richards.

Not only was Rhoades the captain of the gold train, he also brought with him a large amount of his own gold dust. Colonel Joseph M. Louck reported:

> Father Rhodes brought several sacks of gold among which there was a 60 pound sack, the largest amount of gold that had been brought into the valley. Father Rhodes turned all the gold over to Brigham Young, who in turn had a home built for Rhodes and allowed him to withdraw from the tithing office all the food supplies he deemed necessary. He also received a herd of cattle . . . Father Rhodes contributed the en-

tire amount to accelerate the progress of the Mormon people. The famous 60 pound sack of gold was the chief topic of the people in the Valley at that time and for quite some time after. [16]

The amount of gold Rhoades brought with him cannot be proved. However, at $16 an ounce (with 16 ounces to the pound), 60 pounds would be valued at $15,360. The story of Thomas Rhoades and his barrel or sack of gold is also given credence by an address of Brigham Young in September, 1850. He said: "I declare openly and boldly, there is no necessity for any man of this community to go to the gold mines . . . we have more property and wealth than we are capable of taking care of . . . Before I had been one year in this place, the wealthiest man who came from the mines Father Rhodes, with $17,000 could not buy the possessions I had made in one year." [17] This was an unfair comparison because Brigham Young had access to Church funds as a source of capital. While it does not say that Rhoades gave or deposited all of his gold with the prophet-statesman, the fact that Rhoades had tithed earlier that year (the next to largest tithe payer in California and one of the largest tithe payers in the Church) and the fact that he had left his prospering gold diggings at the height of the gold rush, indicates that Rhoades was responsive to the will of the Prophet. If Brigham Young asked him for his gold, he probably gave it up. The fact that gold was scarce and certainly needed in Utah in 1849, leads to the conclusion that he probably was asked for and did turn his gold over in response to the Church leader to help "build the kingdom." But in return he received compensation in land, house, cattle and supplies.

A recently located record in the Church archives gives some detail on Rhoades' responsiveness. While he did not make a gift of his money, he did deposit it to be used as the Church leaders saw fit. In Brigham Young's Gold Accounts, Rhoades had sufficient activity to warrant a separate account. While his account does not record a deposit of $17,000, it does list $10,826 as deposited by Rhoades (Rhodes). [18] Apparently, he deposited the money, drawing against it primarily for the construction of a home. [19]

Apostle John Taylor received $100, apparently being paid for a building lot on the southwest corner of First South and West Temple where Rhodes built a home. Taylor and Rhoades were to be neighbors for several years. His other neighbors were such notable Church leaders as George Q. Cannon, who soon left on a gold mission for John Taylor and who several years later would become an Apostle and a member of the First Presidency; Thomas Bullock, clerk to Brigham Young; Apostles Parley P. Pratt, Orson Pratt, Franklin D. Richards, Wilford Woodruff; and W. W. Phelps, of earlier Church notoriety.

In Deseret, Rhoades became a public figure for at least a decade. He was soon named as a counselor to the President of the Salt Lake Stake, lived in the midst of the General Authorities, was granted several wives, named as a Regent for the Schools of Deseret and the first treasurer of Salt Lake County, accompanied Brigham Young on at least two of his outings to distant settlements (one to Southern Deseret and one into Salmon River country in Idaho), secured Kamas Prairie or Rhodes Valley as a cattle ranch in partnership with Brigham Young, served as a guide into the Uintah Basin and became the principal character in the Mormon tale of the Lost Rhoades Gold Mine. [20]

William Glover brought at least $3,301.01 with him, $2,623.85 of it in American coin and $676.16 in dust. Three thousand of this went to Brigham Young "towards the store," while $300.01 was due Glover in "valley coin." Out of this, he made presents of $50.00 each to Lorenzo Snow, Erastus Snow and F. D. Richards, three recently named apostles. Samuel G. Ladd evidently brought with him at least $105.80 in coin and dust, making a deposit of that much to the Gold Accounts.

While the Rhoades company is the only organized group so far to be documented as coming to Utah from California in 1849, others also found their way east that fall. Appendix 10c contains a list of those depositing a total of almost $10,000 in gold dust to the Gold Accounts over the next few months. However, it is not known which of the depositors were actually in the gold fields. [21]

The $40,000 or so dollars in gold infused into the Utah economy, mostly by Rhoades and his company, in the fall of 1849, was of critical importance. It probably saved the Mormon money system and provided much of the liquid capital essential for continued economic growth.

NOTES

1. The beginning roster for the Rhoades gold train reported by Thomas Bullock is given in Appendix 11a. Curiously, some names are absent from the roster. Perhaps some joined the train as it moved beyond Sacramento or they moved with it but were independent of it. For example, Thomas Grover, Levi Riter, and Hervey Green are not listed in the roster.

2. See Appendix 11b for list of contributors.

3. Gold Accounts.

4. His wife was able to put away enough gold to extricate the family from a financial crisis some years later.

5. Green's given name was Hervey. He is often mistakenly referred to as Harvey. Neither Hervey Green nor Levi Riter are listed in the Bullock roster.

6. Helen S. Griffin, The Diaries of Peter Decker, 283 n142.

7. Read and Gaines, ed., *Gold Rush*, 554.

8. *Ibid.*, 164. This account, the source of some of the Rhoades-Boren assumptions, seems to be at variance with other sources. Reva Scott, *Samuel Brannan and the Golden Fleece*, 260-266, places Brannan in California in August through September making a fortune at his merchandising business. No known source substantiates the assertion that Brannan commanded this group.

9. Read and Gaines, *Gold Rush*, 554.

10. William Glover, "The Mormons in California," 23-29. This statement appears anachronous, San Bernardino not being settled until 1851. There are at least two possible explanations.

Glover, a devout Mormon who was to write of the experience in 1884 after Lyman's problems with the Church, may have confused two different experiences. On the other hand, Lyman may have already determined in his mind that he was going to establish a major colony in the Southland, the location of which had not yet really been determined, and was unofficially beating the bushes for settlers—especially those with money. He and Rich were promoting such a colonizing effort in 1850.

11. Carter, *Heart Throbs of the West*, 7:401-408.

12. Gold Accounts.

13. Journal History. October 12, 1849.

14. Lyman Papers.

15. Ibid., Attempts were made in Deseret to have men devote a portion of their labor to public works. (See Arrington, *Great Basin Kingdom*, 54-55.)

16. Carter, *Our Pioneer Heritage*, 9:479.

17. Roberts, *Comprehensive History*, 3:347-348. It had actually been two years since his first arrival.

18. It was at this point that confusion as to the spelling of Rhoades name was added. In Missouri and California it was "Rhoads." It was changed by way of this account to "Rhodes." A later change would combine the two, it becoming "Rhoades," at least in Utah.

19. See Appendix 11c.

20. For a somewhat fanciful tale see Rhoades and Boren. *The Lost Rhoades Mines*. A more accurate story of Rhoades is found in the self-published work by this author (JKD), *Thomas Rhoades, the Wealthiest Mormon Gold Miner*.

21. See Appendix 11d.

APPENDIX 11a (Note 11:1)
Roster: Rhoades Gold Train
Sacramento City July 14th 1849

"Report of the number of California Saints together with the number of Waggons, Cattle and other property in their possessions which Company was organized by Elder Amasa Lyman at Sacramento City: Thomas Rhoades was appointed Capt. by the Unanimous voice of the Company.

"Thomas Rhoades, Age 55 years, 1 Waggon, 2 Horses, 3 Yokes oxen
Caleb Rhoades
Lucinda Rhoades 4
Sam (Indian)
Turner Elder, 1 Waggon, 5 Horses, 2 Yokes oxen, 2 Cows
Polly Elder
Martin Elder
Elizebeth Elder
Thomas Elder
Turner Elder
John Elder
Nancy Elder
Alondas D.L. Buckland, Age 24 years, 2 Waggons, 2 Horses, 9 Yokes oxen, 1 Cow 1 Mule.
Nancy L. Buckland
Alondas L. Buckland
Nancy L. Buckland
Prudence Aldredge
Henry L. Dolton, Age 23years, 2 Waggons, 1 Horse, 5 Yokes oxen, 1 Cow, 4 Mules.
Elizebeth J. Dolton
John G. Dolton
Daniel Henry , 2 Horses
Aaron Stow
Wm. Rittlman [Kittleman], 2 Waggons, 1 Horse, 5 Yokes oxen, 1 Cow
Eliza Rittlman [Kittleman]
James Rittlman [Kittleman]
Mary Ann Rittlman [Kittleman]
George Rittlman [Kittleman]
Sarah Rittlman [Kittleman]
Hannah M. Wm. Glover
Jane Glover
Jane Jr. Glover
Katharine Glover
Joseph Glover
Wm. Glover
Sarah Glover

Zelnora Snow
Eliza Savage
Samuel Ladd
Henry Hoskins, Age 40 years, 1 Waggon.
Thomas Treat, 1 Waggon, 2 Horses
Ashbel Green Haskel Disseased on the road July 27th 1849. "

Source: LDS Church Archives;
Also http://www.lds.org/churchhistory/library/source/0,18016,4976-18376,00.html

APPENDIX 11b (Note 11:2)

Tithes and Offerings
California Saints 1849

Brooklyn Saints
Buckland, A. D. L.
Cades, Jonathan
Evans, William
Glover, William
Harris, Henry G.
Knowles, Richard
Mowery, Barton
Nicols, Mrs. V.
Petch, Robert (Peters)
Pool(e), Peter J.
Serrine, G. W.
Serrine, John
Stark, Daniel
Wimmer, G. K.

Battalion Boys
Cheney, Alpheus
Gribble, William
Hunter, Jesse D.
Keysor, Guy M.
Treat, Thomas W.

Others:
Lincoln, Seth (from Honolulu, 1847)
Rhoads, Thomas (Rhodes, Rhoades) (overland from Missouri, 1846)

Sources: Amasa Lyman Papers. Also Gold Account.

APPENDIX 11c (Note 11:19)
Thomas Rhodes Gold Accounts
1850 (1849)

		$ Received	$ Paid
Oct 9	Received from Thomas Rhodes	dust 10,826	
Oct 16	Paid Thomas Rhodes by		
	Thomas Tomkins (Thompkins)		75.
	Paid Thomas Rhodes by John Taylor		100.
	do Silver		200.
	do Perpetual Poor Fund		25.
Oct 18	do T. Tomkins do		50.
Nov 20	do by T. Tomkins		600.
Nov 26	do		200.
Dec 19	do order on Livingston Store		100.
1850			
Feb 14	do by T. Tomkins		5.
Apr 11	do		200.
Apr 15	do by T. Tomkins		240.
May 27	do do		30.
May 27	do do thro Shepherd Hutchings		2.
Jun 1	do by John Stewart		350.
Jun 28	do		50.
Aug 10	do by John Stewart		170.
Jun 27	Paid for labor on Rhodes House		6.75
Jun 29	Furnishing store (stone), etc.		21.12
Aug 10	200 adobes (extra)		27.50
	6 loads of clay and sand extra		6.
	laying and attending the above		25.
Aug 23	Cash paid T. Rhodes		100.
Sep 6	do by J. Stewart		100.
Oct 1	do do		100.
Oct 9	do by J. & E. Reese		103.
Oct 15	do by Stewart		100.
Oct 15	do by Livingston and Kincaid (Kinkead)		19.88
	Amount of contract for building house		1101.
Oct 24	Cash paid T. Rhodes by Stewart		50.
Oct 30	Due bill paid do		10.
Nov 5	Cash paid T. Rhodes by Stewart		40.
Nov 7	Alexander		37.
Nov 26	Paid Thomas Rhodes by T. J. Thurston's order 30.		
Dec 24	Paid Thomas Rhodes		50.
	rd. forward		4,274.25

Source: Gold Accounts.

Note: The accounts in Appendix 11c and 11d use the word "by." Today, it would be more clear what they meant if they had used the word "to."

APPENDIX 11d (Note 11:21)
Deposits to Gold Accounts
October 9-December 31, 1849

Oct. 28	
*Charles Shumway	40.00
*Abner Blackburn	384.00
*Albert G. Fellows	199.00
John Lowry	38.50
Jemima Young	63.00
H.C. Kimball	10.00
John Van Cott	44.00
*Jacob L. Workman	233.00
Sister Young	25.50
Oct. 29	
*William Brown	60.00
A. L. Lamoreaux	6.00
*Thomas Blackburn	200.00
H. C. Kimball	392.00
Nov. 1	
*P. H. Allred	982.00
*Ira J. Willis	4.90
Nov. 2	
Heber C. Kimball	200.00
Brigham Young by	
John Bettel	72.80
Thomas Bullock	3.35
Nov. 5	
*Alexander Stephens	5.80
Allen F. Smithson	20.00
H. C. Kimball	221.00
Ezra T. Benson	105.70
*Levi E. Riter(tithing)	147.64
Brigham Young	21.00
Nov. 6	
*William Lewis	41.35
Nov. 12	
William Clayton	146.85
E. T. Benson	100.00
*William Empey	13.40
Nov. 13	
*Andrew L. Lamoreaux	90.00
T. Bullock	2.50
Ezra T. Benson	90.00
Nov. 16	
*Moses Deming	17.00
*Gilbert Hunt	173.00
Nov. 17	
William Black	1.56
*Wm. C. Staines	1.12

Nov.20	
*Wm. Insfeldt	27.00
*Chancey W. Porter	.66.00
*Jerome Zabriske	330.00
Thomas Bullock	5.00
*Henry W. Jackson	125.00
*John P. Porter	334.00
*Wm. C. Staines	31.50
(Old Mormon Coins)	
Nov. 21	
*Louisa Calkins	988.00
(from deceased husband)	
William W. Casper	7.90
*Fredick Froerer	5.90
H. C. Kimball	
by *H. W. Jackson	100.00
Nov. 22	
George Morris	23.80
Nov. 24	
*John Oakley	32.75
Nov. 26	
H. C. Kimball	200.00
*John S. White	29.80
*Edwin Walker	84.00
Dec. 1	
B. Young by Horace Gibbs	476.15
Dec. 5	
*William H. Ewing	51.20
Dec. 6	
Daniel H. Wells	35.30
Dec. 7	
*Isaace F. Carter, Bishop	1,038.00
Dec.10	
D. H. Wells	1.20
Dec. 21	
Livingston	485.17
Dec. 24	
*Thomas W. Treat	124.00
*Edwin Walker	148.00
Dec. 31	
*Elijah Thomas	9.36
*Urban V. Stewart	1.30
*Walter Barney	8.55
*William Kay	11.12

*Those starred serve as the most likely candi-
dates as emigrants from California though some
may have received their gold from others.

Source: Gold Accounts.

Again, "by" should be understood as "to."

Charles C. Rich (1809-1883)

Charles C. Rich was born in Campbell County, Kentucky. The family moved to Indiana where they were visited by missionaries and baptized into the Church in 1832. He was quickly recognized as a obedient servant, a devoted leader, "a firm but understanding counselor, an effective missionary, and a dauntless colonizer." "He was laconic in his manner, modest and deferential, . . . but intelligent and practical." (Arrington. *Charles C. Rich*, xv-xvi.)

At age 39, in February of 1849, Charles C. Rich, was called to be an Apostle in the Church of Jesus Christ of Latter-day Saints. In October 1849, he was called by Brigham Young to go to California and assist Apostle Amasa Lyman who by then was already in California. He had to leave his family in the care of others. His wife at the time was sick in bed with a child three days old. Because of the many Mormons in California working the mines and supplying the miners in supportive occupations, he and Apostle Lyman were to gather and organize the members for spiritual support. In addition, Rich carried written instructions giving him authority to "investigate Sam Brannan, collect tithing, receive donations for the perpetual emigrating fund for the gathering of the poor of the church, and not to neglect the preaching of the gospel."

Apostles Rich and Lyman traveled back to Salt Lake City in October and early November 1849. The next morning after their arrival, he learned that he and Apostle Lyman had been appointed to make a settlement in the lower part of California as soon in the spring as weather would permit travel. That began their project to settle the San Bernardino Colony. (For a definitive biography, see Arrington, *Charles C. Rich: Mormon General and Western Frontiersman*, 1974.) *Courtesy LDS Arhcives.*

12

Apostle Charles C. Rich and the Gold Missionaries

THE ARRIVAL IN THE FALL of 1849 of the Mormon gold train and other Mormons with approximately $40,000 in gold supported the view that great wealth was available on the west coast, wealth that could be of inestimable value in establishing Zion in the Great Basin. Transported into Deseret, it would make unnecessary the open development of the troves of precious metals said to have been discovered within a few miles of the Mormon headquarters. Local mines would undoubtedly attract numerous gentile miners and their unsavory camp-followers, a probability which Church leaders had no desire to court.

More Mormon manpower was needed in California if its wealth was to be fully exploited for the Saints. In addition, Mormon leaders became engaged in negotiations which would result in a political need for more representation on the coast. For these reasons, companies of intended gold miners were organized in the Salt Lake Valley and sent to California in 1849. There was still the danger that those who went might lose their testimonies and dedication to the kingdom. However, if carefully chosen, and if under apostolic leadership, the dangers would be minimized. The stalwart Charles C. Rich, one of the newest apostles, therefore, was called to accompany the miners. Rich had actually been called to go to California the previous spring, but the call had been postponed.

At least four Mormon companies would leave Salt Lake that fall for the gold fields via the southern route. While not all the men of these companies were "called" as missionaries to mine gold, many were. While not all were dedicated to the kingdom, many were. And while not all would be obedient to apostolic leadership, many would be. Chapters 12 through 15 will deal with each of these four companies. [1]

1. The first Mormon company to leave Salt Lake City for California in the fall of 1849 was a group consisting of Apostle Charles C. Rich, twenty gold missionaries, and a few others. They mostly used pack animals (but two wagons) and would choose James M. Flake as their captain. The Flake company interacted on the trail with a much larger group, mostly of non-Mormons passing through from the East, who contracted Jefferson Hunt of the Battalion as captain. Some Mormon missionaries going to the Society Islands also travelled with Hunt. The Hunt party (consisting of 107 wagons, over four hundred persons, and about one thousand horses, mules, and oxen) assembled near what is now Provo, Utah and began leaving October 2. The Flake company assembled in the same area, chose their captain, and left October 14. The Flake party caught up with the Hunt party near Beaver Creek (in southern Utah). Another group, consisting of some twenty non-Mormon packers, left at about the same time

as the Flake party. They chose the non-Mormon, Orson Kirk Smith, as their captain and travelled variously with or near the Flake party until they also overtook Hunt in the Beaver Creek area.

2. The second group to leave Salt Lake, the Pomeroy Company with trade goods, was led by the non-Mormon Pomeroy brothers, using mostly Mormon drovers. They left November 3.

3. The third company to leave was led by a recent convert, Captain Simpson D. Huffaker. They began leaving November 10.

4. The fourth, the Salt Lake Trading Company led by the veteran Mormon, Captain Howard Egan, went to establish a trading network in the California gold fields. That company left November 18.

Introducing Some Members of the Flake Company

On February 12, 1849, Charles C. Rich, recently appointed president of the Salt Lake Stake, was ordained an Apostle. On March 31, "The First Presidency and the Twelve discussed the propriety of sending a good responsible man to settle on the coast at or near San Francisco bay." At the April conference Rich had been sustained as an Apostle and "appointed to go and establish a settlement or stake." On the 12th he was given the objectives of his call—"to gather the Saints, preach the gospel, and preside over the affairs of the Church on the Western Coast." [2]

If one did not have the advantage of later developments, it would be easy to conclude that it was the intent of the Church leaders at that time to establish a permanent Mormon presence in the San Francisco area. It is uncertain how widespread this conclusion may have been held among the Saints.

Toward the end of May, it was resolved that Elder Charles C. Rich and Addison Pratt (veteran missionary in the Society Islands on his way back to the Islands) should prepare to start for the western coast by the first part of July, if possible." James S. Brown and Hirum H. Blackwell were to travel with Addison Pratt to the Society Islands. In June more names were added for gold missions. However, a few days later, "owing to the heavy emigration of gold-diggers to California," the appointments of some were cancelled, while the others were apparently postponed.

There had been great concern over having Mormon companies travel in general proximity to Gentile companies, often heavily laced with Missourians and Illinoisans. The Saints were convinced that these continued to harbor intense hatred toward them, feelings remaining from the Mormon difficulties in those states in the 1830s and 1840s. Therefore, they felt that the lives of Saints traveling with them would be unduly endangered.

On September 5th, the First Presidency had written to Elder Lyman: "Bros. C. C. Rich, Addison Pratt & Co. will not leave here this fall, it not being considered safe for them to do so while the route west was so full of emigrants. They will probably start in the Spring." [3]

However, General John Wilson arrived in Salt Lake in early September with a request from President Zachary Taylor that the Mormons assist him in achieving statehood for California. Because of this, the Church leader's again changed their minds. On September 20th, Rich and a few others were "counseled to go with Captain (Jefferson) Hunt" the following Monday. However, the start of Rich's trip was delayed once again until after the October conference, allowing time to organize a substantial party of men to leave for California with him.

At the October conference, Elders Lyman (already in California) and Rich were "appointed to gather up funds in California, as agents for the Perpetual fund." [4] Rich was also "assigned to assist Elder Amasa Lyman in the duties of his office, to succeed Elder Lyman when he returns here; to receive tithings and donations . . . and to perform all other duties, as an Apostle . . ."

Rich carried with him a certificate issued by the First Presidency and dated October 1, 1849. In it, Rich was certified as an official representative of the Church, to visit the "Saints in Western California," and to assist Apostle Lyman until he

Henry W. Bigler (1815-1900)

Henry Bigler was at the site when gold was discovered at Coloma, but he was happy to leave the gold fields and return to his family and friends in the Salt Lake Valley. In the Valley, John Smith, uncle to Joseph Smith, was sorely in need of money, Brigham Young gave John Smith permission to select and outfit someone to go to California to mine gold in his stead. John Smith selected Henry Bigler. Bigler was very reluctant to go, but accepted the "chore." Father Smith gave Bigler a blessing, and Bigler had a dream that he was not going to mine gold, but was going to preach the gospel in the Pacific Islands.

From the mines, Bigler was called to go preach the gospel in the Hawaiian Islands. He and his companions boarded a ship in San Francisco in October of 1850. Three years later, in October 1853, Bigler recorded that the Church had fifty-eight branches on the Islands, twenty-nine elders, seventy-two priests, and many teachers and deacons. He was president of the Church branch on Oahu Island. Bigler was released from his mission in 1854 and reached Salt Lake City in 1855 after an absence of almost six years. Those six years were spiritually profitable for the Islanders and for Bigler, but it is not likely he brought back much gold for father Smith. (See Gudde, *Bigler's*

Chronicles and Bishop, *Henry Willam Bigler*.) *Courtesy LDS Archives.*

returned to Salt Lake. The importance of the *California Star* was recognized, with Rich assigned to direct and counsel its publication as well as any other product of its press. He was charged with the responsibility to "preach the gospel as he has an opportunity" and to counsel the Saints "by way of going and returning." All who received Rich as a "messenger of the Most High and administer to his necessities" were assured that they would be blessed and prospered. [5]

Elder Rich also carried with him a letter to Lyman. The instructions show a qualified support for a continued Church presence in California. The letter read in part:

> We wish you and Brother Rich to take into consideration the propriety of continuing to hold our influence in Western California by our people remaining in that region. Our feelings are in favor of that Policy unless, all the offscouring of Hell has been let loose upon that dejected land, in which case we would advise you to gather up all that is worth saving and come hither with all speed. Yet if good can be accomplished by continuing to have a presidency located there, you will continue to gather the people in good and healthy locations in communities together that they may act in concert and receive instruction from those that may be sent among them and from each other . . .[6]

James M. Flake had entered the Valley the previous fall, having been the clerk for the Amasa

Courtesy Pioneer Memorial Museum, International Society Daughters of Utah Pioneers.

Francis Martin Pomeroy (1822-1882)

Francis Martin Pomeroy was born in Somers, Connecticut. At fourteen he was apprenticed to his uncle. Thinking that life was hard, at sixteen, he signed on to a whaler. He was a whaler for six years, learning what "hard" really was. He was swept overboard from a whaler in a storm off the coast of Peru. Francis saved himself, making it to shore hanging on to an oar. He recovered and lived for a while with Spaniards, long enough to learn to speak the Spanish language. He made it back to New Salem, and married Irene, the daughter of Ashbell Green Hascall (Haskell). From the Hascalls he learned of Mormonism and was baptized by Brigham Young. Francis and Irene had a daughter, Francelle, September 21, 1845.

As Ashbell was getting ready to leave on the *Brooklyn* for San Francisco Bay, the Pomeroys (Francis, Irene, and Francelle) made their way to Nauvoo, and were in the first group to leave that city overland for the West. They were also among the first Mormons to reach the Salt Lake Valley. In 1849 Francis went to California with Charles C. Rich, to assist him. He returned the next year. Francis died in Mesa, Arizona at age sixty.

M. Lyman company of pioneers. Born in North Carolina in 1815, the former plantation owner had disposed of his slaves upon joining the Church and emigrated to Deseret, three of his former slaves coming with him. He left his wife and child behind in Deseret as he entered his first and last mission for the Church.

At least five extant personal accounts from Flake company members provide details of the adventures of this unique group in California. These are the accounts of George Q. Cannon, Henry Bigler, James Keeler, William Farrer, and Charles C. Rich. The first four of these writers were gold missionaries. [7]

George Q. Cannon was destined to become the president of the California Mission, editor of the Church's *Western Standard* newspaper in San Francisco, an Apostle, a counselor to four Church presidents (in the First Presidency for three) and a wealthy mining investor. He maintained a diary and also, years later, wrote an article telling of some of his California experiences. [8]

On October 6, 1849, at the Church conference held in Salt Lake, the 32-year-old Cannon informed his readers, "Brother Brigham . . . said that a man that thought when he came back from a mission that he would live at ease was not in the path of his duty; or that lusted for farms, horses, cattle, Gold or anything were not doing what was right." [9]

Lusting after gold or not, a few days later he was sent on a trip to California as a gold missionary. He was sponsored by his uncle, John Taylor, a senior member of the Quorum of the Twelve

Apostles and future Church President, whom he, years later, served as a Counselor.

Years later, in 1869, Cannon wrote of the call to which he and others had been "selected." They were "joined by some few whose only motive was going to enrich themselves by digging gold." He said, "There was no place I would rather not have been at the time than in California. I heartily despised the work of digging gold. There is no occupation I would rather not follow than huntin and digging for gold." But, he continued, "My instructions were to go to California, and be guided by the counsels of Elders Amasa Lyman and Charles C. Rich." [10] Cannon became a special counselor to Brigham Young in 1873 at the peak of the Mormon campaign against mining.

The second account was maintained by Henry Bigler, the Mormon Battalion veteran, already discussed in connection with his first-hand account of the initial discovery of the gold at Coloma. Bigler had left the gold fields the summer of 1848, settled in the Salt Lake Valley, and used up his supply of gold. He did not welcome a recall to California. Bigler recorded in his journal "I was not looking for any such mission. Indeed it had been the President's counsel not to go to the gold mines and those who went after such counsil had been given was looked upon as jack Mormons as they were called." Indeed he was filled "with sorrow to think of leaving, for I am attached to this place and this people, for they are my brothers and sisters and my friends, and it was with considerable struggle with my feelings that I consented to go." [11]

Bigler was called and sponsored by 68-year old Patriarch John Smith, uncle of the Mormon prophet, Joseph Smith, and recent President of the Salt Lake Stake. On October 8th, as Bigler prepared to leave the valley, he recorded that Smith, who had been "kicked and cuft about and finally drove out of the United States because he worshipped God according to the dictates of his own conscience and become poor," had been "counciled to fit out some person and send them to the Gold mines and he has called on me to go and is now fitting me out to go with Brother C. C. Rich and others who are sent. Brother Rich leaves today."

On the 11th, Bigler recorded that "Last evening Father Smith sent for me he wanted to bless me, he then laid his hands on my head and blest me and also Brother (James) Keeler in the name of the Lord. Brother Keeler is a going for Thomas Calister (Smith's son-in-law) we will go in the same wagon together." Bigler's torment on leaving was evidenced: "I experienced what I shall not here attempt to describe. I walked back and forth across my floor and my feelings was spent in a complete shower of tears, everything I looked upon seemed to sympathize with me and say go in peace only be faithful and all will be right." Just before leaving the Valley, Bigler wrote, "Last night I dreamed I was not going to the mines but was on my way to the Pacific Islands to preach the gospel." [12] Little did he realize the prophetic, though slightly inaccurate, nature of his dream.

The third account is that of James Keeler. According to Laura Ann Keeler Thurber, her father, James, and Henry Bigler went to California under the sponsorship of the Callisters, evidently Thomas and Smith O. Quoting her father, she said, "They were to furnish us the means to get to the mines and on our return we were to devied with them. We arrived at the mines the 1st of March of 1850 and stayed there until the last of October and while we were there we were called on a mishion (ten of us)." [13]

The first entry of Keeler's journal says that he and Bigler "were sent in company by Father John Smith and family by the councel of the presidency of the Church to go and (undecipherable) Gold in the mines." [14] This appears to contradict the previous account, but not when one realizes that the Callisters were related to John Smith. John Smith made a small deposit to the Gold Accounts the following fall. Thomas and Smith O. Callister made substantially larger deposits. [15]

The fourth account, of a gold missionary, is that of William Farrer. In a biographical sketch prepared by Farrer's daughter, his descendants were assured that he was sponsored on his gold mission by Joseph Horne, a prominent Mormon in Salt Lake. Horne, who had been called to go to California the previous fall with Amasa Lyman, had evidently not gone (unless he had gone and returned). He was to provide the provisions for

Courtesy Pioneer Memorial Museum, International Society Daughters of Utah Pioneers.

James S. Brown (1828-!902)

In 1849, James S. Brown was called to do missionary work in the Society Islands. He was accompanied by Addison Pratt and Hiram H. Blackwell, and they travelled with the Jefferson Hunt group. On reaching Southern California, Addison Pratt had pressing business to conduct in San Francisco, so he took pack animals and went on ahead, following the Camino Real up the coast. Brown and Blackwell, with wagons and the remainder of their supplies, accompanied Apostle Rich and Howard Egan up the Central Valley, visiting mining sites as they went. They came out of the hills to Stockton, the supply center for the mining communities of the South.

After conducting business at Stockton and taking note of some of the unseemly social life, Brown boarded the steamboat *Captain Sutter* and rejoined Addison Pratt in San Francisco. After enjoying the association of friends in San Francisco, Pratt, Brown, and Blackwell boarded the brig *Frederick* on the April 21 and sailed to the Society Islands (Tahiti). (Brown, *Giant of the Lord*, 138-166.)

Farrer and receive half of all his earnings. [16]

Campbell lists all the gold missionaries in the Flake company, using Bigler's Diary and Cannon recollections as his source. [17] At least four and possibly five of the men had been in the Mormon Battalion.

Break Up of the Hunt Wagon Train Near Beaver Creek

Hunt's train moved slowly south-westward to the Old Spanish Trail, slowly because Hunt was trying to bring up laggers and keep the large company together and was trying to preserve the animals' strength for the difficult desert passage ahead. An error in the route at Beaver Creek caused some loss of time. Many in the company became impatient with the rate of travel and the loss of time, and therefore with Hunt. Given their

displeasure with Hunt, their attention turned to a map Captain Orson K. Smith claimed to have received in Salt Lake showing a short cut west, by way of Walker Pass, leading directly through the Sierra Nevada into Northern California. The Smith company of packers decided to take the short cut.

Many of the Hunt party and also the Flake group became excited about the map. They were moving south into the desert, but they knew that the gold fields were in the northern part of California. They could see that the further south they went, the more backtracking they would have to do. What Smith's map failed to show was the water-short wasteland to the west of their trail. Hunt would not depart from the trail he knew, but Smith unfortunately influenced most of the wagon train to leave Hunt and follow the map into the trackless desert. Only seven wagons remained with Hunt. Unfortunately, the Flake-Rich party also decided to try the illusory short cut. The results from turning west were disastrous and life threatening. Most (including the Smith group) realized their mistake and turned back to the original trail. The Flake-Rich party returned by turning south and following the Muddy until reconnecting with Hunt. A few of those who left Hunt did not turn back, but persisted west into Death Valley. According to accounts, those of the Hunt-Flake-Smith entourage who broke away—and turned back—survived. Southworth claims fourteen of those who persisted into Death Valley perished. Those who persisted into Death Valley and yet survived, did so by turning south when reaching the Sierra and going south and west into Los Angeles County or by crossing Walker Pass. Whichever route they took, they arrived to safety long after Hunt reached the Williams Ranch, and arrived "more dead than alive." [18]

Discovering Gold
and Reaching the Williams Ranch

The trip to California will not be detailed here. However, In eastern California, near the border of present-day Inyo and San Bernardino Counties, Rich recorded on November 10th that a member of the company discovered gold at Salt Springs. James S. Brown, one of the six Battalion Boys at Sutter's Mill when gold was discovered, told the same story. [19] Mormons are usually credited with the first discovery at that location, though Mexicans and Indians had probably been mining there for years. [20]

The Flake company (moving faster as packers) reached the Williams Ranch, the Southern California recouping station for most Mormons at that time, on December 11, 1849. Jefferson Hunt's group arrived Dec. 22. Both remained at the ranch for a month, being joined by Howard Egan and his Salt Lake Trading Company pack train (to be discussed in a later chapter). While there Bigler recorded that Brother Rich received a letter from Apostles George A. Smith and Ezra Taft Benson. This letter demonstrates a naive but probably representative view of the ease with which gold could be secured. Bigler said that the two Apostles wanted "Brother Rich to raise them $5,000 from the brethren who are on a mision to

get goald (gold) that their hands may be liberated and be able to return to their fields of labor (missions) and they pray the Lord to lead the brethren in some nook or corner where it lays." Bigler continued, hoping for Divine help, "as for my part, I shall be glad to help raise it for them and have their prayers and blessings on my head." [21]

A similar letter to Apostle Lyman dated November 11, 1849 was evidently carried by someone in either the Egan party or the Thurber (Huffaker) group which followed the Hunt and Flake Companies. In it Apostles Smith and Benson, who had just reached the Salt Lake Valley from the east, informed their brother Apostle, Amasa M. Lyman, of their poverty and debt, having had to purchase their wagons for their trip west on credit and needing to repay the debt, it seems, in gold.

The Apostles went on to say that they had

discovered for the first time some slight simptoms of the Gold fever . . . we thought of asking you and through our friends in the Mines inasmuch as Providence Blesses your labours with a supply of the Yellow Dirt to give us **a** kind of lift or hoist in the way of a few thousand D ollars by way of relief to us if this assistance can be granted without injuring you or the Brethren with you, we will half venture a prediction that the reward would be certain and the blessing sure to rest on your heads at some future time it will liberate us as well as others from oppression. [22]

Except for Apostle Rich, all accounts of the gold mission were suspended either at the Williams ranch or shortly before reaching that resting place. They did not pick up again until the fall. Perhaps they were too busy mining.

North to the Gold Fields

At the Williams Ranch, Hunt, Flake, Rich, and Egan coordinated their groups for the trip north. Leaving the ranch by January 12 of 1850, the combined group reached the Catholic mission

Facsimile of an oil painting of Stockton by W. H. Cressey (Cressy). The Cressey painting was painted for Charles M. Weber, the founder of Stockton, while Cressey was a guest at his home. It captured one of the earliest images of the city (1849), when Stockton was a port city with many tents and warehouses. The role that Sacramento played for supplying the northern mining region, Stockton played for the southern region; that is, the mining regions of the Calaveras, Stanislaus, Tuolomne, Merced, and Mariposa Rivers. Supplies to both ports could be sent in easily by steamboat from San Francisco. (The facsimile appeared in Townsend and West's *History of San Joaquin County, California* (1879). The original Cressey painting, in color, is presently in the San Joaquin County Historical Museum, Lodi, California.)

of San Gabriel on the 14th. Rich recorded that it was the "most beautiful location that I have seen in this country, and the mission garden was filled with oranges and olives and other fruit trees." [23]

Proceeding to a point a mile or so north of the Mexican Pueblo (village of Los Angeles), the party provisioned up for the northward journey. The group then separated, some wanting to go quickly to San Francisco on business. On January 20th, Rich reported that "having organized the company with Howard Egan as captain to remain with the wagons, Capt. Hunt and myself, together with Brother Addison Pratt and ten or twelve others left the wagons and started ahead, with packs."

Proceeding to the coast, they arrived at the "San Buenaventura" mission January 21. Rich recorded: "This is the first place my eyes had ever held the ocean. We witnessed a school of whales near the shore spouting. Considerable of them could be seen above the water . . . We bought a mess of the finest fish ever caught in the sea by an Indian."

Elder Rich and his group continued northwesterly along El Camino Real passing consecutively through the following additional missions and ranches, noting that a number of them were either abandoned or in a bad state of decay: Santa Barbara Mission, Ortegas Ranch, Los Ojitos Ranch,

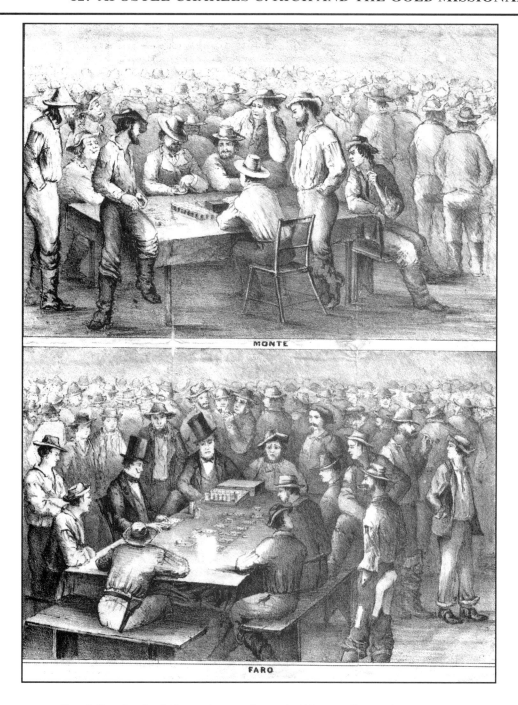

Gambling in the Mines: (upper image): Monte; (lower image): Faro.
Lithography and printing by Britton & Rey of San Francisco, California.
Courtesy Bancroft Library.

As Bayard Taylor observed concerning early California, "Wherever there is gold, there are gamblers." Professional gamblers could earn in an evening what a gold miner would need a week to accumulate. Samuel Coleville wrote of such a scene: "Almost the only comfortable places of resort were the gambling saloons, which were warm and dry, though fetid with the fumes of tobacco, gin, and other liquors, and the poisonous air which has done its duty in turn to a hundred set of lungs. . . . Few could see the heaps of gold on the gambling tables and breathe the air, and resist the influences around and before them. Men entered to avoid the rain and get warm, or through curiosity, saw, bet, and were ruined." (See discussion in Kurutz, "Popular Culture on the Golden Shore," in Star and Orsi. *Rooted in Barbarous Soil*. 281-287.)

Santa (Ynez) Mission, Artemas Ranch, Doney Ranch, Branch Ranch, Santa Margarita Mission, San Miguel Mission, San Antonio de Padua Mission, Maria Santisima (San Juan Bautista?) Mission, Gilroy Ranch, and Pueblo de San Jose.

On February 12th at San Jose, continued Rich, "Captain Howard Egan and two of the boys overtook us having left the teams at San Juan (Bautista) Mission and having traveled all night. We concluded to stay here and try to raise means for Captain Egan and company, which we did." A loan was secured by the Apostle from William H. Eddy. [24] Egan returned to his teams at San Juan (Bautista) Mission. The Rich party proceeded to San Francisco, arriving on February 15th. Rich found that Lyman had "gone to the lower pueblo [Los Angeles] on business," and possibly to meet him. [25]

On February 22nd six days before Lyman's return, having tired of waiting for the senior Apostle and not knowing just when he might return, Rich, probably in company with Jefferson Hunt, James S. Brown, Francis M. Pomeroy and James H. Rawlins (Rollins), returned south, staying at the (Dolores) Mission on their way. On February 25th, the group "stopped at San Jose; repaid Eddy and was kindly treated by him." Rich had evidently secured funds in San Francisco under local banking arrangements. From San Jose, the group proceeded south and eastward, passing through Pacheco Pass into the San Joaquin Valley. They passed the fresh grave of John Bills, a member of the Flake Company, who had died February 19th.

On Sunday, March 3rd, the company "started for the ferry on the San Joaquin" but got lost in the process and had to camp on the plain. [26] The following day, striking the river, they traveled 12 miles downstream, camping at Woods' Ferry. [27] Rich observed that it was "one of the finest plains to look at that mine eyes ever beheld . . ." From the river he "had a full view of the Sierra Nevada Mountains, her lofty peaks pointing upwards towards the sky above the clouds which lay against the mountains."

The company crossed on the ferry on the 5th, traveling up the Merced River about 25 miles. The following day they continued up the river about 15 miles, camping at Wottens. [28] On the 7th, after traveling 15 more miles, they reached Burns' Diggings where they found the brethren camped. [29] They discovered that Captain Egan had gone to Stockton, probably gone with the funds he had received through Rich to obtain supplies for the Salt Lake Trading post.

Rich also discovered that some of the boys had gone up to Mariposa, or Mormon Bar. The Bar was on the Mariposa Grant, purchased from the Mexicans by Col. John C. Fremont. According to Gudde and Gudde, gold was discovered at Mormon Bar by Mormons in 1848. Although Gudde and Gudde maintain that the Mormons soon left for Salt Lake, some may well have remained for a year or so. After Mormon withdrawal, the Chinese took over the camp and the richness of the gold findings drew considerable attention. [30]

At this point, Apostle Rich's diary became silent for 19 days, picking up again on the 26th when he left for Stockton with Captain Egan and Elder James S. Brown. The little group reached French Camp on the 30th, there discovering the Hickerson element of the Pomeroy Train. [31] After five-and one-half months on the road, this party was going into the mines "in destitute circumstances." Rich counseled them to go to Mariposa where they fell in with the Battalion Boys who had gone west with him.

On Sunday, March 31st, Rich took passage on a small boat for Stockton, arriving and staying there overnight. He gave no description of the place, but James S. Brown did, though his dates differ from those of the Apostle. The young missionary who accompanied Rich, but may have separated from him, was not always as circumspect as might be expected from a missionary. He described his experience upon arriving on March 28 in that inland port city:

> There were a few trading establishments and warehouses, and three or four large gambling houses in and around which were gathered freighters, packers, and one of the most motley gangs it has ever been my lot to see. Bands of music were in the gambling

halls. At one of these I noted twelve tables, four men at each, armed with bowie knives and revolvers; and to me it looked as if there were more gold and silver exposed on those twelve tables than six mules could draw. On the street and around the door, calling on the passers-by to come in and have a free drink and listen to the music, were men whom I soon learned were called cappers, or ropers-in, to the gambling hall; they would steam men up with drink, get them to gambling, and rob them. Sometimes men would come in from the mines with their buckskin wallets containing three to four hundred dollars' worth of gold. They would stand around with perfect strangers and drink free whisky until they became dazed, then would set down their wallets of gold on a card, and the next moment their money would be taken up by the gambler, who would continue dealing his cards as unconcernedly as he would knock the ashes from his cigar. The poor, silly miner would turn away with a sickly look, having not even enough left to get him a change of clothing. He would go into the street with his old miner's clothes on, without a dime to pay for his supper or to get a night's lodging. Sometimes thousands of dollars would change hands in a few moments. This was in the spring of 1850, when the strong, with revolver and bowie knife, were law when gamblers and blacklegs ran many of the towns in California. [32]

Candidly revealing some of the temptations facing Mormons in the fleshpots of California in 1850, Brown continued:

By this time I imagine that the reader asks what, as a missionary, I was doing there. I might answer by quoting the saying of Christ, that it was not the righteous but the sinners that He had come to call to repentance. But I will not offer this excuse, for it was not applicable; and as open confession is good for the soul, I will make one, hoping that it may be not only good for my soul, but be a warning to all who read it. I was twenty-one years old at the time, and was alone on the street. I did not know where to go or what to do. My companions had left on business, and as I started along the street I met with an old time friend who appeared very much pleased to see me. His pleasure was reciprocated. He asked me to go in and have something to drink; I thanked him and said that I was not in the habit of indulging. He said, 'Oh, come in, and have a little wine for old friendship's sake. There is no harm in a little wine; come, go in and hear the music, anyway.' With that I turned in with him to the largest gambling den in the town. The place was packed with men of almost every nationality. This was the house I have described. [33]

Failing to tell his reader about the final disposition of the invitation to have some wine, Brown continued:

In the time of great excitement, it must be confessed, the writer was tempted to lay down a purse of one hundred dollars, as he had that amount with him. But the next instant the thought came to him, Would you try to beat a watchmaker or a gunsmith at his trade? The idea was so absurd that he then thought how foolish it was to try to beat these professional gamblers at their own game. Then the disgrace that attached to the act became so repulsive to his nature, that he felt ashamed that he ever had been tempted; and to this day, in the life of seventy-two years, he has never gambled. He has always felt thankful that that simple thought came to him at that time and place. [34]

Rich took passage on the steamboat *Captain*

Sutter, leaving for San Francisco on April 1st. Brown followed a day or so later aboard the same vessel, paying $25 for the passage to San Francisco. The Apostle's party reached Benicia, the major river port between San Francisco Bay and Sacramento, about two o'clock, landing alongside the steamer *El Dorado*. Aboard the other steamer was "Brother Lyman with a company of about 30 brethren, who had come up the coast with him." Rich left the *Sutter* and boarded the *El Dorado*, and headed for the gold fields with his long appointed companion. [35]

NOTES

1. The history of the Southern Route is reviewed definitively in Lyman, *The Overland Journey*. He also summarizes the Hunt train story, 58-69. Edited accounts of those on that trail going to the gold fields in 1849 is found in Hafen and Hafen, eds. *Journals of Forty-Niners*.

2. Journal History, February 12; March 31; April 8, 12, May 27; June 3, 10, 1849.

3. Amasa Lyman Papers.

4. Journal History. September 20, October 6, 1849. The Perpetual Fund, later known as the Perpetual Emigration Fund, was established to help finance the move to Zion of needed but destitute Saints.

5. Rich Certificate, October 1, 1849.

6. Letters of First Presidency.

7. At least for that part of the journey down the southern route to Los Angeles, a copy of the accounts can be found in Hafen and Hafen, eds. *Journals of Forty-niners*, 141-272.

8. Cannon, Diary; Cannon, "After Twenty Years," (1869) 4:13-14; Landon, ed., *The Journal of George Q. Cannon.*

9. Cannon, Diary (Emphasis is the author's.)

10. Cannon, "After Twenty Years," 13.

11. Bigler, Diary. Book B, MS, October 9-16, 1849.

12. Ibid.

13. Laura Ann Keeler Thurber, Journal.

14. James Keeler, Journal.

15. Gold Accounts.

16. William Farrer, Biographical Sketch.

17. See Appendix 12a. Charles C. Rich and Francis M. Pomeroy were in the Flake company, and possibly some others, but are not on the list because they were not gold missionaries. James S. Brown, Hiram S. Blackwell, and Addison Pratt went as proselyting missionaries and travelled with the Hunt company.

18. For accounts of those who went into Death Valley, see Southworth, *Death Valley in 1849, (80-82, concerning the deaths);* also Lingenfelter, *Death Valley and the Amargosa,* 32-51, including the works listed on pages 480-487.

19. Rich, Diary, November 11, 1849; and, Brown, *Giant of the Lord*, 153.

20. Bunje and Kean. *Pre-Marshall Gold in California.*

21. Bigler, Diary, January 6, 1850.

22. Amasa Lyman, Papers.

23. Rich, Diary, January 12, 14, 20, 21, February 12, 1850.

24. Eddy was one of the survivors of the ill-fated Donner Party, who had lost his entire family in that tragedy. He had moved to the vicinity of San Jose, remarrying and prospering well. Bancroft, *Pioneer Register*, 788-9.

25. Rich, Diary, February 15, 22, 25, 1850.

26. From this point on, the day-to-day account of Rich will be used, interjecting as necessary to clarify obscure points and to enrich the material. Unfortunately, after a few days, Rich did not add

the kind of detail to his diary that he had earlier furnished and he leaves a 19 day gap in his day-to-day account immediately after his arrival in the gold fields.

27. Ibid., Gudde and Gudde, *California Gold Camps,* maintain that Woods' Ferry (Tuolumne County) was a major crossing of the Tuolumne River. From the Rich account, it would appear to have been a crossing of the San Joaquin. However, there may have been two Woods' ferries.

28. Wotten not listed in Gudde and Gudde.

29. Burns' Diggings on Burns' Creek was settled in 1847 and gold was discovered there in 1848. Located a few miles southwest of Hornitos, it was an important gold mining camp into the 1950s. (Gudde and Gudde, *California Gold Camps,* 53.)

30. Gudde and Gudde, *California Gold Camps,* 224.

31. This French Camp, but five miles from Stockton, was not one of the several "French Camps" identified by Gudde and Gudde. The Hickerson Group, probably connected with the Pomeroy Train treated later, had taken a most circuitous route having taken over five months for the trip. They might well have attempted to take the legendary Walker "short cut" across the Nevada deserts and Sierra Nevada Mountains. George W. Hickerson Letter, dated August 12, 1850, LDS Church Archives.

32. Brown, *Giant of the Lord,* 163-164.

33. *Ibid.*

34. *Ibid.*

35. Rich, Diary.

APPENDIX 12a (Note 12:17)
Gold Missionaries of the Flake Company

Bankhead, George
Berry, John W.
Bigler, Henry, MB (Mormon Battalion)
Bills, John
Cain, Joseph

Cannon, George Q.
Chase, Darwin, MB
Dixon, Joseph (John) (1)
Farrer, William
Fife, Peter, MB
Flake, James M.
Gibson, Henry
Hawkins, James
Hoagland, Peter
Keeler, James
Morris, Thomas, MB
Peck, Joseph
Rollins, J. Henry (James H. Rawlins) (2)
Stewart, Boyd, MB (3)
Stoddard, Judson Sheldon (4)
Whittle, Thomas

Source: Campbell, "The Mormon Gold Mormon Mission," 26.

(1) Campbell gives the name of Joseph Dixon; however, other evidence indicates it to have been John Dixon.

(2) The Rollins (Rawlins) referred to by Campbell was probably not J. Henry Rollins. While there was a J. Henry Rollins in Utah, after the arrival of the group in the gold fields James H. Rollins was a close companion of Charles C. Rich. A Henry Rollins was in the *Brooklyn* Company while a John Rollins is listed as in the Battalion. James H. Rawlins, who was born in New York in 1816 and was baptized in 1832, entered Utah in 1848 as did a Henry Rollins. It is believed that this person was James H. Rawlins, though his name was frequently spelled Rollins.

(3) Boyd Stewart was probably not in the group when it left the Valley in 1849. A Robert B. Stewart was in the Battalion. A Boyd Stewart entered the Valley in 1847. Boyd was in the Huntington Company that was to leave Salt Lake in the spring of 1850. He may have become attached to the Gold Missionaries after his arrival in El Dorado County in July of that year. Excluding him from Campbell's list makes exactly the twenty gold missionaries referred to by Cannon.

(4) A Stoddard had been called on a mission to California in the fall of 1848, but he was not further identified, and he may not have gone. Judson Stoddard entered the Valley in the Brigham Young Company of 1848.

Salmon Falls

Salmon Falls, Mormon Island, and other important gold-rush sites on the American River are now covered by Folsom Lake, that is, the body of water fed by the North and South Forks of the American River and backing up from a complex of dykes and dams near Folsom, California. This aerial view of the site of Salmon Falls was taken in the summer of 2008 when the water level of the lake was extremely low. The view shows a denuded, light shaded area along the river that goes out to darker shaded land with vegetation. The vegetation line corresponds to the extension of the full lake or reservoir. A similar denuded area branching to the lower right represents a part of the lake that has shrunk to a small creek, Sweetwater Creek, that fed into the South Fork. The old town of Salmon Falls was near the mouth of the Sweetwater (indicated by a vertical arrow). It can be seen that the full lake would cover what was the town. Upstream from the Sweetwater, north of the town, Salmon Falls Bridge crosses the South Fork. This bridge is a more recent construction and also is visible only during low water levels. The site of the actual falls, for which the town was named, was down river from the town, to the left.

Salmon Falls was about six miles upriver from Mormon Island. Gold was discovered there apparently by Mormons in early 1848. The full richness of the site did not become widely appreciated until 1851, after which the population jumped to about 3,000.

The site of the former town is about 1500-2000 ft. from the closest present road, branches of Old Salmon Falls Road to the south. *Imagery Courtesy of Jason R. Brown and Aerials Express.*

And he received them at their hand,
and fashioned it with a graving tool,
after he had made it a molten (golden) calf,
and said, these be thy Gods.

Bible. Exodus 32:4

13

The Gentile Pomeroy Wagon Train

While the general attitude of the Mormon leadership toward the involvement of Mormons in California-bound gentile wagon trains was a negative one, the urgency of the need for more Mormons on the west coast was felt so strongly in the fall of 1849 that exceptions were made. On the third of November, a wagon train consisting of 100 wagons left Salt Lake—largely composed of Mormons, but under the captaincy of the gentile Pomeroy brothers. [1]

Francis Martin Pomeroy was introduced in the last chapter. He had entered the valley in 1847 as one of the original Mormon pioneers and traveled to California earlier that fall as an appointed companion to Elder Charles C. Rich. Thus far, no genealogical connection has been found between Francis and the Pomeroy brothers of the present chapter.

Accounts of two known Mormon subgroups of the Pomeroy Company have been identified, giving some detail of this wagon train. One account was written by Goudy Hogan, the other by David Seeley (Seely). A third possible subgroup was apparently led by George W. Hickerson and consisted of nine men. There is little detail of this latter group, but it is known that George W. Hickerson was a gold missionary, sent by Willard Richards, counselor to Brigham Young.

The Hogan Subgroup

A native of Norway, Goudy Hogan and his family immigrated to the United States about 1837, living consecutively with the Church in Illinois, Iowa, Salt Lake, and then Bountiful. On April 18, 1849, he received a blessing from Patriarch "Uncle" John Smith. Smith blessed him that he should "have riches that was hid in the sand which was fulfilled inside of one year by digging gold in California." [2]

The blessing of riches appeared to be far from being fulfilled as that year proceeded, Hogan having to sell his "fine boots for 1½ bushels of wheat for seed." He and his family made a common mistake in selecting land to cultivate in the Bountiful area north of Salt Lake, as "much of it proved to be mineral where crops would not grow. Then the crickets came down off the mountains apparently on purpose to destroy our crops that were growing." The Hogans were able to save a portion of their crops by "faithful struggle and the aid of seagulls." However, when the harvest time came, his father became ill, and "having no

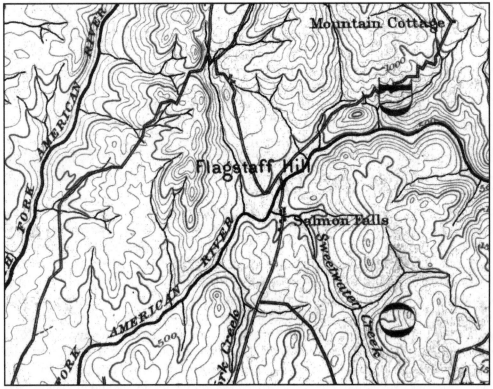

Upper: Lithograph of Salmon Falls and the Natoma Water Works. *Courtesy California State Library.*

Lower: U.S. topographical map from 1892 showing the site of the town Salmon Falls at the location where Sweetwater Creek joins the South fork of the American River. *Courtesy University of California, Berkeley, Earth Sciences & Map Library.*

View showing the origin of the name "Salmon Falls." Indians would spear salmon in the falls and swing them up to the upper rocks, where the salmon could dry in the sun.
Sketch by William N. Bartholomew based on a daguerreotype by J. Wesley Jones. [ca. 1850's]
Courtesy California Historical Society.

reapers or cradles, my oldest sister, Caroline, and myself took each a butcher knife to harvest what wheat there was left . . . 20 bushels. The corn, beans, and other garden truck was destroyed by the crickets."

Although having been counseled by Brigham Young not to go to California, once the meager harvest was over Hogan became anxious to participate in the rush to the gold fields. A Brother Browning from Farmington, just to the north, visited the family revealing that his boys were going to California. [3] Once the Hogans learned that Apostles Rich and Lyman would be there to preside over the Mormon gold miners and receive their tithing, Goudy was able to get his father's consent and then to secure the blessings of the Prophet for the trip.

The two Pomeroy brothers had come to Salt Lake with one hundred wagons with three or four pair of oxen to each. After selling out, "they wished to get teamsters to drive through to California by the southern route." There were so many Mormon boys who wanted to go down that the Pomeroys were easily able to secure their services, the boys receiving only their board as pay. Assuming that all 100 wagons went, with one Mormon each, there must have been at least 100 men associated with this group, a sizable addition to the Mormons already in California.

The Pomeroy wagon train, levaing Salt Lake the 3rd of November, followed the Hunt company by a month and the Flake company by two weeks. Before leaving, Hogan was advised by a good friend to "attend to your secret prayer regularly. Do not associate with bad company nor drink strong drinks or play cards and pay your tithing regularly and if you will remember and observe all these things and be a good boy, I will promise to you, Goudy, that you will be blessed on your gold mission and you will come back being satisfied with your trip."

David Seeley (1819-1892)

David Seeley was born in Whitby Township, Ontario, Canada. In 1846 he moved to Iowa, married, and joined the Mormon Church. The Church was moving west at that time, and the Seeleys moved with them. In 1849 he joined the Pomeroy Company going to Southern California, continuing on to the mines in Northern California. He worked a short time in the mines and returned to Salt Lake Valley over the northern route. In 1851 he was part of the group that went to Southern California and settled San Bernardino. In San Bernardino, he was a city treasurer and became the first San Bernardino Stake President. He had a sawmill and had business dealing with the Salt Lake Valley and other Mormon communities. However, an adverse relationship developed between Seeley and Brigham Young because of Seeley's unwillingness to accept Valley paper currency. Seeley raised his family in San Bernardino and remained there until his death at age 72 years. (Hafen, *Forty-Niners*, 296, and Lyman, *Overland Journey*, 160.) *Courtesy San Bernardino Historical Pioneer Society.*

It was expected that the trip would take but two months to reach the Williams Ranch. Supplies were taken and rations allocated accordingly, there being no place of settlement or re-supply en route. Rather than two months, the trip took four and the rations gave out. The beef was so tough that even though boiled all night by the guard, it was still "tough as shoe leather" the next morning. Two of the men with whom Hogan was associated ran out of flour. To secure more from the Pomeroys, they had to sign a note (reportedly for $1,000) to be repaid in California. Hogan observed: "If we had not been Mormon boys there would have been mutiny in camp, but having just lately been driven from our homes in the United States because of the Gospel of Jesus Christ we had learned to be patient in times of tribulation." He claimed that he paid on the note but made no claim to it having been paid off.

The train reached Williams' Ranch on February 27th, two months after Captain Jefferson Hunt ar-

rived. It had been a miserable trip. In addition to the food problems, the oxen, already pretty well spent by the time they reached Utah, had given out rapidly. Wagons were consequently abandoned en route and used for firewood. Upon reaching what Hogan named the Ruddy (Muddy River), most of the men left the train, taking packs on their backs. Hogan was not one of them.

To Hogan, Lower California was "the finest country that we had ever seen." He reported that while "most of the boys went to Upper California by land, ten of us took the ship at San Pedro and sailed up the coast on a barge (barque, bark?), the *Freemont (Fremont)* to upper California." Their "fare was paid out of the joint note previously spoken of."

After their arrival in Greenwood Valley to the north in present-day El Dorado County, they began "to work at surface digging with rockers," making from $5 to $10 a day a piece "working in small companies." Dissatisfied with their earnings and hearing of "companies making larger wages other places," they moved to the North Fork of the American River five weeks later, paying $25 per hundred weight to have their provisions and tools packed over the mountain.

In their new location they built a double wall dam, filling in dirt between the walls, and dug a race to re-channel the river, expecting to "find gold because there was thousands of dollars taken out of the same place the year before. After six weeks labor as a company, [they] found no gold at the bottom of the river." They were not the only miners to invest great amounts of time and money on the theory that gold would settle in deep holes in the river bed.

Having expended $2,000 on the attempt, the boys were both broke and discouraged. The decision was made for each to go "on his own hook." Hogan made it a matter of prayer as to what he should do and was "impressed to go where there was a company of ten men of the Mormon Battalion who had been working" at a place a little above Mormon Island." This might well have been in the vicinity of Salmon Falls a few miles upstream or at McDowell's Hill.

After working "a few days up and down the river with a shovel and pick and pan" he camped near the Mormon company. He got acquainted with Abraham Woolf who took him in. [4] Becoming ill, Goudy's benefactor offered him "half of his share if" Hogan would work for him. He took up the offer, staying the six weeks Woolf was ill. He also cared for the sick man, often administering to him with a unique Mormon blessing. Woolf had such great confidence in Hogan that he put him in charge of "his sack of gold dust" containing about $2,500.

On September 23rd, Hogan, in company with others, [5] paid tithing to Apostles Rich and Lyman, their location at the time probably being at or near Slap Jack Bar near Murderer's Bar on the Middle Fork of the American River a few miles above present-day Auburn.

One night Hogan had a dream that a member of his family was dead. A few days later he received a letter from his father telling of the death of his three-year-old brother and requesting some money, if he could spare it. Having but $100 at the time, he read his letter to Brother Gordon Beckstead, formerly of the Mormon Battalion, with whom he had become closely associated, remarking that he wished he had more to send home. Beckstead said that he could have "all the money I needed in reason." Hogan borrowed $200, sending $100 home, possibly with Apostle Lyman when he departed in August. He also sent $296 which was deposited in the Gold Account in Salt Lake City on October 3rd. [6]

In October, Hogan learned that Apostle Rich was leaving in a few days for Salt Lake. Even though he was making between $20 and $50 a day, he was "very anxious to go home." He had a dream in which a heavy rain "came and washed our dam down and after that we made no more money." Impressed that the dream was a warning, he informed the men that he was planning to leave. They offered him a full partnership if he would stay, assuring him that he "would make [his] independent fortune." However, he decided to go home, selling out his interest for $500, which satisfied him.

Having made the decision to return home, Hogan went to San Francisco, where he purchased a saddle and mule and returned to join the Rich train, which left the gold fields in October. After crossing the mountains, Indians stole some of their horses, including some belonging to Porter Rockwell, making him "out of patience with the red men." While crossing the 40 Mile Desert between the Carson and Humboldt Rivers, a wind storm hit, and many more of the horses wandered off. Enraged, Porter took off after some Indians with two of the company, taking from them ten head of horses to make up for those lost in Carson Valley.

The intrepid and vindictive Porter did not stop with the horses. One night an Indian walked into camp with "his gun on his shoulder making out he was [the] relief guard." When Porter spoke to him he ran, and the scout "fired two shots with his dragon pistol." The hapless Indian was found dead the next morning, 300 yards from camp.

Reaching home November 8th, Hogan "was received with open arms." He was convinced that his dream had been a warning from the Lord. He reported that he had "obeyed the advice given by [his] friend before leaving and had a very profitable trip in which I gained a great deal of experience." "This was" he said, "the beginning of paying tithing with me and I felt exceedingly well in so doing."

The Seeley Subgroup

The second known subgroup of the Pomeroy train was that to which David Seeley (Seely) was attached. Seeley was born in Canada. Entering Utah in 1847 in the Edward Hunter Company, he reported that the crickets had gotten most of their crops in 1849. On November 3, 1849, he, his brother (Justice Wellington Seeley,) and a brother-in-law (Edwin Pettit) left the valley with the Pomeroy train over the southern route. He reported that:

> The trip was long and many cattle died on the trip at Iron Springs in Cole Country, [7] Utah we picked up nine men that had one time formed part of the company that suffered and perished in Death Valley, Nevada they was trying to get back to Salt Lake they had experienced much suffering for want of food and shoes we brought them safe to California. [8]

Seeley and company left the Pomeroy Train at "Amargosa" near the present day Nevada-California border. Arriving at civilization some ten days in advance of the main body, they camped at Jose Maria Lugo's "famous ranch of San Bernardino," to which the Seeleys returned as settlers a year later. As the Pomeroy Train reached the Williams Ranch on February 27th, the arrival of Seeley and company must have been about the 17th of February.

The Lugo family welcomed the small group warmly, killing a beef and organizing a fandango dance, which the boys "enjoyed to the utmost as a number of the Dark Eyed Senoritas favored us

with their presence." They also experienced the first waltzing that Seeley had ever seen. They remained two weeks "to give rest to us teams and take in the beauties of the country." It is not certain whether the beauties were scenic or female.

The desire for gold eventually overtook them, and they headed for Los Angeles, stopping at the John Roland ranch in El Monte or Puente. "The Boys for the first time partook of the pure California Wine which was taken in by the gallon and we all drank to the Health of our Wives, sweethearts, and Country."

Reaching Los Angeles, they witnessed the brutality often meted out to the Indians. It being Sunday, both Indians and ranchers were in town, the latter on horseback with sabers at their sides. They charged the Indians, drunk with bad whiskey, "with terrible results," the latter having only stones and clubs and coming out second best. Beef was being sold for a dime for a large piece, unweighed because of the lack of scales. This seemed like a great bargain, as beef had been in short supply in Salt Lake and especially on the trip across the deserts.

Some of the boys proceeded to the seaport at San Pedro where they took passage on the brig *Placer of Monterey* for $19 a head. It was "a rather disagreeable passage of twelve days" to San Francisco, landing there on March 22nd. They remained there one week and took passage for Sacramento. At that growing center, they engaged "a pack train to carry (them) to the Mines . . . on the west Bank of Coloma Hill," where they arrived on April 6th.

On May 21st, David and Justice Wellington Seeley, as well as Edwin Pettit paid tithing at Greenwood Valley along with several members of the Huffaker Party. They tithed again on July 16th at Sacramento, again in connection with several Huffaker company members. [9]

By August 14th, they had had their fill of the gold fields even though they had met "with good results." They purchased pack animals and returned to Salt Lake City, arriving the middle of September. They must have found someone to bring some of their earnings home in advance of their return, as Sister Seeley deposited $98.35 in gold to the Gold Accounts on August 12th. Justice deposited $200 on October 4th, followed by David on October 14th with $47.06.[10] A few days later than the Seeleys left (August 17), Lyman left Mormon Tavern, reaching Salt Lake City at the end of September.

In March of 1851, the Seeleys left Utah for California again. This time they went as settlers, going in the company of Apostles Lyman and Rich to help establish the San Bernardino colony. David would become the Stake President, but would later leave the Church.

The Hickerson Subgroup

The third subgroup probably associated with the Pomeroy Train was that led by George W. Hickerson. Born in Tennessee in 1813, he was baptized in 1840 in Illinois. He was sponsored as a gold missionary by President Willard Richards,[11] counselor to Brigham Young, and carried with him a letter from the First Presidency to Elder Lyman. His brother, Andrew Jackson Hickerson, evidently accompanied him; at least he was living with him in the fall of 1850. No detailed record of this group's adventures en route has been found, but as the group reached the southern mines on April 10th after five months and five days, they must have left the valley about the time of the Pomeroys, possibly traveling with them at least part of the way.

As already mentioned, on March 30, 1850, Elder Charles C. Rich came across the Hickerson Party at French Camp near Stockton. They were "just getting in from the lake [and] met with us going to the mines in destitute circumstances."[12] In a letter of August 11, 1850, George W. Hickerson succinctly summarized the ordeal to his sponsor, President Richards, with the statement that it was "a long and tedious ordeal of five months and five days"[13] from Salt Lake to the Mariposa Mines.

The gold missionary's letter reported that, having been counseled by Brother Rich to go to Mariposa, they had done so, digging there for "six weeks without the least success." They then moved to the northern mines, "prospecting as we went." About the 20th of July they made a claim on the Middle Fork of the American River, and had since labored "with our might in the banks and bars," but were earning no more than $8 or $10 a day which was "considered good wages in the mines" at that time. However, they had hopes of "making their raise" once the waters went down and the stream beds became accessible.

Hickerson was embarrassed by the fact that they had so little to show for their labor but said that he would have felt worse if the brethren were not all in "the same order." He added that "even those who have been here since the first discoverings of the mines are but little better off."

While in the Mariposa mines, Hickerson paid a very small tithing on May 1st. He appears to have been in partnership with his young brother-in-law, William Woolsey, who also modestly tithed.[14] It is presumed that the latter had been in the Hickerson party. Hickerson and Woolsey also later paid a substantial joint tithing on August 9th, in the vicinity of Slap Jack or Murderer's Bar.

George and William remained in California over the winter, being found by the census taker in Louisville in El Dorado County that winter. They were then identified as "gardeners" with Andrew J. Hickerson and several others, each listed as having $1500 in real estate.[15] Living next to the Hickersons were several Mormon miners.[16] It is possible that some of these had been associated with them and the Pomeroy train.

On October 1, 1850, President Willard Richards made a deposit of $202 to his credit in the Gold Accounts, the initials GWH being noted,[17] evidence that Richards and George W. Hickerson were associated in the gold mining venture. It was only one of several deposits made by Richards that fall, indicating that he probably had other partners.

George, at least, returned to Utah. He was operating a small store at Kanosh, Utah, in 1854 when he was called on a mission to the states. Listed as a farmer in 1863, he died in the faith at Kanosh, in 1884.[18]

NOTES

1. The Pomeroys have not been identified with certainty, but the 1850 California census included Horace, Ebenezer and Samuel. An S. D. Pomeroy is listed by Bancroft as a California resident as of 1848. If this was Samuel, the other two may have been the leaders of this wagon train.

2. Hogan, Journal. Many short extracts of the journal follow.

3. This family has not been identified. A James G. and Mary Browning entered Utah in 1848 with a one-year-old daughter. According to Carter, the prominent Browning family (including their boys), did not enter until 1850 and 1851.

4. This was probably John A. Woolf, who came to Utah in the Edward Hunter Company of 1847. He made a deposit to the Gold Account of $101 in October of 1850. See Gold Accounts.

5. Samuel Miles, William Boyd, Abraham Boswell and David Smith. Boswell was in the same Group of Ten as John A. Woolf in 1847. Lyman, Papers.

6. Lyman, Papers, and Gold Accounts.

7. Probably present-day Iron County.

8. Seeley, Journal. These were probably remnants of the ill-fated Smith Company.

9. Lyman, Papers.

10. Seeley, Journal, and Gold Accounts.

11. Richards made a deposit showing the initials GWH. Gold Accounts.

12. Rich, Diary, (Word in brackets is the author's.)

13. George W. Hickerson, Letter, August 11, 1850.

14. Lyman, Papers, G. W. Hickerson was married to Sarah Woolsey, sister of William Woolsey.

15. Jeremiah F. Evans, William Whittle and Samuel Buniard. California Census, El Dorado County, 1850.

16. Living next to the Hickersons at Louisville were Erastus and Willard Bingham, and next to them Lucas and Peter Hoagland, Israel West and Richard Robinson, Ibid.

17. Gold Accounts.

18. Carter, *Our Pioneer Heritage*, 12:247, 366.

View of gold miners at work, a typical scene of miners exploring one of the many tributaries of the American River. This lithograph was used in the book *The First Forty-Niner* by James A. B. Scherer (New York: Milton, Balch & Co., 1925). Scherer gave the scene a Mormon interpretation, using the title: "Where Sam Took Tithes from the Miners." It was used again in Arrington, *Charles C. Rich*, with the title "Mormons in the California Gold Mines in 1850." However, it originally appeared in *Mountains and Molehills, or Recollections of a Burnt Journal* by Frank (Francis Samuel) Marryat (London: M. & N. Hanhart, 1855). Lithography was by J. Brandard. The original title was "Where The Gold Comes From," Apparently Scherer and Arrington took some liberties interpreting the scene. *Courtesy Utah State Historical Society.*

Greenwood Valley

Greenwood Valley is located between the Middle and South Forks of the American River. Along with neighboring Louisville, it became a major center of Mormons in El Dorado County in 1849-1850. In 1850 the population was between 1,000 and 1,500. Greenwood was said to be named for the famed mountain man, Caleb Greenwood, or his son. Louisville was said to be named for the first born child in the township, the son of Louis B. Meyers, a Mormon. (Gudde, *California Gold Camps*.)

Several dozen Mormon individuals and families were in Greenwood Valley at the time of the 1850 Census. *Above Courtesy California State Library, Below Courtesy Bancroft Library.*

And it came to pass as soon as he came nigh unto the camp that he saw the calf, and the dancing; and Moses' anger waxed hot.

Bible. Exodus 32:19

14

The Huffaker Company

THE HUFFAKER COMPANY followed the Pomeroy Train by a week. Elements of the company departed Salt Lake November 10th-13th, rendezvousing in Utah Valley, to the south of Salt Lake at the newly established Fort Utah (the future Provo). The group elected Simpson D. Huffaker as captain. Two accounts tell in part the story of the Huffaker Company, the details differing somewhat. Campbell [1] used the account of Albert K. Thurber as his principal source, [2] evidently not having access at that time to other documents. A second, partial account, is that of William Carruth, [3] who was sponsored as a gold missionary by Benjamin F. Johnson, a prominent pioneer and community leader. Neither Thurber nor Campbell mention Carruth.

Campbell claims that there were 31 men in the Huffaker Company, naming 23 of them. [4] While he asserts that the group under Huffaker was largely a group of gold missionaries, it is not altogether certain that this assertion is true, nor is the composition of the group itself positively identified. A number of those listed by Campbell were probably not in the original party, but were people Thurber met in California.

The leader, Huffaker, was a wealthy cattleman who came to Utah in 1847 as a Captain of Ten in the Jedediah M. Grant Company. He was a na-

tive of Kentucky or Tennessee, born in 1812 and baptized a Mormon in 1842. Thurber, the diarist, was born in Rhode Island in 1826 and was a self-described world traveler who stopped off in Salt Lake on a trip to California. In Salt Lake, he became converted to Mormonism. He was baptized and received from Father John Smith a patriarchal blessing in which he was promised that if he was faithful the time would come when he would "possess riches until thou are satisfied." [5]

On November 4, 1849, Thurber returned to Father Smith's (at his invitation) and was ordained an Elder. He also received a certificate to the effect that he was "authorized to preach the gospel agreeable to the authority of that office," although there is no record of his using it for that purpose. A copy of this certificate was sewn into his belt and taken with him when he went to California.

The Albert K. Thurber Account

In his story, written sometime after the events, Thurber revealed that he left for California on November 12, 1849 in one wagon with four yoke of oxen in company with the others. Upon reaching Fort Utah, a company consisting of 31 persons was organized, and Simpson D. Huffaker was appointed captain. This approximate number was later confirmed by Amasa Lyman as the

Courtesy of Craig Dalton.

Albert K. Thurber (1826-1888)

Albert Thurber was born at Foster, Rhode Island. He caught the gold fever in 1849 and took to the trail with some companions, getting as far as Salt Lake City. While his companions went on to California, he became fascinated with Mormonism. In his words, he "felt thunderstruck." He stayed in Salt Lake City to learn more about the religion. He soon accepted the message of Mormonism and was baptized.

Albert went to work for Benjamin F. Johnson. When men were being chosen to go on gold missions to improve the financial situation of the Saints, Johnson offered to sponsor Albert on such a mission. Johnson would outfit Albert. On Albert's return, Albert would give one third of his earnings to Johnson, and Johnson would give one third of his over the same period to Albert.

Albert left for California in 1849 by the Southern Route. He had limited success gold mining, and returned in the summer of 1850. When Brigham Young asked how he fared, he told him he left California with "a pair of pants, a shirt and hat, pair of old boots, $4.50 in gold dust and mules and provisions enough to take me home." (From Thurber, Journal.)

number in the company which he escorted into San Francisco.

The company proceeded to Salt Creek (present day Nephi, Utah) where they were unexpectedly hit by an early season snowstorm and traveled in the snow to the "rim on the head of Clarra (Santa Clara River)." Thurber complained that they had been informed that the trip would take eight weeks. It actually took "three months and five days." The same misinformation was transmitted to other companies that fall.

Upon reaching the Little Salt Lake Valley in southern Utah (Parowan), the Company came upon Captain Smith and 13 men who had started out with the Hunt train the previous month but had broken off, seeking the legendary Walker Cutoff to California. They had wandered around

for 23 days, living on nothing but mule and horse meat. This added group, plus the unexpectedly longer travel time, made it necessary to place the company on one-third rations. At Bitter Springs, in the Mojave Desert, they came across elements of the Pomeroy party, which had "lost so many cattle that (they) left 13 big freight wagons which his drivers burnt."

Sixteen miles north of Salt Springs, the company was destitute of water and chased a mirage so frequently found in the desert. Fortunately, however, one of the company, Berrill Covington, came across an ox in good condition. Reasoning that it must have found a supply of water, parties were sent in search of it, almost miraculously finding what appeared to be a transient water hole with all the sweet water they wanted (Resting Springs).

According to Thurber, his part of the company left Salt Lake on November 12th. It took them three months and five days to reach the Williams Ranch, about February 17, 1850—ten days in advance of the Pomeroy party which had departed Salt Lake on November 3rd. At Bitter Springs Thurber "beat up for volunteers, packs on our backs, got 12 to go" with him and his partner, Jacob Burnham. They proceeded ahead of the main body to secure help. With "one small skillet full of biscuits" and "2 quarts of brandy," they traveled the 145 miles to the Grape Vines, probably near present-day Barstow. They also took the remnants of Captain Smith's "gave out animals."

After camping overnight and cleaning up, they left with a member of Smith's Company, [6] heading for Indian Town four miles away. Losing their way, they ended up at Isaac Slover's Ranch. They replenished their internal supply of liquor with "argadent" (aguardiente) and were fed by a Scottish girl. The meal (beef, squash, bread and coffee with sugar) cost 40 cents. Securing more whiskey and some beef and squash, they returned to the rest of their advance company at the Grape Vines or Cajon Pass.

The recombined group went to Indian Town. Influenced by the potent liquor, David Cade and Thurber put on an "exhibition of ludicrous dancing and handsprings that regaled the Indians." Their antics were interpreted as a begging dance and the rather unorthodox missionaries were rewarded with a much-needed meal of parched corn. [7]

Thurber and his company proceeded to the Lugo Ranch (near Slover's) where they were well received. This was the ranch purchased by the Mormons a year later, becoming known as San Bernardino. After attending a "fandango" or Mexican dancing celebration at the ranch, Thurber returned to the Grape Vines again, waiting there two weeks for the rest of the company to arrive.

The William Carruth Account

Differing somewhat from the Thurber story, the William Carruth account [8] refers to 40 men being in the Huffaker Company and includes several men not included in the Campbell list. Carruth began his record book in Birkenhead, Scotland, on January 1, 1847, reporting the reason he kept a journal, "it being the counsel and advice of the authorities of the Church of Jesus Christ of Latter-day Saints that each member of said society keep a history or record of his/her life and the correspondence of it."

Carruth left Scotland in 1848 in company with his brother-in-law, Andrew Cahoon, who had been there on a mission. He reached the Salt Lake Valley that fall with his wife, Margaret, as a member of the Willard Richards Company. After receiving a patriarchal blessing, with but a few days of meditation on the matter, and after making arrangements for their families, he and James Gordon [9] left for the "land of gold." They left Cottonwood on November 13th with "about 40 of our Brethren" and Brother Huffaker as Captain, going the southern route.

Later Carruth and a Samuel Wilson [10] left the rest of the group on foot on what was supposed to be a cut off. "Instead of that it was a cut on" as they traveled with some other emigrants "bound for the gold digins." [11]

Going North to the Mines

According to Thurber's account, after "recruiting" (resting) at the Williams Ranch, their group proceeded to San Pedro and met up with Apostle Amasa Lyman and Jesse D. Hunter, who had come from San Francisco by ship. They took passage on the "old and creaky" 70 ton schooner, *Placa*, on March 2nd. Delayed by storms and adverse winds, the trip which should have taken five days took fourteen. [12]

Arriving in San Francisco, their rough garb and travel-worn "fitouts" were so unusual that they created quite a stir. When asked what hotel they were staying at, they laughingly replied that they intended to "camp on the beach" as they would not "know how to deport (themselves) in a house." Besides, they feared they might catch cold if they did so. Their observers remarked, "them fellows will stand the mines."

In the meantime Carruth and his traveling companion, James Gordon, worked for Williams to get a fitout, and reached the gold mines by land the latter part of March. [13]

Thurber and another traveling companion, Brother Washington N. Cook, found employment in San Francisco "digging out a foundation for a house at $5 per day each." One day they were approached by a stranger. Upon learning they were Mormons, "with great astonishment he arose and with wonder depicted in his countenance exclaimed, `You Mormons. Why you look like other folks.'" [14]

Thurber reported that "politics was running high in San Francisco, the sherifality being the contest." This was the state election. One of the candidates, "Col. Jack Hays of Mexican War notoriety," evidently appealed to the Mormons, securing their voting block and winning the election. [15] Thurber observed that, "Gamblers held dominion and ruled the city. Saloons were open day and night where men and women were continually gambling. They were generally furnished with an orchestra of splendid music, a bar of liquors and the side walls hung with life size obscene pictures." He also reported that, "A Cargo of women from New Orleans or Sidney were sold by the capability [captain?] of the vessel who brought them to pay their passage. This set the gamblers in a social capacity."

Working in the Mines and Returning Home

On April 1st the Huffaker company left San Francisco for Sacramento on board the *El Dorado* in company with Elder Lyman, joining up with Elder Rich at Benicia. Reaching Sacramento, the group decided to go to Lewisville [Louisville], the Mormon enclave in Greenwood Valley. They employed a Mormon High Priest and Utah immigrant of 1847 by the name of E. G. Cherry to pack their fitouts to the mines. As seen in the previous chapter, Goudy Hogan and his companions may have been in the company with the group, evidently also working in San Francisco for a month at $5 per day to secure an outfit for mining. He, too, went to Greenwood Valley. [16]

Carruth and his companion, Wilson, went by

land to "Murphy's Digins" on Angel's Creek in Calaveras County, where they worked for about six months, but "made little more than our board."[17] Carruth remained in the mines for another six months, working with only two unnamed partners, and saved $1,070. In the spring of 1851, homesick, ill at ease about his wife and friends in far away Deseret, and having heard no news from Salt Lake, he went to San Francisco where he found a group of eight men headed for the Mormon headquarters with the mail. He joined them, leaving the sin-ridden city. Carruth reached his destination on the 2nd of June, having spent ten days in the snows of the Sierra Nevada. In June he deposited $618.50 in Brigham Young's Gold Accounts. [18]

Carruth later reflected: "Ever since my return I have felt as if that was the last trip I should make on such an errand, unless called upon by those over me in authority." He found all well at home, his wife having delivered a son in his absence. There he learned that his brother-in-law and former traveling companion, Andrew Cahoon, and his wife Mary (Carruth's sister) had left for the gold fields in the spring of 1850, "also . . . in search of gold." [19]

Meanwhile, Thurber reported that while prospecting in Greenwood Valley, he and others bought a gold washer from a Mormon, Jacob Gates, for $64. With five men working, they made but $2.50 the first day. Deciding that there were too many men involved, he and Burnham bought out the others, making a respectable $40 their first day. "The gold was beautiful, mostly nuggets." They were so excited about their success. Thinking it was still only the usual take, they foolishly let others know about their find. Before they knew it "the creek bed was nearly claimed and the place was alive with miners, leaving (them) with small claims." [20]

Thurber maintained that at Greenwood a man offered a reward of one and a half ounces of gold for the return of a "noted horse," that several others had failed to catch. With his choice sense of humor, he revealed that one morning the horse "ran into a lariat that was tied to a pine tree." Franklin Dewey and Henry Gibson took the horse into town to collect the reward. "The man paid the reward and desired Dewey to ride the horse. He offered to do it for 2 oz. which high rate saved his reputation. He bought potatoes for the mess (company) with the money, 20 lbs." [21]

Thurber attended an election in Greenwood Valley in which he voted for two Mormons, Jacob Gates (who was running for Justice of Peace) and Bradford W. Elliot(t) for Recorder. The outcome of the election was not recorded. [22] Gates and Elliott were two of those reported by Campbell as being in the Huffaker party, but it is believed that they were already in California before Huffaker arrived.

Thurber, with Albert Dewey, David Cade, and Willard and Erastus Bingham, took a prospecting trip to Otter Creek, a tributary to the Middle Fork of the American River passing Missouri Canyon on the north slope of Mameluke Hill. Hoping to find mines and provisions at their destination and arriving tired and hungry, they found none. "Discouraged the next morning started over Boll (Bold or Bald?) Mountain for home, got weary. Came to the camp of Jeremiah C. Stone and S. B. Hill. Got one pt. of Santa Cruz rum and some molasses and made 'blackstrap' and started for Georgetown in high life." [23]

The seven-man "mess" decided "the mines were getting too thick, and as soon as the water got down, "they started for their claim" high upon the North Fork of the Middle Fork of the American River." [24] They went with a company totaling 30 men, suggesting that the Huffaker Company may well have stayed quite intact.

Reaching their claim, they built a dam across the 60-yard wide river with two walls "6 feet apart and packed dirt in sacks on their backs" to fill the space. They dug a race to turn the water off and then dug a hole 30 feet long "but failed to reach bed rock" where they had hoped to find a primary source of gold. Working one month, they earned a total of $1.50 or five cents each.

One of their company, John W. Berry, a member of the Flake Company who had evidently joined them, became very ill and they decided to leave. They first posted a notice for any who might follow: "This is to certify that all persons are forbid to violate the right of a damned claim." On the way back to their base camp, the prospecting group crossed "El Dorado Canyon" passing "a tent in the woods in which was a woman which was a curiosity as we had not seen one for three months." Said Thurber, "I thought that I would like to eat some bread that she had made."

The group reached Slap Jack Bar, a Mormon enclave on the Middle Fork of the American River a short distance above present-day Auburn. Jacob Burnham continued along to their old diggings at Greenwood. Thurber went "to work in a hole in much water" working for nine days and taking sick. The group was visited about that time, on May 21st, by Apostles Rich and Lyman who collected their tithing. [25] Of the 21 men listed, six have been tentatively identified by Campbell as in the Huffaker Company. [26] Others may have been likewise associated.

The men were counseled by the Apostles that those who had not found "good claims or found a good chance to make a lot of money in a few days" should go home. When Thurber told Brother Rich of his situation, the Apostle placed his hands on his shoulders and said "the valleys are the place for you, go home with Brother Amasa." [27]

Thurber related a rather complicated tale of losing some mules that were to be taken to Utah for members of his mess (group). After hunting for the mules for several days, they were located and Thurber rode into camp. Upon reaching camp he reported, "I drank the most wine this day of my life so far." [28]

Thurber started the following day for Lathrop's Tavern, the fitting-out place for the Lyman company. Stopping at the old diggings at Greenwood he found his messmate, Jacob D. Burnham, who was "working in a hole alone." While they had planned to return to Utah together, Burnham wanted just $45 more. He was unable to borrow the money and remained behind to mine for a spell, planning to take another company heading east in about ten days. However, according to Thurber "He took sick and died in about 2 weeks after."

On July 16, a number of the Huffaker Company, along with others, paid tithing again. [29] Included in the group were Edwin Pettit and the Seeleys who had probably been with the Pomeroy Train. It is believed that one of them, Anthony Blackburn, who reached Utah in 1848, may have gone to California in the spring of 1849 with his cousin, Abner Blackburn. Huffaker and Thurber were in the Huffaker Company. How or when the others reached California is not known.

Thurber arrived at Lathrop's Mormon Tavern too late to get into a mess, so went it alone, cooking for himself. As the company moved into the mountains he found that "The Sierra Nevada road was infected by robbers and it was conjectured that they were watching for us as there was known to be in Lyman's hands a great amount of tithing gold. Amasa sent me, J. H. Robbins (James Henry Rollins), Frank Dewey, Kiser and Isaac Brown over the mountains with 22 animals. . . . Kiser was too lazy to tie his up one night or could not desist from eating (an occupation that he employed himself of most of the time) to do so and lost the best mule in the company." [30]

On their way, they came across a destitute group of three men from Ithaca, New York headed for Hangtown. While Lyman's group was wary of them, the New Yorkers were nevertheless fed. They offered to trade their pistols for the food and provisions supplied them, which offer was refused. They then wanted to know who their benefactors were. Thurber reported: "We told them we were Mormons going to Salt Lake. They were surprised to think anything good could come from a Mormon . . . Parted with tears of gratitude in their eyes."

Having broken into several parties for the transit, the group rendezvoused in Carson Valley, east of the Sierra Nevada, at Edmunds Station. The bulk of the money they were transporting was hid in a barrel of flour in the wagon being driven by Daniel Clark who was traveling alone. The company consisted of some 40 men, 8 wagons, 2 or 3 women and about 100 animals. [31] Two members of the group, John Gould and Barnum Kinyon, died of cholera on the way.

After arriving in Salt Lake, Apostle Amasa Lyman asked Thurber to go with him to South-ern California where he intended to establish a settlement, wishing Thurber to ride for him on a proposed southern mail route. Thurber reluctantly agreed to the proposal, but in counsel with Bishop William Crosby changed his mind.

The next year, going to Brigham Young to be married, Thurber was asked by the Prophet if he was not the man Brother Benjamin F. Johnson had sent to California to mine gold. Thurber answered that he was, amazed that he should have remembered from an earlier one-minute encounter. When asked how he had fared, Thurber replied, "first rate." When asked if he had gotten rich, he replied that he had returned with a pair of pants, a shirt and hat, $4.50 in dust "and mules and provisions enough to take me home." The Church leader asked how he felt coming home with so little. Thurber replied that he didn't know, upon which Brigham Young "arose, came up and placed his hand on (his) shoulder producing a most singular sensation" and said, "You have entered into a good work, the work of the Lord Almighty."

It appears that Thurber was a gold missionary for Johnson. However, while Thurber made a small deposit of $20 to the gold account on November 5, 1850, Johnson made none. [32] Where Thurber got the gold, unless he had understated his earnings to Brigham Young, is a mystery.

Thurber thought he might as well talk with the Prophet about Lyman's call while he was with him. He was informed that he had "done right, in refusing to go" that "Brother Lyman was sent to California to build up the Church, that he was not authorized to take the Church with him, but a few persons as guides to insure his safety, but instead that he was taking a great portion of the wealthiest men in the Church with him." Thurber "returned home feeling first rate." [33] This interchange indicates that Lyman did not have full approval of the Church president, at least with respect to the size of the settlement of San Bernardino. From the men listed by Campbell as being in the Huffaker Company, and others associated with it at one time or another, ten deposits were made to the Gold Accounts in the fall of 1850. [34]

Thurber went on to become a bishop and the

president of the Spanish Fork branch of the Zion's Cooperative Mercantile Association about 1869 or 1870. This was a Church-owned merchandizing operation, and this position was usually reserved for Church leaders. In 1873 he was called by Brigham Young to go to Grass Valley to make peace with the Indians after the Black Hawk War, during which time he served as a general in the state militia. Finally, he served in the Sevier Stake presidency from 1874 until 1887, then was stake president until his death in 1888. [35]

NOTES

1. Campbell, "The Mormon Gold Mining Mission."

2. Thurber, Journal.

3. Carruth, Journal.

4. See Appendix 14a.

5. Thurber, Journal. Thurber was accompanied by J. D. Burnham, Hyrum Curtis and William P. Goddard.

6. This man, named Beach, was identified as one of Smith's men. However, a man named Rufus Beach (Beech) had entered Utah with his wife and three children in 1847. He was referred to as a Mormon transient and tithing contributor in California in 1850. Lyman, Papers.

7. Thurber, Journal. Their performance was a far cry from what might be expected today of men called on missions for the Mormon Church. It is possible that it was a momentary, if apparently oft repeated, lapse of decorum, at least on Thurber's part. However, the Mormon health code, the Word of Wisdom, which counsels against the use of strong drink, was not as important a feature of the religion at that time as later became true. Then, too, as Thurber was a relatively new convert, he may not yet have been converted to the code itself.

8. Carruth, Journal.

9. Gordon is known to have come to Utah as early as 1848 and returned to Utah at least by 1854. He was listed as a California Mormon transient in 1850.

10. There has been no further identification of Wilson.

11. Carruth, Journal. This sounds much like the experience of David Seeley. It could be that the Seeley group, leaving the Pomeroy Train, had become attached to elements of the Huffaker Company.

12. Thurber, Journal.

13. Carruth, Journal.

14. Thurber, Journal. Cook, a Seventy, was still in the mines in 1852. He died of consumption while on another mission for the Church in the East in 1858 among the Creek and Cherokee Indians.

15. Ibid. Apparently the Mormons tended to vote in blocks as they had in Nauvoo and would in the Utah Territory. Block voting gave them some political influence with the winners, but also evoked difficulties with those they voted against.

16. Hogan, Journal.

17. Carruth, Journal.

18. Gold Accounts.

19. Carruth, Journal; See reference to the Cahoons. Journal History. June 2, 1851.

20. Thurber, Journal. (Word in brackets is the author's.)

21. Ibid. Gibson had probably been in the Flake Company.

22. While Campbell lists Gates and Elliot as members of the Huffaker Party, it would appear that both were already in California. Bradford (White) Elliott was born June 12, 1824, ordained a Seventy in 1845, and became a President of the Second Quorum of Seventy. The family history says that after he arrived in Salt Lake he "was called to be an apostle." However, before he was ordained he went to Montana to visit a brother.

While there he was thrown from a horse and died from the injuries in 1852." If this is the same Bradford W. Elliot encountered by Thurber, it was California, not Montana where he went and where he probably died. (See Bradford White Elliott, Biographical Sketch.) Neither Gates nor Elliott have been located in the 1850 California census. Elliott was reported by Lyman as a transient in 1850. Jacob Gates at thirty-six years of age had entered Utah in 1847 with his wife.

23. Stone and Hill have not been identified as Mormon pioneers. Hill may have been the same Hill who was an acquaintance of Thurber from Rhode Island. Georgetown was a few miles away on top of Mameluke Hill. (Words in brackets are the author's.)

24. This was probably in what would become Sutter and later Placer County.

25. Lyman, Tithing Accounts, May 21, 1850. See Appendix 14b.

26. See Appendix 14a.

27. Thurber, Journal.

28. Ibid. The other members of the mess were John W. Berry, Henry Gibson, and Joseph Peck of the Flake Company as well as Samuel Miles and H. Alexander of the Huffaker Company.

29. Lyman, Papers. See Appendix 14c for list.

30. Thurber, Journal. The "Kiser" referred to was probably Guy M. Keyser of the Mormon Battalion and Isaac Brown of the Huffaker Party rather than Kiser Brown listed by Campbell.

31. The group included Berrill Covington, James C. Sly (who had helped pioneer the road in 1848), John Murray, D. D. (P.?) Richardson, a man named Thompson, Peter Fife, Judson L. Stoddard and Isaac Morley, Jr.

32. Gold Accounts.

33. Thurber, Journal. See Chapter 21 on the San Bernardino Saints.

34. Appendix 14d.

35. Carter, *Our Pioneer Heritage*, vols. 1, 5, 9, 10, 12, and 13.

APPENDIX 14a (Note 14:4)
Possible Members-Huffaker Company 1849

Alexander, H., MB
(Horace M.)
Bingham, Erastus, MB
Bingham, Willard
Bird, William, MB
Brown, Isaac
Brown, Kiser
Burnham, Jacob D.
Cade, David
Cook, Washington N.
Covington, Berrill
Curtis, Hyrum
Dewey, Albert
Dewey, Franklin
Elliott, Bradford W.(1)
Gates, Jacob (1)
Goddard, William
Gould, John, MB
Huffaker, Simpson D.
Kinion (Kinyon), Barnum
Miles, Samuel, MB
Murray, John
Sly, James C., MB
Thurber, Albert King

(1) Probably not in the Huffaker Company but later associated with some of its members.

Source: Campbell, "The Mormon Gold Mormon Mission," 27. (See Note 22 above.)

APPENDIX 14b (Note 14:25)
California Tithe payers-May 21, 1850

Alexander, Horace M. (1)
Bailey, James
Boyd, George
Burnham, Jacob (1)
Burton, Charles E.
Cade, David (1)
Dewey, Albert
Dewey, B. Franklin (1)
Hoagland, Lucas

Miles, Samuel (1)
Pettit, Edwin
Richardson, Darwin
Robinson, John
Seeley, David
Seeley, Justice W.
Thurber, Albert K. (1)
West, Ira
West, Israel

(1) Members of Huffaker Company as reported by Campbell.
Source: Lyman Tithing Accounts, May 1, 1850.

APPENDIX 14c (Note 14:29)
California Tithe payers-July 16, 1850

Blackburn, Anthony
Cherry, Ebenezer G.
Huffaker, Simpson D.(1)
McMurtrey, Samuel
Pettit, Edwin
Phelps, Henry
Seely, David
Seely, (Justice) Wellington
Thurber, Albert K. (1)
Whitney, Ephraim

(1) Members of Huffaker Company as reported by Campbell
Source: Lyman Tithing Accounts.

APPENDIX 14d (Note 14:34)
Deposits to Gold Accounts
Huffaker Company and Associates – 1850

Brown, Isaac	10/07/50	$ 41.36
Covington, Berrill	10/01/50	99.70
Cherry, Ebenezer G.	10/05/50	244.80
Gould, Samuel	10/03/50	100.00
(possibly some for John Gould)	10/07/50	220.50
Keysor, Guy M.	10/25/50	87.30
Rawlins, James H.	10/07/50	108.36
Seeley, Justice W.	10/04/50	200.00
Seeley, David	10/14/50	47.00
Thurber, Albert K.	10/05/50	20.00

Source: Gold Accounts.

Howard Egan (1815-1878)

Howard Egan was born in Tullamore, Kings County, Ireland. After the death of his mother when he was eight, the family emigrated to Canada. Egan began working on the boats and docks of the St. Lawrence River at thirteen. From there, he spent time at sea and settled in Salem, Massachusetts, working as a rope maker. He married Tamson Parshley from New Hampshire. In 1842 they were taught by Mormon missionaries and were baptized into the LDS Church. They moved to Nauvoo, where Howard ran a rope making business and served as a Major in the Nauvoo Legion. They were among the first to leave Nauvoo in the migration west in 1846 and among the first to enter the Salt Lake Valley in 1847. While the Saints were crossing the plains, he acted as a liaison between Brigham Young and the Mormon Battalion.

Howard led the last Mormon wagon train going to Southern California in 1849. His group then went north to the mining regions, but he was only partially successful in mining and business ventures. He suffered some because of illness and returned to the Salt Lake Valley in 1851.

Egan explored and mapped a mail route from Salt Lake City across central Nevada to Sacramento long before the U.S. government Simpson Expedition established a wagon road along essentially the same route. The Pony Express also followed that route. Egan had a major responsibility for sections of the Pony Express route, operating a station, recruiting riders, and sometimes riding the line himself.

Egan settled in the remote Deep Creek region near the Utah-Nevada border, where he raised cattle, developed mining, and supplied a stage line. The Egans eventually moved to Salt Lake City where Howard worked for the police department. From a guard assignment in the rain, he caught pneumonia and died in 1878, at almost 63 years of age. (See Egan, *Pioneering the West*.) *Courtesy Pioneer Memorial Museum, International Society Daughters of Utah Pioneers.*

And he took the calf which they had made,
and burnt it in the fire and ground it to powder,
and strewed it upon the water,
and made the children of Israel drink of it.

Bible. Exodus 32:20

15

The Salt Lake Trading Company

THE LAST KNOWN Mormon train headed for the gold fields in 1849 was that of Captain Howard Egan. [1] It was also known as the Salt Lake Trading Company. Having first arrived in Salt Lake Valley in 1847, Egan re-entered in September of 1848 in company with Brigham Young and Heber C. Kimball, this time bringing his family with him.

On Sunday, November 18, 1849, two weeks after the Pomeroy Train pulled out, Howard Egan left Fort Utah reportedly with a company of forty persons, three wagons and fifteen animals. Like Hickerson, Egan carried a letter to Elder Amasa M. Lyman from the First Presidency. In fact, it was a second copy of the same letter, sent by way of Egan to assure delivery.

Contradicting his diary entry of the previous day, Egan said on the 15th that his company at that time consisted of "fourteen men and boys" which is more consistent with the number of wagons in the company. As no list was made of the company, it is uncertain as to how many persons were actually involved in the train. [2]

As the company moved south, Egan recorded reaching campgrounds, which he identified by numbers. [3] For example, at present-day Payson was located Campground No. 6, which the company bypassed on the 20th moving on to Campground No. 10. The company was joined by Brother (Rodney) Badger and Brother Burnett, [4]

who also came with a letter from Salt Lake. These men are not mentioned again, and it is uncertain as to whether they stayed with the company or returned to Salt Lake. However, if "Burnett" was Bird B. Barnett, he was in California in the fall of 1850.

By the 27th, the company had reached the Beaver River and Campground No. 25, at which point Egan noted "our company is now organized. H. Egan is captain, and Brother Orlando Hovey has joined our company. Brothers Granger and Egan take his provisions." Two days later, "Brother John Hills (Bills?) broke his wagon tire in two places" in the vicinity of Campground No. 26, and on the 30th, the company was "in sight of the Little Salt Lake." [5]

They overtook a company that may possibly have been an element of the Pomeroy Company that had left Salt Lake on November 3rd. The company had "laid up to do some blacksmithing, and kindly offered to have our wagon tire welded, and any other work we wanted." The following day, they "met (and were joined by) four men belonging to Captain Smith's company, who had lost their road and had been living on mule flesh for sixteen days," [6] (probably in Death Valley).

Traveling along the Santa Clara River, one of Egan's wagon tires broke and in company with Granger, he went back to the blacksmith. His return took three days, during which time his company had proceeded on ahead. As the group traveled down the Rio Virgin, the weather moderated, becoming "pleasant." Near the Muddy River, they came up to a "very steep mountain" or ravine which could be negotiated only by removing part of the load, doubling up the teams, and using a 250-foot rope with "twenty men to assist the teams." If starting with only 14 men, the company had grown by at least six men.

The road became very difficult. "The animals sank to their knees every step." Reaching some springs at two o'clock in the morning, several men "left their wagons, bunching up with those with lighter wagons." [7]

The following day, Mr. Noyle [8] "left his wagon and packed" while "We, [Egan and Company], left our wagons and took his, it being lighter." On the 23rd, two of the company were "run by some Indians who were behind," and a day later the Indians fired at the animals, scattering them. "Two of our men pursued them so close they got all but three belonging to Mr. Carr, which the Indians killed and quartered. Here I left the wagons and took Mr. Carr's." [9]

A few days later an unidentified man was found "with an arrow stuck in his side." On the 29th they "passed a number of cattle today and some wagons that were left." On the following day, "three wagons with nearly all their loading in, left by some of the company ahead." The company reached the Mojave Desert on the last day of the year, having traveled all night. The following day they came across more wagons and dead cattle, as well as a mule "in pretty good order." By that time, some were running out of provisions, and "[we] divided all that we had to spare." On the 2nd of January, 1850, they came upon an abandoned campground, the fires of which were still burning. Three of the packers remained in camp. [10] The following day they came upon Captain Davis and his company that "had laid up for the day." [11] On the 4th, they reached "Cahoon" (Cajon) Pass. The following day, as they descended, the water "was rushing through the pass about three feet deep . . . Some places the water would roll our horses over." That day they reached a ranch—the first habitation since leaving Utah. [12]

On the 6th, they reached the Williams Ranch where they camped and where Egan found Brothers Charles C. Rich and Jefferson Hunt with "some eighteen or twenty of the brethren all well." They had taken but seven weeks for their journey. Two days later, Brother (Judson Sheldon) Stoddard arrived with word that the remainder of the company was just ten miles away, the company arriving a day later.

On the 10th, Brother Rich's company, with two ox teams, left the ranch, being joined by Egan and company the following day. Joining up with the Apostle, the camp was organized with Hunt as captain. Stopping for a short visit at the San Gabriel Mission on the 14th or 15th, they camped a mile and a half from "the City or Pueblo de Los Angeles."

The following day, while laying up groceries, "Brother Davis and some two or three others arrived from the Tormage Train, and reported them in distress, and they sent in for assistance." [13] This group must have attempted a different route into Los Angeles than over the Cajon Pass.

Proceeding north and west along the old Spanish Camino Real, the combined company split up. "Brother Rich, Hunt and some others are preparing to pack and go ahead of the wagons. The brethren who were to remain with the wagons, were called together, and Howard Egan was elected captain by a unanimous vote of the company." Before leaving, Brothers Rich and Hunt gave Egan $53 "for the use of the company."

The Egan Company made good progress in spite of the illness of Brother John Bills. At a ranch on the St. Miguel River, they purchased "two beeves and paid $25.00 for them." They reached the San Juan (Bautista) Mission on the 11th, where Egan received a letter informing him that Rich was just one day ahead of them. With Brothers Staden and (Franklin) Edwards, [14] Egan rode at full speed, catching up with Elder Rich and company at San Jose, where they also "made arrangements to get provisions" for the establishment of a trading post in the southern mines.

Egan sent Edwards back to meet the company, stop the ox teams, and send the other teams up to San Jose after the provisions. Brothers Rich, Pratt, Hunt and Rollins (James H. Rollins) started for San Francisco. Securing their provisions, Egan and Company backtracked to the Patghes (Pacheco) pass "on the road to Marapars (Mariposa) Diggins." On the 19th, Brother John Bills died and was buried. [15]

Accompanying the group was Elder James S. Brown, one of the original discoverers of gold at Coloma. Hc had been called on a mission to the South Pacific with Elder Addison Pratt, and had been traveling with Apostle Rich. He apparently joined the Salt Lake Trading Company, probably at San Jose. Being an experienced hand at gold mining, he had delayed his arrival at San Francisco to serve as an advisor to Egan.

As the company moved east from Pacheco Pass toward the San Joaquin River, Elder Brown observed that there was no discernible road. So, they decided to "hit the San Joaquin River plenty high" and then travel downstream so as not to miss the crossing. Night overtook them and they camped near a slough where bear tracks were "in great abundance." Fearing Indians, they "dared not make much fire." They were anxious about comrades who had separated from them. Adding to the gloom, the "night was intensely dark and a drizzling rain was falling. [16]

Suddenly the horses broke loose and the men, following their sound, sloshed through the swamps and sloughs, finally rounding them up. However, one man with their pack provisions was missing—showing up much later in the night. How he found them without "much fire" was a mystery.

As morning dawned and the rest of the company were still missing, they moved down the sloughs toward the river. To Brown, it seemed that the "whole feathered tribe had met over (their) heads and all around in one grand carnival, to consult over the advent of the white man into that swampy country." He had never, and would never, see "its equal." Their next surprise was a herd of about 500 elk which they were not able to take advantage of because of the sloughs.

Fortuitously, they finally fell in with their lost

friends, who had been fortunate enough to find the ill-defined wagon trail to the river. At the river they found a man named Woods who had arrived but three days earlier with a row boat. He had a supply of provisions, including salt pork and sea biscuits which he sold at an "exorbitant" $.75 a pound.

The company disassembled all of the wagons except Brown's which was heavily loaded and fitted with a roadameter. The others were taken across in Woods' rowboat (described by Egan as a whaleboat) at a cost of $87.50. Brown's wagon had a cable rope attached to be used to tow it across. However the cable broke in mid-stream and the wagon overturned. Stoddard jumped in and reattached the broken cable to the axle, but the wagon pole had become lodged in the riverbed. Brown joined Stoddard and the two finally managed to dislodge it, rescuing their precious load.

The next day they swam their livestock over and proceeded up the Merced River. Six of the company went ahead on horseback to survey the country, followed by another four a day later. [17]

On the third day of travel up the Merced, Brown's advance company came to Burns' Diggings on the south side of the river. They "struck a very good prospect" and stopped until the main company came up. Further progress up the river was nearly impossible because of the soft mud. They also found that they could make $12-15 a day per man mining. Brown, the experienced gold miner, advised them to stay put. [18]

Brown observed in a superior way born of experience that his companions' performance became "quite laughable." "Those who had been the very worst drones in camp were now the first with the pick and washpan. They pitched into the creek as if they expected to scoop up the gold by shovelfuls, leaving their teams hitched to their wagons; while those who had been on hand early and late, taking a more methodical view of things, first formed the camp, got their dinner, and then went quietly to prospecting up and down the creek. By this time our drones decided there was no gold there, and that they would go where there was some. What a lesson we learned there of human nature." [18]

The next day things settled down and men began to mine as much as $10-$100 a day each. Egan appointed Brown and five others to head into the mountains to prospect. The remaining men continued mining, keeping track of their earnings to be shared equally with the prospectors.

As the latter moved into the mountains, rain and then snow storms stopped them. After ten days of misery they returned to camp to find that Apostle Rich had arrived and sent all of the accumulated gold with Egan to Stockton for supplies, leaving them nothing. Rich also brought word from Brother Addison Pratt that Brown was to join him in San Francisco as soon as possible so that they could proceed on their mission to the Pacific Islands. Brown packed his gear, sold his oxen to Captain Hunt for $200, and "bade adieu to the rest of the camp. They owed (him) one hundred dollars" which 30 years later was still owed.

The Salt Lake Trading Company was probably located a few miles upriver from present-day Merced Falls near where the Old Highway from Mariposa crosses the Merced River. The probable location of the post is indicated by the Mormon Way Bill, which gives routes to various locations in the gold fields as noted in Chapter 8. It identified the Marsedes (Merced) store as being nine miles from Waters Ferry on the Merced River and six miles from Burns' Diggings near Hornitos.

Information on the operations of the Salt Lake Trading Company have been elusive. However, a hint about problems with the trading post is given in the later account of George Q. Cannon. [19] Cannon had been a member of the Flake Company which had traveled with Egan north from Los Angeles to the southern mines. If he went there, he probably soon left for the northern mines, as he was not listed by Rich and Lyman in connection with their return to Mariposa the first of May, 1850.

That fall, when Apostle Rich called Cannon along with others on a proselyting mission, Cannon recommenced his diary. He recorded that he went to see the ailing Egan, probably sick with cholera, who was recuperating at Lathrop's Mormon Tavern. They had a long talk about the affairs of the store that Cannon had been managing at Slap Jack Bar. They also discussed store business in the southern mines which had fallen on hard times, possibly due to the dishonesty or ineptness of one or more of the employees. Egan's illness probably also played a role. By the 30th of October, Egan had recovered sufficiently to go to San Francisco to purchase flour to take to Stockton.

Egan's sequel is tragic. He returned to Salt Lake the next year only to find that an interloper had come between him and one of his wives. Egan, responding to an unwritten code of honor, killed the man, for which he was disfellowshipped from the Church but not disowned. He retreated to the deserts on the Utah-Nevada border where he farmed, mined and maintained a stage coach way station in or near Egan Valley. At the death of Brigham Young in 1877, he became a guard over his prophet's grave.

The subsequent history of the Salt Lake Trading Company itself is uncertain, but it probably died with its financial problems, with the long illness of its leader, and certainly with Egan's return to Utah in early 1851. However, it established commercial ties which remained functional at least until the Mormon exodus in 1857. A substantial Mormon community flourished at Stockton as late as that pivotal year.

NOTES

1. This account is largely taken from Egan, *Pioneering*, 169-181. Egan, born June 15, 1815 in King's County, Ireland, emigrated with his family to Canada in 1823. Some time after the death of both parents, he went to sea until an adult, eventually settling in Salem, Massachusetts, where he married in 1838. In 1842 he and his wife were converted to Mormonism. They moved to Nauvoo, Illinois, where he became a member of the police force, one of Joseph Smith's many guards, as well as a major in the Nauvoo Legion, the city's standing army. The family left Nauvoo in 1846 and settled first at Winter Quarters on the Missouri River. Egan was chosen as a Captain of Ten in the original band of pioneers that entered the Valley of the Salt Lake on July 24, 1847. After assisting in the planting of a few late crops, and

various construction and exploration projects, on August 26 Egan left the Salt Lake Valley with Brigham Young and most of the advancred pioneer company to return to their families in Winter Quarters.

2. Among the company were Brothers (Lafayette) Granger and John Hill. The following day they were joined by Brother Orlando Hovey with four yoke of cattle and an additional four men. LaFayette Granger went to Utah in the A. O. Smoot Company of 1847. Hill has not been further identified. Hovey had come to Utah in the Henry Harrison Company the previous year. He held the office of Seventy and returned to Utah by 1854. Egan, *Pioneering*, 169.

3. Of the diaries and journals consulted by the author, this is the only one to give numbers to camping sites. It would indicate an extensively mapped-out route more developed and known than generally assumed.

4. Probably Rodney Badger who has not been further identified. An Ephraim and a John Badger came to Utah in 1848. Burnett has not been further identified. However, Bird B. Barnett, who was later in the gold fields, entered Utah in 1848 with an 18-year-old son, William W. He was at White Oak, California with a large family in 1850.

5. Egan, *Pioneering*, 171. "Hills" was probably John Bills, who later died in California.

6. *Ibid*. Smith had been largely responsible for a large part of the train under Jefferson Hunt leaving to search for the Walker Cutoff. Most of those leaving the Hunt group backtracked to continue on the Los Angeles or Old Spanish Trail.

7. The men were Loot (unidentified), Parks and Granger. Parks may have been the Parkes referred to later. It is possible that this was William A. Parke, formerly of the Mormon Battalion. No other Park or Parke has been identified in Utah at that time. A William H. Parks was in Yuba at the time of the census. Egan, *Pioneering*, 173.

8. Because of the use of "Mr.," this may have been a member of the Smith Company remnant.

Or it may have been John C. Naele (Naegle) referred to in chapter 7. No Noyle has been identified in Utah.

9. It will be assumed that Carr may have been a part of Smith's Company. No Carr has been identified in Utah at that time. Egan, *Pioneering*, 174.

10. Parke, Naegle, and Fair.

11. This could have been Captain Daniel C. Davis, a veteran of the Mormon Battalion and the leader of the Mormon Volunteers. Or it could have been another Mormon, Captain Davis, not yet fully identified and yet who appears to have been associated with the southern route. There was later a Mormon, Captain Joseph Davis, in the gold fields. This reference opens up the possibility that another company, in addition to those discussed in detail, left Salt Lake that fall. As will be seen later, Davis was associated with an unidentified "Tormage" party.

12. Egan, *Pioneering*, 175-76. This was probably either the Lugo or the Cucamonga Ranch, depending on the route taken at the Sycamore Grove.

13. *Ibid*. No Tormage is listed in the California 1850 census. Neither has the name, nor even one similar, appeared in any account consulted by the author. These may have been among those attempting a shortcut through Death Valley.

14. Staden has not been identified. Franklin Edwards had come to Utah in 1849 in the Egan Company. Therefore he might well have been the Edwards in the Salt Lake Company as he was later listed in California.

15. There is some confusion on Bills, as will be seen later.

16. Brown, *Giant of the Lord*, 145-147.

17. Egan, *Pioneering*, 181.

18. Brown, *Giant of the Lord*, 161.

19. Cannon, Diary.

Benicia

Benicia, California is located at the Carquinez Strait between Upper San Francisco Bay (that is, San Pablo Bay) and Suisin Bay. From Suisin Bay, one enters the mouth of the Sacramento River. Above, looking southeast, is seen the Barracks in 1850. Below, also looking southeast, is a birds-eye view of Benicia in 1851. In both views, the peaks of Mount Diablo are in the distance. *Courtesy Bancroft Library.*

Benicia was an important port, military center, and arsenal when Amasa M. Lyman and Charles C. Rich met there on April 1, 1850 to begin their first joint tour of California's El Dorado.

And the city was pure gold, like unto clear glass.
  Bible. Revelations 21:18

16

The Joint Apostolic Gold Mission

THE HAPPY COINCIDENCE of the two Apostles, Amasa Lyman and Charles C. Rich, meeting at the river port of Benicia on April 1, 1850, was no April Fool's joke—it was either fortuitous or divinely ordained. In the Apostles' minds there could be no question as to what produced the coincidence. It was divine intervention. The two, finally united as the Church leaders had intended, could travel about the business of the kingdom in mutual support, gathering names of Mormons, as well as financial contributions. [1]

Benicia to Sacramento
and to Communities Just Beyond

On Tuesday, April 2, the Apostles reached Brannan's Sacramento City, putting up at Brother John S. Fowler's City Hotel. [2] The following day they left with the Huffaker company which was headed for Greenwood Valley, where hundreds of Mormons were gathering. The Apostles stopped at Brother [George W.] Rosecrans', about five miles up the river, and spent the night with him.

George W. Rosecrans was a former officer in the Mormon Battalion and a Seventy in the Church. He had gone east from California in 1847 with other members of the Battalion, spending the winter of 1847-48 in Utah. He returned to California in the spring of 1849 with Abner Blackburn. By or near the fall of 1850 he moved with his wife, Elvira, and family up the North Fork of the American River to Doton's Bar in Sutter County. He

remained in California for many years, becoming separated from the Church.

On April 4 the Apostles visited Brother [Pierson B.] Reading [3] and Brother [Jeremiah] Root a mile upstream at or near Six Mile House. This much frequented inn was located on the road along the south bank of the American River leading to both Mormon Island and the Mormon Tavern. Root, a Mormon of unidentified origins, lived at or near Six Mile House with his wife, Elizabeth, and his six children aged two to nineteen years. The children were born successively in Ohio, Illinois and the last in Iowa, paralleling much of the Mormon experience. They ran a hotel or boarding house, possibly the Six Mile House itself. [4] Visiting others in the area, the two Apostles returned to Rosecrans' to spend the night. The following day, they returned to Sacramento and then San Francisco aboard the steamship *Senator*. The fare was $30. Captain Jesse D. Hunter of the Battalion accompanied them on April 9th, returning to a home he maintained in San Francisco.

Back to San Francisco
and Other Bay Communities

Lyman and Rich remained in the Bay area for several days, meeting with some of the brethren in a "council meeting pertaining to making a settlement in the Lower California country, which we concluded to do, if things worked to our minds." This they accomplished the follow-

Mission San Jose ca 1850
Courtesy The Seaver Center for Western History Research

Mission San Jose was founded in 1787 and was secularized in 1835. It was in a state of disepair in 1847 when John Horner settled near by and began farming. The Mission was rebuilt in 1985.

Earl Marshall
[From Wood, *History of Alameda County*]

Earl Marshall (above right) and John Horner (opposite page) came to California on the *Brooklyn*. John Horner settled in the region of Mission San Jose and started farming. Soon many other passengers of the *Brooklyn,* including Marshall, and former members of the Mormon Battalion joined him, also settling near the Mission and developing farms. Horner established a grain and vegetable farm; Marshall a dairy farm. When gold was discovered, both Marshall and Horner went to Mormon Island and joined in the search for gold. Soon they both decided mining was not for them, and they returned to their farms. Marshall's wife Letitia kept their dairy farm going while Earl was at the mines. When Earl returned, and he and Letitia compared accounts, they found that Letitia had netted more income than Earl for the same time period. It was at Earl Marshall's adobe that Apostles Lyman and Rich organized a local branch of the LDS Church in 1850. Mission San Jose and the neighboring farmlands are now in Fremont, California. ;

ing year but at the Lugo rather than the Williams Ranch then being contemplated. [5] They also gave instructions and blessings to Elders Addison Pratt and James S. Brown, missionaries on their way to the Society Islands. They organized the Saints in the area, and started plans for construction of a chapel, which unfortunately was never built. The two Apostles left San Francisco April 19, heading for the southern mines of the Mariposa country.

On Monday, April 22, they reached San Jose, dining with their old benefactor, Mr. William H. Eddy. They went to East San Francisco Bay and Brother John M. Horner's, lodging. Horner ar-

rived on the ship *Brooklyn* and settled near Mission San Jose, located across the Bay, where he farmed. [6] On April 23, Lyman and Rich gathered the Saints living in the Mission San Jose area into Earl Marshall's adobe and organized the Saints of that region into a branch of the LDS Church. Earl Marshall and his wife, Letitia, had also been passengers on the ship *Brooklyn*. Other Mormons who had settled in the area were Zacheus and Mary Ann Fisher Cheney, Origin Mowry, Joseph and Jerusha Nichols, Horace A. and Laura Ann Skinner, Simeon Stivers, Thomas and Jane Elizabeth Tomkins, and Isaac Goodwin, all passengers of the *Brooklyn* except Zacheus Cheney.

John M. Horner (1821-1907)

John Horner reached California aboard the ship *Brooklyn* and immediately explored the San Francisco Bay area for a suitable farming site. He settled and farmed in the region of Mission San Jose in the East Bay.

Horner was credited with being most influential in changing the original, prevailing perception that California was not suitable for significant agricultural production. He introduced large scale farming to California. By raising vegetables and grains of sufficient quality and quantity, he demonstrated that California had great agricultural potential. Horner not only sold food directly to miners in the Sierra foothills, but he bought a steamboat, the *Union*, and shipped produce across the Bay to San Francisco. He did this at about the time the yield in the gold mines was beginning to diminish significantly. Therefore, Horner was influential in turning many would-be miners to agricultural pursuits.

Because of a banking panic and because of being overextended, Horner became bankrupt and lost his large farm holdings. At the time, he even became ill with lock jaw and almost died. In an effort to return to prosperity, Horner made contri-

butions to the early development of the combine harvester. [From Horner, "Personal History."]

Visiting the Southern Mines

Passing through Pacheco Pass, the Apostles camped near Grayson's Ferry [7] on the San Joaquin River. They traveled upriver 12 miles, crossed at Harden's Ferry and camped on the Merced River. On the 27th, they moved 30 miles up the Merced to the Salt Lake Trading Company and the following day were joined by Brother Howard Egan of the Trading Company who returned from Stockton, where he had found the brethren in that growing commercial and trading center "generally well." They proceeded to Mariposa or Mormon Bar in company with Egan, tarrying there with the brethren for a couple of days, teaching them at night, collecting $272.34 in tithing, [8] and making arrangements for future payments of tithes. They made no reference to the means established for collecting the money, no Church organization being apparent in their entries. The contributions

of the first group ranged from $30 to $36 each. All but one of the other contributions, were under $11. Of the group of twenty-one men, seven were known members of the Flake Company, two from the Hickerson Company, and two from the Battalion. The remaining ten were of unknown origin.

The Apostles returned to the Salt Lake Trading Post and found Captain (Jefferson) Hunt there. The following afternoon they left with Hunt and a company of men including Brothers (James Henry) Rawlins (often spelled Rollins) [9] and (Wm. Henry) Bills, heading north. They crossed the Merced for $1.25 and camped that night on Dry Creek, a tributary to the Merced.

Crossing the Tuolumne, their mules stampeded, and they had to lay over Sunday to recover them. The trail wise Captain Hunt located and returned all of them safely to the camp that day. On Mon-

Mormon Bar in the Southern Mines

The Mormon Bar in the southern mines is on Mariposa Creek in Mariposa County and one mile southeast of the town of Mariposa. Gold was discovered there in 1848 by Mormons, who then moved on. There were Mormons at the site later, but the site was exploited mostly by others. The deposits were rich, and by late 1852 had already yielded $2 million in gold. *Courtesy California State Library.*

day they proceeded to Mormon Diggings located on what became known as Mormon Creek running down Mormon Gulch, a few miles west of Sonora. Sonora was the unofficial capital or center of Mexican activity in the southern mines. [10]

Located in what would become Tuolumne County, the rich Mormon Diggings were reportedly first developed by Mormons in 1848. While there is no reason to question this tradition, the names of the Mormons involved have yet to be discovered. Even the Mormons living in the Gulch in 1850 when visited by the Mormon Apostles are not known with certainty. The Apostles dined with the several brethren and took their names, [11] but it is not known whether any of them tithed. At that point Hunt and Egan left the group and headed for Stockton on business. The

Apostles proceeded the same day to the Stanislaus River, crossing it.

Continuing to travel northward, they crossed the Calaveras River, stopping at Brother and Sister William and Emily Atherton's place, finding them not at home. The Athertons had been members of the *Brooklyn* Company. They are not listed by Lyman as either transients or tithe payers and do not even appear on the census rolls. They appear to have become lost to the Church until the 1870s, when Atherton presided over a group of Saints in Sacramento. Their residence may have been located at the place identified by Gibbes [12] in 1852 as "Davis & Atherton" on the Calaveras River near the intersection of the Stockton-to-Mokelumne Hill road with the main route from the south, at the base of the mountains.

The Church emissaries also visited Brothers (Reuben W.) Allred and (Henry) Russell nearby, collecting a substantial amount of tithing. Allred, a Battalion veteran, later became a resident of Salmon Falls, where he associated with several relatives in his activities. Russell was a Utah pioneer of 1847. The party there learned of a major fire in San Francisco and waited a day hoping to catch Atherton. He did not return, and on Thursday the 9th the Apostles split up. Lyman remained at Atherton's, indicating that this may not have been his first visit. Rich's departure with Rawlins and Bills perhaps indicated a sense of urgency to his mission.

The reduced group passed Double Springs (the future county seat of Calaveras County, located on a branch of Cosgrove Creek near Mokelumne Hill), crossed the Mokelumne in a double canoe, proceeded to "Dry Creek" (in future Amador County), and camped there. This was the general area in which the Rhoades family lived. They are mentioned in Lyman's account, but there is no mention of them in Rich's account at that time. Crossing the Cosumnes River (swimming their mules) on the 10th, they reached (Asahel) Lathrop's Mormon Tavern at 2:00 p.m. that day.

Lathrop, a 40 year old native of Connecticut, had been the spiritual leader of the relief party sent to the southern settlements the winter of 1847-48. He had been clerk of Apostle Jedediah M. Grant's Fifty in 1847 as it entered Utah. The family in California consisted of at least his wife, Jane, and four children ranging from eight years down to two, the oldest two born in Illinois, the four year old in Missouri and the youngest in Utah. The Mormon Tavern was located on the main road from Hangtown (now Placerville) to Sacramento via Shingle Springs. It was a favorite stagecoach stop for many years.

The following day Rich and Lathrop, along with Judson Stoddard, a member of the Flake Company, went over to see Brothers (Jefferson) Edmunds and "Brown." "Brown" was the alias for Porter Rockwell. Stoddard had come to Utah in 1848, and was a close associate of Rockwell, being his business partner in a tavern at Murderer's Bar the previous year. [13] Rockwell and Edmunds were partners in a tavern located at Brown's settlement on Deer Creek which became known as the Deer Creek House. Edmunds was the manager. He may also have established Edmunds Station in Carson Valley. Spending the day on unidentified business, the Apostle and his companion returned to Mormon Tavern for the night.

Rich Continues North
while Lyman waits for Atherton's Return

Sunday was spent by Rich once again hunting a strayed mule. On Monday the 13th he started for Sacramento, spending the night with Brother Root at Six Mile House. Later described by Cannon as a "den of apostates," it nevertheless became a major stopover station for both Apostles.

While Rich was going about his business, Lyman waited for Atherton, who finally returned home on the 14th. There is no record of the Athertons making any financial contributions. Leaving the following day Lyman crossed the Mokelumne, camping at Jackson's Creek, a favorite watering place between Mokelumne Hill and Sutter Creek. In 1850, there were reportedly 100 tents situated around the springs located there.

The Apostle traveled to the Cosumnes, camping at Coats Ferry. The following day he went to see Brother John Rhoades at a place later called Slough House, located between Dry Creek and the Cosumnes River. John was the oldest son of Thomas Rhoades Senior, and came to California with his father, mother, and family in 1846. He had been a prominent hero in the attempted, partially successful, rescue of the Donner-Reed Party in 1846. Family members had also been quite successful in their gold mining efforts in the interim, Thomas reportedly took $17,000 with him when he left for Deseret the year before (1849).

Apostles Rejoin at Mormon Tavern
and Tour El Dorado County Together

Leaving Rhoads, Lyman reached the Mormon Tavern the same day. The Apostles were reunited, spending the following day with (Jefferson) Edmunds and the shadowy figure of Orrin Porter Rockwell, unmentioned by Rich and identified by Lyman only as "O.P."

On Sunday, May 19th, the Apostles started on a tour of the gold fields of El Dorado Country, spending the night at Edmunds'. The following day they reached Grand or Green Springs, Rich's and Lyman's accounts differing as to its name. Lyman was the more correct. Green Springs was located on Weber Creek "where the trails to Coloma and Mormon Island crossed." This was probably in present-day Green Valley, just east of Mormon Island. There they visited Brother (Myron) Tanner at the Mormon enclave at McDowell's Hill near the South Fork of the American River and between Mormon Island and Salmon Falls.

Tanner, a Battalion veteran, had been sponsored to the gold fields by Apostle George A. Smith, who provided him with a team of oxen and a wagon. Tanner repaid him $400 in gold in 1850. He worked the mines at McDowell's Hill and by 1852 had saved $1,250. He then went to San Bernardino, eventually moving to Provo, Utah where he became a Bishop. [14]

After a short visit, the Church leaders traveled to Coloma. They crossed the American River and proceeded to Greenwood Valley where they "met the brethren who had recently arrived from the [Great Salt] Lake." This may have been the mail company which left Salt Lake the first of April.

They tarried "with the brethren" collecting "tithing and dues" [15] from 21 men, a number of which are known to have gone to California with the Huffaker and Pomeroy companies. None are known to have been with Flake. None were found in the census taken later that year, most having returned to Utah. The tithing of this group totaled $618 and ranged from $10 to $100 per person.

On the 22nd, the Apostles traveled to Captain (Jesse D.) Hunter's and stayed overnight. Hunter had evidently moved up towards the mountains from the Sacramento area. He may have maintained two residences—one in the city for his family and one upriver for his mining operations. The following day they visited and dined with Samuel McMurtrey. [16] After eating, they went to see the 45-year-old (William) Leffingwell, staying overnight. Born in Connecticut in 1805, Leffingwell was a Captain of Ten in 1847 and a Mormon High Priest. He had built and maintained a threshing

mill on City Creek in Salt Lake in 1848. Leffingwell was living with a large group of Mormons in 1850 at Pilot Hill in Greenwood Valley, where he and his wife ran a hotel or boarding house. At the time of the census they had only three of their older children with them, ranging in age from 15 to 18. The rest of the family later joined him. By 1857 they moved to the area west of the Sacramento River where he was a mill owner. The family in the interim became disaffected from the Church.

On the 24th, the Apostles crossed the South Fork at Salmon Falls, a Mormon enclave several miles upstream from Mormon Island. Mormons had first discovered gold and settled there in 1848, but it was soon overrun by non-Mormons. They dined with A. C. Brower who maintained a hotel with his wife, Margaret E. Bower had been a Captain of Ten in the Edward Hunter Company of 1847. They may have had their three children with them. The family returned to Utah with either Lyman or Rich that year (1850). Brower became the head printer of the Deseret News established that same year. [17]

After dining, they traveled to White Rock Springs on the road from Mormon Tavern to Sacramento where they put up with Brother H. (Henry) Jacobs. Jacobs had played an interesting and unique role, though little known today, in early Mormon history. A prominent Seventy in Nauvoo, he was married to Zina Diantha Huntington, evidently for "time only." She was a "spiritual" or "sealed" wife of the Mormon Prophet Joseph Smith. Following the death of the prophet, she became one of the many wives of Brigham Young, having divorced Jacobs. [18] Jacobs was disfellowshipped from the Church in 1851, [19] along with several other Mormons in the gold fields. He returned to Salt Lake in his old age to be taken care of by his ex-wife until his death. [20]

After an abortive trip to Sacramento to see Fowler, Lyman and Rich crossed the American River north into what became Sutter County, traveling to Brother (William L.) McIntyre's where they lodged. Dr. McIntyre, who had been a member of the Mormon Battalion, reached Utah in 1849, but evidently soon returned to California. He was probably located on the North Fork of the American River in the vicinity of Mormon Bar.

On the 28th the Apostles went to see James Harmon. [21] Harmon had entered Utah with his family in 1847 with the Mississippi Saints. He evidently moved to California in 1849, eventually settling in Long Valley or Mormon Ravine, two miles southwest of what became Auburn. He and his wife ran a hotel, and he mined. He later contracted a fever, probably cholera, on a trip across the Isthmus of Panama, leaving his wife a widow. She remained in that location, running the hotel and hosting Mormon missionaries until 1857, eventually returning to Utah with a stopover in Carson Valley. [22]

Lyman and Rich stayed that night at Rosecrans', who had moved north. On the 29th they visited Brother Anthony (and Hester) Blackburn, staying overnight. The Blackburns, from Pennsylvania, had come to Utah in Brigham Young's Company of 1848. Their daughter Matilda went with them to California.

Back to Sacramento

On May 30th, the Apostles went to Sacramento where they learned of the death of Captain James M. Flake, who was killed by a fall from his mule in Hangtown on the 22nd. They lodged again at the Root's. The following day they went to Lathrop's Mormon Tavern, Rich returning to Sacramento on business. Lyman met up with Captain Hunt and a man identified in his journal only as O.P. This was no doubt Orrin Porter Rockwell. Lyman continued on to Hangtown (Placerville) on the 1st to "meet with the brethren from the south." This group of at least nine men,[23] mostly from the Flake Company, paid $382 in tithing. It appears that they had given up on the southern mines, gathering to El Dorado where most of the Saints were assembling. They were headed for the Mormon claim, Slap Jack Bar, on the Middle Fork of the American River, a few miles upstream from Murderer's Bar.

On June 2nd, Rich went to Salmon Falls with Charles Groves taking dinner with "Brown." Groves was a resident of Sacramento and may have been in the teamstering business. He is not known to have been a Mormon. There was a John Brown, possibly of the Mormon Battalion, living in the vicinity of Salmon Falls that fall. However, this Brown may have been the ubiquitous and incognito Rockwell.

At Salmon Falls, Rich met a man by the name of Abraham Tymmin who claimed to have been a Jewish Rabbi in Jerusalem, to have been baptized a Mormon, and ordained an elder in London. Rich returned to Lathrop's to spend the night. The same day, Lyman returned to Brother Edmunds' with whom he deposited Brother Flake's gun, leaving the Captain's mules with Brother (John or William) Beers. [24] Lyman also retrieved some of Flakes' earnings. The latter's widow, Agnes, depositing $42.06 in gold and $47.00 in silver to the Gold Account that fall. [25]

Lyman and Rich were reunited at Lathrop's on the 3rd and spent the 4th with Captain Hunt. Hunt and a Brother Clark left the following day. Clark may have been William O. Clark, part of a Mormon messenger system between Salt Lake and California. Rich and Lyman "tarried."

On the 6th, the Apostles went to Salmon Falls, dining at Brother Brower's and going on to Leffingwell's where they spent the night. On the 7th, they went on to Greenwood Valley, tarrying with the brethren and collecting tithing, the contributors being unidentified. On June 8th they crossed the Middle Fork of the American River on a bridge a little above Spanish Bar, going to the camp of the "California Company" headed by David Smith, probably of the Mormon Battalion. A David Smith was on the Middle Fork in El Dorado County later that year. A David Smith had also entered Utah in the Isaac Higbee Company of 1848 causing speculation that he may have been sponsored to California by Bishop Higbee who deposited $1,000 to the Gold Account on December 7, 1849. [26]

The following day they visited George Boyd's camp, meeting with "Brother (Thomas) Morris, who deposited with (them) $178 for [Apostle] Parley P. Pratt." Boyd, a Battalion veteran, was one of those called to go to California in the fall of 1848. He was a California tithe payer in 1850. Pratt deposited the money from Morris to the

Gold Account on October 14th. [27] It therefore, appears that Morris, a Battalion veteran and member of the Huffaker Company, was mining for Elder Pratt.

The following day the Apostles went to Brother McMurtrey's and on the 11th to Hunter's, the latter accompanying them on foot to the Harmon's. They crossed the river "below the junction of the North and Middle Forks of the (American) river" in the vicinity of present-day Auburn. They remained until the 13th when they returned to Hunter's and on the 14th went to Lathrop's.

On June 15th Lyman and Rich went to Edmunds', meeting Mrs. D. P. Crofton, the grown daughter of "Father Bosley," possibly G. Bosley who had come to Utah in 1849. They remained, Elder Lyman becoming ill with what he called "Dispepsy." When Lyman recovered sufficiently, on the 19th, they returned to Lathrop's, where he and Rich met with some of the brethren, including a Brother Blackburn. This could have been Anthony, or it could have been Thomas or Abner Blackburn who reached California about that time. The latter two came in from Utah via Carson Valley where they had done some gold mining. They discovered it the previous year at what became Gold Canyon.

On June 20th, still at Lathrop's, they met Captains Egan, Hunt, and Hunter, as well as [Joseph] Cain "on business." Cain had been a member of the Flake Company. He was the co-author of "The Mormon Way-Bill to the Gold Fields," published the next year by Willard Richards, counselor to Brigham Young. Because of his close ties to Richards, Cain may well have been mining for the Church leader.

Again to the Bay Area

The following day Elders Lyman and Rich headed for San Francisco, again spending the night at Root's. Lyman deposited with "Brother (Judson) Stoddard three parcels of gold belonging to the Brothers Crosby, Rollins (Rawlins) and Clark" [28] which had been left with Brother Root.

On the 22nd they reached Sacramento where they met Hervey Green and (Abner) Blackburn who had come in from Salt Lake. Both Hervey Green and his son (Henry?) [29] lived in Salmon Falls where they were partners with Father Hezekiah Thatcher in running a hotel. It was probably the younger man who was met in Sacramento. The Apostles split up, Lyman to go on to San Francisco on the *Hartford* and Rich to go to Weaverville to get some news and letters which had been left there. He reached the mail outpost on June 24th and met Hervey Green, who had brought the mail in and was ready to return to Salt Lake City. Rich wrote a letter home and returned to Lathrop's for the night.

The junior Apostle left for San Francisco on the 25th in company with Dr. (Darwin P.) Richardson, a Utah pioneer of 1847 and a California tithe payer in 1850. They took the steamer, *Gold Hunter*, leaving Sacramento at 2 o'clock for a fourteen hour trip to San Francisco.

Lyman and Rich remained some time on the peninsula—San Francisco, Santa Rosa, Santa Cruz, Mission Dolores, San Jose—usually traveling separately. On June 28th, the two Apostles met with the rebellious but prospering Sam Brannan, and left different impressions on this confrontation:

> Lyman: Spent the day in Francisco and we visited Samuel Brannan who made me a present of $500.00 made an arrangement for the books in his possession.

> Rich: We paid Mr. Samuel Brannan a visit and learned from him that he stood alone and knew no one only himself and family. He agreed to turn over some books.

Rich, of the two, was the much more formal, referring to Brannan as "Mr." while Lyman merely alluded to him as Samuel Brannan. Lyman must have maintained a reasonably positive relationship with his former traveling companion, Brannan, to be given such a gift. Lyman deposited $621.50 to his own account in the Gold Account that fall. Even in reference to the books, Lyman's version is softer—arrangements being made rather than Brannan agreeing to turn them over.

Evidently the mail brought in by Green and Blackburn, having left Salt Lake about April 1, carried a message for the Apostles to come home with the tithing as soon as possible. for they began shortly to prepare for the return. Because of what was to come, there is less certainty that the message was clear as to what was expected of the junior Apostle. In fact, that uncertainty may have been what precipitated his quick trip to Weaverville. On Monday, July 1st, Rich recorded that they did some trading while Lyman "remained in the city made some purchases of goods for home, dined with Mr. Brannan today heard of gold diggins on the east side of the (Sierra Nevada) mountains." [30] Lyman was evidently still on good terms with the rebellious Sam Brannan, but not good enough to induce him to come to Zion nor to return the tithes he had collected in the name of the Church.

The three months (April 1, 1850 to July 1, 1850) had seen the Apostles in almost constant travel from Mormon Bar in the south to the North Fork of the American River in the north, and from San Francisco in the west to Weaverville in the east. Their principal activity was gathering tithing gold for the Church, but they also provided a conduit for private gold being transferred to families and Church leaders in Salt Lake. They organized a branch of the Church in the Mission San Jose area and found time to do some planning of a settlement in the southern part of the incipient state. However, they seemed to do little teaching or preaching in the area of the mines. Certainly the traffic in gold was the dominant activity of the Apostles, evidence of its importance to the fledgling Mormon economy in Deseret.

NOTES

1. Rich, Papers and Lyman, Papers. All quotes and most detail to follow in this chapter unless otherwise credited, come from these two sources without being footnoted. See Appendices 16a-d for lists of Church members in California.

2. See Chapter 9 for more detail on the City Hotel. Brannan was the dominant force in the development of the Embarcadero or waterfront of the infant Sacramento in competition with Sutter's Fort, two miles up the American River. They expanded toward each other, eventually becoming the city of Sacramento.

3. While Rich referred to Reading at that time as "Brother" there is no other indication that he was a Mormon. With the rank of Major, he had played a prominent role in the war with Mexico, having come to California in 1843. He worked for Sutter as a clerk and also worked as a trapper and miner. In October of 1850, he was a partner in a store in Sacramento.

4. The Roots were not on the Utah Immigration list, nor was Jeremiah a Battalion or *Brooklyn* member. Like a number of other Mormons, they probably came directly to California, bypassing Utah. They do not even appear on Lyman's tithing or membership rolls, though they are referred to in various accounts as Mormons.

5. See Chapter 22 for the details of this settlement effort.

6. Horner had mined for a short time at Mormon Island but with little success, prospering primarily in the Mission San Jose area from his farming operations. He assisted missionaries going to the Pacific missions. He committed to invest in the San Bernardino colony, but had gone bankrupt before he could help that colony. He remained in California after the Mormon exodus of 1857, in 1879 moving to Hawaii where he raised sugar cane and eventually served in the Queen's House of Nobles. See John M. Horner, "Personal History" and "Adventures of a Pioneer."

7. All name places were checked with Gudde and Gudde, *California Gold Camps*. They will not be further footnoted. If listed, they will be given additional identification in the text. If not listed, there will not be any further identification.

8. See Appendix 16e.

9. James Henry Rawlins and others spelled his last name in two ways—Rawlins and Rollins. He

entered Utah in 1848 with Henry Rollins (Rawlins) and was possibly the member of the Flake Company referred to by Campbell as John Henry Rollins. A Henry Rollins came to California on the *Brooklyn*.

10. The antagonism of "Americans" toward dark visaged "foreigners" had resulted in so much violence in the northern mines that Spanish speaking residents, whether newcomers or pre-war "Californeos" had been driven into the southern mines, locating especially at Sonora. See Jackson, *Gold Rush*, 286-289 for more complete details on this development.

11. It is believed that these included C. D. Hovey, Franklin Edwards, Lafayette Shephard, Albert Duey (Dewey) and John Robinson.

12. See Gibbes' California Map of 1852.

13. Stoddard is reported to have been a partner with Brown at Murderer's Bar in 1849, but also a member of the Flake Company. To be both, he would have had to take a quick trip to Utah in the later summer of 1849, something entirely possible.

14. Myron Tanner, Manuscript.

15. See Appendix 16f.

16. Once again the Apostles differed, Rich recording it as McMaster, Lyman as McMurtrey. The more experienced and knowledgeable Lyman was probably correct. McMurtrey had been among the Utah pioneers of 1848 together with his wife, Amanda. He may well have been the Wm. S. McMurtrey living with Jas. H. McMurtrey on the lower end of the South Fork of the American River that fall.

17. J. Kenneth Davies, *Deseret Sons of Toil*, 53.

18. Dean C. Jessee, "Brigham Young's Family," also, "All Things Move in Order in the City," 289-320.

19. Journal History, January 26, 1851.

20. Interview of a descendant, Brian S. Jacobs,

June 15, 1980.

21. Again the Apostles differed, Rich spelling it "Harmon" and Lyman "Hammond." This time Rich appears to have been the more correct.

22. See Chapter 23.

23. See Appendix 16g.

24. John Beers was listed by Lyman as a transient. William Beers, a member of the Battalion, was a tithe payer.

25. Gold Accounts.

26. Ibid.

27. Ibid.

28. Crosby was probably Jonathan Crosby, a missionary en route to the Society Islands, and at the time with the Huntington Company which was a month to the east. Rollins (Rawlins) was possibly James H. Rawlins. Father James Clark was also with the Huntington Company. Although there were other Mormon Clarks in the area, James Clark had sons mining in the area to the north of the North Fork of the American River.

29. Hervey Green had reached Salt Lake City with his family in 1848. He came to California shortly after the discovery of gold with his sons Henry and Ammon. Hervey was born in 1806, Henry in 1830 and Ammon in 1833. Since Henry at this time was 20 and Ammon 17, it was probably Henry that Hervey had as a business partner.

30. Thomas Blackburn must have failed to tell the Apostles earlier of his gold mining activities in the Carson Valley area.

Appendices for Chapter 16

About the first of July, 1849, Apostle Amasa M. Lyman began a list of Church members in California who contributed to the emergency fund sent to Church headquarters with the Rhoades Company that summer. In 1850, Lyman began systematically to list the names of Church members whom he met in California, maintaining separate lists for those in San Francisco, San Jose, and what he called "Transients." He also maintained a running list of financial contributors, most of whom are found on the lists of members. The listings generally do not include the children, if any, and often not the women. In addition, Lyman's journals include names not included in his or Apostle Charles C. Rich's lists. The following appendices, 16 a-c, use these lists and journals, as well as other sources with names rearranged alphabetically for ease of reference. The names of apparent women and children (probably adults) have been indented. As Lyman and/or his scribe were not always consistent or accurate, and as some individuals did not know how to spell their names, alternative versions are provided in brackets. Also included in brackets is the priesthood of men where identified.

NOTES:

1. Priesthood Abbreviations

Eld - Elder	Dea - Deacon
Sev - Seventy	Tea - Teacher
HP - High Priest	Pr - Priest

2. Starred names also made financial contributions.

3. Hannah's husband, William Evans, of the *Brooklyn* had been excommunicated.

4. Names with a "U" were tentatively identified in the Utah 1850 Census.

APPENDIX 16a (Note 16:1)

San Francisco Mormons 1849-50

(Samuel and Elizabeth Brannan are noted by their absence, though Elizabeth's mother, Fanny Corwin, is listed.)

Bates, Morgan (Eld) (1)
Brown, Hetty C.
*Cade, Jonathan (Eld) (2)

Cade, Sarah (Susannah)
Corwin, Frances (Fanny) M.
*Crisman (Chrisman), Charles (High Priest)
    Crisman, Mary
        Crisman, George
        Crisman, Ester Ann
*Evans, Hannah (3)
Farnsworth. Alphonzo M. (Eld)
*Griffith, Sarah D.
U Hamilton, Mary (4)
*Hyatt, Elisha
        Hyatt, Matilda
Ira, Cyrus
U *Jones, Sarah
Knowles, Richard (Dea)
Lee (Leigh), Isaac
U   Lee, Mary
*Lewis, John M.
Lincoln, Seth S. (Eld)
        *Lincoln, Priscilla H.
*Meder, Moses A. (Pr)
        *Meder, Sarah D.
*Morey (Mowry), Martin (Barton)
        *Morey, Ruth
Nichols, Joseph
        Nichols, Jerusha L.
Pell, E. W. (Elder)
        Pell, Seba
*Peters, (Petch), Robert (Eld)
        Peters, Mary
Pool(e), Elizabeth
        Pool(e), Mary
Robins (Robbins), John R.
        Robins, Phebe A.
Sirrine (Serrine), Geo. W. (Elder)
Skinner, Horace A. (Eld)
        Skinner, Laura Ann
Sparks, Quartus S.
        Sparks, Mary H.

Source: Lyman, Papers, Utah 1850 Census.

APPENDIX 16b (Note 16:1)

(San Jose Mormons 1849-50)

It should be noted that diaries, journals, and letters of that day often refer to the area around Mission San Jose simply as "San Jose." It is the area of the present city of Fremont. The present city of San Jose (about 15 miles to the south) grew up around the pioneer settlement of "Pueblo San Jose," which was sometimes referred to at the time simply as "Pueblo." The whole region about Southeast and South San Francisco Bay (Fremont and San Jose), even out into the Livermore Valley, was sometimes referred to as the "San Jose Valley." The settlement Lyman refers to here is the one that existed in the Mission San Jose area. The only Mormons in the Pueblo San Jose area at that time were Joseph R. Fisher (brother of Mary Ann Fisher Cheney, both passengers of the *Brooklyn*) and perhaps William Stout, also of the *Brooklyn* (after he left the New Hope Colony).

Baldwin, Dan L.
            Baldwin, Almira
*Cheney, Zacheus
            Cheney, Mary Ann
*Horner, John M.
Marshall (Martial), Earl (Pr)
            Marshall, Salisha (Letitia)
Naile(e) (Naegle) John C. (Eld)
Starks, Dan (Eld)
            Starks, Anna
Stivers, Simeon

NOTES: See Appendix 16a Notes.

Source: Lyman, Papers, Utah 1850 Census.

APPENDIX 16c (Note 16:1)

California Transient Mormons 1849-50

U *Alexander, Horace M.
U *Algar (Alger), John U
*Allred, Reuben W.
Atherton, William
            Atherton, Emily
U *Bailey, James (Tea)
U Bankhead, George
Beckstead, Orrin W.
*Beech, Rufus
U Beer (Beers), John
U *Berry, John M. (W.)
*Bigler, Henry (Sev)
U Bingham, Erastus

Bingham, Willard
Binley, Harriet
*Blackburn, Anthony (HP)
            Blackburn, Esther
                        Blackburn, Matilda
Blackwell, Hiram (Sev)
Bombridge, Frederick
Boswell, Abraham (Sev)
U *Boyce (Boice, Boyes), George
U *Boyce (Boice, Boyes), William
U *Boyd, George W. (Sev)
*Brooks, James H.
U Brower, A. C.
            Brower, Martha E.
Brown, Alexander
U Brown, Daniel
Brown, E. L.
U   Brown, Mary
Brown, Jesse
U Brown, John (Sev)
*Burnham, Jacob F.
*Burton, Charles E.
*Cade, David J.
U Cain, Joseph (Sev)
U Calkins, Sylvanus (Eld)
*Cannon, George Q. (Sev)
Carruth, William
U *Cherry, Ebenezer (HP)
U Clark, Dan P.
U Clawson, John R. (Sev)
*Condit (Conduet), Jeptha (Eld)
Cook, Washington O. U
Coon(s), William (Sev)
Coray, William B.
*Covington, Berril
Crow (Croso), Benjamin B.
            Crow, Harriet
Crow, Hamilton
U   Crow, Mary Jane
U Davis, Joseph
Davis, Nancy
U *Dewey, Albert
U *Dewey, Franklin B.
Dixon, John
Edmunds, Jefferson
Edmunds, ?
Edmunds, Franklin
Egan, Howard
Elliot, B. W.
*Farrer, Wm. (Sev)
*Fife, Peter M. (Sev)

Flake, James M.
Fletcher, Philander (Sev)
Follett, Wm.
U Freeman, John M. (Sev)
Gates, Hiram
       Gates, Emily
Gibson, David
*Gibson, Edgar
U *Gibson, Henry
Gifford, William B.
U Gordon, James
U Gould, John C.
Granger, Fayette
*Harmon, James (Sev)
Harmon, Mary
Harmon, Lorenzo F. (Sev)
Harmon, Oliver N. (Sev)
Harrison, Kathrine
Harte, James
Hawk, Nathan
       Hawk, Elizabeth
*Hawkins, James
U *Hickerson, Geo. W. (Sev)
U *Higbee (Higby), John M. (Pr)
*Hoagland, Lucas
*Hoagland, Peter
Hovey, C. D. (Sev)
U *Huffacker, Simpson D.
U Hunt, Jefferson (HP)
Hunter, Jesse D. (HP)
       Hunter, Keza
       Hunter, Asa
       Hunter, Mary
Hunter, William
*Jacobs, John
Judd, Riley
*Keeler, James (Sev)
Kibby, James (Sev)
Kinney, Patrick
Lanier, Allen
Leffingwell, Anthony B.
Leffingwell, Joseph L.
       Leffingwell, Matilda
Leffingwell, William (HP)
       Leffingwell, Eunice
Marick, Thomas
McMines, William A.
*McMurtrey, Samuel (Eld)
McMurtrey, Julia
U *Miles, Saml.
U Mount, Joseph (HP)

Mowrey, John T.
U *Oakley, James
*Olmstead, Hiram
*Peck, Joseph
U *Pettit, Edwin
U *Phelps, Henry
U *Pomeroy, Francis M.
U Quail (Quayle), James H. (Sev)
Rhoads, John P.
       Rhoads, Matilda G.
*Richardson, Darwin P.
U *Robinson, John
U *Robinson, Richard
Root, Jeremiah
       Root, Emeline
*Rosecrans, Geo. W. (Sev)
       Rosecrans, Elmira
U *Russell, Henry
St. John, Stephen M. (Sev)
       St. John, Folly
       St. John, Kenerva
Saltar, Calvin
U *Seely, David
U *Seely, J. Wellington
U Shepherd, M. Lafayette
Shumway, Aurora
U *Sly, James C.
U *Smith, David
Stone, Edgar
U Swarthout, George N.
U Taft, Seth
*Thomas, Nathan T.
*Thompson, Miles
*Thorpe, Marcus B.
U *Thurber, Albert K.
U *Tuttle, Hubbard
U *Webb, John
*West, Ira E.
*West, Israel
*Whitney, Ephraim B.
Whitney, Harriet
U *Whittle, Thomas (Sev)
Williams, James
U *Wolsey (Woolsey).Wm.
Workman, A. G. (Sev)
U *Young, Alfred D.
U *Young, William
       Young, Emily

Notes: See Appendix 16a Notes.

Sources: Lyman, Papers; Utah 1850 Census.

APPENDIX 16d (Note 16:1)

Additional Possible and Probable California Mormons Unlisted by Lyman

Arnold, Josiah
U Barnard, John
U Beers, (William)
U Billings, George D.
Bills, John
U Bills, (William)
Blackburn, Thomas
U Bradshaw, Abraham
U Brown, Isaac T.
Brown, James S.
U Clark, Hiram
Clark, W. O.
U Colby, Alonson
Cox, Andrew Y.
Dorety (Dougherty), Levi
Douglas, James
U Emmett, James
Everett, Mary Jane
Foot, George H.
U Forsyth, George
Fowler, (John S.)
Goodall, James Goodall, M. T.
Goodwin, Isaac
Green, Ammon
Green, Henry
U Green, Hervey
Hanks, Alvarus
Hanks, Ebenezer
U Hogan, Goudy
U Horne, Joseph
Jacobs, H(enry)
Kimball, Hazen
U Kittleman, William
Knowles, Sarah
Lathrop, (Asahel A.)
Lewis, Richard
U Martin, (Moses)
Matthews, Benjamin F.
U McIntire, Dr. William L.
Morris, Thomas
U Peacock, William
U Philips, John
Porter, (possibly Porter Rockwell)

Powell, U. B.
U Rockwell, O. P.
Seaton (Sutton), James
Stewart, Boyd
U Stoddard, (Judson)
Stout, William
Tanner, (Myron)
Thorpe, Caroline M.
Tymmim, Abraham
U Warrick, Thomas
Wimmer, Moroni

NOTE 1. These individuals are identified within the Lyman and Rich diaries, but are not found in the lists prepared by Lyman and presented in Appendices 16a, b, and c.

NOTE 2. See Appendix 16a Notes

Source: Lyman, Papers; Rich *Diaries*.

APPENDIX 16e (Note 16:8)

Tithe payers at Mariposa May 1, 1850

Thomas Whittle--Flake Co. (1)
James Keeler--Flake Co.
Joseph Peck--Flake Co.
Henry Bigler--Flake Co.
Peter Hoagland--Flake Co.
Geo. W. Hickerson--Hickerson Co. (1)
William Woolsey--Hickerson Co.
Henry Phelps
Alfred D. Young (1)
Wm. Young
Wm. Farrer--Flake Co. (1)
Joseph Horne(e) (2)
Nathan T. Thomas--MB
James Douglas--MB (1)
Richard Robinson
James Hawkins--Flake Co.
John Algar
John Webb
John Bills (3)
Marcus B. Thorpe
John Jacobs

NOTE 1. Groupings represent mining partnerships.
NOTE 2. While Horne is listed here and later, there is no record yet located of him going to

California. He possibly was a sponsor staying in Utah with tithing paid for him in California, or he may have been both a sponsor and an actual miner, the record being unclear.

NOTE 3. If previous accounts are accurate, John Bills was dead. William Bills would appear shortly in the record. It may be assumed that this account should either read "William Bills" or that this was tithing paid for John posthumously. William Andrew Bills came to Utah with John Bills in the Brigham Young Company of 1848.

Source: Lyman, Papers.

APPENDIX 16f (Note 16:15)

Tithe payers - Greenwood Valley
May 21, 1850

Alexander, Horace M.--MB Huffaker Co.
Baley (Bailey), James--MB
Boice (Boyce), George--MB
Boice (Boyce), William--MB
Burnham, Jacob--Huffaker Co.
Burton, Charles E.
Cade, David D. (J)--Huffaker Co.
Dewey, Albert--Huffaker Co.
Dewey, Franklin B.
Hogland (Hoagland), Lucas--MB
McMurtrey, Samuel
Miles, Samuel--MB, Huffaker Co.
Pettit, Edwin--Pomeroy Co.
Richardson, Darwin
Robison, John
Seely, David--Pomeroy Co.
Seely, Justice W.--Pomeroy Co.
Thurber, Albert K.--Huffaker Co.
Tuttle, Hubbard
West, Ira
West, Israel

APPENDIX 16g (Note 16:23)

Tithepayers - Hangtown (Placerville)
June 1, 1850

Bigler, Henry--MB (Mormon Battalion), Flake Co.
Boyd, George--MB
Cade, Jonathan -- *Brooklyn*
Gibson, Edgar
Gibson, Henry--Flake Co.
Keeler, James--MB, Flake Co.
Olmstead, Hiram--MB
Rollins (Rawlins), James H.-- Flake Co.
Shepherd, M. L.-- MB

Source: Lyman, Papers.

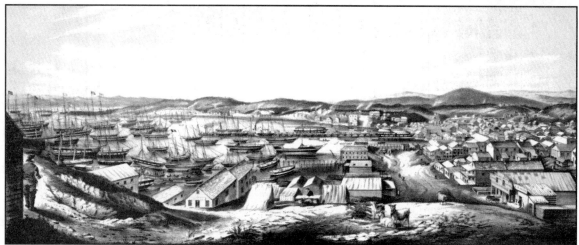

San Francisco (1849-1851)

Two views of San Francisco at about the time the Mormon gold miners called by Apostle Charles C. Rich assembled there to depart on their mission to the Sandwich Islands, November 1850.

UPPER (1849): Lithograph by H.S. Crocker & Co. of painting by George Henry Burgess, looking northward across Yerba Buena Cove toward Telegraph Hill. *Courtesy California History Center, The Louis E. Stocklmeir Regional History Library.*

LOWER (1851): Lithograph by Nathan Currier of painting by William B. McMurtrie, looking in the opposite direction, southward from Telegraph Hill. *Courtesy Bancroft Library.*

Both views show a rapidly growing city of hastily constructed wood buildings and temporary canvas tents. The lower view shows the many ships in Yerba Buena Cove, abandoned by their crews while they joined the search for gold. The lower view also shows the Long Wharf, constructed because the Cove was shallow, and at low tide ships could not get close to shore. The Wharf was initially (in 1849) 800 feet long, but (in 1850) was extended another 2,000 feet. Ships were sometimes permanently tied to the wharf, to function as floating warehouses, for example the *Apollo* and the *Niantic*. The Cove was eventually filled in and is the location of present day Chinatown.

The wood construction of the buildings made the city susceptible to fire. The first fire occurred in December 1849 and devastated a city block. A second occurred in May 1850, a third in June 1850, and a fourth in September 1850. However, a much larger devastation occurred in May 1851, shortly after the missionaries left. It burned eighteen city blocks, as well as the *Apollo* and *Niantic*.

The law of thy mouth is better unto me
than thousands of gold and silver.
  Bible. Psalms 119:72

17

From Gold to the Word

IT IS INTERESTING to note that the Bigler, Cannon, Farrer, Keeler, and Egan accounts of the Flake Company Gold Mission and Salt Lake Trading Company are completely silent on Mormon religious activity in the southern mines. The detailed account of Apostle Rich continued to March 7, 1850 when he arrived in the area of the southern mines. A 19 day gap follows, with sketchy entries thereafter. Cannon's diary has a large number of blank pages for this period which he probably had intended to come back to, but never did.

The next direct reference to the Flake Company is on May 1, 1850, when Elder Rich returned to the southern mines from San Francisco with the senior Apostle, Amasa Lyman. On that date, several members of the Flake Company, among others, paid tithing. [1]

The disposition of the remainder of the Flake party at that time is unknown. It is possible that there were some present who paid no tithing. But it would also appear that most of the men had by that time gone north, some perhaps to Slap Jack Bar near Murderer's Bar on the Middle Fork of the American River where elements of the Huffaker group had settled earlier. This group probably included Cannon who had not been among

the tithe payers in the southern mines. He was appointed to establish and/or manage a store in that vicinity (Slap Jack Bar) which appears to have been connected with the Salt Lake Trading Company store on the Merced River.

On September 23rd, journal keeper Bigler picked up the thread of the story. He said: "I have not written for many months . . . I have exposed myself to both Indians and wether more than I ever want to do again, living out in the snow and storms and rain without shelter, some of my brethren have died . . . all of my brethren have been sick having been much exposed working in gold . . . I am tired of mining and of the country and long to be home among the saints." [2]

On the following day, Keeler's renewed diary reveals that Brother Rich came to their place on the Middle Fork, unexpectedly calling several of the Boys on proselyting missions to the Sandwich Islands. Keeler's reply was that he "was on hand to do as he (Rich) should direct." [3] The missionaries largely came from the Flake Company of gold missionaries.

Apostle Rich had earlier hinted to Cannon of such a call, saying that some of the brethren, including Edgar Gibson (who died before receiving his mission call), would be asked to go to the Sandwich Islands "for the winter." [4] Berry's call was conditional. He was to go only "if he wished." For a Mormon mission call, it was quite unusual, but was probably conditioned by the fact that Berry had been seriously ill, most likely a victim of the dreaded cholera.

Added to these was the aging Father Hiram Clark, who had just that summer come to California via the northern route with the William D. Huntington Company. He was sent to assist Elders Lyman and Rich. Clark (a veteran missionary), however, was called to preside over the missionary group. Boyd Stewart, (who was called to go to Oregon), had also just arrived with the Huntington Company. [5]

Bigler gave his version of the proselyting mission call, saying it was the Apostle's opinion that it would cost no more to spend the winter there than it would in the gold fields, that the men could make nothing in the wintertime in consequence of so much water in the streams. In addition, provisions would be much higher in the mines and it "would cost us more money to stay here and make nothing than if we went to the Island and preach." [6] On the following day Cannon wrote out the "certificates of good standing" [7] for Apostle Rich to sign.

On September 25th, Bigler reviewed his experiences in the mines. He said that he had been mining since February, exposing himself "to living out in the rains, and snow, traveling and prospecting, building and repairing dams, working up to my neck in water and for weeks in water up to my waist and arms, have made but little . . . The expenses overrun the gain." [8]

On August 1st, Bigler had sent $100 to his sponsor, Father John Smith, by way of Apostle Lyman, who was leaving for Salt Lake. He also paid almost a hundred dollars in tithing for himself, indicating earnings of close to a thousand dollars—a lot of money for that day. However, he complained that he had so little to show for it that it made "the hair fairly stand upright" on his head when he thought about it.

On September 25th, Elder Rich gathered the missionaries together, "set them apart" for the mission and gave them a blessing. On Saturday, the 28th, after a respite of several days from mining, "The brethren thought the water sufficiently low to commence work at building the dam" [9] Keeler added "for the third time." [10]

In his renewed diary, Cannon reported that he was occupied in the store over the next few days even though business was "falling away very fast." The rest of the "boys" were engaged building the dam, finishing it on October 2nd. They then "went to work" and towards the "close of the day they struck it pretty rich." On October 6th, they divided the proceeds, receiving $200 a piece. Again on the 13th, they each received $444. The next day "diggings failed." Bigler observed, probably tongue in cheek, "O what a pity." [11] It was not before they took out an additional $92 each. Cannon spent the 17th "settling up the concern making acs. (accounts), etc." [12] The boys began preparations to leave on their missions.

Bigler included in his account some of his expenditures during this period, such as a shovel and pick for ten dollars, four wash pans for eight dollars, and one pair of boots for ten dollars. He also mentioned that he had to borrow the one hundred dollars that he sent to Father John Smith with Amasa Lyman. [13]

Several of the missionaries left the river on the 16th. Keeler recorded on October 17th that they traveled to Greenwood, staying the night in that Mormon community, and traveling to the Mormon enclave of Salmon Falls the following day. At Salmon Falls they stayed at the hotel or inn taken over from Ariah C. Brower by Hervey Green and Hezekiah Thatcher. They then went on to William Huntington's camp, [14] probably at Mormon Island.

Huntington, the leader of the last known Mormon train for the gold fields, [15] had arrived shortly before. The missionaries inquired for Father Hiram Clark, their mission leader, but found that he had gone north to join his sons in mining on the Bear River, 40 miles north of Sacramento City. They waited for the rest of the "boys" who had gone a different route, finally receiving word that they were at Six Mile House, where they joined them, arriving at sundown on the 22nd.

In the meantime, Cannon and the rest of the "boys" did not leave the bar until the 18th. John Berry was so ill that they stopped at Greenwood where Andrew Cahoon, his wife Mary, and Andrew's younger brother, Mahonri, were living. Andrew was not there, but Cannon visited with Mary, learning that she was discouraged and "anxious to get home," being "very tired of the country." [16]

Cannon told Mary of their recent good fortune, having "been blessed to exceed our expectations." He informed her that they were leaving on missions but had no books. She let him take her hymnal and said that Andrew might let him have his *Book of Mormon* when he returned. She refused his offer of $5, but he left it on the table when he departed after accepting an invitation for breakfast the next morning.

Cannon and Henry Gibson went over for breakfast, finding Andrew in "very good spirits" in spite of the failure thus far of his mining ventures in a couple of dams. Cahoon let Cannon have his *Book of Mormon* and a Synopsis, refusing to accept any pay. Cannon was told he could return them upon completion of his mission, but "if not it would make no difference."

Taking leave of the young couple, Cannon and his companions went to Salmon Falls where they put up at the Green-Thatcher hotel. On Sunday, the 20th, Green harnessed his mules and took the missionaries to Lathrop's Mormon Tavern where Brother Howard Egan lay ill, no doubt with cholera. In the fall of 1850, a devastating cholera epidemic struck the Mormon Tavern area, killing about half the population.

Cannon had "a long talk with Egan about the affairs of the store, and the concerns South," evidence that the two stores were connected in some way. Egan informed him that with "his sickness every thing had gone to wreck that Phin(eas) Kimball had acted the scoundrel with him" and that "[Fayette] Granger was bad," blaming the latter for much of whatever trouble the store had experienced. [17] The reference to the "concerns South" could have been about the projected colony in the Southland, Southern California.

Cannon, Dixon and Bigler wanted to send some money to Utah, but (there being "some doubts about a company going home") they left their money with Captain Egan to "send if a company should go." If none went, Cannon's money, at least, was to be used by Egan as he saw fit. On the 21st, the missionaries went by wagon to Root's Six Mile House, "a regular apostate nest," according to Cannon. He claims that Root, "apostate," had sold out to his brothers-in-law, Eleazer and Stirling Davis, and to Henry Fairbanks, "all of the same stripe." [18] Cannon spent some time in conversation with Fairbanks, whom he had known before the latter went into the Battalion. He had known him then as "a fine young man," but he had "changed since then." Fairbanks reportedly told Cannon that "he would not believe anything in religion or God or anything else unless 'Old Christ' himself would come down and tell him." Cannon doubted that he would believe even then.

Fairbanks reportedly swore that he would "kill Bro. Erastus Snow," a recently ordained Apostle, "if he ever came across him." Understandably, the orthodox missionary was shocked and disgusted, remarking "when the light that is in you becomes darkened how great is that darkness."

On the 23rd, Cannon's missionary group left for Sacramento, meeting Brother Hiram Blackwell who told them that President Clark had sent word that he would be down from Bear River in three days. The missionaries sent the messenger back to Clark to hurry him along. On the way they came across Brothers William Squires and Jeptha Condit, both of the Battalion, who "had rented a saloon and were fitting it up." They accepted the Mormon saloon keepers' invitation to spend the night. By November 5th, Squires was dead of cholera.

In the meantime, Bigler left the river in a separate group, going a slightly different route. He and his companions stopped at Brother (Samuel or Benjamin) Crow's in Greenwood to get some copies of the *Book of Mormon* and *Doctrine and Covenants*. They had dinner at Brother [William] Leffingwell's at Pilot Hill for $1.25 a piece, and slept under a tree at Brother Hezekiah Thatcher's at Salmon Falls. Then they paid Brother (Henry) Green of Salmon Falls $2.00 a piece to carry them in a wagon to Brother Lathrop's Mormon Tavern. [19]

Tired of waiting for Brother Clark to show up, and needing to have new underclothing, most of the missionaries decided to leave for San Francisco where there was a community of Mormons available with women seamstresses who could help them. They would then be "nearer ready" when Brother Clark came down. [20]

The Elders had intended to go to San Francisco together but got separated—Whittle, Keeler, Dixon, Hawkins and Farrer going on the *West Point* and Bigler, Cannon and Blackwell on the *Senator*. They arrived in San Francisco that night. Before leaving, Cannon found himself busy "disposing of the *Doctrine and Covenants* with [Section] 75" [21] and copies of the Mormon newspaper, *Times and Seasons*. Unable to dispose of all of them, he left them for William Huntington, who had promised that he would sell all he could.

On October 29th, Cannon witnessed the celebration of California's admission into the Union—without more comment. He met with Captain Egan the following day finding him "looking better." "Egan had purchased a load of flour to take to Stockton," his trading ventures still not over.

On November 5th, Cannon learned of the death of Squires from cholera and that Brother Hiram Clark himself was in bed at Brother Huntington's. He reported that Sacramento was becoming depopulated as people fled the city and that San Francisco itself was also increasingly feeling the "ravages" of the dreaded disease.

While in the hotel in San Francisco preparing to go to the Islands, Cannon was visited by several Saints. One of them was William Patten who had been sick in the hospital and wanted help to go to the Islands. According to Cannon, Patten had "come out of the Valley in our company and had been with us in the Southern Mines." It would, therefore, appear that he had been an unnamed member of the Flake Company of gold mission-

aries. Patten, who had been a Captain of Ten in the G. A. Smith Company of 1849, had been a good Mormon, Cannon claimed, but was by then a complete apostate. Cannon refused to help him, saying that others needed help more.

Cannon saw the cholera scourge as a fulfillment of the prophecies of the Elders of the Church. He observed that "since Joseph's [Smith] death there has been nothing but war and pestilence among the nations of the Earth."

On Wednesday, November 6th, Cannon met with Brother and Sister [Joseph] Nichols (of the *Brooklyn*) who were "good folks but very little of the spirit of Gathering about them . . . In fact, you speak to the majority of the folks professing to be Latter-day Saints here about going to the Salt Lake Valley and it is an after consideration to be done when it was the only resort." He also reported that "Brother Clark and B [Blackwell] arrived."

Hiram Blackwell had originally been called to go to the Society Islands earlier with Addison Pratt. However, he had not been observing the Word of Wisdom on his trip to California earlier that year and had been left behind by the mission leader. John W. Berry, who had been told that he was called "if he wished" and who had become ill, probably with cholera, was not in the group. He returned to Utah within a year.

The various Sandwich Island missionaries rendezvoused in San Francisco, setting sail for the islands on November 15-17, 1850. They had difficulty getting out of the Bay because of adverse winds.

The mission to the Society Islands would break the spirit of the aging Hiram Clark, but made the reputation of George Q. Cannon as a vigorous, successful missionary and a translator of the *Book of Mormon* into the Hawaiian language. Some of the missionaries soon left the field. Others returned with Cannon in 1854 and became involved in the proselyting of Northern California in 1855-57, with Cannon as their mission president. Cannon would go on to become an Apostle and counselor to Church Presidents. He would also become a wealthy mining entrepreneur in

Utah.

NOTES

1. Lyman, Tithing Record. See Appendix 16e

2. Bigler, Diary. September 23, 1850.

3. Keeler, Journal, September 24, 1850. See Appendix 17a for list of Sandwich Island Missionaries. (Word in brackets is the author's).

4. Cannon, Diary, September 24, 1850.

5. See Chapter 18 for detailed account of the Huntington Company.

6. Bigler, Diary, September 25, 1850.

7. Cannon, Diary, September 25, 1850.

8. Bigler, Diary.

9. Cannon, Diary,

10. Keeler, Journal, September 28, 1850.

11. Bigler, Diary.

12. Cannon, Diary, September 29 - October 7, 1858. (Word in brackets is the author's).

13. Bigler, Diary, October 6-16, 1850.

14. Keeler, Journal, October 17, 1850.

15. See Chapter 18. Huntington had shortly before arrived as the leader of a wagon train containing proselyting missionaries headed for the Society Islands, as well as gold diggers and Mormon settlers.

16. Cannon, Diary.

17. Ibid. The next year, Kimball, a disaffected Mormon, was living at Curtisville in Tuolumne. He had probably come to California in 1848, avoiding a stay in Utah. Later that year (Fayette) Granger became a resident of Louisville in El Dorado County.

18. Ibid. All three of these men were Battalion veterans. Henry was living at Mormon Island later that year.

19. Bigler, Diary, October 19, 20, 1850.

20. Cannon, Diary, October 24, 25, 1850. The term "underclothing" probably referred to certain garments considered by Mormons to be sacred. These garments are worn by the more faithful Saints who have participated in special rites performed in Mormon temples.

21. The reference to Section 75 (of the 1844 edition) of the *Doctrine and Covenants* is interesting. It constituted what is now Section 66 of the contemporary edition of that volume of Mormon scripture. That section is a revelation given in 1831 in which the recipient was praised for "receiving mine everlasting covenant, even the fulness of my gospel . . ." These phrases, to the initiated, related to the covenant of "eternal marriage" peculiar to the more faithful Latter-day Saints, a more complete reference to which is found in a revelation of 1843, Section 132 of the *Doctrine and Covenants,*

APPENDIX

Appendix 17a (Note 17:3)

Sandwich Island Missionaries Called

Berry, John W. (Seriously ill, did not go.)
Bigler, Henry
Cannon, George Q.
Clark, Hiram
Dixon, John
Farrer, William
Hawkins, James
Keeler, Henry
Morris, Thomas
Whittle, Thomas

Source: Keeler, Journal

Weberville (Weaverville)

Weberville became important as the western terminus of the Mormon-Carson Pass Emigrant Trail (that is, the original Mormon Emigrant Route.) However, Weberville began as a very rich gold site. The sketch is by William Pearson from a pantoscope daguerreotype by J. Wesley Jones. [ca. 1850's] *Courtesy California Historical Society.*

In July 1848, recently appointed to military command in California, Colonel Richard Barnes Mason visited the site and described what he found to his superior in Washington, D.C.:

"I struck the stream [now known as Weber's Creek] . . . They had about thirty Indians employed, whom they pay in merchandise. They were getting gold of a character similar to that found in the main fork, . . . From this point we proceeded up the stream about eight miles, where we found a great many people and Indians, some engaged in the bed of the stream, and others in the small side valleys that put into it. These latter are exceedingly rich, two ounces being considered an ordinary yield for a day's work. A small gutter, not more than 100 yards long by four feet wide, and two or three deep, was pointed out to me as the one where two men . . . had a short time before obtained 17,000 dollars' worth of gold. Captain [Charles M.] Weber informed me, that he knew that these two men had employed four white men and about 100 Indians, and that, at the end of one week's work, they paid off their party, and had left 10,000 dollars' worth of this gold. Another small ravine was shown me, from which had been taken upwards of 12,000 dollars' worth of gold. Hundreds of similar ravines, to all appearances, are as yet untouched. The country on either side of Weber's Creek is much broken up by hills, and is intersected in every direction by small streams or ravines which contain more or less gold. Those that have been worked are barely scratched, and, although thousands of ounces have been carried away, I do not consider that a serious impression has been made upon the whole." [Mason, "Mason Report, August 17, 1848," available in Castro, *Carson's California*, 220-240.]

We'll build on the rock they planted A palace to the King.
Into its shining corridors, Our sons of praise we'll bring,
For the heritage they left us, Not of gold or worldly wealth . . .
    Mormon Hymn, "Firm as the Mountains Around Us"
    (1985) #255.

18

The Last Trains West

THE ORGANIZED MOVE of Mormon wagon trains to California had reached a peak during the winter of 1849-50. However, the success of the Mormon gold missionaries during that spring and summer was limited and would be reflected in the lack of organized movement in the fall of the latter year. That spring, before the disappointing word could reach Church leaders and the Mormon people, at least three and probably four Mormon companies, leaving Deseret apparently under the direction and approval of Church authorities, pulled out of the City of the Great Salt Lake for the gold fields. In addition, many went unrecorded on their "own hook."

The concerned attitude of the First Presidency toward the massive spring exodus of Saints to California was mixed. In their General Epistle to the Saints, dated April 12, 1850, they complained that many brethren had gone and many more were planning to go, no doubt claiming that they went "by counsel." Only a few, they said, had actually "gone according to the advice of those whose right it is to counsel the Saints, and such are right, inasmuch as they do right." It was felt that those who went without counsel could have done more for Zion if they had stayed in Utah.

However, as long as they had gone, it was "not too late for them to do good and be saved, if they will do right . . . although they will not get so great a reward." [1]

The only hope of the defiant ones lay in listening to "those . . . appointed to counsel them" and then when they returned to "work righteousness." However, if they failed to heed counsel and instead made "gold their god" and did not use their wealth to help "their poor brethren . . . ," it would be "better for them if a mill stone had been hanged about their necks, and they had been drowned in the depths of the sea." They were accused of saying as an excuse that "Gold is good in its place . . . to do good with." but, continued the epistle, "in the hands of a wicked man it often proves a curse instead of a blessing."

Evidently sufficient brethren had returned to Zion in 1849 who used their new wealth selfishly enough to occasion a tongue lashing. The California Saints were informed that Apostles Rich and Lyman would continue to collect tithing, keeping a record "of the faithful brethren," but they were also to keep a "perfect history of all who profess to be Saints and do not follow counsel" and who refuse to "do their duty in all things." These were to be reported on every mail, that "their works may be entered in a book of remembrance in Zion." The leaders went on to say that such "are not wanted in our midst . . . Let such leave their carcasses where they do their work, we want not our burial grounds polluted with such hypocrites." Of course, these could acceptably repent if they did it "speedily."

Of those who went that season "by counsel," it is believed that they included at least a mail company leaving about April 1st, as well as the companies of Thomas Orr, Sr., Ephraim Hanks and William D. Huntington.

The Mail Company

A company assigned to take the first mail of the season to California was scheduled to leave April 3, 1850. [2] The mail company probably traveled on horse or mule back without wagons and, therefore, had an easier time crossing the snow packed mountains that held up the Orr Company, following them by three weeks.

The company probably included Hervey Green and Thomas Blackburn, who Apostle Rich reported on June 22nd had reached Sacramento "from the lake" having left mail at Weaverville. (This indicates that they must have traveled the Mormon Trail through Carson Pass, Weaverville being its western terminus.) The Apostle, upon learning of the mail's arrival, traveled to Weaverville to get it and to send a letter east. Green and Blackburn also brought word of "gold diggins on the east side of the mountain," revealing it to Elder Rich in Sacramento on July 1st. [3] The company may have included John Barnard and George H. Foote, mail carriers who also made the trip that spring and who were residents of El Dorado County that fall. It may also have included the 62-year-old Solomon Chamberlain, who left Iowa with the original band of pioneers of 1847, but did not reach Salt Lake until 1848. He went to the Land of Gold early in the spring of 1850, and returned to Utah after only two weeks of abortive prospecting. [4]

The Thomas Orr Company

Probably the first wagon train to enter California on the Mormon Trail that season was that of Captain Thomas Orr, Sr. [5] He had entered Utah in 1847 as a Captain of Ten in the Edward Hunter Company, his family being among the first to settle in Utah Valley to the south of the Salt Lake Valley. Members of his family participated in putting down the Indian resistance to the Mormon encroachments in the area. By the spring of 1850, they had made the decision to move on. While there is no firm evidence that they were sent to California by Brigham Young, nor even that they went with the leader's blessing, the fact that they were to remain loyal to the Church for many years would seem to indicate that their departure was at least not opposed.

The family record indicates that Orr was the captain of a wagon train composed of some 35 families which included his own. [6] The pilot was William Prouse, a Battalion veteran who remained in California for several years, as did most of the Orr family. Also in the company was Nicholas Kelly of the Mormon Battalion, who eventually settled near the Mormon Tavern. Other members of the company have not yet been identified.

The company traveled north and west to the California Trail using the Salt Lake Cutoff, then along the Humboldt River dropping south at either the Sinks or the Truckee to Carson Valley. Stopping at Mormon Station (which became known as Genoa), the company had to wait three weeks for the mountain snow to sufficiently melt. It, therefore, appears that the company left Salt Lake well in advance of the Huntington Company which left Salt Lake May 7th. While there, Thomas Orr Jr. later maintained that John Orr, Bill Prouse, and Nick Kelly went prospecting and found "the first piece of gold ever found on that side of the mountains." [7] However, as shown in a later chapter, Abner Blackburn, a frequent associate of the Orrs, reported that he had found gold in the same general location the previous year.

While waiting for the snow to melt the Thomas Orr group made preparations for going up Carson Canyon by building some bridges. Thomas Orr Jr. later recalled what happened when they

Thomas Orr (1802-1893) and Catherine Jackson Orr (1797-1879)

Thomas Orr was born in Cumberland, Lanark, Scotland, and Catherine Jackson was born in Kilbrine, Ayrshire, Scotland. Thomas and Catherine married, started a family, and in 1835 emigrated to New York. They farmed a short time in New York and emigrated to Illinois, settling along the Mississippi River a few miles northeast of what became Nauvoo. When the Mormons were driven out of Missouri, many of them settled in the region where the Orrs had settled. The Orr children, for the first time, were able to go to schools, ones the Mormons had established. The Orrs were Presbyterian, but soon converted to Mormonism. Thomas' son wrote in an autobiography that his parents were "so pious they wouldn't even let us children whistle on Sunday." When the Mormons left Nauvoo for the West, the Orrs went with them, Thomas acted as captain of his wagon train, and they entered the Salt Lake Valley in the latter part of the 1847 season.

The Orrs suffered and struggled to survive through the first two seasons in the Valley. They decided in 1850 to go to California. Thirty five families joined them, and Thomas was elected as their captain. They went by the Carson Pass Route. The Orrs settled at New York Ravine near Salmon Falls. Thomas rented a hotel and started a hotel and bakery business. He later bought the hotel and still later let others manage it while he turned to farming his homestead land.

Thomas and Catharine had five children. Thomas died in Shingle Springs, California November 15, 1893. Catharine died in Salmon Falls, California July 3, 1879. *Courtesy El Dorado County Chamber of Commerce.*

resumed their journey.

"Alter this delay we left Mormon Station (now Genoa) and heard that the men ahead of us were exacting a toll from travelers on the three bridges we had built across the Carson River. When we arrived at that point, we put an end to that practice and left the bridges open for the travelers following us." [8] Orr does not say who the interlopers were.

Thomas King Tomkins (1817-1885) and Jane Elizabeth Rollins Tomkins (1821-1865)

Thomas was born in Walcott, Lincolnshire, England. Jane Elizabeth was born in Boston, Lincolnshire, England. Their two families emigrated to America on the same boat in 1828. Thomas and Jane were married in Dansville, New York in 1839. They had two girls, joined the LDS Church, and sailed on the ship *Brooklyn* for San Francisco Bay in 1846. They farmed for a time in the region of Mission San Jose, and when gold was discovered, tried mining gold for a short time. They joined the Ebenezer Brown Company that went to the Salt Lake Valley in 1848.

Brigham Young called the Tomkins family, along with the Crosby family and Louisa Pratt, to go and do missionary work in the Society Islands (Tahiti, Louisa's husband, Addison Pratt, had gone there the previous year). They left the Salt Lake Valley in 1850 and recorded events as they journeyed through the California gold mining communities later that year, Those records give us a glimpse into the people and the places of the gold rush era. The Tomkins family only stayed about a year in the Islands and returned, settling in the new San Bernardino colony. Years later, in 1857, when Brigham Young called on the Saints to leave San Bernardino and come to the Salt Lake Valley, the Tomkins stayed and lived out their lives in the San Bernardino area. *Courtesy of Blanche Lane Tomkins and Alma Lee of San Bernardino, California.*

After ascending Carson Canyon, they moved through Hope Valley, crossed the mountains over West Pass (bucking 20 foot snowdrifts), and followed the Mormon Emigrant Trail, down through Leek Springs, Sly Park, and Pleasant Valley. They arrived at the latter place on July 4, 1850, eight days in advance of the Huntington Company.

The company camped at Shingle Springs near the Planters House, five miles west of Mud (Diamond) Springs. They then moved on to Deer Creek, about halfway between Shingle Springs and Mormon Tavern where they met up with Porter Rockwell, who was keeping a trading post and tavern. The senior Thomas had known Rockwell in Illinois and Salt Lake and called him by his real name. Alarmed, Porter asked Orr to use the name Brown, informing him that his life would be worth nothing if the Gentiles knew who he was. He advised the Orrs to settle there, and they remained, but only for a short period.

Thomas, Sr. and his son, John, soon moved on to New York Ravine above Salmon Falls, where they purchased a trading post from two old mountain men, the McKenzies, for $500. [9] The deal included two quarter sections of land on which the seller had squatter's rights. The family followed, being there at the time of the census that fall.

Mining fever was soon caught by some of the family. They went to mining at Mormon Island several miles down the river from Salmon Falls, renting the trading post to a man named McFarland.[10] However, Thomas, Sr. also purchased a hotel at Salmon Falls from Henry Larkin for $2,500, adding to it to accommodate more guests and to establish a bakery. [11] Meals cost $1.00; pies sold for $1.00 to $1.50 each; and whiskey sold for $.25 a drink. The family had taken a dozen chickens with them from Salt Lake, and they sold eggnogs for $.50 each, milk punch selling for the same. Thomas Sr. was later Deputy Sheriff to both Larkin and Dave Buell. Having what they claimed to be the only bakery, store, hotel, and feed stable in town, they took in as much as $1,000 to $1,500 a day. They stayed in business until about 1862, and reportedly over the years grubstaked newly arrived gold miners to the tune of $85,000, receiving no payments in return. About 1862, the family business was returned to the McKenzie brothers, later of French Creek, and the Orrs started farming near New York Ravine where they still had their mining claims.

According to Thomas Jr., all of the children were raised as Mormons, though some appear not to have been baptized. James and John ran a stage line from Sacramento to Marysville in the north, and also in Placer and in El Dorado Counties, in competition with the California Stage Company. Thomas Jr. became the proprietor of the Meyers Hotel in Shingle Springs. The youngest daughter, Lillie Jane, married William G. Taylor. [12] Isabella married Isaac Russell, a disaffected Mormon. The elderly Orrs were frequent hosts to Mormon missionaries in the 1853 to 1857 period, but did not make the exodus to Utah in 1857. They died in Salmon Falls. The graves of some of the fam-

ily along with other Salmon Falls residents, were later moved when the town was reached by the expanding Folsom Reservoir.

The Ephraim Hanks Company

Little is known about the Ephraim Hanks Company. It evidently left about three weeks in advance of the Huntington Company, or about April 20th. This may have been another mail company, as Hanks the next year secured the contract for the mail between Salt Lake and Fort Laramie.

Hanks was born in Ohio in 1827, following his brother, Sidney Alvarus Hanks, into the Church in 1844-45. Having been at sea for three or four years, he had joined the Mormon Battalion and went to the Salt Lake Valley from California in 1847. He became a frequent messenger and trouble shooter for Brigham Young, being accused by some of being a Danite leader in Utah. His trip to California in 1850 was a short one, as he was back in Utah at the time of the Utah census of that year.

Eph, as he was often called, may have been accompanied by his kinsman Ebenezer Hanks, who had been called on a mission to the Society Islands (Tahiti) while on a visit to Utah from his home in Salmon Falls. While in Salt Lake, Ebenezer had a judgment against him for $50 in a Salt Lake Court. He did not go on his mission, probably because of the ill health of his wife. Eph's brother, Sidney Alvarus, was called on a Society Island mission, but is listed as traveling to California in the Huntington Company that followed. Unfortunately, Sidney Alvarus' diary became lost in the course of his travels. It might well have supplied much valuable detail.

The company probably included Benjamin F. Stoddard, Ashel Thorn[e] and Myron Tanner, since the three of them were living together at McDowell's Hill near Salmon Falls that fall. It appears that they were sent to California on a gold mining mission for Apostle George A. Smith, who had the previous year admitted to a touch of gold fever and had requested Mormon gold miners in California to send him some gold to help pay off the personal debts he had incurred in coming to Zion in 1849. Thorne had been his Captain of the

Guard for the trip west. Stoddard, also a member of Smith's company, had been sent ahead on October 27, 1849, with dispatches for Brigham Young. The stories of Stoddard and Thorne subsequent to 1850 are presently unknown, except that at least Thorne was an active member of the Church in 1855.

Tanner's story is much clearer. He later informed his descendants that Brother George A. (Smith) had furnished him with a yoke of oxen and a wagon worth $40 for a trip to California. Upon his arrival in the gold fields, he settled with his traveling companions at McDowell's Hill, a Mormon enclave "about four miles up from Mormon Island." [13] In the two and a half years of mining there, he accumulated $1250 and sent Elder Smith $400. A Seventy, Tanner was a native of New York, having been born in 1826. He was a member of the Mormon Battalion, but dropped out at Santa Fe because of illness and wintered at Pueblo. He came to the Salt Lake Valley with the pioneers in 1847, but returned to Winter Quarters that year, returning to Utah again in Apostle Smith's company of 1849. In 1852 he moved from McDowell's Hill to the Mormon colony at San Bernardino and remained there until 1855. At that time Tanner returned to Utah and settled in Payson. He later moved to Provo where he was a mill owner, eventually becoming the mayor. Tanner also served as a bishop from 1864 to 1891.

On August 4, 1850, Stoddard wrote a letter to his sponsoring Apostle saying that they were all well except for Ashel Thorn, but he was expected to recover soon. They had "commenced ascending the mountains on July 1 camping that night on the summit, with snow from one to six feet deep." They crossed the last ridge on July 4th, "the coldest Independence Day" he had ever seen. They struggled through snow sometimes 15 feet deep and reached McDowell's Hill on July 8th. He said "mining is bad, and we have made but little progress in gold digging as yet; but I hope by the assistance of your prayers, to be able to make a decent outfit." Thorne was not certain that he would "be able to return to the States" that season, but importuned his sponsor to pray for them that they might reach their objective "and leave this country." [14]

If the trio were with the Hanks Company, it must have proceeded again ahead of the Huntington Company (which had caught up to it on June 28th). The Orr Company reached Pleasant Valley ahead of them on the 4th of July, the same day that Stoddard was "crossing the last ridge." Hervey Green and Thomas Blackburn may have been members of the Ephraim Hanks group, proceeding ahead of the main company after reaching Mormon Station in Carson Valley.

The William D. Huntington Company

The last known company of approved Mormon gold miners to leave Utah was led by William D. Huntington. Differing from the gold missions of the preceding fall, this one was public, its leaders called at the April Conference. No evidence has yet been located to indicate whether the "gold diggers" were specifically called to mine gold for Church leaders or other prominent men of the valley, but as others in the companies leaving earlier that spring were so called, it is certainly possible that some of the Huntington Company were also.

On April 7th, the aging Hiram Clark and William D. Huntington were called to lead the company to California and upon arriving to assist Apostles Lyman and Rich. [15] Hiram Clark was a Captain of Ten in the Silas Richards Company of 1849. He was born in 1795 in Vermont and had already served two missions for the Church in Great Britain. William Dresser Huntington was the son of the illustrious William Huntington, a stake president who had died in Iowa in 1846. The son had played a significant role at the death of Joseph Smith, helping to prepare the bodies of the slain prophet and his brother, Hyrum, and secretly burying them. William D. had also entered Utah in 1849 as a Captain of Ten in the Silas Richards Company.

When they left they carried a letter from the First Presidency dated April 23rd, which indicates that the "gold diggers" of the company went with the blessing of the Church leaders. The letter also gave counsel on gathering the Saints, collecting tithing, holding religious services among themselves, Sabbath observance, and prayers which would assist them in the discovery of gold. The letter said that if "they will have the Spirit of God and rejoice therein . . . it will instruct them where to find gold and how to get it." [16] Perhaps this letter induced what appeared to be a change in a policy by Lyman and Rich leading them to hold religious services in the gold fields.

On May 7th, the combined group of Mormon proselyting missionaries [17] (led by Thomas Tomkins), the Mormon "gold diggers," some non-Mormons, and possibly some who were going to California on their own initiative left the old fort, headed north past the Salt Lake, and then west. Captain Huntington was the leader, with Frederick Mills, a non-Mormon, serving as clerk. The "gold diggers," an array of Mormons and non-Mormons, consisted of 39 persons. [18]

Fortunately for this story, there are two proselyting missionary diaries [19] that detail the trip—those of the two sisters, Louisa Barnes Pratt and Caroline Barnes Crosby, the first known LDS female Mormon missionaries. According to Pratt, the journey west was without great consequence or note until the company came to the Salmon Trout or Carson River in Western Deseret (Nevada). On June 19th, she remarked that Bader (a socialist) and Mills (a phrenologist) who were traveling together, had failed to lay in sufficient supplies. While they were not Mormons, "the brethren will not see them want for food." On June 28th, the Huntington party overtook the Ephraim Hanks Company, which had left the Valley about three weeks before the former. Pratt observed that "they have traveled on the Sabbath, we have not, and we have gained on them."

On June 29th, while some of the men "were sent ahead to explore the road over the mountains," the main body camped in the Carson Valley. Crosby prophetically observed it was an ideal location for a Stake of Zion, a place of "gathering." Pratt observed that "emigrants are coming to our camp half starved. Elder (Julian) Moses delivered a lecture on the doctrines of our church, to which the strangers listened with apparent interest." No mention was made of either the Mormon or Edmunds Station.

Upon the return of the men, the company started over the snow-topped mountains. Pratt remarked,

"Oh, the crowds that throng this highway, going in search of gold; crowding about our wagons to be fed. We must feed them either for pay or without. They must have starved to death had we not been here with provisions." On the 8th the company passed Tragedy Spring.

On the 9th, as the Huntington party descended into the valley of the Cosumnes, they ran into a Mormon trading expedition carrying supplies headed for what Caroline Crosby named Salmon Trout Valley (probably for Mormon or Edmunds Station in Carson Valley). With the leading group was Father (Solomon) Chamberlain who reached California about two weeks earlier but was leaving home discouraged. [20]

Chamberlain was one of the earlier converts to the Church, joining about 1830. He had started for Utah with the original pioneers in 1847 but became ill and returned to Winter Quarters. After his wife died over the winter, he made the trip to Utah in 1848. Chamberlain met with little success in supporting himself and family.

By 1850 the lure of the gold mines was too great. Chamberlain went, using the northern route, hoping to be able to make himself and family comfortable. He made his "stand on Weber Creek, making but a dollar a day with meals costing a dollar." Running out of money and nearly out of provisions, he feared that if he stayed any longer he would have to sell his mule. The streams were high and effective digging would be delayed a month or more so, he decided to "ask the Lord what (he) should do." He did so and "the voice of the Lord came unto (him) as plain as though a man spake" telling him to go home and "nothing shall harm [him]." [21]

Telling no one, he took his mule, traded off his chest of clothes and rifle for provisions, and headed home, armed with only his pocket knife. While the Indians were "more trouble-some than ever they were before" he put his "trust in God" and the Priesthood, which carried him home safe. Exaggerating a bit, he says that he came through all alone, except for his mule. He evidently took a little poetic license as he recounted the story years later, since he went at least as far as Carson Valley with the trading company. The fact that he had been in California for two weeks in advance of July 9th would indicate that some party had reached the gold fields about June 26th, possibly the mail train.

The Huntington Company "passed a trading post" consisting of "a table set under a tree with liquors, groceries and provisions of almost all kinds," stopping for lunch on a stream nearby. Proceeding over a very rough, dusty, unstable road, they camped for the night in the woods with "poor feed and little watering." The next day they came upon some houses made of "posts set in the earth and covered with cloth" looking "very comfortable for summer." [22]

On the 12th they came down into Pleasant Valley, meeting "lots of traders going up into the mountains to speculate off the immigrants." Caroline Crosby described the valley as "in reality a pleasant place, such beautiful groves and splendid shade trees" she had scarcely seen before. There were three or four trading posts, one of which belonged to Mr. (L. C.) Bidamon from Nauvoo, who lived in "quite an extensive house." William Steed of Keokuk, Iowa and others were living with him.

Bidamon had married Emma Smith, the beloved widow of the martyred Mormon Prophet Joseph Smith. On April 20, 1850, he wrote [23] to Emma Smith from the Dry Creek Mines in the gold fields. He said that he had come to California overland in 1849, reaching Goose Creek near the City of Rocks about August 16, 1849. He there addressed an earlier letter which was posted from "Salt Lake, California." In his second letter he informed his wife that the tent in which he had spent the winter was about 100 miles southeast of Sacramento. He said that gold was not as plentiful as thought in the States. "It is obtained," he said, "by the hardest of labour, harder than my constitution is able to bear. The acquisition of gold in the mines is something like a lottery, there is sometimes large amounts obtained in a short time with but little labor, but these are few occurrences and far between."

Bidamon and a companion-brother, John, had mined not more than $15 to $30 in a day, with many days securing no gold at all. His diet was poor—sour flour bread and pickled meat (pork, venison, or beef) with no fat and seldom any vegetables. The result was a considerable lowering of his vitality. He gave the price of supplies, with eggs selling at $6 to $12 per dozen. He informed Emma that he had received but one letter from her via Babit (possibly Almon Babbit, a Mormon sent to Washington in 1849 to seek statehood for Deseret).

Bidamon also informed his wife that there were good prospects 25 miles further into the mountains where they would go once the snow was gone. If unsuccessful, the plans were to go to the City (Sacramento) and get into some speculation activity. To that point in time, he and John had accumulated about eight pounds of gold. At $16 an ounce, it would be valued at about $2,048. Nathan King, from Nauvoo, was also in the same camp and would be in the Mormon enclave at Greenwood that fall. Bidamon either prospered very quickly or he was a great exaggerator, since he was in Sacramento on October 5, 1850 where he was the proprietor of an eating house and claiming property worth $200,000. Living with L. C. Bidamon, and in business with him, was J. C. Bidamon (probably his brother John) who claimed $4,000 in property. [24] Bidamon treated the missionaries in a "very friendly and sociable" way, accompanying them back to their camp that night, staying for prayers, and joining them in their singing. He was "delighted with some of (their) hymns." Father (Samuel) Burton and his wife (Hannah S.), who had come to California with Hanks, were cooking for Bidamon, who paid them a share of his profits.

Planning to stay over the weekend, the missionaries accepted an invitation from an "old gentleman" to come to tea on Saturday. They returned at that time and were "entertained in a very good style for this wilderness country" at a long bower covered table filled with biscuits, butter, cheese, sweet cakes and pies "made of sugar pears," as well as "dried beef and good tea" and "plenty of good brandy for those who chose to partake of it."

On Sunday the company "had singing and prayers after breakfast," but, "the brethren concluded best to discontinue our meeting as Brothers Rich and Lyman we understand hold none here."

On Monday the 15th, they pursued their journey, passing through Weaverville and reaching Mud Springs where Brothers (Sherman) Gilbert and (Henry H.) Harrison and their families concluded to stay. Harrison, with a large family of little children, lost his only milch cow, a severe blow as he had depended on it for "nearly half (his) living." The Gilberts soon moved on to Sacramento and the Harrisons were found at nearby Ringold at census time.

Leaving the Springs the next morning, they passed "several comfortable looking houses" and arrived at Brown's Settlement on Deer Creek in mid-afternoon. During the day they met up with Father (Hiram) Clark and (William) Huntington who left them a week before to reach Lathrop's Tavern, where they hoped to find Elders Lyman and Rich.

The Huntington Company camped in an oak grove near Brown's, "a fictitious name for Porter Rockwell." Finding a "spring of clear, cold water," they decided to wait there until the Apostles arrived to give them instructions. On the 17th, Tomkins and Bushby left for Sacramento to locate a place to camp while making preparations for their trip to the Islands.

The Apostles arrived late in the day, bringing a letter to Louisa Pratt from her missionary husband that had been posted the day he had sailed. The missionaries were counseled to go directly to San Francisco where they would be received kindly by the Saints. That night the Apostles preached. It was "comforting to see and hear Apostles so far from home."

The missionaries were visited at Brown's by several old friends. Brown (Rockwell) and the Stewards (Stewarts) treated the missionaries well, presenting them with several gifts. They made their money "selling liquor and provisions to emigrants." On Friday evening the Apostles joined the missionaries in their evening devotions, telling them of "their travels in California." They were warned of the "great wickedness and corruption of the people," which increased the

missionaries' "anxiety to pursue (their) journey as soon as possible." Pratt observed: "Men are reckless in this country. There is a great want of woman's influence: filth and confusion throughout the whole country." [25]

Deciding to stay at Brown's over the weekend, on Saturday morning Caroline and Louisa, accompanied by Iris Chase (possibly the wife of Darwin Chase, who ran a hotel in Mud Springs), walked into the tiny settlement to trade and inspect. They were well received by Sisters Edmunds and Jacobs, two sisters of Henry Jacobs.[26] Caroline and Louisa spent the day sewing for the sisters and being liberally rewarded with supper and money.

Tomkins returned from Sacramento having sold his oxen and wagons for $1,075. On Sunday, the Apostles instructed the missionaries and "counseled those who expected to stay in California to disdain from the vices of the country, viz, gambling, drunken[n]ess, and every other that can be named."

On Monday they proceeded to White Rock in Sacramento County, about nine miles west of Brown's, where Henry Jacobs "had previously kept a public house." They did not linger but pressed on an additional days journey to another "Brown's" establishment, located between White Rock and the American River. Caroline's husband was not so fortunate in the sale of his wagon and oxen as Tomkins, selling it to Brown (Rockwell) for only $225. Tomkins received $100 down and the remainder when Brown took the teams.

They reached the American Fork on the 23rd, watering their teams at Ten Mile House. This popular inn was run by (J.) Lewis and (A.D. and Wm.) Patterson. Mrs. Lewis, a Mormon and former resident of Nauvoo, came out and spoke to them. She told them that if she lived, she hoped to go to Salt Lake. They then proceeded to the Roots' at Six Mile House, where they camped. The following day Tomkins went into Sacramento to engage passage and the sisters stayed behind to wash and bake, being visited for supper by Apostles Lyman and Rich who were staying at Roots'.

On the 24th, Louisa recalled the "great celebration in Salt Lake Valley" the previous year, hoping they would be remembered with "a toast." She reported that "the brethren who went back to the mountains after ice and snow for Stewart's market" returned, but that the price had fallen "from one dollar to five cents per pound. [27]

On the 25th "the mules were missing." Tied up close to camp through the night, they had been loosened in the morning and were missing in 15 minutes. The missionaries searched for them as far back as Brown's, but all they heard of them was that two men had been seen "riding bareback towards the mines."

The Crosbys left their oxen and wagons at the Roots'. Putting their things in Tomkins' wagon along with Louisa's, They drove to Sacramento, observing "some very pretty houses on the way." Carolyn described the Five Mile House, which they passed, as "a splendid building." A short distance below it they halted and there met several ladies from Missouri. [28]

They reached Sacramento finding an "irregularly built dirty place full of dead creatures' bones and all manner of uncleanness." They stopped in the shade of a tree while the men went to secure passage to San Francisco. Caroline's husband borrowed a tent from Levi Dority (Dougherty), [29] a Mormon who traveled to Utah with the Crosbys. They camped there for two days awaiting passage. Shortly before, the Doritys (Doughertys) had reached California and were living in a new unfinished house. They were the proud owners of five cows from which they were selling $8 to $10 worth of milk a day.

The missionary camp was visited by a number of young men from the east coast who brought them a "dozen bottles of wine and beer with as many mince and apple pies and made (them) a present of them." The gifts were well received as the "day was very warm and (they) were fatigued." They were also visited by Mr. Hughs (the husband of a Mormon acquaintance, Mary Parker), who had just landed in California and was homesick. He had been living in cholera ridden St. Louis. He sent his wife to live in Nauvoo, hoping she could avoid the disease while he went to "California to make his fortune."

On the 26th, their wagons were unloaded and taken away by the purchasers. Louisa's "faithful old carriage" was sold for only $30. It had been the sleeping quarters for her children for four years, had taken her 2,000 miles and "was the last piece of property that remained of all the labors of (her) youth, and that of (her) husband."

The missionaries, preparing to embark on the bark *Alden*, were visited by some of their "gold digger" companions of the trip west. All were saddened by the dirty appearance of the ship. They boarded the bark looking forward to a good night's rest, but found their quarters filled with ravenous mosquitoes. They fled to the decks, but in vain. There was no escape. Louisa wrapped herself in a thick blanket but the insects were unhindered. Her ankles and feet becoming swollen and inflamed. To find relief she wrapped them in vinegar soaked bandages. To make matters worse, the sailing vessel, could not leave the harbor because of contrary winds. The captain sent to town several times for a steamer to tow his vessel out, but to no avail.

Finally Tomkins went to see what he could do. Soon a steamer appeared with instructions to take 20 passengers. When the steamer's captain was asked where Tomkins was, he replied that Tomkins had been left by mistake. The missionaries, anxious to be rid of the mosquitoes, assumed that they were the ones to board the steamer and transferred their goods, all except Jonathan Crosby who thought it to be a deception.

Free of their tormenters, the missionaries went to their staterooms but found they had "only made an exchange in the nature of (their) foes." Their new enemies were bed bugs. Fortunately, they were in San Francisco in a few hours. Four days later Tomkins arrived in a foul mood because they had left the bark. He had shown up with a steamer to take it into the bay where it could proceed on its own and found his companions gone.

True to the promise made earlier, the San Francisco Saints received them warmly, especially Sam Brannan's mother-in-law, Fanny Corwin. Sister Corwin lived with her daughter in "a king's palace." Brother John Lewis carried them in his carriage to his home at Mission Dolores where they were entertained by the Saints for two weeks. "A better class of citizens never lived in San Francisco; a city for money and business."

While many ships lay in the harbor, their crews had deserted them for the mines. "They looked like a funeral procession." The city was busy rebuilding after the fire of a few months earlier. It took the bark, which the missionaries had left, 14 days to arrive, it having "baffled about" in the Bay trying to reach San Francisco. They felt fortunate, but Brother Tomkins, (whose wife had stood the expense of the transfer) felt that "his expenses had been too great." Letting the others know of his displeasure added another sour note to their journey.

Several of the Society Island bound missionaries did not go to San Francisco in July. Among these was Simeon A. Dunn, who remained in the gold fields until the end of August or the first of September, probably attempting to raise money for his passage. He arrived in San Francisco on September 5th. In a letter to Brigham Young of that date, he informed the Church President that the journey had been prosperous and that peace, harmony, and goodwill prevailed in the company all the way. Only Julian Moses experienced any sickness (mountain fever). He reported that one of the company, Uriah B. Powell, a Seventy, had come up missing and "whose whereabouts was not then known." [30] Rich reported that Powell paid tithing on September 25th in Greenwood Valley, after the missionaries set sail. [31] He evidently remained in the gold fields, at least until 1854.

Sidney Alvarus Hanks also remained in the gold fields for awhile, probably visiting his prospering relative, Ebenezer Hanks, at Salmon Falls. He, like Dunn, eventually found his way to San Francisco and went on to serve a mission. Josiah Bushby may not have gone to the Islands, for he returned to Utah in September of 1851, with "a number of brethren arrived from California." [32]

On July 23rd, Father Hiram Clark, co-leader of the Huntington Company, had written Brigham Young to advise him of their safe arrival. He informed the Prophet that Apostles Rich and Ly-man were "making arrangements to forward the mission to the Islands and had counseled some of those remaining to put up a temporary boarding-house near Sacramento." He reported that most of the Saints "were in the mines, but not doing much and a very poor prospect of doing better." He maintained that "many of the boys here would give their old shoes to be back" with the body of the Saints and that many would be better off if they went back "to learn Mormonism from its beginning again." Nevertheless he said that, "there are many as good Saints here as we found anywhere, most of whom belong to the class who came out with Brothers Rich, Egan, Huffaker and Mr. Pomeroy's trains." Clark went on to support Brigham Young's prediction that the Saints who remained in Utah would be better off than those who went off to the mines. [33] All of this was before Clark caught gold fever himself, going off with his sons to mine for a while on the Bear River.

The other members of the Huntington Party who were not bound for the Society Islands spread themselves over the gold fields. [34] Except for the proselyting missionaries, very few of the Huntington Party have been identified with the subsequent history of the Church. [35]

The Demont Company

Another company leaving Salt Lake that spring was led by the gentile, Joseph DeMont (Dumont) and Hampton S. Beatie, whose stories are told later. It was members of this company, including Abner Blackburn and Beatie, who are credited with establishing the first white settlement in Nevada. The Mormons who went with this company by and large may have gone without the blessings of their religious leaders—if Blackburn's story presented later is given full credit.

Thus, the last known organized and authorized Mormon trains going west were in the spring of 1850. They consisted of mail carriers, settlers, gold diggers (Mormon and non-Mormon), and proselyting missionaries bound for the Society Islands. Many of the settlers and gold diggers eventually became lost to the Church. The missionaries as well as mail carriers for the most part remained faithful to the kingdom. The missionaries were aided by California gold (directly or indirectly) in reaching their fields of labor (as was true of the missionaries going to the Sandwich Islands that fall). Some of this group became involved in mining. Others were aided by Mormon miners, and still others made money from economic activities made profitable by gold miners.

NOTES

1. Journal History, April 12, 1850.

2. Journal History, April 3, 1850.

3. Rich, Papers, June 22 and July 1, 1850.

4. Caroline Barnes Crosby, Diary. The Diary is found in: Lyman, Payne, and Ellsworth, eds. *No Place to Call Home.* Chamberlain will be discussed in greater detail later.

5. The account of the Orrs is taken largely from Yohalem, *"I Remember . . ."* 127-133.

6. This included his wife, Catherine, his sons, John (25), James (22), and Thomas Jr. (10), along with two daughters, Isabella (17), and Mary Ann (13).

7. Yohalem, *"I Remember . . ."* 133.

8. Orr, Thomas J., Jr., *Life History*, 20-21. Orr's account is extensively quoted and briefly discussed in Owens (*Gold Rush Saints*, 292-297) and Bagley (*Frontiersman*, 160-161).

9, Probably Bernard and Daniel McKenzie. The former is credited as one of the original discoverers of gold at Placerville. The latter lived on the South Fork of the American River in 1850.

10. This may have been Daniel McFarland who resided nearby on the South Fork.

11. The Hezekiah Thatcher family also ran a hotel in or near Salmon Falls probably in connection with Hervey Green and his son, Henry Green. The Orr homestead itself, was a mile or so above Salmon Falls on the hill road to Mormon Island. It became identified as Mormon Hill, a small community of Mormons being established there. It is also identified as "Orr's" on some maps. Henry Larkin, may have been a kinsman of Thomas Larkin, one of California's early American political leaders.

12. A William Taylor was the Captain of the Fourth Ten in the Edward Hunter Company of 1847, Orr being the Captain of the Fifth Ten. It is not known if the two Taylors were the same person.

13. Tanner, Biography, 15-16.

14. Journal History, August 4, 1850.

15. Journal History, April 7, 1850.

16. Letter of the First Presidency, April 23, 1850.

17. The original group included Joseph Bushby, Simeon A. Dunn, (Sydney) Alvarus Hanks, Julian Moses, George Pitkin, Uriah B. Powell, and Thomas Tomkins. By the time the group left, Pitkin had evidently dropped out. However, to the Society Island missionaries had been added one Jane Tomkins, Jonathan and Caroline Barnes Crosby, and Caroline's sister, Louisa Barnes Pratt and her three children. Louisa was the stalwart wife of the veteran Society Islands missionary, Addison Pratt. Thomas Tomkins appears to have been the leader of the missionary subgroup.

18. See Appendix 18a.

19. Louisa Barnes Pratt's diary is published as: Ellsworth, ed. *The History of Louisa Barnes Pratt.*

20. The group included Albiston Tyler (probably Allen Benedict Tyler who came to Utah in 1848), Judson and Ervin Stoddard (Judson being one of Rockwell's partners), and William Bears (Beers) of the Battalion and others.

21. Porter, "A Study of the Origins of the Church," 360-364. (Word in brackets is the author's.)

22. The following diary quotes are from Crosby, *No Place to Call Home,* unless otherwise noted.

23. Bidamon Papers.

24. Living with Bidamon, with age and state of origin indicated, were Samuel Brown (20 In), Louisa Smith (38 NY), Louisa Smith (2 Ca), and Andrew P. Mallery (26 NY), California Census, 1850.

25. Pratt, *History of Louisa Barnes Pratt*, 1998. The Stewart referred to was possibly Boyd Stewart, a reported member of the Flake Company, who is reported by others to have been a business associate of Rockwell. As he was in the Huntington Company leaving Salt Lake, he may have been on a visit to Utah.

26. These two sisters have not been positively identified. Jefferson Edmunds, one of Porter Rockwell's partners, was operating a tavern in the Deer Creek House area as late as 1853 when he was visited by Sandwich Island-bound missionaries. He gave them money for their mission. No Jacobs women were in the 1850 census of the area.

27. This could have been the store run by Boyd Stewart.

28. Meg (Isabell) White who lived there with her husband, (William T.) and their daughter, one year old Kate, born in Missouri.

29. This was probably the Levi Dority (Dougherty) with whom Rich and Lyman stayed on July 25. He returned to Utah in 1857. While Crosby said that the Doughertys originally came to Utah with them, they are not so recorded by Carter.

30. Dunn, Letter to Brigham Young, September 5, 1850.

31. Rich, Papers.

32. Journal History, September 12, 1851.

33. Journal History, May 7, 1850.

34. See Appendix 18b.

35. See Appendix 18c.

APPENDIX 18a (Note 18:18)
Gold Diggers of the Huntington Company – 1850

Albion, Moreland
Arnold, Josiah and Elizabeth
Bader, John B.
Carter, John and Mary
Clark, George S.
Clark, Samuel G.
Clawson, George
Clawson, William and Mary
Gay, H. (Hail) K.
Gheen, John
Gilbert, Sherman (A) & Elysabeth
Goodwin, Lewis
Hall, Samuel and Semanthy
Harrison, Henry H., Lydia & Elizabeth
Hewlitt, Sylvester
Huntington, William D. and Harriet
Kimball, Charles
Leonard, Moses C.
Lewis, William C. (Crawford)
McCoy, Daniel
McCrow, George
Mills, Frederick
Pendleton, Andrew
Stewart, Robert Boyd
Tarley, Joel
Thurston, Moses
Tubbs, Amos
Wheeler, Ammon G.
Willard, David
Williams, Norman S.
Woynarski, Thomas

APPENDIX 18b (Note 18:34)
California Locations of Huntington Company Gold Diggers -- 1850

Note: age and place of origin given in the parentheses.

1. Moseland (Moreland) Albon (Albion) (33 Oh), was located in Placerville in El Dorado County.

2. Josiah Arnold, and his wife Elizabeth (50 Ct), along with Orson (12 NY), and Joseph (10 NY), were in Placerville in El Dorado County.

3. While there was no John Bader, there was a John Bondine (20 Md) at Georgetown in El Dorado County.

4. There were two John Carters: (40 Great Britain), in Ringold, and another (25, Oh), in Placerville, both in El Dorado County.

5. There were three George Clarks in El Dorado County:(18, Cn), Mathinias Creek; (18, NY), Dutch Creek; and (30, Oh), Georgetown.

6. There were two Samuel Clarks in El Dorado: (25, Ma) and (21, Mo) as well as one in Sutter County, (29, NY), and one in Sacramento County, (20, In).

7. George Clawson, (19, Mo), was located in El Dorado County, at Lathrop's Mormon Tavern.

8. Jno W. Ghee (Gheen?), (Va), was located in Sacramento that fall.

9. Sherman A. Gilbert (41, GB), with Elizabeth, (28, I1), and Sherma (9, NY) were in Sacramento with a James Gilbert, (23, In) nearby

10. A Lewis H. Goodwin, (32, I1), was on the Cosumnes River with a George Goodwin, (30, In).

11. Samuel Hall, (38, GB), with Simanthy, (29, Oh), and Thomas, (30, Ky), were near Mormon Island in Sacramento County with George M. Hall, (20, Ky), nearby.

12. Henry A. or H. Harrison, (49, Va), was at Ringold with Lydia, (33, In), William H., (14, Ia); Elizabeth 13, Il); Sara J. (12, Ia); Mary C., (9, Ia); Francis C., (7, I1); Lucinda, (4, Ia); Mary A., 2; and Rachel S., (8 mos, Ca).

13. Henry Hewitt was found in Yuba county in 1850.

14. William Huntington, (34, NY), was located at Louisville in El Dorado County but Harriet was not listed with him.

15. There was a Charles Leonard (possibly Moses C. Leonard), (44 NY), at Placerville.

16. There were several William Lewises scattered throughout the gold fields.

17. George McCrown, who could have been George McCrow, (28, Ma), was in Sutter County at Rattlesnake Bar.

18. Frederick Mills, (32, GB), was near Sacramento City.

19. Andrew Pendleton, (28, NC), evidently went south to Mariposa County (85) being there with John Pendleton, (28, NC).

20. There were several Robert Stewarts in Calaveras, El Dorado, and Mariposa counties: 23, in Calaveras County; (26, Oh), in Pilot Hill in El Dorado county; and (21, Mo), in Mariposa County.

21. A. Tubs (probably Amos Tubs), (58, Ct), was associated with George Clawson at Mormon Tavern. In addition, there was a Tubs family nearby at Mormon Island: W. R., (25, Oh); Sarah, (21, NY); Henry,(2, Ca).   W. R. Tubs may have been William Tubs of the Mormon Battalion.

22. A. Wheeler (possibly Ammon G. Wheeler), (42, NY), was at Nicolaus in Sutter County, with Barabara, (27, NY); and Mary, (7, NY).

23. N. L. Williams (possibly Norman S. Williams), (26, Ma), lived in Stockton in San Jose County.

NOTE: Those Gold Diggers not identified above were not listed in the 1850 Census.

APPENDIX 18c (Note 18:35)
Later Identification of Members of
Huntington Company of 1850
With Mormon History

Josiah Arnold became a member of the Green River Expedition in December of 1853 as did George Clawson and Andrew Pendleton. Arnold was still there in June of 1854. Pendleton was sent on a mission to Carson Valley in 1856. Clawson was an active Utah Mormon in 1855 and 1859, as was Pendleton. John Gheen, who had earlier been involved in a homicide, had his life subsequently taken.

William Huntington was living in Springville, Utah in 1853, where he died in 1887. He arrived in Utah from California in 1851 with a Brother Pickett, possibly William A. Pickett. He was an active Utah Mormon in 1855 and 1859.

Moses C. Leonard was killed on his way to Utah in 1851. He was possibly traveling to Utah in connection with Huntington who returned that year.

Moses Thurston was called on a mission to England in 1852, going with several others who had been gold miners: William Glover, Thomas W. Treat, Darwin Richardson and Ephraim Green.

Thurston was released in 1854. He was an active Mormon in 1859.

Norman S. Williams either was still in California or there again in 1856.

Of the Society Islands missionaries, the subsequent association of the following is known:

Bushby returned to Utah in 1851. In 1853 he was operating a ferry for California emigrants at Haws Ford and was an active Mormon in 1859.

Louisa Barnes Pratt returned to Utah with her husband and remained faithful. Her missionary husband moved back to California to live near his daughter.

Jonathan and Caroline Crosby were active Mormons in 1859.

Julian Moses was an active Mormon in 1855.

Simeon A. Dunn was an active Utah Mormon in 1855.

Only Esshom, Jensen, the Journal History, and Church records for 1855 and 1859 were used to trace these individuals.

Great Salt Lake City in 1853, looking South

From the book *Route From Liverpool to the Great Salt Lake Valley*, illustrated with steel engravings and wood cuts from sketches made by Frederick Piercy. Narrated by Piercy and edited by James Linforth. Liverpool: Franklin D. Richards, 1855; 108-110. *Courtesy Utah State Historical Society.*

Piercy writes: "By the time we entered Great Salt Lake City darkness had enveloped it, shutting out from my straining and inquiring eyes all details. I could see that the streets were broad, and hear the refreshing sound of water rippling and gushing by the road side. Occasionally a tall house would loom up through the gloom and every now and then the cheerful lights came twinkling through the cottage windows — slight things to write about, yet noticed with pleasure by one fresh from the Plains. A happy meeting with relatives, and a few moments of wakefulness ended [the day] and also ends my hastily sketched and simple narrative."

Joy and nostalgia must have been deeply felt by those coming from the East over the Plains, reaching their destination, and being with friends, family, and co-religionists. This elation and relief could easily be matched by those coming from the West, meeting family and friends after surmounting the daunting Sierra, skirting past the edges of the Carson and Humboldt Sinks, and crossing the desolate expanse of the western territory. In addition, many of those coming from the West had often preceded this final leg of the journey with another, an incredible march to open a road through the parched southwest with the Mormon Battalion or with one of the longest point-to-point pilgrimages by sea in the voyage of the *Brooklyn*. The travelers must have been impressed with the final grand scene of the Great Salt Lake Valley nestling the modest but tidy fledgling community. However, after so many dangerous miles, so many obstacles, and so many intervening momentous experiences, the reunion with friends and family must have been most sweet.

He brought them forth also with silver and gold.

Bible. Psalms 105:37

19

Home to Zion

WHILE THE MORMON Argonaut companies of 1850 were heading westward, Elders Lyman and Rich were preparing to go home to Zion. On Thursday, July 11, 1850, while still in San Francisco, they began preparations for their trip and on the 15th took passage for Sacramento on board the steamer *Hartford.* They took with them $1,007, which they had collected between July 4th and July 15th from the Saints, most of whom lived on the peninsula. [1]

On July 15th, Apostle Rich continued the account of his gold-field odyssey. On that day, he and Apostle Lyman reached Sacramento, meeting with Brothers (Jesse D.) Hunter and (Anthony) Blackburn. Hunter and Blackburn were ready to go to "Lower California" where others would join them to prepare the way for a Mormon settlement the following year. [2] The Apostles spent the night with the Hunters and while there received $422 in tithes ranging from $5 to $100 from ten men. [3]

On the following day the two Apostles met "Brother Hiram Clark from Salt Lake with the mail." Learning of the arrival of Huntington's wagon train, they left to meet them, traveling as far as Henry Jacobs' place at White Rock, lodg-

ing there. The next day they went on to (Jefferson) Edmunds' at Brown's Settlement at Deer Creek where they "met the company of Saints on their way to the Society Islands," finding them in "good health and spirits." [4]

They spent the three days writing letters to the First Presidency and to their own families, counseling the missionaries, and holding a meeting in camp on Sunday the 21st. The letter they had received from the First Presidency, instructed them to be attentive to the spiritual needs of the Saints, which provoked them to change their policy against holding Church meetings in the region of the mines.

Apostle Lyman felt that the tithing they had received thus far was inadequate, especially having come from the wealthy brethren who had "paid little or none." He was also convinced that the only location suitable for a permanent settlement on the coast was in Southern California. [5] He had already become committed to the Southland, having sent one group of Saints to San Diego and another to the Williams Ranch in Los Angeles County.

On Monday they finished with their correspondence home and sent the mail off with Barnard and Foote, [6] lodging that night at Lathrop's Mormon Tavern on their return to Sacramento. They detoured south going to "Brother John Roads (Rhoades) on the (Cosumnes)" but failed to find him home. Notwithstanding, they spent the night there before traveling on. [7]

On July 24th, the 3rd anniversary of the arrival of the Saints in Salt Lake Valley, the Apostles traveled north to the American River, reaching the Root's at Six Mile House (Brighton), meeting with the Society Island missionaries, and staying overnight. They made no mention of the anniversary in their journals. The following day they were forced to go "on foot 6 miles to Sacramento to finish matters with the Society Island missionaries," Elder (Sidney) Alvarus Hanks, one of the Society Island missionaries, having lost their mules (a not uncommon occurrence it would appear). They stayed the night with Brother Levi (Dougherty) and his family.

Finishing their "business with the missionaries," they returned to the Roots', staying the night, moving on to Lathrop's the following day. On their way they came across their mules "tied up by Mr. Boles, who found them fast in the brush by their halters." On Sunday they left the Tavern headed for the Middle Fork of the American River, stopping for dinner with Brother (A. C.) Brower, who maintained a hotel at Salmon Falls. While there they met with the (Samuel) McMurtrey family on their way to the Society Islands. After dinner they crossed the South Fork, reaching Pilot Hill where they stayed with Brother (William) Leffingwell. The next day they reached (Murderer's) Bar (near which Rockwell maintained a tavern) located on the Middle Fork, and went on to "Brother (David) Seeley's camp where they visited Brother Hazen Kimball who was ill." [8]

On the 30th they returned to the Middle Fork, going to (George) Boyd's camp, staying the night with Joseph Cain. They stayed a couple of days, counseling with the brethren in the evening after their day's work was done. There were reportedly between 100 and 200 Mormons working in the area, some of them being found experimenting with a "submarine press" in the river. [9]

Leaving the river, the Apostles "climbed the steepest mountain" that at least Elder Rich had ever experienced. Returning to Greenwood, Elder Lyman remained while Elder Rich went on to Salmon Falls where he stayed, once again, with the Browers. Lyman dined with Brother (Benjamin) Crow who lived at Louisville (adjacent to Greenwood), traveling on to Coloma where he lodged. [10] His business at Coloma is unrevealed, but that is where Peter Wimmer and his wife, Elizabeth, lived.

The Apostles rejoined each other at Lathrop's meeting with Brothers (James H.) Rollins (Rawlins) and Clark from Carson Valley on the other side of the mountains. [11] The following day they headed for Sacramento, to buy "stores for the journey home." Making some purchases on Sunday, they left for a return to Lathrop's, stopping overnight at the Root's. They spent the next few days packing, each of the Apostles returning to Sacramento for additional supplies.

They remained at the Tavern, receiving tithing and preparing for the trip over the mountains until August 16th. Lyman, however, left for the North Fork of the American River with Brother (Hiram) Clark whose sons were working mining claims near there, stopping at Mr. (Moses) Martin's near Murderer's Bar. They may have gone there to inform him of his excommunication, announced at the previous April Conference in Salt Lake. While Martin maintained a residence at Pilot Hill, he evidently also had a mining claim down on the Middle Fork. [12]

From Martin's camp they went to "Brother Hamond's" (James Harmon's) lodging at Brother (William L.) McIntires in Long Valley (or Mormon Ravine) near Auburn. On the 23rd, Lyman reported collecting $201 in tithing from seven men. [13] It is not certain just where these men were living at the time. Bigler could have been at Slap Jack Bar up the Middle Fork. Hickerson and Woolsey were living together at Louisville in January of 1851, classified by the census taker as gardeners. Robinson lived next door to them. It is possible, therefore, that Lyman collected tithing at Long Valley, Slap Jack Bar, and Louisville.

Apostle Lyman's account stops abruptly at that

point, not picking up again until October 1st, after he had arrived home in Salt Lake. However, there was a record made of tithes totaling $312, collected on the 13th. [14]

Rich continued his diary saying that his party left Lathrop's for Salt Lake on August 17th, staying that night at Mud Springs, about 16 miles east of the Tavern. Several Mormon families lived there at the time of the 1850 census, including Thomas Blackburn (Abner Blackburn's brother) and his wife who ran a hotel, along with Darwin Chase of the Mormon Battalion, and Calvin Saltar who also maintained a hotel.

They reached Pleasant Valley, the staging area for the Battalion Boys' journey over the mountains in 1848, on the 18th. The Apostles separated at that time, Rich taking the money and traveling with packs ahead of the slower moving wagons led by Lyman. Rich crossed the summit on the 20th, camping in Lake Valley, going a "half mile on snow." [15] He reached Carson Valley camping at Edmunds Station on the 25th.

On August 28th Lyman came up with the wagons. The following day he proceeded on to Salt Lake with about 34 men while Rich returned to California having received some letters, presumably from Salt Lake, via William O. Clark, instructing him to return to California to conduct some Church business.

One member of Lyman's company, Joseph Cain, wrote a letter for the *Deseret News* describing this return trip. He wrote that for the first 15 days they met on the average a thousand emigrants headed for California, and "most of them were in a state of starvation." The Lyman company found the feed for their animals "good, in consequence of the overflowing rivers in the early part of the season." However, as a consequence the river bottoms were "miry." [16]

"On the desert . . . between Salmon Trout or Carson River, and the sink of the Marys (Humboldt) River", he continued, they "found an awful destruction of property. Wagons, carriages, harnesses, etc. were strewed from one end of the desert to the other . . . the dead animals were so numerous that the stench was almost intolerable."

One of the company "counted fourteen hundred head by the roadside." Upon reaching the sink, "Brothers John Gould and Kenyon (Farnum Kinion) were attacked with Cholera and died." [16]

Lyman and his company reached Salt Lake on September 29th, the Apostle bringing with him "a most unfavourable account from the gold region." He anticipated that things would only get worse, the country "swamped in blood" and "depopulated by ravages of cholera." He announced that Brother Rich would leave California with "most of the brethren" about October 1st. He observed that "Gold is not the god of the Saints." Rather they "seek to build up the Kingdom of God by industry, by building cities." [16a]

Having heard rumors of gold mines in Salt Lake Valley and a consequent "overplus of metal imported from California," Lyman stated that the rumors were "entirely unfounded." He continued, "A coal mine would be a welcome sight to us, but a gold mine we neither have found nor seek to find." It would appear that he was attempting, along with the other leaders of the Church, to downplay the importance of gold in the minds of the body of the Saints. [16a]

This report by Lyman is an interesting comment on the policy on gold being developed at that time. The acquisition of gold had certainly assumed a position of prominence for the past two years. It would be less important after this season. The comment raised the possibility that the gold of Bingham Canyon (near Salt Lake) had been discovered by that date, possibly by Thomas Bingham who is usually credited with the find by Utah folklore. Other Binghams, Erastus and Willard, were in California at the time of the 1850 census, both being located at Pilot Hill that fall. [17]

Unfortunately, a record was not kept as punctiliously for the companies of Mormons coming from California as for those arriving from the East and there is no certainty of who was included in the Lyman Company. However, entries in the Gold Accounts between September 29th (when Lyman reached Utah) and November 11th (when Charles C. Rich reached the growing Mormon town) give some indication of who may have been involved. The complications arise in that some of the en-

On the Trail Back to Zion

Twin Sisters, at the City of Rocks, near the southern border of Idaho, where the Salt Lake Cutoff meets the California Trail.

Wagon trains going east from California, in the region of the Twin Sisters would veer to the right and take the Salt Lake Cutoff south to Salt Lake City.

The Cutoff was first used by Saints returning to Zion by the Holmes-Thompson party in 1848, just after the Cutoff was established by the Hensley party going west out of Salt Lake. (See chapter 4.) *Courtesy Utah State Historical Society.*

tries were possibly for women who were either the widows of men who had died in California, the wives of men who had remained behind, the wives of men who returned with Lyman, or other women who were with Lyman in his return home. Other entries are those of Church leaders and prominent men who had sponsored gold missionaries the preceding winter. In addition to those listed, there were probably some who did not deposit their gold at all and others who may have deposited it later. [18]

In the meantime, Rich returned to Sacramento Valley in company with (William) Peacock and others by much the same route as he had just traveled—Pleasant Valley, Brown's Settlement, and Salmon Falls, where he stayed with Brother (Boyd) Stewart on September 5th. [19] Rich received tithing from Alanson Colby. His company proceeded to Lathrop's and Sacramento, catching the steamer *Senator,* and landed in San Francisco on September 7th. He conducted business, visiting the Saints in both San Francisco and San Jose (Mission San Jose area), and was present on September 17th when four blocks in the heart of San Francisco were destroyed by fire. While there he collected tithing from Zacheus Cheney and Quartus Sparks.

Rich returned on September 19th to Sacramento where he paid a Church obligation of $1,000 and conducted other Church business. On Sunday, September 22nd, he "traveled by stage 35 miles to the Mountaineer House," thence to Lathrop's, collecting tithing en route from James Emmett."[20]

Rich then proceeded to Murderer's Bar, collecting tithing on the way. [21] On the 24th he went to Greenwood, and then to Slap Jack Bar where he "met with the boys." After counseling with them a number were "appointed to go on missions" to the Sandwich Islands and Oregon. After laying his hands on them and blessing them, he traveled to (William) Leffingwell's at Pilot Hill where he stayed the night. Before leaving Slap Jack Bar, he collected $248 in tithing from all but two of them.

On Thursday the 26th, the Apostle went to Lathrop's, "calling at different places on the road" and collecting $150 in tithing from John Higby (Higbee) and Rufus Beach (Beech). From there he proceeded to Sacramento to purchase his "fitout for home," conducting other undisclosed business while in the growing commercial center, and collecting tithing from Marcus B. Thorpe, some of it for the previous year.

On Sunday, Rich set Hiram Clark and Hiram H. Blackwell apart for missions to the Sandwich Islands, "Clark to be president." Evidently Blackwell had overcome his Word of Wisdom problem which had kept him from going to the Society Islands with Elder Addison Pratt. Rich went by way of (John) Roads (Rhoades) on the (Cosumnes) River. The following day found him at Lathrop's, where he "arranged for getting started" for the Valley again.

However, more business detained him. On the 2nd he "met Mr. Eskell with two drafts" which he paid, then proceeded to Salmon Falls where he stayed with (Ebenezer) Hanks, and collected $150 in tithing from Francis M. Pomeroy and William Peacock. According to Rich, the following day he went to the South (actually the North) Fork of the American River visiting (William L.) McIntire, (James) Harmon, and (George W.) Rosecrans, staying at (Benjamin F.) Matthews, and collecting $150.00 in tithing from Matthews and Harmon.

He returned to Lathrop's by way of Salmon Falls where he received $50 in tithing from Ebenezer Hanks and Hervey Green, partners in a 'hotel in that Mormon enclave. At Lathrop's he made final preparations for going home, leaving the Mormon Tavern on Saturday, October 5th, with six brethren—the rest "having gone ahead over the mountains." They camped that night at Pleasant Valley, Rich having collected during the day $353.50 in tithing. [22]

Unfortunately, as with Lyman, Apostle Rich did not include a complete list of the persons accompanying him home. However, the Journal History entry of November 12th records his arrival that day with Orrin P. Rockwell) and "fifty-one others, mostly brethren." Obviously, some women accompanied the predominantly male group. [23]

Rich's return will not be detailed, except to note that he reached Salt Lake on November 11th. The November 12th Journal History entry records that he had not lost a single man. However, James Seaton did die at Ogden, having been ill most of the trip. On the 13th, Rich met with Willard Richards of the First Presidency discussing "California matters." The unfavorable accounts of Rich's companions corroborated those of Lyman's company. They reported that "[m]any murders had been committed for which no punishment had been attempted." On their return trip they "had been dogged by Indians for a distance of over four hundred miles." En route they had "found the bodies of Hyrum Gates and his two sons with throats cut by Indians." [24]

It may be remembered that Gates was one of two men for whom an arrest warrant had been issued to Porter Rockwell on April 11, 1849, on charges of having kidnapped Rockwell's daughter. Their throats having been cut raised the speculation that Rockwell might have been involved in their execution rather than Indians. The other man named in the warrant, Levi Fifield, returned to Salt Lake by the southern route with Jefferson Hunt, arriving on January 27, 1851. [25]

A number of individuals made deposits to the Gold Accounts after Rich's arrival in Salt Lake on November 11, 1850, and before the end of that year. [26] Two women depositors, Sarah Hawkins and Mary Whittle, were possibly the wives of two of the Sandwich Island missionaries. Several depositors were probably sponsors of gold missionaries.

On January 21st, Captain Jefferson Hunt reached Salt Lake, via the southern route having left Sacramento on the 25th day of November, 1850, Stockton on the 30th, the Williams Ranch on December 15th, and reaching the southern colonies of Deseret on January 11th. [27] He reported on February 2nd to Brigham Young that the diggings were not as prosperous as they had been and that "the brethren employed around the gold mines in California were anxious to return home." [28] Deposits by or for Amasa Lyman and Brigham Young were made to the Gold Accounts shortly after Hunt arrived in Salt Lake.

Other groups of Mormons filtered back into Utah. For example, on January 27, 1851, John D. Lee, adopted son of Brigham Young, recorded that "[a]bout noon a small company of brethren (six in number) arrived from California. [29] They brought with them "a package of letters from Mr. Williams of California to President Brigham Young containing propositions relative to the sale of his ranch." According to Lee, "The brethren reported that times were dull in California and that many who had made independent fortunes and as much gold as a mule would pack were now as a rule poor and miserable." He went on to say that "many of them have not credit for a meal or victuals and have sunk into all manners of vice and intemperance. The consummation of their folly," he said, "will stand registered against them to testify of their acts of disobedience and confirm in the strongest terms which language can express that Brigham Young and Heber C. Kimball are Prophets; for they plainly warned the bretheren who went to California of the evils into which they were led." [30]

That was John D. Lee's view. However, the fact that it was selected for inclusion in the Journal History reflected a policy that was being forged and in itself probably had some influence in the establishment of a negative public policy toward gold mining. While a hundred or so Mormon Argonauts returned to Zion in 1850-51, hundreds remained in the California Babylon, the Land of Gold.

NOTES

1. See Appendix 19a.

2. The Cades, Whitneys, Crismans and Lewis'. 1850 U.S. Census, San Diego County.

3. See Appendix 19b.

4. Rich and Lyman, Papers.

5. Journal History, July 23, 1850.

6. Barnard, 40, of Kentucky, and Foote, 26, of Connecticut, were living at Granite Creek at the time of the census. While Granite Creek is not identified by Gudde and Gudde, it appears to have

been between Georgetown and Louisville. Evidently their mail run only took them to Edmunds (Edmonds) or Mormon Station in Carson Valley, as they were listed in California at the time of the census. Both had entered Utah in 1848.

7. Rich and Lyman, Papers.

8. Kimball, a Captain of Ten in 1847, was a kinsman of Heber C. Kimball, a Counselor to Brigham Young. He had apparently become disaffected or discouraged, going to California the previous year. He was later rebaptized in San Francisco.

9. This group of 100-200 Mormons in or near Boyd's camp has not been located in the 1850 census. In fact, not even Boyd has been located. They may have been at Mormon Gulch, just north of Georgetown. There were two Boyds, James and William of Kentucky, located at Louisville just a few miles west of Georgetown, in 1850. On the other hand it is possible that Rich was referring to the total number of Saints living in the area between Greenwood Valley and the Middle Fork, rather than at a single location.

It is not clear what is meant by a "submarine press." Underwater mining techniques used during the California gold rush go by the generic name of "dredges." Spense, "Gold Pans to Dredges," reviews these techniques and mentions such approaches as scoops, spoon dredges, bucket lines, diving bells, augers, vacuum pumps or suction dredges, pressure tubes, etc.

10. Benjamin Crow, 30, of Missouri, resided at Louisville with his wife and two children at the time of the census. He was a member of the Robert Crow family that had been associated with the Mississippi Company at Pueblo in 1846-47.

11. On the 8th, Lyman received $78.00 in tithing from George Boyd, Zacheus Cheney, John M. Higby (Higbee) and Darwin Richardson at Lathrop's Tavern.

12. California Census, 1850, El Dorado County.

13. Lyman, Papers. Henry Bigler, James Douglas, George W. Hickerson, John Jacobs, William L. McIntire, Richard Robinson and William Woolsey.

14. Horace M. Alexander, John Alger, George D. (P.) Billings, Isaac T. Brown, Berrill Covington, Peter M. Fife and James C. Sly. Ibid.

15. Rich, Papers.

16. *Deseret News,* October 5, 1850. The Cain letter is also found in Journal History, September 29, 1850.

16a. Having received a personal report from Lyman, George A. Smith and Ezra T. Benson related the report in a letter dated September 29, 1850 to Orson Pratt and Franklin D. Richards in England, who then published the letter in the *Latter-Day Saints Millenial Star,* vol. 13, no. 2, January 15, 1851. The letter is also found in Journal History, September 29, 1850.

17. California Census 1850, El Dorado County.

18. Gold Accounts; Appendices 19c, d.

19. Rich, Papers.

20. This Mountaineer House visited by Rich was apparently located in El Dorado County, near Mormon Tavern. There was another Mountaineer House in Mormon Ravine in Sutter (Placer) County. In 1857 a Mountaineer House in the general area was run by some reportedly disaffected Mormons by the name of Anderson.

21. Abraham Boswell, William Boyes (Boice), Goudy Hogan, Samuel Miles, and David Smith.

22. Jeptha Condit, James Oakley, William Kittleman, and James Seaton.

23. Journal History, November 12, 1850. See Appendix 19e for list of some members of the Rich Company.

24. Journal History. November 13, 1850. Descendants of Hyrum Gates maintain the two sons were not killed, though they did leave the Church and stay in California. Hyrum Gates (Bates) apparently was killed, because the next we read of Rockwell's daughter is as a widow, in 1851

in California, marrying Henry W. Brizzee of the Mormon Battalion. See Schindler, Rockwell, 184 and 184 n.1. A colorful account of the wedding is in Ham, *A Buckeye in the Land of Gold* 136-37.

25. Journal History, January 27, 1851.

26. See Appendix 19f.

27. Journal History. January 27, 1851. With Hunt were John W. Berry, James Brooks, Isaac Brown, Levi Fifield and son, Henry E. Gibson, Marshall Hunt, and John Mackay. An Isaac Brown had made a deposit to the Gold Accounts in October raising the possibility of two Mormon Isaac Browns in California unless he sent his gold home earlier with others.

28. Ibid., February 2, 1851.

29. Gordon S. Beckstead, William Bird, Henry Cook, James Davidson, William P. Goddard, and Jacob Winters."

30. Ibid., January 27, 1851 — taken from Lee, Journal.

APPENDIX 19a (Note 19:1)
San Francisco Area Tithe payers
July 4-5, 1850

Cade, Jonathan (1)
Cade, Susanna
Cheney, Zacheus (1)
Chrisman (Crisman), Charles
Hyatt, Elisha
Lewis, John
Meder, Moses
Morey, Barton
Petch (Peters), Robert
Phillips, John

1. Cade and Cheney of the *Brooklyn*, also paid tithing in the Gold Fields.
Source: Lyman, Papers.

APPENDIX 19b (Note 19:3)
Sacramento Tithe payers
July 15, 1850

Blackburn, Anthony
Cherry, Ebenezer G.
Huffaker, Simpson D.
McMurtrey (McMarty), Samuel .
Petit, Edwin
Phelps, Henry
Seely, David
Seely, Wellington (Justice)
Thurber, Albert K
Whitney, Ephraim B.

Source: Lyman, Papers

APPENDIX 19c· (Note 19:18)
Gold Depositors
September 29 - November 10, 1850

Women - Probably Widows and Wives of Gold Miners

Beach, Mrs. (Rufus?)
Bills, Sister (John or William)
Flake, (James M.)
Hogland (Hoagland), (Peter or Lucas)
Rawlins, Sister Agnes (James H.)
Rich, Sister (Charles C.)
Seely, Sister (David or J. W.)

Church Leaders and Prominent Men Some of Whom Probably Sponsored Gold Miners on Missions

Clayton, William
Callister, Smith O.
Glover, William
Higby (Higbee), Isaac
Horne, Joseph
Kay, John
Pratt, Parley P.
Richards, Willard
Smith, John
Wells, Daniel H.
Young, Brigham
Young, John

Likely Returning Gold Miners

Babcock, George
*Brown, Isaac F.
*Boyce, George
*Burr, Charles C.
Cherry, Aaron B.
*Cherry, Ebenezer
*Covington, Berrill
Gardner, Elias
*Gould, Samuel
Hale, Aroet
Hatch, Ira S.
*Hogan, E. G. M.
Lewis, Carleton
Morse, Brother
*Oakley, John
*Rawlins (Rollins), James H.
*Seeley (Seely), Justus W.
*Seeley (Seely), David
*Thurber, Albert K.
*Woolf, John A.
* Those starred are known to have been in California.

Source: Gold Accounts

APPENDIX 19d (Note 19:18)
Some Men Known to Have Been in Lyman-
Salt Lake Bound Company
July - December 1850

Brown, Kiser
Clark, Daniel
Dewey, Frank
Fife, Peter
Morley, Isaac, Jr.
Murray, John
Richardson, D. P.
Sly, James C.
Stoddard, Judson S.
Thompson, _____

Source: Lyman, Papers.

APPENDIX 19e (Note 19:23)
Some of Apostle Rich's Salt Lake Bound
Company
October-November 1850

Bradshaw, Abraham
Forsyth, George
Goodall, James
Goodall, M. T.
Lewis, Richard
Pomeroy, Francis M.
Rockwell, Orrin P.
Stoddard, Judson
Seaton, James

Source: Rich, Diary.

APPENDIX 19f (Note 19:26)
Depositors to Gold Accounts
Nov. 11-Dec. 31, 1850

Callister, Thomas*
Hatch, Ira S.
Hawkins, Sarah
Ladd, S. G.
Lambert, Charles*
Lyman, Amasa
Oakley, James
Richards, Willard*
Spencer, Daniel*
Wells, Daniel H.*
Whittle, Mary
Young, Brigham*

* Those starred were probably Gold Missionary Sponsors

Source: Gold Accounts.

Abner Blackburn (1827-1904)

Abner Blackburn was born at St. Clair Township, Pennsylvania. His father's family moved to Ohio and joined the LDS Church in 1836. The family's attachment to the Church fluctuated. That is, they moved with the Mormons to Missouri. Then Abner's father became disenchanted with Mormonism and moved the family to Carlinville, Illinois. The Mormons were driven from Missouri and settled Nauvoo, Illinois, some 160 miles to the northwest of Carlinville. The Blackburns then had a change in their feelings and moved to Nauvoo to rejoin the Mormons. Abner was striking out on his own at that time. He worked at steamboating, trading on the Mississippi River, and did some lead mining. He returned to Nauvoo to help in the exodus west and on that trek joined the Mormon Battalion. He didn't reach California with the Battalion. Instead, he became part of the Willis detachment, the sick who were sent back from the Rio Grande River, who spent the rest of the winter in Pueblo. He continued on to the Salt Lake Valley in 1847.

Abner went to California four times. The first trip was in 1847, sent by Brigham Young to settle issues with the Army concerning mustering out and pay. The second trip was in 1849, after hearing about the gold discovery. On that trip he was the first to discover gold at Gold Canyon on the east side of the Sierra. He and his brother mined in California, toured the mining regions, and returned to Salt Lake City. On a third trip, in 1850, Abner went as far as Genoa in Carson Valley where he and some partners set up a temporary trading post. They obtained their trading supplies from California. At the end of the travel season, they went back to Salt Lake City. On the fourth trip to California, in 1851, Abner went with the Jefferson Edmunds company by the northern route. It was during this trip he discovered his father had been killed in Northern California. Abner finally went south to the new San Bernardino colony and lived out his life there. *Courtesy Mattiott Library, University of Utah.*

And . . . will try them as gold is tried.
Bible. Zechariah 13:9

20

A Maverick Mormon Argonaut

WHILE HUNDREDS OF MORMONS were sent or given permission to go to the California gold fields between 1848 and 1850, enough went in defiance of the Mormon prophet to give a renegade or maverick reputation to Mormon gold diggers in general. In fact, it is not always clear who were the obedient and the disobedient among the Mormon Argonauts. Abner Blackburn is an example of those who admitted to, if not gloried in, defiance. [1]

Born January 13, 1827 in Bedford County Pennsylvania, Abner was the third child and first son of Anthony and Hester Rose Blackburn. Abner joined the Mormon Church with his family in 1837, and the family moved to Missouri in 1839, just in time to be involved in the final stages of the Mormon Wars. That was a difficult year for the faithful Latter-day Saints in the Missouri Zion. A number of the leaders of the Church deserted. Others were imprisoned, including their Prophet, Joseph Smith. Furthermore, the persecution of the Saints ended in their expulsion, as a result of the infamous Extermination Order issued to the state militia by Governor Boggs.

The Blackburn parents appear to have been caught up in the turmoil, becoming disaffected for a period but returning to the fold in the 1840s, and settling in the Nauvoo area where the Church was headquartered. Abner was said to have been a member of the Nauvoo Legion, the military arm of the city-state government.

With the death of the Prophet Joseph Smith in June of 1844 and the subsequent turmoil within the Church, Abner became somewhat disillusioned. While others worked intensely to complete their temple and perform the ceremonies of the new temple, Abner refused the invitation to participate. Also rejecting the competing claims for the leadership of the Church, Abner left Nauvoo and went to work in the nearby lead mines, learning skills he would use later.

In 1846, the adventurous Abner, drawn back to the Saints, found himself in the exile and responding to the call for volunteers for the Mormon Battalion, more for the adventure, he said later, than for religious duty.

By the time the Battalion reached Santa Fe in New Mexico, approximately 150 had been detached for various reasons, but primarily because of sickness. Abner was among these, moving north to winter in Pueblo in present-day Colorado. He learned there that the Mormon pioneers would not leave the banks of the Missouri that season.

In the spring, the sick detachments' Battalion boys and families set out about the same time as the Mississippi Saints who also wintered in Pueblo. They met up with the pioneer company led by Brigham Young, following him into the Salt Lake Valley in July of 1847. Abner's name is not found among those recorded as entering the valley that year, though he did enter.

Abner to California and Back

A few weeks later a small group of men was mustered to accompany Sam Brannan and Captain James Brown [2] to California. The latter was charged with the responsibility of collecting the army pay due the detached soldiers and attending to the business of formally mustering them out. Abner was selected to be a member of the company. His narrative records the conflict between Brannan and Brown, which caused them to reach Sutter's Fort in California in separate parties. After the Battalion business was attended to, Blackburn returned to Utah in the fall and left for Missouri to assist his family in the move to the Valley of the Great Salt Lake. [3] Before leaving, however, he took action through the Church legal system against his captain, James Brown, for "not supplying beef as per agreement" [4] on their trip to California.

Learning of Gold, Abner goes back to California

Abner's narrative continues. He says that, upon learning of the "great gold discovery" following his return to Utah in 1848, many who had intended to go to Oregon "changed their minds and went for the diggings." However, because the family's cattle and horses were "worn down," they decided to winter in the Salt Lake Valley.

In the spring of 1849, Abner joined a pack train headed for the mines, leaving his folks to come along later when the grass would be better. They apparently took the Salt Lake Cutoff, striking the California Trail at the City of Rocks, which trail he had taken, he claims, two years earlier. If true, it was one of the earliest uses of that cutoff.

About halfway along the Humboldt, he and a companion, William Lane, were riding alongside each other when Lane's gun accidentally discharged, tore through Abner's pant leg, cutting the stirrup leather and killing the horse which belonged to Lieutenant George W. Rosecrans of the Battalion (who presumably was going with him to California). [5] Rosecrans had secured the horse at a Pima Village on the Gila River in Arizona as

the Battalion marched through that area in 1846. Abner "saddled another horse and went on ready for something els[e]."

Upon reaching the Sinks of the Humboldt River, the party took a new route to California made since he had been there almost two years before. It would become known as the Mormon Emigrant Trail. They crossed Forty Mile Desert, striking the Carson River. Going up the river for two days, they stopped to "recruit" (rest) their animals.

Some of the company had been to the mines before and when Abner asked them why no gold had been found east of the mountains, they said "no one had looked for it." The next day while others were playing cards, the inquisitive Abner went out with a bread pan and butcher knife to a nearby ravine to prospect. He found "gold in small quantities," going on to a larger ravine with water running down it. Digging down to slate, he "found a fair prospect."

After an hour or so, he took his findings to camp showing them to his traveling companions, who promptly "grabbed up pans, knives and kettles and started out." They worked until sundown, taking out "nine or ten dollars worth of gold." Having inadequate tools and supplies they felt compelled "to abandon the place, but calculated to return some time in the future." Abner maintains that the location was up Gold Canyon a few miles below what would later become Virginia City. This means that they had stopped to recuperate near present day .

The company traveled up the Carson River in the snow, stumbling around, looking unsuccessfully for a road. Their horses "nearly starved and some of our party . . . snowblind," they finally descended the mountain and found a valley of "green grass and wild flowers." They stopped for a day to rest and tried once again to find the road. Unable to locate it, they proceeded down the divide between the American and Cosumnes Rivers, paralleling the Mormon Emigrant Trail in the valley several miles to the north. Wondering whether or not they would ever reach the mines, they finally came upon "some miners crevicing in a raveine for gold." According to Abner, we "jum[p]t off our horses and began to do as they [the miners] did and let our horses eat grass." After three hours of working "several small gulches wit[h] our knives and bread pans" we had enough "course gold" to buy some of our most "pressing needs."

To Sacramento for Supplies and back to the Mines

Abner and his group went over a ridge into Weaverville, where they purchased tobacco, whiskey, and other provisions, but found it necessary to go back to Sacramento or Sutter's Fort to buy the outfit needed for mining. At the Fort, Abner got a job cutting a hole for a doorway, being paid an ounce of gold for his labor. They also sold some of their horses and purchased the needed tools and provisions for the mines.

Hearing of "a big strike at the Auburn raveine" near the juncture of the North and Middle Forks of the American River, they packed their horses and headed up the northwest side of the American River. Upon reaching the ravine they found that the Sonorans and Chileans had "gutted the raveines of the cream." They "dam[n]ed them some what" and went down to the river but found the water too high to work the bars, forcing them to establish camp and work up higher until the water fell.

They broke up for the day, Abner and his friend, Nat (Nathaniel) Fairbanks, going upriver. Fairbanks was a young Mormon whose family entered Utah in 1847. He settled with William Lane at Louisville in El Dorado County as early as the fall of 1850, working and living there as a butcher with Louis Myers and his young family. Also living with them was William Crow who, like Myers and Blackburn, had been associated with the Mississippi Saints.

As they moved upriver, they "found a little [gold] all a long." However, it was not enough to be very encouraging. Stopping in a ravine for lunch they "felt down in the mouth because [they] could not strike it rich and [their] luch had souerd on [them]." Abner looked down and there beneath his feet was "something yellow about a half inch long." He picked it up handing it to Nat who sang out, "Gold! by my life!" They stopped

eating and began to make "the gravel fly," working until sundown and staking out two claims. In about five hours of work they took out "about four hundred dollars in coarse gold," which they took back to their base camp.

The next morning they took two friends with them and staked out two more claims. The four of them took out $2500 in gold in eight days. Having run out of pay dirt, they "left to find other diggins." They heard that miners were "shoveling it up rich in other places," but intended to come back when the river was lower.

Going to Coloma, they purchased some lumber with which to make rockers, crossing the river at Spanish Bar on the Middle Fork of the American River. Numerous Mormons were mining where they crossed, "taking it out big," a real "bonanza." Finding themselves in a good place, Abner and his friends went to work.

Hearing that his folks were coming over the mountains, Abner decided to go meet them. He sold his "interest in the claim" and started out, finding them coming down the mountain. (Presumably his brother Thomas came with his parents.) They went into Sacramento where they purchased another outfit, then headed for the area below Auburn. Abner, with his father and Thomas, returned to his old ravine. The water had fallen low and they "found the ground richer than at first." Going "down into the river bed as low as possible" they "realized about eighteen hundred dollars from the place."

They moved to a place about three miles above Auburn. Finding good grass, they camped. Two enriched miners came up from the river, headed for home in Oregon. They struck up a friendship and the miners suggested that the Blackburns go where they had been successfully mining for six weeks.

Abner and Thomas went down to the river and found miners "cleaning up their rockers," the bottoms of "their pans covered with gold." The brothers saw "enough to sattisfy the most greed of mortals." They made two rockers and established themselves alongside the diggings of the others before they "had their breakfast." The min-

"Miner's Cabin," lithograph published in the *Illustrated News* from New York on Feb. 18, 1853 on page 117. *Courtesy California State Library.*

ers "come chargeing down to (them) with pistols in hand to drive (them) off." But the brothers "did not scare worth a cent" and they were given two claims being asked to "keep it quiet from others." Once they got started they took out from "eighty to one hundred fifty dollars a day to the hand."

They worked as long as they could, but the "excitement of mining" caused them "to overwork themselves." They had to lay off to recuperate. Selling their claims, they came up from the river to rejoin their father, who had established a very successful "miners store, boarding house, and a general trading station" three miles north of Auburn.

Abner and Thomas
Decide to Tour California

After a rest, and having more money than they had seen in their entire lives, the two brothers and three friends decided to see California and the mines. They "fitted out Spanish stile and started for Sacramento," stopping at all of the places along the road. They came across "a bar for liquor, gold scales for weighing gold, cards and dice, [and] banking games" with "players of all nations." They saw "packers going to the mines" on foot and horse as well as "Chinamen with their bamboo poles loaded with all they could carry," and "Sonorans with their little mules. All wanted to get their before it was too late."

Coming to Sacramento or "embarkadero as some called it," they found it the "Cap Shief of all places." Everybody was in "hot hast[e] about something." "The great gambling houses were doing the best business. Monte was the favorite game." Tables were stacked with "doubloons, Mexecan dollars and gold dust by the sack," and a band played. Free liquor was dispensed to "all the house." There were Brazilians, Chileans,

Mexicans, Kanakas (Hawaiians) and (according to Abner) "all the skum of the earth."

Going on to San Francisco, they found the bays "crowded with shipping and forgheners from all nations." The ships were "used for storehouses and lodging places," their crews having deserted them for the mines. A more "conglomerate set of mortals was never seen on earth."

They soon tired of the "clatter and confusion" and started for the Spanish ranches to the south. Purchasing Sonoran mules, they "struck out over the mountains to Santa Cruz" and then to the San Juan mission. Reaching a large Spanish ranch, they rested for several days being treated to a "fandango" (Mexican dance) with wine flowing freely. Impressed by the "seneretoes," they admired the simple lives of the people "with no lame backs or rheumatism to complain about."

After making some purchases, they headed for the Southern mines, going through the Pacheco Pass to the San Joaquin River and then up the Merced, taking much the same route as Apostle Rich and the Salt Lake Trading Company would take the next spring. Coming to the mountains, they headed north, finding "considerable mining all along the creeks and the raveines." Crossing the Tuolumne and Stanislaus Rivers, they came to Sonora, the liveliest place they had seen and "the richest of all the southern mines." It also had "too manny cut throats," and they soon left, heading for the Calaveras River. Blackburn makes no mention of Mormon Diggings which he must have at least passed near by.

As they moved north, they came upon an old man and his son with a very rich claim, just coming under attack by some Portuguese miners. They pitched in and helped the father and son drive their attackers off. Offered half of the old man's claim as a reward, they accepted, finding it "rich but shallow and worked it out in a week." Deciding to leave, the old man followed suit, fearing he would be murdered.

As they headed north, Abner came across Lou Devon (the pilot on his trip to California in 1847) and his Indian wife, Leaping Faun. They had arrived two weeks earlier from Fort Hall, had found

a rich claim and were working it with their little son. A young daughter was running around, while an older girl was lending a hand now and then with the mining operation.

Spending but a day or so with them, and listening to a long narrative about their journeys, the travelers "started home to (their) camp on the American river, They felt they had visited the best portion of the mines." While gone, a company had been formed to "turn the river across the bar" where there was a deep hole, hoping to find it filled with gold. However, Abner and Thomas sold out "for a good price." Abner had learned that "gold does not stop in deep places." Abner does not make it clear whether or not this was learned before or after participating in the construction of the dam.

Returning to Salt Lake City

Abner states that he and his brother started back over the mountains on October 29, 1847. However, he must have meant 1849. [His narrative being written a half century later.] They headed east to assist family members somewhere on the road. Reaching Carson Valley, they came across many emigrants, but none knew of their relatives. They crossed the desert to the Humboldt where they learned that the family had remained in the Salt Lake Valley for the winter. Abner wanted to return to California, but his brother was "attracted to a girl in Salt Lake" and wanted to go there. Abner bowed to young love and accompanied Thomas to the "City of the Saints," where they found their kindred.

"With [their] pockets full of the needful" they "had a splendid time," finding that they, or "at least [their] gold," was "just as good as the Elders of Israel." Thomas found his love and on Christmas day was wedded. Abner does not reveal her name but the next year Thomas and Emily, the latter aged eighteen, were living in El Dorado County in California.

Abner's report of the date of his and Thomas' departure from California is in conflict with other evidence. On October 28, 1849, Abner is listed as a depositor of $384 into the Church's Gold Accounts; Thomas deposited $200 the fol-

Abner Blackburn and his wife Lucinda Harris Blackburn about 1880.
Courtesy San Bernardino Historical Pioneer Society.

lowing day. Both received back equal amounts in Mormon valley currency. [6] The fact that the two brothers deposited gold in the Gold Accounts would seem to indicate that they were not completely detached from the Church at that point in time.

After the marriage, Abner headed south where he participated in some bloody battles with Indians in Utah Valley, in company with James Orr with whom he had lived as neighbors in Illinois. This was the area where his kin folk, Anthony (his father), and Jehu and Elias Blackburn (his uncles) settled.

Abner and Thomas again to California, but stop at Genoa

In the spring of 1850, Abner and his brother

Thomas and bride joined a company headed for California, "ready to leave the Saints for good." Joseph DeMont (Dumont), not a Mormon, was their captain with Hampton S. Beaty (Beatie), secretary. Beatie, also a non-Mormon, later joined the Mormon Church.

They traveled to Carson Valley "with out anny thing happening of note." They reached the place where Abner had mined the previous spring but found that others had also found it and had "worked out the best places," not realizing they were on the fringes of an incredibly rich gold and silver deposit. Going back to the Carson River, they followed it to the mountains. Hearing of thousands coming on the road, they "concluded to start a station for trade." [7]

DeMont, Thomas, Abner and four others went

back to the location of present-day Genoa. There was "no better place on the river," there being pine trees, cold clear water and "oceans of good feed." They built a station "out of pine logs and a large log coral." Taking several teams, Abner headed over the mountains for supplies and provisions for the station.

Crossing the mountains, they came upon wagon teams from Sacramento loading up with snow which was selling for $80 a ton in the city. Abner and his companions also loaded up with snow, covering it with wagon sheets and pine boughs and headed for the city. Disposing of the snow, they bought their supplies and returned to Carson Valley, the roads crowded with emigrants headed in the opposite direction.

Upon reaching the station, Abner's partners asked him to "make up a company" to go "work Gold Canion," while they ran the station, giving them "two strings to the bow." With two teams and 14 men, they headed for the canyon, encountering an Indian war party, supposedly led by the famous Chief Winnemucca, on the way. However, they were able to scare the Indians off. Reaching the canyon, they prospected for a week without success, returning to the station. Abner later observed, "If we had known the rich mines higher up the canion the outcome would be different. We mist the great Bonanza," known later as the silver rich Comstock Lode.

Thomas to California, Abner to Salt Lake

Business was good at the station and the company "put in the sum[m]er and fall to good advantage." They divided the proceeds, all satisfied. Thomas went over to California and Abner and the rest of his group headed for Fort Hall to trade off his 25 head of horses and six mules. They had to fight renegade Indians from many tribes all along the way, losing some of their livestock.

Disposing of his remaining stock at the Fort, he headed south to "winter with the Saints." Abner was at least a nominal Mormon and was well received in Zion, but as Abner summed up the hospitality, "they were real good while our money lasted." However, the Saints did not like "the gay

uniform of the Spanish Hidalgo whitch the California boys brought with them." He wrote that "The boys took delight in pestering the leaders with their California customs" which included taking a girl to a dance seated on the horse in front of the man. However, "the boys did not care and the girls did not mind it." The authorities lectured the girls saying that the "indecent proceedings must stop." No evidence is presented which shows the lectures to have been particularly effective.

Abner goes Back to California

In the spring of 1851, Blackburn joined the company of Jef (Jefferson) Edmonds (Edmunds) who was returning to California after a trip to Utah. Edmunds was Porter Rockwell's partner in a tavern at Deer Creek and possibly the proprietor of a station at or near Mormon Station. Having skirmishes with Indians, they went to Mormon Station. As the snow was still too deep to cross the mountains with their wagons, they killed time by following an old Indian on a wild goose chase looking for gold north of the Truckee River. Returning to Carson Valley, they headed into the mountains. The snow still very deep, but they struggled through, passing Tragedy Spring.

Abner reached San Francisco, hoping to find his parents. Instead, he learned his father had been killed (and family tradition says skinned)[8] by Indians on the Klamath River on his way to visit Thomas and his wife, who were running a ferry. Taking the first steamer north, Abner landed at Trinidad and headed inland to find his brother. Locating him, they joined the local miners in a reprisal "war on the savages," the gold diggers showing no mercy. Settling up their business, they returned to San Francisco and then went south. [9]

Moving South to settle finally at San Bernardino

Abner settled in the newly established Mormon colony of San Bernardino where he married Lucinda Harris in 1851. The marriage was performed by Elder Amasa Lyman, co-founder of San Bernardino. Abner remained when the Saints were recalled to Utah in 1857. Many of those who stayed were either disaffected from the Church at the time or became such. No known official Mormon Church organization existed there for many years after the recall. A number of ex-Mormons later joined a branch of the Reorganized Church of Jesus Christ of Latter Day Saints, which rejected the leadership of Brigham Young. However, Abner is not found on the rolls of that Church.

In 1897, Abner was invited to return to Salt Lake to help commemorate the arrival of the pioneers of 1847. He wrote asking for financial assistance, saying, "California is not a land of gold and we are nearly all poor." [10] He died November 2, 1904, at 72 years of age having resided in San Bernardino for 53 years.

Thomas R. (Abner's brother) and his wife Emily were operating a hotel, or more likely a boarding house at Mud Springs, El Dorado County, in October of 1850. [11] Thomas and his wife then moved to San Bernardino, where he was listed as residing at the Fort (as was Abner) in 1851. He became numbered among the dissenters there, for in 1855 he voted in opposition to the Mormon party. Thomas died in San Bernardino June 15, 1863. [12]

NOTES

1. The account of Abner Blackburn comes largely from Abner's "Narrative of Experiences," written later in life. A copy and informative commentary is conveniently available in Will Bagley, ed. *Frontiersman*. Only those events most pertinent to this story are recounted here. Bagley's spellings and annotations (in square brackets) are adopted (and a few of our own are added in brackets.) The narrative used here is found in Bagley's pages 124-131, 139-150, 168-175, and 181-187. Specific pages for individual quotations are not indicated.

2. The leader of one of the detachments of the Mormon Battalion that spent the winter of 1846-47 in Pueblo.

3. Abner arrived in the Salt Lake Valley in November of 1847. Members of his family had already arrived in September of 1847. Bagley, *Frontiersman*, 121.

4. Carter, ed. *Our Pioneer Heritage*, 17:97.

5. William Lane entered Utah as a 16-year-old in 1847. George W. Rosecrans was a lieutenant in the Mormon Battalion, probably going to Utah from California in 1847. He returned to California in 1849, probably as a member of Abner's company. He would remain in California.

6. Gold Accounts; The date given in the gold accounts contradicts the date given by Abner for starting back over the mountains, unless someone else made the deposits for them.

7. This is usually accredited as the first white habitation in Nevada. However, if others had mined out the best places in Gold Canyon, they should be given the credit even if their identities are unknown.

8. Bagley, *Frontiersman*, 186 n29.

9. Abner penned at the end of his story "to be continued." However, no additional narrative of this interesting character has been located.

10. Carter, *Our Pioneer Heritage*. 4:441.

11. California Census, El Dorado County, 1850.

12. See Bagley, *Frontiersman*, 199, 203, 214.

Wagon trains going to California followed the Carson River in Carson Valley along the eastern foothills of the towering Sierra Nevada Range, the Range they would be required to surmount. Painting by Albert Bierstadt, untitled. *Courtesy Bancroft Library.*

Orson Hyde (1805-1878)

Orson Hyde was born in Oxford, Connecticut. His mother raised him while his father was away fighting in the War of 1812. His mother died and he was then raised by neighbors, who took him with them when they moved to Ohio. While in Ohio, Orson became acquainted with Mormonism and joined the Church in 1831, shortly after the Church was organized. He was ordained an apostle at age thirty and served in that capacity for forty-three years, twenty-eight as president of the Quorum of Twelve Apostles. He was "a farmer, supervisor of Utah immigration, wagon-train master, irrigation specialist, founder of new Utah settlements, railroad planner, sawmill operator, participant in the Utah War councils, regent of the University of Deseret, legislator, newspaper editor, Indian fighter, peace-maker, lawyer, judge, and statesman."

"He helped start the LDS British Mission . . . He is best remembered for his solo mission to Jeru-salem in 1841, where he dedicated the land of Palestine for the return of the Jews . . . He headed the Mormon colony at Winter Quarters (Iowa/Nebraska) from 1847 to 1852 . . . and led two large pioneer wagon companies across the plains to Utah in 1850 and 1852 . . . He established an outpost on the western edge of the Utah Territory [Carson Valley] from 1855 to 1857. As the presiding officer and probate judge, he led the colony and built and operated a sawmill . . . In 1860 he was called to preside as stake president over the settlements in Sanpete County, Utah . . . He served twelve years in the Ter-ritorial legislature, the last part as the president of the Utah Senate. He died at the age of 73 in Spring City, Utah." (From an article by Lynn M. Hilton and Hope A. Hilton in *Utah History Encyclopedia*, edited by Allan Kent Powell. Salt Lake City : University of Utah Press, 1994.) *Photo Courtesy Utah State Historical Society.*

Forasmuch as ye know that ye were not redeemed
with corruptible things as silver and gold . . .
  Bible. I Peter 1:18

21

Mormon Station
and the Carson Valley Saints

AT THE TIME of the discovery of gold at Coloma, present-day Nevada and Utah were part of Upper California, recently secured from Mexico. When the State of California was created by Congress in 1850, the area to the east of the Sierra Nevada mountains became part of the Territory of Utah. It was also included in the provisional State of Deseret, an abortive Mormon attempt to have their envisioned western empire made a sovereign state. The state of Nevada was progressively carved out of Utah Territory.

In those early years, what is now Nevada was mostly an area one traveled through in order to get somewhere else. The Spanish, for many years, had used the southernmost tip of present day Nevada as a major route from Santa Fe to California. The earliest known traversing of the northern portion of Nevada by Anglo Americans was in the 1820s when Peter Skene Ogden and later Jedediah Smith traveled along the Mary's or Humboldt River. John C. Fremont and Kit Carson traversed the area in 1844 and crossed over what is now Carson Pass. Emigrant trains began to move through the northern area in the 1840s using the Mary's (Humboldt) and Truckee River route for their primary entrance into and out of Mexican held California. The Humboldt River moves west and the Truckee east, reaching sinks in a most desolate area of the region. The Carson River begins about 50 miles to the south in California, moving mostly north but increasingly east through the Carson Valley. It reaches a sink in about the same general area as the Humboldt and the Truckee, a few miles to the south.

One study of the Carson Valley Saints, by Page, [1] incorrectly identified the first Mormon to pass through the Carson Valley as Sam Brannan. Brannan actually went east via the Truckee River route, to meet Brigham Young in 1847. He returned to California that same year and same way, having failed to induce Brigham Young to come to California. So Page was using the term "Carson Valley" rather loosely. The closest Brannan would have come to Carson (River) Valley was to pass a few miles north of the Carson Sink. [2] On Brannan's return, he took with him a small company of Battalion Boys led by Captain James Brown. Among them was Abner Blackburn.

The same study identifies two other companies with Mormons in the "Carson Valley." The first was the group of Battalion Boys led by Captain Jefferson Hunt who moved east to meet up with the Saints in 1847. The second group consisted of Battalion members accompanying General Kearny as he took John C. Fremont east that same year for a court martial. However, the evidence again indicates these groups used the Truckee route. They were preceded by the Thomas Rhoades, Harlan-Young and the Donner-Reed parties of 1846, which included Mormons, which

Hampton S. Beatie

In June of 1850, Hampton S. Beatie and his party, a group of five including Abner and Thomas Blackburn, camped at a location in Carson Valley now known as Genoa. They established a temporary trading post to profit from sales to emigrants heading to California that season. They built a two room, log house for themselves and also a corral for their animals. They traded horses and mules with the emigrants. Members of the party brought in flour, dried fruit, bacon, sugar and coffee from California to sell. Abner Blackburn also checked and mined again the site where he had discovered gold the year before (near what is now Dayton).

At the end of the season, the party returned to Salt Lake City, Beatie to work for J & E Reese Mercantile, (John and Enoch Reese). *Courtesy Pioneer Memorial Museum, International Society Daughters of Utah Pioneers.*

Colonel John Reese

The first "permanent" settlement in Carson Valley was established in the spring of 1851 by Colonel John Reese, a proprietor of J & E Reese Mercantile in Salt Lake City. Reese apparently built his trading post about a mile south of Beatie's temporary post and continued the trade with the emigrants of the 1851 season.

Reese, intent on a permanent settlement, joined with the other settlers in setting up an ad hoc, squatters government, with rules for taking possession of land. John Reese was elected recorder and treasurer, and his first recording was a land claim for himself. He called the settlement Mormon Station. Orson Hyde would come later to establish official government for the area, authorized by the governor of the territory, Brigham Young. Hyde renamed the settlement Genoa. *Courtesy Nevada Historical Society.*

took the Truckee River route going west.

The first known Mormon involvement in Carson Valley (rather than just the fringes) consisted of the Battalion veterans the summer of 1848.

These veterans, who had been mining in the Mormon Diggings from Mormon Island to Coloma in the spring of 1848, decided to go to the Salt Lake Valley and wished to avoid the 27 tortuous crossings of the Truckee River, They had learned of

Carson's crossing in 1844 of the Sierra Nevada mountains to the south of the Mountain Lake (which became known as Lake Bigler and later Lake Tahoe). Based on that information, they decided to established a new road, crossing the summit in the region where Carson had crossed (now called Carson Pass). As they descended the eastern slopes, they struck the Carson River and followed the river north through Carson Valley probably to the vicinity of present-day Silver Springs (or just beyond). From there they went northwest to the Truckee river, most likely joining the traditional California Trail near present-day Fernley.

One of the first westward wagon or pack trains entering California in 1849 was that of Apostle Amasa M. Lyman and Porter Rockwell, though it is not known whether their company used the traditional but more difficult Truckee route or the unproven but easier Carson Valley route; there is yet to be discovered a detailed account of this trip. Lyman probably had with him one or more Battalion Boys returning to the gold fields who served as guides and they could well have led him via the Carson Valley route.

The first documented California-bound, Mormon-involved wagon train to pass through Carson Valley came in the spring of 1849 and included Abner Blackburn. [3] His story is already told in the preceding chapter. There is no indication of a trading post or building being constructed by this company, nor of any other building in the area at that time. They were evidently nothing more than transients. As soon as the snows permitted, Abner's pack train moved over the mountains and into the gold fields. He spent the summer and early fall prospecting, mining and touring the California country, returning to Utah in the fall, going over Carson Pass and through Carson Valley on his return. In the late summer of 1849, the Mormon gold train led by Thomas Rhoades, passed through Carson Valley on its way to Salt Lake, carrying $25,000-$30,000 in gold and silver for the Mormon money system.

In the spring of 1850, Blackburn joined the DeMont Company, with Hampton S. Beatie as secretary, leaving Salt Lake for Carson Valley.

Upon reaching Gold Canyon, Blackburn said that they "stopt at the place i found the year before . . . but their had been some miners their and worked out the best place . . . We concluded to start a station for trade" where Genoa now is. [4] A successful summer was spent at the post, Abner returning to Salt Lake the following winter.

A more detailed account of the DeMont-Beatie Company of 1850 is found in the recounting of Hampton S. Beatie made in 1884. [5] Beatie maintained that his ventures took place in 1849, but they actually occurred in 1850. Therefore, care must be taken in accepting at face value his dating, though his dates will be accepted in this account unless other evidence would seem to indicate that he was in error.

Beatie's account, in general, confirms Blackburn's story. While he claims 1848 as the date of his arrival in Utah, he probably did not arrive until 1849, which is when Kate B. Carter [6] established his arrival in the E. T. Benson Company of that year. He served as the company's clerk even though he was not a Mormon at the time.

A Trading Post is Established in Carson Valley

In the spring of 1850, Beatie joined the California-bound train of Captain Joseph DeMont, again serving as clerk. There were approximately 80 persons with about 15 Mormons, including Thomas and Abner Blackburn, in the company. Abner, having been over the route several times, was probably the guide for the trek west. Beatie stated that upon their arrival in Carson Valley, "The Mormon portion of the company went to mine temporarily, leaving their families here [Salt Lake]. I don't think they asked the advice of the Church authorities before going." [7]

Ten of the Mormons went over the mountains to mine, five remaining in Carson Valley with Beatie. He says that most of the Mormons, including two men by the name of Smith and Brown, were from Farmington (Utah). Another man by the name of Parson (possibly Harmon Parsons) was also included in the Mormon group. [8]

Mormon Station (Genoa)

The first permanent building in Carson Valley, was built by John Reese and his party in the summer of 1851 for the purpose of trading with the gold seeking emigrants on their way to California. It was a two room, double logged, two story house. *Courtesy Nevada Historical Society.*

Arriving in Carson Valley early in June of 1850 (he says 1849), Beatie built what he maintained was the first "house" in the valley at what later would become Genoa. It was actually a log structure without a roof or a floor. He remained there with DeMont, the Blackburns, a man named Carter, (possibly John S.), and two others. Once the "house" was built, Beatie and Thomas Blackburn were commissioned to go over the mountains to Placerville for supplies.

In September Beatie sold out to a man identified only as Moore, who it was thought sold out to John Reese the next year. Beatie maintained, "Our party was the first to discover gold in Nevada." and specified that Abner "was the first to find it." The discovery was made in July while Beatie and Thomas were in California for supplies. This would have been in 1850. However, "When Abner Blackburn first went over the mountains (he had done so in 1847 and 1849) it

seems he had an idea that there was gold in the vicinity of what is now Virginia City; and . . . it appears that he went out prospecting and discovered gold," all of which appears to support Blackburn's claim of discovering gold in 1849.

According to Beatie, DeMont and a man named Kimball went to California, and he had "never seen them since." Kimball may have been Hazen Kimball, the Mormon Captain of Ten of 1847 mentioned earlier who had become disaffected and gone to California from Salt Lake. In the fall, five of the men in Carson Valley were rejoined by ten more from California, making 15 in all. They journeyed together back home to Utah.

Page (writing the history of Mormons in Carson Valley) helped perpetuate a common myth when he stated that those who went to California were generally not "very stalwart members," making special reference to the "likes of Abner

Blackburn." He said that "Beatie recorded that he was under the impression that those Mormons who went along did so without the permission of, and in fact, in opposition to Brigham Young's counsel." [9] This conclusion goes beyond Beatie's who only said, "I don't think they asked the advice of the Church authorities." [10] Page also cast doubt on Abner's membership in the Church, despite the latter's written specification to that effect. Until evidence proves otherwise, Blackburn must be assumed to have been a Mormon, even though perhaps later a "ragtail" one.

In 1850, several "authorized" Mormon trains passed westward through Carson Valley, including a mail train, and the companies of Thomas Orr, Ephraim Hanks and William D. Huntington. Caroline Crosby, one of several missionaries attached to the Huntington Company, observed, "This afternoon we traveled through the richest valley I have seen since we came to the western country, such tall, thrifty grass, and beautiful streams of cool soft water pouring down from the mountains, which are covered with lofty cedars and pine, and whose tops are white with snow, was enough to make our hearts dance for joy. Our brethren think it will be a splendid place for a stake of Zion," [11] a "stake" being considered a permanent place of Mormon settlement.

Elder Lyman, who returned to Utah from California in the summer of 1850, and Elder Rich, who returned in the fall of that same year, also passed through Carson Valley, stopping at Edmunds Station en route. [12] By this time, it appears their interests had been relocated to the southern part of California and they had paid little attention to the potential of the country through which they passed.

Another resident of Carson Valley was the man named Moore to whom Beatie sold out. Several Moores had entered Utah in 1847-49, however, no more of this man is known. The next of whom there is some record was one nicknamed Virginia, who wintered (1850-51) in Gold Canyon. He was busily engaged in washing out gold using water from a reservoir he had constructed when Colonel John Reese became acquainted with him. This would have been in 1851, when Reese entered the Valley. Reese claimed that Virginia City

was named after this man, who was probably not a Mormon. [13]

Colonel John Reese was what was then called a jack-Mormon—meaning originally a non-Mormon who associated with the Mormons. He and his brother, Enoch, who was a Mormon, had come to Utah in 1849 with trade goods, establishing the firm of J. and E. Reese. John soon went east for more goods, returning to Utah in 1850. In 1851, he took 13 wagon loads of goods to Carson Valley. He said that only he and his driver went, but as he had 13 wagon loads he must have had more than one driver. At the same time he was joined in the operation by his nephew, S. A. Kinsley, a non-Mormon. Leaving Salt Lake the fifth of April, John Reese arrived in the area (Genoa) on the first of June. According to his story the first thing he did was to secure a ranch at the location and to build a house, which he called Mormon Station. "It was a kind of a hotel or store" with "a dining room." The building was originally of unhewn logs, was two stories high, and measured 50 by 30 feet.

Reese had 17 men working for him cutting timber and building log houses at a salary of $75.00 a month. He fenced a 30-acre field raising wheat, barley, corn, and watermelons. Also, hearing of an anticipated heavy emigration the next year, he planted turnips, getting $1.00 a bunch. People in Utah paid only $.10. He had taken many eggs with him and "sold them well." He secured pigs from California.

A Community Begins to Develop

Mormon Station became a full-fledged commercial operation and attracted others to the area, Mormon and non-Mormon alike. According to Reese, Beatie established a trading post about a mile away with about a half dozen men, mostly Battalion veterans, but most of them went on to California. Reese later bought Beatie's property for $15.00 to $20.00 from a man, who "pretended to own it." Though unmentioned by Blackburn, Beatie, or Reese, the Edmunds Station was also established in the area in 1849 or 1850.

With Reese, settling nearby were John and Rufus Thomas from Salt Lake and a man named

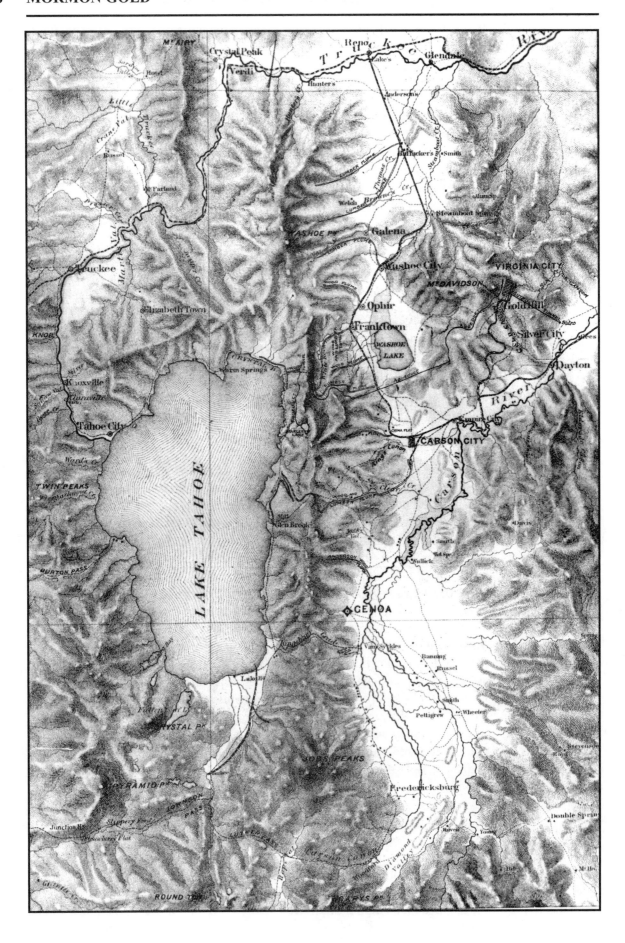

Brown. A man by the name of (N. R.) Haskell put up another trading post. He was shortly followed by (Hirum) Mott from American Fork. William Thorington (Thorrington) started a ranch nearby. He was followed by a man by the name of (Joseph?) Williams from Utah, and one named (Moses) Job, who established a store ten miles from Reese. Reportedly, a man named Condi and another, Gibson, from Salt Lake settled nearby, and John Redding settled the area which became known as Jacks Valley.

Others, mostly non-Mormons, came in 1851: the Van Sickles, (Walter) Crosser and Dr. (Charles A.) Daggett. Many went to Gold Canyon to mine over the winter, having come over the mountains from California. Because the streams dried up in the summer, the canyon could only be mined during the wet winter months. Reese kept them supplied with beef in 1851-1853.

Of the persons listed by Reese, only Mott, and possibly Haskell and Williams, have been identified with the Mormon migrations of 1847-1851. However, a Scot by the name of Gibson Condie went to Utah with his family in 1850. He may have been the man who came to Carson Valley rather than the reported Gibson and Condi. As Reese was later deprived of his membership in the Church, he must have at some time during the intervening years been baptized a Mormon.

In the spring of 1851, Abner Blackburn joined the company of Jeffrey (Jefferson) Edmunds (Edmonds) who was returning to California from a trip to the Valley of the Saints, going by way of Mormon Station. While waiting for the snow pack to permit passage through the mountain, they encountered a group of five old acquaintances from California who had picked up an old Indian claiming to know of a canyon "where they could find all the gold they wanted in a day or two." [14] Taking two men from the westward bound company, Abner's acquaintances followed the Indian north of the Truckee River but found no gold. The disappointed group returned to Carson Valley and crossed the mountains on the Mormon Trail by way of Tragedy Spring. As far as is known, this was the last visit of either Abner or Thomas Blackburn to Carson Valley.

The Community Establishes Self-Government

In November of 1851, a series of meetings was held at Mormon Station to set up a squatter government with Col. A. Woodward, a non-Mormon, initially acting as chairman. Of the group of ten men listed as serving in some official capacity, only Reese, John Porter Barnard, and possibly E. L. Barnard and N. R. Haskell have thus far been identified tentatively as Mormons.

In 1852, Western Utah (Nevada) was divided among several counties of the Territory, with county seats in present-day Utah. This made effective political administration impossible. On December 1st, the first land claims authorized by the squatter government were made. John Reese was the first to secure such, but was followed the same day by six men not identified with the Mormons. In addition, Reese and Mott were authorized to construct a bridge across the Carson River and to repair and collect tolls on a road into the mountains. This toll was an irritant to those who wanted to use their "improved" road via the southern edge of Lake Bigler (Tahoe).

Mott and his wife (Elizabeth) had shortly before arrived from Utah, having come there with

LEFT: Topographical Map (using hachures) of Carson Valley, Nevada from a United States Geological Survey, Eliot Lord in charge. The Mormon-Carson Pass Emigrant Trail (and the West Fork of the Carson River) exited Carson Canyon at Woodfords at the bottom center of the map. The Trail followed the Carson River north and went northeast from what is now Dayton (upper right of the map). Gold Canyon was west of north out of Dayton. The Comstock Lode was primarily between Gold Hill and Virginia City. A slight variation of the map was printed in Eliot Lord, *Comstock Mining and Miners.* 1883, pl. III (U.S. Geological Survey. Monographs, v. IV.). *Courtesy University of California, Berkeley.*

members of his family in 1850. Hiram, his wife Elizabeth, his son Israel and Israel's wife Eliza Ann settled in an area that became known as Mottsville, about four miles south of Mormon Station. They remained in 1857, when most other Mormons left.

Thompson and West [15] list about 30 other residents of Carson, Jacks, Eagle, and Washoe Valleys, as well as Gold Canyon. None of these have yet been identified with the Mormons.

Henry Van Sickle, a non-Mormon en route to California, reached Mormon Station September 24, 1852. He later reported that all the owners of Mormon Station and the inhabitants of the valley were Mormons with the possible exception of Reese's nephew, S.A. Kinsley, who had joined the firm. [16] This may have been true (but probably wasn't) for Carson Valley itself, but must not have been of Washoe Valley and Gold Canyon to the north and east. If Carson Valley was Mormon dominated, all were not happy with it being governed by Salt Lake, 500 miles or so away.

In 1852, Thomas S. Williams, a Mormon trader and Battalion veteran on his way to California with Church cattle to market, reported to Governor Young that all was not well in Carson Valley. He said that "the citizens of this valley declare in language too strong to utter that they will no longer be governed or tried by Mormon law, that they are chiefly organized here to redress the wrongs inflicted on United States citizens who had the good luck, or were fortunate enough to escape with life and limb from Utah." [17]

Williams had evidently been served a writ or attachment of property by a constable appointed by the local citizens in Carson Valley, which writ he refused to honor, "as the matter had been fully settled by a legal process in G. S. L. City." He was supported in his position, he said, "by Major Holeman, Holliday, Warner Livingston, Kinkade and others." [18]

Williams went on to urge official, separate organization of the area saying that "if there are no legal steps taken to organize this part of the territory, the safety of the inhabitants will always be in danger while sojourning in these parts." Wil-liams went on, "I myself know that Col. Reese and his nephew Mr. Kinsley who are both so good and accommodating while in Salt Lake have been ringleaders in opposing the organization of the territory of Utah and declare they will pay no taxes that are levied on them from that source and advise others to hold out in like manner until they get this valley annexed to California. [19]

This letter, written in June, was followed by a statement from California's Surveyor General concluding that the valley was outside of California. Dissatisfied with this opinion, the dissidents fruitlessly petitioned the California legislature to officially annex them, at least for judicial purposes, until Congress could act. [20] In spite of Williams' suggestion, and the activities of the Carson Valley residents, the Utah territorial government did not act until January of 1854 when the legislature finally provided for the creation of Carson County by authorizing the appointment of a probate judge authorized to organize it. [21]

In the meantime, the loyalty of Carson Valley residents, who were becoming increasingly dominated by Gentiles and at least semi-apostate Mormons, was being called into question by loyal Mormons in the area. Edwin D. Wooley, one of the early Bishops of the Church, wrote of Carson Valley to Joseph Cain in June of 1853: "It is the most God-forsaken place that ever I was in, and as to Mormonism, I can't find it here. If the name remains, the Spirit has fled. I have my doubts whether Mormonism can exist in the country as far as I have seen." [22]

The time and distance involved in the traditional route to Carson Valley via the Humboldt encouraged the establishment of a new, more direct route from Salt Lake. Such was given a boost when Lt. Col. Edward J. Steptoe of the U.S. Army arrived in Salt Lake in August of 1854 with a goal of establishing a new road to Carson Valley south of the Great Salt Lake and the salt desert. He appointed John Reese, who had recently pioneered a new road from Carson Valley to Salt Lake, to assist him. This was accomplished in the fall when Reese led a group of four men from Salt Lake to Carson Valley via the Beckwourth Cutoff, shortening the trip by 150 miles, reducing the total time to about four weeks. [23]

Apostle Orson Hyde
sent to Carson Valley

Governor Brigham Young cannot be accused of acting hastily to implement the legislative action of January 1854. The appointment of a probate judge did not take place until January of 1855 when he appointed Apostle Orson Hyde to that position. From the Church's point of view, Hyde's appointment would take care of two needs. He could protect Church interests as he organized the new county, and he could also provide the Mormons in the area with strong, apostolic leadership, something sorely needed by the Saints.

Hyde left the Great Salt Lake City on May 17, 1855, with a company of about 35 missionaries called to help maintain a Mormon foothold in Western Deseret. The party arrived in Carson Valley on June 17th, finding a community still divided over whether the area should be under the jurisdiction of the Gentile-dominated State of California or the Mormon-controlled Territory of Utah. Hyde soon left for California to confer with Governor John Bigler about conducting an official survey to determine the boundary between California and Utah, hopefully resolving the dispute.

Before leaving, the apostle judge wrote to Brigham Young, the prophet-governor, recognizing it as a "great and valuable country . . . Its mineral wealth, though of minor consideration, is hardly exceeded by any portion of California if they can manage to get water to it, which they are now endeavoring to do." He recognized that to accomplish what he had been sent out to do would require time, "patience and perseverance."[24]

Hyde's responsibilities were complicated by the fact that he was given "financial oversight" for the establishment of a Mormon newspaper, the *Western Standard*, in the San Francisco area. The paper would be published by Apostle Parley P. Pratt with the help of the ex-goldminer, missionary and future Apostle, George Q. Cannon. He felt that the dual mission (in California and Carson Valley) was impossible, and so informed Brigham Young. The *Western Standard* subsequently became an important link between the Saints in California and those in the Carson Valley area.

Upon his return to Nevada from a trip to California to confer with that state's leaders, Hyde found the people still agitated over the question of governance. Mott appears to have been a ringleader of the opposition to Utah connections. Hyde was able to forestall a vote on the subject until the boundary line question could be resolved.

The survey work finally commenced in the late summer of 1855. Hyde, along with three other Mormons—Christopher Merkley, Seth Dustin and George W. Hancock—participated in the work. Learning from the California surveyor, George H. Goddard, that most of Carson Valley (including Mormon Station) was definitely in Utah (though barely), Hyde called for an election to be held at Mormon Station on September 20, 1855. A slate of county officers did not include any Saints known to have entered Salt Lake Valley between 1847 and 1851.[25] Hyde and his missionaries had not been able to turn the political tide.

Mormon Station was designated as the county seat and was renamed (possibly at the suggestion of Hyde) Genoa, after the birthplace of Columbus. While Carson Valley was primarily agricultural and commercial, the growing exploitation of the ores of Gold Canyon raised the hopes of the residents of Carson Valley. On October 27th a meeting was held at John Reese's in Genoa in which eight men were granted exclusive rights to the water of Carson River for use in mining Gold Canyon. Of this group, only John Reese, Christopher Merkley and Apostle Orson Hyde have been identified as Mormons.

As winter approached, Hyde saw little to be accomplished by keeping his corps of missionaries in the isolated area. He returned a substantial number of them to their families in Utah, some of them being missionaries, others not. Hyde remained for the winter in the western outpost with one of his newly arrived polygamous wives. While he was the only official political or religious authority, he saw that he must govern "for the present with a gentle hand."[26]

The year of 1856 was one which would see a

substantial increase in both Mormons and non-Mormons, as each sought to establish and maintain political power. [27] As many as two or three hundred Mormons were called as missionaries. The purpose of the intended mission is not altogether clear—whether they were to be settlers or transients. Communications between Salt Lake and Carson Valley indicated both. One signal that seemed to indicate some degree of intended permanence was the designation of Carson County as a Stake of Zion and a secondary gathering place along with San Bernardino in Southern California, a place for the Saints coming from the West Coast and the Pacific Islands. The Mormons did establish small communities from Genoa northward to the Truckee River. A Stake was formed with William Price as Stake President, Chester Loveland as President of the High Council, and Richard Bentley as Bishop of the Stake with organized branches in Carson and Jack Valleys (William Nixon, President) and Washoe Valley (Seth Dustin, President). Franktown in Washoe Valley (Meltiah Hatch, President) became a flourishing Mormon town. Orson Hyde settled there. Another small Mormon community existed at Eagle Valley (Carson City).

In August of 1856, Carson County elections were held, the "Mormon" ticket running against the "Human" ticket. The Mormon ticket, which included three non-Mormons out of 12, won handily. While the Gentiles and apostates, by and large, still opted for attachment to California, as long as the Mormons and their friends maintained political control that was not a viable option. As the communities in Carson Valley grew, the polarization between the non-Mormon settlers who wanted attachment to California and the Mormon settlers who had allegiance to Salt Lake City also increased.

The conflict between Mormons and non-Mormons is sometimes pictured as one between the Mormons and miners. While it is true that Brigham Young's policy against running off to mine gold (unless counseled to do so) periodically became more and more strident, substantial numbers of Mormons engaged in the activity in Carson Valley, as they had been doing in California. Even Apostle Hyde's attitude appears to have been ambivalent. On one hand he had

benefitted, at least potentially, from the attempt to establish a monopoly on Carson River water for, among other things, mining purposes. On the other hand, he reported to Brigham Young that, "Not a man among us wishes to go nearer the mines than one hundred miles." Yet he went on to say that John Dilworth and possibly Peregrine Sessions were involved in mining, and that there was "some little murmuring for a time" [28] when he attempted to put down this minor [miner?] rebellion. In addition, William Jennings, one of the Carson Valley missionaries of 1856, in a rather disjointed account stated that when the missionaries reached Carson Valley "there was little to do, and most of the people went to digging gold. I also went there, having nothing else to do and done very well . . . I carried across [to] Slippery Fall [in California] that spring in a pair of saddlebags between $6,000 and $7,000 of gold dust about as much as I could pack." [29]

Orson Hyde Recalled and Replaced by Chester Loveland

Hyde received a letter in November of 1856 recalling him to Salt Lake City. He was instructed to appoint a successor, apparently assured that Mormons would continue to dominate Carson County politics. He appointed Chester Loveland, president of the High Council. The community grew and unity seemed also to improve under Loveland's leadership. He divided the region into four (later enlarged to five) school districts:

"At the April 1857 annual stake conference the Mormon membership was reported as the following: Carson Valley Branch, 116 members . . . ; Washoe Branch, 111 members . . . ; and Eagle Valley Branch, 60 members . . . . The members included William Jennings, a butcher and meat dealer whose enterprise is suggested by the fact that he later became Utah's first millionaire and was a principal organizer of Zion's Cooperative Mercantile Institution (ZCMI) . . . ; Chester Loveland, who later became the first mayor of Brigham City, Utah . . . ; Christopher Layton, founder of Layton, Utah and of Layton, Arizona; and Abraham Hunsaker, a prime colonizer in northern Utah who was one of the best stockmen in the territory." [30]

The Church Abandons Carson Valley

In the summer of 1857, the Mormons of Carson Valley had the feeling that they were part of a community that was thriving economically and improving politically. They were not prepared for what came next. At 6:00 am on September 5, 1857, Loveland heard a knock on his front door. He opened it find Peter W. Conover, Oliver B. Huntington, and Samuel Dalton with an express message from Brigham Young. They were told that Salt Lake City was being invaded by the United States Army, and that all available manpower, guns and ammunition were needed to defend the Saints. Brigham Young wanted the members to abandon Carson Valley and to bring back all the guns and bullets they could buy.

The Nevada Saints responded to the call, joined by Mormons leaving Northern California under a similar call. While most of the Carson Valley Saints responding to the call sold their assets and headed to Salt Lake City, Conover went into California and bought guns and ammunition in Stockton. He bought so much he ran out of money and didn't have enough to buy wagons and teams to haul it back to Salt Lake City. Fortunately, he met a wagon train headed by Zacheus Cheney composed of Saints from San Francisco and the Mission San Jose area, also heading back in response to a call from Brigham Young. Cheney provided the extra money needed to buy the wagons and bring the supplies to the Salt Lake Valley.

Not all Mormons left Carson Valley immediately. Some remained, hoping to dispose of their properties at higher than the forced sales prices prevailing in 1857. Some remained for years with the hope of eventually "gathering to Zion," whose borders had been severely drawn in. Others became absorbed into the gentile mining population as the silver of the Comstock became a dominant drawing card for disillusioned California gold miners and others. A few eventually became associated with the Reorganized Latter Day Saint Movement of the late 1860s. [31]

Although direct Mormon influence came to an end, the effects of that initial influence remained. They were the first to discover gold on the East Sierra. They had brought "the first organized civic government [to Nevada], the first courthouse, the first school house, the first store and hotel, the first legal records, and the first modern-day irrigation system." [32] With the removal of most Mormons from Carson County in the fall of 1857, however, those desiring separation from Utah came into power. A constitutional convention was called the next year, meeting in Genoa, but its efforts to secure statehood failed. As the rich ores of the Comstock became generally known following their discovery in 1859, additional thousands inundated the area, and in 1861 the Territory of Nevada was sliced off from Utah at 39 degrees west from Washington, D.C. Statehood itself was delayed until 1864 when Nevada (which had generally remained faithful to the Union cause) was rewarded by being admitted to the Union. Successive additions to Nevada at the expense of Utah took place in 1862 and finally in 1866, when the present boundary was established.

NOTES

1. Page, "Orson Hyde and the Carson Valley Mission," 6-10.

2. Page accepts that Brannan traveled over the Truckee route and still calls that "going through Carson Valley," thus using a rather expansive definition of "Carson Valley." However, there is a tradition of Brannan having a connection to upper Carson Valley in 1847. The following comes from a booklet put out by the Centennial Book Committee for the Alpine County Museum (of California) called "ALPINE HERITAGE: One Hundred Years of History, Recreation, and Lore in Alpine County California, 1864-1964."

> Established as an outpost in 1847 by Samuel Brannan, Woodfords was the first white settlement in this area. Brannan, a Mormon on his way from the west coast to Salt Lake to meet with Brigham Young, left two men and a cache of supplies at the spring which is close to the present Woodfords store. The men remained there throughout one winter and built dugouts with log facing for shelter and a storage cabin. The place was soon referred to as Brannan Springs; and

although this settlement project was abandoned in the spring, other squatters arrived and the spot continued to be called Brannan Springs. In the year 1848 a stopping place for travelers was built.

Woodfords is in California at the Carson River and at the head of Carson Valley. It is possible that Brannan, before his return to California in 1847, no longer needing two of his guides, instructed them to find a more southerly route across the Sierra. The site of Woodfords, where the Carson River emerges from the Sierra, would have been a likely place to begin that search. If they waited at "Brannan Springs" and attempted the crossing in early spring, they would have been going west at the same time the Holmes-Thompson party was going east over the same region. Nothing more is known about the men or even if what we have of the story is entirely correct.

3. Page, "Orson Hyde and Carson Valley," 14-15. There has been considerable confusion over the account of the first discovery of gold in Nevada by Abner Blackburn. The traditional account gives Abner this credit. Page challenges that account asserting that the event supposedly taking place in 1849 actually took place in 1850. Page appears to be in error, having evidently failed to read Abner's account carefully enough, and thereby confusing two visits by Abner to the area in 1849 and 1850 as being only one visit—that connected with Captain DeMont in 1850. This confusion perhaps occurred because Hampton S. Beatie made the initial error when he told his story in 1884 of the DeMont Train, claiming that it went through Carson Valley in 1849, when it actually did not go until 1850.

4. Bagley, *Frontiersman*, 171-172.

5. Beatie, "The First in Nevada," 168-171.

6. Carter, *Heart Throbs of the West*, 10:494.

7. Beatie, "The First in Nevada," 168. (Words in brackets are the author's.)

8. Numerous Mormon Smiths and Browns had entered Salt Lake in 1848, as had John S. Carter.

Harmon Parsons came in 1850.

9. Page, "Orson Hyde and Carson Valley," 14-15.

10. Beatie, "The First in Nevada," 168.

11. Crosby, *No Place to Call Home*, 104-105.

12. Probably established by Jefferson Edmunds who also was in business with Porter Rockwell in California.

13. Reese, "Mormon Station," 187.

14. Bagley, *Frontiersman*, 185.

15. Thompson and West, *History of Nevada*, 1881, 31-55.

16. Henry Van Sickle, "Utah Desperadoes," 190-91.

17. Journal History. June 24, 1852, quoted in Page, "Orson Hyde and Carson Valley," 20.

18. These were largely non-Mormon merchants of Salt Lake.

19. Journal History. June 24, 1852, quoted in Page, "Orson Hyde and Carson Valley," 20.

20. Page, "Orson Hyde and Carson Valley," 21.

21. *Deseret News*. January 26, 1854. See Page, "Orson Hyde and Carson Valley," 24-25.

22. *Ibid.*, July 30, 1853. See Page, "Orson Hyde and Carson Valley," p. 22.

23. Page, "Orson Hyde and Carson Valley." 26.

24. Letter, Orson Hyde to Brigham Young, June 19, 1855. Page, "Orson Hyde and Carson Valley," 34-36.

25. See Appendix 21a for list of Carson County Officers, 21b for those granted water rights in Gold Canyon and 21c for missionaries accompanying Hyde.

26. Letter, Orson Hyde to Brigham Young, November 17, 1855. Page, "Orson Hyde and Carson Valley," 51.

27. With the exception of the last paragraph and as noted otherwise the remainder of this chapter is a very brief digest of the presentation of Page, "Orson Hyde and Carson Valley." This is the most complete work yet found on the Carson Valley Saints.

28. Letter, Orson Hyde to Brigham Young, August 8, 1856. See Page, "Orson Hyde and Carson Valley," 79.

29. William Jennings, "Carson Valley." 179.

30. Arrington, *Mormons in Nevada*, 18.

31. Membership Records, Reorganized Church of Jesus Christ of Latter Day Saints.

32. Jensen, "Mormon Settlements in Nevada," 25.

APPENDIX 21a (Note 21:25)
Carson County Officers
Elected September 20, 1855

Fain, James C.--Sheriff
Niles, Henry W.--Surveyor
Daggett, Charles D.--Prosecuting Attorney
Sides, Richard D.--Treasurer
Hodges, H. M.--Constable
Williams, James A.--Constable
Ambrosia, Nicholas--Justice of the Peace
Van Sickle, Henry--Justice of the Peace
Sears, Henry D.--Selectman
Allen, William P.--Selectman
McMarlin, James—Selectman

Source: Thompson and West, *History of Nevada*, 38.

APPENDIX 21b (Note 21:25)
Grantees of Carson River Water
October 1855

Fain, James C.
Fitzgibbon, Morris
Hyde, Orson

Kinsey, Stephen A.
McMarlin, James
McMarlin, John
Merkley, Christopher
Reese, John

Source: Thompson and West, *History of Nevada*, 38.

APPENDIX 21c (Note 21:25)
Mormon Groups Returning to Salt Lake, 1855
From Carson Valley Area

October Group:
Dustin, Seth
Edmonds, Jefferson
Hancock, George W.
Hutchins, Shepherd
Loveland, Chester
Pitt, P. D.
Potter, Amasa
Reese, Enoch

Source:
Deseret News, October 31, 1855, 50.

November Group:
Dodge, Nathaniel
Merkley, Christopher
Merkely, Nelson
Riddle, James
Riddle, Simpson
Steward, Riley

Source:
Deseret News, December 19, 1855.

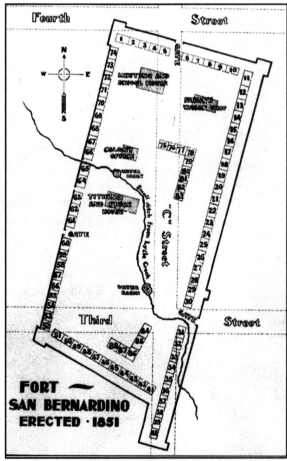

Fort San Bernardino

Above: Fort San Bernardino as seen from a distance from the northeast, sketch by William R. Hutton. *Courtesy Huntington Library*.

Below: Layout of the fort, viewed from above [From Luther Ingersoll's *Annals of San Bernardino*.]

and because some of you have obtained
(gold) more abundantly than that of your brethren
ye are lifted up in the pride of your hearts . . .
and persecute your brethren because ye suppose
that ye are better than they.

    Book of Mormon. Jacob 2:13

22

The San Bernardino Saints and Gold

WHILE THE SAN BERNARDINO Mormon Colony was not established because of Mormon participation in the gold fields, the history of the colony is nevertheless intrinsically entwined with the theme of this volume, the story of *Mormon Gold*. San Bernardino was established as a Mormon gathering point and way station near the coast, important for both California and the whole Pacific region. It became the southern terminus for Mormon winter travel over the southern route between California and Salt Lake. Therefore, during the gold rush, San Bernardino became an important relief and supply station for winter travel to and from the mines. More important to San Bernardino itself, the search for gold and the solicitation of funds coming from gold rush activities became part of their scheme to pay for the land upon which their colony was built. [1]

The story of Mormon involvement in the San Bernardino area began with a detachment of the Mormon Battalion sent to secure supplies from the Robidoux Rancho (Riverside) shortly after their arrival at Mission San Luis Rey in February of 1847. Battalion Boys were also employed in timbering and intercepting marauding bands of desert Indians who periodically spilled into the lush valleys of Southern California. These men

undoubtedly learned of the Old Spanish Trail which headed east to Sante Fe via the southern part of the Great Basin. They may even have explored some of the western reaches of the trail.

Jefferson Hunt became acquainted with Colonel Isaac Williams, proprietor of the Chino Ranch which became popularly known as the Williams Ranch, a haven for many immigrant trains, especially those of the Mormons, over the next several years. Williams had become discouraged over the constant depredations of Indians and renegade whites. He wanted to sell out, offering his ranch and its stock for $500 down and the rest (an undisclosed amount) at the convenience of the buyers. The offer was transmitted to Brigham Young by Captain Hunt when he met his Prophet leader later that year. However, the Church was in no financial position to purchase the land at that time, even had Young been so disposed.

Earlier chapters have recorded how men of the Mormon Volunteers, upon discharge in the spring of 1848, went to work for Williams, having contracted to build a fence. However, when it was only about three-fourths done the rumors of gold were verified and they left for the gold fields in July. It was one of the few recorded instances of the failure of an organized group of Mormons to meet contractual obligations. That Fall, several groups of Mormons passed through Williams' ranch on their way to or from the gold fields. In the winter of 1849-50, several companies of Mormons went to the gold fields via the southern route. Included in these companies were Mormon gold missionaries being sent to mine gold on behalf of prominent sponsors in Utah. In the vanguard was Captain Jefferson Hunt who had been employed to guide a non-Mormon wagon train. With him was Apostle Charles C. Rich, as well as James S. Brown. Rich was being sent to assist Apostle Amasa M. Lyman who had gone to California the previous spring via the northern route. The 21-year-old Brown was being sent on a proselyting mission to the Pacific in company with the veteran missionary, Addison Pratt. A member of the Battalion, Brown had been one of the six Mormons at Coloma when gold was discovered. His story, told later in life, claimed that members of his party discovered gold en route at or near the Amargosa, usually identified as Salt Springs, near the juncture of what became Inyo and San Bernardino counties and the state of Nevada.

Henry Bigler (of the Flake Company and also one of the Mormons at Coloma) reported that Williams told Rich he would now sell his ranch for $200,000. Bigler, aware of the high price of land and beef when he had left the gold fields in the summer of 1848, was convinced that the sale of the cattle alone would pay for the ranch.

When Apostle Rich eventually teamed up with Apostle Lyman in the gold fields in the spring of 1850, some of their time was spent in meetings with Jefferson Hunt, Charles Crisman, Porter Rockwell and Captain Jesse D. Hunter discussing the possibilities of settlements in the southern part of California. While Rich and Lyman returned to Utah via the northern route that fall, Hunt went by way of the southern route, stopping to see his old friend Col. Williams. Crisman also went south with his family and others, including the E. B. Whitneys and the John M. Lewises, establishing residences on or near the Williams Ranch, which was part of Los Angeles County at the time. [2]

Jefferson Hunt left the Rancho on December 15th, reaching Salt Lake on January 21st and reporting to Brigham Young on February 2nd. Three days after Hunt left, Williams sent an offer to Rich to sell out for $150,000, his letter going with a company of six Mormon ex-gold miners headed for Salt Lake. This group reached the city on January 27th with "a package of letters from Mr. Williams of California to President Young containing propositions relative to the sale of his ranch." [3] Perhaps it was the "dullness" of the times that induced the reduction of price from $200,000 to $150,000 — evidence of a "good bargain." It is uncertain as to whether Williams was communicating to Young through Rich, or whether he was "covering his bets" making two offers, a private one to Rich and one to the Church. The fact that San Bernardino appears to have been the private venture of Rich and Lyman supports the latter possibility.

Upon his arrival in Salt Lake Valley from California in the early fall of 1850, Apostle Lyman undoubtedly began to promote the cause of his projected Southern California colonization effort. It was probably at that time that he pressured William Glover of the *Brooklyn* and some of the Mississippi Saints to join with him. While he failed to win over Glover, he found more receptive recruits among the Mississippi Saints, who had settled on the Lyman Tract at Holladay a few miles south of Salt Lake. He was still their patron Apostle. Then, too, the harsh Utah winters and sparse harvests which these Southern Saints had been experiencing since their arrival could be avoided in a land already flowing with "milk and honey" and gold. [4]

Wagon Trains Leave
for Southern California

The San Bernardino-bound company which left Salt Lake in March of 1851 did so under a cloud. President Young had only authorized or expected a small advance group to go into the "Babylon" of California. However, Lyman's recruiting efforts had succeeded, perhaps beyond his expectations, 437 persons with 150 wagons responding to his importunings. When Brother Brigham went to Peeteetneet (present Payson) to inspect the company, he "was sick at the sight of so many of the Saints running to California, chiefly after the god

Daniel Stark (1820-1907)

Daniel Stark was born at Windsor, Nova Scotia, Canada. It was there he attended school and honed his talent for mechanical skills. He went to Boston and got a job working for a cabinet maker. While there, he became acquainted with Mormonism, was baptized, and met Ann Cook, whom he married. They had a child and in 1846 boarded the *Brooklyn* to go to California. Before sailing, Daniel bought surveying tools in New York, and he taught himself to use them while on the *Brooklyn*.

Daniel put his skills to work on building projects in San Francisco, including building his own home. When gold was discovered, he mined for short periods between building projects. When the pioneers in San Bernardino came north to encourage the northern Saints to invest in San Bernardino to help them meet the mortgage payments, Daniel and John Horner went down to examine the colony. John Horner committed to help them, but about the time he was to fulfill his promise he had gone bankrupt and could not.

Daniel bought property in San Bernardino, made improvements on the property and moved there. He had fencing put in, developed a vineyard, brought in potato and other seeds, mules, and a thresher. He intended to make it a permanent home. When the call came in 1857 for the Mormons to abandon San Bernardino, Daniel and his family left with the others and settled near Payson, Utah. There he continued his farming, surveying, and building activities.

Ann passed away in 1865 in Payson. Daniel married a second wife, Elizabeth Baldwin, and later married Priscilla Ann Birkenhead. Brigham Young called on the Stark family to help settle land on the Muddy River, land now under Lake Mead. That mission was later abandoned. The Stark family went to Mt. Carmel and then returned to Payson. Daniel died there in 1907. *Photo Courtesy of Wade Fillmore.*

---

of this world (gold?)." [5] In fact, he was so sick that he could not address the group—one of the few recorded instances when he was without words. His disappointment undoubtedly left him with a distaste for the San Bernardino venture and may have helped to establish the reputation of California Saints as generally being luke-warm and apostate—a reputation that may have contributed to the later 40 year abandonment of the Golden State by the Church. It is interesting to note that at least seven of the nine company "captains" in

the move had been in the gold fields. [6]

The advance group of the main body reached the Sycamore Grove (near Devore) on the edge of San Bernardino Valley on June 11, 1851. The Saints remained there for three and a half months until a permanent location could be established. Rich and Lyman proceeded to the Williams' Rancho to close the bargain with Williams, staying with the Charles Crisman family—Mormon immigrants of 1847. However, their offer was either

Andrew Lytle (1812-1870)

Courtesy San Bernardino Historical Pioneer Society.

Andrew Lytle was born in Milton, Pennsylvania. He joined the LDS Church and was with the Mormons in Missouri, then Nauvoo. In Nauvoo, he was part of the city police force. In the exodus from Nauvoo, he was appointed a second lieutenant in Company E of the Mormon Battalion. His wife camped at Winter Quarters until he returned. On discharge, he was a leader of a group of veterans going to the Salt Lake Valley by the northern route. He went on to Winter Quarters to reunite with his wife.

In 1851, Lytle led one of the companies going south to settle San Bernardino. When they arrived in the area, they camped beside a creek, which became known as Lytle Creek. He worked as a blacksmith. When the Church was organized there he was on the first High Council. Lytle also served in the militia and as a justice of the peace. He was elected as San Bernardio's third mayor.

When the Mormons left San Bernardino and went back to Utah, Lytle went with them and lived for a short time in Beaver, Utah and Salt Lake City. In 1860, he returned to San Bernardino. Lytle Creek, at the time, was proving to be a rich source of gold.

Lytle passed away and was buried in San Bernardino in December 1870.

too low or Williams changed his mind. Williams kept his ranch.

No doubt disappointed, the Apostles left, taking word to their flock. They then went to seek the advice of Captain J. D. Hunter who had moved south from the gold fields the previous fall. The record does not show any help rendered. They returned to the grove on June 20th, camping en route on the Lugo rancho. They left almost immediately for the Pueblo de Los Angeles to confer with Antonio Maria de Lugo, who was generally in residence there rather than at his ranch. On their return they inspected the Lugo ranch with its abandoned and decaying mission and dilapidated

buildings more carefully, returning to the grove on June 29th. The decision was made to purchase the Lugo property, which became known as San Bernardino.

The Southern Californians were at first apprehensive over the arrival of this large body of strange religionists on their borders. However, they soon saw the Mormons as advantageous to the Southland and as a source of flour, wine, lumber, and protection from the Indians.

On July 5th, a Church conference was held to organize a stake. A stake presidency, high council and bishops were called—a sign of intended permanence. Two days later Lyman and Rich left for San Francisco to secure financial aid for the purchase. Arriving in San Francisco, they took a river steamer to Sacramento and a stage to Mormon Island, staying there with Battalion veteran William Simmons on the 15th. Walking to the Mormon enclave at Salmon Falls, they traveled on to the Edmonds' at Brown's Settlement and stayed with the Darwin Chases (probably at Mud Springs) on the 17th. They proceeded into Calaveras (later Amador) County to see W. O. Clark on Dry Creek (Drytown). Clark was a missionary companion of Lyman in the early 1840s. They possibly informed Clark and Chase they had been disfellowshipped in Salt Lake in January.

Returning to Salmon Falls on the 19th, the Apostles met with "a number of the brethren from different parts on business." [7] Traveling by private conveyance to Mormon Island, they caught a stage for Sacramento and then a steamer for San Francisco. No record was made of what help they received from these brethren.

In San Francisco, on the 26th, they "held a council at Brother Morey's [Barton Mowry's] to take into consideration the buying of a ranch in the south part of the state." [8] Two weeks were spent purchasing $8000 worth of provisions. Lyman remained in San Francisco to finalize the financial arrangements for the purchase of a ranch at San Bernardino. He returned with the needed cash on the 29th. The purchase was finally concluded on August 31st with $7,000 down on the purchase price of $77,500. The Mormon company took possession of the ranch the first of October.

The organization of the San Bernardino Stake of Zion which had taken place on July 5th was the first such organization in the west outside of present day Utah. The stake president was the ex-gold miner David Seeley. A school was soon established with J. H. Rollins as one of the teachers. Rollins had been associated with Rich in the gold fields the previous year.

The deed to San Bernardino Rancho was in the name of Lyman and Rich, the Church itself evidently having no part in the legal ownership. It, therefore, appears to have been a purely private enterprise of the two Apostles—with Brigham Young's reluctant permission. Many difficulties over title, the amount of land involved in the purchase, and the subsequent payments ensued. The high interest rate (3 percent per month) on the outstanding debt made a reduction in the principal very difficult. Sales of land to individual Mormons were slow and payments even slower. In fact, the colony was in a precarious position from its very beginning. However, the Saints went to work vigorously in the cultivation of the land, growing fruit trees, grape vineyards and wheat, and in the extraction and milling of timber. They produced butter, cheese, and eggs, and fattened thousands of oxen, built roads into the mountains and established a new, shorter road to Los Angeles. Shortly after its founding, *Brooklyn* Saints, Battalion Boys, and others from the north began to filter into the growing Mormon community.

Among the *Brooklyn* passengers were Quartus Sparks, Jonathan Cade, and William Stout. Among the Battalion Boys was Abner Blackburn, who was elected constable in 1851. At the same time, Battalion veteran J. D. Hunter was elected Justice of the Peace. Many Battalion Boys came, some of whom are either known or believed to have been at some time involved in the gold fields to the north. [9]

Payments on the mortgage were so slow that by 1854 the colony was in danger of foreclosure when their $52,000 note became due. At the first of the year, Lyman, Seeley, and Sparks went to San Francisco, securing an extension loan from the firm of Burgoyne and Ness.

Search for Funds by a Gold Mission in Kern River Country

Several programs were initiated to secure the needed money. California newspapers in early 1855 carried stories of gold discoveries in the Kern River Basin just to the north of the colony. To raise money for payments, a substantial number of men were called early in 1855 to go into the gold fields of Kern River country under the supervision of Theodore Turley and President David Seeley. In return for their services, the men were provided with provisions and paid a moderate daily allowance—to be met by Lyman and Rich. Henry G. Boyle of the Battalion provided an account of at least a portion of these gold missionaries. [10]

Boyle said that on Sunday, March 4, 1855, Brother Lyman "requested a number of us boys to go to Kern River mines to prospect for gold" saying that the Apostle was "using every exertion to secure the funds to pay for this ranch and it is for this purpose we are called." Two days later found Boyle "fitting up for our golden expedition," though he had "little confidence in this expedition." Explaining that he had never had "gold fever," he would rather "stay home among the Saints than to go mingle with the Gentiles," yet he said that he would "go cheerfully" even if he did "not make one cent" and would "not murmur about it either."

The expedition left San Bernardino on March 8th, stopping at the Cucamonga Ranch and the San Gabriel River on the way and arriving at Los Angeles on the 11th. As they moved northward through "Cahonga Canyon," men they met returning from the mines shared "variable" reports. Boyle's group prospected unsuccessfully as they went, the boys "cheerful and full of life."

On the 15th, they repaired the rain-damaged road as they went through the San Fernando Pass. Turning off at the Kern Road trail, they "followed up" Gold Canyon. They found gold "in every place that have been prospected, but in such small quantities that it will not pay."

They soon moved on into the mountains. One party took the trail up San Francisco Canyon with "two parties out in the mountains each side of the road prospecting," but with no reported success. "News from the Kern River Mines" was "very discouraging." They met "old miners" every day returning from the mines, disheartened and disgusted with the "great humbug" of the Kern River Mines.

The canyon was 20 miles long, with 84 crossings of the stream, but "altogether it (was) a good canion road." At the summit they met a group of Mormon prospectors including Cyrus C. Canfield, Hervey Green and Ellis Emes (Elijah Eimes). Canfield and Eimes were Battalion veterans. Green had gone to Utah from California

in the Rhoades Gold Train in 1849. The Mormon prospectors gave "a very discouraged account of the Kern Mines." The gold missionaries, nevertheless, pushed on, camping at Elizabeth Lake on the 18th.

Leaving the lake, they crossed a narrow "neck of the desert," nooning at Willow Springs and camping for the night at Oak Creek. They then crossed "land very high and destitute of timber, but covered with the finest grass, the same kind that grows in Utah," camping at Morehead's Station in Tehachipi Valley. They divided into four or five parties to go out prospecting in the mountains in different directions but with "little success." They found only one place with any hope at all. There was, however, "considerable game," (deer and bear). On the 23rd, some messengers arrived from San Bernardino with the news that "no more teams or men will be sent out here until we can send good news in relation to the gold mines. [11]

On the 24th, Boyle reported that he and his companions traveled 30 miles on foot, carrying their prospecting tools. They had not yet found anything "that will pay 50 cents to the man per day." Continuing to hear discouraging news from the Kern mines, 30 miles distant, the company "upon mature deliberation" decided to return to San Bernardino, only to receive encouraging word about a gulch two miles from their base camp.

They finally rested on Sunday, the 25th, their first such rest. Some of the boys came in during the day "highly pleased and encouraged." The company divided up, 24 (including Boyle) returning to San Bernardino, ten remaining at their "find" and eight to continue on to the Kern River Mines. [12]

On the 31st, Boyle recorded: "Thus ends our expedition without much benefit to anyone. It is all right we have made the exertion according to Brother Lyman's request and I for one feel as though I had done my duty, and I feel all right."

Search for Funds in Northern California

Boyle and others were not allowed to rest long.

Quartus Sparks (1820-1891)

Quartus Strong Sparks was born in Northampton, Massachusetts. He joined the Church and immediately became involved in missionary work. He was a gifted speaker.

Quartus sailed on the *Brooklyn* with his wife, son, and mother-in-law. In California, he was part of the group that settled New Hope in the San Joaquin Valley to raise food for the *Brooklyn* emigrants. Quartus returned to San Francisco because his wife was expecting another child, and was in San Francisco when the discovery of gold became known. Quartus went alone to the mines for a time and had some success. He returned to take his wife to the San Joaquin Valley where they ran a ferry and trading post. Eventually he sold that and moved with his family to San Bernardino.

In San Bernardino, Quartus taught school and became City Attorney. He went with the group of men who went north to obtain refinancing for San Bernardino. Friction gradually developed between Quartus and the Church leaders of San Bernardino as well as with his wife. When the Mormons pulled out of San Bernardino, his wife went to Utah and Quartus stayed. He became a lawyer and lived the rest of his life in San Bernardino and Los Angeles. Quartus died in San Bernardino in August 1891 at age 71.

Courtesy San Bernardino Historical Pioneer Society.

On July 4th, a large group of men were called to go into the northern counties. Of this group at least 12 had probably been involved previously in the gold fields. [13] In the course of two months, Boyle and his companion, David Holladay, visited Saints and former Saints scattered from Petaluma on the north end of San Francisco Bay northward to Dry Creek, a tributary to the Russian River in Mendocino County near the coast. [14]

The missionary work apparently had five objectives, top priority being given to the first two:

> 1) Secure funds for meeting the mortgage debt of the San Bernardino colony.

2) Encourage the Saints "to gather" to San Bernardino.

3) Obtain subscriptions to *The Mormons*, a Church periodical published in the east.

4) Reconvert, rebaptize and reconfirm Mormons.

5) Where possible, preach to non-Mormons.

There appears to have been some resistance by non-Mormons, as well as some Mormons to the missionaries. After his initial visit to the northern Dry Creek, on a subsequent visit Boyle was informed by George W. Sparks, one of the members, that at a recent meeting of the Settlers' Union "some folks talk[ed] of hanging us or driving us out of the country." However, no overt action was taken against the missionaries.

Boyle's importunings with the Leffingwell family (formerly hotel keepers at Pilot Hill) had negative results. Upon presenting William Leffingwell (a High Priest and a Captain of Ten with the Mormon pioneers of 1847) with the purpose of his visit, the latter "refused to do anything for the cause and insinuated that the authorities of the Church could not be trusted." This could have referred to the recent loss by a number of California Saints of their investment in shipping ventures sponsored by Apostle Parley P. Pratt. No great success in raising money was recorded by the indefatigable Boyle, whose only recorded success was $200 from Sparks.

David M. Stuart, a proselyting missionary, reported that he and John Holladay were sent to visit the southern Dry Creek (in Amador County) where he had lived and mined in 1851 and still owned a quarter section of land in the area. Captain Hunt accompanied them. They were well received by Doctor William McIntire, a Mormon physician in the area, and set up a meeting in the chapel in that place. He reported that the meeting was overflowing, filled with his old friends. [15]

Stuart traveled in the mine fields with Holladay from July 29th to September 22, preaching and converting . . . all the old Mormon[s] we could find." They also were able to sell a number of lots in San Bernardino but found a great deal of prejudice against the Saints among the populace. The San Bernardino missionaries returned home after two months of not very effective effort in the north.

Still having financial problems, a special conference was held March 15, 1856, at San Bernardino with Elder Charles C. Rich presiding. A number of men were called on missions to the Society Islands, Australia, and the California

Coast, including Upper California, Oregon and Washington, Southern California, and the Southern California Indians. Those going to the Northern California Coast included the faithful Henry G. Boyle. He at times served in the gold fields, though his work was concentrated in Yolo, Sonoma, and Mendocino counties. Of the 12 members of the Stake High Council sustained at the conference, six men have been identified as having been in the gold fields at some time. [16]

At the conference, President Rich addressed the Saints on the "effort necessary to rid ourselves from the indebtedness that hangs over us." The following day, he also spoke upon "the gathering of Israel," [17] San Bernardino being one of the "gathering places." These continued to be the two primary themes of the missionaries going into the northern counties from San Bernardino in 1856.

Boyle, in reporting the Conference to the *Western Standard*, emphasized the exertions of Brother Rich "to raise the funds to liquidate the debt yet remaining against the Rancho." Optimistically, he reported that they were "raising a drove of cattle to drive into the mines, this will lift the bulk of the debt from our shoulders, or at least reduce it until it will be bearable." [18]

While the intent of Apostle Rich may have been to "liquidate the debt" on San Bernardino and to recruit new residents, the missionary effort of 1856 became absorbed into the general proselyting effort. However, in October Ebenezer Hanks and the Elders from San Bernardino visited the North Country again to raise money for the Rancho. [19]

Dissension Arises in the Colony

In addition to its many other problems, the unity that the San Bernardino Colony experienced in the beginning years began to disintegrate. The burden of the debt, problems over land titles, and the colony becoming a magnet drawing the dissidents and the less committed away from central Zion, began to erode the feelings of the community. Internal dissension reared its ugly head. "Apostates" combined with the Gentiles to oppose the Mormon hegemony that had prevailed.

Rich and Lyman were recalled to Utah on April 18, 1857. They left their new partner, Ebenezer Hanks (the successful Mormon miner and businessman from Salmon Falls) to handle the remaining business details of extinguishing the mortgage. In June, Hanks was notified that he must make a $15,000 payment by August, and a campaign began to raise the money from the Saints in the community. However, the effort to raise the money internally was insufficient. Help from the "upper country" was still needed. Hanks had written to the *Western Standard* earlier that he hoped to reduce the ranch debt by $10,000 by the first of October. He hoped to "get some assistance from the brethren in the upper country" enabling him to raise the needed mortgage money. He could then soon repay them. However, as long as the mortgage was on the ranch, "those half-hearted Mormons and unbelievers have an excuse for not paying us what they owe us." "We have," he said, "sold land enough to pay all our debts, if we only had our pay." He said that anyone helping him would be making "a safe investment" and would at the same time be "doing a substantial good in the Kingdom of God." [20] However, the following day the stake clerk (Hopkins) wrote: "[T]here is but little general interest to pay the ranch debt, though Elder Ebenezer Hanks exerts himself to keep it before the people." [21]

Complicating the picture for San Bernardino was the Utah War. President James Buchanan had been told the Mormons were in rebellion. Without investigating and without attempts at communication or warning, he dispatched 2,500 troops and as many support personnel to Salt Lake to put down the so called "rebellion." In California, because of the polygamy announcement in 1852, anti-Mormon feelings were becoming rampant. Newspapers attacked the Mormons day after day as enemies of the United States. As Buchanan's army was approaching the Saints from the East, there were threats of a gentile army forming in Southern California and invading Deseret from the South.

There had been a long standing call to the Saints to gather to Zion. Because of that and the usual traffic back and forth, parties had been arriving regularly at San Bernardino to take the Southern route to the Great Basin. However, on October 30,

1857, word was received from Brigham Young that, because of the invading armies, all the faithful should return. The San Bernardino Colony was to be abandoned. An exodus began in earnest with forced sales of properties being made at bargain prices. The exodus continued over the winter and by the spring the community was largely in the hands of non-Mormons and their disaffected Mormon allies.

According to Beattie and Beattie, about 55 percent of the Mormons returned to Utah, but many of these soon returned to San Bernardino. While many of those remaining merged with the general population, eventually losing their Mormon identity, others continued to look upon themselves as Mormons, faithful to Joseph Smith, but disavowing Brigham Young and the Utah Church. Disaffected Mormons, by and large, made up the membership of the San Bernardino Branch of the Reorganized Church in 1868-1869. It was the largest such RLDS body in the West. [22]

Hanks was eventually able to pay off the indebtedness with a little money left over to share with his Apostle partners. He returned to Utah where he became the founder of Hanksville, which later became a mining community in the center of the Utah territory. Jefferson Hunt, who had represented Los Angeles and then San Bernardino counties in the California State Legislature, also returned to Utah. David Seeley (the gold miner turned stake president) was involved in a physical fight, and was dropped from his leadership position, becoming disaffected to the point of remaining in San Bernardino to look after his timbering interests. Abner Blackburn (the maverick Mormon gold miner) also remained, still living there when he was invited to join in the Jubilee Celebration of Utah's founding in 1897.

Mormon San Bernardino and the gold rush story surrounding it came to an end after 1857. Shortly after the Mormons officially left, however, in San Bernardino County, gold was discovered in Bear Valley and just to the north in Holcomb Valley (in 1859 and in 1860 respectively.) The Holcomb Valley strike has been the largest in Southern California history. As with the northern discoveries, the resulting Holcomb gold rush frenzy was short lived, but gold is still being drawn from the area. Interestingly, some 30 years after leaving San Bernardino, Church members and Church officials once again, in the 1890s, became engaged in gold mining to help alleviate serious fiscal problems. This time it involved the Stirling mines to the northeast of San Bernardino, at the California-Nevada border. That endeavor, like San Bernardino, was not entirely successful, and the Church finally liquidated those holdings.[23]

NOTES

1. This chapter, draws extensively from William's and Beatie's *Heritage of the Valley*, 77-89 and 170-318. Since the first edition of the present work, a definitive account of Mormon San Bernardino has become available: Lyman, *San Bernardino*. Lyman had previously published a summary of that story in "The Demise of the San Bernardino Mormon Community," which was later reprinted as "The Rise and Decline of Mormon San Bernardino." These latter works by Lyman have been useful for confirming and expanding the present account.

2. See Appendix 22a.

3. Journal History, January 27, 1851.

4. Rich, Diary, April 20, 1851. While the Mississippi Saints were exceptionally well represented among the California-bound company recruited over the winter, according to Rich all but two states were represented, as well as Upper and Lower Canada, England, Wales, Ireland, Austria, New Brunswick, Sweden and France.

5. Brigham Young Manuscript History.

6. See Appendix 22b.

7. Rich, Diary. July 19, 1851.

8. Ibid., July 26, 1851. Morey (Barton Mowry) was one of the more successful Mormon businessmen in the area. He had been a passenger on the *Brooklyn*.

9. See Appendix 22 c.

10. All quotes dealing with the Kern River Expe-

dition, the story of which follows, came from the diary of Henry G. Boyle. See text for dates. In addition to those later identified was David Marshall Stuart who would continue to figure in this story of gold. (See David M. Stuart, Journal).

11. (Ambrose P.) Alexander, (Andrew) Goodwin, and (Reuben or James) Bryent.

12. See Appendix 22d

13. See Appendix 22e.

14. See Appendix 22f.

15. David M. Stuart, Journal.

16. Jefferson Hunt, Andrew Lytle, M. L. Sheppard (Shepherd), Charles Crisman, Daniel Stark, James H. Rawlins (Rollins).

17. Rich, Diary.

18. *Western Standard*. April 12, 1856.

19. *Western Standard*. October 4, 1856.

20. *Ibid.*, August 28, 1857.

21. Richard P. Hopkins, Journal.

22. Record of Membership of the Reorganized Church of Jesus Christ of Latter Day Saints.

23. Arrington and Lyman, "When the Mormon Church Invested in Southern Nevada Gold Mines."

APPENDIX 22a (Note 22:2)

Probable and Possible Mormon Residents at Williams Ranch 1850 Census

It appears that at least three Mormon families were situated at Williams Ranch at the time of the 1850 Census. (The Census entries give ages, state of origin, and occupations.)

Living next door to Isaac Williams were:

E. B. Whitney   31 NY Laborer

| Mary | | 30 Mi | |
| | Sara | 2 Mi | |

Next to the Whitneys in the census were:

Charles Crisman (Chrisman)		45 Ky	Farmer
Mary		33 SC	
	Geo.	17 Il	Laborer
	Hester Ann	14 Il	
	Cemantha	10 Il	
	Mary	8 Il	
	Charles	6 Il	
	Emily	5 on the road	
	Ellen	1 Ca	

Living with the Crismans were:

John M. Lewis		22 Il	Laborer
Jane		18 Il	
William Lewis		20 Il	Laborer
Leonard Ellege		22 Il	Laborer

Note: Most of these were listed by Amasa Lyman as among the San Francisco Saints in 1850. Lewis' wife, Jane, 18, might well have been the older child of the Crismans. A William Lewis, about the right age to be the father of John and William Lewis, entered Utah in 1849, though neither of the latter are listed by Carter as Utah immigrants. In addition to the above family units, a William Workman lived nearby. A William Workman came to Utah in 1848.

A large contingent of Whitneys entered Utah in 1848. A male E. B. Whitney is not listed among them, though an Emmaline B. Whitney is. Lyman lists E. B. Whitney and Harriet Whitney as Transients and E. B. Whitney as a financial contributor in 1850. E. B. Whitney was possibly the Elijah B. Whitmer identified by others.

Source: 1850 Census

APPENDIX 22b (Note 22:6)

Captains of Ten
San Bernardino Pioneers, 1851

Hunt, Jefferson*
Lytle, Andrew*
Lyman, Amasa M.*

Mathews, Joseph*
Pratt, Parley P.
Rich, Charles C.*
Rolfe, Samuel
Seely, David*
Seely, Justice Wellington*

*Note: Those starred are known or believed to have been in the gold fields.

Source: Boyle, Journal.

APPENDIX 22c (Note 22:9)

Some Battalion Boys in the
San Bernardino Colony
Approximately 1851

Allen, Elijah
Bailey, James*
Beckstead, W. E.
Bickmore, Gilbert
Bingham, Thomas*
Boyle, Henry G.*
Button, Montgomery*
Clift, James
Clift, Robert
Curtis, Foster*
Egbert, Robert C.*
Hanks, Ebenezer*
Harris, Silas*
Hirons, James P.*
Hoagland, Lucas*
Hunt, Gilbert*
Hunt, Jefferson*
Hunt, Marshall*
Hyde, William*
Jones, David H.*
Lytle, Andrew*
McIntire, William L.*
Mesic, Peter J.*
Morey, Harley*
Reed, Calvin *
Rawlins, James H. (Rollins)*
Rollins, John Henry
Runyon, Levi*
Shepherd, M. L.*
Stewart, James*
St. John, Stephen M.
Stoddard, Rufus*
Swarthout, Nathan

Tanner, Albert

*Note: Those starred are known or believed to have been involved in the gold fields.

Source: Boyle, Journal.

APPENDIX 22d (Note 22:12)

Members of San Bernardino Gold Mission Remaining in Gold Fields, March 1855

Group A

Alexander, Ambrose P.
Bryent, Reuben
Bryent, James
Cowel, Mark H.
Duell, Ezekiel
Jennings, H.
Johnson, Thomas
McLymont, Alexander
Ridly, Edward
Wilkins, Leonard

Group B

Carter, Philo
Goodwin, Isaac
Jones, William
McBride, (Albert)
McBride, (Alvin)
Sanderson, James
Stoddard, Dr. (Shelburn or Sheldon)
Waits, John (Watts, Wattis)

Source: Boyle, Journal.

APPENDIX 22e (Note 22:13)

Partial List of San Bernardino Saints Called as Short Term Missionaries to Northern California, July 4, 1855

Allen, Brother
Allred, (Redick P.)
Baker, Charles G.
Boyle, Henry G.
Bryent (Bryant), R(euben)*
Casteel (Casto), J(ames) and Son*
Clark, D(an)*
Crosby, W(illia)m. and Son
Egbert, Robert*
Fairbanks, Brother (Nathaniel)*
Frost, B.
Goodwin, Isaac
Haiks, Collins
Holladay, David
Holladay, John
Hyde, J(ohn)
Jackson, Henry*
Jones, David*
Lytle, Andrew*
Mathews, James*
McClemont, Father
Morey, Harley (Mowry)
Morse, Riley
Nelson, Price
Olmstead, H(iram)*
Owen, (James)
Parkerson, Thomas
Reed, (Calvin)
Seely, (David or Justice)*
Stapley, Charles
Starks, Daniel*
Stoddard, Shelburn (Sheldon)*
Sullivan, Archy
Wandell, (C. W.)

*Note: These men had probably previously been in the gold fields.

Source: Boyle, Journal.

APPENDIX 22f (Note 22:14)

**Northern California Mormons Visited by
Elders Boyle and Halladay--1855**

*Sebert C. Shelton and his wife Elizabeth at Stoney Point about eight miles east of Petaluma (with seven children).

*Andrew Jackson Mayfield and Benjamin Franklin Mayfield, sons of Sister Elizabeth Shelton, at Petaluma on the Bay. One or both of these may not have been Mormons.

*William Leffingwell and his wife Eunice and their large family of boys and girls at Leffingwell Mills, about 12 miles east of Stoney Point.

**George W. Sparks and his wife Luana at Dry Creek.

**John Roberts, Sparks' brother-in-law, at Dry Creek.

George W. Chicks and his wife at Dry Creek.

*William Prows (Prouse) and his wife Lodesky at Dry Creek.

John Davenport and his brother (James)--probably at Stoney Point.

John Powell and his wife, probably at Stoney Point.

*Moses Martin and his wife Julia--at Petaluma.

James Marfee (?)

George W. Oman--probably at Petaluma.

Note: Those starred once are known or believed to have been involved in the gold fields. Those with two stars became associated with the Reorganized Latter Day Saints in the late 1860's.

Source: Boyle, Journal

Parley P. Pratt (1807-1857)

Parley P. Pratt was born in Burlington, New York. He joined the LDS Church shortly after it was organized and was part of the Church's first Quorum of Twelve Apostles. He was very influential as a writer and missionary in the early years of the Church.

Elder Pratt entered the California story when in 1851 he was sent on a mission to preside over the Pacific Islands and Coast, and "to open the door to every nation and tongue, as fast as the way is prepared." Traveling via Southern California, Elder Pratt arrived in San Francisco in July of 1851. His traveling companions in a party captained by David Seeley were Elders Lyman and Rich and eight missionaries. He reorganized the Church in San Francisco, formally disfellowshipped Sam Brannan from the Church, and left on a mission in September to Valparaiso, Chile. In Chile, Elder Pratt worked at learning the language and assessing the possibilities for proselyting missionary work. He found the situation very difficult and abandoned the effort after only four months in the country, boarding a ship back to San Francisco in March 1852. He arrived back in San Francisco in May of 1852 and left for the Salt Lake Valley in July, again by the southern route.

In May 1854, Elder Pratt was again sent by the Church on a mission to California, this time to preside over the Pacific Mission (including California) from San Francisco. He arrived in the bustling city July 1854. He was involved mostly in missionary work in the Bay Area, and debated in the local newspapers the newly announced Church practice of polygamy. Elder Pratt left San Francisco, again for the Salt Lake Valley in June 1855, setting apart Elder George Q. Cannon as his replacement before leaving the area.

Elder Pratt was shot and killed in Arkansas in 1857 by an angry man whose estranged wife Pratt had taken in plural marriage. Pratt felt he was rescuing a woman who was trying to escape an abusive relationship. The man judged that to be interference and retaliated. (The story of Pratt's life can be found in his *Autobiography*. For the circumstances of his death, see Steven F. Pratt, "Eleanor McLean and the Murder of Parley P. Pratt," *BYU Studies* 15 (Winter 1975) 225-56.) *Photo Courtesy LDS Archives.*

We saw the Lord standing upon the breastwork
of the pulpit, before us; and under his feet
was a paved work of pure gold . . .

Doctrine and Covenants 110:2

23

Proselyting the Gold Fields

WHEN APOSTLE RICH left Salt Lake for his mission to California in the fall of 1849, he was charged to "preach the gospel as he has the opportunity." [1] This injunction to "preach the gospel" can either be considered a charge specific to Rich or the signal of a change in the Church policy. In 1847, instructions to the Saints in California had read: "We do not desire much public preaching or any noise or confusion concerning us or our religion in California at the present time." [2]

The difference in instructions, as well as the way those instructions were followed, no doubt came from differences in time and place. In 1847, the Church members were trying to establish themselves, having been driven from their homes in the East. Becoming settled and self sustaining was of primary importance. By 1849-50 the Saints were settled in the Great Basin and in significant numbers in the San Francisco Bay area. In the gold fields, they were still scattered and continually in transit. Apostle Charles C. Rich joined with his senior companion, Apostle Amasa M. Lyman, in California in the spring of 1850, and they responded to the situations they found. They held council with the Saints in San Francisco, organized a branch of the Saints in the Mission San Jose area, and made a rapid tour of the Saints in the gold fields. The latter were scattered from Mormon Bar in Mariposa country in the south to Rough and Ready on the Yuba River to the north. Scattered as they were, spiritual en-

couragement had to be more person to person than to sizable groups. The spiritual encouragement was combined with collection of tithes in gold to feed the Mormon mint, to support Mormon paper currency, and to purchase supplies and capital goods in the Great Basin. The Apostles did not record group meetings taking place in the gold fields. However, the company of proselyting missionaries on their way to the Society Islands, who arrived in California in the summer of 1850, did record some religiously oriented meetings.

Judging from the evidence, and as far as the Apostles were concerned, preaching of the Gospel to the Gentiles (non-Mormons) would have to wait. The Apostles completed their three month grand tour and were back in San Francisco in July. By mail they were asked to return as soon as possible to Salt Lake. There had been a spiritual vacuum in the gold country, which became even worse after the Apostles returned to Utah. Hundreds of Mormons remained after the Apostles left, and those were continually being added to by more who, rather than looking for gold, were fleeing the weather, crickets, Indians and/or the strong discipline of Mormon Church leaders. There is no evidence of religiously oriented Mormon activity in the gold country between 1850 and 1853.

The on-site leadership from Salt Lake was about to change in Northern California as Apos-

Office Staff of the *Western Standard*

In the photograph, left to right, are: Joseph Bull, David H, Cannon, George Q. Cannon, William H. Shearman, and Matthew F. Wilkie. The photograph was taken in 1857 by R. H. Vance. *Courtesy Utah State Historical Society.*

tles Rich and Lyman were replaced by Apostle Parley P. Pratt and then George Q. Cannon. With the latter, the emphasis changed from the need for gold to sustain the Utah financial system to sustaining the members spiritually, organizing the members, and getting the Church message out to non-members. How did those in the gold fields factor into this?

Parley P. Pratt
as President of the Pacific Mission

Apostle Parley P. Pratt, President of the Pacific Mission, reached San Francisco on July 11, 1851 and organized a branch of the Church again after the disorganization that had resulted from the movement of the San Francisco Saints into the gold fields in 1848-50. After a short, abortive mission to Chile, Pratt held a Church court which withdrew fellowship from the illustrious Sam Brannan, not for apostasy or misuse of Church funds but for participating in vigilante activities.

Soon after his return from Chile, Pratt left for Deseret, but returned to California in 1854 when he was reappointed to leadership of the Saints in Northern California. [3]

Pacific Missionaries Seek
Support in the Gold Fields

In 1853, a large group of missionaries bound for Pacific and Indian Ocean missions reached San Francisco. They did not come financed from Salt Lake City, but were expected to make their way on their own, "without purse or script." They met with some of the more affluent Saints in the Bay area, soliciting financial help in reaching their fields of labor. It was decided that they should first go among the dispersed Saints, including those in the gold country, to raise what they could. Two of these missionaries, Reddick N. and Reddin A. Allred, headed for Salmon Falls where they had relatives. [4]

En route they visited the J. (John or James) Davenport family [5] at Mormon Island. At Salmon Falls they found their ailing cousin, Reuben W. Allred, formerly of the Battalion. A younger brother, James Riley Allred, was off mining about eight miles distant. Sending for James to come in, the missionaries visited several Mormon families located in the area. Among these was (Hezekiah) Thatcher, a Captain of Ten in 1847, "who had once been a member." He gave them $20 each, "expressed his unshaken faith in the work, and wished to be readmitted to the Church." He apparently left for California without permission or Brigham Young's blessing and assumed he had forfeited his membership in the Church. The missionaries counseled him to "report to the presidency at San Bernardino." [6]

When James returned, Reddick "could not refrain from tears for he had been toiling in the mines till he had lost his health and almost his voice, and only living from hand to mouth." James indicated a desire to return to Utah and was counseled to quit mining and go to work by the month until he could secure the means to go.

They visited Brother (James) Smith, a friendly apostate, and the faithful Brother Thomas Orr telling them of their mission. Both appeared willing to assist them financially. While visiting with the Orrs, missionaries Chauncey West and William F. Carter arrived from San Francisco informing the Allred brothers that they were to "gather all the means" they could by donation and that "Brothers Horner, Sparks and others (in San Francisco) would make up the deficiency."

Having left West and Carter at the Falls, the following day the Allred brothers split up. Reddin crossed the river and headed north for Mormon Ravine where the Crows, Harmons, and other Mormons lived. Reddick went southeast to visit Father Chase about 10 miles away, stayed overnight with him and was given $10. [7]

From the Chases, Reddick went to Deer Creek House, between Mormon Tavern and Shingle Springs. It was still owned by Jefferson Edmonds, but he had rented it out and was living at his mill nearby. Edmonds presented Reddick with $25. While there the missionary met a number of other Mormons, [8] who made only small contributions to the cause as "most of them were only able to buy their daily food." The Elder spent the night with the Arnolds and "advised them to settle their business as soon as possible and return to the Salt Lake Valley."

Reddick returned to Salmon Falls with a lame, inflamed foot. He found that Elder West had "preached to an attentive congregation" the previous day. Reddin returned from the north with $90 which he had received from Brother (Robert) Crow and others.

John Orr, a son of Thomas Orr, made Reddin and Reddick a gift of his silver watch and was told that "the Lord would reward him for his kindness." He replied that he "did not know for he had never been baptized in the Church." Reddick was shocked, counseling him "not to delay for we had no claim on the promises of God till we first obeyed his command."

The four missionaries remained at Salmon Falls a couple of days, held several meetings and preached "upon the order of the Church and Kingdom." Following one meeting, a Mr. Cheasman "said he had been well entertained" and he moved that a collection be taken up to "forward" the mission. Sixty dollars were collected, fifty of it, however, coming from prospering Brother Ebenezer Hanks.

The missionaries reluctantly left and were taken down to the river by Brother Orr who was "going after a load of goods." They arrived at Sacramento that night after wading through "mud and water" to their knees. Putting up at a rooming house, they met two men, Mssrs. Goode and Cosgrove, who had "a very favorable opinion" of the Mormons and wanted to learn more of the divinity of the work. The missionaries talked well into the night, teaching them and bearing testimony. They reached San Francisco the next day, pleased to find that the Saints [9] had come through with over $4000, enough money to pay their passages to the mission fields. Reddick also learned of the death of his daughter four days after he had left on his mission.

Auburn

A group of French gold miners (Francois Gendron, Philibert Courteau and Claude Chana) came through the area of Auburn on their way to Coloma in the spring of 1848. While camping in the ravine adjacent to what became the town, Chana discovered gold. The deposits were rich enough that the miners decided to stay and not go on to Coloma.

The location went through various names. At first it was called North Fork Dry Diggings. When John S. Woods settled and began to mine the ravine, the name was changed to Woods Dry Diggings. By mid 1849, several settlers from Auburn, New York began working the ravine and the name changed again to Auburn. The lithograph shows miners digging even at the edge of town.

The area quickly developed into a well established mining camp. By 1850 the population had grown to about 1500, and in 1851 Auburn became the seat of Placer County. Elders Shearman and Stuart preached in the courthouse in Auburn. This was a small wood structure in the middle of town. The present Courthouse turned Museum came later.

The artist was C. Langdon and publisher Gregory's Express. *Courtesy Bancroft Library.*

Attitudes toward Saints in the Gold Fields

There appear to have been at least three concentrations of Mormons in the gold fields of El Dorado and Sutter counties in 1853. One was at Long Valley or Mormon Ravine, near Auburn. The second was at Salmon Falls and Mormon Hill. The third was located between Mud Springs (El Dorado) and Deer Creek, with Shingle Springs as the central location. It would appear that there were sufficient Saints in these locations for a substantial Church organization. However, while some preaching took place, there is no evidence of any formal Church organization, although there may have been a meetinghouse at Dry Creek. If all 36 missionaries spread throughout Northern California in a way similar to the Allreds, Carter, and West, there may well have been other still unidentified sizable groupings of Saints in the gold fields of California in 1853.

The Church leaders did not have a high opinion of the level of spirituality in California, particularly in the gold fields. In a report of Elder Lyman to the Church leaders in July of 1850 as he was leaving the gold fields, he said, "The only place suitable for a colony of the brethren is in the southern part of the state . . . to strike hands with a man in California (northern, that is) having the spirit of God was a rare treat." [10] Lyman's view of gold miners was in harmony with that of Brigham Young and may have helped to form it. By 1852, the latter was threatening disfellowshipment to those who went to California on their own. He said "Saints, you cannot go to California, as you have done in years gone by, and still retain your fellowship in the Church. It is getting too late in the day for children of the kingdom to trifle." [11] Also in 1852, the Church had made a public announcement concerning the practice of polygamy. With that announcement the mood toward California in 1852 turned decidedly negative.

This negative attitude of Brigham Young toward California was reinforced by a letter from Captain Jefferson Hunt who was serving as the Representative in the California Legislature from San Bernardino. He said that the people in San Bernardino were doing more to open up the country "than is a thousand and fifty old Rag tag and bob tail Mormons scattered all over the country heare what wil be the end of them it would take a profit [prophet] to tel they are all agoing back when they get rich and they are geting power [poorer] every day to hear is more distress heare for monney than anny place . . ." [12]

Missionaries Return from Hawaii
George Q. Cannon Replaces Parley P. Pratt

In August of 1854, George Q. Cannon, the former Mormon gold miner missionary turned proselyter, returned to San Francisco from Hawaii. Returning with him were Elders James Hawkins, Henry Bigler, and William Farrer, who had also served gold mining missions. Cannon remained with President Pratt for several weeks, helping the Apostle with his autobiography. In October, he returned to Utah via San Bernardino and was married shortly after to Elizabeth Hoagland, whose brothers, Peter and Lucas, had been involved in the gold fields in 1850. [13]

In the meantime, President Pratt urged the Church authorities in Salt Lake to establish a newspaper in San Francisco, and requested that Cannon return from Utah to assist him. In May of 1855, Cannon was finally called to return to the Bay Area. By the time Cannon had reached San Francisco, however, Pratt had already left San Francisco to return to Utah. Pratt had crossed the Bay, and had stopped for a while to visit in the East Bay at John C. Naegle's. Cannon, hoping to overtake Pratt, crossed the Bay and took the stage to Mission San Jose. Nearing the Mission, he got off at the Naegle adobe in time to intercept Pratt. During their visit, Pratt laid his hands on Cannon's head and "set him apart" (commissioned Cannon) to replace him as President of the Pacific Mission and then Pratt continued on his trip back to Utah.

Cannon's priority goal was to publish the *Book of Mormon* in the Hawaiian language, into which he had translated it. This task was completed on January 26, 1856, when 2,000 copies finally came off the press. However, the establishment of a press cost money. Little if any help could be expected from a hard-pressed Church headquarters. The Saints and friends in Northern California had to be relied on to obtain the press.

On September 22, 1855, a conference was held at Sacramento with Elders Lyman and Rich present. Elder David M. Stuart (a missionary from Utah and former gold miner) maintained that the Saints in the area were "in the wrong environment, and have no business there: they should be gathered out of the mine[s] and take[n] to the home of the Saints [presumably Salt Lake]." He was called to remain in the mission field to help accomplish this task. Other missionaries were released. Stuart was assigned as a junior companion to William H. Shearman, a former Baptist minister. They were set apart to "labor in the mining regions," specifically Sacramento, Amador, El Dorado and Placer Counties, "without purse or script." [14]

With the Hawaiian edition of the *Book of Mormon* published, President Cannon turned his attention to the establishment of a Church-oriented newspaper. Elder Orson Hyde, who was stationed in the Carson Valley east of the mountains, had been given ecclesiastical authority over Cannon. Hyde suggested the name, *Western Standard*. It was to be more than a secular paper, such as had been published by Sam Brannan. The *Western Standard* was to become the voice of Mormondom on the West Coast and in the Pacific, established to "correct the misrepresentations of Mor-

Courtesy Pioneer Memorial Museum, International Society Daughters of Utah Pioneers.

David M. Stuart (1826-1898)

David Marshall Stuart was born in Irvine, Ayreshire, Scotland. He listened to missionaries, was converted, joined the Church, and immediately wanted to emigrate to "Zion." He worked his way to Zion, going by way of Memphis, St. Louis, and Winter Quarters, and reached the Salt Lake Valley in 1847.

David went to California and found he didn't like hunting for gold. He also tried his hand at buying, raising and selling cattle. In a visionary answer to prayer he felt instructed to devote his life to missionary work. David was called to do missionary work among the northern gold mines. He encouraged members to go to San Bernardino or the Salt Lake Valley and sold subscriptions to the *Western Standard*. He also was sent on a mission to the Oregon and Washington Territories.

After returning to the Salt Lake Valley, he continued to be involved in missionary work. David Stuart died in Ogden, Utah at 72 years of age.

monism," and to defend polygamy. [15] The first issue came off the press on February 23, 1856, and was distributed by a number of agents, some of them in the gold fields. [16]

Missionary Activities of Stuart and Shearman

On March 1, 1856, the paper included a letter from Elders Stuart and Shearman, posted from Cold Springs, located three miles northwest of Placerville near the junction of Hangtown and Weber Creeks. The letter stated in part:

> Since we saw you we have been greatly blessed, and have the pleasure of knowing that we have been the means of convincing some of the truth, of sowing seed, which, we trust, will yet bring forth fruit. We have raised quite a stir throughout the country I assure you, considering we are but beginners.

> We expect to go from here to Mud, and Diamond Springs, and about Placerville, Georgetown, etc. Since we saw you we preached in Auburn, in the Court House, and were invited to come again. We also obtained the Court House to speak in at Coloma, and at other places we had churches . . .

> We believe there is yet a good work to be in California if the right men can be sent out.

In the meantime, Shearman wrote from the Homestead House in Long Valley or Mormon Ravine. [17] It was not the first visit, as the missionary report said that they had a "truly hospitable welcome from our friends, Brother (Robert) Crow and Sister Harmon, with whose families we always find a pleasant quiet home, and a cheerful retreat from the bustle and anxiety of active life . . . it is with pleasure we visit this

William H. Shearman (1831-1892)

William H. Shearman was born in England, emigrated to the U.S., and crossed the plains in 1849 to go to the gold mines in California. He encountered Amasa Lyman in crossing the plains and met Brigham Young when he arrived in Salt Lake City. Because of the influence of these men, Shearman converted to Mormonism and joined the Church. However, he continued on to California.

William had literary talents and in California worked on the staff of the *Western Standard*. Shortly before the leadership left in 1857 because of conflicts in Utah, he was called to do missionary work under the direction of George Q. Cannon.

In Utah, William Shearman was involved in mercantile ventures. He was a leader in the movement to start Sunday Schools in Cache Valley. He went on a mission to England, served as president of the Liverpool Conference, wrote for the *Millennial Star*, and led 636 Saints emigrating to Utah. His relationship with the LDS Church became strained when he became caught up in the

Godbeite movement, and was business manager for a time for the dissident *Mormon Tribune*, a forerunner of the *Salt Lake Tribune*. He eventually left the Godbeite movement and returned to better relations with the LDS Church. He died in 1892 in Salt Lake City, Utah.   (See Walker, *Wayward Saints*.) *Courtesy Utah State Historical Society.*

---

mountain 'Homestead.'" [18] They also met with Brother George P. Dykes "with whom we have spent many pleasant hours, and who appears to sincerely desire the welfare and prosperity of Zion." [19]

The Elders had preached at the Courthouse in Auburn on the preceding Sunday "through the politeness of the gentlemanly Sheriff, Mr. Henson." A small but "highly intelligent" audience consisting of the "leading men of the county" had attended. While some "lasting impression" may have been made, Shearman opined to the *Western Standard* that "few of the great, the learned, or rich men, can make up their minds to sacrifice their honor, reputation, influence and wealth, for the sake of their soul's salvation."

Shearman reported that he and his companion had recently visited Salmon Falls where the Orr family had received them with kindness, express-

ing the desire to "gather with the Church as soon as practicable." Shearman also referred to "brother (William) Lunceford who might successfully compete with Elder Ross for the cognomen of 'The Walking Bible.'" He added that the missionaries had spent a week with the Luncefords, who had a large farm at Pleasant Hill, preaching four times.

From Pleasant Hill the missionaries continued south into Amador County. Writing from Drytown on June 23rd, Shearman reported a visit with Brother (Robert) Plunkett's family in that town, where they were "kindly welcomed by all the friends here." [20] They preached in the local church and also visited Sutter Creek and Jackson. Going on to Pleasant Vale on Dry Creek, residents there listened to their gospel message as they taught in the school house. [21] While the people had administered to their needs and had been attentive, Shearman wrote, they "manifest such

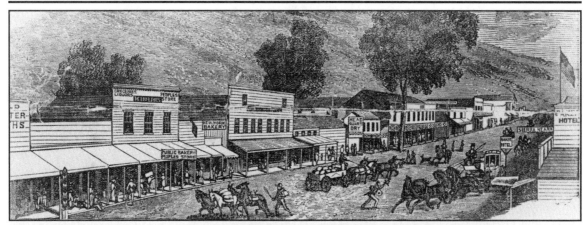

Coloma ca. 1853

At the beginning of 1848, Coloma was just an advantageous sawmill site near a Maidu or Nisenan Indian village of the same name. In the Maidu language, Coloma meant "beautiful vale." With the discovery of gold on January 24, 1848, everything changed. By the fall of that year, the influx of people had brought only three stores to the site. In six more months, however, the area was covered with hundreds of tents that gradually gave way to more permanent structures. The town grew to a population of 600-900. The extent of mining that could be done at Coloma did not justify such a large town, but there were large numbers just passing through. Coloma became a place one had to see for historical reasons, and a social and recreational center for the northern mining district. It became the county seat when El Dorado County was created in 1850. As early as 1852 farmers were planting vineyards. It began to appear that vineyards might overshadow gold as the primary industry of the community.

"By the early 1850s, Coloma had opulent hotels and restaurants with fine china, silverware, and white tablecloths. Menus offered everything from oysters to ice cream. There were saloons and gambling halls. In the Coloma Theater, La Petite Susan did her "Spider Dance" and "Highland Fling," Mademoiselle Thierry starred in ballet, John Kelly played his violin and sang in a sweet tenor, and the Potter, Chapman, and Robinson family troupes played everything from Shakespeare to "The Hunchback." . . . There were [also] a couple of breweries, a candy store, and two bookstores." (Dillinger, *The Gold Discovery*, 39.)

The upper view (*Courtesy California State Library*) is of the main street in 1853. The lower view (*Courtesy Bancroft Library*) shows how that street closely followed the river.

an indifference to the principles, that I confess I sometimes feel rather discouraged." No branches of the Church were reported organized, nor were new members baptized.

On July 26th, Shearman reported on a trip he and Stuart had taken to the Mormon settlements in Carson Valley. They had been warmly received by Judge [Apostle] Orson Hyde and treated to a tour of the numerous Mormon settlements just getting off the ground in Washoe, Eagle, Carson and other valleys. Shearman observed that many of the gentile farmers wanted to sell out as the Mormons moved in and would probably trade for property west of the Divide. Promoting the opportunities there, he cautioned "let those who go, be sure to take their winter's provisions with them, for all who are there have as much as they can do to provide for themselves." Constant and certain communication with Salt Lake was assured with an express soon being put into operation. Shearman saw many advantages there over Salt Lake itself and but "a few days travel distance from that city, [a gross exaggeration] which can be visited at almost all times of the year." [22] Shearman's detachment from San Bernardino is evident. Finally, he informed those in Carson Valley that should they have business in California, Brother William Lunceford invited them to stay at his place, Pleasant Hill, "free of expense." [23]

Shortly after their return from Carson Valley, Stuart and Shearman had a temporary parting of the ways. The latter, a fastidious person, proposed to go mining to earn a new set of clothes, as he was threadbare. The stalwart Stuart opposed that course, proposing that they should put their faith in God, that He would open the hearts of the people to meet their needs. Shearman refused and went to work in the mines. Stuart traveled alone. Lonely and concerned about their separation, he prayed that they would soon be reunited. Traveling to a new field, Stuart found a group of miners who were interested in his message, as well as his threadbare condition. They were baptized, along with a number of women, and furnished him with the needed new clothes.

On September 5th, the missionaries were reunited at White Oak Springs where Shearman had been mining. He had evidently also been do-

ing some missionary work, reporting that he had "continued preaching to the best of my ability as opportunity offered" in Drytown, French Town, Pekin and Coloma. [24] But, he observed, "politics just now occupies so much of the time and attention of the people, that it is difficult to get an audience together . . . they care very little for any religion, much less for a religion which like Mormonism, requires the sacrifice of all." Explaining himself, he said that "they are here to make money, honestly if they can, but to make it any how, and until their minds can be diverted from this one all-absorbing, engrossing idea, it is impossible that religious truth can make any lasting impression upon them." The missionary then cried to the Saints, "If those who are professedly Mormons would only live up to their religion, abide by their principles and strengthen our hands, things would not be so bad as they are." [25]

The missionaries preached again in the courthouse at Coloma, the El Dorado County seat, on the doctrine of the "New and Continued Revelation," probably including the revelation on celestial and polygamous marriage, uniquely Mormon doctrines. Referring again to the Saints, Shearman observed: "it seems to me, that a great many are trying to secure the favors of both God and Mammon. They want to be remembered among the Saints, but they don't want any body to know it outside of the Church."

On October 6, 1856, a semi-annual Conference of the Church in Upper California was held at the Philharmonic Hall in San Francisco. President Cannon reported that while there had been few baptisms, the Elders had "imparted new life to many of those already in the Church, who had lost their love, and have removed much prejudice from the minds of the communities . . . opening the way for the spreading of the gospel, and the gathering out of the honest in heart." [26]

Elders Shearman and Stuart reported their travels through the mining counties where they had preached from "pulpit to bar" to good congregations, but that "the people seemed hardened against receiving the truth." They reported that in the gold fields there were about 60 members generally in good standing, with 11 baptized and two re-baptized since the last conference. The Elders were assigned to continue their labors in the mining counties, "as wisdom and the Spirit of the Lord shall direct." The Elders were split up with Shearman going with Elder Boyle to the counties north of the Bay and Stuart returning to the mining counties.

President Cannon asked Stuart to make a detour on his return to the gold fields into Yolo County to visit the Thatcher family. Traveling to Sacramento by steamer, he headed for the Thatcher's on foot, their home being 20 miles to the north. En route, he was picked up by a jolly, young, 26-year-old native of Virginia, William B. Preston, to whom he preached. Staying overnight at his log cabin, he was asked to hold several public meetings in the area on Sunday, November 2, 1856. Attending one of these were W. F. and Dr. Washington Anderson. [27] After visiting the Thatchers he proceeded to Father Crow's at Mormon Ravine, where he was well received as always.

On December 30th, Stuart reported from Union Town, a mile or so from Coloma, that he was at Brother Plumtree's. "[A] neat little cottage home, the spirit of God broods over the dwelling, a fit habitation for angels or the priesthood of God to visit." The local Methodist minister had warned Sister Plumtree to leave the Church but she, "like the Biblical Ruth," had declared that "the Mormon people henceforth should be her people, and their God would be her [G]od." [28]

On January 3, 1857, Elders Shearman and Boyle joined Elder Stuart and Sister (George Q.) Cannon at Salmon Falls, where they stayed with the Orrs and held a meeting. Both Boyle and Shearman had shortly before "renewed their covenants" through re-baptism. A Reformation and such renewals were sweeping through the Church and President Cannon was pressing a corresponding program in California. Stuart had evidently shown some resistance but had finally acquiesced and was re-baptized and re-confirmed so that he "could continue in the service of God." The re-united companions went on to Folsom, where they preached twice.

At one of the meetings a Methodist minister, the Reverend Dryden, mockingly engaged the missionaries in verbal combat. With tongue in cheek, he said that he and the congregation had been pushed into a "close corner—with no escape except through Mormonism." However, before he joined, he wanted to know "how many wives he should be allowed to have—whether if he should be fortunate in obtaining a large number, it might not excite Brigham Young's jealousy and displeasure. Secondly, what would the Danites do with John Hyde, Jr., if they should catch him." [29]

A local Mormon businessman in attendance, S. G. Higgins, defended the Elders, charging the reverend with failing to give "one word of testimony of any kind in elucidation of the doctrine which he teaches." He continued, "we have reason to rejoice in the opposition that is offered and in the wisdom of God, which is able to turn the evil designs of the devil to His own Glory . . ."

Moving up the west bank of the North Fork of the American River toward Auburn, the missionaries preached at Rattlesnake Bar, at Ophir to a "crowded house," and at Secret Ravine (near present-day Roseville). They then returned south, visiting the Luncefords and Rabbles (Raihles) at Pleasant Hill, staying there over two Sabbaths, preaching seven times, re-baptizing, and baptizing one. They sold several copies of a pamphlet on polygamy, adopting "the plan of offering them for sale every time we preach, saying a few words in explanation of our reasons for publishing such a work." [30]

Shearman reported that John Hyde "has been round stirring the people up, and causing a little excitement. Poor John—he is doing a work which was needed. Undoubtedly he is a chosen instrument as he professes to think—yet for his own sake I could have wished he had left the dirty job to somebody else." [31]

On March 16th, Shearman reported from Pleasant Hill that he and his companions had just returned from a tour to Drytown, Fiddletown, Sutter Creek, etc., being especially well received at Drytown. They were able to preach every day, He observed: "As to those who are strangers to the power and spirit of the gospel of Christ in these parts, they are indeed an ungodly generation who neither fear God, regard man, nor dread the devil . . . How Latter-day Saints can find any enjoyment in associating with them I cannot conceive." However, in a forgiving, if not condescending, tone he added, "When I meet with one who has given his time, his means, and even risked his life itself for the work of God—let he be ever so degraded and ruined, be he ever so dear to honor or ambition, so that he does not entirely turn away from and fight against the truth—my heart warms towards him." [32]

In summary, between 1848 and 1853, the Mormons of the mining area were essentially seen as a source of funds to support the proselyting activities of the Church. However, from 1853 to 1857 the emphasis changed to reconverting the Saints and former Saints who had lost contact with the Church, at the same time pursuing missionary work among persons never affiliated with the Church.

NOTES

1. Rich, Certificate.

2. Journal History, August 7, 1847.

3. Holdaway and Camp, eds., "A Mormon Mission to California in 1851." Reva Stanley, *The Archer of Paradise*.

4. The story of this effort is from Carter, *Treasures of Pioneer History*, 5:322-326.

5. This family later lived near the Sheltons at Stoney Point.

6. Thatcher later led a group of Saints to Salt Lake via Carson Valley. Several of his sons a few years later became missionaries to the gold fields and one of them, Moses, still later became an Apostle.

7. Darwin Chase, of the Battalion, had maintained a hotel at Mud Springs in 1850. In his thirties he was a bit young to be referred to as "Father Chase." Darwin, who had been disfellowshipped in 1851, may have had either Isaac or Ezra Chase living with him. These two men in their late fifties and early sixties had entered Utah in 1847 and 1848. While at the Chases, the Elders received $5 each from Clark Huband and W. Shaw.

8. Father Duston, Brother (Josiah) Arnold and his sons Orson and Joseph, as well as brothers R. Stevens, G. Dibble, Young, Dodge and two others unnamed. Josiah Arnold had been a resident of nearby Placerville in 1850, living there with his wife, Elizabeth and his two sons, Orson (age 12) and Joseph (age 10), both born in New York.

9. Brothers Horner, Williams, Sparks and others.

10. Journal History. July 12, 1850.

11. *Deseret News*, January 24, 1852. Disfellowshipment was a less severe form of Church discipline than excommunication.

12. Hunt, Letter, April 2, 1854. (Words in brackets are the author's) Hunt's political activities in California are described in Sutak, "Jefferson Hunt: California's First Mormon Politician."

13. Flake, *George Q. Cannon*, 91-93; California Census.

14. Stuart, Journal. (Words in brackets, author's). Two missionaries had penetrated as far north and east as Nevada City, baptizing the Carlow family. In 1857, N. H. Carlow, a miner, wrote to President George Q. Cannon in San Francisco summarizing the Church activity in the mining community of Nevada (Nevada City, Yuba County) since September 1855. He said, "There has been seven baptized in Rock Creek, about four miles north of Nevada (City); others are convinced but are holding back some for a parent or companion, or a good name, etc. My son and I are the only elders here that I know of, and we are but children." He went on to say: "We have no place for holding meetings but perhaps there might be a place obtained; my house is not as convenient in location as would be wished, but, such as it is, it is at all times open to the use and accommodation of the Saints."

15. *Western Standard*. Feb. 23, 1856.

16. The agents consisted of the Honorable Jefferson Hunt in Sacramento; Thomas Orr, a resident of Salmon Falls in El Dorado County; David M. Stuart and William H. Shearman "throughout the

mines;" Horace Morse in Columbia (probably the major mining community of Columbia, near Mormon Gulch in Tuolumne County). John Harris in Coloma and George P. Dykes of Auburn, in Sutter County, were not included at the time, but later became agents. The following were agents in other areas of the mission. Many of them had been involved in the gold fields: J. M. Horner and John C. Naile of Mission San Jose, William Hopkins of Union City, Zacheus Cheney of Centerville, Eli Whipple of Redwood City, and Joseph Mount of Napa City.

17. This hotel was owned or managed by Sister Mary Ann Harmon, one of the Mississippi Saints and the widow of James Harrison who had died of fever contracted while crossing the Isthmus of Panama on his return from a visit to the East.

18. *Western Standard*. May 31, 1856. While the Crows were legal landowners in Placer County, Sister Harmon is not recorded as a property owner. Placer County Deeds, Placer County Courthouse.

19. Dykes, the agent for the *Western Standard* at Auburn, had been a not-too-popular officer in the Mormon Battalion. He was a long-time Church member and frequent missionary, having recently returned from a mission to Scandinavia and Germany. However, he soon left the Church. His influence may have contributed to Shearman's estrangement from the Church.

20. *Western Standard*, June 28, 1856.

21. Pleasant Vale has not been identified. (Gudde and Gudde).

22. *Western Standard*, August 9.(Words in brackets are the author's)

23. Pleasant Hill appears to have been in the vicinity of the intersection of French Creek and French Town roads about two miles south of Shingle Creek. It is not yet known when the Luncefords settled there. William had come to Utah at 54 years of age in 1850, with his wife, Rowsey, a Mary Lunceford, (possibly a second wife), age 56, and eleven children ranging from 3 years to 29 years of age.

24. Gudde and Gudde list a White Oak Springs only in Nevada County, but a White Oak Flat in White Oak Township, just south of Salmon Falls. Drytown is well established in Amador County between Plymouth and Amador City. French Town, was located south of Pleasant Hill near the junction of Sawmill and Forty Mile Creeks. Pekin has not been identified, though nearby Fiddletown had one of the largest "Chinatowns" (Peking?) in the gold fields.

25. *Western Standard*, September 20, 1856.

26. *Ibid.*, October 11, 1856.

27. Dr. Washington Anderson, who may have remained unbaptized, became one of Brigham Young's physicians. Both W. F. Anderson and Preston joined the Church and they, with Washington, moved to Utah the next year. Preston married a daughter of Thatcher and he was ordained a Bishop three years later, becoming the Presiding Bishop of the Church in 1884. One of Thatcher's sons, Moses, became an Apostle in 1879.

28. *Western Standard*, January 10, 1857.

29. Higgins, Letter, January 8, 1857, in *Western Standard* on January 17, 1857. Hyde was an apostate Mormon causing quite a stir in California by his personal crusade against the Church and its leaders.

30. *Western Standard*, February 7, 1857.

31. *Ibid.*, March 13, 1857.

32. *Ibid.*, March 27, 1857.

Appendix

The following is a condensed version of a letter from William H. Shearman to George Q. Cannon, reporting conditions in the gold fields, which appeared in the *Western Standard,* 1:4, March 15, 1856.

SALMON FALLS, FEB 29TH, 1856
Dear Br. Cannon:

This morning br. David M. Stuart and myself arrived at this place, and were cordially welcomed by the generous and hospitable proprietor of the American Hotel, br. Thos. Orr, and his agreeable and warm hearted family whose kindness we are enabled to appreciate as none can but those who like ourselves have no abiding place or home, and have been traveling for weeks and months among strangers, without purse or scrip . . .

Perhaps a brief account of our travels may not be entirely uninteresting to some of your readers . . . . Since we left Sacramento, the 27th of last November, we have visited upwards of forty towns, including the County seats of Amador, Eldorado and Placer counties, at which places through the courtesy of some of the officials, we obtained the use of the Court Houses. We have had but little difficulty in obtaining places to preach in, as we speak in Court Houses, Theatres, Temperance Halls, Churches, Ballrooms and Bar rooms. We find the people generally very willing to hear us, which after they do once, they frequently invite us to stay and speak to them again, and we have preached as often as five times in one place.

The miners are, generally speaking, an intellectual, independent, and generous hearted set of men, who are accustomed to think as well as act for themselves, but who care very little about any religious faith. They however listen to us with attention and respect, with but few exceptions, . . . We have of course not been without trials and some opposition, but hitherto personal violence has been withheld, and we have found all the promises of God verified, for we have not gone hungry, nor have we been once without lodging, although our way has sometimes appeared very dark . . .

We have also met with much kindness from some members of other churches, and from many of those who adhere to no particular religion; and we pray God our heavenly Father to bless all those who show any favor to His cause or His servants, and to return their kindness into their own bosoms a hundredfold.

We have not yet baptized any, nor organized any branches, but we have the satisfaction of knowing that we are doing some good, and that God is blessing our humble efforts to build up His Kingdom . . . A general spirit of gathering seems to prevail, and we had many who regret that they ever left the Valley, and most of them intend to return either to San Bernadino or Salt Lake as soon as possible. You speak in your first number of organizing the scattering members into branches. This is a very difficult matter; and in most cases almost impracticable; for the few who would unite and form a branch, are separated so widely from each other, and by such a rugged country, that it would be almost impossible for them to meet together. Under these circumstances we concluded the best counsel we could give them, was, to gather to the body of the Church as fast as practicable, which duty we urge upon them whenever we find them . . .

Notwithstanding the flattering and exaggerated reports of newspapers, etc, the mines are becoming poorer and poorer every day, and thousands of the miners in various portions of the State can scarcely make a living. There are many men who will never be able to return to their homes; and we meet with hundreds of men, who at home were useful members to society, who have given up the hope of ever being able to return, and have yielded to the recklessness of ruin and despair; and we honestly believe that in five years there will be more destitution and poverty in the mines than in any other part of the Union . . . .

Your humble brother to the New and Everlasting Covenant.
WM H SHEARMAN

George Q. Cannon (1827-1901)

George Q Cannon was born in Liverpool England. His parents converted to Mormonism in 1840, and the family emigrated to be with the main body of the Church. His mother died at sea on the way to America, and George's father was left to raise six children. George was the oldest. They settled in Nauvoo and went west with the exodus in 1846, arriving in the Salt Lake Valley in 1847.

In 1849, George was called on a gold mining mission to help alleviate the currency crisis in the Salt Lake Valley. While on that mission in 1850, obtaining his gold by working in a trading store, he was called by Charles C. Rich to go on a proselyting mission to the Sandwich Islands. He learned the Hawaiian language and started the translation of the *Book of Mormon* into the Hawaiian language. He returned to California and then to Salt Lake City in 1854. On Parley P. Pratt's second mission to California, he requested that George Q. Cannon be sent back to California to help him with publishing the *Western Standard*. Cannon was sent to replace Pratt, who then returned to Salt Lake City. It was during Cannon's leadership of the California Mission that the last proselyting and "call to gather" took place.

In 1857, George Q. Cannon closed down the official branches of the Church in California and organized wagon trains for the emigration to Utah. He also left California and reached Utah in January of 1858 by the Southern Route. Cannon was ordained an Apostle in the LDS Church in 1860. He had a long career in business, political, and Church leadership and died in Monterey, California at age 74. *Courtesy LDS Archives.*

Think not when you gather to Zion, Your troubles and trials are through,
That nothing but comfort and pleasure Are waiting in Zion for you:
No, no, 'tis designed as a furnace, All substance, all textures to try
To burn all the "wood, hay and stubble," The gold from the dross purify.
From Mormon Hymn, "Think Not When You Gather" (1948) #21.

24

Missionaries and the Final Exodus

THE LEISURELY "GATHERING" of the Saints from the gold fields to San Bernardino, Carson Valley, and Salt Lake in the summer of 1857 was accelerated that fall when the impending arrival of Johnston's Army in Deseret occasioned the general call of the Prophet for them to in-gather to the reduced Zion—Utah. However, before this development, the tempo of missionary work had increased.

At the conference of the Church in San Francisco in April of 1857, the missionary work of the northern settlements, especially that of the gold fields, was expanded. Fredrick W. and Clement C. Hurst, two New Zealanders, had been converted to Mormonism while working the gold fields of Australia. Having worked in the California redwoods over the winter and planning to go to Zion in the spring, they were among a number of men called to serve as missionaries in Northern California. As they noted, "the conference thought it best, as the field was large and the laborers few, to send us to the mines to preach . . . " [1]

The Call to Accept the Gospel and Gather

According to reports, the Saints were "beginning to wake up, and to realize their true position and the necessity of giving heed to all principles and obeying all the ordinances of the gospel instituted for the salvation and exaltation of the human family." Elder William H. Shearman was

sustained as President of the El Dorado Conference (district) with his companion David M. Stuart, and Elders John B. and Aaron Thatcher, as well as F. W. and C. C. Hurst, to serve as missionaries under him. The Saints were counseled to "gather to Salt Lake but if not prepared to gather to that place, to gather either to Carson Valley or to San Bernardino, or as near to Head Quarters as possible." [2]

Reaching Sacramento on the 15th of April, and lacking the money to go by railroad car to Folsom, Elders Shearman and Stuart walked "the railroad without the cars." There they met with Brother S. G. Higgins in his little backroom, partaking of the Sacrament. They visited Carrolton, Auburn, Salmon Falls, Union Town, Pleasant Hill, and Drytown, finding the Saints better disposed, but with greater opposition from the populace. Had they had the time, Shearman felt they could have organized a branch of the Church. While a meeting at the Temperance Hall in Union Town was less than successful, the missionaries' trials were "more than compensated for" by a visit with the Plumtrees, who were planning to move to Utah once Mr. Plumtree could sell out. [3]

On May 5th, Elder F. W. Hurst and his brother left Sacramento, walking 20 miles to Brother Brown's near Alder Creek (two miles south of Folsom). There a Captain Hammond furnished them with a lighted hall. After preaching on the "first principles of the gospel" to about 60 people an "old man, sinner, and former Methodist preacher" rose and "went on with a long tirade against the Mormons." After a retort by Hurst, "The old Gentleman got wrathy and abused the missionaries," cheered on by the audience. The congregation finally got to quarreling among themselves, and the Elders "thought it high time to leave." [4]

The following day the missionaries walked to Salmon Falls, staying at the Orr's hotel and visiting Orr's daughter (Elzada Allred), whose daughter Jane was very ill. Elzada was the wife of Reuben Allred of the Battalion. Holding a meeting with 30 people in the school house, they administered to and blessed the Allred child, but Fredrick observed, "there are so many unbelieving spirits around here saying 'oh dear, the poor child will surely die'." [5] The child soon passed away.

Sister Orr laundered their shirts and sent them on their way to visit with the Luncefords at Pleasant Hill on May 8. While there, they visited Sister William Johnston (Johnson), an English sister, [6] and Sister Rabbles (Raihles), a married daughter of the Luncefords, both of whom were planning to go to San Bernardino with their families as soon as possible. The following day, they went two miles south to French Town, posting notices of meetings from Shingle Creek to French Creek. On the 10th, they held meetings in French Creek, Pleasant Hill, and Pleasant Grove, a number of unnamed Saints attending. [7]

The principle of tithing was being given increasing attention since the previous conference. Shearman said: ". . . the law is just as binding on us in California as in Utah." He proclaimed that exaltation in the Celestial Kingdom of God could not be obtained without the "endowments and blessing of the House of the Lord (temple)," and that these "could not be received unless one was a tithepayer." Presidents of the conferences were personally to attend to the "collecting of tithing in their various districts." [8]

On May 12th, the Elders walked to the vicinity of Walls Diggings, 14 miles away, writing and posting notices on the way, "much to the derision of the bystanders." They there met with the Joseph Outhouse family. Outhouse was "an apostate," but friendly to the missionaries. [9] It is not known just when he came to California. Two other "apostates," James Smith and Mr. Goodenough, provided the missionaries with a room and lights for a meeting attended by "quite a large congregation." Following the meeting, Mrs. (W. L.) Ball (Bell), a Mormon from Salt Lake, told the missionaries how sorry she was for having left the (Salt Lake) Valley. [10]

Moving northward into Sutter County, the missionaries found Lacklunt Tale Kemper, a "jack Mormon" [11] at Michigan Bar, where they held a meeting with almost a hundred people present. They were informed that a Methodist had been invited to come and oppose them but that he had declined the invitation. Moving to nearby Drummersville (Drummondsville), they found Sisters Simmons and Panel and held a good meeting.

Meanwhile, the Hurst brothers moved south to Drytown in Amador County, staying with Brother Robert Plunkett and holding three meetings. They organized the Drytown Branch the following day (Sunday) with nine members. Thomas Hindley of Willow Springs was called to preside with John Carter to act as clerk. [12]

At Hangtown on the 20th, they held a meeting attended by seven people, staying at the home of Brother George F. Hendry (Hendricks). At Union Town, near Coloma, they were able to secure a Baptist chapel and held a well-attended meeting, though some of the congregation "tried to make a row and disturb the meeting by strongly calling out, (tongue in cheek) `We believe'." [13] The missionaries were comforted and protected by the Plumtrees.

Reading in the *Western Standard* that Elders John B. and Aaron Thatcher were heading for Salmon Falls, the Hursts started out for that Mormon enclave, staying with Sister (Charlotte) Heckies (Hecks) at White Oak Springs. There they held a meeting and going on to Salmon Falls the next day for a "time of rejoicing" with the Thatcher brother missionary team. [14] The Hursts and Thatchers split up, Clem (Charles Clement Hurst) going north with John B. Thatcher to Whiskey Bar in the Horseshoe Bend of the North

Fork of the American River, near Rattlesnake Bar. Fredrick went south with Aaron Thatcher to the Luncefords' at Pleasant Hill, which they used as a base of operations to nearby communities. It also served as a place of spiritual and physical refreshment from encounters with bitter apostates and antagonistic Gentiles.

On June 1st they postponed a public meeting at White Rock Springs, meeting instead with a group of disaffected Mormons. The disfellow-shipped Henry Jacobs, whose estranged wife had married Brigham Young, had (at least earlier) lived there and might well have been the leader of the dissidents. Hurst recorded, "But such an evening I never wish to spend again as long as I live." He understood that they had refused to renew their covenants, "through rebaptism and reconfirmation." "They talked about Brother Brigham [Young], the Twelve, etc., concerning the evil that existed in Salt Lake." One of them said if he met a certain Brother, calling him by name, that "he would put his knife to him. To speak plain I never want to be in a greater Hell than to be with such characters." [15]

On May 29th, William H. Shearman, whose literary ability had been displayed in his letters to the *Western Standard*, was called to San Francisco to replace the ailing Matthew F. Wilkie on the staff of that newspaper. It was hoped by Shearman that the call would only be temporary "as the prospects for a good work being done in the field of labor assigned him (El Dorado Conference) were never more promising . . . ." Wilkie was in turn assigned to take charge of the El Dorado Conference, it being hoped that the "bracing air of the mountains, with plenty of out-door exercise, would restore his health." [16]

On June 3rd, the missionaries visited Mr. (James) Pollick (Pollock) on the Cosumnes River. While he received them kindly enough, he informed them that they were "not to mention anything about Mormonism." [17] The Pollocks later became residents of Slough House, the home of the Rhoades family, where he was eventually buried.

On Sunday, the 7th, the Elders held four meetings and organized a company consisting of 11 people (most of them members from the recently organized Drytown Branch) to go to San Bernardino. [18] The Church members took up a collection for the missionaries, contributing $28.50 from those going to San Bernardino. Brother Robert Plunkett, who with his family evidently remained behind, also contributed.

Following the meeting, the missionaries walked to the mining camp of Volcano in Amador County. With great difficulty they obtained a Baptist chapel for a meeting attended by about a hundred people. However, when Elder Aaron Thatcher began to speak, the people "would not hear him and the meeting broke up in an uproar." [19] The following day, they headed for the Jackson Mines, passing through Aqueduct City, which they found "almost deserted." Unable to obtain either a hall to preach in or a bed, the Elders "slept out in the mountains all night." [20]

Returning to Drytown, they found that the "brethren had all started for the south" (San Bernardino). Going to the little branch chapel, they "pulled out the staple with a pick, then opened the other door from the inside and then replaced the staple and lock as before." Finding some flour, they fixed a meal of biscuits. While there, "a man came down to see who had broke into the house." They preached Mormonism to him and on the following Sunday (June 14th) "baptized him and confirmed him, etc." and held two meetings. [21]

On June 12th, Elder Wilkie began a tour of the El Dorado Conference. Leaving from Salmon Falls for Shingle Springs, he traveled over the cooler hills. He visited the Hicks (Heckies or Hecks) at White Oak Springs, moved on to the Luncefords' at Pleasant Hill, and on to White Rock Springs (the apostate hotbed) where he stayed with some brethren. Upon inquiry, he was informed that Walls Diggings and Alder Creek, nearby, were the toughest places to preach in, so he decided to begin his preaching ministry at the former. He held a meeting with 17 present and stayed with Joseph Outhouse, forming "a very favorable opinion of him." In a meeting at Alder Creek, no questions were asked during the meeting, but afterwards several began to attack the Prophet Joseph Smith. From there he proceeded north into Sutter County and the Mormon enclave

Courtesy Pioneer Memorial Museum, International Society Daughters of Utah Pioneers.

Hezekiah Thatcher (1809-1879)

Hezekiah was born in Gano Town, West Virginia. He married Alena "Alley" Kitchen, and they farmed first in Ohio and then in Illinois. In Illinois they learned about Mormonism, joined the LDS Church in 1843, and moved to Nauvoo. They left with the exodus in 1846, reached the Salt Lake Valley in September 1847, and after they learned of the gold discovery went as a family to California.

Hezekiah and Alena had eight living children at the time. All but their married daughter accompanied them to California. The Thatchers ran a hotel in Salmon Falls, ranched, and did freighting. Their sons, John B. and Aaron were called to assist in the missionary work and to encourage members of the Church to emigrate to Zion.

When Johnston's army marched on Salt Lake City in 1857, the call to emigrate to the Salt Lake Valley became more urgent. The Thatcher family returned to Utah and settled in Cache Valley, Utah. Hezekiah died in 1879 in Logan, Utah; Alena in 1889 in Salt Lake City. (Linda Thatcher, The Thatcher Family.)

---

at Mormon Ravine (Long Valley), holding well attended meetings en route at Mormon Island, Negro Hill, and Condemned Bar. [22]

A week or so later Wilkie wrote from Sister Harmon's Homestead House that he had preached in the schoolhouse at nearby Ophir by early candlelight, with 25 to 30 people present. Shortly after he began to preach, two or three people left and a few minutes later the building was pelted with eggs, some entering the room itself and narrowly missing Wilkie. Brother (Jesse?) Brown, a known member of the Church, was hit three times on the head but with no serious injury. In addition, Sister Laughlin's bonnet was hit. Wilkie was able to calm the frightened congregation, even though rocks were being thrown onto the building. Wilkie felt that the experience had actually redounded to their benefit, gaining some friends. Proceeding on Sunday to Auburn, he preached at the court house and engaged in a discussion with a spiritu-

alist about John Hyde (the Mormon apostate) and the "Philosophy of Nature." They spent the next day or two with the family of Sister Harmon, the Crows, and Brother George P. Dykes. Wilkie reported that "miners were doing but little. Water is scarce, and what there is is evaporating very fast. There will be hard times this fall. The majority of the crops are not worth harvesting." [23]

Meanwhile, at Mud Springs to the south, Elder F. W. Hurst and companion secured a meeting place. However, only "two miserable cusses of apostates showed up" talking about how good they were. They also talked about the brethren of the Church, saying that Mormonism is true, and when the Church first started it was pure but now the head of the Church was like a man with a long stick and as long as they stirred up the mud the stream would be impure." No bed or food was given the Elders. [24] Walking to Jeany Town, they did "considerable fireside preaching" but secured

Moses Thatcher (1842-1909)

Moses Thatcher was born near Springfield, Illinois, the fifth son of Hezekiah and Alena Kitchen Thatcher. The family went to California, and Moses, in 1857 (only fifteen years old), was called to assist Henry G. Boyle in the missionary work there. His family returned to the Salt Lake Valley in 1857. He and his two brothers, John B. and Aaron, returned shortly after.

Moses attended the University of Deseret and worked mostly in family mercantile and banking businesses. He served as director and secretary of the Utah Northern Railroad and on trade boards.

Moses served on a mission to England and France, 1866-1868. In 1877, he was called to serve as a stake president, and was called to be an Apostle in the LDS Church in 1879. He was sent to Mexico to proselyte, to serve as a mission president, and to establish refugee polygamous colonies.

Moses died in Logan, Utah at age 57 (See entry in *Utah History Encyclopedia*.)

Courtesy Pioneer Memorial Museum, International Society Daughters of Utah Pioneers.

---

no "public place to preach in." Going back to Diamond Springs, the Temperance Union Hall was secured, but was then denied them by one of the trustees. [25]

The discouraged missionaries proceeded to the haven of Pleasant Hill where they ran into a Brother Walker with word from Salmon Falls. They were informed that all missionaries were to gather at Mormon Slough in Stockton, the major supply center for the southern mines, for an important conference with President Cannon. The missionaries hastily departed, stopping at members' places on the way.

The main purpose of the meeting was to coordinate plans for the movement of the Saints to the gathering places of San Bernardino, Carson Valley, and Salt Lake. A group of members headed by Hezekiah Thatcher from Yolo County was headed for Utah via Carson Valley, by way

of the northerly Harry James route. Others were going to Carson Valley by the southerly Big Tree road. The latter group was to be asked to take Sister (Sabrina) King and her four children with them, requiring that some luggage be left behind. The missionaries were asked to contact Brother Thatcher, asking him to take Sister King on to Utah from Carson Valley. President Cannon finally counseled the missionaries to concentrate their activities rather than to walk all over the country. Future events would make that counsel impossible to keep. [26]

Leaving Stockton, the Elders walked the 60 miles to Pleasant Hill in 25 hours. They found Elder Henry G. Boyle and his companion, Moses Thatcher, with the folks from Yolo County. The Utah-bound company was organized on July 3rd, with Hezekiah Thatcher as captain and Oliver N. Harmon as sergeant of the guard. They planned to take the Hangtown route. Brother Thatcher agreed

Placerville

Placerville was about two miles to the northeast of Weberville. It also was a rich gold site. Weberville was the western terminus of the original Mormon Emigrant Trail. However, when the traffic shifted to the Johnson Cutoff, the western terminus of the adjusted route became Placerville. Placerville was originally known as Dry Diggins. When Ziba Peterson, the sheriff of the town, hung some escaped and recaptured prisoners, the town became known as Hangtown. Not being happy with such a negative name, in 1851, the town voted to change its name to Placerville. *Courtesy Bancroft Library.*

to take Sister King on from Carson Valley. [27] The following day, Dr. Washington Anderson splinted and bandaged the leg of Brother Thatcher's best mare, worth $300.00. [28]

Boyle and his companion, on their way to Yolo County, stopped off at the Orr's in Salmon Falls where they were, as usual, treated very kindly. However, Boyle recorded "I confess that it was with sadness I bid farewell to the folks this morning. Yesterday morning when I parted with the folks (at Pleasant Hill), it was with different feelings for they are doing right in going to Deseret while the folks here are not doing so well." [29]

On the 12th, Hurst and his companion held two meetings at Brother Lunceford's, baptizing Edward Barnes and meeting a Mr. Bigler who had left Salt Lake in '53, with hope of enriching himself. Hurst remarked, "He is a wiser man than when he first came here. So much for California."[30] The missionaries ordered the *Western Standard* for John Clinton and some books for Brothers Barnes and Thomas Todd. They waited for word from Brother Wilkie but, failing to receive it, went on. At Mr. Niswanger's, who was "packed up ready to start in the morning for Carson Valley to trade dry goods," Hurst read a copy of the *Missouri Republican* which contained "an awful account about the Mormons, Brother (Parley P.) Pratt, etc." [31]

Going to Walls Diggings, the Elders rebaptized Sister Ball in Carson Creek. Brother Outhouse, who attended the service, confessed that "he had got to believe that there was neither God nor Devil nor a hereafter. Yet he said if he only knew whether (the Gospel) was what it professed to be nothing would prevent him from living and dying a Mormon." [32]

On the 16th, Elder Hurst and his companion found Brother Thomas Hindley at Willow Springs "selling out in order to start immediately for San Bernardino en route to Utah." Walking to Drytown, they "found the brethren and sisters well" and held a meeting in the chapel, Brother Griffins speaking. The following day, Robert Plunkett, Jr. was re-baptized and Hindley left for San Bernardino.

Meanwhile, a special conference was held in San Francisco July 16th-18th, at which time Elder Wilkie was released to go home. A number of the Sandwich Island Elders, former gold miner missionaries, most of whom had returned from the Islands with Cannon two years earlier, were assigned to continue their proselyting efforts in California. These included Henry W. Bigler, James Keeler, James Hawkins, and William Farrer. The latter was assigned to the El Dorado Conference, where he had once mined. Shearman was sent back to El Dorado to preside.

Passing through Pleasant Valley, New Town, and Fort Jim on their way to Cedar Ravine (near Placerville), Elder Hurst and his companion stayed at Brother Hendry's [Hendricks] and family on the 18th. They held a street meeting which ended up in a melee, having rocks and mush melons thrown at them, but without injury. Hurst reported, "I can truly say I knew no fear . . . . Brother [Aaron] Thatcher got up and spoke with power but they would not let him continue longer than five minutes. The meeting then broke up in an uproar." A Brother Taylor gave the elders enough money to pay for a room at Sister Bird's, she needing the money. [33]

The first of August, the El Dorado Conference meetings commenced at Salmon Falls. Presidents Cannon and Shearman were present, as were other missionaries. "Father and Mother and Sarah Lunceford came over in their wagon with a number of others from different parts of the Gold Mines" to attend the conference that was intended to last until Monday. However, "the people began to get quite hostile. Brother Cannon said if we kept conference on a day or two longer, we might get mobbed out . . . However, Brothers and

Sisters Orr and Allred treated us very kindly and hospitably." [34]

Another meeting was scheduled to be held at the Lunceford's and Hurst was commissioned to "go around to White Rock Springs, Prairie City, Walls Diggings, Deer Creek, etc. to inform the Saints." He reported that he had recently "baptized 10 new members and rebaptized four old members . . . both Brother Cannon and Brother Shearman were highly pleased with us boys." [35]

Although Elder Hurst was sick with the chills, he left for his tour on August 6th, reaching Brother Miller's at White Rock Springs, then Brother Niswanger's. However, his high fever finally got him down and he reached Father Lunceford's almost unconscious, the family taking care of him. On Saturday, Brothers Cannon, Shearman, Aaron Thatcher and William Farrer arrived for the planned meeting. However, it was delayed while everyone went out to fight a fire "at the other end of Father Lunceford's ranch." Administered to by Brothers Farrer and Barnes, Elder Hurst recovered. A few days after the conference, Samuel Lunceford arrived from Utah "to assist the folks over the plains as Father Lunceford is feeble, and in fact almost helpless." [36]

A letter to the *Western Standard* entitled "A trip through El Dorado Conference" reported the missionary travels over the previous two weeks of Elders Shearman, F. W. and C. W. Hurst, and John B. and Aaron D. Thatcher. After the aborted El Dorado Conference at Salmon Falls, the missionaries had gone to Union Town, near Coloma, where they held two evening meetings. They went to Coloma visiting Mr. Peter Wimmer, one of the original co-discoverers of gold. They partook of some of his peaches and were shown a piece of gold, said to be the first piece of gold found in the race of the sawmill. It was observed that "Mrs. Wimmer values the specimen very highly, and has refused several extravagant offers for it." [37]

At Auburn, a Brother Miller and Father Robert Crow furnished the missionaries with horses for too brief a trip to Grass Valley and Nevada City to the north where they probably visited the Carlows. Elder Henry M. Morgan wrote from Grass Valley that El Dorado was a hard field to labor in but that things were better than in earlier days. While there was hostility, it was viewed as an indication of the success of the missionaries, who were a threat to Satan's Kingdom. While the anti-Mormon excitement caused the "rancor and hatred" of some, it also awakened the people to investigate the Gospel. [38]

On August 28th, Elder Morgan and his unnamed companion baptized one person, with prospects of another as soon as they could get in to see him. He said there were three other young men who were investigating the gospel. Two of them were already converted and planned to join the Church and go to Utah the next fall. He continued:

> The people in the mining regions generally speaking feel favorable towards us, and offer us their houses and saloons to preach in from time to time, as we come round for say they, 'we want to hear the other side of Mormonism now, as we have one . . .' On Sunday, they preached at Brush Creek. All the miner(s) in that place came to hear us and paid good attention to what we said.

In the meantime, on August the 21st, Elder Shearman left for Stockton with the Allreds who planned to join the August Company to Utah. Elders Hurst and Thatcher rode in the Orr's wagon to Salmon Falls, going to Union Town the following day. At Coloma, they called on "old father and mother Wimmer." They tried to hold a public meeting but were pelted with rocks, which ended the meeting. [39]

At Irish Creek, northeast of Coloma, they found a group of Kanakas (Hawaiians). Having learned their language while on his mission in Hawaii, Hurst was able to preach to them in their own tongue. "One of them prayed and thanked the Lord for sending His servants to them." [40] These might well have been Hawaiian Saints on their way to Utah.

After preaching again to the Hawaiians on the 24th, the Elders walked to Georgetown, securing the town hall for a meeting. However, no one showed up, possibly owing to "a large political meeting to be held in the upper part of town." Walking to Union Town the following day, the

Elders (four of them) ate at Sister Plumtree's and then went to Coloma where they again visited Mr. Peter Wimmer, who invited them to eat all the peaches they could. They continued on to Hangtown where they found Brother Bird and family ill. [41]

Headed for Drytown, they were overtaken at Logtown by two brethren from French Town, Brothers John Clinton and Thomas R. Ezzal, who wanted some advice on going to Utah in the August Company. They continued on to the Plunketts at Drytown, where they borrowed a horse from Mr. W. O. Clark [42] for a ride to French Creek.

Animosity Increases

Pressures on the Saints, which had accelerated in August, reached a fevered pitch in September. The mounting pressure was contributed to by developments in Utah and the inflammatory newspaper reports on those developments in California. From the *Weekly Placer Herald* [43] published at Auburn, the following unevaluated items of fact and fiction for 1857 appeared — here summarized:

> April 25th. John Hyde, Jr. late of the Mormon Church lectured in San Francisco on the despotic power of Brigham Young. The article was a reprint from the *Sacramento Bee*.

> June 13th. A large emigrant group reached Carson Valley. It consisted mostly of Mormons and their families "escaping" from Utah.

> August 15th. Taken from the *Marysville Herald* of August 11th. A large wagon train and cattle herd arrived from Salt Lake camping at Honey Lake. It was "confirmed" that the Mormons had destroyed the U.S. District Court Records in Salt Lake and committed outrages against the U.S. officials. (This charge was later discovered to be false.) It was also reported that "a Scotch Mormon and his family came through with the train, also thirty-five Mormons who obtained leave of absence from Brigham upon the

Peter Wilson Conover (1807-1892)

Peter W. Conover was born at Versailles, Kentucky. Before joining the LDS Church, he had military experience as a captain in the Illinois militia. Because of that experience, he was made an officer in the Nauvoo Legion and was a commander of the Utah Military District. He fought in the Black Hawk Indian War. When Johnston's army began marching on Salt Lake City in 1857, Brigham Young sent Conover to California to bring back arms and ammunition so the Saints could defend themselves if necessary. Conover died in Richfield, Utah after reaching his 85th birthday. *Courtesy Pioneer Memorial Museum, International Society Daughters of Utah Pioneers.*

condition that they would act as missionaries in California."

August 22. Some 50,000 head of cattle were reportedly on their way from Utah. An address by Brigham Young to the Nauvoo Legion on June 28 was reportedly calling for the expansion of cavalry units. The *Deseret News* was quoted as calling for the U.S. government to send "intelligent and honorable men" to Deseret.

September 5th. An emigrant train of 100 persons was reported. "Professors of the Mormon faith," they had left Utah "because of the tyranny and injustice of the Brigham Young oligarchy." It was also reported that 1000 persons left Utah at the same time, 400 of them going to Oregon. "It was with great difficulty and some peril that they were able to make their escape."

In July, Brigham Young had been notified by a fast rider from the plains of the U.S. troops approaching the Salt Lake Valley. Since the troops had not been officially announced or prearranged, and considering past interactions with eastern government authorities, he felt required to assume they could be hostile. He immediately sent Peter W. Conover to California to obtain sufficient guns and ammunition, so they could defend

themselves if required.

On August 25, Cannon went across San Francisco Bay to Centerville to organize a company of Saints leaving for Salt Lake City. Many LDS from Centerville were in this wagon train, along with some Latter-day Saints from San Francisco. The captain of the company was Zacheus Cheney, formerly of the Mormon Battalion. They left August 31 from Centerville, made their way along what is now Fremont and Washington Boulevards in Fremont, went over Mission Pass, and on to the Mormon Emigrant Trail, joining up with other groups along the way. Near Genoa they met Conover, who had spent so much on guns and ammunition that he did not have enough wagons and teams to haul it back to the Salt Lake Valley. Zacheus examined the supplies and gave some money to help pay for another wagon. From the Genoa area, they traveled together back to the Valley.

Elders Shearman and James Keeler went to Stockton toward the end of August to assist the Saints emigrating to San Bernardino, camping for a period of time on Mormon Slough. The company left on August 31st. While in Stockton, no public meetings were held as the Elders could not secure a hall. In addition, the last time an attempt had been made (by Elders Keeler and Samuel Miles) to hold a street meeting, a serious disturbance took place. Bloodshed was threatened when the editor of the *Argus* drew a knife on the Elders.

They concluded that the majority of citizens were opposed to the Mormons doing any preaching in that city and the decision was made not to preach there again. [44]

In the countryside, things were not quite as tense. Shearman and Keeler had been able to preach in the Mokelumne River country at Staples Ranch, Atheam's Ferry and Woods' Ferry, but without any apparent success. Between the 5th and 16th Shearman and Hurst preached at Ione City, and were furnished food and a room at the Veranda Hotel. They walked to Ione Valley, preaching at the schoolhouse and staying with the Streeters. Moving northward they visited Sister Plunkett at Drytown, Homer Clarke at Michigan Bar, and Brother J. Cottam. They went to see Dr. Rutherford but found him not in. Going to Rock Springs, they stopped at Rhodes Diggings, seeing Sister Bell (Ball) and Brother Jeremiah Thomas, and staying at Brother Miller's. On their way to the Lunceford's they stopped at the Niswanger's and Wagner's, holding a meeting. At French Creek, they baptized Owen Williamson, who was 63 years of age, and held meetings at the Luncefords' on Sunday.

Preparations for Going to Zion

On September 18th, Hurst observed, "There is quite an excitement about the Mormons. We hear they are all leaving Carson Valley. That all the Elders are called in." [45] The Elders left for Auburn, stopping at the Orrs' at Salmon Falls on the way. Stopping with Brother Crow near Auburn, they found the Elders gathering there—Shearman, John Thatcher, and Clem Hurst. President Cannon and James Orr arrived, confirming the news already received. The faithful were going to Zion. The missionaries were sent on a special mission to warn all of the Saints to be ready to gather at a moment's warning. Cannon reported to the Elders that U.S. troops ordered to Utah were abusing handcart companies and ravaging women. Several companies of men had gone east to meet the "Hell Hounds and give them what they justly deserved." [46]

The Elders split up. Clem Hurst and Shearman headed north to Grass Valley in Yuba (Nevada) County. John B. Thatcher went to Yolo County; Fred Hurst and Aaron Thatcher started out to warn the Saints in El Dorado and Amador counties. Arriving back at Salmon Falls, Aaron Thatcher was done in, coming down sick. Other missionaries were in and out.

The plans were to leave for Utah on October 9th but they failed to make that date. Brother Hendry of Placerville purchased a horse from the Orrs, who planned to remain in California. Hurst assisted the Luncefords to fix their wagons, somewhat self-consciously on the Sabbath. Hurst observed: "I do not know what the pharisees around here will think of us Mormon men. Preaching one day and working another. This is Sunday and I have painted a wagon, in fact, worked hard all day. I have been trying all I can to get the folks off." [47] However, Shearman reduced the pressure by informing the Elders that the departure date had been put off until the 20th of October—a date so late in the season that they were almost required to go by way of San Bernardino to avoid the danger of being caught in the snows of the High Sierra.

Even non-member friends were caught up in the spirit. Hurst wrote, "Mr. Waters, who had been friendly with us, was very much excited. Said if he could see [his way] out he would go by water and meet us at San Bernardino." Gentile enemies were also caught up but in a different way. "Quite a few fellows got together here drinking and swore vengeance regarding us young Elders. However, we escaped out at the back door."

Strained Relationships and the Final Exodus

This threatened attack may have been precipitated by rumors of the Mountain Meadows massacre [48] or even from a newspaper report of it from another locality. However, the local *Placer Herald* did not report the terrible incident until October 17th. The editors at that time reported that the massacre was instituted by the Mormons, allied with the Indians. It was also reported that U.S. troops were approaching Utah and that the Mormons would undoubtedly resist, leading to acts of hostility. The massacre was said to have been the result of the "turbulent demoralized and aggressive spirit" of Mormonism and to have been in revenge for the death of Apostle Parley P. Pratt who had been killed in Arkansas. [49]

On October 12th, a small company of hard pressed Saints headed south. It consisted of Sister Lunceford and daughters (Nancy) Emeline, Sarah and Siritts (Cynthia); James Lunceford, a son, Samuel, who had come from Utah to help the family; Edmund (Edward) S. Barnes; Charles Clement Hurst; Fredrick W. Hurst; Marion Outhouse; as well as George F. Hendry and an adopted Indian son, William. Brother Lunceford stayed behind to sell his ranch, accompanied by Owen Williamson, the new convert. Lunceford never made it to Utah, dying en route.

The company, traveling "in cognito," crossed the Cosumnes River on the wire bridge, 22 miles south of Pleasant Hill. Some suspicious-looking men came into camp, but were met with loaded guns. The people along the route were most curious, wanting to know if they were Mormons. On the 13th they forded the Mokelumne River at Staples Ferry and camped on the ranch of Mr. Carpenter, a reported apostate, but one whose wife was happy to see them. Traveling on to Stockton, they camped on Mormon Slough. Traveling west, they met up with a company from Grass Valley consisting of Nathaniel Carlow, his four sons, a daughter and her suitor, Michael Wahlen, who planned to join the Church. [50]

On the 19th, they met up at the San Juan Mission with Brother Marion Shelton, who informed Hurst that William H. Shearman was coming in from Yolo County with a company consisting of John B., Aaron, and Moses Thatcher, William B. Preston, and others. They were joined by Henry G. Boyle. The combined company traveled south to San Bernardino, reaching that outpost on November 13, 1857. [51] There, the company split up. Some remained until spring; some permanently stayed there. On November 27th, a new company set out for Deseret. [52]

Back in the north, the local editorial attacks on the Mormons grew in frequency and vigor following the departure of the last known Mormon wagon train. There is little doubt that these and the resulting community antagonism provided problems for Mormons remaining in California,

forcing some "underground."

Elder Cannon soon left Northern California, returning to Utah where he became an Apostle and special counselor to Brigham Young and a Counselor in the First Presidency for three subsequent Church presidents. While Cannon supported the policy of the Church leadership opposing precious metal mining in the late 1860s and early 1870s, by the 1890s he was a member of the board of directors of the famous and prosperous Bullion-Beck silver mining operation in the Tintic fields. Interestingly enough, Apostle Moses Thatcher was the president, with his son-in-law, Presiding Bishop William B. Preston, as the treasurer of the Mormon, privately owned company.

Apostles Rich and Lyman had already left the Southern California outpost of San Bernardino. Many of the San Bernardino Saints soon followed. Apostle Lyman would be associated with mining efforts in Southern Utah in the 1860s. The vigorous and talented William H. Shearman returned to Utah. Unstable in his loyalties, he became a leader in the apostate Godbeite movement [53] in the later 1860s and 1870s. This defection was in part generated by Brigham Young's policy of at least public opposition to the mining of precious metals.

It is uncertain how many of the Saints in California, more or less responsive to the call of Brigham Young, ended up in Utah. However, it appears that only between 30 to 50 percent so responded. As California Mormons no longer had any known official leadership or missionary activity until the 1890s, those remaining were essentially cut adrift, to wander in a spiritual Sinai for 40 odd years, but without a Moses or even an Aaron to lead them.

NOTES

1. Hurst, Diary, April 6, 1857.

2. *Western Standard*. April 10, 1857.

3. *Ibid.*, May 15, 1857.

4. *Ibid.*, May 29, 1857, Hurst, Diary., May 4, 1857. "Captain Hammond" may have been Fran-

ces Asbury Hammond or Leonard Hammond, or he may have been a southern Harmon. In 1850, Apostle Rich referred to a Brother Hammond while Lyman apparently spelled the same person's name as Harmon.

5. Hurst, Diary, May 7, 1857.

6. A William and Elizabeth Johnson had entered Utah from England in 1850.

7. Hurst, Diary, May 8-10, 1857.

8. *Western Standard*, May 8, 1857. (Word in brackets is the author's) The "endowment" is a special ceremony in the Mormon temples reserved for the more faithful Latter-day Saints. Actually there was no temple in operation at that time, endowments being temporarily given in a special building, the Endowment House, in Salt Lake City. Endowments had been performed in the Nauvoo Temple in 1846.

9. *Ibid.*, May 12, 1857. In 1852, Outhouse had been chosen to lead a group of 225 Saints to Salt Lake from the East. However, after a few days, he became offended and quit. Journal History. September 6, 1852.

10. Hurst, Diary, May 12, 1857.

11. *Western Standard.*, May 13, 1857. The term "Jack Mormon" at the time referred to friendly non-Mormons rather than an inactive Mormon (the 20th Century definition).

12. *Ibid.*, May 16, 17, 1857.

13. *Ibid.*, May 22, 1857.

14. Hurst, Diary, May 24-25, 1857. Most of the Thatchers lived at Buckeye in Yolo County but had been residents of nearby Salmon Falls in 1850. Two Thatcher brothers were serving missions in the gold fields in 1857. Moses Thatcher was to become an Apostle.

15. Ibid., May 31, 1857. (Words in brackets are the author's)

16. *Western Standard.* May 29, 1857.

17. Pollock, his wife Priscilla, and two children had entered Utah in the Asa Barton Company in 1847.

18. *Western Standard.* June 7, 1857.

19, *Ibid.*

20. *Ibid.*, June 10, 1857.

21. *Ibid.*, June 11-14, 1857.

22. *Ibid.,* June 26, 1857.

23. *Ibid.*, July 3, 1857.

24. Hurst, Diary, June 15, 1857.

25. Ibid., June 16, 1857. Jeany Town not identified.

26. Ibid., June 17-21, 1857. Sabrina Curtis King entered Utah with George King and two small children in 1849. As the Curtis and King families were together in Stockton at this time, this "Sister King" was probably Sabrina.

27. Hurst and Boyle, Diaries, July 3, 1857. (See Appendix 24a for list.)

28. Dr. Washington Anderson, probably not a Mormon, was the son of W. F. Anderson, a recent convert. In Utah, he became one of Brigham Young's physicians.

29. Boyle, Diary, July 7, 1857.

30. Hurst, Diary, July 12, 1857. This does not sound like Henry Bigler, one of the original discoverers of gold at Coloma. He had served as a missionary in Hawaii and was soon called to serve in California. Either Hurst was misinformed or there was another Bigler in the area.

31. Ibid., July 13, 1857. (Words in brackets are the author's) 32. Ibid., July 15, 1857.

33. Ibid., July 21, 1857. (Words in brackets are the author's.)

34. Ibid., July 31 -- August 3, 1857. The *Western*

Standard, in reporting the meeting, made no note of the disturbance.

35. Hurst, Diary, August 2, 1857.

36. Ibid., August 6-15, 1857.

37. *Western Standard*. August 21, 1857.

38. *Ibid*., September 4, 1857.

39. *Ibid*., August 22, 1857.

40. *Ibid*., August 23, 1857.

41. *Ibid*., August 24, 1857.

42. Clark had been disfellowshipped in 1851. He was later a leader in the California temperance movement.

43. *The Weekly Placer Herald*. Placer County Library. See dates in text.

44. *Western Standard*. September 11, 1857.

45. *Ibid*., September 18, 1857.

46. *Ibid*., September 19, 1857. Lot Smith, a former Battalion Volunteer and California gold miner, with others was sent into present-day Western Wyoming to harass General Johnston's westward moving troops by running off their cattle and burning their wagons and grasslands.

47. *Ibid*., October 9, 1857.

48. Earlier that year a large train of Arkansas and Missouri emigrants, aggressively passing through Utah, was attacked at Mountain Meadows in Southern Utah by a group of Indians and Mormons. All except the younger children were killed. By and large the Mormons looked on the massacre as a wartime act, the non-Mormons as wanton murder. See Brooks, *The Mountain Meadows Massacre*, and Walker, Turley, and Leonard, *Massacre at Mountain Meadows*.

49. *The Placer Herald*, October 17, 1857.

50. *Western Standard*, October 12-17, 1857.

51. *Ibid*., October 19 — November 13, 1857.

52. See Appendix 24b for a list of the company.

53. Walker, *Wayward Saints.*

APPENDIX 24a (Note 24:27)

Yolo County Saints En route to Utah, 1857

Hezekiah Thatcher and wife, Alley
W. F. Anderson and his doctor son, Washington
Levi Dougherty
Joseph Thatcher
Harriet Ann Thatcher
George Washington Rogers (Thatcher?)
Oliver N. Harmon
James Bell
George and Cyrus Snell

Source: Hurst, Diary.

APPENDIX 24b (Note 24:52)

Utah-Bound Company
from San Bernardino, November 27, 1857

Father Cram* (Robert Crow) with Minda and John
Charles W. Wandell
Branner Cran (Crow)
Sergeant of the Guard
Mother (Rosey) Lunceford
Sister (Doetis) Whitlock
Silas Smith
Joseph Smith
Edward Partridge
Joseph E. Pack
Fredrick W. Hurst - Chaplain
George F. Hendry
Clement Hurst
Henry G. Boyle
W. B. Preston and Company
Brother (Myron) Tanner and Company
Sister (Matilda) Hyatt
Brother Hamblin (Indian Missionary)
Brother (Charles) Crisman
Brother (James W.) Lemon
Brother (Robert) Collins

Source: Hurst, Diary.

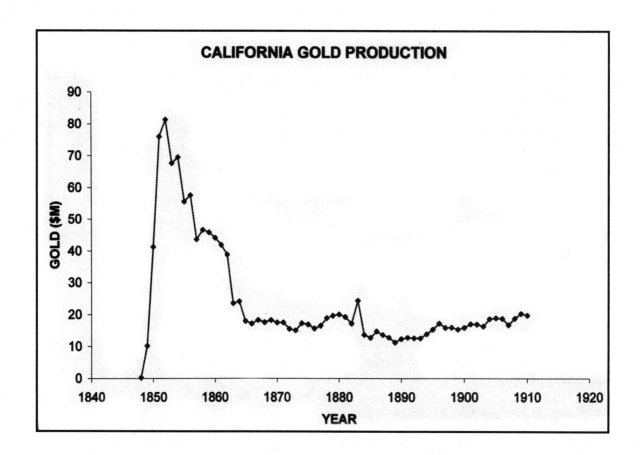

CALIFORNIA GOLD PRODUCTION

From the discovery of gold in 1848, the population of California grew at a fast rate, primarily because of the gold rush, Correspondingly, from 1848 on, the total yearly gold output climbed abruptly, as shown in the above figure. However, the gold output from the mines quickly showed limitations, peaking out about 1854. Even the abrupt rise to the peak gold output involved a weakening of the yield. In 1848, 6,000 miners extracted $10 million worth of gold. In 1852 over 100,000 miners extracted $80 million worth of gold, a factor of eight increase in gold, but about a factor of two reduction in the yield per miner.

Also, by 1853 hydraulic and other more efficient mining methods were being introduced, so large numbers of miners and more efficient methods were involved in reaching the peak of gold output. Despite those factors, gold production dropped precipitously after 1854. By the 1860s, gold mining was becoming primarily the work of well financed companies using advanced techniques, and the yearly gold yield continued relatively low.

The easy-to-get gold was taken in a very short time, so the "get rich" dream of the individual Argonaut, including the Mormon gold miners, came and disappeared rather quickly.

Gold data from Robert Glass Cleland, *March of Industry* (Los Angeles, Calif.: Powell Pub. Co., 1929), 276.

Happy is the man that findeth wisdom,
and the man that getteth understanding.
For the merchandise of it is better than the merchandise of silver,
and the gain thereof than fine gold.

Bible. Proverbs 3: 13-14

25

Mormon Argonauts: Some Reflections

The story of the Mormon Argonauts is a story of incongruity. Brigham Young and his Saints were more interested in creating a permanent, self-sufficient, economically independent kingdom based on agriculture and home industry than in becoming dependent upon will-o'-the-wisp wealth based on what was seen as the "God of this world"—gold and silver. Yet, despite that primary interest, the mid nineteenth century Latter-day Saints were thrust center stage into the great California gold rush.

The truth is that the pragmatic Brigham Young, while recognizing the dangers to the budding Kingdom of Deseret of a single-minded concentration on precious metal mining was willing—even anxious—to exploit California gold, but under his control. While there have been many historians who have reached and promulgated negative conclusions about Brigham Young's forceful leadership style, few (if any) have seen him as economically irrational. To have foregone the opportunities provided by the fortuitous discovery of California's golden treasure would have been supreme economic irrationality.

The Mormons believed that they are a "chosen people" divinely led through a Prophet, with all things working toward the building of a kingdom ready to receive the resurrected Christ at His Second Coming. That world view can fully accommodate the thesis of this volume—that the gold industry was important, if not essential, to the kingdom goal. Brigham Young was aware of that importance, and he took full advantage of the opportunities California gold provided. The result was that hundreds of Mormons were involved in mining California gold, as an official assignment from the Church, or by consent of the Prophet on an individual basis, or without that consent, "on their own hook."

From the Mormon perspective, consider the history of the Mormon people from 1846 to 1857. By the winter of 1845-46, it became apparent to the Mormon collective leadership—the Quorum of the Twelve Apostles with Brigham Young as their President—that Nauvoo was untenable as the new Zion. The United States itself was an inhospitable, unsympathetic host. Their only hope was removal from the states to someplace in the west—they knew not where. The most likely possibilities were Texas, Vancouver Island, Washington, Oregon, coastal Upper California and the

Rocky Mountains.

The sudden fury of the Illinois mobs over the winter of 1845-46, and threats of what might happen from federal interference in the spring, cut short Mormon investigations of locations in the West and preparations for the journey. In February of 1846, in the middle of winter, they headed west like the children of Israel escaping Egypt under the leadership of Moses—in whose image they cast themselves. Some of the scattered Saints who had not yet gathered to Nauvoo and its environs were also ordered to head west that spring in anticipation of meeting up with the main body of Saints somewhere in Indian Country along the Oregon-California Trail. Others in the East were instructed to reach the West by sailing around Cape Horn.

Fortunately, in a sense, the main body proved to be too cumbersome—bogged down by poverty, inadequate preparation, and Iowa mud—to proceed much beyond the Mighty Missouri. They remained there in the area of Council Bluffs over the winter of 1846-47. The delay at the Missouri provided the opportunity for events to evolve which would provide a more hospitable environment for the re-establishment of Zion in the seemingly inhospitable climate of the Great Basin in the Mexican territory of Upper California.

Four vanguard groups outpaced the main body of the Church and went beyond or around the Great Basin to establish themselves on the west coast by 1847. They became strategically located to take advantage of the unfolding developments. The first group was the William B. Ide family in 1848, who went first to Sutter's Fort and then settled in the north Sacramento Valley. The second was the 238 or so *Brooklyn* Saints, under the leadership of Sam Brannan, who became headquartered at Yerba Buena (San Francisco). The third group consisted of the Mormons (such as the Thomas Rhoades family) who traveled the Oregon-California Trail in 1846, locating in the general area of Sutter's Fort. The fourth group was the 200 or so Battalion Boys reaching California in 1847, most of whom remained in California and located in the general area between Yerba Buena and Sutter's Fort (Sacramento). These four groups of Mormons were in a position to receive the main body of Saints, should the decision be to come to the "Land of Everlasting Spring." They would also be in a position to provide logistical support from the western seacoast should the body locate in the Great Basin. Of course, unbeknownst to them, they were in an ideal position to take advantage of the events unfolding with the discovery of gold at Coloma.

As many as 200 from these three groups were involved in gold mining in the relatively halcyon days of 1848—headquartered at Mormon Island (a few miles down stream from Coloma), but spread from Mariposa (Mormon Bar) on the south, to the North Fork of the American River on the north. While the mining operations were arduous, almost anyone could be involved, since the process required little capital or advanced technology. Luck and/or divine direction plus hard work were the main ingredients of success.

Members of the Mormon Battalion, who had worked in the mines, were contracted to spread the news of the gold discovery eastward by delivering Sam Brannan's *California Star* to stage points leading east. On their way, they announced their news to the Saints in the Great Basin and to Brigham Young, who at the time was still bringing Saints into the Valley from Winter Quarters. He received the news in July, 1848, in eastern Wyoming on a trip back to the Valley. The astute leader, recently sustained by the Saints in Iowa as the President, Prophet, Seer and Revelator of the Church, undoubtedly received the news with mixed feelings. The decision had been made in the summer of the previous year to locate on the shores of the great inland salt sea. Successful colonization would require rapid infusion of manpower to subdue the land and the Indians. Also needed were large additions of capital. The general poverty of the Saints, worsened by the losses incurred in their precipitous and repeated expulsions, precluded them as a major source of immediate liquid capital that could be easily translated into livestock, seed, mills and equipage.

California gold could well serve this purpose, but it could at the same time siphon off the manpower needed to subdue the wilderness. The solution was to play down the significance of the gold to the general populace, discouraging general emigration to the gold fields, while at the same time confidentially calling selected, trusted men to go to California to add to those Saints still remaining there. Their primary purpose was to exploit the gold fields for the benefit of the kingdom. Shortly after his arrival at the Salt Lake village in September of 1848, the leader saw the disruption created in the community by those who had come from California with their gold pokes, flaunting them in the faces of those who had suffered the privations of the first valley winter, and whose misery was added to by the threat of a poor harvest again that year. He saw the need to defuse the situation, while at the same time providing a much needed currency. First, he called a substantial number of men to go to California to obtain critical supplies and assess the situation—to see if the gold was more than simply a "flash in the pan." Second, he called on those having gold to deposit it with him, to be minted into gold coins—a little less exhilarating than bags of gold and much more practical as a medium of exchange.

Fortuitously, the crucibles used to mint the first gold bars were soon broken. This provided an excuse to print paper currency backed by gold. The gold was to be deposited with Brigham Young, and an equivalent amount in paper money was to be issued to the depositors desiring it. Or, it could be retained either as an interest free savings account or paid as tithing. The gold could then be used in external trade. Unfortunately, that trade became a negative balance of trade in goods and services which resulted in an outflow of gold. The paper money and savings accounts were also not as acceptable as gold, and were soon reconverted into gold. By the spring of 1849 the gold operation was in trouble. When the outstanding valley currency exceeded the gold on hand, there was a need for larger infusions into the gold fund. Brigham Young sent Apostle Amasa Lyman and Porter Rockwell with a company of men to California that spring to secure all of the gold possible. The most immediate method was to collect the tithing of the California Saints as well as to induce some to bring or send their treasure troves to the Salt Lake Valley.

Arriving in California in early summer, Lyman collected several thousand dollars in tithes and offerings and induced Thomas Rhoades (over-land California pioneer of 1846) and William Glover (a *Brooklyn* leader) to bring their accumulated gold to the valley. He failed to induce the prospering Brannan either to send the tithing he had been collecting and that which he personally "owed," or to come himself.

The aging Father Rhoades captained the eastward-bound Mormon gold train encountered by so many incredulous westward-bound '49ers across the wastelands of Nevada that summer. The $25,000 - $30,000 in gold which they transported (using the Consumer Price Index, worth about $800,000 in 2008) temporarily saved the Mormon money system. It infused that system with new hope of the riches available in California. It also pacified the "greed" of the Saints that was siphoning them off to the gold fields. Therefore, at least temporarily, the influx of gold helped assure the success of the Mormon colonizing endeavor.

The policy established the previous year of down playing and keeping as secret as possible the extent of the gold troves was adhered to that fall. Several groups, totaling as many as two to three hundred men were confidentially called (many as mining missionaries) by Church leaders to go to California under the general spiritual leadership of the newly-called Apostle, Charles C. Rich, with Captain Hunt as their guide. This large influx of Saints on the west coast could also serve a political purpose—hopefully to help secure statehood for California, to be followed quickly and automatically by statehood for Deseret. Not only would these gold missionaries help provide gold for the Mormon money system, but as they were personal missionaries of Church-community leaders, grubstaked by them and expecting half of the proceeds of their mining surrogates, the leaders could have their material needs met. The Church too, would benefit from the tithes of these Mormon Argonauts.

Unfortunately, by the time these gold missionaries arrived in the gold fields in the spring of 1850, the easy-to-get gold had been pretty well mined out. It was only the luckiest who found substantial quantities of gold and even then their accumulation was greatly diminished by the high cost of living, as well as the depredations of armed highwaymen. More unfortunately for the spiritual well-being of the California Saints, the temptations of the wild living that usually characterized the gold camps and towns also took their toll on Church membership.

Nevertheless, Apostles Lyman and Rich prodigiously went about the gold fields collecting the tithes of the faithful, paying the Church debts in California, gathering the Saints into small communities for mutual support and taking gold to Salt Lake to feed the voracious appetite of the Mormon mint, which had recommenced operations in the fall of 1849 to back their paper currency. They also encouraged many of the miners to abandon the gold fields. Lyman that summer and Rich that fall (1850) returned with those who were successfully encouraged. By the spring of 1851, a total of over $80,000 (mostly gold) had been funneled into the Mormon mint. (According to the CPI, $80,000 in 1851 would be equivilent to over $2,000,000 in 2008.)

When the Apostles returned, they took with them plans for the establishment of a colony in Southern California. They considered the gold fields a lost cause and therefore had spent some of their time laying the plans. They had already sent a number of families south to prepare the way for Rich and Lyman to return to the South the following year, assuming the Apostles could get the blessings of the Prophet as well as the support of some colonizers. As they passed eastward, through Carson Valley, they failed to see either the gold or the potential of that area for a Stake of Zion.

Before their return to Deseret, the Apostles assisted in converting some gold missions into proselyting ones in the islands of the Pacific. Elder Addison Pratt and others had met with substantial success in their efforts in the South Pacific. In the spring of 1850, a group of missionaries from Salt Lake (males and females) was called to assist Pratt. They traveled to San Francisco in association with a substantial number of gold miners and colonizing families. The discouraging reports of Lyman and Rich had not yet reached Brigham Young. The missionaries in the group were assisted on their way by the California Saints, who had either prospered by their own mining efforts or as businessmen selling goods and services to others.

In the fall of 1850, the success of most of the gold missionaries being limited and faced with an anticipated sterile winter with high expenses, Apostle Rich called a number of the more faithful on proselyting missions to the Sandwich Islands (Hawaii). One of these was George Q. Cannon, who developed into the leader of the mission. He later served as the mission leader in Northern California. Cannon eventually became an Apostle and a counselor to several Church presidents. He also became a successful mining entrepreneur in Utah toward the end of the century.

In the meantime, an informal, non-sponsored community of Mormons filtered into the Carson Valley area of Northern Nevada, following the Mormon discovery of gold in Gold Canyon in 1849. These Saints settled just below what would become the silver mining capital of the west, the future Virginia City, where the Comstock Lode was discovered there in 1859. These Mormons were in a position not only to benefit from gold mining, but also to profit from trade with gold seekers, as well as from their agricultural pursuits.

In the spring of 1851, Apostles Lyman and Rich led several hundred Mormons to Southern California, establishing San Bernardino. The purchase of the Lugo rancho was made with money borrowed from sources in San Francisco at a high rate of interest. The Apostles went with the reluctant, unenthusiastic acquiescence of Brigham Young. His lack of support, the high rates of interest, the dullness of the times, and the inability of the colonizers to pay for their land as fast as needed doomed the colony. However, the end of the Mormon community did not occur before it was intimately affected by the search for gold. Prospecting missionaries were called, abortively it turned out, to locate a golden bonanza in Central California. Other men were called to visit the Northern California Saints, including those in the gold fields, to solicit their financial and colonizing support. This latter attempt was more fruitful, but was not enough to save that community, torn asunder by internal strife.

In Carson Valley, Orson Hyde was appointed by Territorial Governor Brigham Young as secular probate judge in 1855. Being an Apostle, he also served as a spiritual leader to the local Mormons. He took with him a large number of colonizers in an attempt to maintain Mormon control of this strategically located mining, agricultural, and trading area.

However, Mormon involvement, direct and indirect, in the gold fields of California and Western Nevada was cut short in 1857 by the invasion of Mormondom by Johnston's Army. The Saints were ordered to in-gather to Zion's center—essentially present-day Utah. By and large, it was the more faithful Saints who gathered. Most of those remaining, bereft of apostolic leadership, soon became absorbed into the gentile communities, losing their Mormon identities or becoming associated some years later with the newly emerging Reorganized Church of Jesus Christ of Latter Day Saints.

While Mormons had participated in the establishment of numerous camps and towns in the gold fields of California, their contributions were short-lived and soon forgotten. They left no permanent buildings and few identifiable tombstones. When the histories of the gold fields were being written a half century later, there were few remaining Mormon California residents who would identify with their Mormon beginnings or even admit to having once been affiliated with such an unpopular religious group. Within Mormondom, there were few who would admit to having been participants, fearing that they would be branded as rebellious apostate spirits.

The result was the general conclusion that "good" Mormons were not much involved in the gold fields—a conclusion belied by the true story. "Good" Mormons were substantially involved between 1848 and 1857 in the discovery and exploitation of California gold. It was the first successful export industry for the staggering Mormon economy, providing both a domestic money and a "foreign" exchange which could be used for the much needed capital improvements of Deseret. Their gold played a significant role in Deseret, a crucial element in the survival of the colony, until domestic production could be built up to provide the needed capital. Nevertheless, the public versus the confidential views of Church leaders toward gold mining produced an ambivalence in the body of the Church toward mining—especially mining of gold and silver—that would be reflected in Mormon consciousness.

Sutter's Coloma Sawmill

In January 1848, James Marshall discovered gold in the mill race of the Coloma sawmill which he was building for John A. Sutter. The mill used diverted water from the American River to power the saws, and the race carried the water back into the river. Several Mormons, formerly of the Mormon Battalion, were assisting in the construction of the mill, and therefore were present at the time of the discovery. The above is a sketch by George Mathis, one of his many masterful sketches of California gold rush scenes. The Mathis Collection can be found in the archives at Washington State University, Pullman, Washington. *Courtesy John Davies, grandson of George Mathis.*

Appendix A:
The Mormon Argonaut Communities

BY THE TIME of the 1850 Census, Mormons had been substantially involved in the settlement of many communities in or contiguous with the gold fields of California. More communities of Mormons were added by 1857, a number of which have already been discussed. In this chapter all known communities of Mormon Argonauts are identified or re-identified in greater detail. Most have become obscured by time, the impermanence of many of the early mining camps, and the winnowing-out process that takes place as history is written and rewritten.

Three types of Mormon Argonaut communities are included:

1. Those places which at some time have carried the name "Mormon," the assumption being that Mormons must have played a significant role in the area. Except for Quaker City Mine, Puritan Camp, and Methodist Reserve Hill, the Mormons constitute the only known religious body to be so honored. There were at least ten such places, half being listed in Gudde and Gudde. [1] Others have been added from various maps of the gold fields.

2. Those communities which, according to the 1850 Census, contained at least five persons from two or more family units who have either been definitely or tentatively identified as Mormon. [2] (Almost all of the communities of that day were rather small.)

3. Those additional communities in the establishment of which Mormons have been given substantial credit by various sources.

Brighton (Six Mile House, Natoma)

Six Mile House was a favorite stopping place, especially for Mormons in 1850. It was located on the American River about six miles upstream from Sutter's Fort in Sacramento County at or near Sutter's flour mill site, Natoma. Gudde and Gudde do not identify it. The census does not identify the place as such. However, various Mormon sources have located the Root family and the Davises there in 1850, [3] which reasonably assures the existence of a Mormon Argonaut community at that location. Later records indicate that Brighton was located in the general vicinity of Five and Six Mile Houses.

The Roots are not shown as innkeepers in the census, however, since Apostles Rich and Lyman and various missionaries stayed there in 1850, the Roots probably did maintain a public accommodation.

Neighbor to the Roots was the Lansford W. Hastings family consisting of Lansford (a lawyer), his wife Charlotte C., and a son, William W. No direct connection with the Mormons has been found, though Lansford was on at least friendly terms with them. He also favored the Mormon position or interests at the California Constitutional Convention. It may be remembered that it was he who had pioneered and promoted the Hastings Cutoff, the western portion of which crossed the Salt Flats of Utah, and was used by the Donner-Reed Party in 1846. The eastern portion was the route used by the Pioneer Mormon Company of 1847.

Brown's Settlement

This was probably the location of one of Porter Rockwell's three taverns. It was located where Deer Creek crosses the Placerville-Sacramento Road, between Shingle Springs and the Mormon Tavern in El Dorado County. It was frequently visited by Elders Charles C. Rich and Amasa M. Lyman, the Society Island-bound Mormon missionaries in the summer of 1850, as well as missionaries to the Pacific in 1853. It included Rockwell's partner, Jefferson Edmunds and his wife (a sister of Henry Jacobs, a disaffected Mormon of White Rock), and an unmarried sister. Edmunds was still the owner of the Deer Creek House and a mill in 1853. Neither Jacobs nor Evans has been located in the 1850 census, and this Brown's Settlement is not identified by Gudde and Gudde.

Coloma

On the South Fork of the American River in El Dorado County, Coloma was the site of Sutter's timber mill and the location of the first documented discovery of gold by Anglo-Saxons in California. At least six Mormons were living and working at the site when gold was discovered in 1848. Other Mormons were employed there, but not present at the time of discovery. Peter Wimmer (Weimer), who may have been a Mormon and who was also involved in the initial discovery, remained there with his family for many years, being there in 1850. [4] He was a prominent land owner and hotel keeper as late as 1857. Mormon missionaries visited the Wimmers until that year. Peter's aged parents (who were Mormons) were living with them at the time. Nathan Hawk of the Mormon Battalion and a member of the *California Star* Express Company, whose riders carried Brannan's publicity about the gold discovery to eastern newspapers, is buried there with members of his family.

Diamond Springs

Located about three miles south of Placerville, Diamond Springs was included in the 1850 Census for El Dorado County. [5] One account claims the town was given its name by a Mormon resident, George W. Sparks. [6]

Dry Creek - (Slough House--Rhoades)

There were numerous Dry Creeks, but this one was in Calaveras (later Amador) County. In 1846, Thomas Rhoades and members of his family [7] settled in the area between Dry Creek and the Cosumnes River in an area that came to be known as Rhoades or Sloughhouse. It was there that the Utah branch of the family claims gold was discovered in 1847, but mined secretly in agreement with Captain Sutter. Thomas Rhoades, Sr., left for Utah in 1849 with his younger children, at least Caleb and Lucinda. His older children, including most of his daughters, a number of whom had married prominent, old-timer Americans, remained in the area. Rich and Lyman visited a son, John Rhoades, and his wife in 1850. John Rhoades remained associated with the Mormons at least until 1857. Most of Thomas' California children evidently became alienated from their father and his religion when he became polygamous in Utah. The Slough House Pioneer Cemetery contains the remains of members of the Rhoades family and other early Mormons.

Also located at Dry Creek or Sloughhouse in 1856-57, was James Pollock, who was buried there with members of his family. The family was located at McDowell Hill in 1850. Pollock Pines above Placerville could well have been named after this prominent family. James Bailey, possibly of the Mormon Battalion, was also buried there.

Drytown - Calaveras County

Located on Dry Creek in Calaveras County, later Amador County, Drytown was settled as early as 1849. One of its prominent permanent citizens was W. O. Clark, a Mormon involved for a period in the mail service between Salt Lake and the gold field. He was listed as a merchant in the Calaveras District at the time of the 1850 Census. [8] Living with him were B. B. Clark and

Lyman Curtis.

Mormon missionaries, William H. Shearman and David M. Stuart, were in Drytown as early as June 23, 1856, while visiting the Robert Plunkett family. Plunkett, a native of Scotland, had entered Utah in 1849 with his wife, Sarah K., of Ireland, and a daughter, Mary M., born in Canada. They also had a son named Robert who was with them in 1857. It is not known when they entered California.

When Shearman and Stuart visited the area they were "kindly welcomed by all the friends." The Mormon apostate, John Hyde, had preached there in February of 1857, "stirring the people up," but in March the missionaries reported that they were well received, preaching every day. On May 15th, the Hurst brothers missionary team held three meetings in Drytown and organized a branch of the Church consisting of:

William Staines (probably with five sons),
Robert and Sarah Plunkett,
Robert Plunkett, Jr.,
W. L. Ball,
Abel and Alice Royle (probably with a son).

Evidently, by the time the branch was organized, W. O. Clark had ceased to be associated with the Church, having been disfellowshipped in 1851, though he did remain friendly and helpful to the missionaries. On June 7, 1857, the missionaries held four meetings at Drytown and organized a company of 11 people to go to San Bernardino. The group included the Staines, the Royles, John Carter, and W. L. Ball.

The Elders visited the town again on the 11th of June and managed to get into the house or chapel abandoned by the emigrating members. A suspicious neighbor came to investigate. The Elders preached to him and administered baptism. They held two meetings. In August, the Plunketts were visited by the missionaries, and W. O. Clark loaned the Elders a horse. In September the Saints remaining in Drytown were warned by the missionaries that they should be prepared to leave on moments notice because of the impending invasion of Utah by U. S. troops. The fate of those who remained after the October exodus is not known.

Eagle Valley

Eagle Valley, part of the larger Carson Valley in Western Nevada, was part of California in 1850. Settled by Mormons in the 1850s, a branch of the Church was established in 1856. Soon known as Carson City, it was abandoned by most of its Mormon population in 1857.

Folsom (See Negro Bar.)

Franktown

Located in Washoe Valley to the north of Eagle Valley (Carson City) in present-day Nevada, Franktown was the home of the Mormon Apostle Orson Hyde in 1855-56 when he served as probate judge and the organizer of Carson County in 1855. It had a Mormon ward or branch in 1856-57, which was abandoned in the latter year. About two miles north is the Bowers Mansion. Mrs. Eilley Bowers was a Mormon who stayed on after the Mormon exodus of 1857. She and her non-Mormon husband, Sandy Bowers, became Nevada's first millionaires. They soon lost their fortune made in nearby Virginia City.

Genoa (See Mormon Station.)

Gold Canyon

Descending to Carson Valley from Virginia City is Gold Canyon, the site of the discovery of gold by the Mormon Battalion veteran, Abner Blackburn, and other Mormons in 1849. The Orrs are also given credit for discovering gold there in 1850. Gold Canyon usually is credited as the site of the first discovery of gold in Nevada. Mormons were involved in mining the area at least until 1857 when most of them left.

Greenwood-Louisville

The Greenwood-Louisville town is located between Georgetown and Auburn Ravine in the northern part of El Dorado County. Now known simply as Greenwood, at the time of the 1850 Census it was two contiguous communities. [9]

John and/or Caleb Greenwood—father and son old-timers in California—are usually given the credit for establishing the community in 1849. However, a Mormon by the name of Gates was evidently involved with them. It is suspected that this was Hiram Gates, a Mormon Utah immigrant of 1848 who escaped Utah for some crime (reportedly the kidnapping of a young lady) in the spring of 1849, along with a man by the name of Fifield, probably Levi. Louisville (Lewisville) was named after the son of Lewis B. Myers, a Utah immigrant of 1847. He is said to have been the first white child born in the area of present-day El Dorado County. There were three Gates teenagers living with Mormons in the area at the time of the 1850 Census (January, 1851). About 50 out of 700 persons in the census for the area, have been tentatively identified as Mormons.

Hangtown (Placerville)

Originally known as Dry Diggings (one of many), Hangtown had become officially known as Placerville by the 1850 Census, when approximately 57 possible Mormons were in the area.[10] As early as November of 1848, four old-time Mormons, not associated with the Utah migration, had become short-term residents of the expanding village. They were Jesse Hitchcock, Joshua Hitchcock, John Killion, and Ziba Peterson.

Ziba was important enough in the early Church to have been mentioned in the Mormon scriptures, the *Doctrine and Covenants* (32:3, 58, 60). None of the Petersons were in Placerville at the time of the 1850 Census. When Ziba died in 1849, Rebecca moved to Sonoma with their seven children. This family lived at that time close to Silas G. Higgins, a Mormon member of the New York Volunteers, and later a businessman in Folsom.

James M. Flake, the captain of one of the companies of Mormon gold missionaries in 1849-50, died from an accident there in 1850. Apostle Lyman visited the area on June 1st of that year to meet with some of the brethren who had come up from the Southern Mines. While a substantial number of Mormons, mostly Battalion Boys, appear to have been located in the Placerville area at the time of the 1850 census, no record has been found of tithing paid there, although several of those identified did pay elsewhere. If all or even most of those named in the appendix were Mormons, it appears to have been the largest such concentration in the gold fields.

Placerville was visited by Mormon missionaries, Shearman and Stuart, possibly as early as March of 1856. The following are some of the Saints of the area who were contacted by various missionaries in 1856-57: Brother and Sister Bird (from Australia); George F. Hendry (Hendricks) and family; William Cooke, Jr.; as well as Brother and Sister Taylor.

Higgins Point (See Salmon Falls.)

Hudson Gulch (See Mormon Gulch-North.)

Jacks Valley

Jacks Valley is just north of Mormon Station (Genoa) and is a part of the larger Carson Valley in present-day Nevada. It had Mormons living in it in 1856-57 as a part of the Carson Valley-Jacks Valley Ward. Probably named after John (Jack) Redding, a possible Mormon, it was seemingly abandoned by most of the Mormons in 1857.

Logtown

Logtown, located two miles south of Mud Springs (El Dorado), had 420 inhabitants in 1850. Thirteen residents have been identified as possible Mormons located in that area of El Dorado County. [11]

Long Valley (See Mormon Ravine.)

Louisville (See Greenwood.)

Lytle Creek

The Lytle Creek placer mines were located about 13 miles northwest of San Bernardino. They were named for Andrew Lytle of the Mormon Battalion, one of the pioneers who settled in the San Bernardino area in 1851. Lytle was involved in the area in the 1850s, probably in the logging business. He may also have been involved in mining there, having been a miner in Mud Springs or Logtown in El Dorado County in 1850.

McDowellsville (McDowell Hill)

Gudde and Gudde describe McDowellsville (McDowell Hill) as on the South Fork of the American River, below Salmon Falls. It at one time had 4 stores and 100 residents. A Mormon, Myron Tanner, says that he worked the mines on the hill, located four miles above Mormon Island. Tanner appears in the 1850 Census of El Dorado County (appearing on page 384, enumerated on October 29, 1850). Located on the same and following page were 18 tentatively identified Mormons. [12] If all were actually Mormons, and McDowellsville had but 100 residents, this probably constituted the greatest per capita concentration of Mormons in California in 1850, being close to 20 percent.

One of the residents, Asa Barton, was a Captain of Ten in 1847. Sarah Dewitt, his and Polly's daughter, was the wife of Martin Dewitt who has not been located. The Pollocks entered Utah in company with the Bartons in 1847. The Thatcher family, at Salmon Falls nearby, were also with the Bartons in that year. It may have been contiguous with Mormon Hill, identified later.

Middle Fork, American River

There were evidently numerous Mormons mining along the Middle Fork of the American River in the summer of 1850. On July 29, Apostles Rich and Lyman went to Murderer's Bar, located on the Middle Fork a couple of miles upstream from its confluence with the North Fork. On the 30th they visited George Boyd's Camp nearby, going to Joseph Cain's and talking "with the Brethren at night." At the time, according to Rich, there were "one or two hundred (Mormons) working there." No such community has been found in the 1850 Census, however. Many of these may have returned to Utah before the census was conducted in January of 1851. It is known that Cain (a hotel owner) returned, becoming the co-author of the Mormon Way Bill. Boyd was not in the 1850 Census for California, but was for Utah.

The census [13] does show a reasonably well concentrated group of 25 identified possible Mormons along the Middle Fork of the American River. While the maps usually show the Middle Fork to be upriver from Auburn, the fact that the numbering of the census ends near Salmon Falls, near the confluence of the South and North Forks, leads to the speculation that some of these may have actually been located downstream from Auburn, on the El Dorado side.

Mormon Bar – North

The northern Mormon Bar was located between Beals and Laceys Bars, on both sides of the North Fork of the American River in Sutter (Placer) and El Dorado Counties. By the time of the 1850 Census, the Mormon participation had evidently been largely dissipated. The only resident tentatively identified as a Mormon in 1850 was Arnold Stevens of the Mormon Battalion. The bar is now covered by Folsom Reservoir and has long since been excluded from the maps of the area.

Mormon Bar - South
(and Mariposa County)

This southern Mormon Bar was located in the southern mines on Mariposa Creek, two miles downstream from Mariposa in present-day Mariposa County. Gudde and Gudde maintain that gold was discovered there in 1848 by Mormons who soon left for Utah. The discoverers have yet to be identified by name. They may have been members of the Mormon Volunteers who were discharged in the spring of 1848, some of whom passed through the general area on their way north to the gold fields that summer. It is also possible that some of the other Battalion Boys remaining in Northern California over the winter of 1847-48 found their way that far south. A third possibility is that some of the *Brooklyn* Saints who had participated with John C. Fremont in his Central California campaigns were rewarded with the right to mine on his "floating Mexican land grant" in Mariposa. A fourth group may have been Mormons of the New Hope colony on the Stanislaus, not far distant.

Mormons may have been involved at the bar as late as May of 1850 when Apostles Lyman and Rich visited the Mariposa area, preaching and collecting tithing from at least 21 Mormons listed in

Chapter 16. Of this group, at least 11 were recent arrivals with the Flake and Hickerson Companies. Only two of those remaining had been members of the Battalion and neither of these was associated with the Volunteers. At the time of the census in the fall, a substantial number (20) of possible Mormons were in the county, their exact location being uncertain. [14] It may be noted that few were grouped together, eliminating the possibility that they were at Mormon Bar as a group. Among the more prominent of these was M. E. Button, a Seventy and Battalion veteran, along with his family which he had brought from Utah.

Mormon Gulch. North - Hudson Gulch

Little is known about the northern Mormon Gulch. Gudde and Gudde maintain that it was located on Mameluke Hill, which is just north of Georgetown in present-day El Dorado County. Its exact location is uncertain, but it may have also been called Hudson Gulch in Oregon Canyon as the gold of both was reportedly discovered by a man named Hudson in the summer of 1849. This was probably Wilford Hudson, of the Mormon Battalion, who is credited with being one of the co-discoverers of gold at Mormon Island. Hudson Gulch is identified on a geological survey map.

It is possible that the 100-200 Mormons mining in the area of the Middle Fork, referred to by Rich in 1850, may have included those mining in Mormon Gulch, North. The Gulch was a short distance upstream from Slap Jack Bar.

Mormon Gulch, South
(Mormon Diggins, South, and Tuolumne County)

The southern Mormon Gulch was located in present-day Tuolumne County adjacent to Tuttletown. It was northwest of Sonora and a few miles west of Columbia, the "Queen of the Southern Mines," a reconstructed ghost town as of 1984. Mormon Creek finds its way down the Gulch. It may also have been known as Morinose Gulch and Mormonitos.

Little is known about the identity of the Mormons who discovered gold there in the fall of 1848. One reference gives a Colonel Graham and a William Bailey the credit for being the leaders of the group. Neither has been identified. There were three Baileys in the Battalion: Addison, James, and Jefferson, the latter being one of the Mormon Volunteers. The article cited above refers to the Battalion Boys as having a "reputation of being reckless, wild, and lawless all up and down the Gulch." [15]

The Gulch was visited by Apostles Rich and Lyman in May of 1850 when they collected names and tithing from the Mormons in the area. These are believed to have included Franklin Edwards, C. D. Hovey, Albert Duey (Dewey), John Robinson, and Marcus Lafayette Shepherd. Of these, only Shepherd was in the Battalion. Only Robinson possibly remained in the county at the time of the census, there being two men by that name.

Peter Justesen, as recounted by Gudde and Gudde, later wrote that in 1851 Mormons were taking gold out of Mormon Gulch (South) by the mule load. If true, they are unknown. No concentrated group of Mormons was found in Tuolumne County at the time of the census except for a small group associated with the Davis family. [16] There were, however, about 26 possible Mormons in the county.

Mormon Hill (Orr, & Salmon Falls or New York Ravine)

Mormon Hill is located just south of Salmon Falls. Its residents were often considered part of the Salmon Falls community. A cemetery is located nearby, evidence that at one time a community was probably located on the hill. Mormon Hill was likely the area also identified on an 1860 map as Orr's. It is located on a tributary to New York Ravine on the hill road from Mormon Island to Salmon Falls. If this is true, the Orr family probably lived there along with other tentatively identified Mormons. [17]

One of the residents, Elzada Allred, was one of Thomas Orr's daughters. The birthplaces for a number of the residents, as recorded on the 1850 census, undoubtedly gave New York Ravine its name. Ebenezer Hanks was known as a prominent Mormon businessman in Salmon Falls in the early 1850s. The Orrs continued to entertain

Mormon missionaries into 1857, but did not go to Utah that year. Some of their descendants are buried in the relocated Mormon Island-Salmon Falls cemetery.

Mormon Island (Mormon Diggings - North, Lower Diggings)

Mormon Island is located on the South Fork of the American River in the northeast corner of Sacramento County. Gold was first discovered there by Wilford Hudson and Sidney Willis on February 2, 1848, as they returned to Sutter's grist mill from a visit to Coloma. Now covered by the waters of Folsom Reservoir, it was the site of California's first gold rush, there being 200 to 300 persons by June of 1848. Some of the gold mined there was in the sample sent east that summer to support the claim of a substantial gold discovery. Sam Brannan established a store at the Island in 1848 with Charles C. Smith as the manager. Lip service was given to keeping the discovery of gold a secret; however, the Battalion Boys and some of the *Brooklyn* Saints in San Francisco probably learned of the gold in April. According to William Glover's account, Sam Brannan announced the find to the Saints in San Francisco at the last meeting he attended there. The Saints responded immediately and began to flock to the Diggings at that time. Brannan attempted for awhile to collect 30 percent of the mined gold, but with the influx of non-Mormons and the disillusionment of the Mormons with him, his collection broke down. Apostle Lyman and Porter Rockwell were there in 1849, Lyman evidently supervising the Mormons in their mining activity. By the time of the 1850 Census, few Mormons remained. [18] It was visited by Mormon missionaries in 1857, but they had no reported success in their preaching.

Mormon Ravine (Long Valley -- Auburn)

At least four Mormon families lived in Long Valley on the Sacramento Road two miles west of Auburn in Sutter (Placer) County, probably giving it the name of Mormon Ravine. While not identified in the 1850 Census, it is known that James and Mary Ann Harmon and Dr. William L. McIntire, were there in the summer of 1850 when they were visited by Apostles Rich and Lyman on August 12th. They were joined by the Robert Crow and the Threllkill families after the census.

Dr. McIntire had entered Utah in 1849. The others had been associated with the Mississippi Saints entering Utah in 1847. While the Harmons have not been identified in the census, a 26 year old black by the name of Harmon was living in the vicinity of Auburn with two other blacks named Moses and John Dowty, all from Mississippi.

In May of 1856, Elders Shearman and Stuart stayed at the Homestead House in Long Valley (a hotel run by Mary Ann Harmon, widow of James Harmon). They also visited long-time Mormon missionary, George P. Dykes, agent for the *Western Standard* in Auburn. They preached in the courthouse in Auburn and were well treated—though making no known converts. The following June the Crows hosted Elder Matthew Wilkie, district mission leader. A week later, after an aborted meeting at nearby Ophir, the widow Harmon and the Crows received the Elders and they preached again in the courthouse at Auburn (a simple wooden structure).

At the time of the Mormon exodus in October of 1857, several of the Crow family went south to San Bernardino, some going on to Utah. Others remained in San Bernardino, and still others in the area of Auburn along with the Threllkills. Several became members of the Reorganized Church. Most of the Harmons went to Utah, some by way of Carson City.

Mormon Slough (See Stockton.)

Mormon Station (Genoa -- Edmunds (Edmonds) Station)

Mormon Station, later named Genoa, in Carson Valley, Nevada, was established in 1850 by Hampton S. Beatie, Abner and Thomas Blackburn, and others. The Blackburns were Mormons. Beatie later became a Church member. Others unnamed may have been Mormons. John Reese, who later became a Mormon, was the chief resident for several years. While it was not established under the official aegis of the Church, Mormon Station/Genoa nevertheless had a substantial number of Mormons (including Apostle Orson Hyde) involved with it over the years. It is known as the first white habitation in present-day Nevada and became the county seat for Carson County. It has been restored and is maintained as a site of historical interest. Edmunds (Edmonds) Station (which may have been another name for the place) was located in the area, possibly established by Jefferson Edmunds.

Mormon Tavern (Lathrop's Tavern)

The Mormon Tavern was located in El Dorado County on the road from Placerville to Sacramento and between Shingle Springs and White Rock near the Sacramento County Line. It was run by Asahel A. Lathrop, who lived there with his family in 1850. [19] Lathrop had been a Captain of Ten in the Mormon migration of 1847. He probably moved to California with Lyman and Rockwell in the spring of 1849, establishing his tavern a few miles west of Rockwell's tavern (Deer Creek House) which was on or near Deer Creek.

Apostles Rich and Lyman used it as a base of operations in 1850, planning meetings with Jefferson Hunt and Rockwell for the southern colony. It later became a major stage coach station. Clarksville was located nearby. A historical marker is located on power company property alongside the Placerville-Sacramento freeway. Lathrop may well have been living with three polygamous wives: his identified wife, Jane (Peacock) and her sisters, Hannah and Sarah.

Mud Springs (Mathinias Creek -- El Dorado)

Mud Springs was located about four miles south of Placerville in El Dorado County. It officially became El Dorado in 1855, but unofficially retained its former name for many years. Contiguous to it was Mathinias (Matheney's) Creek, which had as many as nine tentatively identified Mormons in 1850. [20]

Murderer's Bar (See Middle Fork, American River.)

Natoma (See Brighton.)

Negro Bar (Folsom)

As early as 1849, mining commenced at Negro Bar on the American River, about 20 miles upstream from Sutter's Fort, Its location between Sutter's grist mill (under construction in 1848) at or near Six Mile House (Brighton) and Mormon Island, makes it an extremely likely candidate for early Mormon involvement, even though no positive documentation of such exists at the present time. The fact that there is a Mormon Street in present-day Folsom, contiguous to Negro Bar, enhances the possibility. The Bar is not identified in the 1850 Census, but several possible Mormon family units, including two Crow families, were in the general vicinity. [21]

Folsom itself was not established until about 1854 with the coming of California's first railroad which originated at Sacramento. Folsom grew as the eastern terminus of the line. S. G. Higgins was a Mormon businessman in the area in the 1855-57 period, and missionaries frequently held meetings there, not all of them well received. Walls Diggings and Rhodes Diggings (where Mormon families lived between 1850-1857) were located a mile or so to the south.

Negro Hill

Negro Hill was located on the South Fork of the American River in El Dorado County across the river from Mormon Island. Gudde and Gudde claim that it probably was developed at the same time as Mormon Island in 1848, which probably means that it was first settled by Mormon Battalion Boys. Benjamin Hawkins and Fayette Shepherd of the Battalion, accompanied by "old man" (Ashbel) Haskell of the *Brooklyn*, were probably the discoverers of the first gold at this site.

Nevada City (Rough and Ready. Grass Valley – Nevada, Yuba Counties)

Nevada City, or Nevada, as it was frequently called, is located on Deer Creek in Yuba (Nevada County). Gold was discovered by a man named Hunt in the fall of 1849. In 1850, 21 possible Mormons resided in the county. [22]

Missionaries were active in the area as early

as September of 1855. Between then and 1857, at least seven persons were baptized in the Rock Creek, about four miles north of Nevada City. N. H. Carlow and his son were the only Mormon Elders in the area. The Saints had no meetinghouse but probably used the home of Brother Carlow, despite its inconvenient location on the south slope of Bold (Bald) Mountain near the Flying Cloud Tunneling Company, four miles north of Nevada. In June of 1857, Elder Matthew F. Wilkie intended to visit "the northern division of the El Dorado Conference." On August 24, 1857, the Elders secured horses for a brief trip to Grass Valley and Nevada City to recruit Saints to move to Utah. The visit apparently bore fruit in August when Nathaniel Carlow, his four sons, a daughter, and Michael Wahlen joined a Mormon group headed for San Bernardino, that being the terminus for the winter route to Utah.

Established in 1849, Rough and Ready is located about seven miles southwest of Nevada City. Gudde and Gudde credit William H. Folsom as mining there in 1850, though he was listed in the census for Nevada City. However, Folsom referred in his memoirs to his mining activities at Rough and Ready. Folsom was one of the builders of the Nauvoo Temple, later an architect on the Salt Lake Temple and builder of the Manti Temple.

Newton (New Town)

Located in El Dorado County on the south side of Weber Creek, Newton was first settled by Mormon Battalion Boys as they worked their way into the mountains from Mormon Island in 1848 on their way to Utah. They built a corral there in July and mined successfully while waiting for word that the snow would allow them passage over the Sierra Nevada. The following year a small group of men returned and began to mine in earnest. Some of them are believed to have been in the 1848 company and led by a man named Russell, possibly Henry. Russell remained a resident of the community for many years.

New York Ravine (See Mormon Hill.)

Orr (See Mormon Hill.)

Pilot Hill

Pilot Hill was a camp located on the northeast side of Pilot Hill, halfway between the South and Middle Forks of the American River. It may have had an earlier name of Centerville, but was called Pilot Hill at the time of the census. Mining began as early as 1849, but according to Gudde and Gudde, water was not available until 1854. The Census of 1850, conducted in January of 1851, shows that among the 546 residents lived 40 possible Mormons, 5 of them noted as hotel keepers. [23]

Placerville (See Hangtown.)

Pleasant Hill - French Town

A community of about 300 persons at the time of the 1850 Census, Pleasant Hill in El Dorado County became a center of Mormon activity and a base of missionary effort, by 1855 or 1856. It was located about two miles south of Shingle Springs on the Cosumnes Road, which put it very close to Frenchtown. The Lunceford family was the nucleus of the Mormon community. The Luncefords had entered Utah in 1850. At that time, the family consisted of 15 persons. Which of these came to California is not apparent. It is known, however, that at least William, Rawsey, Sarah, and Cynthia did.

Pleasant Hill was visited by William H. Shearman, Mormon missionary and leader in the gold fields, as early as May of 1856. Baptisms were frequent. In addition to the Luncefords, several residents of the area were or had become Mormons by October of 1857. [24]

In July of 1857, Pleasant Hill was the gathering place for the Saints from Northern California who were emigrating to Deseret via Carson Valley. They departed the farm on July 7th.

In August of 1857, Samuel Lunceford arrived to help his family in the move to Utah. By October, the outside pressures in the wake of the news of the Mountain Meadows Massacre began to build up. Mob action was threatened. On October 12th, most of the Lunceford family and Brother Barnes, along with other Saints and missionaries, left Pleasant Hill. William Lunceford and Williamson stayed behind to dispose of the Lunceford farm. Father Lunceford apparently never made it to Utah, dying in California.

Pleasant Valley

Located between the North Fork of the Cosumnes River and Weber Creek in El Dorado County, Pleasant Valley was the scene of the assembling of Mormons between June 17th and July 4th in 1848 for their trek east. While waiting, they mined successfully in the area.

Rhodes Diggings - El Dorado County

Rhodes Diggings in El Dorado County was located between Diamond Springs and Placerville. This may have been one of several mines established by the family of Thomas Rhoads (Rhoades).

Rhodes Diggings – Sacramento County

Rhodes Diggings in Sacramento County, was located three miles southeast of Folsom, on Alder Creek and near Prairie City. This was probably one of the mining claims of the Thomas Rhoades (Rhodes) family.

A number of Rhodes (Rhoades) have been identified as living in Sacramento County in 1850. [25] It is not certain which were members of Thomas Rhoades' family, but from their places of origin it would appear that most were at least related.

Rosecrans Quartz Lode

This may have been a mine belonging to George W. Rosecrans, an officer in the Mormon Battalion. He had gone to Utah in 1847, returning to California, probably with Abner Blackburn, in 1849. While he maintained a hotel at Dolores Bar on the North Fork of the American River, he may also have had his mine located a mile and a half northwest of Garden Valley in El Dorado County. He lived at the Bar with his wife Elmira and their son G. W., Jr. in 1850. He apparently remained in California after the Mormon exodus.

Rough and Ready (See Nevada City.)

Sacramento

While not in the gold fields proper, Sacramento was the major supply center for the northern mines. There were two locations in present-day Sacramento in which Mormons played a significant role. One was Sutter's Fort, established by John Sutter. Samuel Brannan and his Mormon partner, Charles C. Smith, maintained a store at the fort. Numerous Mormons worked for Sutter as craftsmen, herdsmen and laborers after their arrival in 1847. The fort was located on high ground adjacent to a slough of the American River, about a mile south of the river itself, and two miles east of the confluence of the American and Sacramento Rivers.

The Embarcadero or waterfront of Sacramento at the juncture of the Sacramento and American Rivers was developed to a considerable extent by Sam Brannan, who built the City Hotel, the area's first. A Mormon immigrant to Utah (1847), John S. Fowler, went to California in 1848, becoming the manager of the hotel constructed that year. While the area had the advantage of being on the two rivers, it was on low land and subject to frequent flooding. It became necessary to raise the land at least one story above the natural elevation. Brannan owned much of the land, subdividing and selling it over the years. It was there that he made most of his wealth. In 1850, some 26 possible Mormons resided in the city's environs. [26]

Salmon Falls (Higgins Point – See Mormon Hill.)

Salmon Falls in El Dorado County was located several miles upstream from Mormon Island on the South Fork of the American River. Gudde and Gudde credit the Mormons as probably being its founders before July of 1848, having discovered gold there by that time. While non-Mormons soon inundated the area, it remained a Mormon enclave for at least a decade. The 1850 Census showed 14 probable Mormons. [27]

Higgins Point was located a quarter of a mile below Salmon Falls. It was named after an Australian who opened its first store. The credit for discovering gold there in 1848 is given by Gudde and Gudde to the Mormons. It may well have been merged with Salmon Falls in the census. Both Salmon Falls and Higgins Point have been at least partially covered by Folsom reservoir. The local cemeteries were merged with that of Mormon Island and all the interred moved to the new Mormon Island Memorial Cemetery in advance of the rising water of the Folsom Reservoir.

The Orrs, who lived a mile or two up the hill from Salmon Falls in 1850, were later known as residents and hotel keepers. They hospitably received missionaries as late as the fall of 1857.

A. C. Brower and his wife maintained a hotel in the area from 1849-50. It was probably taken over at that time by Ebenezer Hanks and his wife who prospered there until 1855-56, when they moved to San Bernardino. The Thatchers and Hervey Green also maintained a hotel there in 1850.

Salt Lake Trading Company

The Salt Lake Trading Company established a store on the Merced River in the spring of 1850, a few miles upstream from present-day Merced Falls. Captain Howard Egan, one of Brigham Young's bodyguards, was the leader. It is uncertain that other Mormons located there. If they did, they probably included those accompanying Egan to California, as well as some members of the Flake Company.

Salt Springs

Located far to the south of the major gold mining areas of California was Salt Springs on the Amargosa River in San Bernardino County, north of present-day Baker. Mormons, on their way to California in 1849, discovered gold in this general area. They may have returned over the next few years to mine the area, since one account places them there in 1854.

San Bernardino

Located far to the south of the major gold mining areas, San Bernardino was settled by Mormons in 1851 when they purchased the Lugo Ranch. Until 1857 when it was abandoned by the Mormon faithful, San Bernardino was a favorite stopping place for Mormons going to and from

the gold fields to the north during winter months. Financed to a considerable extent by money from the gold fields, it was the base from which a Mormon gold mining expedition was sent to the Kern River mines in 1855, but with little success, as well as the home of proselyting missionaries sent into the northern gold fields in 1855 and 1856 to raise money to meet that colony's mortgage obligations.

Six Mile House (See Brighton.)

Slap Jack Bar

Located on the Middle Fork of the American River in Sutter (Placer) County, a substantial number of the Mormon gold missionaries mined here in 1850. Especially prominent were members of the Flake Company. George Q. Cannon—later a Mormon Apostle, special counselor to Brigham Young, and in the First Presidency for three other Church presidents—maintained a store, possibly a branch of the Salt Lake Trading Company. A number of the men mining there were called on proselyting missions in the fall of 1850, happy to leave their arduous and only minimally rewarding physical labor for one more in keeping with their religious proclivities.

Slough House (See Dry Creek.)

Sly Park

Sly Park, a name still retained for the area, was east of Placerville in El Dorado County. Sly Park Creek flowed into Camp Creek east of Placerville in El Dorado County. It is now covered by a reservoir. It was the part of Pleasant Valley reportedly found by James C. Sly of the Mormon Battalion on July 5, 1848, and named after him.

Stockton (Mormon Slough --Mormon Levee -- Mormon Channel)

While technically not in the gold fields, Stockton was the major supply center for the southern mines. It was originally called Tuleberg and was settled by Charles Weber in 1848.

Mormons played a role in Stockton since as early as 1848 when, according to Hammond and

Morgan, [28] a group of them on the way from San Francisco to the Stanislaus River transported their goods up a channel of the San Joaquin River. It was later named Mormon Channel. Mormons probably played a more important role in the area than just transporting goods through it. There was a Mormon Levee protecting the southern flank of the village. One of the four major avenues running east and west, toward the southern edge of the city, was named Mormon Avenue, and alongside it was Mormon Slough.

No record has yet been found of actual Mormon activity in Tuleberg (Stockton), but in the 1850-1851 census covering Stockton in San Joaquin County, nineteen men, with a number of children and possibly one wife, had names either the same or very close to the same as Mormons either known or believed to have been in California. [29] Most had been involved with the Mormon Battalion.

One of the earliest branches of the Reorganized Church of Jesus Christ of Latter Day Saints was organized in Stockton in the late 1860s.

Sutter's Fort (See Sacramento.)

Weaverville (Weberville) and Ringold

Weaverville (a name corruption for Weberville) and Ringold in El Dorado County were essentially the same town, though listed separately in the 1850 Census. The towns were about halfway between Placerville and Diamond Springs. Weaverville, a mail terminus, was frequently referred to as the first place of habitation after coming from the east over the Mormon-Carson Pass Emigrant Trail. (The properly named Weaverville is in Trinity County.)

Charles M. Weber of Tuleberg (Stockton) is credited with having been the pioneer gold miner between the Cosumnes River and the South Fork of the American River. He worked in partnership with William Daylor who had the land grant from Sutter. Daylor, in turn, was a son-in-law of Thomas Rhoades. The Rhoades family probably maintained a gold mine in the general vicinity. When Governor Mason visited Weberville, then consisting of about a dozen cabins, in July of 1848, he was enthusiastic about the gold in the streams.

In 1850, 14 possible Mormons were in the village. [30] It is interesting to note that a James J. Strang lived next door to a Mormon, William A. Simmons. A James J. Strang was the leader of an offshoot of the Mormon Church which was centered in Illinois and Wisconsin. However, there is no known connection between the two Strangs.

White Oak

White Oak Flat or Springs in White Oak Township in El Dorado County was located south of Salmon Falls, Its original name was Cartwheel Valley. Missionaries visited the Heckies (Hicks or Hecks) family at White Oak Springs in 1857, making special reference to Sister Heckies or Hecks. This was probably the Charlotte C. Hix who entered Utah in the migration of 1848, who was living with Christian and Constantine Hick in White Oak in 1850. A total of 29 residents of White Oak have tentatively been identified as Mormons. [31] One of the family units, that of Bird Barnett (Burnett), a hotel keeper, appears to have brought several slaves or former slaves with them from Utah, probably in 1849.

Family Units

The usual view of California Argonauts is that they were single—at least they did not go as family units. So far as the Mormon Argonauts are concerned, this view seems to be reinforced by examining the stories of the gold missionaries and even proselyting missionaries in the gold fields. However, this is a distorted view. While, without question, most Mormon Argonauts were in California as lone males, there were substantial numbers of family units. Defining a family unit as consisting of a husband and wife; father, mother, and children; father and children; or mother and children, there were at least 72 tentatively identified Mormon family units in the gold fields, consisting of 308 persons. [32]

Occupational Characteristics

The possible or probable Mormons in California during the period covered by this volume constituted a cross section of occupations. [33] The greatest number were miners, of course, but in addition there were the following:

Hotel or tavern keepers	42
Traders or merchants	34
Carters or teamsters	14
Farmers or ranchers	14
Laborers	10
Carpenters	5
Woodchoppers	4
Butchers	3
Clothiers or merchants	3
Mariners or seamen	3
Mill owners	2
Physicians	2
Shoemakers	1
Livery stable owners	1
Express office managers	1
Blacksmiths	1
Grocers	1
Tinners	1
Bakers	1
Coopers	1
Restaurateurs	1
Ten Pin Alley operators	1
Gamblers	1

NOTES

1. Gudde and Gudde, *California Gold Camps.*

2. See Explanation, Appendix B.

3. See Appendix B, Census 1.

4. See Appendix B, Census 2.

5. See Appendix B, Census 3.

6. Carter, *Our Pioneer Heritage.* 2:455.

7. See Appendix B, Census 4.

8. See Appendix B, Census 5.

9. See Appendix B, Census 6.

10. See Appendix B, Census 7.

11. See Appendix B, Census 8.

12. See Appendix B, Census 9.

13. See Appendix B, Census 10.

14. See Appendix B, Census 11.

15. *Sacramento Union,* June 20, 1848.

16. See Appendix B, Census 12.

17. See Appendix B, Census 13.

18. See Appendix B, Census 14.

19. See Appendix B, Census 15.

20. See Appendix B, Census 16.

21. See Appendix B, Census 17.

22. See Appendix B, Census 18.

23. See Appendix B, Census 19.

24. See Appendix B, Census 20.

25. See Appendix B, Census 21.

26. See Appendix B, Census 22.

27. See Appendix B, Census 23.

28. Hammond and Morgan, "Captain Charles M. Weber." Bancroft Library.

29. See Appendix B, Census 24.

30. See Appendix B, Census 25.

31. See Appendix B, Census 26.

32. See Appendix B, Census 27.

33. See Appendix B, Census 28.

**Modern View of Sutter's Fort, Sacramento Civic Center in the Background.
(Black and white version of a water color by Udo Schroeder.)**

"Construction on Sutter's fort was begun in 1841 after John Sutter received a grant of land from the Mexican government. This grant by 1844 encompassed an area of over 225 square miles. Sutter's settlement thrived and soon he employed some 450 workers, mostly Native Americans, raising cattle, as well as such crops as grapes and wheat. Although California changed hands in 1846 as a result of the war between Mexico and the United States, nothing changed dramatically until the discovery of gold at Sutter's newly constructed sawmill at Coloma in 1848. Soon squatters had occupied most of Sutter's land, stolen most of his cattle, and destroyed his crops. Consequently he sold the fort in 1849 for $7,000 and moved to a farm near what is now Marysville. The fort fell into disrepair as Sacramento grew around it. In 1890 it was purchased and reconstructed, then presented to the state of California. In 1947 it became a state park." *Illustration and Caption Courtesy of Udo Schroeder.*

This and other watercolor sketches by Udo Schroeder are available at the Marshall Gold Discovery State Historic Park, Coloma, California.

Appendix B: Mormon Argonauts in the Census Records

Possible and Probable Mormons in the U.S. Census, California 1850, for various Counties.

Explanations

In all subsequent listings from the census, those individuals have been included whose names lead to the belief that they were or may have been Mormons. Some of them are relatively certain. Others are very tentative, with names that are close enough to persons associated with the Mormon migration that they are at least likely candidates. Spelling cannot always be relied on nor even the given year or place of birth (origin) to identify persons. The same person often spelled, caused, or allowed to have spelled the name differently. Some even gave differences in date of birth. There were frequently different people with the same name. Some Mormons may even have used pseudonyms or purposely obscured their place of origin to avoid identification.

In the census listings, the three digit numbers on the left are keys to the census, indicating the page number for that particular county in which the names are found. Following the name is the age and recorded place of birth or origin (as abbreviated in the census). That is followed by the occupation. The last column is a key to tentatively identifying the person with particular Mormon groups: MB–Mormon Battalion, *Brook–Brooklyn*, Ut (year) entered Utah, Ca (year) entered Califor-

nia, etc. Census abbreviations for the states are used throughout, which if capitalized would correspond to modern postal abbreviations. "Can" is used for Canada, "GB" for Great Britain, "It" for Italy, "Ind. Terr." for Indian Territory, "Rus" for Russia, and "UnK" for unknown.

As the means of tentatively identifying the individuals as Mormons, the lists of Utah immigrants published by Kate Carter, a microfilm listing of Utah immigrants, the lists of Mormon Battalion Boys and *Brooklyn* Saints, the lists of tithe payers and California Saints maintained by Apostle Amasa M. Lyman, and miscellaneous diaries and accounts have been consulted. Association with various individuals, records, or groups are indicated: Boyle, Egan, Flake, Lyman, Lyman-Rich, Huff. (Huffaker), and Hunt. (Huntington). Some relevant years are indicated.

Individuals from the census have been grouped into what were apparently family units and those at the same residence, with the father first, followed by the mother (indented), the children (indented) and others. Where they had the same last name as the father, it has not been repeated.

A few have been included who are very speculative in that they have not yet even tentatively been tied to a Mormon group. They were, however, living at the time of the census in proximity to known Mormons and their names make them likely candidates as Mormons. These are designated with a question mark (?) in the additional identification column. To illustrate, under Brighton or Six Mile House is A. Cheney and his family. They were living near the Roots, known to be Mormons. Known Mormons by the name of Cheney were in California and Utah in 1847 and 1849. Next to them was the Lathrop family group. Living with the latter was E. A. Cheney. Lathrop himself might well have been related to, but is apparently not the same as Asahel Lathrop of the Mormon Tavern.

Included in parentheses are possible or probable first names. For example, the census only lists J. Foxall at Brighton. From other sources it is known that a James Foxall came to California with other Mormons in 1850. Therefore, J. (James) Foxall is listed.

The census systematically excludes occupational information on women and those under 15 years of age; therefore, that column has been left blank for those individuals.

CENSUS 1
Possible or Probable Mormons–Brighton, 1850

Census Page	Individuals		Age/ Origin	Occupation	Additional Identification
199	J. (James) Foxall		22 GB	none	Ca 1850
199	E. (Eleazer) Davis		23 NY	Laborer	MB
	M. Boyd		28 De	none	?
199	J. (Jeremiah) Root		48 Va	(Innkeeper)	Lyman & Rich
	E. (Elizabeth)		37 NY		
		Alex	19 Oh	none	
		Abner	17 Oh	none	
		Jno	15 Oh	none	
		Geo.	13 Oh		
		Samuel	9 Il		
		C. A.	2 Ia		
199	A. (Alpheus) Cheney		45 In	(Innkeeper)	
	Eliza		40 In		
		Mary	4 In		
		Lucy	2 In		
199	Mr. Lathrop		43 Mo	(Innkeeper)	
	Jane		43 Mo		
		Jno	9 Mo		
		Eliza	5 Mo		
		Jane	3 Mo		
	E. A. Cheney		12 In		
200a	Wm. R. Tubs		25 Oh	Rancher	MB
	Sarah		21 NY		
		Henry	2 Ca		
200	L. (Levi) Fifield		46 NH	Blacksmith	MB
	B.		17 Vt	Laborer	?
200	James Davis		25 Ma	Miner	MB

NOTE: a. It is not altogether certain that the "200" listing was at Six Mile House. It may have been at Negro Bar (what was later Folsom), or near Mormon Island (201).

CENSUS 2
Peter Wimmer Family–Coloma, 1850

396	Peter L. Wimmer	39 Oh	Hotel	Ca1846
	Elizabeth J.	28 Va		
	Elijah	20 Mi	none	
	John	19 Mi	none	
	Geo	17 Mi	none	
	Sarah	12 Mi		
	Wm	10 Mo		
	Benj. F.	2 Ca		

CENSUS 3
Possible or Probable Mormons–Diamond Springs, 1850

344	Jesse T. (Taylor) Jackson	38 Pa	none	Ut1850
	Fanny	23 NY		
	Nephi	8/12 Ut		
344	Jesse W. Johnson	30 Oh	Miner	MB
344	Wm. J. Johnson (Johnston)	25 Oh	Miner	MB
	Elizabeth			
349	John Roberts	45 Ga	Miner	Ut1847
	Martha	35 Al		
	Richard T.	14 Ms		
	Elnidra	13 Ms		
	Harriet L.	11 Ms		
	Francis E.	8 Ms		
	William B.	5 Ms		
	Catherine	2 Ut		
	Matthew Roberts	34 Al	Miner	?
349	Joseph Roberts	19 Mo	Miner	?
349	Geo. W. Sparks	31 Al	Merchant	Ut1847
	Luana	31 Al		
	Wm. T.	7 Ms		
	Mary A.	5 Ms		
	Geo. F.	2 Ut		
	Harriet C.	1/12 Ca		
350	Orrin Hatch	20 NY	Teamster	MB

CENSUS 4
Possible or Probable Mormons–Dry Creek

(a)   The Thomas Rhoades Family
Thomas Rhoades
   Elizabeth Forster Rhoades
      Isaac (23)   Foster (15)
      Thomas (21)   George W. (13)

Elizabeth (19)	Henry (11)
Sarah Pierce (17)	Caleb Baldwin (10)
William Baldwin (17)	Lucinda (8)
Catherine (15)	

(b)   The following were also in the Rhoades company in 1846:
John Pierce Rhoades
      Matilda Fanning Rhoades with six children
Joseph House
Isaac House
Christine Forster Patterson and baby
Turner Elder
      Polly Rhoades Elder
            The Fanning Boys
Daniel Rhoades
      Amanda Esrey Rhoades
      and one son
The Astray Boys (note 1)
Mr. Whitman

(c)   The Pollocks moved to Dry Creek after 1850:

James Pollock	38 GB	Miner	Ut1847
Priscilla	22 Pa		
Clarinda	10 Il		
Thos	5 Il		
John	3 Ut		
Mary	2 Ca		

NOTE 1. The Esrey boys probably consisted of Justin, James, Thomas, and Jonathan, all of Illinois living together on the El Dorado side of the Cosumnes River in 1850.

CENSUS 5
Possible or Probable Mormons–Drytown and Calaveras County, 1850

The 1850 Census does not identify Drytown. However, the following individuals listed in the census for Calaveras County may have been Mormons.

74	William Hunter	27 NY	Miner	MB
83	Samuel Campbell	21 GB	Miner	MB
91	Wm. Wood	28 Ma	Miner	MB
97	Wm. Muir	34 Can	Miner	MB
100	Wm. T. Follett	31 NY	Teamster	MB
106	James Dunn	29 Ky	Merchant	MB
	J. R. Dunn	29 Ky	Merchant	?
	Robt C. Dunn	27 Ky	Merchant	?
109	Dan. Brown	24 GB	Miner	MB
116	O. M. Beckstead	16 Il	Miner	MB
123	Wm. Robinson	23 Ma	Miner	MB
127	Chas. Wright	50 GB	Miner	MB

132	John Green	22 Tn	Miner	MB
133	Edward Martin	25 Ca	Miner	MB
136	James Dunn	26 Me	Miner	MB
142	James Dunn	27 Oh	Miner	MB
153	John Snyder	46 Tn	Miner	MB
155	Edward Martin	34 NY	Miner	MB
156	John Allen	26 NY	Miner	MB
159	Wm. O. Clark	33 In	Merchant	?
	B. B. Clark	35 Oh	Merchant	?
	Lyman Curtis	25 Cn	Miner	?
161	Alex Brown	23 Oh	Miner	MB
165	Edward Martin	32 NY	Miner	MB
170	Robert Harris	22 NY	Miner	MB
181	Samuel Lewis	46 Oh	Miner	MB
186	Samuel Lewis	24 Me	Miner	MB
189	Jas. Stewart	27 Pa	Miner	MB
197	G. W. (N.) Haskell	22 Pa	Miner	MB
205	J. M. King	45 Pa	Miner	MB
	Samuel King	21 RI	Miner	?
	George King	23 Pa	Miner	?
205	James Bailey	21 La	Miner	MB
210	James Hampton	21 Il	Merchant	MB
218	John Rollins	21 Ma	Miner	MB
	L. R. Rollins	20 Ma	Miner	?
220	Walter L. Davis	21 Ma	Miner	MB
237	Chas. Jamison	48 Tn	Miner	MB
242	Robert (S.) Bliss	26 Ma	Miner	MB
243	Geo. Allen	27 Ar	Miner	MB
244	Jas. Ferguson	21 NY	Miner	MB

CENSUS 6
Possible or Probable Mormons–Greenwood-Louistown, 1850

440	James Boyd	36 Ky	Miner	?
	Wm. Boyd	33 Ky	Miner	MB
449	Henry A. (H.) Harrison	32 Il	Miner	Hunt.1850
	Geo. A. Harrison	25 Il	Miner	?
	James Willis	40 Il	Miner	MB
450	John B. Lemon (Lemmon)	23 Ia	Merchant	Ut1847
	James M. (W.) Lemon	23 Ia	Merchant	MB
450	Joseph Lisk (Lish)	23 NY	Miner	Ut1850
450	Emily Gates	18 Mo	none	Ut1848
	John (R.) Clawson	24 ?	none	MB
	Fayette Granger	28 NY	none	Ut1847
	Solomon Gates	14 Can	none	Ut1847
450	Lewis B. Myers	36 Pa	Butcher	Ut1847
	Maria	18 Il		
	Lewis L.	9/12 Ca		

	Francis M. Clements	17 Il	Laborer	Ut1847
451	William Lane	20 Il	Laborer	Ut1847,MB
	Nathaniel Fairbanks	25 Oh	Butcher	Ut1847
	William Crow	22 Il	Butcher	Ut1847
451	Andrew J. Hickerson	39 Tn	Gardener	Ut1849
	George W. Hickerson	37 Tn	Gardener	Ut1848
	William Wolsey	20 Ia	Gardener	Ut1848,49
451	Erastus Bingham	28 Vt	Miner	MB
	Willard Bingham	19 Vt	Miner	Ut1847
451	Lucas Hoagland	24 Mi	Miner	MB
	Peter Hoagland	20 Mi	Miner	Ut1847
	Israel West	20 NY	Miner	Ut1847
	Richard Robinson	20 GB	Miner	Ut1847
451	Samuel L. Crane (Crow)	45 Ky	Merchant	Ut1847
	Elizabeth A.	12 Ky		
	Charles H.	8 Ky		
	Mary J.	6 Ky		
	Adam H.	4 Ky		
451	Benjamin B. Croso (Crow)	30 Mo	Miner	Ut1847
	Harriet	22 GB		
	Harriet	3 Ut		
	Wm. D.	10/12 Ca		
	Jessee Brown	21 Mo	Ten Pin Alley	MB
452	Geo. Threllkill	30 Il	Miner	Ut1847
	Jane	25 Il		
	James	5 Il		
	Harriet N.	3 Ut		
	Geo. L.	5/ 12 Ca		
	Philo N. Bechunin (Behunin)	20 NY	Shoemaker	Ut1849
453	William Huntington	34 NY	Merchant	Ut1848
	Mary	21 GB		
	Mahonra (Mahonri) Calhoun	16 Oh	Miner	
	Thomas Gates	16 Can	Miner	?
	M. L. Chapin	45 UnK	Miner	MB
456	Thomas Johnson	29 GB	Miner	Ut1848
456	Miles Miller	29 GB	Miner	MB

CENSUS 7
Possible or Probable Mormons–Hangtown (Placerville), 1850

263	John Lowry	35 Pa	Miner	Ut1847
264	James M. Welch	42 Oh	Miner	MB
268	Robert S. Bliss	43 Ct	Trader	MB
	Mary A.	34 NY		
	Laica C.	9 Dl		

270	John Berry	17 Mo	Miner	Flake
274	David G. Wilkin(s)	49 NH	Miner	MB
	Peter S. Wilkins	24 NY	Miner	MB
274	George Hendricks	22 Oh	Miner	?
	James Hendricks	27 Oh	Miner	Lyman
276	John C. Quayle	27 GB	Miner	MB
278	Lorenzo Clark	46 Vt	Miner	MB
282	James Bailey	23 Oh	Miner	MB
283	John Green	20 Il	Miner	MB
	Mathew Green	38 De	Miner	MB
283	James Brown	24 GB	Miner	MB
284	Samuel Chapin	25 In	Miner	MB
286	Charles Wright	22 Pa	Miner	MB
287	John C. Gold (Gould)	30 NH	Baker	MB
291	William Andrews	27 SC	none	?
296	James (C.) Sly	38 Va	Miner	MB
297	Edgar Stone	20 Ky	Miner	?
298	Wm. H. Walker	30 Ky	Miner	MB
	Andrew J. Walker	34 Ky	Miner	?
299	Andrew J. Cox	17 Il	Miner	Ut1848,49
	John Dixon	20 Mo	Miner	Flake
300	Francis Brown	27 Ma	Miner	MB
302	Seth B. Tanner	22 NY	Miner	Ut1848
	Levi Lamb	25 NY	Miner	Ut1850
303	William Patten	33 Ky	Miner	Flake
303	Josiah Arnold	50 NY	Tavern Keeper	Hunt.1850
	Elizabeth	50 Ct		
	Orson	12 NY		
	Joseph	10 NY		
	Daniel McCay (McCoy)	35 Oh	Tavern Keeper	Hunt.1850
303	Meron (Myron) Tanner	24 NY	Miner	MB
303	Moseland Albon	33 Oh	Miner	Hunt.1850
304	Elijah Stephens	30 Ky	Miner	?
	John Stephens	28 Ky	Miner	?
	Alexander Stephens	23 Ky	Miner	MB
	James H. Stephens	21 Mo	Miner	?
305	Daniel Brown	21 GB	Miner	MB
306	John Steele	25 Ga	Miner	MB
308	Edward Wilcox	32 NY	Miner	MB
	Wm. H. W. Rust	22 NY	Miner	MB
	Calvin E. Wilcox	24 NY	Miner	?
313	Chas. H. Shomway (Shumway)	25 Ma	Miner	Ut1847
	Harrison Shomway	85 Ma	Miner	Ut1848
318	James Gordon	40 Can	Miner	Ut1847
318	Samuel Hall	25 Pa	Miner	Hunt.1850
323	Moses Job	50 Va	Trader	?
324	George W. Saxton	49 Ma	Miner	?
	George B. Saxton	21 Ma	Miner	MB
325	James A. (G.) Browning	23 In	Miner	Ut1848
325	Thomas J. Gibson	22 Ky	Miner	MB
328	James S. Harte	24 NY	Miner	MB

| 372 | Geo. L. Grant | 21 In | Miner | Ut1848 |

CENSUS 8
Possible or Probable Mormons–Logtown, 1850

354	Andrew Lytle	23 Oh	Miner	MB
365	Darwin Chase	32 NY	Hotel	MB
	Calvin W. Saltar	28 NY	Hotel	Lyman
365	Andrew J. Cox	25 SC	Merchant	Lyman
	Elizabeth A.	25 SC		
	Silas	7 Al		
	Thomas Chilesa	12 Mi		
	Ramsey	4 Ind. Ter.		
	Jackson	1/12 Ut		
367	Thomas Blackburn	21 Oh	Hotel	Ut1847,48
	Emily	18 NY		
367	William Gardner (Garner)	20 Pa	Miner	MB
	Jesse Gardner	22 Pa	Miner	?

NOTE: a. The age of Thomas Chiles exempts him from being a child of Cox. Josiah B. Chiles, a former Kentuckian, took his motherless children to California in 1841. There is no known direct connection with the Mormon Church, but one daughter, Elizabeth, married a Daniel Brown. A Daniel Brown was a Mormon in California. Chiles was referred to by at least one Mormon as a "fellow traveler."

CENSUS 9
Possible or Probable Mormons–McDowellsville, 1850

382	Charles (A.) Jackson	20 Me	Miner	MB
382	Geo. Forsyth	50 UnK	Miner	U1850
382	Ashel Thorn	42 NY	Miner	MB,Cal 1850
	Myron Tanner	24 NY	Miner	MB,Cal 1850
	Franklin Stoddard	41 NY	Miner	Ut1849,Cal 1850
382	Wm. Myers	40 GB	Miner	?
	Jerusha	40 Oh		
	Wm. Horner	60 Tn	Miner	?
382	Asa Barton	48 Ky	Miner	Ut1847
	Polly	47 Ky		
	Sarah Dewitt	22 Il		
	Mary	2 Ut		
382,3	James Pollock	38 GB	Miner	Ut1847
	Priscilla	22 Pa		
	Clarinda	10 Il		
	Thos	5 Il		

| | John | 3 Ut | | |
| | Mary | 2 Ca | | |

CENSUS 10
Possible or Probable Mormons–Middle Fork, American River, 1850

458	Horace Whitney	18 Il	Miner	?
458	? Blackburn	30 ?	Miner	Ut1848 or 49
458	Wm. Peacock	35 GB	Miner	Ut1847
459	Luther Tuttle	21 Va	Miner	MB
459	Isaac Blackburn	40 Pa	Miner	Ut1848 or 49
461	Joseph Atherton	26 Vt	Miner	*Brook*(?)
461	John Hills	28 Mo	Miner	Egan 1849
462	Joseph Peck	21 Vt	Miner	Ut48
	Edward Peck	24 Vt	Miner	Ut48
	John Robinson	15 Ma	Miner	Ut47
464	Frank Weaver	31 ?	Miner	MB
465	Wm. Hyde	28 GB	Miner	MB
466	Wm. Burt	36 Me	Miner	MB
468	Isaac N. (A.) Russell	38 Oh	Miner	Ut48
476	John Murray	44 ?	Miner	Huff.1849
477	Capt. C. (C. D.) Hovey	30 NY	Miner	Lyman-Rich
Richard R. Hovey		23 NH	Miner	?
John H. Hovey		25 NY	Miner	?
Samuel W. Hovey		28 NY	Miner	?
477	James Davis	30 NY	Miner	MB
480	Wm. S. Clark	25 GB	Clerk	Ut1849
	Elizabeth	35 ?		
481	William Stoddard	26 GB	Miner	?
482	Hiram Dewitt	28 Ma	Miner	Ut1847
482	Saml Clark	25 Ma	Miner	MB,U1848

CENSUS 11
Possible or Probable Mormons–Mariposa County, 1850

050	J. L. Thompson	26 Pa	Miner	MB
053	David Wilkins)	35 Ky	Miner	MB
061	Alexander K. Brown	43 Pa	Miner	MB
065	Henry Thompson	28 GB	Miner	MB
068	M. (Montgomery) E. Button	37 NY	No occupation	MB
	Mary	34 NY		
	James	14 Oh		
	J.	12 Oh		
	S. M.	9 Oh		
	Saml	6 Il		
071	James Brooks	22 Ct	Trader	Lyman
073	S. (Seth) Lincoln	28 NH	Miner	Lyman

073	John Allen	25 Ma	Miner	MB
074	Wm. Holden	29 NY	Trader and Tavern Keeper	Ut1847
079	E. L. Brown	25 Ga	Miner	MB
083	John Armstrong	25 Ky	Miner	Ut1847
085	John Allen	25 Va	Miner	MB
087	James Hawkins	26 La	Miner	Lyman
090	Charles Wright	28 GB	Miner	MB
097	John Dixon	33 Ma	Miner	Lyman

CENSUS 12
Possible or Probable Mormons–Tuolumne County, 1850

The following possible or probable Mormons have been identified in Townships I and II, one of which probably included Mormon Gulch:

127	J. W. White	50 GB	Miner	MB
135	James Williams	19 Tx	Miner	MB
138	S. R. Davis	24 NY	Miner	MB
138	James Emmett	31 NY	Miner	Lyman
139	Wm. Woods	28 GB	Miner	MB
145	James Douglas(s)	20 Va	Miner	MB
154	John Brown	24 GB	Miner	MB
154	E. L. Davis	28 Vt	Miner	MB
	R. J. Davis	30 Vt	Miner	MB
	J. Davis	26 Pa	Miner	MB
	Saml. Hart	17 GB	Miner	MB
	T. F. Peck	30 Ct	Merchant	MB
167	John Hicknot (Hickmott)	25 GB	Miner	MB
170	Jeptha Condit	22 NJ	Miner	MB
172	Henry Gibson	36 Md	Miner	Lyman
174	W. B. Gifford	24 NY	Miner	MB
174	J. A. Richardson	22 Va	Miner	MB

Other possible or probable Mormons living elsewhere in Tuolumne County were the following:

Curtisville–

100 Phineas Kimball	29 Vt	Miner	?

Louisville–

109 John Allan	20 ?	Miner	MB

Gerote–

111 Danl. M. Hoyt	24 Ma	Miner	MB
T. S. Hoyt	21 Ma	Miner	MB
113 Thomas Morris	27 GB	Miner	MB

Georgetown–

119 Albert Smith	27 Ma	Miner		MB
121 Wm. Maxwell	28 Ma	Miner		MB
122 Henry Bowling	18 Al	Miner		MB

Jamestown–

123 James Doulas(s)	45 Tn	Miner		MB

CENSUS 13
Possible or Probable Mormons–Mormon Hill, 1850

484	Leighton Hatch	23 NY	Miner	?
	Eliza	23 Me		
	Mary I.	6 Il		
	Wm. H.	1 Ne		
484	Reuben Allred	23 Ky	Miner	MB
	Elzada	23 NY		
	Jane	1 Ut		
484	Ebenezer Hanks	35 NY	Miner	MB
	Jane	33 NY		
484	John Freeman	19 Mo	Miner	Ut1847
484	Joshua Abbott	42 Ma	Carpenter	MB
484	Thomas Orr	49 GB	Hotel	Ut1847
	Catherine	48 GB		
	John	25 GB	Miner	
	James	22 GB	Miner	
	Thomas	19 GB	Miner	
	Isabella	17 GB		
	Mary Ann	13 NY		
486	Isaac Brown	31 Il	Miner	Ut1847

CENSUS 14
Possible or Probable Mormons–Mormon Island, 1850

201	G. W. Serine (Serrine)	24 Pa	Miner	*Brook*
201	A. (Amos) Fairbanks)	25 Ia	Miner	?
201	W. Willis	35 Pa	Carpenter	MB
213	John Cox	23 Tn	Miner	MB
213	A. (Abraham) Day	21 Pa	Miner	MB
213	John Robinson	28 Ma	Miner	Lyman
214	George Coleman	29 Ma	Miner	MB

CENSUS 15

Possible or Probable Mormons–Mormon Tavern, 1850

381	Ashel (Asahel) Lathrop	40 Ct		Hotel		Ut1847
	Jane (Peacock)	29 GB				
	Horace H.	8 Il				
	Mary A.	6 Il				
	Ashel A.	4 Mo				
	Sarah A.	2 Ut				
	Hannah Peacock		25 GB			
	Sarah Peacock		22 GB			
	George Clawson		19 Mo	Herdsman		MB
	Wm. Peacock		25 Me	Merchant		Lyman
381	Amos Tubs		58 Ct	Miner		Hunt.1850

CENSUS 16
Possible or Probable Mormons–Mud Springs (Mathinias Creek), 1850

342	Leonard Crow	33 Mo		Miner		Ut1847
	Horton H. Crow	23 Mo		Miner		Ut1847
	Mary	25 GB				
	John	9 Il				
	Alex	5 Il				
	Mary	2 Il				
	Jonathan	6/12 Ca				
	William H. Walker	24 Il		Miner		MB
343	Charles B. Hopkins	40 Vt		Miner		MB

CENSUS 17
Possible or Probable Mormons–Negro Bar, 1850

202	Samuel Hall	38 ?	Dairyman	Hunt.1850
	Semanthy ? ?			
202-3	Robert Crow	56 Tn	Woodchopper	U47
	Elizabeth	56 SC		
	Walter H.	28 Il	Woodchopper	
203	James R. Crow	50 Tn	Woodchopper ?	
	Mary Jane	22 La		
	Jno L.	23 Ar	Woodchopper	
	Benj. S.	18 La	Woodchopper	

CENSUS 18
Possible or Probable Mormons–Nevada and Yuba Counties, 1850

a.   Nevada County

279	Wm. Gifford	41 NC	Miner	MB
283	Wm. Boyd	27 Il	Miner	MB
287	Wm. H. Folsom	27 Il	Miner	Ca1850
294	Henry Hoyt	27 NC	Miner	MB
298	Horace (M.) Alexander	37 NY	Miner	MB
267	James (B.) Casto (Castro)	38 Oh	Cooper	MB
	Abel Casto	33 Oh	Teamster	?
270	Richard Carter	20 Al	Teamster	MB
272	William (Wilmer) Brunson	30 Tn	Miner	Ut1847
272	John Phillips	24 Ms	Miner	*Brook*

b.   Yuba County

205	Henry Gibson	27 Ma	Miner	Lyman
206	Horace A. Skinner	24 Pa	Miner	*Brook*
207	Wm. Patten	20 In	Miner	Ut1848
230	James Brooks	24 NY	?	Lyman
246	James Gordon	22 Mo	Trader	Lyman
251	Richard Robinson	25 Ma	Carpenter	Ut1847
252	George S. Clark	19 NY	Hotel	MB
256	Edward W. Haskell	31 Ct	Merchant	?
	George W. (N.) Haskell	30 Vt	?	MB
311	Joseph Dobson	30 Ky	?	MB
311	Thomas Kirk	60 Pa	Grocer	MB

CENSUS 19
Possible or Probable Mormons–Pilot Hill, 1850

471	Theodore Lytle	18 Oh	Miner	Ut1849
471	Edgar Bliss	20 NY	Miner	?
472	Wm. Robinson	50 NY	Miner	MB
472	James Barrus (Barrows)	23 Ky	Miner	Ut1848
472	Norman Bliss	34 NY	Miner	Ut1849
	Orlay Bliss	10 NY		
	Dezur Bliss	21 NY	Miner	
473	William (F.) Ewell	23 Ms	Laborer	MB
473	Henry K. Jarvis	26 NY	Miner	Ca 1847, Ut1847
474	Moses Martin	36 NY	Hotel	Boyle
	Julia	31 NY		
	Priscilla	11 Oh		
	Rosella	8 Oh		

	Joseph N.	2 Oh		
	Hiram	6/12 Ca		
474	Sebert C. Shelton	57 Va	Hotel	MB
	Elizabeth	45 Tn		
	Benj. F. Mayfield	23 Tn	none	MB
	Andrew Mayfield	23 Tn	Gardener	Ut1847
	John Mayfield	18 Ky	Gardener	
	Sarah Mayfield	16 Il		
	Cooper Shelton	11 Il		
	Thomas Shelton	9/Il		
	Mary O	5/Il		
474	Harriet Mayfield	22 Oh	none	
	Eliza E. Grayham	10/12 Ca		
	Lysander Woodworth (Woodward)	22 Oh	none	MB
474	Wm. Leffingwell	45 UnK	Hotel	Ut1847
	Mrs. (Eunice)	40 UnK		
	Cynthia	18 UnK		
	Joseph	16 UnK	Laborer	
	Matilda	15 UnK	none	
475	Isaac Harrison	35 Oh	Hotel	MB
	Catherine	33 GB	none	
	Daniel Smith	8 Pa		
	Hiram J. Smith	5 Pa		
	Mary C. Smith	2 Ca		
	Sabina Harrison	6/12 Ca		
475	Andrew J. Workman	24 Ky	Hotel	MB
	Cornelius Workman	22 Ky	Hotel	MB

NOTE: a. While the Leffingwell's show only three children in the census when they entered Utah in 1847, they had four more children ages 2-9 who joined them by 1855 when they were living west of the Sacramento River.

CENSUS 20
Mormon Residents of Pleasant Hill Area, 1857

William Lunceford	54 years
Rawsey?	
Mary T. H.	45
George	29
Mary Ann	27
Elizabeth	25
John Dew	24
Martha J.	20
Samuel	18
William T.	12
Nancy E.	10
Sarah M.	6
Cynthia M.	3
Joseph	?

James ?

Brother and Sister Henry Rabble (Raihle) Brother and Sister William Johnston (Johnson)

John Clinton

Owen W. Williamson

Edmund (Edward) S. Barnes

CENSUS 21
Possible or Probable Mormons–Rhodes Diggins (Sacramento County.), 1850

183	Lucinda Rhodes	14 Mo		Ca 1846
196	George Rhodes	? Il	Eating House	Ca 1846
	W. Rhodes	? Il	Herdsman	Ca 1846
	Henry Rhodes	? Il	Herdsman	
196	Jno Rhoades	32 Ky	Ranchero	Ca 1846
	Matilda	31 Ky		
	Thos	12 Mo		
	Jno K.	9 Mo		
	Mary E.	9 Mo		
	G. W.	7 Mo		
	M. M.	5 Mo,		
	And. J.	2 Ca		
	Jno Polk	2 Ca		

NOTE: a. John Rhoades evidently inherited his father Thomas' proclivity for multiple offspring.

CENSUS 22
Possible or Probable Mormons–Sacramento City, 1850

136	Samuel Myers	28 Va	none	MB
136	Geo. W. Hill	29 Rus.	Physician	Ut1847
137	Sam W. Chapin	30 NC	Clerk	MB
140	Francis Brown	26 Mo	Hotel	MB
	Frances	22 Mo		
	Emily	12 Mo		
	Thomas	2 Mo		
140	Willard (William) Dayton	30 UnK	none	MB
141	David H. Mossa	25 Mo	Livery Stable	MB
142	William Patten	33 NY	none	Ut1849
143	Edmund L. Brown	46 Va	Merchant	MB
	Wm. A.	22 Va	Merchant	?
	Edmund L., Jr.	16 DC	Merchant	?
148	Julius Mosey (Moser)	45 It	Carter	*Brook*
151	James Hart	21 NY	Laborer	MB
154	John W. Ghee (n)	39 Va	Laborer	Ut1849
155	Daniel Davis	20 GB	Clothing Store	MB
157	James M. Freeman	27 Me	Express Office	?

Ground Sluicing, at Gold Hill

"A very popular method of mining is that called " ground-sluicing." . . . At Gold Hill, in Placer County, this operation was in very general use, and one of our party, during our short stay there, bought an interest in a company of ground-sluicers, by which he cleared three ounces of gold-dust, and, on our departure, sold out his share at an advance.

"It has been found that the principal deposits of gold are on the great rocky ridge already referred to as the " bed-rock," and extending throughout the mining region, sometimes out-cropping at the surface, and at others sinking to a depth of above a hundred feet. Where the bed-rock is not at too great a depth, the miners, instead of sinking a shaft to reach the deposits of gold, turn a heavy stream of water upon the bank which is to be removed, and with the aid of picks and spades reduce it so as to leave the lower or gold-bearing earth accessible to be worked. The force of the water is such as to carry away the debris, while any gold it may contain remains by its own gravity and is saved with the earth intended to be washed by the ordinary methods. Ground-sluicing is thus, to a certain extent, used as a substitute for shoveling, to remove heavy layers of earth from places where gold is supposed to be deposited . . ."

[From "How We Get Gold, From a Miner in the Year '49," *Harper's New Monthly Magazine*, vol. 20, issue 119 (April 1860) 611-613.]

161	Thomas Kirk	65 Va	Merchant	MB	
164	Sherman Gilbert	41 GB	none	Hunt.Co	
	Elizabeth	28 Il			
	Sherman	9 NY			
168	Thomas Morris	40 GB	Laborer	MB	
	Sarah J.	35 GB			
172	Jno G. Smith	31 Oh	Teamster	MB	
177	Sarni Barris	25 NY	none	MB	

NOTE: a. Living near Moss was Louis C. Bidamon, husband of Joseph Smith's widow.

CENSUS 23
Possible or Probable Mormons–Salmon Falls, 1850

384	Hervey Green	43 NY	Hotel		
	Henry	21 Pa	Miner		
	Ammon	17 Mo	none		
384	Hezekiah Thatcher	41 Va	Hotel	Ut1847	
	Alley	42 Va			
	Joseph	20 Oh	Miner		
	John	15 Oh	Miner		
	Aaron D.	14 Oh			
	Harriett A.	12 Oh			
	Geo. W.	10 Il			
	Moses	8 Il			
	Hiram	6 Il			
	Abraham Boswell	25 NY	none	Lyman	
384	Philip Quail (Quayle)	26 GB	Gambler	Ut1847(?)	

CENSUS 24
a. Possible or Probable Mormons–Stockton, 1850

284	John Blythe	32 Me	Mariner	?	
284	Samuel Campbell	30 Pa	Drover	MB	
	Reuben	15 Mo			
	William	14 Mo			
	Nicholas	12 Mo			
	Joseph	10 Mo			
	Joshua	8 Mo			
285	Samuel Myers	28 Pa	Teamster	MB	
286	Joseph Hunt	26 Il	Tinner	MB	
286	James Davis	29 GB	Teamster	MB	
287	N. L. Williams	26 Ma	Drover	?	
292	William Boyd	45 Mo	Trader	MB	
294	Sarni Thompson	33 NY	Miner	MB	
295	Robert Harris	40 GB	Carpenter	MB	
301	James Davis	31 GB	Seaman	MB	

301	William Kelly	35 RI	Carpenter	MB
306	Samuel Clark	26 Ma	Miner	MB
309	John Freeman	19 Ma	Miner	Lyman
316	John Cox	36 NY	Seaman	MB
319	Henry Hoyt	24 Me	Teamster	MB
320	James Douglas	23 NY	Trader	MB
324	Henry Jackson	38 Pa	Merchant	MB
325	John Gilbert	28 Ky	Farmer	MB

b. Reorganized Church Members–Stockton, 1866-68

The following adult males of the branch in 1866-1868 are listed, none of whom have been identified with those tentatively identified Mormons of 1850-51:

Richard Arner   John D. Jones
John Barrow   Henry Robbins
John Blake   Daniel Thomas
Nathaniel Booth   Charles Youd
William Cunnington   James Youd
Hans Jensen

CENSUS 25
Possible or Probable Mormons–Weaverville, 1850

252	George W. Thrillkeld	28 Ky	Miner	Ut1847
253	Benjamin F. Stewart	30 Ky	Trader	MB
	John Q. A. Stewart	27 Ky	Trader	MB
	Jonathan F. Stewart	35 Ky	Trader	?
254	Alfred (G.) Wilson	29 Oh	Miner	MB
256	Robinson C. Threlkild	25 Ky	Miner	Ut1847
265	John A. Lytle	18 Oh,	none	MB
265	John Allen	26 Ky	Teamster	MB
	David Allen	24 Ky	Trader	?
	James Allen	22 Ky	Teamster	?
	William Allen	20 Mo	Teamster	?
265	James W. Orr	22 Tn	Miner	Ut1847
265	William A. Simmons	22 Can	Miner	MB
	Mary E.	18 Oh		

CENSUS 26
Possible or Probable Mormons–White Oak, 1850

379	Daniel E. Tyler	25 NY	Miner	MB
	John Moon	21 GB	Miner	Ut1850
	Geo. Moon	20 GB	Miner	Ut1850
	Geo. Smith	21 GB	?	Ut1850
379	Benj. L. West	22 RI	Laborer	MB
379	Bird D. (B.) Barnett (Burnett)	40 Tn	Hotel	Ut1848
	Martha	39 SC		
	Wm.	20 Tn	Laborer	
	Henry	18 Tn	Laborer	

	Alexander	16 Tn	Laborer	
	Ann M.	13 Tn		
	Mary F.	12 Tn		
	Francis M.	10 Tn		
	Jasper	8 Tn		
	Joseph	5 Tn		
	John	21 NC	Laborer	
	Sandy	21 Tn	Laborer	
	James (Black)	18 Tn	Laborer	
	Jane (Black)	10 Tn		
	Lucinda (Black)	7 Tn		
	Jourdan (Black)	5 Tn		
380	Christian Hecks	28 Oh		
	Charlotte Hecks	22 Ct		
	Constantine Hecks	35 Vt		Ut1848
380	Nicholas Kelly (Kelley)	26 Il	Hotel	MB
	Sarah	30 Va		

CENSUS 27
Possible or Probable Mormon Family Units in California 1850

Location	# Family Units	# Persons
Brighton (Six Mile House)	5	23
Browns Settlement	1	2
Coloma	2	10
Diamond Springs	4	20
Dry Creek	5	22
Drytown and Calaveras County	4	15
Greenwood-Louisville	5	19
Hangtown (Placerville)	6	21
Logtown	2	8
McDowellsville (McDowell's Hill)	3	12
Middle Fork (American River)	1	2
Mormon Bar and Mariposa County	1	6
Mormon Hill (New York Ravine)	4	16
Mormon Ravine	3	6
Mormon Station	1	6
Mud Springs	1	6
Negro Bar	3	9
Pilot Hill	6	32
Pleasant Hill	2	17
Rhodes Diggins (Sacramento County)	2	12
Rosecrans	1	3
Sacramento	3	10
Salmon Falls	3	14
Weaverville	1	2
White Oaks	3	15
TOTAL	72	308

CENSUS 28

Occupational Characteristics, California Mormon Argonauts, 1850

a. The following are listed in the hotel or tavern business in the 1850 census or from other information:

Peter Wimmer at Coloma.
Josiah Arnold and David (Daniel) McCoy at Hangtown (Placerville).
George S. Clark in Yuba County.
Darwin Chase and Calvin W. Saltar as well as Thomas Blackburn at Logtown.
Wm. Holden in Mariposa County.
Moses Martin, Sebert C. Shelton, Wm. Leffingwell, Isaac Harrison and Andrew J.and Cornelius.
Workman at Pilot Hill.
Asahel Lathrop at the Mormon Tavern.
George Rhodes at or near Rhodes Diggings in Sacramento County.
Hervey Green and Hezekiah Thatcher in Salmon Falls.
Thomas Orr in Salmon Falls, Mormon Hill or New York Ravine.
Bird D. (B.) Barnett and Nicholas Kelly (Kelley) at White Oak on the South Fork of the American River.
Porter Rockwell, in partnership with Judson Stoddard, Boyd Stewart, and Jefferson Edmonds, near Folsom, Murderers Bar, and at Buckeye or Deer Creek, respectively.
Henry Jacobs at White Rock.
John and Enoch Reese and Jefferson Edmunds at Mormon Station.
Samuel Brannan with John S. Fowler in Sacramento.
Jeremiah Root at or near Six Mile House on the South Fork of the American River. He sold out to Eleazer and Stirling Davis along with Henry Fairbanks.
A. Cheney and Mr. Lathrop, possibly Mormons, were also located at Six Mile House.
A. C. Brower and Ebenezer Hanks at Salmon Falls.
James Harmon and Robert Crow in Long Valley (Mormon Ravine).
William Squires and Jeptha Condit, probably in or near Sacramento.

b. The following are those who have been identified as traders or merchants:

George W. Sparks at Diamond Springs.
James Dunn with J. R. and Robert C. Dunn as well as John Allen, William Huntington and Samuel Crow in Greenwood-Louisville.
Moses Job and Robert S. Bliss in Hangtown (Placerville).
George W. and Edward W. Haskell, as well as James Gordon in Yuba County.
Andrew J. Cox in Logtown.
James Brooks and Wm. Holden in Mariposa County.
T. F. Peck in Calaveras County.
Thomas Kirk and Edmund L. Brown in Sacramento.
William Boyd, James Douglas, and Henry Jackson in Stockton (Mormon Slough).
William Peacock at or near the Mormon Tavern.
Benjamin F., John G. A. and Jonathan F. Stewart as well as David Allen in Weaverville.
Sam Brannan maintained stores at Sutter's Fort, the Embarcadero, Coloma and Mormon Island. He probably had a Mormon resident manager at each. It is known that Charles C. Smith managed Brannan's store at Sutter's Fort and then Mormon Island.
George Q. Cannon maintained a store at Slap Jack Bar, Howard Egan (The Salt Lake Trading Company) on the Merced River.
The Thomas Orr's in Salmon Falls.

W. O. and B. B. Clark–at Drytown.

c. There were a substantial number of farmers, ranchers and gardeners:

Andrew and George Nickerson, along with William Wolsey in Greenwood-Louisville.
Andrew and John Mayfield at Pilot Hill.
Jno., George W., and Henry Rhodes at Rhodes Diggings in Sacramento County.
Wm. R. Tubs and Samuel Hall at or near Six Mile House.
John Gilbert in Stockton (Mormon Slough).
George Clawson at the Mormon Tavern.
Peter Wimmer at Coloma.
The Luncefords at Pleasant Hill.

The following engaged as teamsters or carters:

Orrin Hatch in Diamond Springs.
William T. Follet in Drytown.
Julius Mosey (Moser) and Jno G. Smith in Sacramento.
Richard Carter and Abel Casto at Rough and Ready with James Gordon elsewhere in Yuba County.
Samuel Campbell, Samuel Myers, James Davis, N. L. Williams, and Henry Holt in Stockton (Mormon Slough).
John, James, and William Allen in Weaverville.

Other occupations were:

Butchers:
Lewis B. Myers, Nathaniel Fairbanks, and William Crow at Greenwood-Louisville.

Shoemaker:
Philo M. Behunin at Greenwood-Louisville.

Carpenters:
Joshua Abbot at Mormon Hill.
Richard Robinson in Yuba County.
W. Willis at Mormon Island.
William Kelly and Robert Harris at Stockton (Mormon Slough).

Physicians:
Geo. W. Hill in Sacramento.
Wm. L. McIntyre in Mormon Ravine.

Livery Stable:
David H. Moss in Sacramento.

Clothiers and Merchants:
Samuel W. Chapin and Daniel Davis and Thomas Kirk in Sacramento.

Express Office:
James M. Freeman in Sacramento.

Blacksmith:

Levi Fifield at or near Six Mile House.

Woodchoppers:
Robert, Walter H., James R., Jno L. and Benj. S. Crow at or near Six Mile House.

Grocer:
Thomas Kirk in Yuba County.

Tinner:
Joseph Hunt at Stockton (Mormon Slough).

Baker:
John C. Gold (Gould) at Placerville.

Mariners or Seamen:
John Blythe, John Cox, and James Davis at Stockton (Mormon Slough).

Laborers:
William (F.) Ewell and Joseph Leffingwell at Pilot Hill.
James Hart, Thomas Morris and John W. Ghee(n) in Sacramento.
E. Davis and B. Fifield at or near Six Mile House.
Benj. L. West, along with Wm., Henry and Alexander Barnett as well as five Negroes living with the Barnetts--all at White Oak.

Cooper:
James (B.) Casto (Castro) at Rough and Ready.

Gambler:
Philip Quail (Quayle) in Sacramento.

Ten Pin Alley:
Jesse Brown at Greenwood-Louisville.

Restaurateur:
George Rhodes at Rhodes Diggings (Sacramento County.)

Mill owners:
William Leffingwell and Jefferson Edmunds at Deer Creek and Brown's.

Quicksilver Machine, in Mormon Gulch.

"One of the principal tributaries of the Stanislaus is the stream passing through Mormon Gulch, and running within a stone's-throw of Tuttletown. The diggings in this vicinity have been celebrated for their richness, especially to-ward the head of the cañon known as Mormon "Creek." Desirous of ascertaining if our old diggings had been worked out during our four years of absence, we purchased an old quicksilver machine at this place, which we stationed in a certain bend, half-way between Tuttletown and the river. The gold in the bed of this stream is so fine as to escape from the riffles of a long tom, and can only be worked to advantage by the use of quicksilver. Minute particles, in the shape of flakes, are found adhering to the blades of grass in the shallow parts of the stream.

"Our machine, which resembled the "bumper," or Virginia rocker, consisted of a wooden trough, furnished with quicksilver riffles, placed in a framework, and so hung as to be rocked to and fro by hand. This motion was made by one man, and the machine was supplied with earth by the others, who shoveled it in from the bed of the creek. The water was led through canvas hose from a series of rapids above us; and the operation of shoveling and rocking was continued for a week without interruption. At the end of that time the amalgam was taken from the machine and retorted, when we found nearly three hundred dollars as the reward of our labor. Most of this gold was fine as snuff, and could only have been saved by coming in contact with the quicksilver, with which it instantly amalgamates. There were, however, many pieces from the size of shot to that of a pea."

[From "How We Get Gold, From a Miner in the Year '49," *Harper's New Monthly Magazine*, vol. 20, issue 119 (April 1860) 605, 609.]

Helvetia Quartz Mill, Grass Valley.

"At the quartz mill, "[t]he quartz is conveyed to the works by carts or mule panniers from the vein, near which they are generally erected. The machinery is under the cover of a large shed; the apparatus consisting of a series of iron stampers, placed in a line, and made to fit into iron boxes, which receive the quartz, previously broken into egg size. The stampers are moved by cogs or cans, connected with a revolving wheel, which alternately lifts and lets them fall into the boxes containing the quartz . . .

"The quartz operations at Grass Valley, in Nevada County, have probably made the largest re-turns. Some of the richest veins in the State have been discovered in this vicinity, some of them yielding occasionally two hundred dollars to the ton, but by no means averaging as much. The Helvetia quartz mill at this place is one of the principal, working thirty-four stampers, and crushing on an average thirty tons a day. The stamping-box, already described, is supplied with water by a hose or pipe. Through a hole made for the purpose, the quartz, as it is crushed, passes out in the form of a thick, milky water, carrying with it much of the fine gold, which is thus discharged upon a frame-work, across which are placed several quicksilver riffles, where the gold amalgamates in its passage. Any fine particles escaping the quicksilver are arrested below, as they pass over a hide or blanket stretched tightly across a frame. But even these careful preparations for saving the gold are not always success-ful; for the " tailings," or refuse from the mill, is found to pay nearly as well under a second process as by the original crushing."

From "How We Get Gold, From a Miner in the Year '49," *Harper's New Monthly Magazine*, vol. 20, issue 119 (April 1860) 608, 611.

Appendix C:
Mormon Gold Time Line

**Note: Numbers in brackets at the end of entries indicate pages
of the text where the events are discussed.**

May 10, 1845   Ide family left Independence, Missouri, intending to emigrate to Oregon. [2-3]

Oct. 25, 1845   The Ide party reached Sutter's Fort. [4]

February 4, 1846   Ship *Brooklyn* left New York to sail around the Horn, and the Nauvoo Saints began their overland exodus west. [5-6]

April 8, 1846   Under instructions from Brigham Young, a company of Mormon converts left Monroe County, Mississippi, intending to meet the main body of Mormon expatriates in Indian country, then to head westward across Southern Iowa. The group was under the immediate leadership of William Crosby. En route the contingent was joined by the Crow family group. [133]

June 26, 1846   Captain James Allen (representing Colonel S. W. Kearny, U. S. Army, at Fort Leavenworth, Kansas) arrived at the Mormon's Mount Pisgah Camp in Iowa to obtain several companies of recruits for a period of one year. [9]

July 31, 1846   The ship *Brooklyn*, after nearly a six month voyage, landed at Yerba Buena (the future San Francisco). [6]

September 25, 1846   The New York Volunteers embarked on several ships and sailed for California. They anchored off Clark's Point at Yerba Buena on March 5, 1847. [15]

October 5, 1846   Thomas Rhoades and his family crossed Donner Pass into California. [9]

January 29, 1847   The Mormon Battalion camp, 371 men and a few women, who made the

	700-mile march across the southern border regions of present-day New Mexico, Arizona and California, staggered out of the Imperial Desert, and reached the Mexican village of San Diego on the Pacific shore. [10]
July 16, 1847	The Mormon Battalion was discharged at Fort Moore. [45]
July 24, 1847	Brigham Young, leading the Saints going overland, arrived at the Salt Lake Valley.
July 31, 1847	Brannan, having gone east from California and having met Brigham Young on the trail east of the Salt Lake Valley, entered the Salt Lake Valley. [7]
November 18, 1847	A relief party with Asahel A. Lathrop, Orrin Porter Rockwell, and Elijah Fuller left Salt Lake Valley to secure "cows, mules, mares, wheat and seeds" in Southern California. They reached the southern settlements after six weeks travel. [10-11]
January 24, 1848	Gold was discovered in the mill races at Coloma, California. [17]
February 2, 1848	The Treaty of Guadalupe Hidalgo was signed by Mexico, selling the Mexican Cession, including all of California to the United States for $15 million. The treaty was proclaimed by U. S. President James K. Polk on June 19, but the news of the treaty proclamation did not reach California until August 7.
February 14, 1848	The relief party under Jefferson Hunt started north with supplies on the return trip to the Salt Lake Valley, arriving May 15. [63]
March 11, 1848	The Battalion boys working for Sutter at Coloma started operation of the mill, fulfilling their contract. [21]
March 11, 1848	Date given in at least one journal when gold was found by Mormons on a bar and small island on the South Fork of the American River. The site became known as Mormon Island. [46]
March 14, 1848	Mormon Volunteers discharged. [77]
March 15, 1848	The *Californian* first announces the discovery of gold. [32-33]
March 18, 1848	Brannan's *California Star* also reports the discovery of gold. [33]
April 1, 1848	The *California Star* published a special edition with the announcement of the discovery of gold. This was the Express edition carried east. [33, 46]
April 8, 1848,	Henry Bigler and Levi Fifield left Coloma and reached Natoma from a short trip to the Fort to find that several of their mates "were up river getting gold and had been for several days, but how they were making it, no one seemed to know" [27]
April 9, 1848	Some Battalion boys met to discuss the best route for going to Salt Lake City. Brannan was present. They decide to search for a route other than

	the Truckee route. (According to the diary of Samuel Hollister Rogers. Discussions on leaving and using a new route had previously occurred Feb. 13, 1848.) [47]
April 10, 1848	Sutter went over his books to see what he owed his Battalion workmen. He was unable to pay them at the time, but later paid them at least partly "in kind," that is, in animals, wagons, supplies, and tools. [47]
Late spring 1848	The Mormons traveling to the Great Salt Lake Valley in 1848 assembled in an area to the east of Hangtown (Placerville) and Weaverville (Weberville), an area they called Pleasant Valley. [47-48]
April 12, 1848	Orrin Porter Rockwell left the Rancho Santa Ana del Chino in the southern settlements with about 25 of the Mormon Volunteers, including Henry G. Boyle, and John Jacob Riser. They arrived in Salt Lake on June 5 via Cajon Pass and the Spanish Trail. They brought the first wagon over this route. [67, 77]
April 15, 1848	The group carrying the special edition of the *California Star* passed Sutter's Fort with over seventy-five head of horses. A portion of the group reached Salt Lake City about the middle of June. Harris remained in Salt Lake while Jacobs, Slater and Hawk traveled east to meet their families, leaving Salt Lake on July 9 and probably taking with them the Council's communication of that date. They reached Brigham Young on July 27. [70]
May 1, 1848	An advanced group of Mormon Battalion veterans made a first attempt to find a trail over the Carson Route. They encountered considerable snow and turned back to wait a couple of months. [47]
May 1848	Samuel Brannan stirred up excitement about gold. He gathered a bottle full of gold dust at the mines (probably from Mormon Island) and rode to San Francisco, where he then ran up and down the streets shouting, "Gold! Gold! Gold from the American River!" [35, 46]
May 29, 1848	The *Californian* suspended publication, and resumed publication Aug. 14. [35]
June 5, 1848	Porter Rockwell reached Salt Lake City from Southern California. [73]
June 14, 1848	The *California Star* suspended their publication, resuming publication in November. At that time it was combined with the *Californian* to become the *Star and Californian*. [35]
June 21, 1848	Rockwell, with Captain Davis and others, left the Great Salt Lake Valley carrying an epistle from the Stake Presidency to President Young, who they found near Fort Laramie on July 20. [69]
June 25, 1848	Daniel Browett, Ezra Allen, and Henderson Cox started again to search out a route over Carson Pass. [48]

July 3, 1848	The wagon train of emigrating Saints, mostly Mormon Battalion veterans, soon to be known as the Holmes-Thompson party, having gathered together at Pleasant Valley east of Weaverville, began their pioneering trip. [48]
July 11-27, 1848	Brigham Young may have first heard about the gold discoveries in California from the Jefferson Hunt and George W. Rosecrans group on July 11, or from the Rockwell and Davis group on July 20. He certainly heard about the gold from Nathan Hawk and his companions of the "Express" on July 27. [73]
July 21, 1848	The 1848 pioneer emigrant group left Tragedy Spring to ascend Squaw Ridge to West Pass summit. [49-51]
July 24, 1848	The emigrant group crossed West Pass. [51]
July 28, 1848	2000 Express copies of the *California Star* (less those disposed of on the way) arrived at St. Joseph, Missouri.
August 4, 1848	Construction of the road through Carson Canyon was completed. Advanced members of the Ebenezer Brown Company (who had left the mines five days before) overtook the trail blazing Holmes-Thompson company and helped them down through the canyon. August 4 they reached the mouth of Carson Canyon. [51-52]
August 6, 1848	News reached California of the conclusion of the war between Mexico and the United States.
August 7, 1848	Gov. Richard B. Mason officially proclaimed the end of the war at the capital in Monterey.
August 10, 1848	The main body of the Ebenezer Brown Company left Pleasant Valley. [60]
August 19, 1848	News of the gold discovery reached New York and was published in the *New York Herald*.
September 24, 1848	The Ebenezer Brown Company advance elements arrived in Salt Lake City. [54]
September 28, 1848	The Holmes-Thompson Company advance pack train reached Salt Lake City. [54]
Late September 1848	The Brigham Young Company consisting of 1,220 Saints from Winter Quarters reached the Salt Lake Valley about the same time as many of the Battalion Boys were arriving after their short but successful season in the gold fields. They brought with them both tales of gold and the physical evidence to support the tales. [63]
October 6, 1848	The Holmes-Thompson Company's main wagon train reached Salt Lake City. The remainder of the Ebenezer Brown Company also reached Salt Lake City. [54, 73]

Fall 1848	At least two and perhaps three groups of individuals intending to search for gold were either sent to California by Brigham Young or went with his blessings. One left in October immediately following Conference, another in November, having been officially called Nov. 20, 1848. [80]
November 23, 1848	The first recorded receipt of gold by the gold office in Salt Lake City (later called the "Mint" and the "National Bank") was that from Ebenezer Brown, a Battalion veteran. [89]
December 10, 1848	Regular deposits of gold dust began to be made to "Brigham Young's Daily Transactions in Gold Dust" account book. [89]
December 22, 1848	"Many of the brethren came to the office to exchange gold dust for hard money, but no business was done on account of Pres. Young not having any coin. The crucibles had broken, and minting had stopped. [90]
December 28, 1848	A meeting was held "for the purpose of regulating the currency, at which a vote was taken authorizing Pres. Young to issue bills." [90]
January 1, 1849	The first bill, a one-dollar note, backed by gold, was issued. [91]
January 4, 1849	The *Star and Californian* became the *Alta Californian*. On July 4, 1849 it started publication daily on a steam press under the name *Daily Alta California*.
Spring 1849,	En route to California with a pack train, Abner Blackburn discovered gold in what became known as Gold Canyon near present day Dayton, Nevada. [244]
April 12, 1849	The Lyman-Rockwell party departed Salt Lake, taking the northern route, and arrived at Sutter's Fort on May 25th. Elder Amasa Lyman and Orrin P. Rockwell were sent on this mission to California to preach the Gospel, to look after the interest of the Church and the Saints, and to return with those who might be coming to the Valley in the fall. [115, 117]
April 28, 1849	Ferry service to Mormon Island was started by Samuel Brannan.
May 25, 1849	Amasa Lyman arrived at Sutter's Fort. One of his immediate goals was to gather up what gold he could and send it back to the Valley. [117]
July 1849	Brannan's City Hotel, built with timbers from John Sutter's abandoned grist mill, opened at the Embarcadero (Old Sacramento). Construction lasted from June to September. [124]
July 14, 1849.	The Mormon Gold Train assembled at Sacramento to begin the journey to the Salt Lake Valley. [143-145, 150-151]
August 1, 1849	Elections were held for delegates to the California's Constitutional Convention. [125]
September 1, 1849	The Constitutional Convention was called to order at Colton Hall in

Monterey. Five days later the Church leadership addressed a letter to Lyman in California instructing him to get involved. However, considering the time it took for the message to get to California, the request was far too late. The Convention completed its work on October 12th and adjourned the following day. [125]

Early September 1849   The destruction of paper currency began and the minting of gold coins recommenced at the Salt Lake City Mint using the professionally prepared crucibles. On September 10, Daniel H. Wells, Aide-de-Camp to Brigham Young, and Thomas Bullock "spent the day in the office destroying paper, tearing up and burning between three and four thousand dollars." [94]

September 13, 1849   A state constitution was completed for California by the Constitutional Convention. Peter H. Burnett was elected governor. [127]

September 22, 1849   The debate on California's boundaries began at the Constitutional Convention. There were two basic proposals presented. One called for the eastern boundary to be at the Sierra Nevada mountains. This was the proposal of the Committee on Boundaries. The other proposal was to establish the boundary at the Rocky Mountains, which would include all of present day Arizona, Utah, and Nevada in the State of California. The first position prevailed. [127]

September 28, 1849   The Mormon Gold Train arrived in Salt Lake City from the west coast bringing The train brought about $3000 in gold dust and $1280 in coins collected by Apostle Lyman from the California Saints as tithing and contributions, about $17,000 of Rhoades' gold, and $3,300 in dust and coin carried by William Glover. [95, 148]

October 2, 1849   The wagon train, mostly of non-Mormons, led by Jefferson Hunt left from Fort Utah, near the present Provo, Utah to go to California by the southern route. Some missionaries going to the Society Islands (Addison Pratt, James S. Brown and Hirum H. Blackwell) traveled with this train. [75]

October 14, 1849   The Flake Company left for California from Fort Utah, near the present Provo, Utah. They were mostly gold missionaries. Charles C. Rich and Francis M. Pomeroy were also in this group. [75]

November 3, 1849   A wagon train consisting of 100 wagons left the Salt Lake Valley—largely composed of Mormons, but under the captaincy of the gentile Pomeroy brothers. The train reached the Williams ranch on February 27th. [76, 160, 174]

November 3, 1849   A third sub-group probably associated with the Pomeroy Train, led by George W. Hickerson, left for California. [76, 169]

November 10-13, 1849   Following the Pomeroy Train by a week, the Huffaker Company departed Salt Lake City. [76, 179]

November 18, 1849   Howard Egan, leading a wagon train known as the Salt Lake Trading Company, left Fort Utah taking the southern route to California. [76, 189]

January 1850	Ten days of flooding devastated Sacramento. [124]
January 21, 1850	Captain Jefferson Hunt reached Salt Lake City, via the southern route having left Sacramento November 25, 1850, Stockton on the 30th, and Williams Ranch on December 15. He reported on February 2nd to Brigham Young that the diggings were not as prosperous as they had been and that "the brethren employed around the gold mines in California were anxious to return home." [238]
January 29, 1850	Elder Lyman, then in the San Francisco area, met General John Wilson in the belated joint attempt of Presidents Zachary Taylor and Brigham Young to secure statehood for the combined California (what became California plus what was then called Deseret). [125]
Spring 1850	At least three and probably four Mormon companies, left Salt Lake Valley for the gold fields, apparently under the direction and approval of Church authorities. In addition, many went unrecorded on their "own hook." [217]
Spring 1850	Captain Thomas Orr, Senior's wagon train entered California on the Mormon Emigrant Trail. It was probably the first wagon train to do so in 1850, having left Salt Lake well in advance of the Huntington Company. [218]
Spring 1850	The DeMont Company, with Hampton S. Beatie as secretary and Abner Blackburn a member, left Salt Lake City for Carson Valley. Upon reaching Gold Canyon, Blackburn said that they "stopt at the place i found the year before . . . but their had been some miners their and worked out the best place . . . ." [244]
April 1, 1850	By happy coincidence Apostles Lyman and Rich met at the river port of Benicia. [195]
April 3, 1850	A company assigned to take the first mail of the season to California left Salt Lake City. The company probably included Hervey Green and Thomas Blackburn. Green and Blackburn also brought word of "gold diggins on the east side of the mountain," revealing it to Elder Rich in Sacramento on July 1. [218]
April 7, 1850	The aging Hiram Clark and William D. Huntington were called to lead a company to California to assist Apostles Lyman and Rich. [222]
May 7, 1850	A company led by William D. Huntington left Salt Lake City for California. The group consisted of 39 persons, some Mormon proselyting missionaries led by Thomas Tomkins, some Mormon "gold diggers," and some non-Mormons. They left the old fort, headed north of the Salt Lake, and then traveled west. [218, 222]
May 19, 1850	Apostles Lyman and Rich started a tour of the gold fields of El Dorado country. [199]

ca. April 20, 1850	The Ephraim Hanks Company left Salt Lake about three weeks in advance of the Huntington Company. [221]
July 15, 1850	Elders Lyman and Rich left San Francisco by steamer for Sacramento, the first leg of a trip back to the Valley. Rich reached Salt Lake on November 11. [233]
September 9, 1850	California was admitted into the Union as a state (without Deseret) by action of Congress.
September 25, 1850	Elder Rich gathered the miners together at Slap Jack Bar, who were being called as missionaries to the Sandwich Islands, "set them apart" for the mission, and gave them a blessing. [212]
October 18, 1850	The steamer *Oregon* arrived in San Francisco with news that California had been admitted to the Union.
October 29, 1850	George Q. Cannon witnessed the celebration of California's admission into the Union. [214]
November 15-17, 1850	The various Sandwich Island missionaries set sail from San Francisco. Their departure had been delayed because of adverse winds. [214]
1850	The census of 1850 found that 73 percent of California's population was between the ages of 20 and 40, and 92 percent was male.
March 1851	The large San Bernardino-bound company departed from Deseret, but did so under a cloud. Apparently President Young had only authorized a small advance group of 20 or so persons to go into the "Babylon" of California. [268]
Spring of 1851	Abner Blackburn joined the company of Jef (Jefferson) Edmonds (Edmunds) who was returning to California after a trip to Utah. [248]
June 11, 1851	The advance group of the main San Bernardino body reached the Sycamore Grove (near Devore) on the edge of San Bernardino Valley. The Saints remained there for three and a half months until a permanent location could be established. [269]
July 11, 1851	Apostle Parley P. Pratt, President of the Pacific Mission, reached San Francisco and organized a branch of the Church. It had been disorganized since the time San Francisco Saints went to the gold fields in 1848-50. [282]
August of 1854	George Q. Cannon, the former Mormon gold miner missionary turned proselyter, returned to San Francisco from the Sandwich Islands, Hawaii. [285]
January 1855	Governor Brigham Young appointed Apostle Orson Hyde as probate judge for Carson County. Hyde left the Great Salt Lake City on May 17, 1855, with a company of about 35 missionaries called to help maintain a Mormon

foothold in Western Deseret. [260]

March 4, 1855	Elder Lyman "requested a number of us boys to go to Kern River mines to prospect for gold" to help pay for the mortgage of the San Bernardino colony. [272]
May 1855	George Q. Cannon, having gone to the Salt Lake Valley, was called to return to the Bay Area to replace Parley P. Pratt as leader of the Saints on the coast. [285]
September 20, 1855	An election was held at Mormon Station, called by Orson Hyde. The slate of county officers did not include any known Mormons. [261]
September 22, 1855	A conference was held at Sacramento with Elders Lyman and Rich present. Elder David M. Stuart, a missionary from Utah and former gold miner, maintained that the Saints in the area should be gathered out of the mines and take(n) to the home of the Saints (presumably Salt Lake)." He was called to remain in the mission field to help accomplish this task. [285]
January 26, 1856	George Q. Cannon, having previously translated the Book of Mormon into the Hawaiian language, proceeded with the task of printing it. The task was completed when 2,000 copies finally came off the press. [214, 285]
February 23, 1856	The first issue of the *Western Standard* came off the press. [286]
August 1856	Carson County elections were held and the Mormon ticket, which included three non-Mormons out of 12, won handily over the Human ticket. [262]
November 1856	Hyde received a letter recalling him to Salt Lake City. He was replaced by Chester Loveland. [262]
April 18, 1857	Elders Rich and Lyman were recalled to Utah, leaving their new partner, Ebenezer Hanks, the successful Mormon miner and businessman from Salmon Falls, to handle the remaining business details of extinguishing the mortgage. [274-275]
September 5, 1857	Loveland received an express message from Brigham Young. The Carson Valley Saints were told that Salt Lake City was being invaded by the United States Army. Brigham Young wanted the members to abandon Carson Valley and being back all the guns and bullets they could buy to help defend the Saints. [263]
1859	Gold and Silver of the Comstock region was discovered. [263]
April 2, 1860	The first mail by the Pony Express reached Sacramento.
1864	Nevada was admitted to the Union. Sections of Utah territory were used to form the state. Additional land was taken from Utah Territory in 1866 to form the present boundaries of the state of Nevada.

Hydraulic Mining, at French Corral

"At French Corral . . . we visited every place of interest with the gentlemanly proprietors of the Shady Creek Canal, who have become identified with that section of the country. Here may be seen the various works of sluicing, canaling, flaming, and hydraulic mining. A hill of moderate size, which is found to contain gold throughout its formation, but too thinly scattered for cradle-washing, is generally selected for the operation of hydraulic mining. A series of boxes, fourteen inches in length by about three feet wide, called "sluice-boxes," are ' fitted together at the ends so as to form a continuous, strongly built trough as long as may be desired, sometimes extending several thousand feet. This is made of the stoutest boards, and of sufficient strength to allow the passage of any amount of earth and stones forced through by a flood of water. It is lined on the bottom with wooden blocks, like the octagonal street pavement, for the double purpose of resisting the friction of the debris intended to pass through it, and to make place in the interstices for quick-silver which secures the fine gold. Sometimes the bottom is furnished with small transverse gutters or riffles charged with quicksilver for the same purpose. The sluice, thus prepared, is firmly placed in a slanting position near the foot of the hill intended to be attacked.

"To shovel a mass of several million tons of earth into this sluice for washing would, of course, prove a profitless job. It is now that the art of hydraulic mining is called into play, by which the labor of many men is cheaply performed, and the hill torn down to its base. The operation is simply throwing an immense stream of water upon the side of the hill with hose and pipe, precisely as a fire-engine plays upon a burning building, and few who have not witnessed it can imagine the effect. The water is led through gutta percha or oftener double canvas hose, and generally from a great height above the scene of operations. It is consequently thrown with such force as to eat into the hill-side as if it were made of sugar or salt. Neither man nor beast can stand for a moment against the projectile power of the hydraulic hose; they become a weapon of defense, and a miner with a hose-pipe in his hand need not fear the advance of half a dozen adversaries. Several of these streams directed upon a hill-side bring down more earth than a hundred men with shovels and picks could throw. But the art of the miner does not rest here. It is his constant aim to undermine as well as to break down; he consequently works, in a single day, huge caverns into the hill-side with his "water-batteries," until by certain indications he knows that a "cave in" is about to take place. Then every body flies from the spot. The earth far above their heads begins to quake and crinkle, and slowly the face of the precipice topples over and falls to the earth with the noise of an avalanche. Thus the miner makes one of the simplest laws of nature subservient to his will, and hundreds of tons of earth are leveled down for washing.

"Now they return and commence throwing into the sluice. Here again the water becomes their giant servant; for it not only carries the earth through the sluice, completely disintegrating it, and allowing the gold it may contain to lodge in the interstices of the octagonal pavement, but it acts the part of many shovels, and rushes the earth into the sluice with tremendous force. By these means a few men find it profitable to work earth, which, with the discarded, snail-paced rocker, could never have been advantageously washed."

From "How We Get Gold, From a Miner in the Year '49," *Harper's New Monthly Magazine*, vol. 20, Issue 119 (April 1860), 614-16.

The Ox-Cart (Carreta) of Early California

The ox-carts (or carretas), were essentially the only wheeled vehicles in Spanish and Mexican California. Land conveyance at that time was mostly by ox-cart for short distances and pack mule for longer distances. The wheels of the ox-cart were usually sawed from the trunk of a tree, and as a result, ordinarily, were not absolutely circular. The axles were also of tree trunks or branches. The friction of wood against wood produced loud squeaks, rapid wear, and short life. Tallow was sometimes applied to reduce the squeaks and the wear and to extend the life of the wheels and axles. [Coy, *Pictorial History of California*, Plate 97. Photograph by McCurry Co.]

In January 1847, William Tecumseh Sherman, a young Lieutenant, arrived by ship at Monterey. Sherman made a quick assessment of the town, and with quartermaster and commissary responsibilities, noted with some dismay the limited facilities for conveyance: "Not a single modern wagon or cart was to be had in Monterey, nothing but the old Mexican cart with wooden wheels, drawn by two or three pairs of oxen, yoked by the horns." -- *The Memoirs of General W. T. Sherman,* 44.

A decade earlier, in 1835, Richard Henry Dana had visited California towns and had also noted the "large, clumsy ox-carts, with the yoke on the ox's neck instead of under it, and with small solid wheels." Concerning personal transportation in Monterey, Dana wrote, "the men . . . appeared to me to be always on horseback. Horses are as abundant as dogs and chickens were in Juan Fernandez." The men "can hardly go from one house to another without getting on a horse."-- *Two Years Before The Mast,* 118, 109.

APPENDIX D:

TRANSPORTATION AND AGRICULTURE AS HISTORICAL BACKGROUND FOR THE *MORMON GOLD* STORY

THE MAIN CHAPTERS of the present work have focused on the specific people and events of the *Mormon Gold* story. During the decade of that story, the decade of the gold rush, California itself was going through dramatic transformations. Mormons were affected by and played a part in the explosive changes taking place in infrastructure and transportation in California. Mormons were also an influence in important developments in agriculture. To better appreciate the *Mormon Gold* story, therefore, the present appendix summarizes the transformations taking place in transportation and agriculture during that formative decade, and notes examples of Mormon participation. (Page numbers of the text where features of these transformations relate to the *Mormon Gold* story are provided in parentheses.)

A revolution in transportation was essential for the development of the gold rush. A sudden development of an infrastructure was needed to accommodate the sudden increase in population and activity. At the same time, agriculture was developed to feed the miners, was often the occupation of their retreat when they became disappointed at the mines, and in the end agriculture became a more lasting source of California "gold."

When Mormons first came to Alta California in 1845-46, California was one of the most remote, inaccessible parts of the New World (at least from the view of the non-natives). The western part of Alta California, the part that became the state of California, was sandwiched between an ocean on one side and the nearly impenetrable Sierra and southern desert on the other. The region was under Spanish rule from 1769 to 1821, and set-

tlers arrived gradually overland from the south. However, over that period, only four presidios, two pueblos and twenty-one missions were established. Few immigrants were involved. The mission populations, for example, were mostly native.

When Mexican rule began in 1821, this "province to the north" was still considered too remote for desirable residence. The Mexican government decommissioned or secularized the missions starting in 1833, and ownership of most of the Mission lands was dispersed as land grants to induce people to immigrate. By 1840 six hundred ranchos had been established, mostly in the coastal regions. Yet by the gold discovery and the negotiated end of Mexican rule, 1848, the non-native population had still only reached about 14,000.

This 1848 non-native population was sparsely settled, living mostly a frontier pastoral existence. The main industry was cattle ranching, from which they obtained meat and hides and tallow. Except for trading hides and tallow with an occasional ship to obtain other basic needs, the population seemed disconnected from the material progress taking place in other parts of the world.

The population of "foreigners"—that is, non-native and non-Hispanic—was even more sparse. At the end of the Spanish rule, records show only seventeen "foreigners" in Alta California, and by the end of 1845, only 680. They first came as visitors, then some came to stay. There were "foreigners" at Monterey, the capital of the province.

Drawing of Front Street in Sacramento in 1849 by Emanuel Wyttenbach. The City Hotel is to the left, the Eagle Theatre is at the center (to the left of the tree), and S. Brannan & Co. is the large "warehouse" store to the right. The waterfront is behind and to the right. *Courtesy California State Library, from the original art collection: Art, Original-VA-S.*

Thomas O. Larkin, for example, was an American merchant and the U.S. Consul in Monterey. William Richardson and the Hudson Bay Company had established a presence at Yerba Buena. The Russians had a settlement at Fort Ross. A few settlers were trying to build footholds in the Central Valley, such as John A. Sutter near the confluence of the American and Sacramento Rivers, and John Marsh near Mt. Diablo. A few mountain men had crossed the Sierra looking for furs, but they were just passing through. Soon, however, a few permanent settlers began to follow their trails into California.

Limited Infrastructure

Not only was the non-native population in Alta California limited before the gold rush, but the infrastructure also was minimal. The means of transportation was hardly an improvement over what had existed there for centuries. Inland travel often followed old Indian trails or crude trails connecting one rancho or settlement with another. Even the Camino Real connecting the missions, pueblos, and presidios was essentially a bridle and pack trail, sometimes in rainy seasons nearly impassable. Short range, local hauling on land was commonly by the primitive, two-wheeled ox cart, the only vehicle manufactured locally. Long range land travel was by horseback. Long range hauling was mostly by pack animals.

If travel networks within California were poor, reaching California overland from the East was almost impossible. Settlers began reaching California overland only in the early 1840s, and then only by using pack animals. The first wagons over the Sierra came with the Stevens party over the Truckee route in 1844.

The Sacramento City waterfront with contemplated improvements (1856-1860) by artist Thomas C. Boyd and lithographer Victor Hoffman. View shows steamers *Young America*, *Queen City*, and *New World* docking at a floating landing stage that allows for changing levels of the river. The broad Front Street permits easy approach by freighting wagons and a train of the Sacramento Valley Railroad. *Courtesy Bancroft Library.*

Water transportation of the period was also simple. For centuries, the native Americans navigated the waterways of the greater San Francisco Bay in boats fashioned from bundles of tule reeds. When the Spanish settled in the area and the Russians settled at Fort Ross, more sophisticated, ocean-going, sailing vessels began appearing in the Bay, engaging in trade. Accordingly, settlers began to ply the waterways with launches to trade with these larger vessels and to distribute imports. Before the gold rush, William Richardson, for example, used launches to collect produce from around the Bay to supply Yerba Buena with food and to collect hides and tallow for export. The settlers eventually acquired and built a few sloops and schooners, by which they explored the bays and rivers from South San Francisco Bay all the way to what is now Sacramento. John A. Sutter, in 1839, took supplies up the Sacramento River with a small flotilla of two sloops and a third smaller, four-oar boat to begin his settlement in the Central Valley. Sam Brannan, leader of the Mormon group aboard the ship *Brooklyn*, soon after the arrival of the ship in 1846, sent a schooner (filled with supplies) up the San Joaquin River to settle the inland farming community of New Hope (at the Stanislaus, south of what is now Manteca).

Gold Discovery and the Rapid Migration Inland

The gold discovery in 1848, however, triggered a population and infrastructure explosion. The non-native population before the gold rush was about 14,000. With the gold rush, immigration accelerated and the population reached 300,000 by 1853. Some of these immigrants followed occupations that held them to the coastal regions, but most came as gold miners. They wanted to go where the gold was, that is, mostly to the Sierra foothills. Once gold strikes were made in these foothills, tent cities materialized over night. The tents were gradually replaced by cabins and stores. Small towns appeared along almost every river and every ravine. This sudden appearance of inland communities required just-as-sudden robust communication and transportation networks, which followed in rapid order.

Travel on the Bay and the Rivers

The inland bays (San Francisco Bay leading into San Pablo Bay and Suisun Bay) and the hundreds of miles of rivers, creeks, and sloughs complicated land travel to the mines. However, much of these waterways were navigable and provided a convenient network of "water highways" into the interior. After the discovery of gold, sloops, schooners, and schooner-rigged scows were quickly built to begin carrying people and supplies inland. Even some ocean going vessels, on entering San Francisco Bay continued on and were able to reach inland as far as Sacramento and Stockton. These sailing vessels, large and small, responded to the urgent need, but they hardly met the demand. They were mostly too small and, in all cases, too slow. Because of their dependence on wind, they took several days to go some 50-60 miles from San Francisco Bay to Sacramento.

Steam power first came to Alta California before the gold rush (October 1847) when William A. Leidsdorff purchased a small steam powered launch from the Russians. The vessel had been built in Sitka, and Leidsdorff shipped the boat to San Francisco aboard a sailing vessel. He named the steamboat the *Sitka*, after its port of birth, and planned to use it to bring to Yerba Buena the hides and tallow from the shallow rivers and sloughs of San Francisco Bay. It was only thirty-seven feet long, had only a nine-foot beam, and displaced only an eighteen-inch draft. Also it was terribly underpowered. After some test runs on San Francisco Bay in November 1847, the *Sitka* was loaded with nine passengers, one a woman, and sent on a history making voyage to Sacramento. After six days, the *Sitka* had only come within seven miles of Sacramento. The woman decided to get off and walk the rest of the way. She reached Sacramento seven hours before the *Sitka*. To top this stunning performance, a few weeks later the *Sitka* was tethered at the foot of Broadway in San Fran-

cisco, became swamped in a windstorm, and sank. That was in February 1848, thus bench marking the status of water navigation in California at the eve of the gold rush. However, a "tsunami" of progress was about to hit California.

Practical paddle wheel and propeller steamers were introduced to California in 1849, just two years after the *Sitka*, and these boats soon dominated traffic to the interior. The first three were smaller craft, delivered aboard sailing ships in parts, and assembled locally. A fourth, the *Senator*, was the first full-sized steamboat to reach California on its own power. It was a 226 foot, 750 ton side wheeler built in the East and piloted around the Horn. It arrived in San Francisco Bay October 27, 1849, and immediately went into service, reaching Sacramento November 5. The *Senator* made three round trips a week between the two cities. It was capable of carrying 300 passengers and 300 tons of freight. Additional steamers arrived rapidly. It is estimated that as many as 300 steamers were active in California in the gold rush period. Sacramento became the main inland port for the northern mining region. Smaller steam boats went above Sacramento as far as Red Bluff on the Sacramento River and Marysville on the Feather River. Stockton, on the San Joaquin River, became the main inland port for the southern mining region, that is, mines in the southern part of the Mother Lode.

The first steamboats were owned by a multitude of small private concerns. As their number increased and as the shipping and passenger demand was met, they competed fiercely, leading to a period of racing and ruinous price competition on the rivers. Stability and order, however, returned in 1854 when northern California steamboat ownership was largely consolidated into the California Steam Navigation Company.

Amasa Lyman and Charles C. Rich, Mormon leaders of Church affairs in northern California, made frequent use of steamers. When Lyman was escorting the Huffaker Company to the mines in April 1850, he took the *El Dorado* out of San Francisco. When that steamer stopped at Benicia, it berthed next to the *Captain Sutter* coming from Stockton, and Lyman found Rich on board the *Sutter*. Rich had been visiting the southern mines (pages 129 165). The *Captain Sutter* had begun service to Stockton only the previous November. Near the end of their joint mission in June 1850, Lyman went from Sacramento directly to San Francisco aboard the *Hartford*. Rich went to Weaverville (Weberville) for mail and, returning to Sacramento, caught the *Gold Hunter* for San Francisco (page 202). (The *Gold Hunter* was a 435 ton propeller craft, built in 1850 in the East. The *Hartford* was a 251 ton propeller craft, also built in 1850 in the East.) When Lyman and Rich were homeward bound in July 1850, they left San Francisco for Sacramento on the *Hartford* (page 233). From there, Lyman returned to Salt Lake City, but Rich returned to San Francisco aboard the *Senator* to conduct further business, before leaving for Salt Lake City in September.

Other Saints also used steamers in their travels. When the missionaries assigned to Tahiti had to assemble at San Francisco, they went from Sacramento by steamers (page 226). In late 1850, the missionaries to the Hawaiian Islands gathered to San Francisco from Sacramento on the *Senator* and the *West Point,* both side wheelers (page 214). When George Q. Cannon, another Mormon leader, sent David M. Stuart on a missionary assignment from San Francisco to the Thatchers, Stuart first went to Sacramento on a steamer (page 290). Steamers were the standard mode of travel between San Francisco and Sacramento. John Horner, the Mormon farmer in the Mission San Jose region, also ran a side wheeler, the *Union*, on San Francisco Bay to carry produce and people between San Francisco and Union City, the East Bay portal to the Mission San Jose area (page 197).

Steamers were used also for coastal travel. When Andrew Workman (discharged from the Mormon Battalion) wanted to get to the northern mines, he left from San Pedro for San Francisco by steamer (page 79). When Abner Blackburn (also of the Mormon Battalion) needed to go up the north coast to Trinidad to find his father, he went by steamer (page 249). When Rich and Lyman went north to San Francisco to obtain funding for the San Bernardino colony, they went by steamer (page 271).

Steamers would ply the waters of California for a hundred years, but they began to lose their dominance with the coming of the railroads at the end of the gold rush period.

Development of Roads and Bridges

From the inland ports, Argonauts at first made their way to the mining regions forging or following ill-defined trails. They walked or rode horses or mules and brought in their supplies by pack train.

California was not at first self sufficient in either material or food supplies. Continuing supplies had to be shipped in from distant places such as Oregon, Hawaii, or even the East Coast. The supplies came by ship to San Francisco and continued on to inland ports by California waterways. At all receiving points, wharves and other port facilities were built to accept and transfer the shipments. The supplies then went to the mining settlements, at first mostly by pack mules. Horses and mules could pull many times more in a wagon than they could carry on their backs. Wagons were becoming available, brought in by overland immigrants and manufactured locally. So, trails over all but the most difficult mountain terrain were soon expanded to comfortably accommodate wagons. By mid 1849, the more accessible mining towns could be supplied by wagons. Pack trains, however, were the only way supplies could be taken into remote camps in the mountains.

The roads were developed and maintained in the first half of the 1850s, mostly by private parties, sometimes by joint-stock toll road companies. The roads were dusty in the summer, muddy in the rainy seasons, and in many places very rough. Frank Marryat, touring California in the early 1850s, and therefore a veteran of such roads, correctly observed, "No one knows what a wagon will undergo until he has mastered California trails and gulches." [1] As the roads were developed, they were leveled and, when necessary, "planked."

According to records, there were twenty-three toll roads in California by the end of 1857 and sixty-four by the end of 1858. In 1859, the state began appropriating funds for road building. By 1860, all the towns could be reached by passable

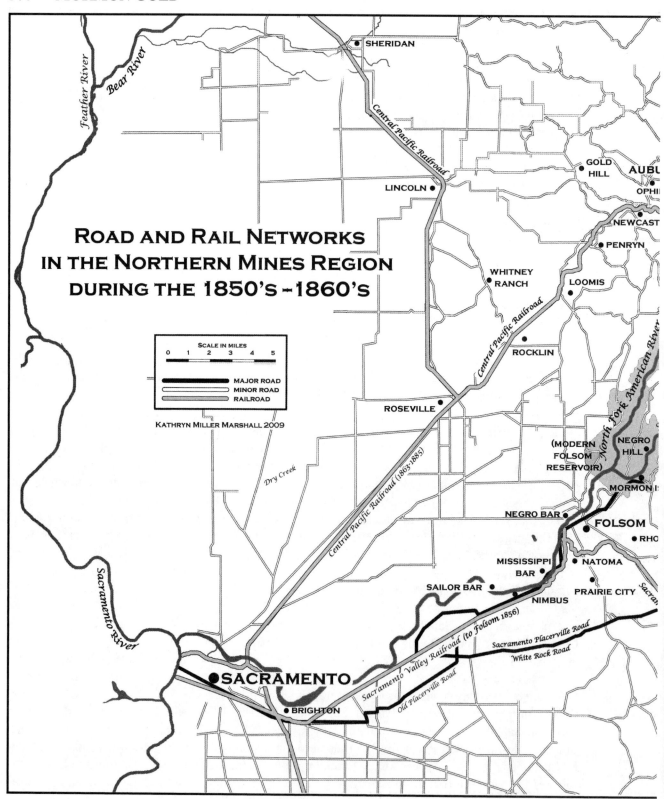

ROAD AND RAIL NETWORKS
IN THE NORTHERN MINES REGION
DURING THE 1850'S – 1860'S

KATHRYN MILLER MARSHALL 2009

Map of the roads, railroad lines, and major rivers in Sacramento and El Dorado Counties as of the late 1850s and early 1860s. Most communities of the gold country could be reached at least by secondary wagon roads by mid 1849. These roads proliferated and became well developed by the 1860s.

The modern Folsom Reservoir, in the region of the North and South Forks of the American River above Folsom, is superimposed on the map as a shaded region. Today many Mormon locations are covered with the

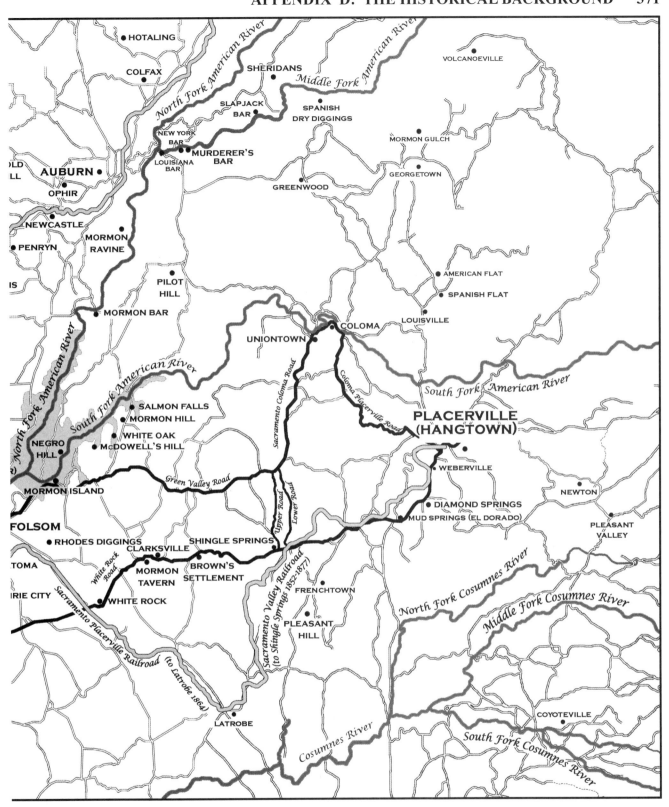

water of Folsom Reservoir, at least during high water periods. A few of the flooded sites, such as Salmon Falls, can be visited only during low water seasons and in years of low precipitation. For the sake of simplicity, the many small rivers and creeks are not shown on the map.

The Sacramento to Placerville road is now approximately the route of Highway 50, which continues across the Sierra, following roughly Johnson's Cutoff from the original Mormon Emigrant Trail.

Rattlesnake Bridge and Tollhouse, Sketch by George Mathis

The Rattlesnake Bridge and tollhouse crossed the American River at the approximate location of Mormon Bar, six miles west of Pilot Hill. The site now appears on maps as Rattlesnake Bar and is at the upper reaches of the Folsom Reservoir.

Wooden trusses were in use by 1850, and the trusses were often housed over (as shown above) to protect them from deterioration. Wire cable came into use by 1854. Despite the careful design and construction, these bridges were often swept away in periods of high water floods. Yet, they were often profitable enough that the construction or reconstruction could be paid for in a few months. A typical charge was four dollars for a loaded wagon, fifty cents for an animal and twelve-and-a-half cents for a person.

The Mathis Collection is now in archives at Washington State University, Pullman, Washington. *Courtesy John Davies, grandson of George Mathis.*

wagon roads. These wagon roads, in constant use, given the expanding population, developed into veritable highways.

Since rivers ran east to west out of the Sierra, traveling north and south on the east side of the Central Valley (along the Sierra foothills) required frequent river crossings. These rivers were often in gorges or not fordable, especially during the spring run-off. As a result, there was a need for many bridges in the region. Both roads and bridges were mostly built as local ventures by cities, counties, small groups, or even individuals. By 1856, there were 117 toll bridges in California.

California style freighting wagons pulled by a mule team in an unidentified location in the Sierra.
Courtesy Society of California Pioneers, from the Lawrence and Houseworth Albums.

Freighting to the Mines

Oxen and horses were used for freighting in early California, but mules were the favored pack animal, even before the Americans arrived. Mules adapted better than horses to the California climate. Their skin was less sensitive to sun and rain. They could survive and work well with coarser feed. They require less water than a horse. A mule could carry 350 pounds with ease. They were more sure footed and fearless on mountain trails. While horses, oxen, and mules were commonly used on the valley floor, mules were required in the mountains.

Packing by mule train is an art that is not obvious and could not be left to amateurs. The acknowledged leaders in this task were the Mexicans/native Californios. From long experience, they knew how to properly load the "aparajos" (pack saddles) and understood the intelligent, self-willed mules sufficiently to control them in difficult situations with deceiving ease. Although the Americans were using pack trains to supply the mining regions, it was often Mexicans/Californios who were actually in control of the mules.

The freighting wagons used initially in California were the wagons brought in by the immigrants, but a local industry of wagon makers and wheelwrights soon developed. In either case, the eastern designs of wagons were soon found to be inadequate for California freighting. Their track was too narrow, their bed was too heavy, and their capacity was too small, especially for mountain

Travel over the early trails and roads began with horses and pack animals. Soon wagons were plying the route. In 1851, stage routes began appearing between the various mining communities. In 1857 when road work improved the Johnson Cutoff, Colonel J. B. Crandall expanded the Pioneer Stage line to include a route between Sacramento and Genoa, Nevada, which carried the great Overland Mail and Wells, Fargo & Company Express. This route followed the Johnson Cutoff deviation from the Mormon Emigrant Trail or Carson Pass Route, and thus skirted the southern end of Lake Bigler or Tahoe, seen in the distance in the above illustration. This is the line taken by Horace Greeley in his famous, wild ride to Placerville with Hank Monk in the driver's box. *Courtesy Bancroft Library.*

freighting.

Californians soon developed their own standard freight wagon. Such a wagon would have a box-like structure sixteen to twenty feet long, forty to forty-eight inches wide, and four to eight feet high. The sides leaned outward at a five degree angle and the ends leaned outward at about a forty-five degree angle. In contrast to the end gates of eastern wagons, these wagons had side gates and were loaded from the side. Front wheels were 3 to 4-1/2 feet in diameter, supposedly so the wagon could be pulled from front axle level. Rear wheels were about seven feet in diameter, supposedly to give the high structure a center of gravity nearer the rear axel for stability; that is, to keep the wagon from being too top heavy. These wagons were usually pulled by mules and often had trailer wagons to carry fodder for the animals. The main wagon, pulled by

an eight-mule team, could carry as much as three to five tons of supplies. Examples of such wagons can be seen on pages 373, 378-381.

At least fourteen Mormons were known to have worked in freighting services (pages 348-349).

Express Companies

In California before 1860, the fastest way to transport supplies and mail was by express. The U.S. government began mail service between the Atlantic and Pacific coasts in 1847, as soon as California became U.S. territory. In fact, it was a mail steamer that brought some of the first Argonauts into San Francisco, having picked them up after they crossed the Isthmus of Panama. Developing U.S. mail service into the interior of California, however, was a slow process. With the flood of miners moving to the Sierra foothills, and with the U.S. mail slow to expand inland, there was an immediate and widespread need for express services. Mail and supplies had to get to the miners, and gold had to get back to depositories. Without a widespread mail service, it was a simple matter for enterprising individuals to contract with others in the interior to deliver items to San Francisco and to bring back mail and packages. A simple decision and an agreement and an express operation was born.

According to Bancroft, the first such express services began in California when C. L. Cady began operations between San Francisco and Sacramento in July 1847. It was an historic but short lived operation. The next attempt at an express business in California was when Sam Brannan, Mormon leader in San Francisco, organized the *California Star* Express—the special mule train to carry mail and the special April 1, 1848 edition of his newspaper to the East. Brannan announced his Express January 15, 1848 in the *Star*, just before gold was discovered. Its intent was to tell those in the East the wonderful opportunities in California in order to encourage immigration. Type for the printing had already been set when Brannan learned of the gold discovery. Room was made in the special edition for brief announcements. That announcement and especially President Polk's confirmation sparked a flood of immigration to California. Brannan had considered another Express, but that did not materialize, no doubt because it was not needed.

Entrepreneurs quickly went into the express business anywhere a need appeared, which was nearly everywhere. The *Daily Alta California* reported in January 1850, "There are so many express companies daily starting that we can scarcely keep the run of them." Miners were moving about, but they could register with an express man, indicating some store or bar where mail could be delivered. Some Express men would even deliver directly to the mines. Alexander H. Todd, for example, set up an office in Stockton with branch offices throughout the southern mines and quickly developed a list of about 2,000 names for whom he was a courier. For a while he was making a thousand dollars a day carrying mail and packages to miners, and gold from min-

ers and merchants to banks in San Francisco. By 1860, even according to what the imperfect records show, there had been over 260 such express companies in California.

The manager of one Express office was thought to be Mormon (page 349). The Mormons operated their own mail service between Salt Lake City and California, making deliveries whenever groups went one way or the other. When the Mormon frontiersman Orrin Porter Rockwell was first in California, he tried to obtain a contract for express mail (page 64). The Mormons W. O. Clark and Howard Egan were also involved in mail service. Clark for a time was involved in carrying mail between Salt Lake City and the mines (pages 316-317). Howard Egan mapped a route across central Nevada (page 188) which was used for mail and the Pony Express. Prior to his return to Salt Lake City, when Elder Rich went back to Weaverville for mail at the "mail outpost" in 1850 (pages 202, 218), prior to his return to Salt Lake City, it was no doubt to a registered express drop. There he picked up the mail recently brought in by Mormon Hervey Green (teacher, farmer, eventually hotel manager and gold seeker) from Salt Lake City.

Early in the gold rush, two express companies from the East (Adams & Company and Wells, Fargo & Company) began serving in California. They operated in San Francisco and offered connections to the East. They also began consolidating and absorbing many of the smaller inland companies in California. By 1853, Adams & Company had become the leading business in California. However, by 1854 the company was beginning to have internal conflicts and suffered from the bank panic of that year. Wells, Fargo & Company began operation in California in 1852 and immediately began setting up offices at major cities in the interior. Mail and packages were delivered by both of these companies, but gold was the most profitable commodity transported. From transporting gold, they drifted into buying and selling gold and then into banking. By 1856 Wells Fargo had established itself as the dominant firm in the field with its 56 branch offices.

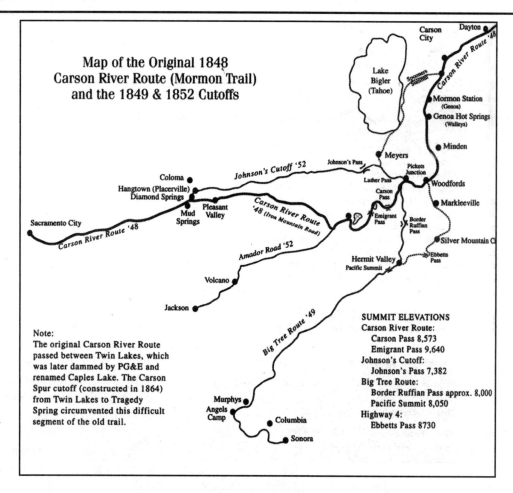

Map showing the relationship of the original Mormon Emigrant Trail (identified in the map as the Carson River Route) to branches and cutoffs developed in 1849 and 1852. Of particular interest is the Johnson Cutoff connecting Placerville to Carson City by skirting the east side and south end of Lake Tahoe. The Johnson Cutoff became the approximate route of present Highway 50. The Amador Road became the approximate route of Highway 88. The connection road between them labeled Carson River Route ('48 Iron Mountain Road) follows approximately present Highway 5. In 1974 that highway was given the official name "Mormon Emigrant Trail."

It is very likely that travel between Salt Lake City and California over the northern route after 1852 was directed along the Johnson Cutoff.

(Map was drawn by Marshall Fey and is contained in his book *Emigrant Shadows: A History and Guide to the California Trail (2002)*, 158, and in that book's recent update, *Emigrant Trails: The Long Road to California* (2008), 156. These and other publications by Marshall Fey are available at the web site LibertyBelleBooks.com. *Map reproduced courtesy of Marshall Fey.*)

Stagecoaches

The first two stage lines in California began in 1849, one connecting San Francisco and San Jose, the other connecting Sacramento to Mormon Island and other towns on the American River. Stage lines were established in 1851 from Sacramento to Placerville (Hangtown) and from Sacramento to Marysville. Since the San Francisco Bay impeded land travel out of San Francisco to the interior, inland travel went from San Francisco mostly by way of steamboats to Sacramento. The town soon became the major stagecoach hub of California. Bancroft estimates that in 1853 twelve stage lines worked out of Sacramento. In that year, one newspaperman counted the coming and going of approximately 300 passengers daily. After 1853, stage lines began to merge again to eliminate ruinous competition, and by 1855 the California Stage Company controlled about five sixths of the stage travel in northern California. Coaching across the Sierra over the Placerville road (from Placerville to Carson Valley), began in 1857. By 1864, the Pioneer Company was operating four stages each way daily.

The first so-called stagecoaches in California were actually just wagons, and given the condition of the early roads, they had to be sturdy. Dame Shirley (Mrs. Louise Clappe) wrote of a ride in such a "sturdy" wagon. Concerning her departure from Rich Bar on the North Fork of the Feather River, in September 1851, she wrote, "I seated myself in the most excruciating springless wagon that it was ever my lot to be victimized in." [2] The more pleasant-riding, traditional coaches started arriving in 1850. They were mostly of two types, the standard "Concord" coaches and the "mudwagons." The Concord stages were developed in Concord, New Hampshire and had the now-famous box structure slung from the axles by leather straps. This attachment gave travel a rolling motion rather than the jerks and jars of the rigid spring wagons. Concord stages could carry nine passengers inside, and if necessary, a dozen on top. The "mudwagons" had half height boxes with a light superstructure covered simply with canvas. This made them lighter and gave them a lower center of gravity, making them more useful for mountain travel and heavy roads.

Mormon Thomas Orr's sons, John and James, ran a stage line from Sacramento to Marysville (page 221). John Horner, also Mormon, set up his own stage line in the Mission San Jose area and hired Charles Allen, a Mormon, as the driver (page 42).

Travel over the Sierra

The Carson Pass was a favorite route over the Sierra for immigrants going west during the gold rush. Reversing the course of the original passage, the immigrants went up through Carson Canyon, through Hope Valley, up Devil's Ladder, and over West Pass. The Carson Pass route was usually chosen because it avoided the many river crossings of the Truckee route and ended in the center of the Mother Lode. However, efforts began early to find variations to the route that would avoid the high pass. This was accomplished using Johnson's Cutoff. Johnson's (or Echo) Pass was over two thousand feet lower than West Pass (7382 ft. vs. 9640 ft.) This route variation (going west) originally went up a steep incline from Carson Valley just south of Carson City, went over Spooner Summit (at 7146 ft.), skirted the east and south shores of Lake Tahoe (at about 6200 feet), went over Echo Pass, and followed the Peavine Ridge down into Placerville. After 1852, much of the later Carson traffic was diverted to the Johnson Cutoff. However, since parts of Johnson's Cutoff were toll roads, the original Carson Pass route was still kept in use.

As the traffic and the importance of the Carson route increased, a variation was sought that could be kept open through the whole year. In 1855, a year round route was found to be achievable. The optimum route, going from east to west, entered the mountains through Carson Canyon, went from Hope Valley over Luther Pass (7300 ft.), on to Echo Summit, then down Johnson's Cutoff to Placerville. Sections of this route gradually improved through the efforts of individual immigrants and toll companies. However, in 1858, El Dorado, Sacramento, and Yolo Counties combined their efforts for further grading or leveling of the route. What began as a trail became a significantly improved highway. Even before that was accomplished, however, J. B. Crandall's Pioneer Stage Company began service over the route connecting Placerville and Genoa, Nevada. The trip took twenty-four hours.

Hoover describes later activity on the Carson route:

> "During the years 1859 to 1866, this "grand artery of travel" witnessed a great era of staging and freighting by horse-drawn vehicles. By day continuous streams of one-to-eight-span teams moved in both directions, while at night from four to six Concord coaches rumbled in and out of

Photographs from the 1860s of wagon caravans on the Johnson Cutoff at Slippery Ford. Slippery Ford was the original name for Kyburz on the Johnson Cutoff from the Carson Pass Trail, located just west of Johnson's Pass (now Echo Summit on Highway 50.) Teams wore a set of bells mounted on an arch above the collar of the animals. The bells could often be heard from teams approaching from the opposite direction before those teams could be seen. Roads were narrow, and such warning allowed teams not having the right of way to get into turnouts. Usually, a team going uphill had the right of way. *Courtesy Society of California Pioneers, from the Lawrence and Houseworth Albums.*

Placerville loaded with bullion, passengers, and mail. Mule trains, filling the canyons with the music of their bells; cumbersome freight schooners, rumbling over the rough roads; aristocratic Concord coaches, rattling at breakneck speed over the narrow, tortuous thread of road; Pony Express riders, filling the night with the clop of galloping hooves—all passed over this great thoroughfare through country once traversed only by Indians.

"An actual check made of this over-land commerce as it passed by Swan's tollhouse during three months in 1864 revealed that 6,667 foot travelers, 833 travelers on horseback, 3,164 stage passengers, 5,000 pack animals, 2,564 teams, and 4,649 head of cattle had gone that way. During the years 1864 and 1865, 320 tons of freight passed through Placerville daily, while the combined freight charges of 1863 could not have been less than $12 million. William H. Brewer, who camped at Slippery Ford in August 1863, says that 5,000 teams were then employed

The "Mule Ballet" sketch by George Mathis was published in 1973 in his pamphlets, "Eldorado Sketches" and "Auburn Lake Trails." In the first pamphlet, Mathis used the title "Mule Ballet At Slippery Ford." Slippery Ford, as already mentioned, was the original name for Kyburz on the Johnson Cutoff. The rendition shown above, taken from the second pamphlet, adapts the sketch from the first pamphlet to represent the hair pin curves on the way to the mining camp, Cool, out of Auburn.

Teams as shown were called "jerk-line teams." They consisted of six to fourteen animals, The name "jerk-line" comes from the fact that such teams were controlled by pulls and jerks on a rein or jerk-line passing through rings on the harness back straps and collars before going to bits in the animal's mouths. These jerk-line signals were reinforced by wagon master shouts and the snap of a "black snake" whip over the animals heads. The animals were well trained, and the signals were especially important on curves (for example, with the mountain on the outside of a curve). In that case (shown in the sketch), tension on the chain would tend to pull and straighten the chain, causing it to pass over the ravine. If the animals did not obey instructions, step over the chain, and pull to the outside of the turn, toward the mountain, they could be pulled off the road into the ravine.

The sets of bells that were mounted on an arch above the collar of the animals can be seen in the sketch. Again, the bells could often be heard from teams approaching from the opposite direction before those teams could be seen, allowing the teams to prepare for passing.

A collection of Mathis art works can be found in the archives of Washington State University, Pullman, Washington. *Courtesy John Davies, grandson of George Mathis.*

Team and Wagons at Webster Station on the Placerville Road

Just west of Kyburz, Webster's Sugar Loaf House was a remount station and horse change station for stage companies. (Historical Marker one mile west of Kyburz on U.S. 50.) *Courtesy Society of California Pioneers, from the Lawrence and Houseworth Albums.*

steadily in the Virginia City trade. Mark Twain's humorous version of Horace Greeley's stage ride over the old Placerville road in the summer of 1859 is one of the choice passages of *Roughing It.*" [4]

Hotels, Taverns, and Boarding Houses

Another consequence of the gold rush was a sudden increase in travelers accommodations. In 1851, Dame Shirley wrote before leaving Rich Bar. "California herself might be called the Hotel State, so completely is she inundated with taverns, boarding-houses, etc." [3] California was bursting with activity, and people were on the move. Often they could not reach their destina-

tions on a single day's travel, or did not plan to remain in one place very long. Travelers needed eating and sleeping accommodations along the way. Teams had to be rested and fed. Many travelers welcomed bars and gambling tables. Accordingly, hotels, taverns, and boarding houses sprang up in mining towns, such as the hotel run by the Mormons Hezekiah Thatcher and Hervey Green in Salmon Falls (pages 202, 212, 228, 297), by Thomas Orr Sr. in Salmon Falls (page 220), by Thomas Orr Jr. in Shingle Springs (page 221), not to mention Brannan's City Hotel in Sacramento and Mormon boarding houses in San Francisco. These stopping places were strung out in great numbers along the major roads. For example, Lathrop's Mormon Tavern (page 109) and Orrin Porter Rockwell's establishments were located

Wagon traffic at the Summit of the Placerville Road
Courtesy Society of California Pioneers, from the Lawrence and Houseworth Albums.

on the Sacramento to Placerville Road. As many as forty-two Mormons worked as hotel or tavern keepers (pages 347-348). Hotels or way stations were also established along the roads over the Sierra (such as Webster Station, page 380).

Railroads

Plans for a railroad in California began as early as 1852 when the Sacramento Valley Railroad (SVRR) was formed as an organization, with Colonel Charles L. Wilson as president. Wilson went east and secured Theodore Judah, an experienced railroad man from the East, as Chief Engineer. Judah began surveying a route east out of Sacramento in 1854 and began construction in 1855. The rail line was completed in February 1856, connecting Sacramento and Folsom (a newly surveyed town just above Negro Bar), covering a distance of 22.9 miles. Mormon Elders William H. Shearman and David M. Stuart walked this route to Folsom shortly after the line

was established, following the tracks on foot, because they did not have any money for a ticket (page 295). The first Bill of Lading on the SVRR carried the name of Thomas Orr, Mormon businessman and farmer of Salmon Falls. [5]

Judah's original intent was to go to Folsom, branching north and south from there to service the entire mining region, but he left the organization just before the section to Folsom went into operation. Others extended Judah's line east to Lincoln in 1861, to Latrobe in 1864, and to Shingle Springs in 1865. These lines continued to multiply and in time were consolidated. When Judah left the Sacramento Valley Line, he began lobbying for a rail line through the Sierra. That dream was realized when the Central Pacific Railroad coming out of Sacramento completed a line over the Truckee route of the Sierra Nevada (1864-1868).

To help the general public become more railroad conscious, a celebration was held when only a short distance of the tracks had been laid in Sacramento. A few people were chosen to take the first ride on the Sacramento Valley Railroad (S.V.R.R.) on August 17, 1855, from the levee to 17th and R Street. The above woodcut commemorating the event appeared in the *Sacramento Union* January 1, 1856. *Courtesy California State Library.*

Industry and Agriculture

As was pointed out in chapter twenty-five (page 308), the easy-to-get gold was taken in a very short time. Nevertheless, gold seekers continued to flood into California. However, gold miners in California were beginning to realize that the mining of gold was more difficult than they had thought, and the rewards for their efforts were diminishing by 1852. Fortunately, Argonauts came to California from other professions, so they had other skills and began looking to those other skills for their livelihood. Varied opportunities abounded. The large population generated a broad demand for general consumer products. Also, the equipment demands of higher technology gold mining and the transportation industry spawned an industrial base in lumber, foundries, machine tool companies, and metal working trades. Although the growth in these industries was slow, impeded by a scarcity of coal and iron, the industries developed steadily through the gold rush period. The greatest opportunity for disappointed Argonauts, however, was in farming.

The general opinion at the beginning of the gold rush was that California had little or no potential for farming. Gold seekers coming across the plains usually reached California in the summer and saw the Central Valley when the landscape was brown, dry, and hot. Many of them came from verdant farms in the East. Compared to eastern farmland, most of California did not look like good farm country. Food was being shipped in from Hawaii and more distant ports. Mormon farmer John Horner played a major role in changing that perception. Horner farmed vegetables and grains in the Mission San Jose area (pages 41-42). After two false starts, he had a productive year in 1849. A flood destroyed half that crop, but still the crop he was able to harvest was worth $8,000. In 1850 Horner increased his acreage planted and grossed $175,000 in crop sales. The third year, with still further increase in acreage, gross sales were about $275,000.

In 1851, during Horner's third productive

The Sacramento Valley Railroad began operation with three locomotives. Their No. 1 locomotive was the *Sacramento*, above, which led the opening run from Sacramento to Folsom on Washington's birthday, February 22, 1856. It was immediately followed by her sister engine, the *Nevada*, which didn't make it to Folsom. Part way to Folsom a flue burned through on the *Nevada*, allowing water to pour onto the grate. The above scale rendition of the *Sacramento* is from a lithograph produced by the locomotive builder, the Boston Locomotive Works. The third engine in service at the beginning of the SVRR line was the *L.L.Robinson*, an engine built in New Jersey. *Courtesy Union Pacific Railroad Museum.*

year, an eminent botanist, Christopher A. Shelton sponsored a fair in San Francisco billed as an "Agricultural and Mineralogical Exhibition." As a botanist, Shelton had reached the opinion that California had agricultural potential, and he wanted to prove it. So, he challenged those attempting farming in California to bring their prized agricultural specimens for display at the Exhibition in October and November of 1851. He also wanted any farm statistics, information about their class of soils, their mode of culture, etc. He offered a silver goblet for the most outstanding display. He wanted to show that California could "beat the world in vegetables and grains, as well as in her gold."

Horner won that contest and was awarded the goblet. His unique specimens of general produce, and especially Horner's overall display and statistics, proved what Shelton believed—that beyond the metal gold, California had great potential in agriculture. In the process, Horner was instrumental in moving California beyond the family farm concept prevalent in the East to farming as a large commercial endeavor.

While gold miners were looking for a second chance doing something else, Horner showed there was also "gold" in California agriculture. So it is natural that the second chance for many miners would involve agriculture. The Spanish missions, when they were in operation, had grown a variety of grains, fruits, and vegetables on a small scale for their own use. Horner demonstrated that those could be produced on a large scale. Unfortunately, raising vegetables was labor intensive and usually required extensive irrigation. Orchards and vineyards required special expertise and took years to develop. Prospective farmers soon recognized that the crops most easily, quickly, and cheaply produced would be the cereal grains. Because of the mild winters and hot summers, they would till the ground in the fall to retain the winter rains and sow by December. The hot, no-rain summers would ripen the mature grain, and it could be harvested at their leisure. Large tracts of land were available in the Central Valley. The waterways of the Sacramento and the San Joaquin Rivers offered easy access and easy shipping to markets. The predominant choice by those turning to farming was to produce wheat.

NOTICE!

There will be a Public Exhibition of the

Traveling Harvester,

MONITOR,

☞ On Thursday, the 3d day of September, commencing at 1 o'clock P. M., MONITOR No. 1 or 3 will be exhibited to the public upon the farm of WM. Y. HORNER, near the Mission San Jose, Alameda County.

We claim that one-half of the expense of harvesting would be saved to the Farmer by using the Harvester; in fact, the entire expense of Threshing is saved.

Three men and twelve horses have Cut Threshed, Cleaned and Sacked, in good workmanlike manner, fifteen (15) acres of grain per day—making five acres per man—a feat, we believe, never performed in America before! One and three-quarter (1¾) acres to the man, working with the most approved machinery, is about the highest figure yet reached—one acre per man being nearer the general average.

☞ Farmers! come and see if our claims are well founded.   JOHN M. HORNER,
v80-5   WM. Y. HORNER.

John Horner built three combines of his own design in the years between 1859 and 1867, which he called Monitors 1, 2, and 3. The above ad appeared in three issues of the *California Farmer*, August 13, 20, and 27, 1868, offering to harvest other people's grain. Only Monitor 1 and Monitor 3 are advertised in this series since Monitor 2 was committed elsewhere. A year later, however, Monitor 2 was burned in its shed, supposedly by arsonists, fearful that the Monitors would displace their labor.

A potential farmer could lease land, obtain machinery on credit, go into business with little risk and have a significant return in one season. Wheat quickly became the principal agricultural product in California and remained so for almost 50 years.

John Horner made another major contribution to California agriculture. At the time, most harvesting of grain was done using multiple machines—headers or reapers for cutting the grain, threshers for threshing the grain, wagons for transporting cut grain to the thresher, and usually a steam engine to drive the thresher. In the eastern states, Hiram Moore of Climax, Michigan, experimented with another approach. In cooperation with John Hascall, Moore was combining several harvesting functions into a "combined harvester," sometimes called, simply, a "combine." Moore's first patent was issued in 1836.

At first Moore's combine was not accepted as a practical approach in the East where farms tended to be too small for the large teams needed to pull the combine, and the weather often required the grain to be cut and threshed at different times.

However, John Horner imported one of the machines. In 1854, Horner used it to harvest grain on 600 acres of his farm and those of his neighbors. Unfortunately, that combine burned in the fields in 1856 because of overheated bearings. Horner continued to build, develop, and promote the combine. By about 1880, harvesting wheat using a combine became the accepted approach in California. Manufacturers, mostly based in Stockton, began producing standard combines in large numbers. Horner did not participate in this 1880 blossoming of the new industry. In 1879, after twenty-five years of developing and promoting the combine, he sold his farm, abandoned his combine machines, moved to Hawaii, and started a new career in raising and processing sugar cane.

John Horner, however, helped usher in two agricultural revolutions. First, he helped turn California to large scale agriculture. With some initial help from him, California went from thinking it had little agricultural potential to eventually becoming the leading agricultural state in the nation. Second, Horner began the implementation of mechanized, combined harvesting in California. California eventually played a leading role in bringing that technology to world acceptance.

Summary

The *Mormon Gold* story began in 1846 with California as a sparsely settled, pastoral frontier having only a primitive infrastructure and minimal industry. Because of the gold rush, the next decade saw California become a state of the Union. Its energies turned from the hide and tallow trade via ox cart to the development of roads, bridges, steamboats, mule team freighting, stage coaches, daily scheduled public transportation over the Sierra, the beginnings of a railroad, and the beginnings of significant manufacturing and agriculture. By another decade, California had a transcontinental telegraph line and was completing a transcontinental railroad. Changes came at a breath-taking rate. That explosive transformation was the historic setting for events of the *Mormon Gold* story, and individual Mormons made significant contributions.

NOTES

Information in Appendix D comes mainly from the following sources:

St. Clair, "Beginning of California Industry," 185-208.

Bethel, "The Golden Skein," 250-275.

Cross. *Early Inns.*

Drago, *Steamboaters.*

Hinckley, *Rails from the West*, 1-52.

Hull, *Up the River*, 48-52.

Jelineck, "Property of Every Kind," 233-249.

Kneiss, *Bonanza Railroads*, 3-29.

McGowan, *Sacramento Valley*, 1:71-102.

McGowan, "Freighting to the Mines," 1949.

MacMullen, *Paddle-Wheel Days.*

Olmstead, *Scow Schooners*, 5-12.

Shirley, *The Shirley Letters.*

Winther, *Express and Stagecoach Days.*

Winther, *Via Western Express and Stagecoach.*

Specific quotations are the following:

1. Marryat, *Mountains and Molehills*, 220.

2. Dame Shirley, *Letters*, First letter, 8.

3. Dame Shirley, *Letters,* Second letter, 23.

4. Hoover, et al. *Historical Spots in California*, 78-79.

5. Orr, *Life History*, i.

Tunneling for Gold at Table Mountian

"Passing through Tuolumne County is a remarkable plateau about twelve hundred feet above the surrounding country, which, from its flat surface and peculiar form, has been named Table Mountain. A few years since, a miner . . . while prospecting here, was led to believe that it had anciently been the course of a river -- a conclusion which has since proved correct, by the alluvial deposit and fossils found there by the miners. Here had accumulated, in distant ages, vast amounts of gold, which however could only be reached by shafts or tunnels. One of these had been commenced by the discoverer, . . . but others carried it through, and struck the interior basin or bed of an ancient river, in which were found deposits of gold of fabulous richness. The news spread, and the adjacent country was quickly "staked off" into claims, according to the local mining rules of that neighborhood.

"One of the largest tunnels which have been driven into the mountain is on its western slope, about six miles from the town of Sonora, and has been worked entirely through a bed of talcose slate and vitreous volcanic matter. It has more than paid its way by the richness of the mass through which it passes . . .The proprietor invited us to enter the tunnel . . . It enters horizontally, and follows the uneven surface of the bed-rock. On each side of us, as we entered, the damp walls reflected the light of our candles, while the roof, which was of sufficient height to allow us to walk upright, was strongly timbered at regular distances, and down the sides the water dripped from numerous subterranean springs, doubtless far above our heads. Passing along the middle is a railroad, upon which cars, loaded with earth, are run out by mule-power. Beneath this is a drain, carrying off, in a large stream, the accumulations of water from the works, and which affords enough for all mining purposes . . .

"While we were exploring a lateral chamber leading off from the main tunnel one of the workmen came upon a pocket, or nest of gold, which had accumulated in a hollow place in the bed-rock. We held the candles, and watched with curious interest the process of gathering the gold. The hole, which was about the size of a common wash-bowl, was filled with a collection of black mud, clay, disintegrated slate, and some black vitreous matter . . . This substance yielded like clay to a few blows of the pick; and as the slices were turned carefully up, they resembled chunks of plumb-cake, the clay being stuffed in every part with the golden lumps. Upon breaking these pieces in the hand like bread, the interior was still found plugged with pellets of gold, and the whole mass was heavy with it."

From From "How We Get Gold, From a Miner in the Year '49,"*Harper's New Monthly Magazine* 20:119 (April 1860) 613-614.

BIBLIOGRAPHY

UNPUBLISHED MATERIALS

Barger, Mrs. William H. Letter written in 1848 from the Winter Quarters. LDS Church Archives.

Bidamon, L. C. Papers, Archives, Community of Christ Church (Formerly Reorganized Church of Jesus Christ of Latter Day Saints), Independence, Missouri.

Bigler, Henry W. Diary. Lee Library, Brigham Young University.

———. Day Book. Lee Library, Brigham Young University.

Borrowman, John. John Borrowman Journals, LDS Church Archives. (Copy in Bancroft Library.)

Boyle, Henry G. Journal (1824-1888). Holograph 14 vols. Lee Library; Typescript 2 vols, Lee Library, Brigham Young University. Photocopy of typescript, LDS Church Archives.

Cannon, George Q. Diaries (1849-1894). LDS Church Archives.

Carruth, William H. Autobiography. LDS Church Archives.

California Census. 1850. US Census Bureau.

Crosby, Jonathan. Biographical Sketch (1807-1852). Holograph and typescript, Utah Historical Society, Salt Lake City, Utah;

Dunn, Simeon, Letter to Brigham Young, September 5, 1850, L.D.S. Church Archives.

Elliott, Bradford White. History of Bradford White Elliott. Lee Library, Brigham Young University.

Farrer, William Diaries and Letters. (1849-1860). Seven handwritten volumes. Lee Library, Brigham Young University. On line access to first six volumes. Seventh volume in Hawaiian language.

Gibbes, Charles Dayton. A New Map of California. Stockton, Calif.: C. D. Gibbes: New York: Sherman and Smith, 1852. Copy available at Bancroft Library. Available on the Internet at at address: http://imgzoom.cdlib.org/Fullscreen.ics?ark=ark:/13030/hb0x0nb3zm/z1&&brand=calisphere

Gold Accounts, See Young, Brigham, "Brigham Young's Daily Transactions in Gold Dust," LDS Church Archives.

Harris, Silas A Sketch of Silas Harris' Life as Written by Himself. Lee Library, Brigham Young University.

Hammond, George P. and Dale L.Morgan, "Captain Charles M. Weber: pioneer of the San Joaquin and founder of Stockton, California / with a description of his papers, maps, books, pictures and memorabilia." Bancroft Library, 1966.

Hickerson, George W. Letter, August 12, 1850. LDS Church Archives.

Hickerson, George W. Letter. August 11, 1850. LDS Church Archives.

Hogan, Goudy E. Journal (1829-1909). LDS Church Archives.

Higgins, S. G. Letter, January 8, 1857. in *Western Standard* on January 17, 1857.

Hopkins, Richard R. San Bernardino Branch Record. LDS Church Archives.

Hunt, Jefferson. Letter, April 2, 1854. LDS Church Archives.

Hurst, Fredrick W. Diary, 1855-1877. Lee Library, Brigham Young University.

Hyde, Orson. Letters, 1855-56. LDS Church Archives.

Jacobs, Brian S. Interview of a descendant by author, JKD.

Journal History of the Church of Jesus Christ of Latter-day Saints. LDS Church Archives.

Judd, Zadock Knapp. Autobiography. Lee Library, Brigham Young University.

Keeler, James. Diaries (1859-1879). Holograph at LDS Archives. Photocopy at Brigham Young University.

Kennedy, William A. Letter to James Ferguson April 2, 1848. LDS Church Archives. Available also in *Army of Israel: Mormon Battalion Narratives*. David Bigler and Will Bagley eds. 404-405.

Lee, John D. Diaries and Official Records. May 1844 - Nov. 1846, and Dec. 1850 -Feb. 1851, and records, 1861-1878.. Provo : Brigham Young University, 1957. See also *A Mormon Chronicle: The Diaries of John D. Lee 1848-1876* Edited and annotated by Robert Glass Cleland and Juanita Brooks. San Marino, Calif., Huntington Library, 1955. (Republished by University of California Press, 2004.)

Letters of First Presidency. LDS Church Archives.

Lyman, Amasa M. Papers. LDS Church Archives.

————. Diary. LDS Church Archives.

Lyman, Eliza Marie Partridge. Diary. Lee Library, Brigham Young University.

Membership Records. Archives, Community of Christ Church (Formerly Reorganized Church of Jesus Christ of Latter Day Saints), Independence, Missouri.

Naegle, John Conrad. Biography. Lee Library, Brigham Young University.

Peters, Charles. The Autobiography of Charles Peters . . . also historical happenings, interesting incidents and illustrations of the old mining towns in the good luck era, the placer mining days of the '50s. Sacramento: La Grave Co. [1915?]

Rich , Charles C. Certificate, October 1, 1849, LDS Church Archives.

————. Diary. LDS Church Archives.

————. Papers. LDS Church Archives.

Riser, John Jacob. Risers' complete Journal has not been released by the Riser family, but his account of the 1848 trip over southern route to Salt Lake City can be found in David L. Bigler and Will Bagley, Army of Israel, 397-400.

Rogers, Samuel Hollister. Diaries and Reminiscences, 1841-1886. Lee Library, Brigham Young University.

Seeley, David. Autobiographical Sketch. Bancroft Library.

Stout, Hosea. Diary, Available in *On the MormonFrontier: the Diary of Hosea Stout, 1844-1861*. edited by Juanita Brooks. v.1. 1844-1848. v.2. 1848-1861. Salt Lake City: University of Utah Press, 1964.

Stuart, David M. Journal excerpts (1820-1877). LDS Church Archives.

Tanner, Myron. Biography of Myron Tanner. Salt Lake City, Utah: Deseret News, 1907. Copies in Lee Library, Brigham Young University, and LDS Church Archives.

Thatcher, Linda. The Thatcher Family: A Case Study in Community and Family Interaction. Unpublished paper presented at the 23rd annual conference of the Mormon History Association, Logan, Utah, 1988

Thurber, Laura Ann Keeler Autobiography (1859-1900). Holograph at Brigham Young University; Photocopy at LDS Archives. (Begins with biographical sketches of her father and mother, James Keeler and Eliza Shelton Keeler.)

Wilson, John N. These Lonely Hills. California State Library, Sacramento.

Workman, Andrew Jackson. Autobiography. LDS Archives, also Lee Library, Brigham Young University.

Young, Brigham. "Brigham Young's Daily Transactions in Gold Dust," LDS Church Archives, abbreviated "Gold Accounts."

————. Correspondence. LDS Church Archives.

————. Brigham Young Manuscript History. LDS Church Archives.

PUBLISHED SOURCES

Achilles. *Destroying Angels of Mormonism, or, A Sketch of the Life of Orrin Porter Rockwell, the Late Danite Chief.* San Francisco: Alta California Printing House, 1878.

Arrington, Leonard J. *Charles C. Rich: Mormon General and Western Frontiersman.* Provo, Utah: Brigham Young University Press, 1974.

———. *Great Basin Kingdom: An Economic History of the Latter-day Saints*, 1830-1900. Cambridge: Harvard University Press, 1958.

———. *The Mormons in Nevada.* Las Vegas, Nev.: Los Vegas Sun, 1979.

———. "Mississippi Mormons." *Ensign* 7 (June, 1977): 46-51.

———. "Coin and Currency in Early Utah" and "Mormon Finance and the Utah War." *Utah Historical Quarterly*, 20 (January and July, 1952): 56-76, 219-37.

Arrington, Leonard J. and Edward Leo Lyman. "When the Mormon Church Invested in Southern Nevada Gold Mines." *Dialogue: A Journal of Mormon Thought* 35 (Summer 2002): 73-87.

Bagley, Will. *Scoundrel's Tale: The Sam Brannan Papers.* Spokane, Wash.: Arthur H. Clark Co., 1999.

Bagley, Will ed. *Frontiersman: Abner Blackburn's Narrative.* Salt Lake City: University of Utah Press, 1992.

Bancroft, Hubert Howe. *History of California*, 7 vols. San Francisco, Calif.: The History Company, 1886-1890.

———. *California Pioneer Register and Index, 1542-1848.* Baltimore, Md.: Regional Pub. Co., 1964. (Also available in Bancroft's *History of California*.)

Beattie, George William and Helen Pruitt Beatttie. *Heritage of the Valley: San Bernardino's First Century.* First ed. Pasadena, Calif.: San Pasqual Press, 1939. (Second ed. Oakland, Calif.: Biobooks, 1951.)

Beatie, H. S. "The First in Nevada," *Nevada Historical Society Papers 1913-1916*, (Carson City, Nevada: State Printing Office, 1917), 168-171.

Bennyhoff, J. A., et al. *Emigrant Summit Trail Historic Background, Eldorado National Forest, Excerpts from Emit Summit Trail, Archaeological Investigations and Historic Research of the Trail from Caples Lake to Maiadens Grave.* United States Department of Agriculture, Forest Service, Amador Ranger District. n.d.

Bethel, A. C. W. "The Golden Skien: California's Gold-Rush Transportation Network," in *A Golden State: Mining and Economic Development in Gold-Rush California.* Editors James J. Rawls and Richard J. Orsi, Published for the California Historical Society by the University of California Press. Appeared as *California History*, 77:4. (Winter 1998/1999), 250-275.

Bigler, David L., ed. *The Gold Discovery Journal of Azariah Smith*. Salt Lake City: University of Utah Press, 1990.

Bigler, David and Will Bagley, eds. *Army of Israel: Mormon Battalion Narratives*. Spokane, Wash.: Arthur H. Clark, Co., 2000.

Bigler, Henry W. Diary. Available in Erwin G. Gudde, *Bigler's Chronicle of the West*. Berkeley: University of California Press, 1962.

Bishop, M Guy. *William Bigler: Soldier, Gold Miner, Missionary.* Logan: Utah State University Press, 1998.

Bitton, Davis. *George Q. Cannon: A Biography*. Salt Lake City, Utah: Deseret Book, 1999.

Blackburn, Abner. "Narrative of Experiences," Available with informative commentary in Will Bagley's *Frontiersman: Abner Blackburn's Narrative*. Salt Lake City: University of Utah Press, 1992. The narrative is found on pages 124-131, 139-150, 168-175, and 181-187.

Brock, Richard K. and Donald E. Buck. *A Guide to the California Trail Along the Humboldt River*. Reno, Nev.: Trails West, 2007.

Brooks, Juanita. *The Mountain Meadows Massacre*. Norman: University of Oklahoma Press, 1970.

Brooks, Juanita, ed. *On the Mormon Frontier: The Diary of Hosea Stout, 1844-1861*, 2 vols. Salt Lake City: University of Utah Press, 1964.

Brown, James S. *Giant of the Lord - Life of a Pioneer*. Salt Lake City, Utah: Bookcraft, 1960 (Originally published as *Life of a Pioneer* by Geo. Q. Cannon and Sons, 1900.)

Brown, James S. *California Gold*. Oakland, Calif.: Pacific Press Publishing Co., 1894.

Brown, John Z. ed. *Autobiography of Pioneer John Brown, 1820-1896*. Salt Lake City, Utah: Stephen and Wallis Press, 1941.

Browne, J. Ross. See California. Constitutional Convention, 1849.

Bullock, Richard. *Biographies of the Ship Brooklyn Passengers*. Web site: ShipBrooklyn.com

———. *Ship Brooklyn Saints: Their Journey and Early endeavors in California*. Self published, available through web site: ShipBrooklyn.com

Bunje, Emil T. H. and James C. Kean. *Pre-Marshall Gold in California*, vol. 2. Sacramento: Historic California Press, 1983.

Cain, Joseph and Ariah C. Brower. *Mormon Way Bill*. Great Salt Lake City, Deseret: W. Richards, Printer, 1851. (Available in Lee Library, Brigham Young University.)

California. *Constitutional Convention, 1849. Report of the debates in the Convention of California, on the formation of the state constitution, in September and October, 1849* by J. Ross Browne. (Washington: printed by John T. Towers, 1850.)

California. Legislature. *Journal of the Proceedings of the Senate and the House of Assembly of the State of California at its first Session Begun and Held at Puebla de San Jose, on the Fifteenth Day of December, 1949* (San Jose, Calif.: J. Winchester, State Printer, 1850),

Campbell, Eugene E. "A History of the Church of Jesus Christ of Latter-day Saints in California, 1846-1946." PhD diss. University of Southern California, 1952.

————. "The Apostasy of Samuel Brannan." *Utah Historical Quarterly* 27 (Apr 1959): 157-167.

————. "The Mormon Gold Mining Mission of 1849." *BYU Studies*. 2:1 (Autumn 1959/ Winter 1960): 19-31.

————. "Authority Conflicts in the Mormon Battalion." *BYU Studies* 8 (Winter 1968): 127-42.

Cannon, George Q. "Twenty Years Ago: A Trip to California." *Juvenile Instructor* 4 (1869): Twelve short installments. 6-7, 13-14, 21-22, 28, 36-37, 44, 52-53, 60, 68, 78-79, 84, 92. Expanded to book format by Michael N. Landon, ed. *The Journal of George Q. Cannon: To California in '49*. Salt Lake City, Utah: Deseret Book, 1999.

Carter, Kate B. ed., *Heart Throbs of the West*, 12 vols. Salt Lake City, Utah: International Society Daughters of Utah Pioneers, 1939-51.

————. *Our Pioneer Heritage*, 20 vols. Salt Lake City, Utah: International Society Daughters of Utah Pioneers, 1958-77.

————. *Treasures of Pioneer History*, 6 vols. Salt Lake City, Utah: International Society Daughters of Utah Pioneers, 1952-1957.

Castro, Doris Shaw. *James H. Carson's California, 1847-1853*. New York: Vantage Press, 1997.

Centennial Book Committee for the Alpine County Museum (of California). "ALPINE HERITAGE: One Hundred Years of History, Recreation, and Lore in Alpine County California, 1864-1964."

Crampton, C. Gregory. "Utah's Spanish Trail." *Utah Historical Quarterly* 47 (Fall 1979): 361-383.

Crosby, Caroline Barnes. Diary. Published in: Edward Leo Lyman, Susan Ward Payne, and S. George Ellsworth, eds. *No Place to Call Home: The 1807-1857 Life Writings of Caroline Barnes Crosby*. Logan: Utah State University Press, 2005.

Cross, Ralph H. *The Early Inns of California: 1844-1869*. San Francisco: Self Published, 1954.

Davies, J. Kenneth. *Deseret's Sons of Toil*. Salt Lake City, Utah: Olympus Publishing Co., 1977.

————. *Thomas Rhoads: The Wealthiest Mormon Gold Miner*. Self published, 1980.

————. "Thomas Rhoads: Forgotten Mormon Pioneer of 1846." *Nebraska History* 64:1, (Spring 1983): 81-95.

Day, Robert O. *March of the Mormon Battalion: Called to Serve*, 2 ed. Oviedo, Fla.: Day to Day Enterprises, 2003. (First edition released as March of the Mormon Battalion, The Lord's Faithful, 1996.)

Dillinger, William C. *The Gold Discovery: James Marshall and the California Gold Rush.* Sacramento: California Department of Parks and Recreation, 1990 (Revised 2006).

Divett, Robert T. *Medicine and the Mormons, An Introduction to the History of the Latter-day Saint Health Care.* Bountiful, Utah: Horizon Publishers, 1981.

Drago, Harry S. *The Steamboaters, From the Early Side-Wheelers to the Big Packets.* New York: Dodd, Mead, 1967.

Durham, G. Homer. *Discourses of Wilford Woodruff.* Salt Lake City, Utah: Bookcraft, 1946.

Egan, Howard. *Pioneering the West*, Richmond, Utah: published privately by his estate, 1917.

Ellsworth, S. George, ed. *The History of Louisa Barnes Pratt: Being the Autobiography of A Mormon Missionary Widow and Pioneer*. Logan: Utah State University Press, 1998.

————. *The Journals of Addison Pratt.: Being a Narrative of Yankee Whaling in the Eighteen Twenties, A Mormon Mission to the Society Islands, and of Early California and Utah in the Eighteen Forties and Fifties.* Salt Lake City: University of Utah Press, 1990.

Fey, Marshall, R. Joe King, and Jack Lepisto. *Emigrant Shadows, A History and Guide to the California Trail*. Virginia City, Nev.: Western Trails Research Association, 2002.

Flake, Lawrence R. *George Q. Cannon: His Missionary Years.* Salt Lake City, Utah: Bookcraft, 1998,

Fleek, Sherman L. *History May Be Searched in Vain: A Military History of the Mormon Battalion.* Spokane, Wash.: Arthur H. Clark Co., 2006.

Garrett, H. Dean. "Ziba Peterson: From Missionary to Hanging Sheriff." Mormon Historical Studies, Nauvoo Journal 28 (Spring 1997): 28-32. Also available at the following web site. http://www. mormonhistoricsitesfoundation.org/publications/nj_spring1997/Garrett.pdf

Gay, Theressa. *James W. Marshall: The Discoverer of California Gold, A Biography*. Georgetown, Calif.: Talisman Press, 1967.

Glover, William. Paul D. Bailey, ed. *The Mormons of California*. Los Angeles, Calif.: Glen Dawson Press, 1954.

Golder, Frank A. *The March of the Mormon Battalion: From Council Bluffs to California.* New York: The Century Co., 1928. (Reprinted Waterbury, Conn.: Brohan Press, 2000.)

Griffin, Helen S. *The Diaries of Peter Decker*. Georgetown, Calif.: Talisman Press, 1966.

————. *Trail-Blazing Pioneer: Colonel Joseph Ballinger Chiles.* San Francisco: John-Howell Books, 1969.

Gudde, Erwin G. *Bigler's Chronicle of the West: The Conquest of California, Discovery of Gold, and Mormon Settlement as Reflected in Henry William Bigler's Diaries.* Berkeley: University of California Press, 1962.

Gudde, Erwin G. and Elizabeth K. Gudde. *California Gold Camps.* Berkeley: University of California Press, 1975.

Hafen, Leroy R. and Ann W. Hafen, eds. *Journal of Forty-Niners*: Salt Lake to Los Angeles. Lincoln: University of Nebraska Press, 1998. (Originally published Seattle, Wash.: Arthur H. Clark Co., 1954.)

Ham, Randall E. *A Buckeye in the Land of Gold: The Letters and Journal of William Dennison Bickham.* Spokane, Wash.: Arthur H. Clark Company, 1996.

Hammond, Francis Asbury. "In Early Days: My Introduction to Mormonism." *Juvenile Instructor* (June-September, 1894).

Hansen, Lorin K. "The Voyage of the Brooklyn." *Dialogue: A Journal of Mormon Thought* 21:3 (Autumn 1988): 47-72.

Hansen, Lorin K. and Lila J. Bringhurst. *Let This Be Zion: Mormon Pioneers and Modern Sainnts in Southern Alameda County.* Salt Lake City, Utah: Publishers Press, 1996.

Harris, E. W. *The Overland Emigrant Trail to California, A Guide to Trail Markers Placed in Western Nevada and the Sierra Nevada Mountains in California.* Fourth Printing (slightly revised). Reno: Nevada Emigrant Trail Marking Committee, Nevada Historical Society, 1980.

Hill, Marvin S. et al. *The Kirtland Economy Revisited.* Provo, Utah: Brigham Young University Press, 1977.

Hinckley, Helen. *Rails From the West; A Biography of Theodore D. Judah.* San Marino, Calif.: Golden West Books, 1969.

Hoover, Mildred B. et al. Revised by Douglas E. Kyle. *Historical Spots in California,* 5 ed. Palo Alto, Calif.: Stanford University Press, 2002.

Horner, John Meirs. "Adventures of a Pioneer" *Improvement Era* 7 (May-Sept. 1904): 571-585, 561-570, 665-672, 767-772, 849-854.

———. "Looking Back" *Improvement Era* 8 (Nov., Dec. 1904): 29-35, 112-117.

———. "Personal History of the Author." in *National Finance and Public Money* (Honolulu: Hawaii Gazette Co., 1898), 247-276.

Hughes, Benjamin M. "William B. Ide, Pioneer, Bear-Flagger & Builder." Dogtown Territorial Quarterly. Issues no. 16 (Winter 1993) 4, 5, 20-23, 54-55; no. 17 (Spring 1994) 46-53; no. 18 (Summer 1994) 6, 24-26, 31, 34-37; no. 19 (Fall 1994) 48-55; no. 20 (Winter 1994) 56-63; no. 21 (Spring 1995) 8-9, 36-47. Paradise, Calif.: Bill and Penny Anderson.

Hull, David, ed. *Up the River: Steam Navigation above the Carquinez Strait.* San Francisco: Book Club of California, 2003.

Hurtado, Albert L. *John Sutter: A Life on the North American Frontier* (Norman: University of Oklahoma Press, 1988).

Hutton, William R. *Glances at California, 1847-1853*, diaries and letters of William Rich Hutton with a brief memoir and notes by Willard O. Waters.

Hyde, Myrtle Stevens. *Orson Hyde: The Olive Branch of Israel*. Salt Lake City, Utah: Agreka Books, 2000.

Ignoffo, Mary Jo. *Gold Rush Politics: California's First Legislature*. Published jointly by the California State Senate, Sacramento California, and Cupertino, Calif.: California History Center and Foundation, De Anza College, 1999.

An Illustrated History of Southern California. Chicago: The Lewis Publishing Company, 1890. 1940?

Ide, Simeon. *A Biographical Sketch of the Life of William B. Ide*. Glorieta, N.M.: Rio Grande Press, 1967.

Ide, William B. *Who Conquered California?* (Otherwise known as the Wambaugh Letter) Glorieta, N.M.: Rio Grande Press, 1967.

Jackson, Donald Dale. *Gold Rush*. New York: Alfred A. Knopf, 1980.

Jelineck, Lawrence James. "Property of Every Kind," in *A Golden State: Mining and Economic Development in Gold-Rush California*. Editors James J. Rawls and Richard J. Orsi, Published for the California Historical Society by the University of California Press. Appeared as *California History*, 77:4. (Winter 1998/1999), 233-249.

Jensen, Chris. "Mormon Settlements in Nevada." *Ensign* 1 (April 1971): 25-29.

Jessee, Dean C. "All Things Move in Order in the City." *BYU Studies* 19 (Spring, 1979): 289-320.

Jessee, Dean C. "Brigham Young's Family: The Wilderness Years." *BYU Studies* 19 (Summer 1979): 474-500.

Kagin, Donald H. *Private Gold Coins and Patterns of the United States*. New York : Arco Pub., c1981.

Kneiss, Gilbert H. *Bonanza Railroads*. Stanford University: Stanford Univ. Press, 1947.

Kimble, Rose. "Newton, Ghost Town and Eldorado County." *Pony Express Courier* 8 (November 1941.)

Lamb, Blaine P. "Emigrant Aid on California Gold Rush Trails: Private Need and Public Enterprise." *Overland Journal* 19 (Winter 2001/2002): 122-35.

Landon, Michael N., ed. *The Journal of George Q. Cannon: To California in '49*. Salt Lake City, Utah: Deseret Book (Published in Collaboration with the Historical Department of The Church of Jesus Christ of Latter-day Saints), 1999.

Letts, John M. *California Illustrated: Including a Description of the Panama and Nicaragua Routes, By a returned Californian.* New York: Wm. Holdredge, Publisher, 1852. (Facsimile available by Ann Arbor: University Library, University of Michigan, 2001.)

Lorenz, Anthony J. "Scurvy in the Gold Rush." *Journal of the History of Medicine and Allied Sciences* 12:4 (1957) 473-510.

Lyman, Edward Leo. *Amasa Mason Lyman, Mormon Apostle and Apostate*: A Study in Dedication. Salt Lake City: University of Utah Press, 2009.

———. *The Overland Journey from Utah to California: Wagon Travel from the City of Saints to the City of Angels*, Reno: University of Nevada Press, 2004

———. *San Bernardino: the Rise and Fall of a California Community*, Salt Lake City, Utah: Signature Books, 1997.

———. "The Demise of the San Bernardino Mormon Community." *Southern California Quarterly* 65 (Winter 1983) 321-39, Later reprinted as "The Rise and Decline of Mormon San Bernardino." *BYU Studies*, 29 (Fall 1989) 43-63.

———. "Larger than Texas: 1849 Proposal for Uniting Mormon Deseret and California to Form One State. *California History* 80:1 (March 2001): 18.

Lynch, James and Francis Clark. *The New York Volunteers in California: With Stevenson in California.* Republished Glorieta, N.M., Rio Grande Press, 1970.

McCready, Clint. "New Hope: A Mormon Colony in Central California." MA Thesis, Brigham Young University, 1976.

McGowan, Joseph A. *History of the Sacramento Valley*, 3 vols. New York: Lewis Historical Pub. Co., 1961.

McGowan, Joseph A. "Freighting to the Mines in California, 1849-1859." PhD diss. University of California, Berkeley, 1949.

MacMullen, Jerry. *Paddle-Wheel Days in California*. Stanford University: Stanford Univ. Press, 1944.

Marryat, Frank, *Mountains and Molehills, or Recollections of a Burnt Journal*, Stanford, Calif.: Stanford University Press, 1952,

Mason, Col. R. B. "Mason Report, August 17, 1848," Exec. Doc. 17, H.R., 31st Cong., 1st sess., 1850. Also available in Castro, Carson's California, 220-240.

Miller, Robert. *Guide to Old Sacramento*. Sacramento, Calif.: River City Press, 1977.

Naegle, Cherrie Gubler. *The Life and Times of John Conrad Naegle and Family*. (Toquerville, Utah: C. G. Naegle, 2003).

Nash, John D. and Mary Ann Nash. *In a Goodly Land: Latter-Day Saints on the Stanislaus*. Fresno, Calif.: Linrose Publ. Co., 1997.

Olmstead, Roger R. *Scow Schooners of San Francisco Bay*. Cupertino, Calif.: California History Center, De Anza College, 1988.

Orr, Thomas J., Jr. *Life History of Thomas Orr, Jr., Pioneer Stories of California and Utah*. Lillie Jane Orr Taylor, ed. Shingle Springs, Calif.: Privately published, 1930.

Owens, Kenneth N. *Gold Rush Saints, California Mormons and the Great Rush for Riches*. Lincoln: University of Nebraska Press, 2002.

————. *Riches for All: The California Gold Rush and the World*. Spokane, Wash.: Arthur H. Clark, 2004.

Paden, Irene D. ed. "The Ira J. Willis Guide to the Gold Fields." *California Historical Quarterly* 32:3 (Sept. 1953): 193-204.

Page, Albert R. "Orson Hyde and the Carson Valley Mission, 1855-57." MA Thesis, Brigham Young University, 1970. (Available digitally from Lee Library, BYU.)

Parmalee, Robert D. *Pioneer Sonoma*. Sonoma, Calif.: Sonoma Index Press, 1972.

Paul, Rodman W., ed. *The California Gold Discovery; Sources, Documents, Accounts, and Memoirs Relating to the Discovery of Gold at Sutter's Mill*. Georgetown, Calif.: Talisman Press, 1966.

Porter, Larry C. "A Study of the Origins of the Church of Jesus Christ of Latter-day Saints in the States of New York and Pennsylvania, 1816-1831." PhD diss, Brigham Young University, 1971.

Pratt, Louisa Barnes. Diary. Published in: S. George Ellsworth, ed. *The History of Louisa Barnes Pratt: Being the Autobiography of A Mormon Missionary Widow and Pioneer*. (Logan: Utah State University Press, 1998).

Pratt, Parley P. *Autobiography of Parley P. Pratt*. Revised and enhanced edition edited by Scot Facer and Maurine Jensen Proctor. Salt Lake City, Utah: Deseret Book, 2000.

Read, Georgia W. and Ruth Gaines, eds. *Gold Rush*. New York: Columbia University Press, 1944.

Reese, Col. John. "Mormon Station," *Nevada Historical Society Papers*, 1917, (Carson City, Nevada: State Printing Office, 1917), 187.

Rhoades, Gale R. and Kerry R. Bowen. *Footprints in the Wilderness : A History of the Lost Rhoades Mines*. Salt Lake City: Dream Garden Press, 1980.

Ricketts, Norma Baldwin. *The Mormon Battalion: U.S. Army of the West, 1846-1848*. Logan: Utah State University Press, 1996.

————. *Tragedy Spring and the Pouch of Gold*. Sacramento, Calif.: Ricketts Pub., 1983.

————. "The California Star Express." *Golden Notes* 28:1 (Spring, 1982). (Published by Sacramento County Historical Society and self published by the author.)

Roberts, B. H. *Comprehensive History of the Church*. 6 vols. Salt Lake City, Utah: Deseret News Press, 1957.

————. *The Mormon Battalion, Its History and Achievements*. Salt Lake City, Utah: Deseret News, 1919.

Robie, Wendell. "At Murderer's Bar, Middle Fork American River – 1849." *The Pony Express*, 25:2 (July 1958): 3-6.) Address delivered before the California Historical Society

Rogers, Fred Blackburn, *William B. Ide, Bear Flagger*. San Francisco, Calif.: John Howell Books, 1961.

Rust, Alvin E. *Mormon and Utah Coin and Currency*. Salt Lake City, Utah: Rust Rare Coin Co., 1984.

St. Clair, David J. "The Gold Rush and the Beginnings of California Industry," in *A Golden State: Mining and Economic Development in Gold-Rush California*. Editors James J. Rawls and Richard J. Orsi, Published for the California Historical Society by the University of California Press. Appeared as *California History*, 77:4. (Winter 1998/1999), 185-208.

Schindler, Harold. *Orrin Porter Rockwell: Man of God, Son of Thunder*. Salt Lake City: University of Utah Press, 1966,

Scott, Reva. *Samuel Brannan and the Golden Fleece*. New York: MacMillan Co., 1944.

Sherman, William Tecumseh. *Memoirs of General W. T. Sherman*. New York: Library Classics of the United States, 1990.

Shirley, Dame. *The Shirley Letters: Being Letters written 1851-1852 from the California Mines*. New York: Alfred A Knopf, 1949.

Slater, Nelson. *Fruits of Mormonism*. Coloma, Calif.: Harmon and Springer, 1850.

Smith, Grant H. *The History of the Comstock Lode: 1850-1920*. Reno: Nevada State Bureau of Mines and the Macckay School of Mines / University of Nevada Press, 1943 (1954 reprint.)

Smith, Joseph, et al., *History of the Church of Jesus Christ of Latter-day Saints*. ed. by Brigham H. Roberts, 7 vols., 2nd ed. rev. Salt Lake City, Utah.: Deseret News, 1948 printing.

Smith, Pauline Udall. *Captain Jefferson Hunt of the Mormon Battalion*. Salt Lake City : The Nicholas G. Morgan, Sr. Foundation, 1958.

Southworth, John. *Death Valley in 1849: The Luck of the Gold Rush Emigrants*. Burbank, Calif.: Pegleg Books, 1978.

Spence, Clark C. "From Gold Pans to California Dredges." in *Riches for All: The California Gold Rush and the World*. Kenneth N. Owens, ed. Published by University of Nebraska Press (2002), 296-316.

Stanley, Reva Holdaway. *Parley P. Pratt, The Archer of Paradise*. Caldwell, ID: Caxton Printers, 1937.

Stanley, Reva Holdaway. "Sutter's Mormon Workmen at Natoma and Coloma in 1848." *California Historical Society Quarterly* 14:3 (Sept. 1935): 268-82.

Stanley, Reva Holdaway, and Charles L. Camp, eds. "A Mormon Mission to California in 1851, From the Diary of Parley Parker Pratt." *California Historical Society Quarterly* 14:1-2, (March 1935):59-73, 175-182.

Starr, Kevin and Richard J. Orsi. *Routed in Barbarous Soil: People, Culture, and Community in Gold Rush California*. Appeared as *California History*, 79:2, Summer 2000. Published for the California Historical Society by the University of California Press.

Stegner, Wallace. *The Gathering of Zion, The Story of the Mormon Trail*. Salt Lake City, Utah: Westwater Press, 1981.

Stewart, George R. *The California Trail*. Lincoln: University of Nebraska Press, 1962.

Stout, Hosea, Diary. See *On the Mormon Frontier: The Diary of Hosea Stout, 1844-1861*, Juanita Brooks, ed. 2 vols. Salt Lake City: University of Utah Press, 1964.

Stuart, David M. *The Stuart Records*, Salt Lake City: David M. Stuart Family, 1998/

Sutak, Tom. "Jefferson Hunt: California's First Mormon Politician." *Journal of Mormon History* 36:3 (Summer 2010): 82-117.

Sutter, Johann August. *Diary of Johann August Sutter*. San Francisco, Calif.: Grabhorn Press, 1932.

Sutter, John A. *New Helvetia Diary*. San Francisco: Southern California Pioneers, Grabhorn Press, 1939.

Taylor, John. "The Upper California: O! That's the Land for Me." *BYU Studies* 20 (Spring 1980): 280.

Thompson and West's, *History of Nevada*, 1881, Reproduction Berkeley, Calif.: Howell and North, 1958.

Thurber, Albert K. Journal. Available in Carter, *Treasures of Pioneer History*, vol. 3, 1954, 253-320.

Tortorich, Frank, Jr. *Hiking the Gold Rush Trail, A Hiking Guide Over West Pass, Caples Lake to Tragedy Spring*. Pine Grove, Calif.: Wagon Wheel Tours, 2004.

―――. *Gold Rush Trail, A Guide to the Carson River Route of the Emigrant Trail*. Pine Grove, Calif.: Wagon Wheel Tours, 1998.

Tyler, Daniel. *A Concise History of the Mormon Battalion in the Mexican War: 1846-1847*. 1881; Reprinted by Glorieta, NM: Rio Grande Press, 1964.

Van Sickle, Henry. "Utah Desperadoes." *Nevada Historical Society Papers,* 1917, (Carson City, Nev.: State Printing Office, 1917), 190-91.

Walker, Dale L. *Bear Flag Rising, The Conquest of California*, 1846. New York: Tom Doherty Associates, 1999.

Walker, Ronald W. *Wayward Saints: The Godbeites and Brigham Young.* Urbana: University of Illinois Press, 1998.

Walker, Ronald W., Richard E. Turley, and Glen M. Leonard. *Massacre at Mountain Meadows.* New York: Oxford University Press, 2008.

Warner, Barbara R. *The Men of the Bear Flag Revolt and their Heritage.* Seattle, Wash.: Arthur H. Clark Publ. Co., Sonoma Valley Historical Association, 1996.

Winther, Oscar O. *Express and Stagecoach days in California, from the Gold Rush to the Civil War.* Stanford University: Stanford Univ. Press, 1936.

Winther, Oscar O. *Via Western Express and Stagecoach.* Stanford University: Stanford Univ. Press, 1945.

Wood, M.W. *History of Alameda Connty, California.* Oakland: M. W. Wood Publ., 1883., reprinted Oakland: Holmes Book Co., 1969.

Yohalem, Betty. *"I Remember…" Stories and Pictures of El Dorado Pioneer Families.* Placerville, Calif.: El Dorado County Chamber of Commerce, 1977.

Young , Brigham. Letter to Sam Brannan, Sept. 15, 1845, *History of the Church*, 7: 444-45.

Yurtinus, John F. "A Ram in the Thicket." PhD diss, Brigham Young University, 1976.

———. "The Mormon Volunteers: The Recruitment and Service of a Unique Military Company." *Journal of San Diego History* 25:3 (Summer 1979): 242-61.

NEWSPAPERS

The Californian. San Francisco.

The California Star. San Francisco.

Deseret News. Salt Lake City.

Deseret. News Weekly. Salt Lake City.

The Nauvoo Neighbor, Nauvoo, Illinois.

Pioneer Sonoma, Sonoma, California

The Placer Herald, Auburn, California.

Times and Seasons, Nauvoo, Illinois.

The Weekly Placer Herald. Placer County Library, Auburn, California.

The Western Standard, San Francisco.

SCRIPTURAL AND RELIGIOUS PUBLICATIONS

Bible, KJV.

Book of Mormon. Church of Jesus Christ of Latter-day Saints, Salt Lake City, Utah.

Doctrine and Covenants. Church of Jesus Christ of Latter-day Saints, Salt Lake City, Utah.

Hymns of The Church of Jesus Christ of Latter-day Saints. Salt Lake City, Utah: The Church of Jesus Christ of Latter-day Saints. Quotations from hymns in chapters 9 and 23 are in the 1948 ed. Quotations from chapters 5, 10, and 17 can be found in the 1985 ed.

Journal of Discourses (Sermons of early leaders of the Church of Jesus Christ of Latter-day Saints). Liverpool, England: F. D. and S. W. Richards, 1854

Flutter-Wheel, on the Tuolumne

"The elevation of many rich mines has given rise to a variety of ingenious inventions for raising and supplying them, with water. Among these is the " flutter-wheel," which the traveler will find erected in every conceivable manner and place; carried, in all cases, by the force of the river currents. It consists of a wheel, sometimes thirty feet in diameter, the paddles of which are furnished with large buckets, made to catch themselves full of water at each revolution, and to discharge into a trough, through which it flows to the tom, or sluice, where the mining operations are being conducted. This contrivance differs little from the common " undershot wheel." They may be seen by the dozens along the Tuolumne and Stanislaus rivers, and supply countless miners with the indispensable water."

[From "How We Get Gold, From a Miner in the Year '49," *Harper's New Monthly Magazine*, vol. 20, issue 119 (April 1860) 606, 609-610.]

Map and Illustration Credits

Maps and Illustrations on the pages listed are reproduced by permission of the following individuals and organizations.

Aerials Express and Jason R. Brown (page 168)

The Bancroft Library, University of California, Berkeley
[pages 6 (I0040632) Brannan, Samuel--POR1;
20 (HN000232a; Marshall Banc 1)
      1963.002:0007--A;
22 (HN001679a) 1963.002:0486--B;
23 (brk00007992_24a) xF865.R4;
31 (brk00040721_8a) 19xx.074--DIG;
118 (BANK PIC 1963 002:0994:18--A);
123 (HN001591a) 1963.002:1537--E;
124 (See 132),
125(cubanc_37_1_00474966a) 1963.002:467-D;
127 (I0040791) Burnett, Peter H--POR1;
132 (HN001437a) 1963.002:1535:01--D;
163 (HN000610a) 1963.002:0042--A;
178 (HN002298a) 1963.002:1305:005--ALB;
194 (HN001620a) 1905.00006:6--B;
194 (I0008396) 1963.002.0203--A;
210 (HN001542a) 1963.002:1495--FR;
251 (HN000101a) 1963.002:1370--FR;
284 (HN000830a) 1963.002:0104--A;
288 (HN000424a) 1063.002:0158--B;
300 (I0041618), 19xx.097:34--A
367 (HN002514a) 1963.002:1535-E; and
374 (HN000065a) 1963.002:0317-C]

California Historical Society, San Francisco
[pages 18, 44 (FN-13638/CHS2009.142.tif),
54 (FN-13637/CHS2009.141.tif), 171 (FN-28873/CHS2009.140.tif), and 216 (FN-19211/CHS2009.139.tif)]

California History Center, Louis E. Stocklmeir Library and Archives, De Anza College. Cupertino, California (page 210)

California History Room, California State Library, Sacramento
[pages 23 (prints coll. #2002-0057),
26 (art coll. #1999-0326);
30 (photo coll. neg. #4552);
132 (lettersheet coll. neg.#24,375);
170 (photo coll. neg. #7346 *Pictorial Union* Jan. 1855, p. 3);
178 (photo coll. neg. #7349 *Pictorial Union* Jan. 1855, p. 4);
198 (From book coll. **fc017.94 P5 Vol. 3, *Photographic Views of One Hundred and Twelve of the Principle and most Picturesque Places of California*, p. 76, image call #2008-2306);
246 (prints coll. #9027);
288 (photo coll. neg. #3684 *Pictorial Union* Jan. 1854, p. 4);
366 (art coll. call #2000-0106 neg. #659); and
382 (photo coll. neg. #650)]

City of San Bernardino Historical and Pioneer Society, San Bernardino, California (pages 172, 248, 270, and 273)

Community of Christ Church (Formerly Reorganized Church of Jesus Christ of Latter Day Saints) Archives, Independence, Missouri (page 145)

Craig Dalton (page 180)

John Davies (pages 314, 372, and 379)

El Dorado County Chamber of Commerce, Placerville, California (page 219)

Wade Fillmore (page 269)

Ed Fraughton (page 8)

Dennis Holland (pages 50 and 53)

The Huntington Library, San Marino, California [pages 29 (HM43214_94) and 266 (HM43214_21)]

The Hurricane Pioneer Heritage Park Foundation, Hurricane Museum, Hurricane, Utah (page 78)

LDS Archives, The Church of Jesus Christ of Latter-day Saints (pages 71, 114, 154, 157, 280, and 294)

LDS Museum of History and Art (page 3)

Marriott Library, University of Utah (page 242)

Jack Marshall (page 144)

Katherine Miller Marshall (Mrs. John Marshall), Woodbridge, California (map touch-ups on pages xvi, xviii, and xx; maps on pages 48-49, 55, 56-57, 106, and 370-371).

Heber and Genevieve Moulton (page 100)

Museum of El Dorado County, Placerville, California (page 109)

Nevada Historical Society, Reno (pages 254 and 256)

Marshall Nye, Liberty Bell Press (page 376)

Douglas Nyholm (coin on cover and pages 86, 88, and 90)

Pioneer Museum, International Society Daughters of Utah Pioneers, Salt Lake City (pages 33, 34, 35, 50, 52, 67, 122, 134, 136, 147, 158, 160, 188, 254, 286, 298, 299, and 303)

Bernie L. Rhoades (pages 7 and 142)

Sacramento Archives and Museum Collection Center (page 68)

San Jose Public Library, California Room, San Jose, California [page 126 (Image digitally altered to remove distracting structures.)]

Udo Schroeder (pages 18 and 328)

Scotts Bluff National Monument, Gering, Nebraska (pages 16 and 81)

The Seaver Center for Western History Research, Natural History Museum of Los Angeles County (page 196)

The Society of California Pioneers, San Francisco [pages 21, 373 (Lawrence & Houseworth image 1064), 378 (L&H image 425), 380 (L&H image 409), and 381 (L&H image 432)]

Blanche Lane Tomkins and Alma Lee (page 220)

Union Pacific Railroad Museum, Council Bluffs, Iowa (page 383)

University of California, Berkeley - Earth Sciences and Map Library (pages 170 and 258)

University of Utah Press, Salt Lake City (page 121)

Utah State Historical Society, Salt Lake City (pages 11, 65, 66, 122, 177, 232, 236, 252, 282, and 287)

Utah State University, Merrill-Cazier Library, Special Collections & Archives, Logan (pages 70 and 122)

SUBJECT INDEX

The letters *m* (-*m*) or *i* following a page number
denotes the entry occurs in a map or an illustration.

PERSONAL NAME INDEX

The letter *i* following a page number denotes the entry occurs as an illustration.
Names of modern authors given in references are not listed.

ABOUT THE AUTHORS

J. Kenneth Davies received a Ph.D. in economics from the University of Southern California and is a distinguished Utah labor historian and active labor arbitrator. He is presently retired, but was a Professor of Managerial Economics at Brigham Young University and taught in the fields of labor and economics. He has been active in the areas of economic education, manpower planning, banking, and labor relations.

The author's interest in the present subject was provoked by his search for the history of Utah's workers. He soon learned of the historically uneasy relationship between Utah miners and Mormons and realized that Mormon antagonism toward miners found its roots in Brigham Young's public policy in the gold mining era. Thus began his re-examination of the role of Mormons in this exciting period.

Professor Davies has authored or co-authored eight books and has written numerous articles in his areas of expertise.

Lorin K. Hansen received a Ph.D. in physics from U.C.L.A., has worked mostly in applied research, and is presently retired. One of his areas of research has been low energy plasmas and their use in the generation of electrical power. He also worked for Xerox Colorgrafx Systems in San Jose, California, helping them develop electrographic color printing.

The author became interested in Mormons in early California from living many years in Fremont, California, the location of an early farming community developed substantially by passengers from the ship *Brooklyn* and some of the men discharged from the Mormon Battalion. His interest was also enhanced because the family had a favorite vacation spot at Silver Lake in the Sierra, where they enjoyed exploring the adjacent Mormon Emigrant Trail.

Dr. Hansen was co-author of *Let This Be Zion*, a history of Mormon activities in the Fremont area, the account beginning with the ship *Brooklyn*, the Mormon Battalion, and the mid nineteenth century farming community. He has published many articles on various subjects, two in particular on the voyage of the ship *Brooklyn*.